Outstanding Contributions to Logic

Volume 1

For further volumes:
http://www.springer.com/series/10033

Robert Trypuz
Editor

Krister Segerberg on Logic of Actions

Springer

Editor
Robert Trypuz
The John Paul II Catholic University of Lublin
Lublin
Poland

ISSN 2211-2758 ISSN 2211-2766 (electronic)
ISBN 978-94-007-7045-4 ISBN 978-94-007-7046-1 (eBook)
DOI 10.1007/978-94-007-7046-1
Springer Dordrecht Heidelberg New York London

Library of Congress Control Number: 2013945289

The photography in the cover taken by Sten Lindström

Printed on acid-free paper

Springer is part of Springer Science+Business Media (www.springer.com)

Contents

Introduction

The concepts of action and agency belong to the category of those concepts which are not easy to deal with. A vast amount of literature on the philosophy of action, the logic of action and agency and broadly understood AI proves these words to be true. The difficulty one encounters when analysing the concepts in question lies in their complex nature manifested by their strong relationship with mental attitudes (such as beliefs, desires and intentions), practical reasoning (consisting of deliberation, means-end reasoning and decision process), plans and routines, will, agent's abilities, time (a well-known problem of temporal extension of actions), responsibility and causality binding mental attitudes with bodily motions and action's results. Thus starting from Aristotle, through Anselm of Canterbury to the new opening in the philosophy of action initiated by Elizabeth Anscombe, we can count many ways of explaining and defining what action and agency are (almost as many as there are philosophers who have been writing about them). It also has to be emphasised that many issues concerning the notions of action and agency studied previously in philosophy, in particular those being in the scope of interest of philosophical logic, have recently found their creative continuation (in some cases got even their second life) in computer science, especially in AI, planning and knowledge representation. Situation Calculus, Dynamic Logic, a family of BDI logics or the insight given by game theory: Alternating-time Temporal Logic and Coalition Logic are just a few examples of artefacts created to solve problems in computer science. Notwithstanding the fact that the aforementioned theories have been developed in the scope of computer science, it is obvious today that they point out problems relevant also to philosophy (frame problem being just one of many examples).

While talking about actions, it is useful from the very beginning to distinguish between real actions and doxastic (or epistemic) actions. Real actions are actions having some manifestation in the environment external to the agent. We may metaphorically call such actions "tangible". Doxastic or epistemic actions are actions changing agents' beliefs and knowledge about the environment as well as about other beliefs. We may also call the actions in question "intangible", since they do not have physical presence in the environment.

Krister Segerberg is a philosopher who for more than 30 years has been analysing intricacies of real and doxastic actions by means of formal tools—mostly modal (dynamic) logic and its semantics. He has had such a significant impact on modal logic that "*It is hard to roam for long in modal logic without finding Krister Segerberg's traces*", as Johan van Benthem noted in [Van-Benthem-Ch, p. 18]. Krister Segerberg himself admits in [24]: "*I am a supporter of formal methods in philosophy. This is not to say that I believe that all philosophy must be made with their help . [...] My own view is that formal methods are important for some parts of philosophy and indispensable for a few.*"

Krister Segerberg was always open to insights and problems coming both from philosophy and computer science. Working on the border between the fields, he built many logical systems and conceptual frameworks, which resolved many issues in the theory of action and agency, contributing both to philosophy and computer science. A characteristic feature of his works is their outstanding philosophical depth connected with perfect logical skills.

For the sake of presentation, the volume is divided into two parts. In the first part there are papers devoted to the real actions. In this part there are also papers taking into account the works of Krister Segerberg on deontic logic which he built upon a theory of real actions. The second part of the volume contains the papers on the doxastic actions. Remaining part of this introduction briefly sketches the content of the two parts. It is also intended to be a sort of roadmap to Krister Segerberg's works on actions and an incentive for many, in particular young, researchers to continue further exploration. In fact it was Krister Segerberg's wish to invite young researchers to contribute to this volume. Thus many chapters, and this introduction as well, have been written by young authors or are co-authored by young researchers. Richmond Thomason's chapter in the first part of the volume and Sven Ove Hansson's chapter in the second part of it can be seen as a much more mature and experienced continuation of this introduction.

Real Actions

Variety of approaches towards actions can be divided into two main streams. The first stream prefers to refer to actions directly and to study them as events of certain kind. In the second stream actions are out of the picture—instead of referring to actions, one studies how the states of affairs (or events) are brought about by agents, or how the agents are responsible for the states of affairs. It should be also mentioned that quite recently there have been attempts to combine the two approaches together by creating formal languages enabling at the same time to refer to actions and express agent's responsibility.

Actions as events. In the first approach towards actions actions are events. "*There is no action without a corresponding event*"—writes Krister Segerberg in [71, p. 303]. In most of the works on the philosophy of action, "action" is synonymous with "intentional action", meaning an action done with intention [4, 45] or done for a reason [13, 6], which is supposed to differentiate it from unintentional behaviour or reflex. Some philosophers researching actions, e.g., Donald Davidson, claimed that actions are events and indeed "*nothing is added to the event itself*

that makes it into an action" [14]. What distinguishes events which are actions from those which are not, is the fact that the former are caused by some pro-attitudes. However, as Davidson puts it, "*this is an addition to the description we give of the event, not to the event itself*" [14]. Therefore it is clear that despite the fact that mental attitudes are necessary for the presence of an action, they are not "part" of it. The other point of view is represented for instance by John Searle. In [46] he stated that "*the whole action consists of two components—the intention-in-action and the bodily movement*". In case of a premeditated action, an action is additionally preceded by practical reasoning.

Similar definition of action we find in [57, p. 161], where Krister Segerberg states "*To understand action both are needed, agent and world, intention and change*". The concept of change for Krister Segerberg, much like for George Henrik von Wright [99], is a transition between two states: prior and posterior ones. Theory of change, developed in von Wright's theory of facts, was formally clarified and compared to classification of verbs [1] by Krister Segerberg in [64, 65]. According to Krister Segerberg, intention is directed towards change (an event) [54, 57]. The intention which triggers an action must be operational, i.e., there is a routine [58] which an agent can run directly in order to fulfil his intention. "*To do something is to run a routine. To be able to do something is to have a routine available. To deliberate is to search for a routine.*" [58, p. 188]. The process of searching for a routine Krister Segerberg calls "deliberation walk", which is in practice a process of specification of the starting intention in order to find the one which is operational. By deliberation walk an agent ends up with the intention set consisting of the intentions linked or ordered in specific way, the last one being operational. In order to find out with which intention an action was carried out, Krister Segerberg introduces the infimum property which states that the last intention in the set is the one with which the agent's action is carried out. In [50] he states that an action triggered on the basis of operational intention cannot usually guarantee in which posterior state an agent will end up. Krister Segerberg sees the role of intention as a function which restricts all possible outcomes of the action to those which are intended. That concept of intention as a function was a source of inspiration for the authors of chapter [Herzig-Ch].

The idea of actions as events found its formal representation in many works of Krister Segerberg.[2] In [50, 51, 54, 55, 57] one can find non-dynamic logics of action. The papers [50, 54, 57] contain an interesting study of the concept of action and intention, where an action is interpreted as an intention-outcome pair. More on this subject one can find in chapter [Elgasem-Ch] of this volume, in Sect. 4, *Segerberg's formal characterisation of intentional actions*.

Another logic with actions, where action complement was interestingly analysed (by referring to the interior operation in topology), has been introduced in

---

[1] Cf. [96].

[2] Please see [63, 80, 88] for the outline of the logic of action and agency from Krister Segerberg's perspective.

[55]. In [34, p. 1203] we find a study of such operators as: "*a* is about to do *e*", "*a* has just finished doing *e*", "because of *a*'s action, *e* is just about to be realized" and "because of *a*'s action, *e* has just been realized".

Other formal systems of Krister Segerberg refer to propositional dynamic logic (PDL) created by Vaughan R. Pratt for describing and analysing computer programs (cf. [42, 43]). PDL was brought to the philosophical ground by Krister Segerberg. In 1980 he wrote about PDL: "*This paper is perhaps the first one to present it to a philosophical audience*" [49, p. 276].

Richmond Thomason describes Krister Segerberg's approach in chapter [Thomason-Ch, p.2] in the following words:

> Krister Segerberg's approach to action differs from contemporary work in the philosophy of action in seeking to begin with logical foundations. And it differs from much contemporary work in philosophical logic by drawing on dynamic logic as a source of ideas. The computational turn makes a lot of sense, for at least two reasons. First, as we noted, traditional philosophical logic doesn't seem to provide tools that are well adapted to modelling action. Theoretical computer science represents a relatively recent branch of logic, inspired by a new application area, and we can look to it for innovations that may be of philosophical value. Second, computer programs are instructions, and so are directed towards action; rather than being true or false, a computer program is executed. A logical theory of programs could well serve to provide conceptual rigour as well as new insights to the philosophy of action.

Krister Segerberg also provided an intuitive and extensive way of understanding programes as actions by referring to the concept of routine [58]. We have already quoted his motto, "*To do something is to run a routine. To be able to do something is to have a routine available. To deliberate is to search for a routine*" [58, p. 188]. Extensive and critical study of the Krister Segerberg's concept of routine is presented in chapter [Elgasem-Ch] of this volume by Dag Elgasem. The chapter introduces central elements of Krister Segerberg's account of routines and relates it to other positions in the philosophy of action. It is argued that the concept of a routine has an important role to play in the theory of action and that Krister Segerberg's own formalisation of the concept of intentional action does not meet the theoretical challenges posed by the routine concept. It is pointed out that to meet the challenges it is enough to bring the concept of a routine explicitly into the semantic framework of the logic of intentions and actions.

Krister Segerberg introduced many interesting dynamic operators and provided adequate (i.e., sound and complete) axiomatisation for PDL (cf. [47, 53][3] and many other interesting formal results in [48, 52]). Language of dynamic logic with operators "after" and "during" is defined in Backus-Naur notation as follows [49, 52]:

$$\varphi ::= p_i \mid \neg\varphi \mid \varphi \wedge \varphi \mid [\alpha]\varphi \mid [[\alpha]]\varphi \tag{1}$$

$$\alpha ::= a_i \mid \alpha^* \mid \alpha \sqcup \alpha \mid \alpha; \alpha \tag{2}$$

[3] Decidability of PDL was proved in [18]. The history of early results in PDL can be found in [20].

where p_i belongs to an infinite set of *propositional letters*, a_i belongs to a set of *action letters*, "$[\alpha]\varphi$"—after the agent's action (according to) α, φ holds; "$[[\alpha]]\varphi$"—always during every agent's action (according to) α, φ holds; "$\alpha \sqcup \beta$"—α or β (action union); "$\alpha; \beta$"—α and then β (action sequence); "α^*"—doing α some number of times (action repetition). Adequate axiomatisation can be found in [49, 53, 63] and other "after" and "during" operators in [49, 56, 80]. Krister Segerberg explains that the basic intuition behind PDL is that the world is always in some total state and its changes can be represented as the sequences of states being results of agents' or nature's actions. An important feature of PDL is that it separates a discussion of actions from a discussion of states of affairs, as presented in the following example. Sentence "Anyone who is killed dies" can be rendered in PDL-like way as "x is left dead at the end of every possible run of the *kill*$-x$ action/program", formally: $[kill{-}x]x{-}\text{is}{-}\text{dead}$ (see [49]).

In [63] Krister Segerberg also postulates that PDL must be extended by the operators expressing intentions and goals. This postulate was reflected in the works of many philosophers and researches working in (broadly understood) AI who have been directly or indirectly inspirited by Krister Segerberg (cf. e.g., [22, 25, 36, 101]).[4]

Summarising what have just been said, we shall refer to [Thomason-Ch, p. 2]:

> There are two sides to Krister Segerberg's approach to action: logical and informal. The logical side borrows ideas from dynamic logic. The informal side centres around the concept of a routine, a way of accomplishing something. Routines figure in computer science, where they are also known as procedures or subroutines, but Krister Segerberg understands them in a more everyday setting.

Agency—a logic of action without actions. Another way of dealing with actions takes its beginning in the works of Anselm of Canterbury who around the year 1100 argued that actions are best described by what an agent brings about, i.e., by action's results/outcomes (see [93]). In this approach it is not important in which way a certain result was obtained; moreover, as noticed by Krister Segerberg, this approach does not clarify what an agent really does, for "*it is a logic of action without actions*" [34, p. 1199].

This view on action was extensively studied by logicians, especially by von Wright [99] and in the scope of so called modal logic of agency. In 1969, Chellas [12] published the first system of modal logic of agency with an explicit semantics based on Kripke models. Since that time many modal logics of agency with different (intended) models have been developed by several authors. Nowadays, the most influential system of modal logic of agency is the family of STIT logics [8]. The first STIT logic was proposed in 1989 by Belnap and Perloff in [9]. As Krister Segerberg writes, "*The theory presented by Belnap and his collaborators is the culmination of a long development in modal logic*; *it surpasses all earlier efforts by its sophistication, power and comprehensiveness.*" [34, p. 1199].

[4] More on Krister Segerberg's understanding of PDL one can find [59, 66, 68, 71].

The primitive operator δ of a modal logic of agency allows to express formula "$\delta_a\varphi$" (sometimes without index a), which can be read as "the agent a brings about that φ", "the agent a sees to it that φ" or "the agent a is causally responsible for the fact that φ". Krister Segerberg treats "$\delta\varphi$" as an action which is interpreted as a set of all (finite) paths p for which there is some action/program α s.t. the following conditions are satisfied:

1. p is the computation according to some program α
2. α only terminates at total state in which it is true that φ

δ operator is often explained by referring to the concepts of choice or action-equivalent histories. In both cases the basic idea is such that $\delta_a\varphi$ is satisfied at some moment m and history h iff for all histories in the choice to which h belongs, or for all histories being action-equivalent with h, it is the case that φ. As some authors (e.g., [34, p. 1198], [89]) pointed out there is an "agency gap" in this approach, because if some fact (e.g., that the door is closed) is true for all histories in the choice to which h belongs (or for all histories being action-equivalent with h), then an agent sees to it that φ at h and m even if he did nothing to bring it about or sustain it.

Bridge between the two approaches towards actions. Krister Segerberg points out the limitations of PDL. He states that it "*lacks resources in the object language directly to express agency and ability*" [63]. Further in [80, p. 365] Krister Segerberg states explicitly that there is a need "*to combine action logic in the Scott/ Chellas/Belnap tradition with Pratts dynamic logic*". He attempted to fill this gap in [60, 62] by adding the "bringing about" operator to action terms in PDL. In [60] Krister Segerberg proposed PDL in which all action terms are of the form $\delta\varphi$. This change in PDL allows for modelling agent's abilities which was not possible in "pure" PDL. In [62], which is the improved version of [60], the two new operators test φ? and **OK**(α)—"α is safe" or "α is OK" have been added to PDL. "δ" operator is also a subject of [61, 69, 73]. This idea appeared to be very inspiring and stimulated many authors to follow this path. In this volume there are two chapters (see [Broersen-Ch, Herzig-Ch]) in which we may find attempts at marrying agency operator with PDL.

In chapter [Broersen-Ch], Jan Broersen refers to *Outline of a logic of action* by Krister Segerberg [80]. He discusses Krister Segerberg's theory of agency and action and compares it with his own view on the concepts in question. Broersen argues that dynamic logic is an inappropriate framework for understanding agency because it has not expressive power to explain the logical differences between an action a performed by agent A, an action a performed by agent B and an action a performed by agents A and B together. To meet the aforementioned challenges, Broersen proposes a theory where the dynamic logic type reasoning is simulated in a STIT framework.

In chapter [Hezig-Ch], Andreas Hezig, Tiago de Lima, Emiliano Lorini and Nicolas Troquard, similarly to Krister Segerberg, start from dynamic logic framework into which they add an operator of agency. A dynamic logic in question is of special kind. First, it lacks sequential and non-deterministic composition, iteration and test; second, its atomic programmes (interpreted as group actions) are sets of (always executable) assignments of propositional variables each of which is of the form $p \leftarrow \varphi$ where p is a propositional variable and φ is a formula. Moreover, they also embed the "situation calculus spirit" into the framework, naming the obtained logic *dynamic logic of propositional control*. The language of the logic has two kinds of dynamic operators: (standard) one expressing the opportunity of performance of an action and the new dynamic operator expressing performance of an action. The semantics of the logic has a repertoire function and a successor function that both associate sets of assignments to agents.

Deontic logic. Among the works of Krister Segerberg there are those devoted to a formal study of such concepts as obligation, permission, prohibition and omission in relation to real actions. A branch of logic concerning the concepts in question was named deontic logic.[5] Research in deontic logic can be divided into two subfields taking into account the kind of "objects" deontic qualifications apply to (cf. [91, 92]). In the first field, deontic operators apply to sentences stating that some states of affairs (sometimes understood as the results of actions, cf. e.g., [27]) are obligatory, permitted or prohibited. The second field is concerned with deontic operators applied to actions. The first approach seems to be more common (it is worth mentioning that in some handbooks, e.g., [38], only this approach is discussed). The second approach, initiated in the 1950s by G. H. von Wright [97] and J. Kalinowski [28], had been almost forgotten until 1982, when Krister Segerberg published his article *A Deontic Logic of Action* [51]. The article has triggered off many new researches on deontic action logic. Thus, Krister Segerberg's work was further extended by Trypuz and Kulicki in [91, 92], developed in deontic first-order theories (see [35, 90]) and deontic logics of action built in connection with PDL. In the latter class of systems, two approaches can be distinguished. In the first, deontic operators are introduced with the use of dynamic operators and the notion of violation or sanction (the approach initiated by J. -J. Ch. Meyer in [40] and continued in e.g., [16]); in the second, at least some of the operators are taken as primitive (see [11, 37, 39]). In the systems of the latter kind we can further distinguish those having a two-layered construction (PDL and logic for deontic operators) [37, 39] and those having a three-layered construction (Boolean algebra for actions, PDL, logic for deontic operators) [11].

In *A Deontic Logic of Action* [51] Krister Segerberg proposed two systems $\mathcal{B.O.D.}$ and $\mathcal{B.C.D.}$ and also provided two classes of models for each of them proving adequacy theorems. The language of $\mathcal{B.O.D.}$ and $\mathcal{B.C.D.}$ is the same and is defined in the following way:

$$\varphi ::= \alpha = \alpha \mid \mathbf{P}(\alpha) \mid \mathbf{F}(\alpha) \mid \neg\varphi \mid \varphi \wedge \varphi \tag{3}$$

$$\alpha ::= a_i \mid \alpha \sqcap \alpha \mid \alpha \sqcup \alpha \mid \overline{\alpha} \mid \mathbf{1} \mid \mathbf{0} \tag{4}$$

[5] State of the art in the field one can find in [1, 5, 19, 38, 41].

where α is an action from Boolean action algebra, "$\mathbf{P}(\alpha)$"—α is permitted; "$\mathbf{F}(\alpha)$"—α is forbidden. Intuitively, for an action to be permitted (forbidden) means "permitted (forbidden) in any *possible* circumstances", i.e., "in combination with any other action". This sense of permissibility was named *strong permission* (cf. [100]). Axioms for "**P**" and "**F**" ensure that they are ideals in Boolean algebra. One of the models proposed by Krister Segerberg for the systems in question is structure $\mathcal{M} = \langle \mathcal{DAF}, \mathcal{I} \rangle$, where $\mathcal{DAF} = \langle \mathcal{E}, Leg, Ill \rangle$ is a *deontic action frame* in which $\mathcal{E}$ is a *non-empty* set of possible outcomes, *Leg* and *Ill* are subsets of $\mathcal{E}$ and should be understood as sets of legal and illegal outcomes, respectively, and $\mathcal{I}$ is an interpretation function assigning to each action its extension, i.e., a set of its possible outcomes. By simply assuming that $Leg \cap Ill = \emptyset$ we obtain an adequate class of models for $\mathcal{B.O.D.}$, with the following satisfaction conditions:

$$\mathcal{M} \models \mathbf{P}(\alpha) \Longleftrightarrow \mathcal{I}(\alpha) \subseteq \mathcal{L}]\}$$
$$\mathcal{M} \models \mathbf{F}(\alpha) \Longleftrightarrow \mathcal{I}(\alpha) \subseteq Ill$$

The models adequate for $\mathcal{B.C.D.}$ must be closed (i.e., $Leg \cup Ill = \mathcal{E}$) and interpretation of each atomic action term a_i should be a subset of *Leg* or *Ill*. More about the deontic action logic of that kind we find in chapter [Castro-Ch] of this volume, where Pablo Castro and Piotr Kulicki review the history of deontic logic before Krister Segerberg and then introduce Segerberg's formalism and describe a lattice of extensions of $\mathcal{B.O.D.}$ and $\mathcal{B.C.D.}$ They also review some contemporary works in deontic logic based on boolean algebra and investigate future lines of research.

In [34, 83, 84, 86] Krister Segerberg explores other possibilities of expressing the deontic operators by means of dynamic and temporal ones. He introduces an interesting notion of understanding simple and complex norms in the semantics as a function N which for particular path h (for simple norms) or for particular path and a set of possible futures (for complex norms) selects a set of legal futures after h. By means of the function Krister Segerberg introduces the satisfaction conditions for deontic operators according to which obligatory action will be carried out in every legal future, permitted action in some legal future, forbidden actions will not be performed in any legal future, and omissible ones will not be performed in some legal futures. Homogeneity condition also guarantees that obligatory and permitted actions will be carried out in some legal futures, whereas forbidden and omissible ones are excluded in at least one legal future. In the chapter [Meyer-Ch] John-Jules Ch. Meyer reviews Krister Segerberg's proposal of dynamic deontic logic, which, as pointed out by the author, is quite expressive and able to resolve a number of classical "paradoxes" in deontic logic in an interesting way.

Deontic actions. Krister Segerberg's framework for dynamic deontic logic appeared to be expressible enough to capture deontic actions as well, i.e., "actions that change the *legal* (*normal*) *position* without changing the *real position*" [86, p. 397]. Among deontic actions Krister Segerberg listed: ordering, permitting, forbidding and making omissible a real action a. Semi-formal understanding, for instance "ordering action a", Krister Segerberg explains as follows ([86, p. 398]):

as long as *a* has not been realised, every legal future includes an occurrence of a path in *a*, and every occurrence of a path in *a* will discharge the obligation to do *a*. In chapter [Meyer-Ch] Meyer stresses that the distinction between two types of actions: "real" actions and "deontic" actions is a very interesting and important aspect of Krister Segerberg's work. The author also notices that it is important not only from philosophical point of view, but also "*from the standpoint of the design of so-called normative systems in computer science*". Meyer argues that it gives yet another meaning to the term "dynamic", because it can state properties of the change of deontic status of actions over time.

The change of normative positions (Krister Segerberg stipulates that "*norms don't change, only normative positions do*" [86, p. 399]) resembles Krister Segerberg's study of belief change being a result of doxastic actions which are the subject of the second part of the volume.

Doxastic Actions

For Krister Segerberg, doxastic actions are actions which—in contrast to real actions—do not change the environment [74], but instead change agents' beliefs (or knowledge) about the environment or other beliefs. There are many known and studied doxastic actions. They are often divided into two groups. In the first group (*postulational approach*) we find three extensively studied doxastic actions such as expansion, revision, contraction. All of them are often referred to as *belief revision*. In the second group (*constructive approach*) there are doxastic actions which are different types of *belief update*.

It is frequently repeated that a belief revision is a "belief change due to new information in an unchanging environment [...]", while belief update is a "belief change that is due to reported changes in the environment itself [...]" [30, p. 183–184]. However, it is also true that there are some authors for whom that way of putting things is not that obvious. In chapter [Lang-Ch, p. 2], Jérôme Lang, inspired by [30], argues that

> although many papers about belief update have been written, including many papers addressing its differences with belief revision, its precise scope still remains unclear. Part of the reason is that the first generation of papers on belief update contain a number of vague and ambiguous formulations

The author tries to identify the precise meaning of belief update doxastic action. In particular he looks for conditions under which update is a suitable process for belief change.

To study doxastic actions, different tools and knowledge coming from different sources are used, for example the already mentioned dynamic logic and other computer science sources (cf. [17, 44]), some works in formal linguistics, "static tradition" in doxastic logic, AGM and KGM theories. The static tradition in doxastic logic was initiated by von Wright [98] and then developed by Jaakko

Hintikka [26]. Within the scope of interest of that tradition is a formal study of static properties[6] of the operator of individual belief ($B_a\varphi$—"a believes that φ") and knowledge ($K_a\varphi$—"a knows that φ") by providing axioms characterising them in the best way. Recently, due to increasing interest in collective phenomena it was shown that the approach is expressive enough to also capture shared knowledge, distributive knowledge and common knowledge. AGM and KGM theories shall be described in more detail below.

Belief revision. In [2], Carlos E. Alchourrón, Peter Gärdenfors and David Makinson have established the so-called AGM approach to belief revision. Paradigmatic AGM-style doxastic actions are:

- expansion—adding (unqualified acquisition of) some belief to the belief set;
- revision—adding (qualified acquisition of) some belief to the belief set and ensuring the resulting theory is consistent;
- contraction—giving up belief in something.

They are represented, respectively, by the following operators:

- $+\varphi$—expanding by φ;
- $*\varphi$—revision by φ;
- $-\varphi$—contraction by φ.

The actions in question are then embedded by Krister Segerberg in his favourite dynamic logic extended by elements taken from"static" tradition in doxastic logic. As a result, Krister Segerberg obtains the atomic formulas[7] of dynamic doxastic logic (henceforward DDL) (see [30, 33, 67, 70, 72, 75, 76, 77, 78, 82, 85, 87]):

- $[+\varphi]B_a\psi$—"a believes that ψ after expansion by φ";
- $[*\varphi]B_a\psi$ —"a believes that ψ after revision by φ";
- $[-\varphi]B_a\psi$—"a believes that ψ after contraction by φ".

From static doxastic logic and AGM to DDL. In order to study the formal properties of the doxastic actions within DDL, Krister Segerberg refers to their properties expressed in AGM. AGM theory (not logic!) provided the rules according to which a set of sentences $\mathcal{B}$—possibly interpreted as a belief set of some agent a ($\mathcal{B}_a$)—changes (cf. the original work [2] or [95, Chap. 3]). We may even say that AGM provides the postulates how to rationally carry out doxastic actions. The postulates establish the meaning of the doxastic actions.

The basic formula of AGM is:

$$\varphi \in \mathcal{B}_a$$

read as "φ is in the belief set $\mathcal{B}$ of the agent a". Here is the way of expressing expansion, revision and contraction in the framework:

---

6 In the sense that a change of beliefs is not taken into account here.

7 The reader is asked to notice that all of them fall under the dynamic logic schema "$[\alpha]\varphi$".

- $\psi \in \mathcal{B}_a + \varphi$ —"ψ is in the belief set $\mathcal{B}_a$ expanded by φ"
- $\psi \in \mathcal{B}_a * \varphi$ —"ψ is in the belief set $\mathcal{B}_a$ revised by φ"
- $\psi \in \mathcal{B}_a - \varphi$ —"ψ is in the belief set $\mathcal{B}_a$ contracted by φ".

It is worth mentioning an opinion of Alexandru Baltag, Virginie Fiutek and Sonja Smets expressed in chapter [Baltag-Ch, p. 2] that AGM theory "*focuses on the way in which a given theory [...] gets revised, but it does not treat "belief revision" itself as an ingredient in the object language under study. Krister Segerberg's work opened up a new perspective by taking the very act of belief revision itself and placing it on an equal (formal) footing with the doxastic attitudes such as "knowledge" and "belief".*" Thus Krister Segerbergs' DDL, is on the one hand, a sentential counterpart of AGM and, on the other hand, "a generalization of ordinary Hintikka type doxastic logic" [79]. Krister Segerberg's dynamic framework enables to say much more than can be expressed separately in each of the systems from which it has emerged, mostly due to representing "*meta*-linguistically expressed" sentences with doxastic operator as "*object*-linguistic" sentences. In [30, p. 171] we read that "*the driving idea of DDL is that formulae such as* $[*\phi]\theta$ *are used to express doxastic actions on the same linguistic level on which also the arguments and the outcomes of these doxastic actions are expressed.*" For instance an iteration of belief operator is possible in DDL, so that one can express positive and negative introspection, respectively:

- $B_a\varphi \rightarrow B_aB_a\varphi$
- $\neg B_a\varphi \rightarrow B_a\neg B_a\varphi$

This cannot be done in AGM (see [Hansson-Ch, p. 10]). It is worth mentioning that DDL allows for formulas expressing change of belief to be arguments of (static) belief operator. For instance, the agent a believes that he believes that ψ after expansion by φ, formally: $B_a([+\varphi]B_a\psi)$ (see [Hansson-Ch, p. 10–11]). Besides expressing a theory in modal logic, DDL has the advantage of providing many interesting meta-properties and techniques "for free" , which gives "*proof- and complexity theoretic control over linguistic expressiveness.*" [30, p. 170].

Revision is known to be defined in terms of expansion and contraction in one of the ways:

$$[*\varphi]B_a\psi =_{df} [-(\neg\varphi)][+\varphi]B_a\psi \text{ (Levi revision)}$$
$$[*\varphi]B_a\psi =_{df} [+\varphi][-(\neg\varphi)]B_a\psi \text{ (Hansson revision)}$$

Krister Segerberg in [70] shows that they are equivalent on the ground of DDL.

"K" is an operator of knowledge or doxastic commitment. It is worth mentioning that Krister Segerberg has shown that it is valid for this operator that

$$K_a\varphi \equiv [*\neg\varphi]B_a\bot$$

which in practice is a way to define a knowledge by revision and belief.

It should be also mentioned that Krister Segerberg himself points out (e.g., in [79]) the works of Johan van Benthem [94] and Maarten de Rijke [15] as containing the idea of expressing a change of beliefs in modal logic. The way of studying belief change initiated by van Benthem is called dynamic epistemic logic (DEL) [7, 10]. Van Benthem in chapter [Van-Benthem] distinguishes DDL and DEL as two approaches to belief change. In his opinion the difference between them lies in the fact that Krister Segerberg's DDL "*has abstract modal operators describing transitions in abstract universes of models to describe changes in belief, and then encodes basic postulates on belief change in modal axioms that can be studied by familiar techniques*". whereas in DEL "*belief changes are modeled* [...] *as acts of changing a plausibility ordering in a current model, and the update rule for doing that is made explicit, while its properties are axiomatized completely in modal terms*". Van Benthem establishes a bridge between the two approaches by using the frame correspondence method. Comparison of expressiveness of DDL and DEL is also a subject of the chapter [Baltag-Ch].

Robert Goldblatt in chapter [Goldblatt-Ch] raises the question "When should two propositions be regarded as equivalent as adopted beliefs?" The author states that φ is doxasticlly equivalent to ψ (for some agent a) in the states s when the set of belief states entered by a from state s after revising his beliefs by φ is identical with the set of belief states entered by a from state s after revising his beliefs by ψ. In other words, two propositions are equivalent for an agent a if the revision of a's set of beliefs by each of them has exactly the same effect.

Belief update. Belief update approach was initiated by Katsuno and Mendelson [29] and Grahne [21]. Krister Segerberg calls the approach initiated by the authors "KGM approach". In the approach an agent learns about some change in the real world and adopts his beliefs accordingly. That is when "*we are informed that the real world has changed in a certain respect, we examine each of the old possible worlds and ask how our beliefs would have changed if that particular one had been the real world*" [34, p. 1186].

The basic formula of KGM approach is

$$\varphi \bigstar \psi$$

read as "if φ is a knowledge base (each knowledge base consisting of just one formula!) and ψ is a formula (intuitively, the new information) then $\varphi \bigstar \psi$ is the knowledge base that results from updating φ with ψ." KGM postulates for that update operator are listed and discussed in chapter [Lang-Ch, p. 3–4].

KGM formula

$$\varphi \bigstar \psi \to \chi$$

is expressed by Krister Segerberg (see [34, p. 1187]) in DDL as:

$$E_a\varphi \to [\bigstar\psi]B_a\chi$$

where $E_a\varphi$ is Hector Levesque's operator and stands for "the agent a believes exactly that φ (and what follows logically from φ)" or "all that the agent a believes is that φ (and what follows logically from φ). But as stated in [34, p. 1187] "*Unfortunately, Levesque's operator is not easy to axiomatise.*"

Krister Segerberg also noticed that "there is a close connection between the theory of belief change and the theory of conditionals" [34, p. 1189]. He assumes the axiom systems for David K. Lewis's logic VC and VCU of the counterfactual conditional. Then assuming the sign "$\sqsupset$" for conditionals Krister Segerberg introduces in his framework the key axiom of KGM:

$$B_a(\varphi \sqsupset \psi) \equiv [\bigstar\varphi]B_a\psi$$

being in fact a belief update version of the Ramsey test for conditionals. The following formula is also valid for conditionals and belief update:

$$B_a(\varphi \sqsupset (\psi \sqsupset \chi)) \equiv [\bigstar\varphi][\bigstar\psi]B_a\chi$$

It shows that KGM is a theory of iterated belief change and that "*given a body of systematic beliefs and an initial set of particular beliefs, in KGM all future particular beliefs are determined by reports about what happens*" [30, p. 186].

It is interesting to note that Krister Segerberg provides the following equivalence inter-linking conditionals with a real action of "bringing about" (see above):

$$\varphi \sqsupset \psi \equiv [\delta\varphi]\psi$$

Thanks to that equivalence Krister Segerberg obtains a formula:

$$B_a[\delta\varphi]\psi \equiv [\bigstar\varphi]B_a\psi$$

which according to the author gives "*a precise sense in which beliefs, conditionals, and real and doxastic actions correlate in KGM*" [30, p. 183]. We shall get back to the question of interplay between beliefs, conditionals, real and doxastic actions later on when we introduce Krister Segerberg's favourite onion/sphere model for doxastic actions.

Doxastic voluntarism. Sven Ove Hansson argues in chapter [Hansson-Ch, p. 12] that it is not obvious that a change of beliefs as studied in DDL by Krister Segerberg is voluntary or intentional (which, as we have mentioned earlier, would be required to name the change of beliefs action). He points out that the position that recognises existence of doxastic actions is usually called "doxastic (epistemic) voluntarism". Then he tries to explain what kind of doxastic voluntarism underlines Krister Segerberg's DDL. According to Hansson, a doxastic voluntarism suitable for interpreting DDL has to be:

- genetic, i.e., assuming that forming (not holding) a belief is an action-type;
- complete, i.e., assuming that all beliefs are voluntary and;
- direct, i.e., indicating that we can adopt or give up a belief by a simple act of decision making.

Hansson argues that the form of doxastic voluntarism assumed by DDL is "*apparently implausible standpoint with very few adherents*" (Hansson is particularly critical of the directness of doxastic voluntarism, see [Hansson-Ch, p. 14–16]). As a solution he proposes that "$+\varphi$", "$*\varphi$", "$-\varphi$" can be interpreted as representing external influences (not doxastic actions). For instance according to this interpretation the formula "$[*\varphi]B_a\psi$" may be understood as "after receiving the information that φ, a believes that ψ".

Some problems with belief change. We have just mentioned that DDL enables expression of introspective beliefs. In chapter [Enqvist-Olsson-Ch, p. 2], Sebastian Enqvist and Erik J. Olsson state that "*it turns out that this added expressive power comes with a price*". Referring to [32], the authors show that the postulates *Vacuity* and *Success*, adopted by Krister Segerberg in DDL, lead to some "disturbing paradoxes." The Vacuity postulate states that for φ being consistent with the agent's beliefs (formally $\neg B_a\neg\varphi$) and ψ being an element of agent's beliefs (formally: $B_a\psi$), revision by φ results in the proposition being added to the set and, at the same time, no information is lost, formally:

$$\neg B_a\neg\varphi \wedge B_a\psi \rightarrow [*\varphi]B_a\psi$$

Success of revision guarantees that after revision by φ, the proposition belongs to the agent's beliefs, formally:

$$[*\varphi]B_a\varphi$$

Enqvist and Olsson argue that the formula

$$\neg B_a\neg\varphi \wedge B_a\neg B_a\varphi \rightarrow [*\varphi](B_a\varphi \wedge B_a\neg B_a\varphi)$$

—being a consequence of the above-mentioned postulates—is paradoxical:

> To see why, toss a coin, without looking at it when it lands. Presumably, given that the coin is fair, you now have no opinion at all on whether the coin landed heads or tails. Let stand for the proposition that the coin landed heads. Since you have no opinion on whether the toss came out heads or tails, you do not believe that the coin did not land heads. That is, your current belief state satisfies the condition $\neg B\neg\alpha$. But you do not believe that the coin did land heads, and we think that you have the required powers of introspection to be aware of this fact. Thus, your current belief state also satisfies the condition $B\neg B\alpha$. But then, according to DDL, the condition $[*\alpha](B\alpha \wedge B\neg B\alpha)$ should also be true. This means that if you were to take a look at the coin and learn that it did in fact land heads, as a result you should believe that the coin landed heads, but at the same time you should believe that you do not believe it.

The authors present and criticise Krister Segerberg's own solution to the paradox, showing that there are known solutions being more natural than the one proposed by Krister Segerberg. The alternative solutions considered by the authors in the chapter are: a solution proposed by Sten Lindström and Wlodek Rabinowicz, a solution put forward by Giacomo Bonanno and a solution suggested by Johan van Benthem.

Also Alexandru Baltag, Virginie Fiutek and Sonja Smets argue in the second section of chapter [Baltag-Ch] that *Success Postulate* is very problematic in the context of iterated belief revision. Namely, they show that assuming *Success Postulate* and that "there occasionally may exist some agent who is introspective with respect to some fact p, while the fact p itself is currently neither believed nor disbelieved by the agent" we obtain contradiction.

Another problem with DDL is raised by Robert Goldblatt in chapter [Goldblatt-Ch]. The author points out that DDL containing axioms [81, 87]:

- $[*\varphi]B_a\varphi$ (success of revision);
- $\neg B\bot$ (rationality/beliefs consistency);
- $K\varphi \to B\varphi$ (believing is a necessary condition for knowing);
- $K\psi \equiv [*\varphi]K\psi$[8] (persistence of knowledge)

is inconsistent. As a solution, Goldblatt in his chapter proposes a weaker version of DDL.

Onions (*aka hypertheories*). So far nothing has been said about the intended interpretation of DDL. Krister Segerberg's favourite semantic model for belief change and counterfactuals is a frame whose essential component is a slightly modified sphere (or onion) system proposed by David Lewis in [31] and modified by Adam Grove in [23]. We shall give it more attention because it is less popular than Kripke's relational structure. The frame in question, called a revision frame, is a tuple (see [30, 34]):

$$\langle U, T, H, R\rangle.$$

U is a set of all possible states of the world (from some subjective point of view). $\langle U, T\rangle$ is a Stone (topological) space, i.e.,

- $T \in 2^U$ is closed under the formation of arbitrary unions and finite intersections (in this case we say T is a topology on U)
- $\langle U, T\rangle$ is compact:
  If $S \subseteq T$ and $U = \bigcup S$, then there is a finite subset $S' \subseteq S$ s.t. $U = \bigcup S'$
- $\langle U, T\rangle$ is totally separated:
  If $u, v \in U$ and $u \neq v$, then there is $X \subseteq U$ s.t. $X,\ U - X \in T$, $u \in X$, $v \in U - X$.

The sets $X \in T$ are called open. A subset X of U is called closed, if $U - X \in T$. A subset of U, which is at the same time open and closed is called clopen. For any $X \in U$, $\mathsf{C}X$ is called the closure of X and is the smallest closed set that includes X. It is well known that every open set in a Stone space is the union of a set of clopen sets, and hence every closed set is the intersection of a set of clopen sets. Open sets of a Stone space are referred to as *propositions* of the space, whereas closed sets are called *theories* of the space.

---

[8] Its weaker version $[*\bot]K\bot \to K\bot$ is enough, as Goldblatt noticed in his chapter.

H is a set of onions in U. An onion (a hypertheory or a fallback) O is a non-empty family of theories (closed subsets of U) of the space that satisfies two conditions:

1. it is closed under arbitrary non-empty intersection,
2. it is linearly ordered by set inclusion.

Onions describe a *doxastic state* (or *belief state*) of an agent, i.e., his doxastic dispositions "*how he would respond to a new information about the world*" [76, p. 288].

For some onion O, a proposition P is called entertainable or inaccessible in O, if $P \cap \bigcup O \neq \emptyset$. "$O \bullet P$" is a subset of O, consisting of these theories $X \in O$ for which it is true that $P \cap X \neq \emptyset$ (compactness of a Stone topological space guarantees that if P is entertainable in O, then $O \bullet P$ contains a smallest element). Onion commitment states that for all $O, O' \in H$

$$\mathsf{C}\bigcup O = \mathsf{C}\bigcup O'$$

R is a function from P to $H \times H$. It satisfies the following conditions:

(onion seriality)	For every $O \in H$, there is some $O' \in H$ s.t. $\langle O, O' \rangle \in R(P)$
(onion functionality)	if $\langle O, O' \rangle \in R(P)$ and $\langle O, O'' \rangle \in R(P)$, then $O' = O''$.
(onion revision)	For every proposition P, if $\langle O, O' \rangle \in R(P)$, then (1) either P is entertainable in O and $\bigcap O' = P \cap Z$, where Z is the smallest element of $O \bullet P$ (2) or $\bigcap O' = \emptyset$.

A revision model is a tuple

$$\langle U, P, Q, D, V \rangle$$

where $\langle U, P, Q, D \rangle$ is a revision frame and V is a valuation function from the set of formulas to the set of propositions (i.e., clopen sets). $\overline{V}$ is a standard homomorphic extension o V to Boolean formulas. For Boolean formula φ, $[\![\varphi]\!]$ is a set of $u \in U$ s.t. $u \in \overline{V}(\varphi)$.

The notion of truth of a formula in a revision model, symbolised by the symbol $\models$, is defined in relation to a pair $\langle O, u \rangle$, where O is an onion representing the belief state of the agent and $u \in U$ is the state of the environment.

- $\langle O, u \rangle \models \varphi$ iff $u \in [\![\varphi]\!]$ (for φ being a Boolean formula)
- $\langle O, u \rangle \models B_a\varphi$ iff $\bigcap O \subseteq [\![\varphi]\!]$
- $\langle O, u \rangle \models K_a\varphi$ iff $\bigcup O \subseteq [\![\varphi]\!]$
- $\langle O, u \rangle \models [*\varphi]\psi$ iff for all O', if $\langle O, O' \rangle \in R([\![\varphi]\!])$, then $\langle O', u \rangle \models \psi$

In Fig. 1 we see a belief revision by $\neg p$.

Semantics for belief update. An update frame (see [30, 34]) is a triple $\langle U, T, F \rangle$ s.t. $\langle U, T \rangle$ is a Stone space as characterised above and F is a function assigning to each element $u \in U$ and $P \in 2^U$ a selection F_u. For all propositions P, Q and $u \in U$, F satisfies the following conditions:

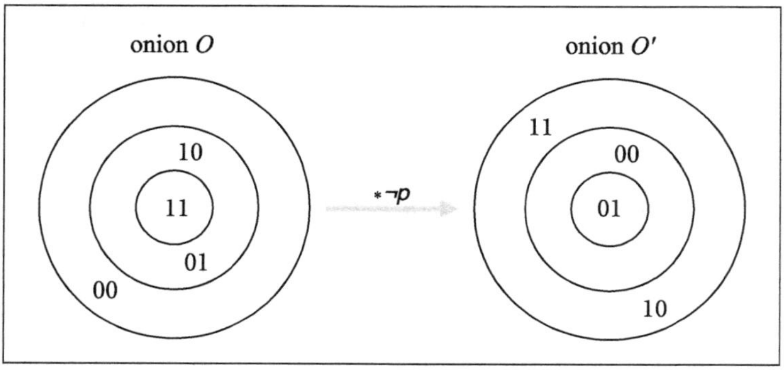

Fig. 1 We have to propositions $[\![p]\!] = P = \{11,10\}$ and $[\![q]\!] = Q = \{11,01\}$. There are also two onions $O, O' \in H$, $O = \{\{11\},\{11,10,01\},\{11,10,01,00\}\}$ and $O' = \{\{01\},\{01,00\},\{11,10,01,00\}\}$. $\langle O, O'\rangle \in R([\![\neg p]\!])$. One can check that because $O \bullet [\![\neg p]\!] = \{\{10,01\},\{10,01,00\}\}$ and the smallest element Z of $O \bullet P$ is $\{10,01\}$, then $[\![\neg p]\!] \cap Z = \{01\} = \bigcap O'$. Onion commitment is also satisfied, i.e., $\mathsf{C}\bigcup O = \mathsf{C}\bigcup O'$. Because $\bigcap O \subseteq [\![p]\!]$, $\bigcap O \subseteq [\![q]\!]$ and $\bigcap O' \subseteq [\![q]\!]$, $\langle O, 11\rangle \models B_a p$, $\langle O, 11\rangle \models B_a q$ and $\langle O', 01\rangle \models B_a q$. It it also true that $\langle O, 01\rangle \models [*\neg p]\neg p$

- $F_u(P) \subseteq P$
- if $P \subseteq Q$ and $F_u(P) \neq \emptyset$, then $F_u(Q) \neq \emptyset$
- if $P \subseteq Q$ and $P \cap F_u(Q) \neq \emptyset$, then $F_u(P) = P \cap F_u(Q)$

Understanding belief update depends on defining and understanding a selection function F. As we have mentioned earlier, it is commonly interpreted as expressing environmental change.

T is closed under the binary operations , where for all propositions P and Q

$$P \quad Q =_{df} \{u \in U : F_u(P) \subseteq Q\}$$

An update model is a tuple $\langle U, T, F, V\rangle$ s.t. $\langle U, T, F\rangle$ is an update frame and V is a valuation defined as earlier. $\overline{V}$ is extended to capture the following condition:

$$\overline{V}(\varphi \sqsupset \psi) = \{u \in U : \overline{V}(\varphi) \quad \overline{V}(\psi)\}$$

Another change considers "$[\![\varphi]\!]$". It is understood as before; however φ is allowed to be a pure conditional formula. Satisfability in the model is relative to a pair $\langle B, u\rangle$, where B is theory and $u \in U$ (so there is not reference to onions).

- $\langle B, u\rangle \models p$ iff $u \in [\![p]\!]$ (for propositional letter p)
- conditions for the Boolean operators
- $\langle B, u\rangle \models B_a\varphi$ iff $B \subseteq [\![\varphi]\!]$
- $\langle B, u\rangle \models K_a\varphi$ iff $K \subseteq [\![\varphi]\!]$, where $K = \bigcup_{v\in B}\{F_v(p) : p \text{isa proposition}\}$
- $\langle B, u\rangle \models \varphi \sqsupset \psi$ iff for all $v \in F_u([\![\varphi]\!])$, $\langle B, u\rangle \models \psi$
- $\langle B, u\rangle \models [\bigstar\varphi]\psi$ iff $\langle B', u\rangle \models \psi$, where $B' = \mathsf{C}\bigcup_{v\in B} F_v([\![\varphi]\!])$.

Now if $[\![\varphi]\!]$ is further extended to cover real actions, the interpretation of bringing about operator is the following:

$$[\![\delta\varphi]\!] = \{(u, v) : v \in F_u([\![\varphi]\!])\}$$

Then its satisfaction condition is defined as below:

- $\langle B, u\rangle \models [\delta\varphi]\psi$ iff for all $v \in U$, if $\langle u, v\rangle \in [\![\delta\varphi]\!]$, then $\langle B, v\rangle \models \psi$

Finally we can easily check that the equivalencies which we have described earlier, i.e.,

$$B_a(\varphi \sqsupset \psi) \equiv [\bigstar\varphi]B_a\psi$$
$$\varphi \sqsupset \psi \equiv [\delta\varphi]\psi$$
$$B_a[\delta\varphi]\psi \equiv [\bigstar\varphi]B_a\psi$$

are satisfied.

Revocable and irrevocable belief revision Krister Segerberg proposed irrevocable belief revision in [76]. In standard belief revision an agent can revoke belief after receiving information that contradicts it. In irrevocable belief revision there are irrevocable formulas which an agent can never unmake. Moreover it also allows for inconsistent beliefs which remain inconsistent after any revision, i.e.,:

$$B_a\bot \rightarrow [*\varphi]B_a\bot$$

is an axiom of irrevocable belief revision. In irrevocable belief revision the onion O' after revision onion O by P is either consistent or inconsistent. It is inconsistent if and only if P is inaccessible to O or O is inconsistent. If it is not inconsistent, then it is the consistent set $\{X \cap P : X \in O \text{ and } X \cap P \neq \emptyset\}$. Therefore, onion commitment condition is not satisfied. It is perhaps the main difference between revocable and irrevocable belief revisions Fig. 2.

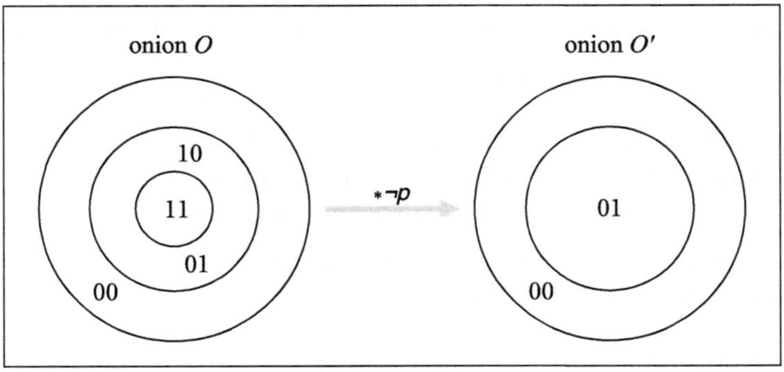

Fig. 2 In irrevocable belief revision onion commitment condition (saying that the background knowledge does not change when beliefs are revised) does not hold. It means that if revising by some proposition we go from onion/hypertheory O to O', then the closure of sum of theories in O is not necessarily identical with the closure of sum of theories in O' (compare with Fig. 1)

In chapter [Van-Ditmarsch-Ch], Hans van Ditmarsch defines revocable belief revision as belief revision for which it is valid that

$$\psi \equiv [*\varphi][*\neg\varphi]\psi$$

Irrevocable means not revocable. Van Ditmarsch provides methodology to judge whether particular belief revision is revocable or not. In order for belief revision to be revocable: (i) the agents should consider the same states possible before and after revision, (ii) states that are non-bisimilar before revision may not be bisimilar after revision (if states are non-bisimilar, they can be distinguished from one another in the logical language), and (iii) it should be possible that states that are not equally plausible before revision become equally plausible after revision. Van Ditmatsch argues that Krister Segerberg's belief revision is irrevocable. He reformulates four well-known belief revision operators (hard revision, soft revision, conservative revision, severe revision) as qualitative dynamic belief revision operators. He also points out that hard revision is Krister Segerberg's irrevocable belief revision.

* * *

In July 2011, Horacio Arló-Costa passed away. In 2010, he was very happy to accept the invitation to contribute a paper on iterated belief revision to this volume. Unfortunately, his chapter was not ready in time. We have decided against transferring his chapter to someone else.

References

1. al Hibri, A. (1978). *Deontic Logic*. Washington, DC: University of America.
2. Alchourròn, C. E., Gärdenfors, P., & Makinson, D. (1985). On the logic of theory change: Partial meet contraction and revision functions. *Journal of Symbolic Logic*, *50*, 510–530.
3. Allen, J. F., Fikes, R., & Sandewall, E. (Eds.). (1991). *Proceedings of the 2nd International Conference on Principles of Knowledge Representation and Reasoning* (*KR'91*), , April 22–25, 1991. Cambridge: Morgan Kaufmann.
4. Anscombe, E. (1957) *Intention*. Ithaca: Cornell University Press.
5. Åqvist, L. (2002). Deontic logic. In D. Gabbay & F. Guenthner (Eds.), *Handbook of Philosophical Logic* (Vol. 8, pp. 147–264). Dordrecht: Kluwer Academic Publishers.
6. Audi, R. (1986). Acting for reasons. *Philosophical Review*, *95*, 511–546.
7. Baltag, A., & Smets, S. (2008). A qualitative theory of dynamic interactive belief revision. In G. Bonanno, W. van der Hoek, & M. Woolridge (Eds.), *Texts in logic and games* (Vol. 3). Amsterdam: Amsterdam University Press.
8. Belnap, N., Perloff, M., & Xu, M. (2001). *Facing the future: Agents and choices in our indeterminist world*. Oxford: Oxford University Press.
9. Belnap, N. D., & Perloff, M. (1989). Seeing to it that: a canonical form for agentives. *Theoria*, *54*, 175–199.
10. Van Benthem, J. (2004). Dynamic logic for belief revision. *Journal of Applied Non-Classical Logics*, *14*, 1–26.

11. Castro, P. F., & Maibaum, T. S. E. (2009). Deontic action logic, atomic boolean algebra and fault-tolerance. *Journal of Applied Logic*, *7*(4), 441–466.
12. Chellas, B. F. (1969). *The logical form of imperatives*. Stanford: Perry Lane Press.
13. Davidson, D. (1991). *Essays on actions and events*. Oxford: Clarendon Press.
14. Davidson, D. (2004). Problems in explanation of actions. In *Problems of rationality*. Oxford: Oxford University Press.
15. De Rijke, M. (1994). Meeting some neighbours. Cambridge: MIT Press.
16. Dignum, F., Meyer, J.-J.Ch., & Wieringa, R. J. (1996). Free choice and contextually permitted actions. *Studia Logica*, *57*(1), 193–220.
17. Fagin, R., Halpern, J. Y., Moses, Y., & Vardi, M. Y. (2003). *Reasoning about knowledge*. Cambridge: MIT Press.
18. Fischer, M. J., & Ladner, R. E. (1979). Propositional dynamic logic of regular programs. *Journal of Computer and System Sciences*, *18*(2), 194–211.
19. Føllesdal D., & Hilpinen, R. (1971). Deontic logic: An introduction. In R. Hilpinen (Ed.) *Deontic logic*: *Introductory and systematic reading* (pp. 1–35). Dordrecht: D. Reidel.
20. Goldblatt, R. (1986). Review of initial papers on dynamic logic by Pratt, Fischer and Ladner, Segerberg, Parikh and Kozen. *Journal of Symbolic Logic*, *51*, 225–227.
21. Grahne, G. (1991). Updates and counterfactuals. In Allen et al. [3], pp. 269–276.
22. Grosz, B., & Kraus, V. (1996). Collaborative plans for complex group action. *Artificial Intelligence*, *86*(2), 269–357.
23. Grove, A. (1988). Two modellings for theory change. *Journal of Philosophical Logic*, *17*, 157–170.
24. Hendricks, V. F. & Symons, J. (Eds.). (2005). Formal philosophy, *aim*, *scope direction*. Copenhagen: Automatic Press.
25. Herzig, A., & Longin, D. (2004). C&L intention revised. In M.-A. Williams, D. Dubois, & Ch. Welty (Eds.), *Principles of knowledge representation and reasoning*. Menlo Park: AAAI Press.
26. Hintikka, J. (1962). *Knowledge and belief*: *An introduction to the logic of the two notions*. Ithaca: Cornell University Press.
27. Horty, J. F. (2001). *Agency and deontic logic*. Oxford: Oxford University Press.
28. Kalinowski, J. (1953). Theorie des propositions normatives. *Studia Logica*, *1*, 147–182.
29. Katsuno, H., & Mendelzon, A. O. (1991). On the difference between updating a knowledge base and revising it. In Allen et al. [3], pp. 387–394.
30. Leitgeb, H., & Segerberg, K. (2007). Dynamic doxastic logic: Why, how, and where to? *Synthese*, *155*(2), 167–190.
31. Lewis, D. (1973). *Counterfactuals*. Oxford: Blackwell Publishers.
32. Lindström, S., & Rabinowicz, W. (1999). DDL unlimited: Dynamic doxastic logic for introspective agents. *Erkenntnis*, *50*(2–3), 353–385.
33. Lindström, V., & Rabinowicz, V. (1997). Extending dynamic doxastic logic: Accommodating iterated beliefs and ramsey conditionals within DDL. In L. Lindahl, P. Needham, & R.Sliwinski (Eds.), *For good measure*: *Philosophical essays dedicated to Jan Odelstad on the occasion of his fiftieth birthday* (Vol. 46, pp. 126–153). Uppsala: Uppsala Philosophical Studies.
34. Lindström, S., & Segerberg, K. (2007). Modal Logic and Philosophy. In P. Blackburn & J. van Benthem (Eds.), *Handbook of Modal Logic*. Amsterdam: Elsevier.
35. Lokhorst, C. G.-J. (1996). Reasoning about actions and obligations in first-order logic. *Studia Logica*, *57*(1), 221–237.
36. Lorini, E., & Herzig, A. (2008). A logic of intention and attempt. *Synthese*, *163*(1), 45–77.
37. McCarty, L. T. (1983). Permissions and Obligations. In *Proccedings of IJCAI-83* (pp. 287–294).
38. McNamara, P. (2006). Deontic Logic. In D. M. Gabbay & J. Woods (Eds.), *Handbook of the History of Logic* (Vol. 7, pp. 197–288). North Holland: Elsevier.

39. Van Der Meyden, R. (1996). The dynamic logic of permission. *Journal of Logic and Computation, 6*, 465–479.
40. Meyer, J. J. Ch. (1988). A Different approach to deontic logic: Deontic logic viewed as a variant of dynamic logic. *Notre Dame Journal of Formal Logic, 1*, 109–136.
41. Meyer, J.-J. Ch., & Wieringa, R. J. (1993). Deontic logic: A concise overview. In *Deontic logic in computer science: Normative system specification* (pp. 3–16). Chichester: John Wiley & Sons Ltd.
42. Pratt, V. R. (1976). Semantical considerations on Floyd-Hoare logic. In *Proceedings of 17th Annual IEEE Symposium on FOCS* (pp. 109–121).
43. Pratt, V. R. (1980). Application of Modal Logic to Programming. *Studia Logica, 39*(2–3), 257–274.
44. Reiter, R. (2001). *Knowledge in action: Logical foundations for specifying and implementing dynamical systems*. Cambridge: MIT Press.
45. Searle,J. R. (1983). *Intentionality: An essay in the philosophy of mind*. Cambridge: Cambridge University Press.
46. Searle, J. R. (2001). *Rationality in action*. Cambridge: MIT Press.
47. Segerberg, K. (1977). A completeness theorem in the modal logic of programs. *Notices of American Mathematical Society, 24*, A–552.
48. Segerberg, K. (1978). A conjecture in dynamic logic. In *Min-essays in honor of Juhani Pietarinen* (pp. 23–26). Abo.
49. Segerberg, K. (1980). Applying modal logic. *Studia Logica, 39*(2–3), 275–295.
50. Segerberg, K. (1981). Action-games. *Acta Philosophica Fennica, 32*, 220–231.
51. Segerberg, K. (1982). A Deontic Logic of Action. *Studia Logica, 41*(2–3), 269–282.
52. Segerberg, K. (1982). "After" and "during" in dynamic logic. In I. Niiniluoto & E. Saarinen (Eds.), *Intensional logic: Theory and applications, acta philosophica fennica* (Vol. 35, pp. 203–228). Helsinki: Philosophical Society of Finland.
53. Segerberg, K. (1982). A completeness theorem in the modal logic of programs. In T. Traczyk (Ed.), *Universal algebra and applications. Papers presented at the seminar held at the Stefan Banach International Mathematical Center 1978, Banach Center Publications* (Vol. 9, pp. 31–46). Warsaw: PWN.
54. Segerberg, K. (1982). The Logic of deliberate action. *Journal of Philosophical Logic, 11*(2), 233–254.
55. Segerberg, K. (1984). A topological logic of action. *Studia Logica, 43*(4), 415–419.
56. Segerberg, K. (1984). Towards an exact philosophy of action. *Topoi, 3*(1), 75–83.
57. Segerberg, K. (1985). Models for action. In B. K. Matilal & J. L. Shaw (Eds.), *Analytical philosophy in comparative perspective* (pp. 161–171). Reidel: Dordrecht.
58. Segerberg, K. (1985). Routines. *Synthese, 65*(2), 185–210.
59. Segerberg, K. (1988). Action in dynamic logic (abstract). *Journal of Symbolic Logic, 53*, 1285–1286.
60. Segerberg, K. (1989). Bringing it about. *Journal of Philosophical Logic, 18*(4), 327–347.
61. Segerberg, K. (1990). Validity and satisfaction in imperative logic. *Notre Dame Journal of Formal Logic, 31*(2), 203–221.
62. Segerberg, K. (1992). Action incompleteness. *Studia Logica, 51*(3/4), 533–550.
63. Segerberg, K. (1992). Getting started: Beginnings in the logic of action. *Studia Logica, 51*(3/4), 347–378.
64. Segerberg, K. (1992). Representing facts. In C. Bicchieri & M. L. D. Chiara (Eds.), *Knowledge, belief, and strategic interaction*. Cambridge: University Press.
65. Segerberg, K. (1994). A festival of facts. *Logic and logical philosophy, 2*, 7–22.
66. Segerberg, K. (1995). Accepting failure in dynamic logic. In D. Prawitz, B. Skyrms, & D. Westerstahl (Eds.), *Logic, Methodology and Philosophy of Science IX, Proceedings of the Ninth International Congress of Logic, Studies in Logic and the Foundations of Mathematics* (Vol. 134, pp. 327–349). Amsterdam: Elsevier.

67. Segerberg, K. (1995). Belief revision from the point of view of doxastic logic. *Logic Journal of the IGPL*, *3*(4), 535–553.
68. Segerberg, K. (1995). Conditional action. In G. Crocco, L. Fariñas, & A. Herzig (Eds.), *Conditionals*: *From philosophy to computer science*, *Studies in logic and computation* (Vol. 5, pp. 241–265). Oxford: Clarendon Press.
69. Segerberg, K. (1996). The delta operator at three levels of analysis. In A. Fuhrmann & H. Rott (Eds.), *Logic, action, and information*: *Essays on logic in philosophy and artificial intelligence* (pp. 63–78). Berlin, New York: Walter de Gruyter.
70. Segerberg, K. (1996). Three recipes for revision. *Theoria*, *62*, 62–73.
71. Segerberg, K. (1996). To do and not to do. In B. J. Copeland (Ed.), *Logic and reality*: *Essays on the legacy of Arthur Prior* (pp. 301–313). Oxford: Clarendon Press.
72. Segerberg, K. (1997). A doxastic walk with darwiche and pearl. *Nordic Journal of Philosophical Logic*, *2*(1), 63–66.
73. Segerberg, K. (1997). Delta logic and brown's logic of ability. In E. Ejerhed & S. Lindström (Eds.), *Logic, action and cognition* (pp. 29–45). Dordrecht: Kluwer.
74. Segerberg, K. (1997). Proposal for a theory of belief revision along the lines of Lindström and Rabinowicz. *Fundamenta Informaticae*, *32*(2), 183–191.
75. Segerberg, K. (1988). Belief revision and doxastic commitment. *Bulletin of the Section of Logic*, *27*(1–2), 43–45.
76. Segerberg, K. (1998). Irrevocable belief revision in dynamic doxastic logic. *Notre Dame Journal of Formal Logic*, *39*(3), 287–306.
77. Segerberg, K. (1998). On the reversibility of doxastic actions. In A. S. Karpenko (Eds.), *Logical investigations. No.5. Proceedings from the section "Symbolic logic" of the 1st International conference "Smirnov Readings", Moscow, Russia, March 1997* (pp. 135–138). Moskva: Nauka.
78. Segerberg, K. (1999). Default logic as dynamic doxastic logic. *Erkenntnis*, *50*(2–3), 333–352.
79. Segerberg, K. (1999). Two traditions in the logic of belief: Bringing them together. In H. J. Ohlbach & U. Reyle (Eds.), *Logic, language and reasoning* (pp. 135–147). Dordrecht: Kluwer Academic Publishers.
80. Segerberg, K. (2000). Outline of a logic of action. In *Advances in Modal Logic* (pp. 365–387).
81. Segerberg, K. (2001). The basic dynamic doxastic logic of AGM. In M.-A. Williams & H. Rott (Eds.), *Frontiers in belief revision* (pp. 57–84). Dordrecht: Kluwer.
82. Segerberg, K. (2006). Moore problems in full dynamic doxastic logic. *Poznan Studies in the Philosophy of the Sciences and the Humanities*, *91*(1), 95–110.
83. Segerberg, K. (2006). Trying to meet Ross's challenge. In E. Ballo & M. Franchella (Eds.), *Logic and philosophy in Italy*: *Some trends and perspectives. Essays in Honor of Corrado Mangione on his 75th Birthday* (pp. 155–166). Monza: Polimetrica International Scientific Publisher.
84. Segerberg, K. (2007). A blueprint for deontic logic in three (not necessarily easy) steps. In G. Bonanno, J. P. Delgrande, J. Lang, & H. Rott (Eds.), *Formal models of belief change in rational agents, Dagstuhl Seminar Proceedings*. (vol. 07351) Internationales Begegnungs- und Forschungszentrum fuer Informatik (IBFI), Schloss Dagstuhl, Germany.
85. Segerberg, K. (2007). Iterated belief revision in dynamic doxastic logic. In A. Gupta, R. Parikh, & J. van Benthem (Eds.), *Logic at the crossroads*: *An interdisciplinary view*. New Delhi: Allied Publishers Pvt. Ltd.
86. Segerberg, K. (2009). Blueprint for a dynamic deontic logic. *Journal of Applied Logic*, *7*(4), 388–402 Amsterdam: Elsevier.
87. Segerberg, K. (2010). Some completeness theorems in the dynamic doxastic logic of iterated belief revision. *Review of Symbolic Logic*, *3*(2), 228–246.
88. Segerberg, K., Meyer, J.-J., & Kracht, M. (2009). The logic of action. In E. N. Zalta (Ed.), *The Stanford Encyclopedia of Philosophy*. Summer 2009 edition.

89. Trypuz, R. (2007). *Formal ontology of action: A unifying approach*. PhD thesis, Università degli Studi di Trento, ICT International Doctorate School.
90. Trypuz, R. (2011). Simple theory of norm and action. In A. Brożek, J. Jadacki, & B. Žarnić (Eds.), *Theory of imperatives from different points of view*, Logic, Methodology and Philosophy of Science at Warsaw University (Vol. 6, pp. 120–136). Warsaw: Wydawnictwo Naukowe Semper.
91. Trypuz, R., & Kulicki, P. (2009). A systematics of deontic action logics based on boolean algebra. *Logic and Logical Philosophy, 18*(3–4), 253–270.
92. Trypuz, R., & Kulicki, P. (2010). Towards metalogical systematisation of deontic action logics based on Boolean algebra. In G. Governatori and G. Sartor (Eds.), *Deontic Logic in Computer Science (DEON 2010)* (pp. 132–147).
93. Uckelman, S. L. (2007). Anselm's logic of agency. ILLC Publications PP-2007-31, University of Amsterdam.
94. van Benthem, J. (1991). Logic and the flow of information. Technical report, University of Amerstam.
95. van Ditmarsch, H., van der Hoek, W., & Kooi, B. (2007). *Dynamic epistemic logic*, Synthese library series (Vol. 337). Berlin: Springer.
96. Vendler,Z. (1957). Verbs and times. *Philosophical Review, 46*, 143–160.
97. von Wright, G. H. (1951). Deontic logic. *Mind*, LX(237), 1–15.
98. von Wright, G. H. (1951). *An essay in modal logic*. Amsterdam: North Holland.
99. von Wright, G. H. (1963). *Norm and Action*. New York: The Humanities Press.
100. von Wright, G. H. (1968). *An essay in deontic logic and the general theory of action*. Amsterdam, North Holland.
101. Wooldridge, M. (2000). *Reasoning about rational agents*. Cambridge: MIT Press.

Part I

Krister Segerberg's Philosophy of Action

Richmond H. Thomason

Abstract In his logic of action, Krister Segerberg has provided many insights about how to formalize actions. In this chapter I consider these insights critically, concluding that any formalization of action needs to be thoroughly connected to the relevant reasoning, and in particular to temporal reasoning and planning in realistic contexts. This consideration reveals that Segerberg's ideas are limited in several fundamental ways. To a large extent, these limitations have been overcome by research that has been carried out for many years in Artificial Intelligence.

1 Introduction

The philosophy of action is an active area of philosophy, in its modern form largely inspired by [1]. It considers issues such as (1) The ontology of agents, agency, and actions, (2) the difference (if any) between actions and bodily movements, (3) whether there are such things as basic actions, (4) the nature of intention, and (5) whether intentions are causes. Many of these issues have antecedents in earlier philosophical work, and for the most part the recent literature treats them using traditional philosophical methods.

These questions have been pretty thoroughly thrashed out over the last fifty years. Whether or not the discussion has reached a point of diminishing returns, it might be helpful at this point to have a source of new ideas. It would be especially useful to have an independent theory of actions that informs and structures the issues in much the same way that logical theories based on possible worlds have influenced philosophical work in metaphysics and philosophy of language. In other words, it might be useful to have a logic of action.

R. H. Thomason (✉)
University of Michigan, Ann Arbor, MI, USA
e-mail: rthomaso@umich.edu

R. Trypuz (ed.), *Krister Segerberg on Logic of Actions*,
Outstanding Contributions to Logic 1, DOI: 10.1007/978-94-007-7046-1_1,

But where to find it? A logic of action is not readily available, for instance, in the logical toolkit of possible worlds semantics. Although sentences expressing the performance of actions, like *Sam crossed the street*, correspond to propositions and can be modeled as sets of possible worlds, and verb phrases like *cook a turkey* can be modeled as functions from individuals to propositions, this does not take us very far. Even if it provides a compositional semantics for a language capable of talking about actions, it doesn't distinguish between *Sam crossed the street* and *Judy is intelligent*, or between *cook a turkey* and *ought to go home*. As far as possible worlds semantics goes, both sentences correspond to propositions, and both verb phrases to functions from individuals to propositions. But only one of the sentences involves an action and only one of the verb phrases expresses an action.

Krister Segerberg's approach to action differs from contemporary work in the philosophy of action in seeking to begin with logical foundations. And it differs from much contemporary work in philosophical logic by drawing on dynamic logic as a source of ideas.[1] The computational turn makes a lot of sense, for at least two reasons. First, as we noted, traditional philosophical logic doesn't seem to provide tools that are well adapted to modeling action. Theoretical computer science represents a relatively recent branch of logic, inspired by a new application area, and we can look to it for innovations that may be of philosophical value. Second, computer programs are instructions, and so are directed towards action; rather than being true or false, a computer program is *executed.* A logical theory of programs could well serve to provide conceptual rigor as well as new insights to the philosophy of action.

2 Ingredients of Segerberg's Approach

There are two sides to Segerberg's approach to action: logical and informal. The logical side borrows ideas from dynamic logic.[2] The informal side centers around the concept of a *routine*, a way of accomplishing something. Routines figure in computer science, where they are also known as *procedures* or *subroutines*, but Segerberg understands them in a more everyday setting; in [23], he illustrates them with culinary examples, in [17] with the options available to his washing machine. Cookbook recipes are routines, as are techniques for processing food. Just as computer routines can be strung together to make complex programs, everyday routines can be combined to make complex plans.

It is natural to invoke routines in characterizing other concepts that are important in practical reasoning: consider *agency*, *ends*, *intentions*, and *ability*, Agency is the capacity to perform routines. Ends are desired ways for the future to be—propositions about the future—that can be realized by the performance of a routine. An agent may choose to perform a routine in order to achieve an end; such a determination

---

[1] Segerberg's work on action is presented in articles dating from around 1980. See the articles by Segerberg cited in the bibliography of this chapter.

[2] See [9].

constitutes an intention. When circumstances allow the execution of a routine by an agent, the agent is able to perform the routine. These connections drive home the theoretical centrality of routines.

Dynamic logic provides a logical theory of program executions, using this to interpret programming languages. It delivers methods of intepreting languages with complex imperative constructions as well as models of routines, and so is a very natural place to look for ideas that might be useful in theorizing about action.

3 Computation and Action

To evaluate the potentiality of adapting dynamic logic to this broader application, it's useful to begin with the computational setting that motivated the logic in the first place.

3.1 The Logic of Computation

Digital computers can be mathematically modeled as Turing machines. These machines manipulate the symbols on an infinite tape. We can assume that there are only two symbols on a tape, '0' and '1', and we insist that at each stage of a computation, the tape displays only a finite number of '1's. The machine can change the tape, but these changes are local, and in fact can only occur at a single position of the tape. (This position can be moved as the program is executed, allowing the machine to scan its tape in a series of sequential operations.)

Associated with each Turing machine is a finite set of "internal states:" you can think of these as dispositions to behave in certain ways. Instructions in primitive "Turing machine language" prescribe simple operations, conditional on the symbol that is currently read and the internal state. Each instruction tells the machine which internal state to assume, and whether (1) to move the designated read-write position to the right, (2) to move it to the left, or (3) to rewrite the current symbol, without moving left or right.

This model provides a clear picture of the computing agent's computational states: such a state is determined by three things: (1) the internal state, (2) the symbols written on the tape, and (3) the read-write position. If we wish to generalize this picture, we could allow the machine to flip a coin at each step and to consult the result of the coin flip in deciding what to do. In this nondeterministic case, the outcome of a step would in general depend on the observed result of the randomizing device.

In any case—although the Turing machine model can be applied to the performance of physically realized computers—Turing machine states are not the same as the physical states of working computer. For one thing, the memory of every realized computer is bounded. For another, a working computer can fail for physical reasons.

Fig. 1 A simple program

$x := 1;$
$y := 0 \mid y := 1$

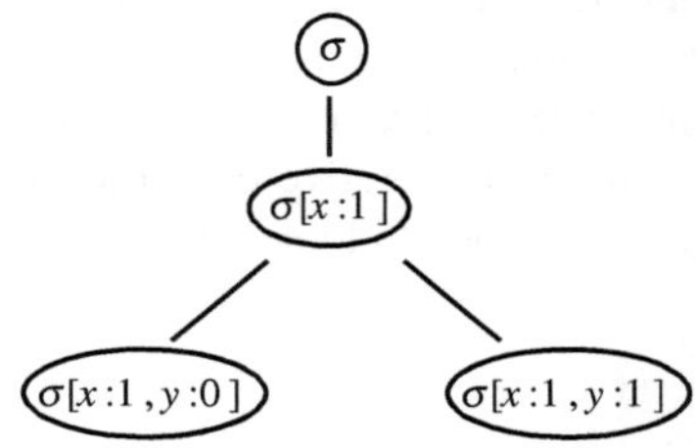

Fig. 2 A computation tree

A Turing machine computation will traverse a series of states, producing a path beginning with the initial state and continuing: either infinitely, in case the computation doesn't halt, or to a final halting state. For deterministic machines, the computation is linear. Nondeterministic computations may branch, and can be represented by trees rooted in the initial state.

In dynamic models, computation trees are used to model programs. For instance, consider the program consisting of the two lines in Fig. 1.[3]

The first instruction binds the variable x to 1. The second nondeterministically binds y either to 0 or to 1. Let the initial state be σ, and let $\tau[x : n]$ be the result of changing the value of x in τ to n. Then the program is represented by the computation tree shown in Fig. 2.

3.2 Agents, Routines, and Actions

Transferring this model of programs from a computational setting to the broader arena of humanlike agents and their actions, Segerberg's idea is to use such trees to model routines, as executed by deliberating agents acting in the world. The states that figure in the "execution trees" will now be *global states*, consisting not only of the cognitive state of the agent, but also of relevant parts of the environment in which the routine is performed. And rather than computation trees, Segerberg uses a slightly more general representation: sets of sequences of states.[4] (See [21], p. 77.)

For Segerberg, routines are closely connected to actions: in acting, an agent executes a chosen routine. Some of Segerberg's works discuss actions with this background in mind but without explicitly modeling them. The works that provide explicit models of action differ, although the variations reflect differences in the theoretical

[3] Now we are working with Turing machines that run pseudocode, and whose states consist of assignments of values to an infinite set of variables. This assumption is legitimate, and loses no generality.

[4] Corresponding to any state-tree, there is the set of its branches. Conversely, however, not every set of sequences can be pieced together into a tree.

context and purposes, and aren't important for our purposes. Here, I'll concentrate on the account in [31].

If a routine is nondeterministic, the outcome when it is executed will depend on other concurrent events, and perhaps on chance as well. But—since the paths in a set S representing a routine include *all* the transitions that are compatible with running the routine—the outcome, whatever it is, must be a member of S. Therefore, a realized action would consist of a pair $\langle S, p\rangle$ where S is a routine, i.e. a set of state-paths, and $p \in S$. In settings where there is more than one agent, we also need to designate the agent. This leads us to the idea of ([31], p. 176), where an *individual action* is defined as a triple $\langle i, S, p\rangle$, where i is an agent, S is a set of state-paths, and $p \in S$. I'll confine myself in what follows to the single-agent case, identifying a realized action with a pair $\langle S, p\rangle$.

Consider one of Segerberg's favorite example of an action—someone throws a dart and hits the bullseye. An ordinary darts player does this by executing his current, learned routine for aiming and throwing a dart. When the action is executed, chance and nature combine with the routine to determine the outcome. Thus, execution of the same routine—which could be called "trying to hit the bullseye with dart *d*"—might or might not constitute a realized action of hitting the bullseye.

This idea has ontological advantages. It certainly tells us everything that can be said about what would happen if a routine is run. It clarifies in a useful way the distinction between trying to achieve an outcome and achieving it. It can be helpful in thinking about certain philosophical questions—for instance, questions about how actions are individuated. (More about this below, in Sect. 9.) And it makes available the theoretical apparatus of dynamic logic. But it is not entirely unproblematic, and I don't think that Segerberg has provided a solution to the problem of modeling action that is entirely definitive. I will mention three considerations.

Epistemology. The idea has problems on the epistemological side; it is not so clear how an agent can learn or compute routines, if routines are constituted by global states. Whether my hall light will turn on, for instance, when I flip the switch will depend (among other things) on details concerning the power supply, the switch, the wiring to the bulb, and the bulb itself. Causal laws involving electronics. and initial conditions concerning the house wiring, among other things, will determine what paths belong to the routine for turning on the light.

While I may need causal knowledge of some of these things to diagnose the problem if something goes wrong when I flip the switch, knowing how to do something and how to recover from a failure are different things. I don't have to know about circuit breakers, for instance, in order to know how to turn on the light.

Perhaps such epistemological problems are similar to those to which possible worlds models in general fall prey, and are not peculiar to Segerberg's theory of action.

Fit to common sense. Our intuitions about what counts as an action arise in common sense and are, to some extent, encoded in how we talk about actions. And it seems that we don't think and talk about *inadvertance* in the way that Segerberg's theory would lead us to expect. Suppose, for instance, that in the course of executing a routine for getting off a bus I step on a woman's foot. In cases like this, common sense tells us that I stepped on her foot. I have done something here that I'm responsible for, and that at the very least I should apologize for. If I need to excuse the action, I'd say that I didn't mean to do it, not that I didn't do it. But Segerberg's account doesn't fit this sort of action; I have not in any sense executed a routine for stepping on the woman's foot.[5]

Logical flexibility and simplicity. A contemporary logic of action, to be at all successful, must go beyond illuminating selected philosophical examples. Logics of action are used nowadays to formalize realistic planning domains, to provide knowledge representation support for automated planning systems.

Formalizing these domains requires an axiomatization of what Segerberg called the *change function*, which tells us what to expect when an action is performed. In general, these axiomatizations require quantifying over actions. See, for instance, [3, 14, 34]. Most of the existing formalisms treat actions as individuals. Segerberg's languages don't provide for quantification over actions, and his reification of actions suggests a second-order formalization.

As far as I can see, a second-order logic of actions is not ruled out by the practical constraints imposed by knowledge representation, but it might well be more difficult to work with than a first-order logic. In any case, first-order theories of action have been worked out in detail and used successfully for knowledge representation purposes. Second-order theories haven't.

For philosophical and linguistic purposes, I myself would prefer to think of actions, and other eventualities, as individuals. Attributes can then be associated with actions as needed. In a language (for instance, a high-level control language for robot effectors) that accommodates motor routines, nothing would prevent us from explicitly associating such routines with certain actions. But for many planning purposes, this doesn't turn out to be important. We remain more flexible if we don't insist on reifying actions as routines.

3.3 From Computation to Agency

Segerberg's approach is problematic in more foundational respects. The assumption that computational states can be generalized to causally embedded agents who must execute their routines in the natural world is controversial, and needs to be examined critically.

It is not as if the thesis that humans undergo cognitive states can be disproved; the question is whether the separation of cognitive from physical states is appropriate or useful in accounting for action. This specific problem in logical modeling, by the way, is related to the much broader and more vague mind-body problem in philosophy.

In (nondeterministic) Turing machines, an exogenous variable—the "oracle"—represents the environment. This variable could in principle dominate the compu-

[5] Further examples along these lines, and a classification of the cases, can be found in [2]. I believe that an adequate theory of action must do justice to Austin's distinctions.

tation, but in cases where dynamic logic is at all useful, its role has to be severely limited. Dynamic logic is primarily used for *program verification*, providing a method of proving that a program will not lead to undesirable results.[6] For this to be possible, the execution of the program has to be reasonably predictable. This is why software designed to interact strongly with an unpredictable environment has to be tested empirically. Dynamic logic is useful because many programs are designed either not to interact at all with the environment or to interact with it in very limited and predictable ways. For this reason, program verification is not very helpful in robotics, and we have to wonder whether the sorts of models associated with dynamic logic will be appropriate.

Humans (and robots), are causally entangled in their environments, interacting with them through a chain of subsystems which, at the motor and sensory interfaces, is thoroughly intertwined. When I am carving a piece of wood, it may be most useful to regard the hand (including its motor control), the knife, and the wood as a single system, and difficult to do useful causal modeling with any of its subsystems. In such cases, the notion of a cognitive state may not be helpful. Indeed, global states in these cases—whether they are cognitive, physical, or combinations of the two—will be too complex to be workable in dealing even with relatively simple realistic applications.

Take Segerberg's darts example, for instance. Finding a plausible level of analysis of the agent at which there is a series of states corresponding to the routine of trying to hit the bullseye is problematic. Perhaps each time I throw a dart I think to myself "I am trying to hit the bullseye," but the part of the activity that I can put in words is negligible. I let my body take over.

Doubtless, each time I throw a dart there are measurable differences in the pressure of my fingers, the angle of rotation of my arm, and many other properties of the physical system that is manipulating the dart. Almost certainly, these correspond to differences in the neural motor systems that control these movements. At some level, I may be going through the same cognitive operations, but few of these are conscious and it is futile to describe them. To say that there is a routine here, in the sense that Segerberg intends, is a matter of faith, and postulating a routine may be of little value in accounting for the human enterprise of dart-throwing.[7] The idea might be more helpful in the case of an expert piano player and a well-rehearsed phrase from a sonata, because the instrument is, at least in part, discrete. It is undoubtedly helpful in the case of a chess master and a standard chess opening.

Of course, human-like agents often find offline, reflective planning to be indispensable. Imagine, for instance, preparing for a trip. Without advance planning, the experience is likely to be a disaster. It is still uncertain how useful reflective planning will prove to be in robotics, but a significant part of the robotics community firmly believes in *cognitive robotics*; see [8, 14].

Reflective planning is possible in the travel example because at an appropriate level of abstraction many features of a contemplated trip are predictable and the number of

---

[6] See, for instance, [7].

[7] Such routines might be helpful in designing a robot that could learn to throw darts, but issues like this are controversial in robotics itself. See [6] and other references on "situated robotics."

relevant variables is manageable. For instance, a traveler can be reasonably confident that if she shows up on time at an airport with a ticket and appropriate identification, then she will get to her destination. The states in such plans will represent selected aspects of stages of the contemplated trip (such as location, items of luggage, hotel and travel reservations). It is in these opportunistic, *ad hoc*, scaled-down planning domains that the notion of a state can be useful, and here the sort of models that are found in dynamic logic make good sense.

But the example of planning a trip illustrates an important difference between the states that are important in practical deliberation and the states that are typically used in dynamic logic. In dynamic logic, execution is computation. The model in view is that of a Turing machine with no or very limited interaction with an exogenous environment, and the programs that one wants to verify will stick, for the most part, to information processing. In this case, executions can be viewed as successions of cognitive states. In planning applications, however, the agent is hypothetically manipulating the external environment. Therefore, states are stages of the external world, including the initial state and ones that can be reached from it by performing a series of actions. I want to emphasize again that these states will be created ad hoc for specific planning purposes and typically will involve only a small number of variables.

With the changes in the notion of a state that are imposed by these considerations, I believe that Segerberg's ideas have great value in clarifying issues in practical reasoning. As I will indicate later, when the ideas are framed in this way, they are very similar to themes that have been independently developed by Artificial Intelligence researchers concerned with planning and rational agency.

Segerberg's approach illuminates at least one area that is left obscure by the usual formalizations of deliberation found in AI. It provides a way of thinking about attempting to achieve a goal. For Segerberg, attempts—cases where an agent runs a routine which aims at achieving a goal—are the basic performances. The theories usually adopted in AI take successful performances as basic and try to build conditions for success into the causal axioms for actions. These methods support reasoning about the performance of actions, but not reasoning about the performance of attempts, and so they don't provide very natural ways to formalize the diagnosis of failed attempts. (However, see [11].)

3.4 Psychological Considerations

Routines have a psychological dimension, and it isn't surprising that they are important, under various guises, in cognitive psychology. It is well known, for instance, that massive knowledge of routines, and of the conditions for exploiting them, characterizes human expertise across a wide range of domains. See, for instance, the discussion of chess expertise in [35].

And routines are central components of cognitive architectures—systematic, principled simulations of general human intelligence. In the SOAR architecture,[8] for instance, where they are known as *productions* or *chunks*, they are the fundamental mechanism of cognition. They are the units that are learned and remembered, and cognition consists of their activation in working memory.

Of course, as realized in a cognitive architecture like SOAR, routines are not modeled as transformations on states, but are symbolic structures that are remembered and activated by the thinking agent. That is, they are more like programs than like dynamic models of programs.

This suggests a solution to the epistemological problems alluded to above, in Sect. 3.2. Humans don't learn or remember routines directly, but learn and remember representations of them.

4 Deliberation

Logic is supposed to have something to do with reasoning, and hopefully a logic of action would illuminate practical reasoning. In [23], Segerberg turns to this topic. This is one of the very few places in the literature concerning action and practical reasoning where a philosopher actually examines a multiple-step example of practical reasoning, with attention to the reasoning that is involved. That he does so is very much to Segerberg's credit, and to the credit of the tradition, due to von Wright, in which he works.

Segerberg's example is inspired by Aristotle. He imagines an ancient Greek doctor deliberating about a patient. The reasoning goes like this.

1. My goal is to make this patient healthy.
2. The only way to do that is to balance his humors.
3. There are only two ways to balance the patient's humors: (1) to warm him, and (2) to administer a potion.
4. I can think of only two ways to warm the patient: (1.1) a hot bath, and (1.2) rubbing.

The example is a specimen of means-end reasoning, leading from a top-level goal (Step 1), through an examination of means to an eventual intention. (This last step is not explicit in the reasoning presented here.) For Segerberg, goals are propositions; the overall aim of the planning exercise in this example is a state of the environment in which the proposition *This patient is healthy* is true.

This reasoning consists of iterated *subgoaling*—of provisionally adopting goals, which, if achieved, will realize higher-level goals. A reasoning path terminates either when the agent has an immediate routine to realize the current goal, or can think of

---

[8] See [13].

no such routine.[9] As alternative subgoals branch from the top-level goal, a tree is formed. The paths of the tree terminating in subgoals that the agent can achieve with a known routine provide the alternative candidates for practical adoption by the agent. To arrive at an intention, the agent will need to have preferences over these alternatives.

According to this model of deliberation, an agent is equipped at the outset with a fixed set of routines, along with an achievement relation between routines and propositions, and with knowledge of a realization relation between propositions. Deliberation towards a goal proposition $\mathbf{p}_0$ produces a set of sequences of the form $\mathbf{p}_0, \ldots, \mathbf{p}_n$, such that $\mathbf{p}_{i+1}$ realizes $\mathbf{p}_i$ for all i, $0 \leq i < n$, and the agent has a routine that achieves $\mathbf{p}_n$.

This model doesn't seem to fit many planning problems. The difficulty is that agents often are faced with practical problems calling for routines, and deliberate in order to solve these problems. We can't assume, then, that the routines available to an agent remain fixed through the course of a deliberation. This leads to my first critical point about Segerberg's model of practical reasoning.

4.1 The Need to Plan Routines

The difficulty can be illustrated with simple blocks-world planning problems of the sort that are often used to motivate AI theories of planning. In the blocks-world domain, states consist of configurations of a finite set of blocks, arranged in stacks on a table. A block is *clear* in state s if there is no block on it in s. Associated with this domain are certain *primitive actions*.[10] If b is a block then $\textsc{Table}(b)$ is a primitive action, and if b_1 and b_2 are blocks then $\textsc{PutOn}(b_1, b_2)$ is a primitive action. $\textsc{Table}(b)$ can be performed in a state s if and only if b is clear in s, and results in a state in which b is on the table, i.e., a state in which $OnTable(b)$ is true. $\textsc{PutOn}(b_1, b_2)$ can be performed in a state s if and only if $b_1 \neq b_2$ and both b_1 and b_2 are clear in s, and results in a state in which b_1 is on b_2, i.e., a state in which $On(b_1, b_2)$ is true.[11]

Crucially, a solution to the planning problem in this domain has to deliver a *sequence* of actions, and (unless the agent has a ready-made multi-step routine to

9 There are problems with such a termination rule in cases where the agent can exercise knowledge acquisition routines—routines that can expand the routines available to the agent. But this problem is secondary, and we need not worry about it.

10 In more complex cases, and to do justice to the way humans often plan, we might want to associate various levels of abstraction with a domain, and allow the primitive actions at higher levels of abstraction to be decomposed into complex lower-level actions. This idea has been explored in the AI literature; see, for instance, [15, 37]. One way to look at what Segerberg seems to be doing is this: he is confining means-end reasoning to realization and ignoring causality. He discusses cases in which the reasoning moves from more abstract goals to more concrete goals that realize them. But he ignores cases where, at the same level of abstraction, the reasoning moves from a temporal goal to an action that will bring the goal about if performed.

11 In this section, we use *italics* for predicates and SMALLCAPS for actions.

achieve its blocks-world goal) it will be necessary to deal with temporal sequences of actions in the course of deliberation. Segerberg's model doesn't provide for this. According to that model, routines might involve sequences of actions, but deliberation assumes a fixed repertoire of known routines; it doesn't create new routines. And the realization relation between propositions is not explicitly temporal.

Of course, an intelligent blocks-world agent might well know a large number of complex routines. For any given blocks-world problem, we can imagine an agent with a ready-made routine to solve the problem immediately. But it will always be possible to imagine planning problems that don't match the routines of a given agent, and I think we will lose no generality in our blocks-world example by assuming that the routines the agent knows are simply the primitive actions of the domain.

Nodes in Segerberg's trees represent propositions: subordinate ends that will achieve the ultimate end. In the more general, temporal context that is needed to solve many planning problems, this will not do. A plan needs to transform the current state in which the planning agent is located into a state satisfying the goal. To do this, *we must represent the intermediate states*, not just the subgoals that they satisfy.

Suppose, for instance, that I am outside my locked office. My computer is inside the office. I want to be outside the office, with the computer and with the office locked. To get the computer, I need to enter the office. To enter, I need to unlock the door. I have two methods of unlocking the door: unlocking it with a key and breaking the lock. If all I remember about the effects of these two actions is the goal that they achieve, they are both equally good, since they both will satisfy the subgoal of unlocking the door. But, of course, breaking the lock will frustrate my ultimate purpose. So Segerberg's account of practical reasoning doesn't allow me to make a distinction that is crucial in this and many other cases.

The moral is that the side-effects of actions can be important in planning. We can do justice to this by keeping track not just of subgoals, but of the states that result from achieving them. Deliberation trees need to track states rather than propositions expressing subgoals.[12]

Consider, now, the deliberation problem posed by Figs. 3 and 4. The solution will be a series of actions transforming the initial state in Fig. 3 into the goal state in Fig. 4.

It is possible to solve this problem by reasoning backwards from the goal state, using means-end reasoning. But any solution has to involve a series of states begin-

Fig. 3 A blocks-world initial state

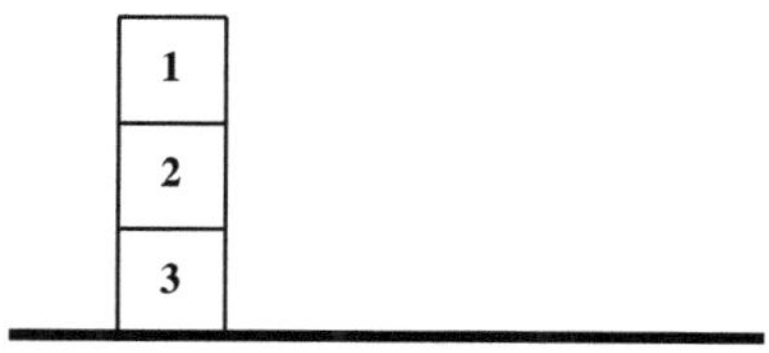

[12] We can, of course, think of states as propositions of a special, very informative sort.

Fig. 4 A blocks-world goal state

ning with the initial state, and at some point this will have to be taken into account, if only in the termination rule for branches.

This problem can be attacked using Segerberg's deliberation trees. We begin the tree with the goal state pictured in Fig. 3. We build the tree by taking a node that has not yet been processed, associated, say, with state s, and creating daughters for this node for each nontrivial action[13] that could produce s, associating these daughters with the appropriate states.[14] A branch terminates when its associated state is the initial state.

This produces the (infinite) tree pictured in Fig. 5. States are indicated in the figure by little pictures in the ellipses. Along the rightmost branch, arcs are labeled by the action that effects the change.

The rightmost branch corresponds to the optimal solution to this planning problem: move all the blocks to the table, then build the desired stack. And other, less efficient solutions can be found elsewhere in the tree.

In general, this top-down, exhaustive method of searching for a plan would be hopelessly inefficient, even with an improved termination rule that would guarantee a finite tree. Perhaps it would be best to distinguish between the *search space*, or the total space of possible solutions, and *search methods*, which are designed to find an acceptable solution quickly, and may visit only part of the total space. Segerberg seems to recommend top-down, exhaustive search; but making this distinction, he could easily avoid this recommendation.

We have modified Segerberg's model of deliberation to bring temporality into the picture, in a limited and qualitative way, and to make states central to deliberation, rather than propositions. This brings me to my second critical point: how can a deliberator know what is needed for deliberation?

5 Knowledge Representation Issues

To be explanatory and useful, a logical account of deliberation has to deliver a theory of the reasoning. Human agents engage in practical reasoning, and have intuitions about the correctness of this reasoning—and, of course, the logic should explain

[13] An action is trivial in s if it leaves s unchanged.

[14] Reasoning in this direction is cumbersome; it is easier to find opportunities to act in a state s than to find ways in which s might have come about. Evidently, Segerberg's method is not the most natural way to approach this planning problem.

Krister Segerberg's Philosophy of Action

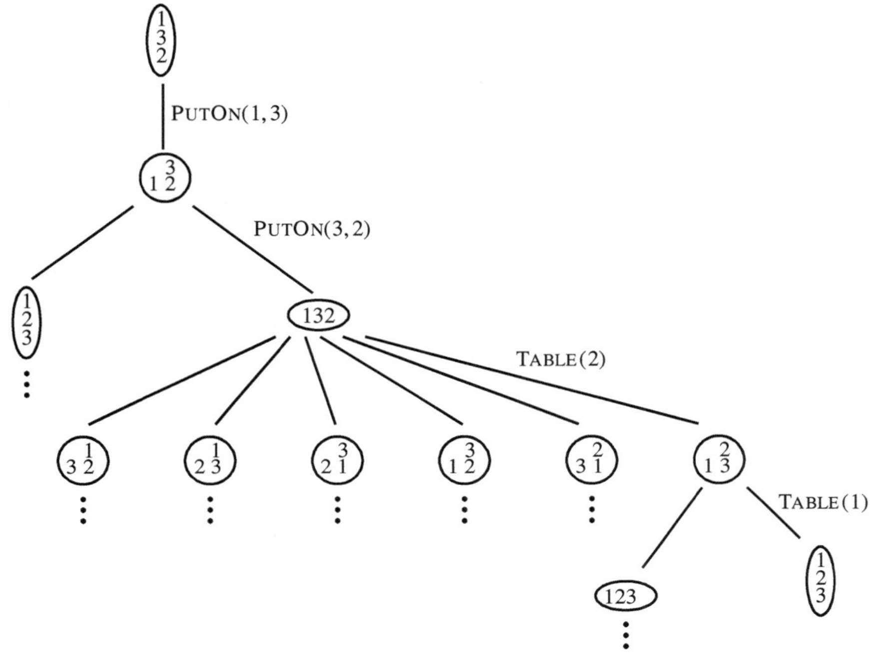

Fig. 5 A tree of subgoals

these intuitions. But AI planning and robotic systems also deliberate, and a logic of practical reasoning should be helpful in designing such systems. This means, among other things, that the theory should be scaleable to realistic, complex planning problems of the sort that these systems need to deal with.

In this section, we discuss the impact of these considerations on the logic of practical reasoning.

5.1 Axiomatization

In the logic of theoretical reasoning, we expect a formal language that allows us to represent illustrative examples of reasoning, and to present theories as formalized objects. In the case of mathematical reasoning, for instance, we hope for formalize the axioms and theorems of mathematical theories, and the steps of proofs. But we also want a consequence relation that can explain the correctness of proofs in these theories.

What should we expect of a formalization of practical reasoning, and in particular, of a formalization of the sort that Segerberg discusses in [23]?

Segerberg's medical example, and the blocks-world case discussed in Sect. 4.1, show that at least we can formalize the steps of some practical reasoning specimens. But this is a relatively shallow use of logic. How can bring logical consequence relations to bear on the reasoning?

In cases with no uncertainty about the initial state and the consequences of actions, we can at least hope for a logical consequence relation to deliver *plan verification*. That is, we would hope for an axiomatization of planning that would allow us to verify a correct plan. Given an initial state, a goal state, and a plan that achieves the goal state it should be a logical consequence of the axiomatization that it indeed does this. This could be done in a version of dynamic logic where the states are states of the environment that can be changed by performing actions, but it could also be done in a static logic with explicit variables over states. In either case, we would need to provide appropriate axioms.

What sort of axioms would we need, for instance, to achieve adequate plan verification for the blocks-world domain? In particular, what axioms would we need to prove something like

$$\begin{aligned}(1)\ &\mathit{Achieves}(\textsc{Table}(1); \textsc{Table}(2); \textsc{PutOn}(3,2); \textsc{PutOn}(1,3),\\ &\quad \mathit{Clear}(1) \wedge \mathit{On}(1,2) \wedge \mathit{On}(2,3) \wedge \mathit{OnTable}(3)),\\ &\quad \mathit{Clear}(1) \wedge \mathit{On}(1,3) \wedge \mathit{On}(3,2) \wedge \mathit{OnTable}(2))?\end{aligned}$$

Here, $\mathit{Achieves}(a, \phi, \psi)$ is true if performing the action denoted by a in any state satisfying ϕ produces a state that satisfies ψ. And $a; b$ denotes the action of performing first the action denoted by a and then the action denoted by b. The provability of this formula would guarantee the success of the blocks-world plan discussed in Sect. 4.1.

Providing axioms that would enable us to prove formulas like (1) divides into three parts: (i) supplying a general theory of *action-based causality*, (ii) supplying specific causal axioms for each primitive action in the domain, and (iii) supplying axioms deriving the causal properties of complex actions from the properties of their components.

All of these things can be done; in fact they are part of the logical theories of reasoning about actions and plans in logical AI.[15]

As for task (ii), it's generally agreed that the causal axioms for an action need to provide the conditions under which an action can be performed, and the direct effects of performing the action. We could do this for the blocks-world action TABLE, for instance, with the following two axioms.[16]

[15] See, for instance, [10, 14, 34, 39]. In this chapter I don't follow any of the usual formalisms precisely, but have invented one that, I hope, will seem more familiar to readers who know some modal logic.

[16] I hope the notation is clear. $[a]$ is a modal operator indicating what holds after performing action denoted by a.

$$\text{(A1) } \forall x \Box[\mathit{Feasible}(\text{TABLE}(x)) \leftrightarrow \mathit{Clear}(x)]$$
$$\text{(A2) } \forall x \Box[\mathit{Feasible}(\text{TABLE}(x)) \rightarrow [\text{TABLE}(x)]\mathit{OnTable}(x)]$$

Task (i) is more complicated, leading to a number of logical problems, including the Frame Problem. In the blocks-world example, however, the solution is fairly simple, involving change-of-state axioms like (A3), which provides the satisfaction conditions for $\mathit{OnTable}$ after a performance of PUTON (x, y).

$$\text{(A3)} \forall x \forall y \forall z \Box[\mathit{Feasible}\left(\text{PUTON}(x, y)\right) \rightarrow$$
$$[[\text{PUTON}(x, y)]]\mathit{OnTable}(z) \leftrightarrow [z \neq x \wedge \mathit{OnTable}(z)]]]$$

Axiomatizations along these lines succeed well even for complex planning domains. For examples, see [14].

5.2 Knowledge for Planning

The axiomatization techniques sketched in Sect. 5.1 are centered around actions and predicates; each primitive action will have its causal axioms, and each predicate will have its associated change-of-state axioms. This organization of knowledge is quite different from the one suggested by Segerberg's theory of deliberation in [23], which centers around the relation between a goal proposition and the propositions that represent ways of achieving it.

Several difficulties stand in the way of axiomatizing the knowledge used for planning on the basis of this idea.

The enablement relation between propositions may be too inchoate, as it stands, to support an axiomatization. For one thing, the relation is state-dependent. Pushing a door will open it if the door isn't latched, but (ordinarily) will open it if it isn't latched. Also, the relation between enablement and temporality needs to be worked out. Segerberg's example is atemporal, but many examples of enablement involve change of state. It would be necessary to decide whether we have one or many enablement relations here. Finally, as in the blocks-world example and many other planning cases, ways of doing things need to be computed, so that we can't assume that all these ways are known at the outset of deliberation. This problem could be addressed by distinguishing basic or built-in ways of doing things from derived ways of doing things. I have not thought through the details of this, but I suspect that it would lead us to something very like the distinction between primitive actions and plans that is used in AI models of planning.

6 Direction of Reasoning

If Segerberg's model of practical reasoning is linked to top-down, exhaustive search—starting with the goal, creating subgoals consisting of all the known ways of achieving it, and proceeding recursively—it doesn't match many typical cases of human deliberation, and would commit us to a horribly inefficient search method.

For example, take the deliberation problem created by chess. If we start by asking "How can I achieve checkmate?" we can imagine a very large number of mating positions. But no one plans an opening move by finding a path from one of these positions to the opening position. Nevertheless reasoning of the sort we find in chess is fairly common, and has to count as deliberation.

As I said in Sect. 4.1, it might be best to think of Segerberg's deliberation trees as a way of defining the entire search space, rather than as a recommendation about how to explore this space in the process of deliberation. But then, of course, the account of deliberation is very incomplete.

7 Methodology and the Study of Practical Reasoning

The traditional methodology relates philosophical logic to reasoning either by producing semantic definitions of validity that are intuitively well motivated, or by formalizing a few well-chosen examples that illustrate how the logical theory might apply to relatively simple cases of human reasoning.

Artificial Intelligence offers the opportunity of testing logical theories by relating them to computerized reasoning, and places new demands on logical methodology. Just as the needs of philosophical logic—and, in particular, of explaining reasoning in domains other than mathematics—inspired the development of nonclassical logics and of various extensions of classical logic, the needs of intelligent automated reasoning have led to logical innovations, such as nonmonotonic logics.

The axiom sets that are needed to deal with many realistic cases of reasoning, such as the planning problems that are routinely encountered by large organizations, are too large for checking by hand; they must be stored on a computer and tested by the usual techniques that are used to validate the components of AI programs. For instance, the axiom sets can be used as knowledge sources for planning algorithms, and the performance of these algorithms can be tested experimentally.[17]

This methodology is problematic in some ways, but if logic is to be applied to realistic reasoning problems—and, especially, to practical reasoning, there really is no alternative. Traditional logical methods, adopted for mathematical reasoning, are simply not adequate for the complexity and messiness of practical reasoning.

My final comment on Segerberg's logic of deliberation is that, if logic is to be successfully applied to practical reasoning the logical theories will need to be tested by embedding them in implemented reasoning systems and evaluating the performance of these systems.

---

[17] For more about methods for testing knowledge-based programs, see [12, 36]. For a discussion of the relation of logic to agent architectures, see ([40], Chap. 9).

8 Intention

Intentions connect deliberation with action. Deliberation attempts to prioritize and practicalize desires, converting them to plans. The adoption of one of these plans is the formation of an intention. In some cases, there may be no gap between forming an intention and acting. In other cases, there may be quite long delays. In fact, the relation between intention and dispositions to act is problematic; this is probably due, in part at least, to the fact that the scheduling and activation of intentions, in humans, is not entirely conscious or rational.

Since the publication of Anscombe's 1958 book [1], entitled *Intention*, philosophers of action have debated the nature of intention and its relation to action. For a survey of the literature on this topic, see [33]. Illustrating the general pattern in the philosophy of action that I mentioned in Sect. 1, this debate is uninformed by a logical theory of action; nor do the philosophers engaging in it seem to feel the need of such a theory.

In many of his articles on the logic of action,[18] Segerberg considers how to include intention in his languages and models. The most recent presentation of the theory, presented in [31], begins with the reification of actions as sets of state paths that was discussed above in Sect. 3.2. The theory is then complicated by layering on top of this a temporal modeling according to which a "history" is a series of actions. This introduces a puzzling duality in the treatment of time, since actions themselves involve series of states; I am not sure how this duality is to be reconciled, or how to associate states with points along a history.

I don't believe anything that I want to say will be affected by thinking of Segerberg's histories as series of states; I invite the reader to do this.

The intentions of an agent with a given past h, within a background set H of possible histories, are modeled by a subset $\text{int}_H(h)$ of the continuations of h in H (i.e., a subset of $\{g : hg \in H\}$). This set is used in the same way sets of possible worlds are used to model propositional attitudes—the histories in $\text{int}_H(h)$ represent the outcomes that are compatible with the agent's intentions. For instance, if I intend at 9am to stay in bed until noon (and only intend this), my intention set will be the set of future histories in which I don't leave my bed until the afternoon.

Segerberg considers a language with two intention operators, $\mathbf{int}^\circ$ and **int**, both of which apply to terms denoting actions. (This is the reason for incorporating actions in histories.) The gloss of $\mathbf{int}^\circ$ is "intends in the narrow sense" and the gloss of **int** is simply "intends." But there is no explanation of the two operators and I, for one, am skeptical about whether the word 'intends' has these two senses. There seems to be an error in the satisfaction conditions for **int** on ([31], p. 181), but the aim seems to be a definition incorporating a persistent commitment to perform an action. I'll confine my comments to $\mathbf{int}^\circ$; I think they would also apply to most variants of this definition.

---

[18] These include [18, 20–24, 30, 31].

$\mathbf{int}^{\circ}(\alpha)$ is satisfied relative to a past history h in case the action α is performed in every possible future g in the intention set $\text{int}_H(h)$. This produces a logic for $\mathbf{int}^{\circ}$ analogous to a modal necessity operator.

The main problem with this idea has to do with unintended consequences of intended actions. Let $\text{fut}_{h,\alpha}$ be the set of continuations of h in which the action denoted by α is performed. If $\text{fut}_{h,\beta} \subseteq \text{fut}_{h,\alpha}$, then $\mathbf{int}^{\circ}(\alpha) \rightarrow \mathbf{int}^{\circ}(\beta)$ must be true at h. But this isn't in fact how intention acts. To adapt an example from ([4], p. 41), I can intend to turn on my computer without intending to increase the temperature of the computer, even if the computer is heated in every possible future in which I turn the computer on.

Segerberg recognizes this problem, and proposes ([31], p. 184) to solve it by insisting that the set of future histories to which $\text{int}_H(h)$ is sensitive consist of all the logically possible continuations of h. This blocks the unwanted inference, since it is logically possible that turning on the computer won't make it warmer. But, if the role of belief in forming intentions is taken into account, I don't think this will yield a satisfactory solution to the problem of unintended consequences.

Rational intention, at any rate, has to be governed by belief. It is pointless, for instance, to deliberate about how to be the first person to climb Mt. McKinley if you believe that someone else has climbed Mt. Mckinley, and irrational to intend to be the first person to climb this mountain if you have this belief.[19]

This constraint on rational intention would be enforced, in models of the sort that Segerberg is considering, by adding a subset $\text{bel}_H(h)$ of the continuations of h, representing the futures compatible with the agent's beliefs, and requiring that $\text{int}_H(h) \subseteq \text{bel}_H(h)$: every intended continuation is compatible with the agent's beliefs. Perhaps something short of this requirement would do what is needed to relate rational intention to belief, but it is hard to see what that would be.

But now the problem of unintended consequences reappears. I can believe that turning on my computer will warm it and intend to turn the computer on, without intending to warm it.[20] I conclude that Segerberg's treatment of intention can't solve the problem of unintended consequences, if belief is taken into account.[21]

Unlike modal operators and some propositional attitudes, but like many propositional attitudes, intention does not seem to have interesting, nontrivial logical properties of its own, and I doubt that a satisfaction condition of any sort is likely to prove very illuminating, if we are interested in the role of intention in reasoning.

We can do better by considering the interactions of intention with other attitudes—intention-belief inconsistency is an example. But I suspect that the traditional methods of logical analysis are limited in what they can achieve here. Bratman's work, as well as work in AI on agent architectures, suggests that the important properties

[19] For more about intention-belief inconsistency, see ([5], pp. 37–38).

[20] If this example fails to convince you, consider the following one. I'm a terrible typist. When I began to prepare this chapter, I believed I would make many typographical errors in writing it. But when I intended to write the chapter, I didn't intend to make typographical errors.

[21] The theory presented in [31] is by no means the only logic of intention to suffer from this problem. See, for instance, ([40], Chap. 4).

of intention will only emerge in the context of a planning agent that is also involved in interacting in the world. I'd be the last to deny that logic has an important part to play in the theory of such agents, but it is only part of the story.

9 The Logic of Action and Philosophy

I will be brief here.

In [22, 27] Segerberg discusses ways in which his reification of actions might be useful in issues that have arisen in the philosophical literature on action having to do with how actions are to be individuated. I agree that the logical theory is helpful in thinking about these issues. But philosophers need philosophical arguments, and for an application of a logical model to philosophy to be convincing, the model needs to be motivated philosophically. I believe that Segerberg's models need more thorough motivation of this sort, and particularly motivation that critically compares the theory to other alternatives.

On the other hand, most philosophers of action claim to be interested in practical reasoning, but for them the term seems to indicate a cluster of familiar philosophical issues, and to have little or nothing to do with reasoning. Here there is a gap that philosophical logicians may be able to fill, by providing a serious theory of deliberative reasoning, analyzing realistic examples, and identifying problems of philosophical interest that arise from this enterprise. Segerberg deserves a great deal of credit for seeking to begin this process, but we will need a better developed, more robust logical theory of practical reasoning if the interactions with philosophy are to flourish.

10 The Problem of Discreteness

I want to return briefly to the problem of discreteness. Recall that Segerberg's theory of agency is based on discrete models of change-of-state. Discrete theories are also used in the theory of computation and in formalisms that are used to model human cognition, in game theory, and in AI planning formalisms. Computational theories can justify this assumption by appealing to the discrete architecture of digital computers. It is more difficult to do something similar for human cognition, although in [38] Alan Turing argues that digital computers can simulate continuous computation devices well enough to be practically indistinguishable from them.

Perhaps the most powerful arguments for discrete theories of control and cognitive mechanisms is that we don't seem to be able to do without them. Moreover, these systems seem to function perfectly well even when they are designed to interact with a continuous environment. Discrete control systems for robot motion illustrate this point.

But if we are interested in agents like humans and robots that are embedded in the real world, we may need to reconsider whether nature should be regarded, as it is in game theory and as Segerberg regards it, as an agent. Our best theory of how nature operates might well be continuous. Consider, for instance, an agent dribbling a basketball. We might want to treat the agent and its interventions in the physical process using discrete models, but use continuous variables and physical laws of motion to track the basketball.[22]

11 Conclusion

I agree with Segerberg that we need a logic of action, and that it is good to look to computer science for ideas about how to develop such a logic. But, if we want a logic that will apply to realistic examples, we need to look further than theoretical computer science. Artificial Intelligence is the area of computer science that seeks to deal with the problems of deliberation, and logicians in the AI community have been working for many years on these problems.

I have tried to indicate how to motivate improvements in the theory of deliberation that is sketched in some of Segerberg's works, and how these improvements lead in the direction of action theories that have emerged in AI. I urge any philosopher interested in the logic of deliberation to take these theories into account.

References

1. Anscombe, G. (1958). *Intention*. Oxford: Blackwell Publishers.
2. Austin, J. L. (1956–57). A plea for excuses. *Proceedings of the Aristotelian Society, 57*, 1–30.
3. Brachman, R. J., & Levesque, H. (2004). *Knowledge representation and reasoning*. Amsterdam: Elsevier.
4. Bratman, M. E. (1987). *Intentions, plans and practical reason*. Cambridge: Harvard University Press.
5. Bratman, M. E. (1990). What is intention? In P. R. Cohen, J. Morgan, & M. Pollack (Eds.), *Intentions in communication* (pp. 15–32). Cambridge, MA: MIT Press.
6. Brooks, R. A. (1990). Elephants don't play chess. *Robotics and Autonomous Systems*, *6*(1–2), 3–15.
7. Clarke, E. M., Grumberg, O., & Peled, D. A. (1999). *Model checking*. Cambridge, MA: MIT Press.
8. Fritz, C., & McIlraith, S. A. (2008). Planning in the face of frequent exogenous events. In *Online Poster Proceedings of the 18th International Conference on Automated Planning and Scheduling (ICAPS), Sydney, Australia*. http://www.cs.toronto.edu/kr/publications/fri-mci-icaps08.pdf.
9. Harel, D., Kozen, D., & Tiuryn, J. (2000). *Dynamic logic*. Cambridge, MA: MIT Press.
10. Lifschitz, V. (1987). Formal theories of action. In M. L. Ginsberg (Ed.), *Readings in non-monotonic reasoning* (pp. 410–432). Los Altos, CA: Morgan Kaufmann.
11. Lorini, E., & Herzig, A. (2008). A logic of intention and attempt. *Synthése*, *163*(1), 45–77.
12. McGuinness, D. L., Fikes, R., Rice, J., & Wilder, S. (2000). An environment for merging and testing large ontologies. In A. G. Cohn, F. Giunchiglia, & B. Selman (Eds.), *KR2000:*

[22] For mixed models of this kind, see, for instance, [16].

Principles of knowledge representation and reasoning (pp. 483–493). San Francisco: Morgan Kaufmann.
13. Newell, A. (1992). *Unified theories of cognition*. Cambridge, MA: Harvard University Press.
14. Reiter, R. (2001). *Knowledge in action: Logical foundations for specifying and implementing dynamical systems*. Cambridge, MA: MIT Press.
15. Sacerdoti, E. D. (1974). Planning in a hierarchy of abstraction spaces. *Artificial Intelligence*, *5*(2), 115–135.
16. Sandewall, E. (1989). Combining logic and differential equations for describing real-world systems. In R. J. Brachman, H. J. Levesque, & R. Reiter (Eds.), *KR'89: Principles of knowledge representation and reasoning* (pp. 412–420). San Mateo, CA: Morgan Kaufmann.
17. Segerberg, K. (1980). Applying modal logic. *Studia Logica*, *39*(2–3), 275–295.
18. Segerberg, K. (1981). Action-games. *Acta Philosophica Fennica*, *32*, 220–231.
19. Segerberg, K. (1982a). Getting started: Beginnings in the logic of action. *Studia Logica*, *51*(3–4), 437–478.
20. Segerberg, K. (1982b). The logic of deliberate action. *Journal of Philosophical Logic*, *11*(2), 233–254.
21. Segerberg, K. (1984). Towards an exact philosophy of action. *Topoi*, *3*(1), 75–83.
22. Segerberg, K. (1985a). Models for action. In B. K. Matilal & J. L. Shaw (Eds.), *Analytical philosophy in contemporary perspective* (pp. 161–171). Dordrecht: D. Reidel Publishing Co.
23. Segerberg, K. (1985b). Routines. *Synthése*, *65*(2), 185–210.
24. Segerberg, K. (1988). Talking about actions. *Studia Logica*, *47*(4), 347–352.
25. Segerberg, K. (1989). Bringing it about. *Journal of Philosophical Logic*, *18*(4), 327–347.
26. Segerberg, K. (1992). Representing facts. In C. Bicchieri & M. L. D. Chiara (Eds.), *Knowledge, belief, and strategic interaction* (pp. 239–256). Cambridge, UK: Cambridge University Press.
27. Segerberg, K. (1994). A festival of facts. *Logic and Logical Philosophy*, *2*, 7–22.
28. Segerberg, K. (1995). Conditional action. In G. Crocco, L. F. nas del Cerro, & A. Herzig (Eds.), *Conditionals: From philosophy to computer science* (pp. 241–265). Oxford: Oxford University Press.
29. Segerberg, K. (1996). To do and not to do. In J. Copeland (Ed.), *Logic and reality: Essays on the legacy of Arthur Prior* (pp. 301–313). Oxford: Oxford University Press.
30. Segerberg, K. (1999). Results, consequences, intentions. In G. Meggle (Ed.), *Actions, norms, values: Discussion with Georg Henrik von Wright* (pp. 147–157). Berlin: Walter de Gruyter.
31. Segerberg, K. (2005). Intension, intention. In R. Kahle (Ed.), *Intensionality* (pp. 174–186). Wellesley, MA: A.K. Peters, Ltd.
32. Segerberg, K., Meyer, J. J., & Kracht, M. (2009). The logic of action. In E. N. Zalta (Ed.), *The Stanford encyclopedia of philosophy*, summer (2009th ed.). Stanford: Stanford University.
33. Setiya, K. (2011). Intention. In E. N. Zalta (Ed.), *The Stanford encyclopedia of philosophy*, spring (2011th ed.). Stanford: Stanford University.
34. Shanahan, M. (1997). *Solving the frame problem*. Cambridge, MA: MIT Press.
35. Simon, H. A., & Schaeffer, J. (1992). The game of chess. In R. J. Aumann & S. Hart (Eds.), *Handbook of game theory with economic applications* (Vol. 1, pp. 1–17). Amsterdam: North-Holland.
36. Stefik, M. J. (1995). *An introduction to knowledge systems*. San Francisco: Morgan Kaufmann.
37. Sutton, R. S., Precup, D., & Singh, S. (1999). Between MDPs and semi-MDPs: A framework for temporal abstraction in reinforcement learning. *Artificial Intelligence*, *112*(1–2), 181–211.
38. Turing, A. M. (1950). Computing machinery and intelligence. *Mind*, *59*(236), 433–460.
39. Turner, H. (1999). A logic of universal causation. *Artificial Intelligence*, *113*(1–2), 87–123.
40. Wooldridge, M. J. (2000). *Reasoning about Rational Agents*. Cambridge, UK: Cambridge University Press.

The Concept of a Routine in Segerberg's Philosophy of Action

Dag Elgesem

Abstract The notion of a routine for acting plays a fundamental role in Krister Segeberg's philosophy of action and he uses it in a series of papers as the basis for the formulation of logics of intentional action. The present chapter is an attempt to provide a critical assessment of Segerberg's program. First, an exposition of the central elements of Segerberg's account of routines is given and its roles in his philosophy of action are discussed. It is argued that Segerberg's notion of routines provides a very productive perspective on intentional agency and that it gives rise to a series of challenges to attempts to construct logics of intentional action. It is then argued that Segerberg's own formal theories of intentional action do not fully meet these challenges. Finally, it is suggested a way in which the challenges can be met if the concept of a routine is brought explicitly into the semantic framework for the logic of intentions and actions.

Keywords Actions · Agency · Intentions · Intentional action · Routines · Action theory · Action logic

1 Introduction

20 years ago I wrote a paper called "Intentions, actions and routines: A problem in Krister Segerberg's theory of action." In that paper I tried to give a critical assessment of Segerberg's proposal for a theory of intentional action as he had formulated it in a series of papers. The concept of a routine was central to the theory. Segerberg motivated his formal account with a number of interesting observations about the relationship between intention, actions and outcomes, and argued that the concept of a routine could be used to clarify and characterize this relationship. On the basis

D. Elgesem (✉)
University of Bergen, 5020 Bergen, Norway
e-mail: Dag.Elgesem@infomedia.uib.no

R. Trypuz (ed.), *Krister Segerberg on Logic of Actions*,
Outstanding Contributions to Logic 1, DOI: 10.1007/978-94-007-7046-1_2,

of this Segerberg formulated a number of proposals for the formal characterization of intentional agency. In my paper I criticized these attempts by showing that if all of the informally motivated assumption underlying the routine theory were made explicit in the semantics of the formal theory, some very problematic properties were forthcoming. In particular, I argued that with all of the assumptions made explicit in the semantics, the agents must realize all of their intentions whenever they act. This is undesirable in a theory of action since agents sometimes fail to realize the intentions they act on. Hence, the theory is not flexible enough as a characterization of the relationship between intentions and actions, I argued. This criticism is still valid, I think, and I will provide some of the details of it below. However, I now think the conclusion I draw from it was wrong. The paper ended with the following sentence: "The proper conclusion to be drawn seems to be that the concept of a routine, as Segerberg develops it, does not provide a suitable basis for action theory".[1] The correct lesson to be drawn, I will argue, is instead that the idea of a routine is a very fruitful one in the theory of intentional agency, and that it can provide the basis for an interesting formal characterization of intentional action.

In this chapter I will try to bring out the role I think the notion of a routine should play in the account of intentional action and also provide a suggestion for what I think the basic elements of a formal characterization of intentional agency should be. In the first section below I will give an exposition of the central elements of Segerberg's account of routines and explain its central role in his philosophy of action. In the second section I will expand on Segerberg's remarks on the notion of routines and relate it to other positions in the philosophy of action. I will argue that the notion of a routine has an important role to play in the theory of action and that, properly understood, provides a series of challenges to the formal characterization of intentional agency. In the third section I will argue that Segerberg's own formalization of the notion of intentional action does not meet the theoretical challenges posed by the routine concept. In the final section I argue that the challenges can be met if the concept of a routine is brought explicitly into the semantic framework for the logic of intentions and actions.

2 Segerberg's Concept of a Routine[2]

The central concept in Segerberg's theory of action is that of having a routine for acting. The importance of this concept for his theory of action is clearly stated in (1985, p. 188):

> It is a thesis of this chapter that that the concept of a routine is a natural one and that a philosophy of action can be built on it. To do something is to run a routine. To be able to do something is have a routine available. To deliberate is to search for a routine.

---

[1] Elgesem [4], p. 174.

[2] This section is excerpted from my paper Elgesem [4].

The concept of a routine is primitive in this theory, and is used to explicate other elements in the theory of action. The obvious starting point for an attempt to make an assessment of Segerberg's program therefore, is to try to understand how this fundamental notion is to be understood.

As the name suggests, a routine is a relatively constant procedure the agent has available for doing an action of a specific sort. The routine, according to Segerberg's conception, is that which makes something into the same action on different occasions of performance, that is, the part of the action that depends on the agent's permanent abilities. But even though the routine is employed on different occasions of acting, the outcome of the execution of the action may vary in certain respects. One of Segerberg's examples here is dart-throwing, where the routine is described in this way: "I aim carefully, inhale deeply, exhale half my breath, keep the rest, hope for the best, 1, 2, 3, and off it goes".[3] This is an intuitive description of the invariant element across all different occasions where the agent's action is one of dart-throwing—a description of what it is for him to throw the dart. But there is another aspect of dart-throwing situations that may vary: the result of the action.

> In order to see that I am doing a different thing each time I throw the dart, just look at the score: now (usually) it is a bad miss, now (sometimes) it is a near miss, now (once in a long while) it is the Bull's Eye. It is true that I am doing the same thing each time I throw the dart, viz. throwing it with the intention of hitting the Bull's Eye. Obviously, there must be an important distinction waiting to be made here. A statistician would say that it is the same experiment that is being repeated but that the outcomes differ. Using the vocabulary introduced above, we may add to this by saying that the reason it is the same experiment is that it is the same routine that is being used.[4]

So even though the outcomes may differ, the routine makes it the same action every time the agent runs it.

This example also illustrates another important aspect of Segerberg's notion of a routine, namely that what makes a routine the routine it is, is the agent's intentions. Their essential role in deliberation and practical reasoning is the second main feature of Segerberg's conception of routines. In all his discussions of the concept, their crucial role in rational deliberation emphasized. A rationally deliberating agent, according to Segerberg, usually starts out with a rather general intention to do something. Further deliberation is then constrained by this general intention, and the agent now tries to find means that will realize the intention he has already adopted. Rational deliberation is then viewed as a step-by-step expansion of the set of intentions with new intentions to do something that are means to the realization of the intentions that were initially adopted, a process Segerberg calls 'deliberation walk'. The process ends when the agent has found an intention that is executable, i.e. he has found a routine the execution of which will realize the whole of his intention set.

As an example of this 'deliberation walk' Segerberg [6] tells the story of a man who wants to give his friend a birthday present, and accordingly forms an intention to

---

[3] Segerberg [6], p. 234.

[4] Segerberg [6], pp. 234–235.

do this. Then he decides to give a book, and as the next step he settles for a book by a particular author. Finally, in the book shop he decides in favor of a particular one of the author's titles, and he buys a copy of this book. By doing this action, i.e. executing the routine that is associated with his most specific intention—picking the book from the shelves, purchasing it, etc.—the whole of his intention set is realized. The point of the example is summed up by Segerberg thus, "A series of, as it happens, strictly monotonically more specific intentions is formed until one is formed until one is reached which can be realized immediately—an intention that is operational".[5]

There are then, two crucial elements in Segerberg's notion of routine. First, to act is to run routine of a certain kind; the action gets its identity from the routine, i.e. it is the act it is in virtue of the routine that is employed. Second, a routine is associated with the intentions of the agent, i.e. the running of the routine is the last step in the agent's 'deliberation walk'. This means that routines can be identified from two perspectives, so to speak, both as part of the agent's performed action and as part of his intention.

According to Segerberg's picture of intentional action the agent forms a coherent set of intentions and the execution of the routine that is associated with the most specific intention both realizes the whole set, and makes the activity the kind of action that it is. Intuitively, then, there is a strong connection between the intention of the agent and the identity of his action, and the role of the routine is precisely to establish this connection. A question that arises is whether there are resources in the theory to describe a situation where the agent fails to realize his intentions through his actions. Such a situation would have to be described, perhaps, as a situation where there is a discrepancy between the routine as seen from the perspective of the agent's intentions and as seen from the perspective of the performed action.

Segerberg does not address this question but such a situation is among those an adequate theory of intentional action should allow for, at least. In the discussion below of his formal theory of intentional action I will show that the theory does not have room for the case of a failing routine. This suggest, I will argue, that the theory of intentional action has to make a distinction between the description of the routine as part of the agent's intention and the routine as described in terms of the consequences of its execution in the world.

3 The Concept of a Routine and the Philosophy of Action

Segerberg's observations and suggestions about the role of routines in our everyday deliberation and action are intriguing and I think he is right that the concept is a theoretically fruitful one. This is a point that I want to argue by way of a discussion four aspect of intentional agency that I think a theory of action action should make sense of and where the concept of a routine could have an important role to play. The

[5] Segerberg [6], p. 235.

discussion will go beyond Segerberg's own reflections on the role of the concept of a routine and it is an attempt to clarify and extend his ideas.

Segerberg's philosophical project is to understand the relationship between the mental and the physical in intentional agency. Importantly, the ascriptions of intentional agency combine the description of some of the agent's mental states and his influence on the world. An agent's actions typically have some external, often physical effects on the world that can be used to describe the action. In the cases where the agent's action is said to be intentional these physical properties are used also to describe some of the agent's mental properties, i.e. his or her intentions. Following Segerberg's line of thought this double use of the action descriptions is possible in virtue of the tight connection between the intention and the action established by the routine. Routines are seen both as the elements of deliberation and as descriptions of physical actions and thus provide a bridge between the action as a mental and as a physical event.

To elaborate on this fundamental point, I think it is crucial to see that with a description of an intentional action, e.g. "Peter turned on the computer", there is a description of a physical process—the causal route from Peter's movement to the lightening of the screen—and this physical description is also used to describe the agent's mental state, i.e. his intention. Call these the agent-relative and the world-relative descriptions of the agent's activity, respectively. The ascription of intentional agency can serve as both agent-relative and world-relative because the physical movements of the agent carry information about his mental states. Using the vocabulary of Barwise and Seligman [1] there is an *infomophism* between the physical system of the world and the mental structure of the agent's intentions. If we think of the world-relative descriptions as classification of states of the world and the agent-relative descriptions classifications of the agent's mental states, ascriptions of intentional agency involves a morphism between the two classifications. The routine can be referred to both in in the agent-relative and in the world-relative descriptions and can thus provide the necessary relationship between these two classifications.

The first point that I want to emphasize about the usefulness of the routine concept is, then, that it can serve as a referent both in the description of the agent's actions and intentions. This will be a central topic in the discussion of the formal modeling of intentional action below.

The second point that I would like to focus on concerns the role of routines in actions that are not intentional. Segerberg does not say much about actions that are not intentional in the reflections about routines but we do encounter them in his formal theory. Here, intentional actions are defined in terms of non-intentional actions plus intention but the role of routines in actions that are not intentional is not. Segerberg thinks of routines as that part of our actions over which we have control. When we act, as exemplified in the example of darts throwing above, conditions in the world of course also influence the outcome. An intentional action can have consequences of which the agent is not aware and that he therefore did not intend to bring about as part of his routine. However, the outcome which he did not intend to bring about, and therefore did not do intentionally, still is a description of what he did. And since

Segerberg individuates actions by the routine that constitutes them it seems that the non-intentional action description also should be seen as a description of the routine by its casual effects. In this case, the description of the effects of the action cannot be used to describe the agent's intention even if it a reference to his routine.

This brings up the question of the individuation of actions which has been given a lot of attention by Donald Davidson and others. An action can be given an infinite number of descriptions, Davidson suggests, but only under a limited number of them is it intentional. Davidson's illustration has become famous: "I flip the switch, turn on the light, and illuminate the room. Unbeknownst to me I also alert a prowler to the fact that I am home" (Davidson [3], p. 4). Davidson's conclusions about the individuation of actions are in line with Segerberg's account of routines, I think. Some philosophers have suggested that this the sentence describes four different actions. Davidson argues, however, that there is only one action here, but one that is given four different descriptions. And under three of the descriptions the action is intentional and under one it is non-intentional, according to Davidson, who argues that the action is individuated by the causal route from intention to behavior. The idea of a routine plays very much of the same role in the way actions are individuated in Segerberg's theory of intentional actions. Furthermore, Davidson thinks that an event is an action in virtue of being intentional under some description. "A man is the agent of an act if what he does can be described under an aspect that makes it intentional" (Davidson [3], p. 46). "A person is the agent of an event if and only if there is a description of what he did that makes a true sentence that says he did it intentionally" (Davidson [3], p. 46). On Segerberg's account, those of an agent's action which are done intentionally are those that are included in his routine. And as in the example about the throwing of darts above, the routine is the activity in virtue of which he does everything else. Now, Segerberg does not comment on Davidson's theory of the individuation of actions. But given that intentional actions by him are individuated by the routines, and not by the outcomes of the actions, I do think that non-intentional actions should be seen as ways of describing the agent's routine by its casual effects.

If this is correct, it provides also a challenge for the formal modeling of intentional agency which should bring out these complex relationships between the agent's intentions, his intentional actions and his non-intentional actions. In the connection with the framework to be proposed below I will argue that it is possible to do this in an intuitive way by bringing in routines explicitly into the semantics.

An important aspect of routines that is closely related to their function in the individuation of actions is that they are the units of deliberation on Segerberg's theory. The example quoted above of the so-called deliberation walk in the connection with the buying of the birthday present illustrates this role. There is something very compelling about this picture. It suggests that intentions—at least rational ones—are formed by considering what abilities and opportunities we have and how the combination of these can be used to realize our goals. In his theory of intentions Michael Bratman [2] has argued that rational intentions have to be means-ends coherent, i.e.

they should be built up in such a way that, given what the agent's beliefs and goals, the structure of the intention as a whole can be realized. In addition, rational intentions should be consistent with what the agent believes about his abilities and about the world he is going to act in, Bratman argues. But it is important to emphasize, with Bratman, that these should be seen as constraints on the rational formation of intentions and the suggestion is not that it is psychologically impossible to form intentions that violates these norms. Segerberg's thinking about routines as the core elements of practical deliberation is very much in line with this, I think. Deliberation is on Segerberg's account essentially to search for a routine that has the agent has the ability and opportunity to perform, and that he believes is means-ends coherent. And only intentions that are rationally formed in this way, Segerberg seems to suggest, will result in an intentional action. Again, the formal characterization of intentions and intentional actions should reflect the rationality constraints on intentions and intentional actions.

There is also a different challenge for the formal characterization of intentions and actions that arises in the connection with the rationality constraints on the formation of intentions. As we have seen the routine is the core component of the agent's intention and the unit in which the agent thinks of what he will accomplish when the routine is executed. But even if the intention is rationally formed, i.e. is both means ends coherent and consistent in the agents mind, it is not always successful. The world sometimes takes a different turn from the one the agent rationally based his intention on. So sometimes what the agent does intentionally is only a subset of that which he intends to do so. This means that even though all of the agent's intentional actions are also in his set of intended actions, his intentional actions cannot simply be identified with his set of intentions. The notion of a routine, then, can be seen to be referring to those of the agent's intentions that were actually realized when he acted. Again, we see that the routine concept is very useful in thinking about the relationship between the agent's intentions, intentional actions and the influence of his actions on the world. A formal modeling of these relationships should be flexible enough to give a characterization also of a situation where the agent fails to realize some of his intentions. Again, in the discussion below I will argue that it is necessary to explicitly represent routines in the formal semantics to be able to meet this challenge.

A further aspect of the notion of routines is that they provide intentions with a recipe for their execution. A central feature of Segerberg's notion of a routine is that it is a structure that can be executed, like a piece of software run on a computer. And the agent can be seen to be acting intentionally in virtue of executing the routine. Importantly, a routine, like a program, is both a prescription for action and the action itself. For an example of an action that is intended but not intentional assume the darts player in Segerberg's example cited above, intends to hit the Bull's Eye, aims, and starts to run his routine of throwing the dart. However, at the moment the dart is about to leave his hand he is distracted by a flash of light and the dart falls out of his hand, hits the wall, changes direction, and lands in the Bull's Eye. In this situation he intends to hit the target, and hits it, but he is not intentionally hitting the Bull's Eye because the causal route to the goal was not the one he intended. The notion of a routine contributes a way to conceptualize that for an action to be intentional it is not sufficient that the outcome is intended—it has to be achieved in "right way", i.e. in the way prescribed by the intention/routine. This is also a challenge for a formal account of intentions, intentional actions and non-intentional actions: to make sense of a situation where an outcome is intended but still not part of the description of what the agent did intentionally. Again, I will argue below that bringing routines into the formal semantics will make it possible to meet this challenge.

There are thus four aspects of intentional agency with respect to the conceptualization of which I think the notion of a routine is helpful:

1. In the understanding of how ascriptions of intentional agency function both as descriptions of the agent's mental states and descriptions of the agent's activity in the world
2. In the understanding of the role of intentions in the individuation of actions
3. In the explication of rationality constraints on the formation of intentions
4. In the explication of the agent's intentions as both recipes for action and structures that are executed in the agent's acting.

These points also constitute challenges for a formal account of intentional agency, which should be able to:

1. Explicate the relationship between the agent-relative and the world-relative perspectives on the action
2. Characterize the logical relationships between the agent's intentions, intentional actions, and the things he brings out without intending to do so
3. Characterize the constraints on a rational agent's formation of intention
4. Explicate the role of intentions as blueprints for acting in "the right way".

Before I turn to the discussion of a framework for the modeling of intentional action that I think meet these challenges to some extent, I will briefly discuss one of Segerberg's own proposals formal theories of intentional action. The theory is based on his ideas about routines but for a number of reasons I think it does not take full advantage of the conceptual resources in the routine idea and for this reason fails to meet the challenges.

4 Segerberg's Formal Characterization of Intentional Actions[6]

Let us now turn to Segerberg's formal theory of action that he develops on the basis of his routine theory. Actually, in Segerberg's work we find two different types of approaches to the modeling of intentional action and I discuss both types in detail in my old paper [4]. Here I will only discuss one of the approaches as I believe my general conclusions apply to both of them.

[6] This section is excerpted from my paper Elgesem [4].

I will argue that the formal accounts run into problems with the challenges posed by the routine theory. There are two major problems. The first is that if all of the assumptions in the theory are made explicit in the semantics, it will be true in the modeling that the agent realizes all of his intentions and that it is not flexible enough to account for a situation where his attempt to realize an intention fails. The second problem is that intentional action is defined as a combination of intention and non-intentional action. By defining intentional action in this way the formalization fails to capture the idea that the intention has to be realized in the right way for the resulting action to be intentional. Segerberg has developed different approaches to the logic of intentional action but I will discuss only the approach from the paper 'The logic of deliberate action'. The aim is not primarily to criticize Segerberg's theory but to use the discussion of one of his suggestions for a formal theory of action to bring out the challenges for attempts to characterize intentional agency. In particular, I think the problems this approach encounters provide an argument for bringing routines explicitly into the semantic apparatus.

It is striking that routines are not represented explicitly as such. Instead, the idea is to model routines and actions through the states that result from the execution of routines. The reason for constructing things this way is that Segerberg, following von Wright, thinks that an action is an agent's bringing about of an event, i.e. the agent brings it about that the world goes from one state to another.[7] This view of the matter suggests the possibility of representing events as the set of states that are the result of state-change of a certain sort. The next step, then, is to characterize a routine by the event that is associated with its execution, i.e. the set of result-states we get from running the routine on different occasions. This event is one half of the construct Segerberg uses to describe actions, the other half is a set of intentions. Again following von Wright, Segerberg thinks of intentions as directed towards an event or a state, i.e. the result of actions. His suggestion, therefore, is to represent the agent's intention by its object, the event or state he intends to bring about. A set of intentions is thus a set of outcomes, each set representing something the agent intends to bring about. No epistemic concepts are brought into the picture in this deliberately simplified representation of the agent's intentions. These simplifications make the approach very instructive because the problems that emerge suggest the ways in which the model needs to be developed further.

There are two kinds of syntactic categories in the language employed, terms and formulas, terms denoting events while formulas denote truth values. There is an infinite set of atomic terms, while atomic formulas are: (a = b), **Int** *a*, **Real** *a*, where a and b are terms. In addition there is a set of propositional letters.

A model M is a triple $\langle$U, **S**, V$\rangle$, U being the set of outcomes, S an intentional action structure and V a valuation, i.e. a function that assigns to each term a subset of U and to each formula a truth value. Truth is defined relative to a model and an action. The interesting truth-definitions here are as follows:

---

[7] von Wright [9].

$\langle \mathbf{S}, x \rangle \models a = b$ iff $V(a) = V(b)$, where a and b are terms
$\langle \mathbf{S}, x \rangle \models \mathbf{Int}\ a$ iff $V(a) \in S$
$\langle \mathbf{S}, x \rangle \models \mathbf{Real}\ a$ iff $x \in V(a)$
$\langle \mathbf{S}, x \rangle \models \Box A$ iff, for every $\langle T, y \rangle \in S$, $\langle T, y \rangle \models A$

The preferred readings of the three operators are, respectively, "a is intended by the agent", "a is realized", and "it is part of the situation that A". Intuitively, the definitions say that an event is intended by the agent if it is in his set of intentions, and that an event is realized by the agent if the outcome of his actions is of the a-type. The construction □A is meant to express a kind of practical necessity for the agent—an aspect of the situation he cannot control.

We will limit the discussion to the action theoretic concepts. Segerberg defines two types of intentional action, reflecting the fact that the agent in some situation has more or less complete control over the outcome while in other situations he may not be sure of success.

The definitions are as follows:

(1) $\mathbf{Do}\ a = \mathbf{Int}\ a \wedge \Box(\mathbf{Int}\ a \rightarrow \mathbf{Real}\ a)$
(2) $\mathbf{Man}\ A = \mathbf{Int}\ A \wedge \mathbf{Real}\ A$

These definitions are not unproblematic as characterizations of intentional action. The second definition is not one of intentional action, in my view. As discussed above, for an action to be intentional, the outcome has to be accomplished in the way the agent intended. In (1), the intentional action with full control, the use of the necessity operator is hard to understand. Segerberg motivates the definition by saying: "The point of introducing □ is to be able to express, by □A, that no matter what the Agent or Umpire may do, it is the case that A" (Segerberg [5], p. 221). There are a number of problems with making intuitive sense of this definition. The main problem is that it seems to say that the situation makes it unavoidable for him to bring about *a* if he intends it. But unavoidability in the situation and control on the part of the agent is not the same. On the contrary, situations where intentions cause un-intended casual chains which trigger the result seem to be precisely of this kind. A famous one is the example of the climber who intends to drop his partner to save himself and this intention causes him to tremble so much that he drops his partner. These problems indicate that it is not a good strategy to try to define intentional action in the seemingly simpler notions of intention and non-intentional action.

A striking fact, given their prominent place in the discussion that motivates the modeling, is the absence of any explicit representation of routines. I will now argue that this implicit way of representing routines leave some of the essential assumptions Segerberg makes about routines unaccounted for. And, furthermore, once these assumptions are made explicit, the undesirable result: (IR) $\mathbf{Int}\ a \rightarrow \mathbf{Real}\ a$, is forthcoming. It is clear that this is an undesirable result in the logic of intentional action. (IR) would, perhaps, have been acceptable if the intended interpretation of '**Int** *a*' was "the agent is intentionally doing a". But this is not the interpretation Segerberg intends, as explained above.

The theory has two semantic types, outcomes and events (sets of outcomes). The strong association between operative intentions and routines, and the fact that intentions are events, makes it plausible to assume that also routine, semantically speaking, also are events. This assumption gets support from an explicit statement to this effect by Segerberg in [8]. This will be important in the argument below where an attempt to construct a coherent picture out of the basic facts about intentions, routines, and actions as this theory conceives of them:

- every action involves the running of a routine
- routines and intentions are events
- an action is semantically represented as a pair of a set of intentions and an outcome
- the set of intentions is closed under intersection
- the routine is associated with the smallest set in the set of intentions—i.e. the non-empty intersection of all the sets in the set
- when the associated routine is run, all the intentions in the set is realized.

An attempt to piece these elements together into one picture yields, it is argued, (IR). Let us suppose there is an action on the part of the agent described on the form $\langle S, x \rangle$. Also, we have a routine Z, associated with the smallest set in S. Note that there must be such a routine, sine on this theory there is a routine involved in every action. Moreover, the agent is in complete control over the execution of this routine, but may not have complete control when it comes to the exact outcome of the action. Which state results after his action, i.e. what the second element in the action description will be, depends also on the agent's surroundings. But the question now arises: is this outcome in Z, the routine-event associated with his operative intention?

If we suppose it is not, this means that the associated intention was not realized. But this would also mean that the routine was not realized, i.e. executed, and could not be represented by any event Z. So the agent did not run any routine when he acted, contrary to the assumption. But this is in strong disagreement with the fundamental assumption of the theory, namely that the performance of an intentional action always involves the running of a routine. For these reasons, the outcome must be in the routine event Z that realizes the intention.

That the outcome is in the routine event Z means, intuitively, that although the agent has not complete control to determine the outcome, he is able to limit the outcome to a certain set. This is, furthermore, a plausible picture given the fact that the pair $\langle S, x \rangle$ is supposed to describe a certain action where there should be a connection with the agent's activity and the outcome. Furthermore, Segerberg explicitly accepts this picture in his ([8], p. 162): "one may think of the agent as excluding all but a set of possible states, for this is in effect what the routine associated with operative intention does: it limits the choice of posterior states to one of a certain set. Which in fact becomes the posterior state is then determined by the world, that is, nature and, perhaps, other agents." The assumption that the outcome is in the set representing the routine seems, therefore, to be in agreement with Segerberg's view of the matter.

With this settled, the problem then arises that this assumption, together with some of the other assumptions about intentions and routines, gives us (IR) **Int** $a \rightarrow$ **Real** *a*. Let us suppose **Int** *a* is true relative to some action ⟨S, x⟩, which means that the event denoted by 'a' is in the set of intentions, S. From the fact that S is closed under intersection we get that S contains a smallest non-empty set, call it Z′, which is the operative intention associated with the executed routine Z. Furthermore, the only option is to take "associated with" to mean that they are identical because the end of point of the deliberating process, the operative intention, is identified with the selection of a routine.[8] The running of the routine Z will now realize all of the agent's intentions, i.e. the whole set S, just because the operative intention Z′ is the non-empty intersection of all the sets in S. So, in particular, a will be realized since it is a member Z, and we get (IR).

Slightly more formally, the argument runs as follows:

> Suppose ⟨S, x⟩| = **Int** *a*, i.e. V(a) ∈ S. Let Z′ be the intersection of all the sets in S associated with the routine Z, i.e. Z = Z′. The outcome of the action is in the routine set: x ∈ Z = Z′. ⟨S, x⟩| = **Real** Z′ because x ∈ Z′. S is closed under intersection, i.e. for all u ∈ S, if x ∈ Z′ then x ∈ u. In particular, x ∈V(a). But then it follows immediately that | = **Real** *a*.

The fundamental problem with the formal modeling is that the agent-relative and the world-relative perspectives are collapsed. Hence, the framework is not flexible enough to give a plausible explication of the relationship between these two perspectives in the description of an agent's activity.

5 Routines in the Semantics of the Logic of Intentional Action

The root of the problem, I suggest, is that routines are not brought explicitly into the semantics. To develop this argument I will suggest a framework which has routines as part of the semantic apparatus. So let us start by defining a model M = ⟨S, R, E, V⟩, where S is a set of situations, R a set of routines, A is an intentional actions structure, and V a valuation. Intuitively, the elements of R, the routines, are functions from action descriptions to the worlds where the agent executes the routines. The elements of S are functions from action descriptions to the set of the agents' routines that are executed in that world. The sets R and S provide the agent-relative and the world-relative descriptions of the actions, respectively. E is an ordered pair consisting of a set of intentions I and an outcome s. The intentions in I are represented as ordered pairs ⟨r, s⟩, where r is a routine that the agent intends to run and s the situation in which he intends to run it.

As we have seen above, the two types of descriptions of actions—the agent-relative and the world-relative—are related in systematic ways in a given case of action descriptions and in the framework proposed here the basic constraint is (C1):

(C1) $r \in s(\|A\|)$ iff $s \in r(\|A\|)$, with $s \in S$ and $r \in R$

[8] I argue this point in more detail in Elgesem [4].

Think of $s(\|A\|)$ as giving the set of routines the agent can execute in order to bring about A in the situation s, and $r(\|A\|)$ as the set of situations where he will execute the routine r. Again, the underlying idea is that you need both the agent-relative and the world-relative perspectives on the agent to describe what the agent does. (C1) states that these two ways of describing the agent's agency have to "match" each other. This relationship is essential in ascriptions of intentional agency, I argued above, where the effects of the agent's activity on the world are used to describe his intentions and the intentions are used to individuate his actions in the world. Note that (C1) is formulated as a basic constraint on all action descriptions in this framework. However, in the present context it only plays a role in the analysis of intentional actions below.

As mentioned above, Segerberg suggests that. "To be able to do something is to have a routine available".[9] This intuition can be given a simple formulation in the present framework:

(Ability) $\langle I, s\rangle | = \mathbf{Ab}\ A$ iff $\exists t \in S, \exists r \in R: t \in r(\|A\|)$

For an agent to have an ability to do A it is not sufficient to have a general capacity, but we also have to envisage a situation where this capacity can be manifested in the world—i.e. where he can run a routine for A. While having the ability to bring about something is a global property the notion of an opportunity for action is a statement about an agent in some specific circumstance. Again, the routine concept makes it possible to explicate the relationship between agent-relative and the world-relative perspective on the actions:

(Opportunity) $\langle I, s \rangle | = \mathbf{Opp}\ A$ iff $\exists\, r \in R: r \in s(\|A\|)$, i.e. the agent has a routine for A that can be run in the present situation.

One aspect of the relationship between the agent-relative and the world-relative descriptions of agency is that an agent cannot be said to have the opportunity to do something if he not also has the ability to do it. In virtue of (C1) opportunity implies ability (but not vice versa) in the present framework:

(i) $\mathbf{Opp}\ A \rightarrow \mathbf{Ab}\ A$

The weaker notion of agency than intentional action can be defined in different ways. Analogous to Segerberg's operator Real we can define what it is for an agent to realize his ability:

(Realize) $\langle I, s \rangle | = \mathbf{Real}\ A$ iff $\exists\, r \in R: s \in r(\|A\|)$

However, above we argued that we should accept the idea that the criterion of agency is that the action is intentional under some description. The definition of action should therefore make explicit reference to the agent's intention:

(Agency) $\langle I, s\rangle | = \mathbf{Do}\ A$ iff $\exists\, \langle r', t\rangle \in I: s \in r'(\|A\|)$

9 Segerberg [7], p. 88.

The definition says that the agent executes in the present situation one of the routines he intends to execute. However, it is not necessarily the case that the present situation is the *situation* in which he intended to execute it (i.e. perhaps $t \neq s$).

(ii) **Do** A $\rightarrow$ **Ab** *A* $\wedge$ **Opp** A

The third challenge for a theory of intentional action suggested above was to characterize the constraint on the rational formation of intentions. In the present framework the basic rationality constraint on intentions is that there is a "match" between the intended routine and the agent's selection of the world in which he intends to act:

(Intention) $\langle I, s\rangle \models$ **Int** A iff $\exists \langle r', t\rangle \in I: r' \in t(\|A\|)$

The idea is to model the requirements that intentions should be means ends coherent and consistent with the way the agent believes the world is.

In the discussion above I argued that, because of the problem of wayward causal chains, it is a mistake to think that all there is to intentional agency is that the agent intended to do it and that he did it. Therefore, intentional action should not be defined as the simple conjunction of intention and agency (**Int** A and **Do** A). However, the formalism should of course make explicit the relationship between intention, intentional action and the weaker sense of agency. The notion of intentional action should therefore be defined separately and in a way that brings out these relationships:

(Intentional action) $\langle I, s\rangle \models$ **IntDo** A iff $\exists \langle r', t\rangle \in I: s \in r'(\|A\|)$ and $s(\|A\|) \subseteq t(\|A\|)$

The first conjunct in the truth definition is identical to the definition of agency:

(iii) **IntDo** A $\rightarrow$ **Do** A

The second conjunct in the definition implies that the agent intended to do it in virtue of the general constraint (C1):

(iv) **IntDo** A $\rightarrow$ **Int** A

If the first conjunct holds, i.e. $\exists \langle r', t\rangle \in I: s \in r'(\|A\|)$, by (C1) we get $r' \in s(\|A\|)$. Because also the second conjunct holds, i.e. $s(\|A\|) \subseteq t(\|A\|)$, we get $r' \in t(\|A\|)$. This is the definition of intention.

The second conjunct is formulated in a way that is meant to model the idea of bringing about the outcome in the way that was intended, i.e. in "the right way". Intuitively, the idea is here is as follows. Remember that the set $s(\|A\|)$ represent the routines that the agent has available for bringing about A in a given situation. As part of his deliberation walk the agent forms more and more specific intentions and also more and more specific ideas about what the world in which he will realize the intention is like. However, it is plausible to assume that the intention is not specified in every detail. On a given occasion where the agent intends to bring about A, he might have different routines for doing this depending on how the situation develops and where he is in his deliberation process. To stick to Segerberg's own example, even when our agent has settled on the intention to give his friend a certain book for his birthday present, there might still be details that are not fixed in his plan: the exact point in time he will give it to him, whether he will hand it over with his left or right hand, etc. Hence, it seems that up to a point an intention will always be agnostic about a lot of details in the way the intention will eventually be realized. But the final realization of the intention in the real world has to satisfy the constraints defined by the intention, hence the requirement that $s(\|A\|) \subseteq t(\|A\|)$. Because of this condition, the following set is consistent:

(v) {**Int** A, **Do** A, ¬ **IntDo** A }

In this way the formalization satisfies the fourth constraint above, i.e. to articulate that intentions and thus routines are blueprints for how the intentions is to be realized and thus to allow for the type of situation described by (v).

6 Conclusion

The point here has not been to develop the details of a new logic of intentional action but, rater, to argue that the notion of a routine should be brought into the semantics of a formal theory of intention and action. The suggestion is that this is required in order for such a theory to be able to meet the four requirements formulated in the connection with the discussion of the strengths of the routine concept as a basis for a philosophy of action.

References

1. Barwise, K. J., & Seligman, J. (1997). *Information flow: The logic of distributed systems*. Cambridge: Cambridge University Press.
2. Bratman, M. (1987). *Intentions, plans, and practical reason*. Cambridge: Harvard University Press.
3. Davidson, D. (1980). *'Causal relations', in his essays on actions and events*. New York: Clarendon Press.
4. Elgesem, D. (1992). Intentions, actions, and routines: A problem in Krister Segerberg's theory of action. *Synthese*, *85*, 153–177
5. Segerberg, K. (1981). Action games. *Acte Philosophca Fennica*, *32*, 220–231.
6. Segerberg, K. (1982). The logic of deliberate action. *Journal of Philosophical Logic*, *11*, 233–254.
7. Segerberg, K. (1985a). Routines. *Synthese*. *65*(2), 185–210.
8. Segerberg, K. (1985b). Models for actions. In B. K. Matilal & J. L. Shaw (Eds.), *Analytical philosophy in comparative perspective*. Dordrecht: Reidel.
9. von Wright, G. H. (1963). *Norm and action*. New York: Humanities Press.

On the Reconciliation of Logics of Agency and Logics of Event Types

Jan Broersen

Abstract This paper discusses Segerberg's view on agency, a view that is heavily influenced by his thinking about dynamic logic. The main work that puts forward Segerberg's ideas about agency is *Outline of a logic of action*. That article attempts to reconcile the *stit* view of agency with the dynamic logic view of event types. Here I discuss Segerberg's proposal. I will argue that the theory lacks some detail and explanatory power. I will suggest an alternative theory based on an extension of the logic XSTIT. Recently, the subject discussed here has attracted renewed attention of several researchers working in computer science and philosophy.

1 Introduction

Over the last 30 years, two different views on the logic of action have emerged in the computer science and philosophical literature. The first view comes from computer science, and I will call it the 'event type' approach. In this view the structures the logic talks about are labeled transitions systems, where the labels denote a type of event (think of a database update, a register update, a variable assignment, etc). Examples of formalisms of this kind are Hennessey-Milner logic [19], dynamic logic (DL) [21] and process logic [14], but I also take the situation calculus [18] to belong to this branch. The other kind of action formalism originates in philosophy, and focusses on the modeling of agency, that is, on the formal modeling of the connection between agents and the changes in the world they can be held responsible for. In this type of formalism, the structures are choice structures. Examples of formalisms of this kind are 'Bringing It About Logic' (BIAT) [17], *stit*-logic [3], Coalition Logic (CL) [20],

J. Broersen (✉)
Department of Information and Computing Sciences, Utrecht University,
3508 UTRECHT, Netherlands
e-mail: J.M.Broersen@uu.nl

R. Trypuz (ed.), *Krister Segerberg on Logic of Actions*,
Outstanding Contributions to Logic 1, DOI: 10.1007/978-94-007-7046-1_3,

and Alternating time Temporal Logic (ATL) [1] and Brown's logic of ability (which is a predecessor to CL and ATL) [9].

Many authors have sought to combine both views on action. Examples are the work of Herzig and Lorini [15], and the work of Xu [29]. Combining the computer science view on action (but from now on I will refer to this view as the event-type view) and the philosophical, agency-oriented view is of central importance to the understanding of the relation between computation and agency, and thus, it seems safe to claim, to the understanding of the possibilities of Artificial Intelligence.

Krister Segerberg, being one of the central researchers working on action formalisms at the time of their emergence, describes the problem as follows in *Outline of a logic of action* [26] (which extends [25] and is the culmination of ideas first put forward in *Bringing it about* [23] and *Getting started: Beginnings in the logic of action* [24].): "to combine action logic in the Scott/Chellas/Belnap tradition with Pratt's dynamic logic". In *Outline of a logic of action* Segerberg then puts forward a language, a class of structures and a semantics whose main aim is to reconcile the two different views on the logic of action.

Here I will explain and discuss Segerberg's theory of agency and action as put forward in *Outline of a logic of action*. In explaining and discussing this work, I will point to the places where I do not agree with the modeling choices made by Segerberg. Then, to explain my view on the matter in a coherent way, I will put forward my own outline of a theory of action.

That there is a problem to be solved here shines through clearly if we look at the practice of computer scientists to claim that agency in dynamic logic is modeled sufficiently by annotating event types with agents or groups of agents. However, this practice does not explain the logical differences between an action a performed by agent 1, an action a performed by agent 2 and an action a performed by agents 1 and 2 together. For instance, in a dynamic logic theory with event types annotated with agents and groups of agents, it is entirely unclear if there are logical relations between $[a_{ag_1}]\varphi$, $[a_{ag_2}]\psi$ and $[a_{ag_1,ag_2}]\chi$, and if there are such relations, it is unclear what they are (e.g.: since all formulas concern the same event type a, should there be a logical relation between the three formulas? What axioms describe this relation? If there is no such relation, then why introduce event type notations in the formulas at all?).

2 Segerberg's Action Theory

In *Outline of a logic of action*, Segerberg puts forward the following syntax for his unifying action formalism.

Definition 2.1 Given a countable set of atomic proposition letters P and $p \in P$, and given a countable set Ags of agent names, and $i \in Ags$, the formal language $\mathcal{L}_{\mathsf{SEG}}$ is:

$$\varphi := p \mid \neg\varphi \mid \varphi \wedge \varphi \mid [H\psi]\varphi \mid [F]\varphi \mid [P]\varphi \mid [NEXT: \psi]\varphi \mid [LAST: \psi]\varphi \mid$$
$$does_i(\alpha) \mid done_i(\alpha) \mid reals_i(\alpha) \mid realled_i(\alpha) \mid occs(\alpha) \mid occed(\alpha)$$
$$\alpha := \alpha; \beta \mid \delta_i\varphi \mid \epsilon\varphi$$

The reading of the event type terms is as follows:

$\alpha; \beta =$ the composite event type of beta after alpha
$\delta_i\varphi =$ agent i bringing it about that φ (see [23] and [27])
$\epsilon\varphi =$ the coming about of φ

The reading of the modalities is as follows:

$[H\psi]\varphi = \varphi$ holds for all histories for which ψ
$[F]\varphi =$ henceforth φ
$[P]\varphi =$ it has always been the case that φ
$[NEXT: \psi]\varphi =$ next time that ψ, φ holds
$[LAST: \psi]\varphi =$ last time that ψ, φ held
$does_i(\alpha) =$ agent i does an event of type α
$done_i(\alpha) =$ agent i just did an event of type α
$reals_i(\alpha) =$ agent i realizes an event of type α
$realled_i(\alpha) =$ agent i just realized an event of type α
$occs(\alpha) =$ an event of type α occurs
$occed(\alpha) =$ an event of type α just occured

It has to be emphasized that all readings are relative to a state and a history (which is a 'timeline' extending infinitely into the past and the future). So 'always in the future' means always in the future *on the current history of evaluation*, and does *not* mean 'always in the future independent of whatever agents will do or whatever events will occur'. So, like in *stit* theory, Segerberg takes the Ockhamist approach to future contingencies [22], which means that truth of formulas is relative to a history. This means that histories or paths are viewed as possible worlds. That insight is essential. In his semantics Segerberg uses triples $\langle h, u, g\rangle$, where u is the current state, h a path from u into the past, and g a path from u into the future. He calls triples $\langle h, u, g\rangle$ 'articulated histories'. All truth conditions are relative to articulated histories.

Figure 1 shows how in Segerberg's framework histories are build from sequences of actions, pictured as triangles. Histories are defined as maximal sets of subsequent actions.

I will not give the formal definitions of the models and the truth conditions, since the semantics is easy to describe in terms of pictures and natural language. In Fig. 1 we see the actions depicted as triangles. In the formal semantics, an action is a triple (i, a, p), where i is an agent, a is an event type, and p a finite sequence of states

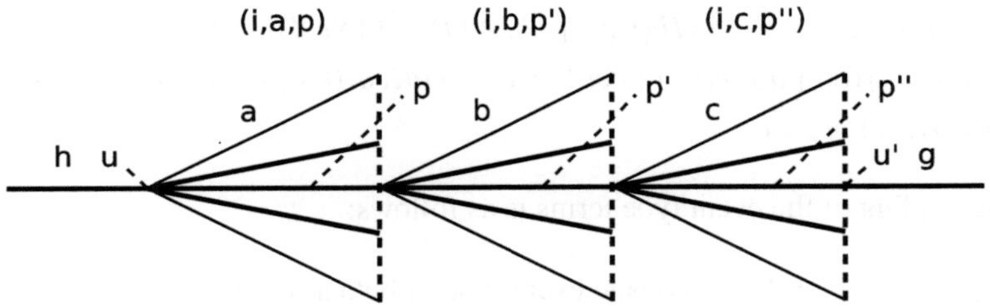

Fig. 1 Histories as sequences of actions in Segerberg's action semantics

representing the way the agent i performs the event of type a. In the picture, events are represented by triangles build from two fine lines and one interrupted line. We see three events, one of type a, one of type b and one of type c. The sub-triangles build from thick lines and parts of the interrupted lines represent the 'ways and means' in which agent i can perform the event types that are associated with the bigger triangles. In terms of this picture the semantics of the action operators is easy to explain. Events of type $\epsilon\varphi$ are those for which φ holds on all the points depicted by the interrupted line of a triangle. Events of type $\delta_i\varphi$ are those for which φ holds on all the points depicted by the interrupted line on a triangle for agent i. Now, $does_i(\alpha)$ holds at a point on the history just in case the event types that agent i 'does' are those interpreting α. For 'doing', the history of evaluation must be contained inside the inner triangles representing the agent's way and means to do the event of the given type. For instance, in point u in the picture it holds that $does_i(a; b; c)$. In point u' in the picture it holds that $done_i(a; b; c)$. But, also we have that in point u in the picture it holds that $reals_i(a; b; c)$ and in point u' that $realled_i(a; b; c)$. For 'realizing' the truth condition is only weaker, and the history of evaluation must run through the outer triangle. It is clear then that one validity of the logic is that doing an event of a given type implies realizing that same event. But the other way around does not hold, which is exemplified by cases where the history of evaluation runs through the part of the bigger triangle that is not included in the smaller triangle. The interpretations of $occs(\alpha)$ and $occed(\alpha)$ are similar to those of $reals_i(\alpha)$ and $realled_i(\alpha)$, the difference being that the agents are quantified out. The interpretation of the modalities $[F]\varphi$, $[P]\varphi$, $[NEXT : \psi]\varphi$ and $[LAST : \psi]\varphi$ is straightforward given their informal reading and the fact that their formal interpretation is relative to individual histories. The interpretation of $[H\psi]\varphi$ is clarified ones we realize that histories like the one depicted in Fig. 1 are elements of trees resulting from the fact that in each state agents in general have multiple event types to choose from and for each event type in general have multiple ways to perform them. Action 'trees' (maybe 'bundles' is a better word) are sets of histories closed under these alternatives for the agents. Now $[H\psi]\varphi$ is true in a state on a history if on all alternative continuations of the path from the past that satisfy ψ, also φ is true.

2.1 Realizing Versus Doing

As explained above, the theory distinguishes between doing and realizing. In particular, $\langle h, u, g\rangle \models does_i(\alpha)$ holds if in state u, along the future history g, along the first part agent i does an event of the type α. In terms of the triangle-based picture of Fig. 1: if the 'inner' triangles (that is, i's possible ways to perform and event of the given type) along future history g are those interpreting α. The semantics of an agent i *realizing* events of a given type is slightly different. $\langle h, u, g\rangle \models reals_i(\alpha)$ holds if in state u, along the future history g, in the first part the agent i realizes an event of the type α. In terms of the triangle-based picture of Fig. 1: if the 'outer' triangles (that is, the events of a given type) along future history g are part of 'outer' triangles that interpret α.

By introducing the difference between realizing and doing, Segerberg aims to accommodate the intuition that an agent can be part of an activity without really contributing to that activity. However, the theory lacks explanatory power here. In what sense can an agent be part of an activity without contributing to it? What is the exact sense in which the agent is still connected to an activity if it is not that it is in some sense responsible for that activity? In *stit* theory, these issue have been resolved quite satisfactory. Either an agent ensures that a condition occurs, or it allows for the negation of that condition to occur. So, by refraining to see to it that the negation of a condition occurs, an agent can play a role in an activity without being the 'author' (as Segerberg puts it) of that activity.

A related problem for the theory is that it does not allow for indeterminism. At least, if it does, it is unclear how. On the one hand it is able to define the *stit* operator (as I will explain later on), so it seems there should be a notion of non-determinism in the system. However, the theory talks about 'ways and means' for the performance of actions as if these are procedures to choose from for the agent. So, it sees the different possible ways of performing an event of a certain type as a choice that is fully under control of the agent, not leaving room for non-determinism.

2.2 More Actions at Once

I think a theory of action should allow for the possibility of single agents performing more than one action at the same time. And indeed, it seems to me that in Segerberg's theory the situation can be as in Fig. 2 (a picture that I will use later on to explain the simulation of *stit* semantics in the theory). The picture shows how along the current history an agent does both an event of type a and an event of type b. However, it is not completely clear if it is actually Segerberg's intention to allow for these situations. For instance can an agent at the same time *do* an event of type a and only *realize* an event of type b? And what would that mean? For instance, would the event of type b be an unintended side effect of the responsibility for event a?

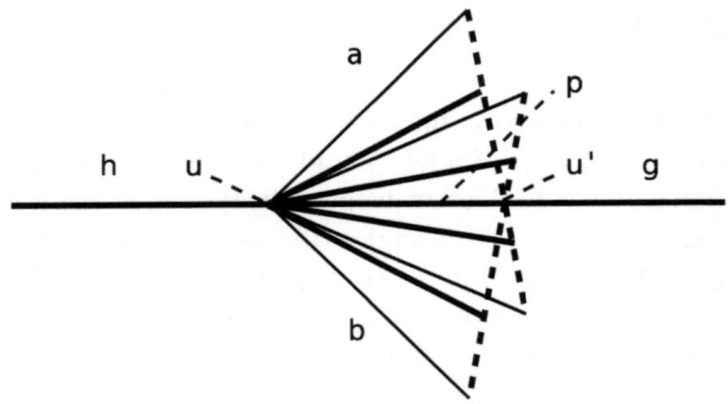

Fig. 2 Explanation of *stit* simulation in Segerberg's action semantics

2.3 Multi-agency and Collective Agency

Branching in action trees is defined in terms of closure of branching under the different possibilities individual agents have to perform an event of a certain type. But the basic theory does not give an answer to how simultaneous actions of different agents relate to each other. As Segerberg admits on page 381, in the base theory, only one agent can act at the time. However, for a theory of agency and action it seems important to ask whether or not one agent, by performing an action, can prevent another agent from performing his action simultaneously. That is, is there, or should there be, a notion of independence of agency like in *stit* theory? A related problem is that it is not clear how branching can occur as the result of collective action. However, Segerberg discusses an approach to this problem later on in the paper (page 375). The idea is to make the ways and means function relative to collectives of agents in stead of individual agents. I believe this is a correct idea, and I will use a closely related idea in my own theory in Sect. 3.

2.4 The Generalization to Complex Action

On page 371 Segerberg discusses a possible generalization of the action theory by allowing regular operations on event types, as in dynamic logic. The suggestion is that this generalization is easy and that, for instance, $\langle h, u, g\rangle \models does_i(\alpha;\gamma \cup \beta;\gamma)$ holds if the first part of the history g is either of the type $\alpha;\gamma$ or of the type $\beta;\gamma$. But, I disagree with that semantics. Assume that indeed in state u there is an alternative of the type β. But also assume that if the agent would have performed an action of type β, afterwards it would not have been possible to do an action of type γ. Then, is it still justified to say that the agent does an action of the type $(\alpha;\gamma \cup \beta;\gamma)$? So, in my opinion, checking if an agent does an action that corresponds with a complex event of the type $\alpha;\gamma\cup\beta;\gamma$ should involve checking that if it would have been β that was performed at the time of choice, afterwards γ is still a possible continuation. The underlying problem is, I believe, that complex actions cannot be interpreted in an Ockhamist way relative to a single history only, because as soon as there is a non-deterministic choice involved (as the result of introducing a binary choice operation $\cup$ and/or the Kleene star *), also alternative histories will have to be considered to determine whether or not a complex action (i.e., a strategy) is actually performed. Also the idea of an agent performing an event of a type that is indeterministic needs much more clarification. What does this non-determinism represent? Uncertainty or practical ignorance on the part of the agent? Lack of agentive control? Intrinsic indeterminedness of the environment? Also, confinement of indeterminism to operators like $\cup$ and * suggests that we can explicitly point to the indeterminism in agency by specifying it in non-deterministic programs. But, in my opinion non-deterministic programs fall far short as an adequate model for agency.

2.5 Simulation of the Stit Operator

Segerberg argues that in his theory the Chellas stit operator is definable through the following definition.

$$[i \text{ cstit}]\varphi \equiv_{def} realled_i(\delta_i\varphi)$$

I will explain this definition using Fig. 2. The definition says (implicitly, using a function $\mathbf{D}(i, P)$ whose formal definition I do not give here) that an agent sees to it that φ if and only if agent i just 'realized' an action (i, a, p) for which it is true that it ensured the outcome φ independent of how the event a was 'done'. In terms of Fig. 2, the *stit* semantics is then as follows. In state u' (and *not* in u) along articulated history $\langle hp, u', g\rangle$, the agent sees to it that φ if either the event of type a or the event of type b (and we assume here that these are the only two events for which the agent i in state u' has a 'way or means' to perform it through p) have as a guaranteed result that φ holds (that is, on each point of at least one of the two dotted lines in the figure, φ must hold).

In my opinion there are three problems with this definition. The first is that since it is unclear what intuitions are behind the distinction between realizing and doing, it is also unclear why the *stit* operator is not defined in such a way that the condition φ is ensured independent of how the agent *does* the event (in stead of guaranteeing the outcome independent of how the agent *realizes* the event). That is, it is not clear why the definition could not be $[i \text{ cstit}]\varphi \equiv_{def} done_i(\delta_i\varphi)$. In terms of Fig. 2 this would amount to the condition that for at least one the two triangles, only the points on the interrupted line part belonging to the inner triangle satisfy φ.

The second problem is the existential quantification that is implicit in Segerberg's version of the *stit* operator. An agent can only see to a condition φ if *there is* an event of a certain type serving as a witness for this. This means that the truth condition for the modal *stit* operator defined in this way has an $\exists - \forall$ structure, which implies that the operator will be weak and will *not* satisfy the agglomeration schema $[i \text{ cstit}]\varphi \wedge [i \text{ cstit}]\psi \rightarrow [i \text{ cstit}](\varphi \wedge \psi)$ (in terms of the picture in Fig. 2: if φ is true on all points of the interrupted line for event of type a and ψ is true on all points of the interrupted line for event of type b, the antecedent of the axiom is true while the consequent is not). However, all *stit* operators in the literature are normal and do satisfy this schema. Another problem with linking agency with the existence of events of a certain type is that events and their types are taken as the starting point for defining agency. I believe this should be the other way around: theories of agency can be used to understand and define the nature of events and their types. This is the approach I will take in Sect. 3.

The third problem for the encoding of the *stit* operator in the theory is that it is unclear how the central *stit* ideas about non-determinism take form in the models. The central idea of *stit* theory is that seeing to it that a condition holds is the same as ensuring that condition irrespective of the non-determinism of the environment (which includes the simultaneous choices of other agents). Now, saying that φ has to hold on all 'realization-alternative' outcomes (that is, the alternatives within the outer triangles) of the realization of an event of a certain type can hardly be seen as ensuring φ modulo *non-determinism* as in *stit* theory. But also if Segerberg would demand that φ would be true on all 'execution-alternative' outcomes (that is, the alternatives within the inner triangles), the semantics would not be one based on the *stit* idea of ensuring a condition modulo non-determism.

2.6 Simulation of the Dynamic Logic Operator

The simulation of the standard basic dynamic logic modality in the theory is as follows:

$$[\alpha]\varphi \equiv_{def} [H : occs(\alpha)][NEXT : occed(\alpha)]\varphi$$

I believe this simulation is intuitive and correct. It defines the modality $[a]\varphi$ as "directly after all possible continuations of the type α it holds that φ". However, it is important to bear in mind that evaluation is still relative to individual articulated histories. And in case $[\alpha]\varphi$ is true on an articulated history $\langle h, u, g\rangle$, it does *not* follow that along the future history g of that same articulated history, the agent i performs an event of type a resulting in φ. The right interpretation is: "for all possible future histories g' whose first part is an event of the type α, immediately after α is finished, φ is true". So it can be that α does not occur on the articulated history $\langle h, u, g\rangle$ relative to which is evaluated. For instance, in Fig. 3 it holds that $\langle h, u, g\rangle \models [a]\varphi$ and $\langle h, u, g'\rangle \models [a]\varphi$ and $\langle h, u, g''\rangle \models [a]\varphi$ in case φ holds on all points of the interrupted line belonging to the triangle of the event of type a. The reason for this interpretation is that $[\alpha]\varphi$ is what Prior [22] calls a Peircian temporal operator, while Segerberg's base semantics is, in Prior's terminology, Ockhamist.

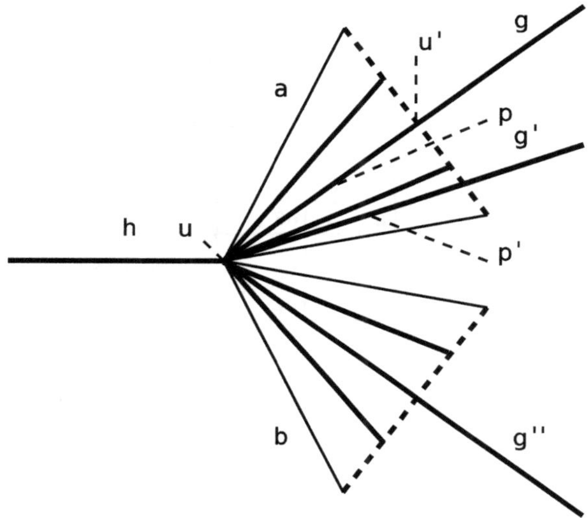

Fig. 3 Explanation of dynamic logic action type simulation in Segerberg's action semantics

3 Outline of an Alternative Theory of Action

I will now put forward an alternative outline for a theory of action. I will take the logic XSTIT as the base logic of agency and add a new operator to it that will enable me to simulate logics of event types (like dynamic logic) within the *stit* framework. This simulation requires a different view on the relation between event types and agency then the one put forward by Segerberg.

It is important, I think, to emphasize that in dynamic logic event types describe characteristics of *transitions*. In dynamic logic, if two transitions are of the same type, they have the same event type name, and using the logic we can specify that they have the same pre- and post-condition relation. For instance, if we want to specify that a-events are of the type whose instances have as a sufficient precondition ψ relative to the postcondition φ, we can write $\psi \rightarrow [a]\varphi$. The semantics of dynamic logic interprets these formulas in a transition system where a transition can only be of type a if in case it is a transition from a state where ψ it leads to a state where φ. As an example we might take the event type of "the closing of a door". Precondition is the door being open, postcondition is the door being closed. If as the result of agentive effort a door is moving from an open position to a closed position, the agent performs an action that is of the type "the closing of a door". But note that that same action or event might also have other types, such as "spending energy", or "producing a slamming noise", etc. But also note that it might take two or more agents to close a door (it might be very heavy). In that case the event of type "closing the door" cannot be linked to one agent exclusively.

The above described view on the relation between agency and event types will be the point of departure for the theory I will put forward here. It will be convenient to

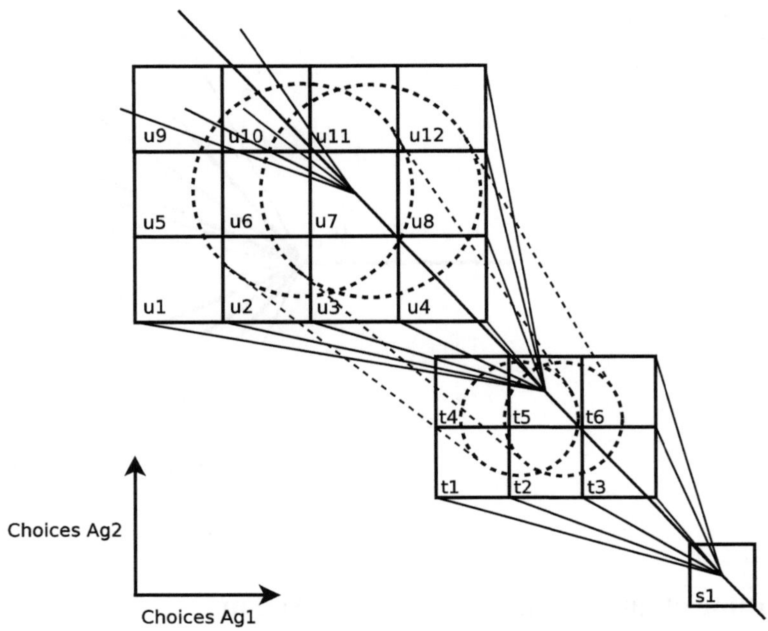

Fig. 4 Event types (*the dotted cylinders*) versus multi-agent choices (the game form structures)

see the central idea in a picture. In Fig. 4 we see the described view on event types pictured inside an XSTIT frame fragment. The XSTIT part gives the states, histories and choices for two agents. Three choice situations s, t and u along one central history are pictured, where in the first situation s, no genuine choices are possible. Of course, the central history (or more correct 'history bundle') pictured is only one of the many histories (bundles) that may result from the genuine choices the two agents have in t and u; the tree of possible histories is closed under the choices that are possible in the different situations. I will extend XSTIT frames to XSTIT.ET frames by adding event types. In the picture these appear as the cylinders build from interrupted line elements. For instance, the right cylinder might picture transitions of type b and the left cylinder transitions of type a. This set-up allows for: (1) different transitions for different situations throughout the frame being of the same event type, (2) single choices realizing more than one event type, and (3) events of a given type for which it takes strictly more than one agent to perform them.

With this conceptualization we arrive at the following ontology. Events are transitions at specific situations at specific moments in time. Actions are events that occur due to agentive involvement of agents.[1] Different agents at different times in

[1] Actually, in the present set-up the difference between events an actions is vacuous, since all transitions in the frames are due to agents. And seeing 'nature' as just another agent is problematic, since it seems natural to demand that nature does not have genuine choices.

different situations can execute an event of the same type. So, an event can be of a certain type α. But, it is never the case that α is the denotation of an action itself (as computer scientists are sometimes inclined to think).

3.1 The Logic XSTIT.ET

I will define a logic with the acronym XSTIT.ET by extending my earlier definitions for the logic XSTIT (first put forward in [7] and corrected, adapted and extended in various ways in [5], [6] and [8]). The characters ET stand for 'Event Types'. The modal language of XSTIT.ET is given by the following definition:

Definition 3.1 Given a countable set of propositions P and $p \in P$, a finite set Ags of agent names with $A \subseteq Ags$, and a countable set of event type names Et with $a \in Et$, the formal language $\mathcal{L}_{\mathsf{XSTIT.ET}}$ is:

$$\varphi := p \mid \neg\varphi \mid \varphi \wedge \varphi \mid \Box\varphi \mid [A\ xstit]\varphi \mid X\varphi \mid [A\ perf\ a]$$

Besides the usual propositional connectives, the syntax of XSTIT.ET comprises four modal operators. The operator $\Box\varphi$ expresses 'historical necessity', and plays the same role as the well-known path quantifiers in logics such as CTL and CTL* [12]. Another way of talking about this operator is to say that it expresses that φ is 'settled'. However, settledness does *not* necessarily mean that a property is *always* true in the future (as often thought). Settledness may, in general, apply to the condition that φ occurs 'some' time in the future, or to some other temporal property. This is reflected by the fact that settledness is interpreted as a universal quantification over the *branching* dimension of time, and *not* over the dimension of duration. The operator $[A\ \mathsf{xstit}]\varphi$ stands for 'agents A jointly see to it that φ in the next state' The third modality is the next operator $X\varphi$. It has a standard interpretation as the transition to a next system state. The new operator introduced in this context is $[A\ \mathsf{perf}\ a]$. It expresses that the group of agents A *performs* an event of the type a.

To give a formal interpretation to the new operator $[A\ \mathsf{perf}\ a]$ we extend XSTIT frames (in their version using functions in stead of relations) with a function A returning the event types of a transition between two subsequent states.

Definition 3.2 An XSTIT.ET-frame is a tuple $\langle S, H, A, E\rangle$ such that[2]:

1. S is a non-empty set of static states. Elements of S are denoted s, s', etc.
2. H is a non-empty set of possible system histories isomorphic to infinite sequences $\ldots s_{-2}, s_{-1}, s_0, s_1, s_2, \ldots$ with $s_i \in S$ for $i \in \mathbb{Z}$. Elements of H are denoted h, h', etc. We denote that s' succeeds s on the history h by $s' = succ(s, h)$ and by $s = pred(s', h)$. We have the following bundeling constraint on the set H:

[2] In the meta-language we use the same symbols both as constant names and as variable names, and we assume universal quantification of unbound meta-variables.

a. if $s \in h$ and $s' \in h'$ and $s = s'$ then $pred(s, h) = pred(s, h')$

3. $A : S \times S \mapsto 2^{Et}$ is a function mapping subsequent states to a set of basic event types characterizing the transition between the two states. We have the following constraints on the function A:

   a. $A(s, t) = \emptyset$ if there is no $h \in H$ with $s \in h$ and $t \in h$ and $t = succ(s, h)$
   b. for any $h \in H$ and $h' \in H$: if $s \in h$ and $s' \in h'$ and $s = s'$ then $A(pred(s, h), s) = A(pred(s', h'), s')$

4. $E : S \times H \times 2^{Ags} \mapsto 2^S$ is an h-effectivity function yielding for a group of agents A the set of next static states allowed by the simultaneous choices exercised by the agents relative to a history. On the function E we have the following constraints:

   a. if $s \notin h$ then $E(s, h, A) = \emptyset$
   b. $succ(s, h) \in E(s, h, A)$
   c. $\exists h : s' = succ(s, h)$ if and only if $\forall h$: if $s \in h$ then $s' \in E(s, h, \emptyset)$
   d. if $s \in h$ then $E(s, h, Ags) = \{succ(s, h)\}$
   e. if $A \supset B$ then $E(s, h, A) \subseteq E(s, h, B)$
   f. if $A \cap B = \emptyset$ and $s \in h$ and $s \in h'$ then $E(s, h, A) \cap E(s, h', B) \neq \emptyset$

In definition 3.2 above, we refer to the states s as 'static states'. This is to distinguish them from what we call 'dynamic states', which are combinations $\langle s, h \rangle$ of static states and histories. Dynamic states will function as the elementary units of evaluation of the logic. This is very much like in Segerberg's semantics, the only difference being that we do no articulate the past of a history. We do not need to refer to the past in our models, since we do not have backwards looking operators in the logical language.

The name 'h-effectivity functions' for the functions defined in item 3. above is short for 'h-relative effectivity functions'. This name is inspired by similar terminology in Coalition Logic whose semantics is in terms of 'effectivity functions'. An effectivity function in Coalition Logic is a function $E : S \times 2^{Ags} \mapsto 2^{2^S}$ mapping static states to sets of sets of static states. Each set in 2^{2^S} then represents a choice. In our h-effectivity functions, choices are always relative to a history (the history that is part of the dynamic state we evaluate against), which is why h-effectivity functions map to sets instead of to sets of sets.

Condition 2.a above ensures that the structure of histories is isomorphic to that of a tree.

Condition 3.a ensures that event types are only assigned to state pairs where one state successes the other.

Condition 3.b ensues that if histories are still undivided, transitions between their subsequent states are uniform, that is, they are characterized by the same set of event type labels.

Condition 4.b says that the next state on the current history is always in the current effectivity set of any group of agents. This gives a notion of success (in instantaneous *stit* semantics [4] the success property is modeled by the truth axiom).

Condition 4.c above states that any next state is in the effectivity set of the empty set and vice versa. This implies the empty set of agents is powerless: it cannot choose between different options and has to 'go with the flow'.

Condition 4.d above implies that a simultaneous choice exertion of all agents in the system uniquely determines a next static state. A similar condition holds for related formalisms like ATL [2] and Coalition logic (CL for short). However, we want to point here to an important difference with these formalisms. Although 4.d uniquely determines the next state relative to a simultaneous choice for all agents in the system, it does not determine the unique next 'dynamic state'. This is important, because dynamic states are the units of evaluation. In ATL and CL, static states are the units of evaluation. As a consequence, CL is not definable in this logic.

Condition 4.e expresses coalition monotony, saying that whatever is ensured by the choice of a group of agents is also ensured by the simultaneous choice of any supergroup of agents.

Condition 4.f above states that simultaneous choices of different agents never have an empty intersection. In *stit* this is referred to as the condition of 'independence of agency'. It says that a choice exertion of one agent can never have as a consequence that some other agent is limited in the choices it can exercise simultaneously.

I briefly explain the formal definition of the frames in definition 3.2 using Fig. 4. The small squares are static states in the effectivity sets of $E(s, h, Ags)$. Combinations of static states and histories running thought them form dynamic states. The big, outmost squares forming the boundaries of the game forms, collect the static (and implicitly also the dynamic) states in the effectivity sets of $E(s, h, \emptyset)$. Independence of choices is reflected by the fact that the game forms contain no 'holes' in them. The semantics is a so called 'bundled' semantics. In a bundled semantics choice exertion is always thought of as the separation of two bundles of histories: one bundle ensured by the choice exercised and one bundle excluded by that choice. In the figure the bundles are depicted as bundles.

We now define models by adding a valuation of propositional atoms to the frames of definition 3.2.

Definition 3.3 A frame $\mathcal{F} = \langle S, H, A, E \rangle$ is extended to a model $\mathcal{M} = \langle S, H, E, \pi \rangle$ by adding a valuation π of atomic propositions:

- π is a valuation function $\pi : P \longrightarrow 2^{S \times H}$ assigning to each atomic proposition the set of dynamic states relative to which they are true.

The truth conditions for the semantics of the operators are fairly standard. The non-standard aspect is the two-dimensionality of the semantics, meaning that we evaluate truth with respect to dynamic states built from a dimension of histories and a dimension of static states.

Definition 3.4 Relative to a model $\mathcal{M} = \langle S, H, A, E, \pi \rangle$, truth $\mathcal{M}, \langle s, h \rangle \models \varphi$ of a formula φ in a dynamic state $\langle s, h \rangle$, with $s \in h$, is defined as:

$$\begin{aligned}
\mathcal{M}, \langle s, h\rangle \models p &\Leftrightarrow s \in \pi(p)\\
\mathcal{M}, \langle s, h\rangle \models \neg\varphi &\Leftrightarrow \text{not } \mathcal{M}, \langle s, h\rangle \models \varphi\\
\mathcal{M}, \langle s, h\rangle \models \varphi \wedge \psi &\Leftrightarrow \mathcal{M}, \langle s, h\rangle \models \varphi \text{ and}\\
& \mathcal{M}, \langle s, h\rangle \models \psi\\
\mathcal{M}, \langle s, h\rangle \models \Box\varphi &\Leftrightarrow \forall h' : \text{ if } s \in h' \text{ then}\\
& \mathcal{M}, \langle s, h'\rangle \models \varphi\\
\mathcal{M}, \langle s, h\rangle \models X\varphi &\Leftrightarrow \forall s' : \text{ if } s' = succ(s, h) \text{ then}\\
& \mathcal{M}, \langle s', h\rangle \models \varphi\\
\mathcal{M}, \langle s, h\rangle \models [A\ xstit]\varphi &\Leftrightarrow \forall s', h' : \text{ if } s' \in E(s, h, A) \text{ and}\\
& s' \in h' \text{ then } \mathcal{M}, \langle s', h'\rangle \models \varphi\\
\mathcal{M}, \langle s, h\rangle \models [A\ perf\ a] &\Leftrightarrow \forall s', h' : \text{ if } s' \in E(s, h, A) \text{ and}\\
& s' \in h' \text{ then } a \in A(s, s')
\end{aligned}$$

Satisfiability, validity on a frame and general validity are defined as usual.

Note that the historical necessity operator quantifies over one dimension, and the next operator over the other. The *stit* modality combines both dimensions.

Definition 3.5 The following axiom schemas, in combination with a standard axiomatization for propositional logic, and the standard rules (like necessitation) for the normal modal operators, define a Hilbert system for XSTIT.ET:

	S5 for $\Box$
	KD for each $[A\ xstit]$
(Det)	$\neg X \neg\varphi \rightarrow X\varphi$
($\emptyset$ = Sett)	$[\emptyset\ xstit]\varphi \leftrightarrow \Box X\varphi$
(Ags = XSett)	$[Ags\ xstit]\varphi \leftrightarrow X\Box\varphi$
(CMon)	$[A\ xstit]\varphi \rightarrow [B\ xstit]\varphi$ for $A \subseteq B$
(Indep-G)	$\Diamond[A\ xstit]\varphi \wedge \Diamond[B\ xstit]\psi \rightarrow \Diamond([A\ xstit]\varphi \wedge [B\ xstit]\psi)$ *for* $A \cap B = \emptyset$
(a-CMon)	$[A\ perf\ a] \rightarrow [B\ perf\ a]$ *for* $A \subseteq B$
(a-Indep-G)	$\Diamond[A\ perf\ a] \wedge \Diamond[B\ perf\ b] \rightarrow \Diamond([A\ perf\ a] \wedge [B\ perf\ b])$ *for* $A \cap B = \emptyset$
(Aa-Lnk)	$[A\ perf\ a] \wedge \Box([Ags\ perf\ a] \rightarrow X\varphi) \rightarrow [A\ xstit]\varphi$

Conjecture 3.1 *The Hilbert system of definition 3.5 is complete with respect to the semantics of definition 3.4.*

The logic of the new operator $[A$ perf $a]$ is very simple. It is not a traditional modal operator, since it works on event type terms and not on arbitrary formulas. Since the event type terms are atomic here, it is close to obvious that the above system is complete. Of course we can get more interesting logics by generalizing to boolean event types or to a regular language like in full propositional dynamic logic. But this is left for future work. Here the central aim is to put forward the central idea about the relation between agency and event types.

Now it is time to explain how in the logic XSTIT.ET we can simulate the basic dynamic logic operator $[a]\varphi$. This is accomplished by the following definition.

Definition 3.6 $[a]\varphi \equiv_{def} \Box([Ags\ perf\ a] \rightarrow X\varphi)$

Proposition 3.1 *Any event type operator* $[a]\varphi$ *as given by definition 3.6 is a normal modal K operator (like in Hennessey-Milner logic)*

The proposition claims that the simulation is indeed a correct simulation of a dynamic logic like operator, and is easily verified by inspection of the semantics. Now I briefly mention three simple properties that follow in the logic.

(a) $\langle a\rangle\varphi \leftrightarrow \Diamond([Ags\ \mathsf{perf}\ a] \wedge X\varphi)$
(b) $[A\ \mathsf{perf}\ a] \wedge [a]\varphi \rightarrow [A\ \mathsf{xstit}]\varphi$
(c) $[a]\varphi \rightarrow \Box[a]\varphi$

Property (a) follows as the dual of definition 3.6. One thing it says is that an event of some type can only occur if the complete group of agents can perform it. Property (b) says that if a group performs an act of a certain type, and if acts of that type, when they occur guarantee that φ holds, then the group sees to it that φ. This property embodies the central relationship between agency and event type reasoning in this theory. Finally, property (c) emphasizes the Peircian character of the dynamic logic operator.

The axiom (a-Indep-G) expresses independence of event types in the sense that if one agent can perform an event of type *a* and another agent can perform an event of type *b*, it is always possible for them to perform these events jointly. It might seem then that here the theory goes wrong. For instance, if *a* is the type 'the closing of a door' and *b* is the type 'the opening of a door', then we cannot have that events of these types can occur at the same time, which means that the axiom does not apply. However, when we say that an agent has the ability to perform an event of the type 'the opening of a door', we never mean that this agent has the ability *under all possible circumstances*. Indeed if another agent obstructs, or if moisture has caused the door to expand the agent cannot open the door even though we would still say that the agent has the ability to open a door. So, an ability is always a conditional: the capacity to perform an action 'under normal circumstances'. Often we are not even aware of what these circumstance are (which relates directly to what in formal theories of action is called the 'qualification problem' [13]). But we know that in most cases we will be able to perform the event associated with the ability.[3] So examples as the one given here are not a counter example to the axiom.

At the end of the introduction I said that a good theory of agency and event types should explain how one agent performing an event of type *a* differs from another

[3] If we model knowledge using probabilities, as in [6], we might also say that an ability is the capacity to significantly higher the chance that an event occurs.

agent performing an event of type a and from both of them performing the event of type a at the same time. Here I will show how the logic makes a difference between these situations. In the logic these three positions can be represented by $[A \text{ perf } a]$, $[B \text{ perf } a]$ and $[A \cup B \text{ perf } a]$ with $A \cap B = \emptyset$ (for the sake of generality we generalize to groups). Because of axiom $(a - CMon)$ we have that the third condition follows from each of the first two conditions. Furthermore we have that this is the only logical dependency there is between the formulas. So, $[A \text{ perf } a]$ can be satisfied while $[B \text{ perf } a]$ is not, and $[A \cup B \text{ perf } a]$ can be satisfied, while neither of $[A \text{ perf } a]$ or $[B \text{ perf } a]$ is.

3.2 Collective Responsibility for an Action

Figure 5 pictures two situations of collective responsibility for an event of type a. In the left picture we have that "$[ag_1 \text{ perf } a] \wedge [ag_2 \text{ perf } a]$" (the grey row is the choice exerted by agent 2 and the grey column is the choice exerted by agent 1). Here both agent ag_1 and agent ag_2 perform an event of type a, and if one of them had chosen differently, the event of type a would still have occurred due to the agentive effort of the other agent. In the right picture we have that "$[ag_1 \cup ag_2 \text{ perf } a]$" and the combined agentive effort of both agents is required for the event of type a to occur.

It is a very interesting question to ask in what sense the collective responsibilities differ in these two situations. Assume that the event of type a is one that is wrong (relative to some normative system) and that we have to decide in which situation the agents are more to blame. Interestingly enough we can argue in two opposite directions. We might say that the individual agents in the left 'full cross' case are more to blame, because each on their own their effort would have been enough to ensure that the bad event occurs. This can be interpreted as pointing to a strong determination on the side of both agents involved. On the other hand we might argue

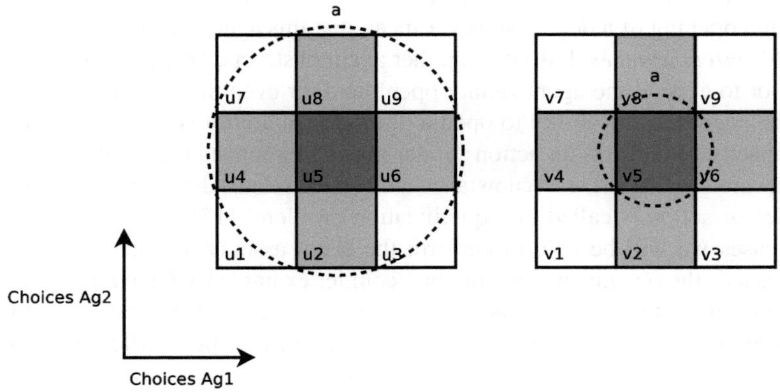

Fig. 5 "$[ag_1 \text{ perf } a] \wedge [ag_2 \text{ perf } a]$" versus "$[ag_1 \cup ag_2 \text{ perf } a]$"

that in the full cross case, both agent's actions are not 'sine qua non', meaning that their effort was not strictly necessary for the bad event to occur. Here the argument would be that each of the agents can claim that the bad event would occur anyway, because the other agent already ensured it. We can make similar arguments starting from the right picture; the one where a is associated with the center of the cross. On the one hand we can argue that relative to the full cross scenario, the agents each individually are more to blame, because each of them had the power to prevent a from happening. On the other hand, we can say that each of them is less to blame in comparison to the full cross case, because their action alone was not enough to ensure a; they both needed the other, and in that sense they could not have been 100 % sure about the outcome.

I believe to analyze this twin example further, and understand how collective responsibility and individual responsibility relate to each other, we need to bring the epistemic dimension into the picture. I will leave this to future work.

4 Related Work

Fairly recently several authors addressed the problem of combining logics of agency and dynamic logic. Here I will mention these works only briefly. Recently Marek Sergot proposed the logic of unwitting collective agency [28]. The adjective 'unwitting' refers to the absence of any epistemic or motivational aspects, which, as is explained in [4], is also a starting point of *stit* theory. However, Sergot is very critical of the *stit* notion of 'independence of agency'. Sergot's semantics takes transitions between system states as the central semantic entities the formulas of his language are evaluated against. There are some similarities with the work of Segerberg discussed in this paper: it departs from dynamic logic intuitions and switches to an Ockhamist view (as Prior calls it) on the evaluation of truth, which enables him to simulate *stit*-like operators. Another work in the same spirit is that of Herzig and Lorini [15]. In this work the central operator is of the form $\langle Ag\!:\!a\rangle\varphi$ and the reading is 'agent Ag does an action of type a resulting in a state where φ'. However, any agent can only do one action of one particular type a at the time, which is a conceptual limitation that inhibits on the explanatory power of the theory (the proposals of Sergot, Segerberg and myself do not have this limitation). Also in this approach, dynamic logic intuitions are the point of departure and *stit* operators are simulated. A third work is that by Ming Xu [29]. Xu studies a slightly different problem though. He does not talk about event types, but aims to reconcile logics of agency with a language that talks directly about events. Xu takes operators $[Ag, e]\varphi$ as the central objects of study, where Ag is an agent and e is an event or action, and not an event *type*. Finally, there are several papers discussing the problem addressed here, without committing to a possible solution, like the papers of Brian Chellas [11], Risto Hilpinen [16] and Mark Brown [10].

5 Conclusion

I have discussed Segerberg's approach to combining two views on action—the dynamic logic view and the *stit* view—within one framework, as put forward in *Outline of a logic of action* [26]. I have placed some critical remarks on the theory. These remarks do not so much concern the fact that the framework lacks certain concepts or makes some oversimplifications (which is, as for any theory, also true, as Segerberg discusses in the final words of the paper), but directly question the idea that a description in terms of dynamic logic event types is appropriate for understanding agency. In stead I suggest to turn this view 180°; I have put forward an alternative action theory outline where it is the dynamic logic event type reasoning that is simulated in a *stit* framework. Further explorations and comparisons in future research will have to shed light on which of the two approaches best explains the relation between computation and agency.

References

1. Alur, R., Henzinger, T.A. & Kupferman. O. (1997). Alternating-time temporal logic. In *FOCS '97: Proceedings of the 38th Annual Symposium on Foundations of Computer Science (FOCS '97)* (pp. 100–109). IEEE Computer Society.
2. Alur, R., Henzinger, T. A., & Kupferman, O. (2002). Alternating-time temporal logic. *Journal of the ACM*, *49*(5), 672–713.
3. Belnap, N., & Perloff, M. (1988). Seeing to it that: a canonical form for agentives. *Theoria*, *54*(3), 175–199.
4. Belnap, N., Perloff, M. & Xu, M. (2001). *Facing the future: agents and choices in our indeterminist world*. Oxford University Press
5. Broersen, J. (2011). Making a start with the stit logic analysis of intentional action. *Journal of Philosophical Logic*, *40*, 399–420.
6. Broersen, J. (2011). Modeling attempt and action failure in probabilistic stit logic. In T. Walsh, (Ed.), *Proceedings of Twenty-Second International Joint Conference on Artificial Intelligence (IJCAI 2011)* (pp. 792–797). IJCAI.
7. Broersen, J.M. (2009). A complete stit logic for knowledge and action, and some of its applications. In M. Baldoni, T. Cao Son, M.B. van Riemsdijk & M. Winikoff, (Eds.), *Declarative Agent Languages and Technologies VI (DALT 2008), volume 5397 of, Lecture Notes in Computer Science* (pp. 47–59). Springer
8. Broersen, J. M. (2011). Deontic epistemic stit logic distinguishing modes of mens rea. *Journal of Applied Logic*, *9*(2), 127–152.
9. Brown, M. A. (1988). On the logic of ability. *Journal of philosophical logic*, *17*(1), 1–26.
10. Brown, M. A. (2008). Acting, events and actions. In R. van der Meyden & L. van der Torre (Eds.), *Deontic Logic in Computer Science, 9th International Conference, DEON 2008, Luxembourg, Luxembourg, July 15–18, 2008. Proceedings, volume 5076 of Lecture Notes in Computer Science* (pp. 19–33). Springer.
11. Chellas, B. F. (1995). On bringing it about. *Journal of Philosophical Logic*, 24, 563–571 (1995). doi:10.1007/BF01306966.
12. Emerson, E.A. (1990). Temporal and modal logic. In J. van Leeuwen (Ed), Handbook of theoretical computer science, volume B: Formal models and semantics, chapter 14, pp. 996–1072. Elsevier Science.

13. Ginsberg, M. L., & Smith, D. E. (1988). Reasoning about action II: The qualification problem. *Artificial Intelligence*, *35*, 311–342.
14. Harel, D. & Peleg, D. (1985). Process logic with regular formulas. *Theoretical Computer Science*, *38*, 307–322.
15. Herzig, Andreas, & Lorini, Emiliano. (2010). A dynamic logic of agency I: Stit, capabilities and powers. *Journal of Logic, Language and Information*, *19*(1), 89–121.
16. Hilpinen, R. (1997). On action and agency. In E. Ejerhed & S. Lindström (Eds.), *Logic, Action and Cognition: Essays in Philosophical Logic* (pp. 3–27). Kluwer Academic Publishers.
17. Kanger, S. (1972). *Law and logic. Theoria*, *38*(3), 105–132.
18. McCarthy, J. & Hayes, P. (1969). Some philosophical problems from the standpoint of artificial intelligence. In B. Meltzer & D. Michie (Eds.), *Machine Intelligence*, 4, pp. 463–502. Edinburgh University Press.
19. Milner, R. (1989). *Communication and concurrency*. Prentice-Hall.
20. Pauly, Marc. (2002). A modal logic for coalitional power in games. *Journal of Logic and Computation*, *12*(1), 149–166.
21. Pratt, V. R. (1976). Semantical considerations on Floyd-Hoare logic. In *Proceedings 17th IEEE Symposium on the Foundations of Computer Science* (pp. 109–121). IEEE Computer Society Press.
22. Prior, A. N. (1967). *Past, present, and future*. Clarendon Press.
23. Segerberg, K. (1989). Bringing it about. *Journal of Philosophical Logic*, *18*(4), 327–347.
24. Segerberg, K. (1992). Getting started: Beginnings in the logic of action. *Studia Logica*, *51*, 347–378.
25. Segerberg, K. (2000). Outline of a logic of action. Technical Report 5–2000, Department of Philosophy University of Uppsala.
26. Segerberg, K. (2002). Outline of a logic of action. In *Advances in Modal Logic, 3*, pp. 365–387. World Scientific.
27. Segerberg, K. (1996). The delta operator at three levels of analysis. In *Logic, action, and, information* (pp. 63–78). De Gruyter
28. Sergot, M. (2008). The logic of unwitting collective agency. Technical Report 2008/6, Department of Computing, Imperial College London.
29. Ming, Xu. (2010). Combinations of stit and actions. *Journal of Logic, Language and Information*, *19*(4), 485–503.

Three Traditions in the Logic of Action: Bringing them Together

Andreas Herzig, Tiago de Lima, Emiliano Lorini and Nicolas Troquard

Abstract We propose a Dynamic Logic of Propositional Control (DL-PC) that is equipped with two dynamic modal operators: one of ability and one of action. We integrate into DL-PC the concept of 'seeing to it that' (abbreviated by stit) as studied by Belnap, Horty and others. We prove decidability of DL-PC satisfiability and establish the relation with the logic of the Chellas stit opertor.

1 Introduction

Krister Segerberg's favourite logic of action is clearly dynamic logic [1–3]. However, there is another important tradition focusing on 'rival' modal logics, such as Pörn's logic of bringing-it-about [4–7] and Belnap et col.'s logic of seeing-to-it-that [8–10]. The latter logics should be called more precisely *logics of agency*: they allow to reason about whether an agent is agentive for a proposition.Beyond dynamic logic and logics of agency, other quite different logical approaches to action were developed in artificial intelligence (AI). There, the aim is to design practically usable formalisms that allow knowledge representation e.g. for automated planning. In Thomason's words, "to formalize realistic planning domains, to provide knowledge representation support for automated planning systems [...] requires an axiomatization of what Segerberg called the change function, which tells us what to expect when an action is performed" [11]. AI formalisms such as the situation calculus [12] focus on the

A. Herzig (✉) · E. Lorini
IRIT, University of Toulouse, 118 Route de Narbonne, 31062 Toulouse Cedex 9, France
e-mail: Andreas.Herzig@irit.fr

T. de Lima
University of Artois and CNRS, Rue Jean Souvraz SP 18,
62307 Lens Cedex, France

N. Troquard
LOA-ISTC, Trento, Italy

R. Trypuz (ed.), *Krister Segerberg on Logic of Actions*,
Outstanding Contributions to Logic 1, DOI: 10.1007/978-94-007-7046-1_4,

problem of defining such change functions, which became known under the denomination 'frame problem' and was considered to be one of the major challenges of AI. By far the most popular solution is in terms of Reiter's basic action theories which axiomatise the change function in terms of so-called successor state axioms [13, 14]. The definition of such axioms requires quantification over actions, which is a feature distinguishing these formalisms from dynamic logic and logics of agency that do not provide such a facility.

It is the aim of the present chapter to bring together the above three traditions in logics of action: dynamic logic, seeing-to-it-that (stit) logic, and situation calculus. We start from dynamic logic, into which we embed the situation calculus à la Reiter and integrate a stit operator of agency. More precisely, we are going to resort to a variant of dynamic logic that we call *dynamic logic of propositional control* (DL-PC).

As far as the embedding of situation calculus is concerned we build on the previous work of van Ditmarsch et al. [15]. There, basic action theories were mapped to a dynamic logic of propositional assignments. Let us call that logic DL-PA. It is a version of dynamic logic whose atomic programs are sets of assignments of propositional variables each of which is of the form $p \leftarrow \varphi$ where p is a propositional variable and φ is a formula. Such an assignment is always executable. DL-PA does not have quantification over actions, thus demonstrating that Reiter's solution to the frame problem actually does not require quantification over actions (contrarily to what Reiter had claimed). While agents play no particular role in DL-PA —that may actually be said to be rather about events than about actions—our logic DL-PC has 'true' actions: assignments performed by agents. An agent can only perform an assignment if he *controls* that assignment, in other words, if it is in his *repertoire*.[1]

Things are more involved if we want to embed logics of agency into our logic. The difficulties are threefold.

- Just as the above DL-PA, dynamic logic is about events rather than actions: agents do not play a role in dynamic logic. As we have said above, this can be overcome by associating repertoires of assignments to agents.
- In stit logic the agents act simultaneously, while (at least in the basic version of) dynamic logic actions are performed in sequence. We therefore need a version of dynamic logic with *parallel* actions. The above DL-PA actually already provides for sets of assignments; in DL-PC these are generalised to sets of authored assignments.
- The dynamic logic operator $\langle\alpha\rangle$ talks about the *possibility* of the occurrence of program α and not about the occurrence of α itself: instead of actual performance of an action, dynamic logic is rather about the opportunity to perform an action.

In order to overcome the third difficulty we are going to add to dynamic logic a second kind of dynamic operator, noted $\langle\!\langle\alpha\rangle\!\rangle$: while $\langle\alpha\rangle$ talks about the opportunity of performance of α, the new dynamic operator $\langle\!\langle\alpha\rangle\!\rangle$ is about the performance of

[1] Our syntax is actually a bit more restrictive: instead of $p \leftarrow \varphi$ it only allows for assignments to either true or false, written $+p$ and $-p$. The more general assignment $p \leftarrow \varphi$ can however be simulated by the dynamic logic program $(\varphi?; +p) \cup (\neg\varphi?; -p)$, where '?' is test, ';' is sequential composition, and '; ∪' is nondeterministic composition.

α. In the semantics we add a *successor function* modelling the next actions that are going to take place.

To sum it up: the language of our dynamic logic of propositional control DL-PC has a language in terms of two kinds of dynamic operators; the arguments of the dynamic operators are group actions; group actions are sets of assignments performed by agents. The semantics of DL-PC has a repertoire function and a successor function that both associate sets of assignments to agents. An obvious requirement is that if a group action α takes place according to the successor function then each of the individual actions in α must be executable, i.e. each individual assignment must be in the repertoire of the agent performing it.

The chapter is organised as follows. Section 2 we introduce dynamic logic of propositional control DL-PC and establish a decidability result. In Sect. 3 we study the fragment without stit operators and give a decision procedure in NP. In Sect. 4 we give reduction axioms for the fragment without the 'next' operator. In Sect. 5 we relate DL-PC to a discrete version of the Chellas stit logic.

2 Dynamic Logic of Propositional Control DL-PC

We now introduce the dynamic logic of propositional control by defining its syntax and semantics.

2.1 Syntax

The vocabulary of the Dynamic Logic of Propositional Control (DL-PC) contains a set P of propositional variables and a finite non-empty set Ag of agent names.

Given a propositional variable $p \in \mathsf{P}$, $+p$ denotes the *positive assignment* of p, i.e., the event of setting the value of p to true, and $-p$ denotes the *negative assignment* of p, i.e., the event of setting the value of p to false. Given a set of propositional variables $P \subseteq \mathsf{P}$, the set of all positive assignments of elements of P is $+P = \{+p : p \in P\}$ and the set of all negative assignments is $-P = \{-p : p \in P\}$. The set of *all* assignments of variables in P is $\pm P = +P \cup -P$. The set of all assignments is therefore $\pm\mathsf{P} = +\mathsf{P} \cup -\mathsf{P}$. We use e for elements of $\pm\mathsf{P}$.

An *individual action* is a couple made up of an agent name and the assignment of a propositional variable. The set of all individual actions is $\mathsf{Act} = \mathsf{Ag} \times \pm\mathsf{P}$. A *group action* is a finite set of actions from Act. The set of all group actions is $\mathsf{GAct} = 2^{\mathsf{Act}}$. The set of sequences of group actions is noted GAct^*. The empty sequence is noted nil, and the typical elements of GAct^* are noted σ, σ_1, etc. For a group action α and a group of agents $G \subseteq \mathsf{Ag}$ we define G's *part in* α as follows:

$$\alpha_G = \alpha \cap (G \times \pm\mathsf{P}) = \{(i, e) : (i, e) \in \alpha \text{ and } i \in G\}$$

In particular, $\alpha_\emptyset = \emptyset$ and $\alpha_{\mathsf{Ag}} = \alpha$. Clearly, every α_G is also a group action from GAct.

The *language* of DL-PC is the set of formulas φ defined by the following BNF:

$$\varphi ::= \top \mid p \mid \neg\varphi \mid \varphi \wedge \varphi \mid \langle\!\langle \alpha \rangle\!\rangle\varphi \mid \langle \alpha \rangle\varphi \mid \mathrm{Stit}_G\varphi \mid \mathrm{X}\varphi$$

where p ranges over P, G ranges over 2^{Ag}, and α ranges over GAct.

The modal operators $\langle \alpha \rangle$ and $\langle\!\langle \alpha \rangle\!\rangle$ are both dynamic operators. The former is about opportunity while the latter is about agency: $\langle\!\langle \alpha \rangle\!\rangle\varphi$ reads "α is going to be performed and φ will be true after updating by α", while $\langle \alpha_G \rangle\varphi$ reads "α_G can be performed and φ will be true after updating by α". The modal operator Stit stands for "seeing-to-it-that": the formula $\mathrm{Stit}_G\varphi$ reads "group G sees to it that φ is true". X is a temporal 'next' operator: the formula $\mathrm{X}\varphi$ is read "next φ".

We use the common abbreviations for $\vee$, $\rightarrow$, $\leftrightarrow$ and $\bot$. When α is a singleton $\{(i, e)\}$ we write the more convenient $\langle\!\langle i, e \rangle\!\rangle\varphi$ instead of $\langle\!\langle \{(i, e)\} \rangle\!\rangle\varphi$. The set of propositional variables occurring in a formula φ is noted P_φ and the set of agents occurring in φ is noted Ag_φ. For example, $\mathsf{P}_{\langle i,-p \rangle q} = \{p, q\}$ and $\mathsf{Ag}_{\langle i,-p \rangle q} = \{i\}$.

2.2 Models

While the semantics of PDL is in terms of Kripke models the semantics of DL-PC is not (cf. [16]). Models for DL-PC are simply valuations of propositional logic that are augmented by two further ingredients: first, every agent has a *repertoire of assignments* that is available to him; second, there is a *successor function* which for every sequence of group actions tells us which group action is going to take place next. Such models consist therefore of tuples $\langle \mathcal{R}, \mathcal{S}, \mathcal{V} \rangle$, where:

- $\mathcal{R} \subseteq \mathsf{Ag} \times \pm\mathsf{P}$
- $\mathcal{S} : \mathsf{GAct}^* \longrightarrow \mathsf{GAct}$ such that $\mathcal{S}(\sigma) \subseteq \mathcal{R}$ for every $\sigma \in \mathsf{GAct}^*$
- $\mathcal{V} \subseteq \mathsf{P}$

The valuation $\mathcal{V}$ provides the set of propositional variables from P that are true. The repertoire $\mathcal{R}$ is a set of group actions: when $(i, e) \in \mathcal{R}$ then agent i is able to perform e. $\mathcal{S}$ associates to every finite sequence of group actions $\sigma \in \mathsf{GAct}$ the group action $\mathcal{S}(\sigma) \in \mathsf{GAct}$ that will occur after σ. So $\mathcal{S}(\mathrm{nil})$ is the group action that is going to be performed now. Our constraint on $\mathcal{S}$ ensures that every $\mathcal{S}(\sigma)$ respects $\mathcal{R}$: for example, when $(i, e) \in \mathcal{S}(\mathrm{nil})$ then according to $\mathcal{S}$ agent i performs e next; we then expect e to be in i's repertoire, i.e., we expect $(i, e) \in \mathcal{R}$. Note that the group action $\emptyset$ is consistent with every repertoire. According to our definitions $(\mathcal{S}(\mathrm{nil}))_G$ is group G's part of the next action, i.e., it is the group action that G will execute now.

2.3 Updating Valuations

Just as in dynamic epistemic logic with assignments [17], the dynamic operators are interpreted as *model updates*.

The language of DL-PC allows for group actions with conflicting assignments, like $\alpha = \{(i, +p), (j, -p)\}$, where two agents disagree on the new value of the variable p; actually these two agents might even be identical. We might stipulate that such a group action cannot be performed. We take a different route: the new value of a variable p changes only if the agents trying to assign p agree on the new value. The other way round, if the agents disagree on the new value of a variable then this variable keeps its old truth value.

The update of the model $\mathcal{M} = \langle \mathcal{R}, \mathcal{S}, \mathcal{V} \rangle$ by the group action $\alpha \in \mathsf{GAct}$ is the new model $\mathcal{M}^\alpha = \langle \mathcal{R}^\alpha, \mathcal{S}^\alpha, \mathcal{V}^\alpha \rangle$, where:

$$\begin{aligned}
\mathcal{R}^\alpha &= \mathcal{R} \\
\mathcal{S}^\alpha(\sigma) &= \mathcal{S}(\alpha \cdot \sigma) \quad \text{(where the symbol $\cdot$ stands for concatenation of lists)} \\
\mathcal{V}^\alpha &= (\mathcal{V} \setminus \{p : \text{ there is } (i, -p) \in \alpha \text{ and there is no } (j, +p) \in \alpha\}) \cup \\
&\qquad \{p : \text{ there is } (i, +p) \in \alpha \text{ and there is no } (j, -p) \in \alpha\}
\end{aligned}$$

Hence $\mathcal{S}^\alpha(\text{nil})$ (the group action that will be executed now in $\mathcal{M}^\alpha$) is the group action that will be executed after α in $\mathcal{M}$; and $\mathcal{V}^\alpha$ (the set of variables that are true in $\mathcal{M}^\alpha$) is $\mathcal{V}$ without those variables that have been set to false by α, plus the new variables that have been set to true by α.

Clearly, the update $\mathcal{M}^\alpha$ of a DL-PC model $\mathcal{M}$ is also a DL-PC model; in particular, the successor function $\mathcal{S}^\alpha$ respects $\mathcal{R}$.

2.4 Varying the Successor Function

The stit operator will be evaluated by varying the successor function.

Given two successor functions $\mathcal{S}$ and $\mathcal{S}'$, we say that *Succ* and $\mathcal{S}'$ *agree on* G's *strategy*, noted $\mathcal{S} \sim_G \mathcal{S}'$, if and only if $(\mathcal{S}'(\sigma))_G = (\mathcal{S}(\sigma))_G$ for every sequence of group actions σ. We also say that $\mathcal{S}'$ is a G-variant of $\mathcal{S}$.

This extends to models:two models $\mathcal{M} = \langle \mathcal{R}, \mathcal{S}, \mathcal{V} \rangle$ and $\mathcal{M}' = \langle \mathcal{R}', \mathcal{S}', \mathcal{V}' \rangle$ *agree on* G's strategy, noted $\mathcal{M} \sim G\mathcal{M}'$, if and only if $\mathcal{R} = \mathcal{R}'$, $\mathcal{V} = \mathcal{V}'$, and $\mathcal{S} \sim_G \mathcal{S}'$. Clearly, when $\mathcal{M}$ is a DL-PC model and $\mathcal{M} \sim_G \mathcal{M}'$ then $\mathcal{M}'$ is also a DL-PC model; in particular, its successor function $\mathcal{S}'$ respects $\mathcal{R}$.

2.5 Truth Conditions

Let $\mathcal{M} = \langle \mathcal{R}, \mathcal{S}, \mathcal{V} \rangle$ be a DL-PC model. The satisfaction relation $\models$ between DL-PC models and formulas is defined as usual for the Boolean operators, plus:

$$\begin{array}{lll}
\mathcal{M} \models p & \text{iff} & p \in \mathcal{V} \\
\mathcal{M} \models \langle\!\langle \alpha \rangle\!\rangle \varphi & \text{iff} & \alpha \subseteq \mathcal{S}(\text{nil}) \text{ and } \mathcal{M}^{\alpha} \models \varphi \\
\mathcal{M} \models \langle \alpha \rangle \varphi & \text{iff} & \alpha \subseteq \mathcal{R} \text{ and } \mathcal{M}^{\alpha} \models \varphi \\
\mathcal{M} \models \text{Stit}_G \varphi & \text{iff} & \mathcal{M}' \models \varphi \text{ for every } \mathcal{M}' \text{ such that } \mathcal{M}' \sim_G \mathcal{M} \\
\mathcal{M} \models \text{X}\varphi & \text{iff} & \mathcal{M}^{\mathcal{S}(\text{nil})} \models \varphi
\end{array}$$

In words, in model $\mathcal{M}$, group G sees to it that φ if and only if φ is true in every DL-PC model that agrees with G's strategy in $\mathcal{M}$. In other words, G sees to it that φ if and only if φ obtains due to the actions selected by G, whatever the other agents choose to do.

Let us consider the two cases when G is empty and when it is the set of all agents Ag. First, $\text{Stit}_{\emptyset}\varphi$ means "φ is true whatever the agents choose to do". This is a modal operator of historic necessity just as in stit logics. Second, $\text{Stit}_{\mathsf{Ag}}\varphi$ means "φ is true given the current strategies of all agents". This is a modal operator of historic possibility.

As usual, a formula φ is valid in DL-PC (notation: $\models \varphi$) if and only if every DL-PC model satisfies φ. A formula φ is satisfiable in DL-PC if and only if $\not\models \neg\varphi$. For example, the schema $\models \langle\!\langle \alpha_G \rangle\!\rangle \top \rightarrow \langle \alpha_G \rangle \top$ is valid (because $\mathcal{S}(\text{nil}) \subseteq \mathcal{R}$). This is a 'do implies can' principle: if α is going to be performed then α can be performed. Moreover, $\langle \emptyset \rangle \top$ and $\langle\!\langle \emptyset \rangle\!\rangle \top$ are both DL-PC valid. If φ is a Boolean formula then $\langle \{(i, +p), (j, -p)\} \rangle \varphi \rightarrow \varphi$ is valid. It is not valid in general; to see this take e.g. $\langle\!\langle (i, +q) \rangle\!\rangle \top$ for φ. Moreover, the converse is invalid, e.g. because $+p$ might not be in i's repertoire. Observe that both $\langle\!\langle \alpha \rangle\!\rangle$ and $\langle \alpha \rangle$ are normal modal diamond operators; in particular the schemas

$$\langle\!\langle \alpha \rangle\!\rangle (\varphi \wedge \psi) \rightarrow (\langle\!\langle \alpha \rangle\!\rangle \varphi \wedge \langle\!\langle \alpha \rangle\!\rangle \psi)$$
$$\langle \alpha \rangle (\varphi \wedge \psi) \rightarrow (\langle \alpha \rangle \varphi \wedge \langle \alpha \rangle \psi)$$

are valid. Observe also that the modal operators Stit_G are normal modal box operators; in particular, the schemas $\text{Stit}_G \top$ and $\text{Stit}_G(\varphi \wedge \psi) \leftrightarrow (\text{Stit}_G \varphi \wedge \text{Stit}_G \psi)$ are valid. A DL-PC validity that we are going to discuss later is $\text{Stit}_i(p \vee q) \rightarrow (\text{Stit}_i p \vee \text{Stit}_i q)$. Note that $\langle\!\langle \alpha \rangle\!\rangle \varphi \rightarrow \text{X}\varphi$ is invalid. (To see this, note that $\varphi \rightarrow \langle\!\langle \emptyset \rangle\!\rangle \varphi$ is valid and that φ should not imply $\text{X}\varphi$.)

2.6 Replacement of Equivalents

The rule of replacement of valid equivalents will be useful in Sects. 3 and 4. It is based on the following proposition.

Proposition 1 (Rules of equivalents for $\langle\alpha\rangle$, $\langle\!\langle\alpha\rangle\!\rangle$, and Stit_G)

1. *If* $\models \varphi_1 \leftrightarrow \varphi_2$ *then* $\models \langle\alpha\rangle\varphi_1 \leftrightarrow \langle\alpha\rangle\psi\varphi_2$ *(rule of equivalents for $\langle\alpha\rangle$)*
2. *If* $\models \varphi \leftrightarrow \psi$ *then* $\models \langle\!\langle\alpha\rangle\!\rangle\varphi_1 \leftrightarrow \langle\!\langle\alpha\rangle\!\rangle\varphi_2$ *(rule of equivalents for $\langle\!\langle\alpha\rangle\!\rangle$)*
3. *If* $\models \varphi_1 \leftrightarrow \varphi_2$ *then* $\models \text{Stit}_G\varphi_1 \leftrightarrow \text{Stit}_G\varphi_2$ *(rule of equivalents for Stit_G)*

Proposition 1 (plus the rules of equivalents for the Boolean connectives) allows to prove that the rule of replacement of equivalents preserves validity. Let $\varphi[p/\psi]$ denote the formula φ where all occurrences of the propositional variable p are replaced by ψ.

Proposition 2 (Rule of replacement of valid equivalents) *If* $\models \varphi_1 \leftrightarrow \varphi_2$ *then* $\models \psi[p/\varphi_1] \leftrightarrow \psi[p/\varphi_2]$.

2.7 Decidability

We now prove that satisfiability is decidable.

Here are some definitions that we need for our results. The *length* of a formula is the number of symbols we need to write it down, including parentheses, '$\langle$', '+', etc. We denote the length of a formula φ by $|\varphi|$. For example, $|\langle i, -p\rangle q| = 2+4+1 = 7$. Moreover, we define the length $|\sigma|$ of a sequence of group actions σ as follows:

$$|\text{nil}| = 0$$
$$|\alpha \cdot \sigma| = \text{card}(\alpha) + |\sigma|$$

where $\text{card}(\alpha)$ is the cardinality of the set α.

The *dynamic depth* of a formula is the maximal number of nested dynamic operators and 'next' operators, defined inductively as:

$$\delta(\top) = \delta(p) = 0$$
$$\delta(\neg\varphi) = \delta(\text{Stit}_G\varphi) = \delta(\varphi)$$
$$\delta(\varphi \wedge \psi) = \max(\delta(\varphi), \delta(\psi))$$
$$\delta(\langle\alpha\rangle\varphi) = \delta(\langle\!\langle\alpha\rangle\!\rangle\varphi) = \delta(\text{X}\varphi) = 1 + \delta(\varphi)$$

We are now going to define the *size* of a finite DL-PC model. At first glance there are no such models because each model is infinite: the function $\mathcal{S}$ is an infinite set of couples $\langle\sigma, \mathcal{S}(\sigma)\rangle$, one per sequence $\sigma \in \mathsf{GAct}^*$. A way out is to consider that a model is finite when $\mathcal{R}$ and $\mathcal{V}$ are finite and the value of the successor function

$\mathcal{S}$ is $\emptyset$ almost everywhere. Such functions can be represented in a finite way if we drop those couples $\langle \sigma, \mathcal{S}(\sigma) \rangle$ where $\mathcal{S}(\sigma) = \emptyset$ and view $\mathcal{S}$ as a partial function. Then the size of the finite DL-PC model $\mathcal{M} = \langle \mathcal{R}, \mathcal{S}, \mathcal{V} \rangle$ can be defined as the sum of the cardinalities of each of its elements, i.e.

$$\text{size}(\mathcal{M}) = \text{card}(\mathcal{R}) + \Sigma_{\{\sigma:\mathcal{S} \text{ is defined on } \sigma\}} |\sigma \cdot \mathcal{S}(\sigma)| + \text{card}(\mathcal{V})$$

Proposition 3 (Strong fmp) *For every* DL-PC *formula φ, if φ is* DL-PC *satisfiable then φ is satisfiable in a model of size* $\mathcal{O}((|\varphi|)^{2|\varphi|})$.

Proof Let $\mathcal{M} = \langle \mathcal{R}, \mathcal{S}, \mathcal{V} \rangle$, let φ be a formula, and let $n \in \mathbb{N}_0$ be an integer with $n \geq 0$. We do two things in order to turn $\mathcal{M}$ into a finite model: we restrict the vocabulary that is interpreted in $\mathcal{M}$ to that of φ, and we restrict the depth of the successor function by setting $\mathcal{S}(\sigma)$ to the empty set when the length of σ is greater than n. So let us define the model $\mathcal{M}_{\varphi,n} = \langle \mathcal{R}_\varphi, \mathcal{S}_{\varphi,n}, \mathcal{V}_\varphi \rangle$ by:

$$\mathcal{R}_\varphi = \mathcal{R} \cap (\mathsf{Ag}_\varphi \times \pm \mathsf{P}_\varphi)$$

$$\mathcal{S}_{\varphi,n}(\sigma) = \begin{cases} \mathcal{S}(\sigma) & \text{if } |\sigma| < n \\ \emptyset & \text{if } |\sigma| \geq n \end{cases}$$

$$\mathcal{V}_\varphi = \mathcal{V} \cap \mathsf{P}_\varphi$$

Each of $\mathcal{R}$, $\mathcal{S}$, and $\mathcal{V}$ is finite (where finiteness of $\mathcal{S}$ is understood as having value $\emptyset$ almost everywhere), and therefore $\mathcal{M}_{\varphi,n}$ is finite. Observe that $(\mathcal{M}^\alpha)_{\varphi,n} = (\mathcal{M}_{\varphi,n+1})^\alpha$ $(*)$; moreover, observe that for every n and φ, the set of models $\mathcal{N}_{\varphi,n}$ such that $\mathcal{N} \sim_G \mathcal{M}$ equals the set of models $\mathcal{N}_{\varphi,n}$ such that $\mathcal{N} \sim_G \mathcal{M}_{\varphi,n}$ $(**)$. Basically, the last property says that 'a G-variant of $\mathcal{S}$ cut at heigth n and restricted to the vocabulary of φ' is the same thing as 'a G-variant of $\mathcal{S}_{\varphi,n}$ cut at heigth n and restricted to the vocabulary of φ'.

We prove that we have $\mathcal{M} \models \chi$ if and only if $\mathcal{M}_{\varphi,\delta(\chi)} \models \chi$ for every formula χ whose language is included in that of φ, i.e. such that $\mathsf{Ag}_\chi \subseteq \mathsf{Ag}_\varphi$ and $\mathsf{P}_\chi \subseteq \mathsf{P}_\varphi$. The proof is by induction on the structure of χ. The only delicate cases are those of the modal operators. We only give those of $\langle \alpha \rangle$ and Stit_G, the others are similar. For the former we prove:

$$\begin{aligned} \mathcal{M} \models \langle \alpha \rangle \chi \text{ iff } & \alpha \subseteq \mathcal{R} \text{ and } \mathcal{M}^\alpha \models \chi \\ \text{iff } & \alpha \subseteq \mathcal{R}_\varphi \text{ and } (\mathcal{M}^\alpha)_{\varphi,\delta(\chi)} \models \chi && \text{(by I.H.)} \\ \text{iff } & \alpha \subseteq \mathcal{R}_\varphi \text{ and } (\mathcal{M}_{\varphi,\delta(\chi)+1})^\alpha \models \chi && \text{(by } (*)) \\ \text{iff } & \alpha \subseteq \mathcal{R}_\varphi \text{ and } (\mathcal{M}_{\varphi,\delta(\langle \alpha \rangle \chi)})^\alpha \models \chi \\ \text{iff } & \mathcal{M}_{\varphi,\delta(\langle \alpha \rangle \chi)} \models \langle \alpha \rangle \chi \end{aligned}$$

For the stit operators we have to apply the induction hypothesis twice:

$$\begin{aligned}\mathcal{M} \models \mathrm{Stit}_G\chi \text{ iff } & \mathcal{N} \models \chi \text{ for every } \mathcal{N} \text{ such that } \mathcal{N} \sim_G \mathcal{M} \\ \text{iff } & \mathcal{N}_{\varphi,\delta(\chi)} \models \chi \text{ for every } \mathcal{N} \text{ such that } \mathcal{N} \sim_G \mathcal{M} && \text{(by I.H.)} \\ \text{iff } & \mathcal{N}_{\varphi,\delta(\chi)} \models \chi \text{ for every } \mathcal{N} \text{ such that } \mathcal{N} \sim_G \mathcal{M}_{\varphi,\delta(\chi)} && \text{(by (**))} \\ \text{iff } & \mathcal{N} \models \chi \text{ for every } \mathcal{N} \text{ such that } \mathcal{N} \sim_G \mathcal{M}_{\varphi,\delta(\chi)} && \text{(by I.H.)} \\ \text{iff } & \mathcal{M}_{\varphi,\delta(\chi)} \models \mathrm{Stit}_G\chi\end{aligned}$$

This ends the proof. ■

Proposition 4 *(Decidability of satisfiability) The* DL-PC *satisfiability problem is decidable.*

Proof This follows by [18, Theorem 6.7] from the above strong fmp (Proposition 3) and the fact that the set of DL-PC models of a given size is recursive (plus the fact that model checking is decidable). ■

We can prove that the satisfiability problem is PSPACE hard by encoding the QBF satisfiability problem: this is already the case for the fragment of the DL-PC language without the next operator, as we will establish in Sect. 4.3. We conjecture that it is also PSPACE complete, but leave a formal proof to future work.

3 The Fragment Without Stit Operators

We now investigate the fragment of DL-PC without stit operators. We provide a decision procedure in terms of reduction axioms.

3.1 *Simplifying* $\langle\langle\alpha\rangle\rangle$, $\langle\alpha\rangle$, and X

The first step is to simplify formulas of the form $\langle\!\langle\alpha\rangle\!\rangle\varphi$.

Proposition 5 (Simplification of $\langle\!\langle\alpha\rangle\!\rangle$**)**

1. $\models \langle\!\langle\alpha\rangle\!\rangle\varphi \leftrightarrow (\langle\alpha\rangle\varphi \wedge \langle\!\langle\alpha\rangle\!\rangle\top)$
2. $\models \langle\!\langle\emptyset\rangle\!\rangle\top \leftrightarrow \top$
3. $\models \langle\!\langle\alpha \cup \beta\rangle\!\rangle\top \leftrightarrow (\langle\!\langle\alpha\rangle\!\rangle\top \wedge \langle\!\langle\beta\rangle\!\rangle\top)$

Proof

1. First, $\langle\!\langle\alpha\rangle\!\rangle\varphi \to \langle\alpha\rangle\varphi$ is valid because $\mathcal{S}(\text{nil}) \subseteq \mathcal{R}$. Second, $(\langle\alpha\rangle\varphi \wedge \langle\!\langle\alpha\rangle\!\rangle\top) \to \langle\!\langle\alpha\rangle\!\rangle\varphi$ is valid because updates are functional.
2. This follows from the observation that for every model $\mathcal{M}$, $\mathcal{M} \models \langle\!\langle\emptyset\rangle\!\rangle\top$.
3. This follows from the observation that for every model $\mathcal{M}$, $\mathcal{M} \models \langle\!\langle\alpha\rangle\!\rangle\top$ iff $\alpha \subseteq \mathcal{S}(\text{nil})$. ■

According to the preceding proposition we can suppose w.l.o.g. that every occurrence of $\langle\!\langle\alpha\rangle\!\rangle$ is followed by $\top$ and that α is a singleton.

The second step is to put formulas of the form $\langle\alpha\rangle\varphi$ without Stit operators in φ in a particular normal form.

Proposition 6 (Simplification of $\langle\alpha\rangle$)

1. $\models \langle\alpha\rangle p \leftrightarrow \begin{cases} \langle\alpha\rangle\top & \textit{if there is } i \textit{ s.th. } (i,+p)\in\alpha \textit{ and there is no } j \textit{ s.th. } (j,-p)\in\alpha \\ \bot & \textit{if there is } i \textit{ s.th. } (i,-p)\in\alpha \textit{ and there is no } j \textit{ s.th. } (j,+p)\in\alpha \\ \langle\alpha\rangle\top\wedge p & \textit{either if there are } i,j \textit{ such that } (i,+p),(j,-p)\in\alpha \\ & \textit{or if there are no } i,j \textit{ such that } (i,+p),(j,-p)\in\alpha \end{cases}$
2. $\models \langle\alpha\rangle\neg\varphi \leftrightarrow (\langle\alpha\rangle\top\wedge\neg\langle\alpha\rangle\varphi)$
3. $\models \langle\alpha\rangle(\varphi\wedge\psi) \leftrightarrow (\langle\alpha\rangle\varphi\wedge\langle\alpha\rangle\psi)$
4. $\models \langle\alpha\rangle\langle\beta\rangle\top \leftrightarrow (\langle\alpha\rangle\top\wedge\langle\beta\rangle\top)$
5. $\models \langle\emptyset\rangle\top \leftrightarrow \top$
6. $\models \langle\alpha\cup\beta\rangle\top \leftrightarrow (\langle\alpha\rangle\top\wedge\langle\beta\rangle\top)$

Proof

1. This is clear from the definition of valuation update.
2. From the left to the right, $\langle\alpha\rangle\neg\varphi \rightarrow \neg\langle\alpha\rangle\varphi$ because updates are functions (as opposed to relations). From the right to the left, suppose $\mathcal{M}\models\langle\alpha\rangle\top\wedge\neg\langle\alpha\rangle\varphi$; then $\alpha\subseteq\mathcal{R}$ and $\mathcal{M}^\alpha\not\models\varphi$, i.e. $\mathcal{M}\models\langle\alpha\rangle\neg\varphi$.
3. From the left to the right, $\langle\alpha\rangle(\varphi\wedge\psi)\rightarrow(\langle\alpha\rangle\varphi\wedge\langle\alpha\rangle\psi)$ is valid because $\langle\alpha\rangle$ is a normal diamond operator. From the right to the left, $(\langle\alpha\rangle\varphi\wedge\langle\alpha\rangle\psi)\rightarrow\langle\alpha\rangle(\varphi\wedge\psi)$ is valid because updates are functions.
4. $\langle\alpha\rangle\langle\beta\rangle\top \leftrightarrow (\langle\alpha\rangle\top\wedge\langle\beta\rangle\top)$ is valid because the repertoire is not modified by the update. ■

For example, the formula $\langle(i,+p),(j,-q)\rangle\langle(i,-r)\rangle p$ can be rewritten as follows:

$$\begin{aligned}\langle(i,+p),(j,-q)\rangle\langle i,-r\rangle p &\leftrightarrow \langle(i,+p),(j,-q)\rangle(\langle i,-r\rangle\top\wedge p)\\ &\leftrightarrow \langle(i,+p),(j,-q)\rangle\langle i,-r\rangle\top\wedge\langle(i,+p),(j,-q)\rangle p\\ &\leftrightarrow \langle(i,+p),(j,-q)\rangle\top\wedge\langle i,-r\rangle\top\wedge\langle(i,+p),(j,-q)\rangle\top\\ &\leftrightarrow \langle i,+p\rangle\top\wedge\langle j,-q\rangle\top\wedge\langle i,-r\rangle\top\end{aligned}$$

The third step deals with the 'next' operator and relies on finiteness of the set of agents Ag.

Proposition 7 (Simplification of X)

1. $\models \mathrm{X}p \leftrightarrow \Big(((\bigvee_{i\in\mathsf{Ag}}\langle\!\langle i,+p\rangle\!\rangle\top)\wedge\neg(\bigvee_{j\in\mathsf{Ag}}\langle\!\langle j,-p\rangle\!\rangle\top))\vee(p\wedge\neg(\bigvee_{j\in\mathsf{Ag}}\langle\!\langle j,-p\rangle\!\rangle\top))\Big)$
2. $\models \mathrm{X}\neg\varphi \leftrightarrow \neg\mathrm{X}\varphi$
3. $\models \mathrm{X}(\varphi\wedge\psi) \leftrightarrow (\mathrm{X}\varphi\wedge\mathrm{X}\psi)$
4. $\models \mathrm{X}\langle\alpha\rangle\top \leftrightarrow \langle\alpha\rangle\top$

Proof The first equivalence is clear from the definition of valuation update. The second and third are familiar from linear-time temporal logic. The last equivalence is valid because the repertoire is not modified by the update. ■

3.2 Modal Atoms and Successor Function Atoms

Rewriting a formula without stit operators by applying the equivalences of propositions 5, 6, and 7 we obtain a Boolean combination of *modal atoms*. A modal atom is either a propositional variable from P, or a *repertoire atom* $\langle i, e\rangle\top$, or a *successor atom* $\langle\langle i, e\rangle\rangle\top$ that is preceded by a sequence of operators either $\langle\alpha\rangle$ or X. We call the latter kind of modal atoms *successor function atoms*, abbreviated SFA, and write $\mu\langle\langle i, e\rangle\rangle\top$ for such successor atoms. The sequence μ of operators $\langle\alpha\rangle$ and X is called a *modality*. The grammar of modal atoms π is therefore:

$$\pi ::= p \mid \langle i, e\rangle\top \mid \mu\langle\langle i, e\rangle\rangle\top$$

For a given SFA $\mu\langle\langle i, e\rangle\rangle\top$, the formula $\mu\langle i, e\rangle\top$ denotes the result of the replacement of $\langle\langle i, e\rangle\rangle$ by $\langle i, e\rangle$.

For a given Boolean combination of modal atoms φ, the set SFA_φ denotes the set of successor function atoms of φ. For example, for

$$\varphi = \neg(p \wedge (\langle i, +p\rangle\top \rightarrow \neg\text{X}\langle\langle j, +q\rangle\rangle\top))$$

we have

$$\text{SFA}_\varphi = \{\text{X}\langle\langle j, +q\rangle\rangle\top\}.$$

Proposition 8 *Let φ be a formula without stit operators. Then φ is equivalent to a Boolean combination of modal atoms of length quadratic in the length of φ.*

Proof Every formula φ without stit operators can be transformed into an equivalent formula by applying the equivalences of propositions 5, 6, and 7 from the left to the right.

All the resulting formulas are equivalent to the original formula due to the rule of replacement of valid equivalents (Proposition 2).

The resulting formula is of length quadratic in the length of φ because the procedure basically consists in shifting the modal operators $\langle . \rangle$, $\langle\langle . \rangle\rangle$, and X in front of the atomic formulas: in the worst case every atom gets prefixed by a sequence of modal operators whose length is in the order of the length of φ. ■

3.3 Decision Procedure

We now translate formulas that are Boolean combinations of modal atoms into formulas of classical propositional logic as follows:

$$
\begin{aligned}
\tau(\top) &= \top \\
\tau(p) &= \nu_p \\
\tau(\langle i, e\rangle \top) &= \nu_{\langle i,e\rangle \top} \\
\tau(\mu\langle\!\langle i, e\rangle\!\rangle \top) &= \nu_{\mu\langle\!\langle i,e\rangle\!\rangle \top} \\
\tau(\neg\varphi) &= \neg\tau(\varphi) \\
\tau(\varphi \wedge \psi) &= \tau(\varphi) \wedge \tau(\psi)
\end{aligned}
$$

where ν_p ,$\nu_{\langle i,e\rangle \top}$ and $\nu_{\mu\langle\!\langle i,e\rangle\!\rangle \top}$ are fresh propositional variables that do not occur in the formula to be translated. Our translation therefore just identifies modal atoms with distinct propositional variables.

Proposition 9 *Let φ be a* DL-PC *formula that is a Boolean combination of modal atoms. φ is* DL-PC *satisfiable if and only if $\tau(\varphi) \wedge (\bigwedge \Gamma_\varphi)$ is satisfiable in classical propositional logic, where*

$$\Gamma_\varphi = \{\nu_{\mu\langle\!\langle i,e\rangle\!\rangle \top} \to \nu_{\langle i,e\rangle \top} : \mu\langle\!\langle i, e\rangle\!\rangle \top \in \mathrm{SFA}_\varphi\}$$

Proof Let φ be a DL-PC formula that is a Boolean combination of modal atoms.

From the left to the right, suppose $\mathcal{M} \models \varphi$. We transform $\mathcal{M}$ into an interpretation $\mathcal{I}_\mathcal{M}$ of classical propositional logic by associating the 'right' truth values to the propositional variables that stand for modal atoms: we set

$$\mathcal{I}_\mathcal{M}(\nu_\pi) = 1 \text{ if and only if } \mathcal{M} \models \pi$$

where π is a modal atom. It is then straightforward to prove by induction on the form of ψ that $\mathcal{M} \models \psi$ if and only if $\mathcal{I}(\tau(\psi)) = 1$, for every DL-PC formula ψ. Moreover, $\mathcal{I}(\bigwedge \Gamma_\varphi) = 1$ because the successor function $\mathcal{S}$ respects the repertoire function $\mathcal{R}$: whenever $\mathcal{M} \models \mu\langle\!\langle i, e\rangle\!\rangle \top$ for some SFA $\mu\langle\!\langle i, e\rangle\!\rangle \top$ then we have $\mathcal{M} \models \langle i, e\rangle \top$.

From the right to the left, suppose $\mathcal{I}(\tau(\varphi) \wedge (\bigwedge \Gamma_\varphi)) = 1$. We may suppose w.l.o.g. that $\mathcal{I}(\nu_{\mu\langle\!\langle i,e\rangle\!\rangle \top}) = 0$ for all those $\nu_{\mu\langle\!\langle i,e\rangle\!\rangle \top}$ such that the SFA $\mu\langle\!\langle i, e\rangle\!\rangle \top$ does not belong to SFA_φ. We build a DL-PC model $\mathcal{M}_\mathcal{I} = \langle \mathcal{R}_\mathcal{I}, \mathcal{S}_\mathcal{I}, \mathcal{V}_\mathcal{I}\rangle$ by setting $\mathcal{R}_\mathcal{I} = \{(i, e) : \mathcal{I}(\nu_{\langle i,e\rangle \top}) = 1\}$, $\mathcal{V}_\mathcal{I} = \{p \in \mathsf{P} : \mathcal{I}(\nu_p) = 1\}$, and by inductively defining $\mathcal{S}_\mathcal{I}$ as follows:

$$\mathcal{S}_\mathcal{I}(\mathrm{nil}) = \{(i, e) : \mathcal{I}(\nu_{\langle\!\langle i,e\rangle\!\rangle \top}) = 1\}$$

$$\mathcal{S}_\mathcal{I}(\alpha \cdot \sigma) = \begin{cases} \mathcal{S}_{\mathcal{I}^\alpha}(\sigma) & \text{if } \alpha \neq \mathcal{S}_\mathcal{I}(\mathrm{nil}) \\ \mathcal{S}_{\mathcal{I}^\mathrm{X}}(\sigma) \cup \{(i_0, +\nu)\} & \text{if } \alpha = \mathcal{S}_\mathcal{I}(\mathrm{nil}) \end{cases}$$

for some i_0 and some fresh ν, where updates of the SFA part of interpretation $\mathcal{I}$ (more precisely, updates of the fresh variables $\nu_{\mu\langle\langle i,e\rangle\rangle\top}$ associated to the SFAs of φ) are defined in the obvious way:

$$\mathcal{I}^{\alpha} = \{\nu_{\mu\langle\langle i,e\rangle\rangle\top} : \nu_{\langle\alpha\rangle\mu\langle\langle i,e\rangle\rangle\top} \in \mathcal{I}\}$$
$$\mathcal{I}^{\mathrm{X}} = \{\nu_{\mu\langle\langle i,e\rangle\rangle\top} : \nu_{\mathrm{X}\mu\langle\langle i,e\rangle\rangle\top} \in \mathcal{I}\}$$

Note that $\mathcal{S}_{\mathcal{I}^{\alpha}} = (\mathcal{S}_{\mathcal{I}})^{\alpha}$ and $\mathcal{S}_{\mathcal{I}^{\mathrm{X}}} = (\mathcal{S}_{\mathcal{I}})^{\mathcal{S}_{\mathcal{I}}(\mathrm{nil})}$. Note also that in the inductive definition of $\mathcal{S}_{\mathcal{I}}$, when $\alpha = \mathcal{S}_{\mathcal{I}}(\mathrm{nil})$ then the 'fresh action' $(i_0, +\nu)$ makes that $\mathcal{S}_{\mathcal{I}}$ is well-defined: it avoids a conflict between e.g. $\mathcal{S}_{\mathcal{I}}(\mathcal{S}_{\mathcal{I}}(\mathrm{nil}))$ and $\mathcal{S}_{\mathcal{I}}(\alpha)$ for some SFA $\langle\alpha\rangle\mu \in \mathrm{SFA}_{\varphi}$ because $\mathcal{S}_{\mathcal{I}}(\mathrm{nil})$ differs from any group action α coming from φ.[2] The triple $\mathcal{M}$ that we have constructed in this way is indeed a DL-PC model: it satisfies the constraint that every $\mathcal{S}(\sigma)$ is included in $\mathcal{R}$ because (1) $\mathcal{I}(\bigwedge \Gamma_{\varphi}) = 1$ and because (2) $\mathcal{I}(\nu_{\mu\langle\langle i,e\rangle\rangle\top}) = 0$ for all those $\mu\langle\langle i, e\rangle\rangle\top$ not in SFA_{φ}. Now we prove, first, that for every modal atom π occurring in φ we have $\mathcal{M} \models \pi$ if and only if $\mathcal{I}(\pi) = 1$. The case of successor function atoms $\mu\langle\langle i, e\rangle\rangle\top$ is proved by induction on its length. In the induction step we use that (1) $\mathcal{I}^{\alpha}(\nu_{\mu\langle\langle i,e\rangle\rangle\top}) = 1$ iff $\mathcal{I}(\nu_{\langle\alpha\rangle\mu\langle\langle i,e\rangle\rangle\top}) = 1$ and that (2) $\mathcal{I}^{\mathrm{X}}(\nu_{\mu\langle\langle i,e\rangle\rangle\top}) = 1$ iff $\mathcal{I}(\nu_{\mathrm{X}\mu\langle\langle i,e\rangle\rangle\top}) = 1$. Second, the formula φ being a Boolean combination of modal atoms it clearly follows that $\mathcal{M} \models \varphi$. ■

3.4 Complexity

We have just defined a decision procedure for DL-PC formulas without stit operators. We are now going to show that that procedure works in nondeterministic polynomial time.

Proposition 10 *The problem of satisfiability of* DL-PC *formulas without the stit operator is NP complete.*

Proof The problem is clearly NP hard, given that DL-PC is a conservative extension of propositional logic.

In what concerns membership, by Proposition 8 we know that every DL-PC formula φ without stit operators is equivalent to a Boolean combination of modal atoms φ' whose length is quadratic in that of φ. According to Proposition we may check satisfiability of φ' by checking satisfiability of $\tau(\varphi') \wedge (\bigwedge \Gamma_{\varphi'})$. The length of $\tau(\varphi')$ is linear in the length of φ', and the length of $\Gamma_{\varphi'}$ is linear in the length of φ'; together, they make up a linear transformation. Overall, the length of the propositional formula $\tau(\varphi') \wedge (\bigwedge \Gamma_{\varphi'})$ is quadratic in the length of the original φ. Therefore DL-PC satisfiability is in NP.

---

[2] To see this, suppose that $\langle\langle i, +p\rangle\rangle\top$ is the only SFA of φ such that $\mathcal{I}(\nu_{\langle\langle i,+p\rangle\rangle\top}) = 1$. Then $\mathcal{S}_{\mathcal{I}}(\mathrm{nil}) = \{(i, +p)\}$. Now suppose $\mathcal{I}$ is such that $\mathcal{I}(\nu_{\mathrm{X}\langle\langle i,+p\rangle\rangle\top}) = 1$ and $\mathcal{I}(\nu_{\langle i,+p\rangle\langle\langle i,+p\rangle\rangle\top}) = 0$: then $\mathcal{S}_{\mathcal{I}}$ would be ill-defined if we hadn't we introduced the fresh action $(i_0, +\nu)$.

4 The Fragment Without the 'next' Operator

We now give a decision procedure for the fragment of the language of DL-PC without the temporal 'next'. The procedure amounts to the elimination of stit operators and uses some of the results of the preceding section.

4.1 G-Determinate Formulas

A formula φ is G-determinate if and only if for all DL-PC models $\mathcal{M}$ and $\mathcal{M}'$ such that $\mathcal{M} \sim_G \mathcal{M}'$ we have $\mathcal{M} \models \varphi$ iff $\mathcal{M}' \models \varphi$. Note that propositional variables are G-determinate, for every group G. The same is the case for formulas of the form $\langle\alpha\rangle\top$. Moreover, $\langle\!\langle(i, e)\rangle\!\rangle\top$ is G-determinate if $i \in G$. Note also that when a formula φ is G-determinate then the equivalence $\text{Stit}_G\varphi \leftrightarrow \varphi$ is valid.

The next two propositions generalise these observations.

Proposition 11 (Some G-determinate formulas) *Let G be a group of agents.*

1. *Every propositional variable is G-determinate.*
2. *Every formula $\langle\alpha\rangle\top$ is G-determinate.*
3. *If $i \in G$ then $\langle\!\langle(i, e)\rangle\!\rangle\top$ is G-determinate.*
4. *If φ is G-determinate then $\neg\varphi$, $\langle\alpha\rangle\varphi$, and $\text{X}\varphi$ are G-determinate.*

Proposition 12 (Properties of G-determinate formulas) *Let φ be G-determinate. Then* $\text{Stit}_G(\varphi \vee \psi) \leftrightarrow (\varphi \vee \text{Stit}_G\psi)$ *is valid.*

Here are some examples of formulas that are not G-determinate. First, when G is the set of all agents Ag then every formula is G-determinate. Second, the formula $\text{X}p$ is G-determinate only when G is the set of all agents Ag. Third, $\langle\!\langle\alpha\rangle\!\rangle\top$ is not G-determinate when α_i is non-empty for some $i \notin G$.

4.2 Eliminating the Stit Operators

Consider any subformula $\text{Stit}_G\psi$ of a formula φ such that ψ is a Boolean combination of modal atoms. We may suppose w.l.o.g. that ψ is in conjunctive normal form, i.e. that ψ is a conjunction of clauses, where clauses are disjunctions of modal atoms or negations thereof. For example, a conjunctive normal form of the above

$$\neg(p \wedge (\langle i, +p\rangle\top \rightarrow \neg\langle i, -p\rangle\langle\!\langle j, +q\rangle\!\rangle\top))$$

is

$$(\neg p \vee \langle i, +p\rangle\top) \wedge (\neg p \vee \langle i, -p\rangle\langle\!\langle j, +q\rangle\!\rangle\top)$$

Given a Stit_G operator followed by a formula in conjunctive normal form, we may apply the following reduction axioms.

Proposition 13 (Reduction axioms for Stit_G)

1. $\models \text{Stit}_G\top \leftrightarrow \top$
2. $\models \text{Stit}_G(\varphi_1 \wedge \varphi_2) \leftrightarrow (\text{Stit}_G\varphi_1 \wedge \text{Stit}_G\varphi_2)$
3. $\models \text{Stit}_G(p \vee \varphi) \leftrightarrow (p \vee \text{Stit}_G\varphi)$
4. $\models \text{Stit}_G(\neg p \vee \varphi) \leftrightarrow (\neg p \vee \text{Stit}_G\varphi)$
5. $\models \text{Stit}_G(\langle\alpha\rangle\top \vee \varphi) \leftrightarrow (\langle\alpha\rangle\top \vee \text{Stit}_G\varphi)$
6. $\models \text{Stit}_G(\neg\langle\alpha\rangle\top \vee \varphi) \leftrightarrow (\neg\langle\alpha\rangle\top \vee \text{Stit}_G\varphi)$
7. *Let* $i \in G$. *Then*

$$\models \text{Stit}_G(\mu\langle\langle i, e\rangle\rangle\top \vee \varphi) \leftrightarrow \mu\langle\langle i, e\rangle\rangle\top \vee \text{Stit}_G\varphi$$
$$\models \text{Stit}_G(\neg\mu\langle\langle i, e\rangle\rangle\top \vee \varphi) \leftrightarrow \neg\mu\langle\langle i, e\rangle\rangle\top \vee \text{Stit}_G\varphi$$

8. *Let* P *and* Q *be two finite sets of successor function atoms that are all of the form* $\mu\langle\langle i, e\rangle\rangle\top$ *with* $i \notin G$ *and that do not contain* X. *Then*

$$\models \text{Stit}_G\left((\bigvee P) \vee \neg(\bigwedge Q)\right) \leftrightarrow \begin{cases} \top & \textit{if } P \cap Q \neq \emptyset \\ \neg \bigwedge_{\mu\langle\langle i,e\rangle\rangle\top \in Q} \mu\langle i, e\rangle\top & \textit{if } P \cap Q = \emptyset \end{cases}$$

Proof As to Item 1, $\models \text{Stit}_G\top \leftrightarrow \top$ is valid because $\text{Stit}_G\top$ is valid (Stit_G being a normal modal box).

As to Item 2, $\models \text{Stit}_G(\varphi_1 \wedge \varphi_2) \leftrightarrow (\text{Stit}_G\varphi_1 \wedge \text{Stit}_G\varphi_2)$ is valid because Stit_G is a normal modal box.

Items 3–6 are valid because Boolean formulas and formulas of the form $\langle\alpha\rangle\top$ and $\neg\langle\alpha\rangle\top$ are G-determinate (Proposition 11, items 1 and 2) and therefore Proposition 12 applies.

For Item 7, let $i \in G$. Then according to Proposition 11, both $\mu\langle\langle i, e\rangle\rangle\top$ and $\neg\mu\langle\langle i, e\rangle\rangle\top$ are G-determinate. Therefore the following schemas are both valid:

$$\text{Stit}_G\ (\mu\langle\langle i, e\rangle\rangle\top \vee \varphi) \leftrightarrow (\mu\langle\langle i, e\rangle\rangle\top \vee \text{Stit}_G\varphi)$$
$$\text{Stit}_G\ (\neg\mu\langle\langle i, e\rangle\rangle\top \vee \varphi) \leftrightarrow (\neg\mu\langle\langle i, e\rangle\rangle\top \vee \text{Stit}_G\varphi)$$

For Item 8 we examine the two cases. First, let $P \cap Q \neq \emptyset$. As P collects the SFAs of the positive literals and Q collects the SFAs of the negative literals, the formula $(\bigvee P) \vee \neg(\bigwedge Q)$ is valid in classical propositional logic; and as Stit_G is a normal modal box, $\text{Stit}_G\left((\bigvee P) \vee \neg(\bigwedge Q)\right)$ is DL-PC valid. For the second case where $P \cap Q = \emptyset$ we prove the two directions of the equivalence separately.

- For *the left-to-right direction*, let $\mathcal{M} = \langle\mathcal{R}, \mathcal{S}, \mathcal{V}\rangle$ be a DL-PC model such that $\mathcal{M} \not\models \neg \bigwedge_{\mu\langle\langle i,e\rangle\rangle\top \in Q} \mu\langle i, e\rangle\top$, i.e. $\mathcal{M} \models \mu\langle i, e\rangle\top$ for every $\mu\langle\langle i, e\rangle\rangle\top \in Q$. Let us define a successor function $\mathcal{S}_Q$ by:

$$\mathcal{S}_Q(\text{nil}) = (\mathcal{S}(\text{nil}))_G \cup \{(i, e) : \langle\!\langle i, e \rangle\!\rangle \top \in Q\}$$
$$\mathcal{S}_Q(\alpha \cdot \sigma) = (\mathcal{S}(\alpha \cdot \sigma))_G \cup \mathcal{S}_{Q^{\langle\alpha\rangle}}(\sigma)$$

where the set $Q^{\langle\alpha\rangle}$ is defined as follows:

$$Q^{\langle\alpha\rangle} = \{\mu\langle\!\langle i, e \rangle\!\rangle \top : \langle\alpha\rangle\mu\langle\!\langle i, e \rangle\!\rangle \top \in Q\}$$

The function $\mathcal{S}_Q$ respects $\mathcal{R}$: clearly, $(\mathcal{S}(\text{nil}))_G$ respects $\mathcal{R}$, and we can prove by induction on the length of σ that $\mathcal{S}_{Q^\mu}(\sigma)$ respects $\mathcal{R}$ for every modality μ, where the set of modal atoms Q^μ generalises the set $Q^{\langle\alpha\rangle}$ in the obvious way.
Let $\mathcal{M}_Q = \langle \mathcal{R}, \mathcal{S}_Q, \mathcal{V} \rangle$. First, we have $\mathcal{M} \sim_G \mathcal{M}_Q$ because $(\mathcal{S}(\text{nil}))_G = (\mathcal{S}_Q(\text{nil}))_G$. Second, we can prove that $\mathcal{M}_Q \models \mu\langle\!\langle i, e \rangle\!\rangle \top$ iff $\mu\langle\!\langle i, e \rangle\!\rangle \top \in Q$, for every successor function atom $\mu\langle\!\langle i, e \rangle\!\rangle \top$ such that $i \notin G$. It follows that $\mathcal{M}_Q \models \mu\langle\!\langle i, e \rangle\!\rangle \top$ for every $\mu\langle\!\langle i, e \rangle\!\rangle \top \in Q$, and as $P \cap Q = \emptyset$ we also have $\mathcal{M}_Q \not\models \mu\langle\!\langle i, e \rangle\!\rangle \top$ for every $\mu\langle\!\langle i, e \rangle\!\rangle \top \in P$. Therefore $\mathcal{M}_Q \models (\bigwedge Q) \wedge \neg(\bigvee P)$, i.e. $\mathcal{M}_Q \not\models (\bigvee P) \vee \neg(\bigwedge Q)$. According to the truth condition for Stit_G this means that $\mathcal{M} \not\models \text{Stit}_G\big((\bigvee P) \vee \neg(\bigwedge Q)\big)$.

- For *the right-to-left direction*, suppose $\mathcal{M} \models \neg \bigwedge_{\mu\langle\!\langle i,e \rangle\!\rangle \top \in Q} \mu\langle i, e \rangle \top$, i.e. $\mathcal{M} \not\models \mu\langle i, e \rangle \top$ for some $\mu\langle\!\langle i, e \rangle\!\rangle \top \in Q$. So either $(i, e) \notin \mathcal{R}$, or $\alpha \not\subseteq \mathcal{R}$ for some dynamic operator $\langle\alpha\rangle$ of the sequence μ. In the first case $\mathcal{M} \not\models \mu\langle\!\langle i, e \rangle\!\rangle \top$ because the successor function respects the repertoire; and in the second case $\mathcal{M} \not\models \mu\top$ because of the truth condition for $\langle\alpha\rangle$, and therefore $\mathcal{M} \not\models \mu\langle\!\langle i, e \rangle\!\rangle \top$, too. The formula $\mu\langle\!\langle i, e \rangle\!\rangle \top$ is actually false in *every* model $\mathcal{M}'$ such that $\mathcal{M} \sim_G \mathcal{M}'$ (in the first case because every $\mathcal{S}'$ respects $\mathcal{R}$; in the second case because when interpreting μ the truth condition for $\langle\alpha\rangle$ checks whether $\alpha \subseteq \mathcal{R}$). It follows that $\mathcal{M}' \not\models \bigwedge Q$ for every model $\mathcal{M}'$ such that $\mathcal{M} \sim_G \mathcal{M}'$. Hence $\mathcal{M}' \models (\bigvee P) \vee \neg(\bigwedge Q)$ for every model $\mathcal{M}'$ such that $\mathcal{M} \sim_G \mathcal{M}'$, from which it follows that $\mathcal{M} \models \text{Stit}_G\big((\bigvee P) \vee \neg(\bigwedge Q)\big)$.

This concludes the proof of Item 8. ■

For example, the formula $\text{Stit}_i\,(\neg p \vee \langle i, +p \rangle \top \vee \langle i, +p \rangle \langle\!\langle j, +q \rangle\!\rangle \top)$ can be rewritten as follows:

$$\begin{aligned} \text{Stit}_i\,(\neg p \vee \langle i, +p \rangle \top \vee \langle i, +p \rangle \langle\!\langle j, +q \rangle\!\rangle \top) &\leftrightarrow \neg p \vee \langle i, +p \rangle \top \vee \text{Stit}_i \langle i, +p \rangle \langle\!\langle j, +q \rangle\!\rangle \top \\ &\leftrightarrow \neg p \vee \langle i, +p \rangle \top \vee \bot \end{aligned}$$

Anticipating a bit, we observe that the first two items of Proposition 13 are also valid in the logic of the Chellas stit, while the third and the fourth item are only valid if the values of the propositional variables are moment-determinate. (Validity in the logic of the Chellas stit and moment-determinateness are going to be defined in Sect. 5.)

Applying the above equivalences from the left to the right allows to entirely eliminate the stit operators. It follows that we can transform every formula without the 'next' operator into an equivalent Boolean combination of modal atoms.

Theorem 14 *Every* DL-PC *formula without* X *is equivalent to a Boolean combination of modal atoms.*

Note that Item 7 of Proposition 13 also holds for the more general case where μ contains the temporal X. Item 8 does not: let $P = \{\langle i, e\rangle\langle\langle i, e\rangle\rangle\top\}$ and let $Q = \{\langle\langle i, e\rangle\rangle\top, \mathrm{X}\langle\langle i, e\rangle\rangle\top\}$. Then the formula $\mathrm{Stit}_{\emptyset}\big((\bigvee P) \vee \neg(\bigwedge Q)\big)$ is not equivalent to $\neg(\langle i, e\rangle\top \wedge \mathrm{X}\langle i, e\rangle\top)$, i.e., to $\neg\langle i, e\rangle\top$. To see this consider any model $\mathcal{M}$ where $\mathcal{R} = \mathcal{S}(\mathrm{nil}) = \mathcal{S}((i, e)\cdot\mathrm{nil}) = \{(i, e)\}$: while $\mathrm{Stit}_{\emptyset}\big((\bigvee P) \vee \neg(\bigwedge Q)\big)$ is true in $\mathcal{M}$, $\neg\langle i, e\rangle\top$ is not. We were not able to find reduction axioms for the whole language of DL-PC.

4.3 Complexity Of Satisfiability: A Lower Bound

Proposition 15 (Complexity, lower bound) *The* DL-PC *satisfiability problem is PSPACE hard even for formulas without the* X *operator.*

Proof We establish the proof by encoding the quantified Boolean formula (QBF) satisfiability problem into the fragment of DL-PC without the next operator. We view an interpretation of classical propositional logic as a mapping $\mathcal{I}$ from the set of propositional variables into $\{0, 1\}$ (that is extended to evaluate any Boolean formula in the standard way).

Let φ_0 be a QBF to be translated. Define a translation t from the language of QBFs to the language of DL-PC as follows:

$$t(p) = \langle\langle p, +p\rangle\rangle\top$$
$$t(\forall p\varphi) = \mathrm{Stit}_{\mathsf{P}_{\varphi_0}\setminus\{p\}}t(\varphi)$$

and homomorphic for the other connectives. (We therefore translate propositional variables into agent names, supposing therefore that there are at least as many agent names in Ag as there are propositional variables in P.)

Define the set Γ_{φ_0} as:

$$\Gamma_{\varphi_0} = \{\langle p, +p\rangle\top : p \in \mathsf{P}_{\varphi_0}\} \cup \{\langle p, -p\rangle\top : p \in \mathsf{P}_{\varphi_0}\}$$

We prove that the QBF φ_0 is satisfiable if and only if $t(\varphi_0) \wedge (\bigwedge \Gamma_{\varphi_0})$ is satisfiable.

From the left to the right, suppose I is an interpretation of classical propositional logic such that $I(\varphi_0) = 1$. We define a DL-PC model $\mathcal{M}_I = \langle\mathcal{R}_I, \mathcal{S}_I, \mathcal{V}_I\rangle$ such that

$$\mathcal{R}_I = \{(p, +p) : p \in \mathsf{P}_{\varphi_0}\} \cup \{(p, -p) : p \in \mathsf{P}_{\varphi_0}\}$$

$$\mathcal{S}_I(\sigma) = \begin{cases} \{(p, +p) : p \in \mathsf{P}_{\varphi_0} \text{ and } I(p) = 1\} & \text{if } \sigma = \text{nil} \\ \mathcal{S}_I(\sigma) = \emptyset & \text{if } \sigma \neq \text{nil} \end{cases}$$

$$\mathcal{V} = \emptyset$$

Clearly $\mathcal{M}_I \models \bigwedge \Gamma_{\varphi_0}$. It then suffices to prove by induction that $I(\varphi) = 1$ iff $\mathcal{M}_I \models t(\varphi)$, for every subformula φ of φ_0.

From the right to the left, suppose $\mathcal{M}$ is a DL-PC model such that $\mathcal{M} \models t(\varphi_0) \wedge (\bigwedge \Gamma_{\varphi_0})$. We define an interpretation $I_\mathcal{M}$ of the propositional variables p occurring in φ_0 by: $I_\mathcal{M}(p) = 1$ iff $(p, +p) \in \mathcal{S}(\text{nil})$. We then prove by induction that $\mathcal{M} \models t(\varphi)$ iff $I_\mathcal{M}(\varphi) = 1$, for every subformula φ of φ_0. ■

5 Relation with Chellas Stit

We now investigate the relationship between our Stit operator and the Chellas stit logic [8–10]. The language of that logic has a stit operator just as DL-PC. It moreover has temporal operators that are not part of DL-PC. We therefore extend the language of DL-PC by the simplest temporal operator, viz. the temporal 'next' operator, and compare that extension with a discrete version of the Chellas stit logic as introduced in [19].

5.1 *Chellas Stit Logic*

The language of the discrete Chellas stit logic is nothing but the fragment $\mathcal{L}_{\text{Stit},X}$ of the language of DL-PC without the dynamic operators. The set of formulas φ is defined by the following BNF:

$$\varphi ::= \top \mid p \mid \neg\varphi \mid \varphi \wedge \varphi \mid \text{Stit}_G\varphi \mid X\varphi$$

The reading of $\text{Stit}_G\varphi$ and $X\varphi$ is the same as before.

The formulas are interpreted in discrete *Branching Time models with Agent Choice functions* (discrete BT+AC models). These models are defined in two steps.

First, a discrete branching time structure (BT) is a pair $\langle \mathsf{Mom}, < \rangle$, where:

- Mom is a non-empty set of moments.
- $<$ is a tree-like partial ordering that is irreflexive and discrete. We recall that an ordering $<$ is discrete if and only if for every $m \in \mathsf{Mom}$ there is a set of closest moments $\text{succ}(m)$ such that for every $m' \in \text{succ}(m)$, $m < m'$ and there is no $m'' \in \mathsf{Mom}$ with $m < m'' < m'$.

Then a *history* is a maximally $<$-ordered set of moments. We use $\mathcal{H}$ to denote the set of all histories and $\mathcal{H}_m$ to denote the set of histories passing through the moment m, i.e., the set of histories h such that $m \in h$. The successor function can be extended to moment-history pairs: $\mathrm{succ}(m, h)$ is the moment m' such that $\mathrm{succ}(m) \cap h = \{m'\}$. Two histories $h_1, h_2 \in \mathcal{H}_m$ are *undivided* at m if and only if both histories have the same successor to m, i.e., if and only if $\mathrm{succ}(m, h_1) = \mathrm{succ}(m, h_2)$.[3]

Second, a discrete BT+AC model is a quadruple of the form

$$\mathcal{M} = \langle \mathsf{Mom}, <, \mathcal{C}, \mathsf{Val} \rangle$$

where $\langle \mathsf{Mom}, < \rangle$ is a discrete branching time structure and where $\mathcal{C}$ and Val are as follows.

- $\mathcal{C}$ is function from $\mathsf{Ag} \times \mathsf{Mom}$ to $\mathcal{H} \times \mathcal{H}$ such that each $\mathcal{C}(i, m)$ is an equivalence relation on $\mathcal{H}_m$.[4] It is assumed that $\mathcal{C}$ satisfies the following constraints:
    1. Independence of agents: for every moment m and for every mapping $H : \mathsf{Ag} \longrightarrow \mathcal{H}_m$ there is a history $h \in \mathcal{H}_m$ such that $(H(i), h) \in \mathcal{C}(i, m)$ for every $i \in \mathsf{Ag}$.[5]
    2. No choice between undivided histories: if two histories h_1 and h_2 are undivided at m then $(h_1, h_2) \in \mathcal{C}(i, m)$ for every agent i.
- Val is a valuation function from $\mathsf{Mom} \times \mathcal{H}$ to 2^{P}.

The constraint of independence of agents says that any individual choice is compatible with the other choices. The constraint of no choice between undivided histories says that if two histories are undivided at m, then no possible choice for any agent at m distinguishes between the two histories: for every agent i, both h_1 and h_2 belong to the same choice cell at m.

Choice functions are extended from agents to groups of agents by stipulating:

$$\mathcal{C}(G, m) = \bigcap_{i \in G} \mathcal{C}(i, m)$$

Note that with this definition the above 'no choice between undivided histories' constraint can be formulated as: if $m \in h_1 \cap h_2$ and $m_0 < m$ then $(h_1, h_2) \in \mathcal{C}(\mathsf{Ag}, m_0)$.

The values of the propositional variables are said to be *moment-determinate* if $\mathsf{Val}(m, h) = \mathsf{Val}(m, h')$ for every $h, h' \in \mathcal{H}_m$.

Let $\mathcal{M} = \langle \mathsf{Mom}, <, \mathcal{C}, \mathsf{Val} \rangle$ be a BT+AC model as defined above. A *pointed BT+AC model* is a pair $(\mathcal{M}, m/h)$ such that where $m \in h$ and $h \in \mathcal{H}$. The satisfaction relation $\models$ is defined between the formulas and pointed BT+AC models as follows:

---

[3] The original definition is equivalent to ours in the case of discrete BT structures: it stipulates that there is some m' such that $m < m'$ and m' belongs to both h_1 and h_2.

[4] The original definition is equivalent: $\mathcal{C}$ is function from $\mathsf{Ag} \times \mathsf{Mom}$ to $2^{2^{\mathcal{H}}}$ mapping each agent and each moment into a partition of $\mathcal{H}_m$.

[5] The original definition is: for every moment m, if H_i is some set in $\mathcal{C}(i, m)$ for every $i \in \mathsf{Ag}$ then $\bigcap_{i \in \mathsf{Ag}} H_i \neq \emptyset$.

$\mathcal{M}, m/h \models p$ iff $p \in \mathsf{Val}(m, h)$

$\mathcal{M}, m/h \models \mathrm{Stit}_G\varphi$ iff for all h' such that $(h, h') \in \mathcal{C}(G, m)$, $\mathcal{M}, m/h' \models \varphi$

$\mathcal{M}, m/h \models \mathrm{X}\varphi$ iff $\mathcal{M}, \mathrm{succ}(m, h)/h \models \varphi$

and as usual for the Boolean operators.

A formula φ is *valid* if and only if $\mathcal{M}, m/h \models \varphi$ for every BT+AC model $\mathcal{M}$, every history h of $\mathcal{M}$, and every moment $m \in h$.

For example, the schema $\mathrm{Stit}_\emptyset\varphi \rightarrow \mathrm{Stit}_G\varphi$ is valid, and the schema $\mathrm{Stit}_{G_1}\mathrm{Stit}_{G_2}\varphi \rightarrow \mathrm{Stit}_\emptyset\varphi$ is valid if $G_1 \cap G_2 = \emptyset$. Each of the modal operators Stit_G is an S5 operator: the schemas $\mathrm{Stit}_G\varphi \rightarrow \varphi$, $\mathrm{Stit}_G\varphi \rightarrow \mathrm{Stit}_G\mathrm{Stit}_G\varphi$, and $\neg\mathrm{Stit}_G\varphi \rightarrow \mathrm{Stit}_G\neg\mathrm{Stit}_G\varphi$ are all valid, and the rule of necessitation preserves validity.

5.2 DL-PC Models as Particular BT+AC Models

We are now going to relate the discrete Chellas stit logic to DL-PC: we show that DL-PC models can be viewed as particular discrete BT+AC models. A similar technique has been used in [20].

Let $\mathcal{M} = \langle \mathcal{R}, \mathcal{S}, \mathcal{V} \rangle$ be a DL-PC model. The translation of $\mathcal{M}$ into a discrete BT+AC model is the structure $\mathrm{tr}(\mathcal{M}) = \langle \mathsf{Mom}, <, \mathcal{C}, \mathsf{Val} \rangle$, where:

- $\mathsf{Mom} = (2^{\mathcal{R}})^*$ (the set of sequences of group actions respecting $\mathcal{R}$)
- $\sigma < \sigma'$ if and only if there is $\sigma'' \neq \mathrm{nil}$ such that $\sigma' = \sigma \cdot \sigma''$ (prefix relation)
- for every agent $i \in \mathsf{Ag}$ and every moment $\sigma \in \mathsf{Mom}$,

$$\mathcal{C}(i, \sigma) = \{(h, h') : \text{ there are } \alpha, \alpha' \text{ such that } \sigma \cdot \alpha \in h, \sigma \cdot \alpha' \in h', \text{ and } \alpha_i = \alpha'_i\}$$

- Val is recursively defined by:

$$\mathsf{Val}(\mathrm{nil}, h) = \mathcal{V} \qquad \text{(for every } h\text{)}$$

$$\mathsf{Val}(\sigma \cdot \alpha, h) = (\mathsf{Val}(\sigma, h))^\alpha \qquad \text{(for every } h\text{)}$$

In the last line, $(\mathsf{Val}(\sigma, h))^\alpha$ is the update of the valuation $\mathsf{Val}(\sigma, h)$ by α as defined in Sect. 2.3.

Note that the successor function of $\mathcal{M}$ does not play any role in the definition. We therefore have the following.

Proposition 16 *Let* $\langle \mathcal{R}, \mathcal{S}, \mathcal{V} \rangle$ *and* $\langle \mathcal{R}, \mathcal{S}', \mathcal{V} \rangle$ *be two* DL-PC *models. Then* $\mathrm{tr}(\langle \mathcal{R}, \mathcal{S}, \mathcal{V} \rangle) = \mathrm{tr}(\langle \mathcal{R}, \mathcal{S}', \mathcal{V} \rangle)$.

Note further that $\mathrm{succ}(\sigma) = \{\sigma \cdot \alpha : \alpha \in \mathcal{R}\}$.

Proposition 17 *If* $\mathcal{M}$ *is a* DL-PC *model then* $\mathrm{tr}(\mathcal{M})$ *is a discrete BT+AC model.*

Proof First, $(\mathsf{Mom}, <)$ is a discrete BT structure because the prefix relation is a tree-like partial ordering. Let us show that $\mathrm{tr}(\mathcal{M}) = \langle \mathsf{Mom}, <, \mathcal{C}, \mathsf{Val}\rangle$ satisfies the two constraints for choice functions: 'independence of agents' and 'no choice between undivided histories'.

Let $\sigma \in \mathsf{Mom}$ be some moment and let $H : \mathsf{Ag} \longrightarrow \mathcal{H}_\sigma$ be some mapping. For every i, let $\alpha(i)$ be such that $\mathrm{succ}(\sigma, H(i)) = \sigma \cdot \alpha(i)$. Let $\alpha = \bigcup_{i \in \mathsf{Ag}}(\alpha(i))_i$. α is composed of the agents' choices at 'their' history $H(i)$. Clearly $\alpha \subseteq \mathcal{R}$, and therefore $\sigma \cdot \alpha \in \mathsf{Mom}$. Let $h \in \mathcal{H}_\sigma$ be any history such that $\sigma \cdot \alpha \in h$. (Such a history exists; take for example the history where none of the agents acts after $\sigma \cdot \alpha$.) Then $(h, H(i)) \in \mathcal{C}(i, \sigma)$. for every agent i. Therefore, $\mathrm{tr}(\mathcal{M})$ satisfies the constraint of independence of agents.

In order to see that the 'no choice between undivided histories' constraint is satisfied suppose that the moment σ is both on h_1 and on h_2, i.e. $\sigma \in h_1 \cap h_2$, and suppose that $\sigma_0 < \sigma$, i.e. $\sigma = \sigma_0 \cdot \sigma'$ for some $\sigma' \neq \mathrm{nil}$. Due to the latter there must be a group action $\alpha \in \mathsf{GAct}$ such that $\sigma = \sigma_0 \cdot \alpha \cdot \sigma''$ for some $\sigma'' \in \mathsf{GAct}^*$. Therefore $\sigma_0 \cdot \alpha \in h_1 \cap h_2$. It then follows from the definition of $\mathcal{C}$ that for every agent i, both h_1 and h_2 belong to the choice cell of i in $\mathcal{C}(i, \sigma_0)$ that is defined by α_i (which is i's part of α). In other words, $(h_1, h_2) \in \mathcal{C}(i, \sigma_0)$. ■

Let $\mathcal{M} = \langle \mathcal{R}, \mathcal{S}, \mathcal{V}\rangle$ be a DL-PC model. We recursively define the history associated to its successor function $\mathcal{S}$ as follows:

$$\begin{aligned} h_{\mathcal{M}}^{\leq 0} &= \{\mathrm{nil}\} \\ h_{\mathcal{M}}^{\leq n+1} &= h_{\mathcal{M}}^{\leq n} \cup \{\mathcal{S}(\sigma) : \sigma \in h_{\mathcal{M}}^{\leq n}\} \\ h_{\mathcal{M}} &= \bigcup_{n \in \mathbb{N}_0} h_{\mathcal{M}}^{\leq n} \end{aligned}$$

The set $h_{\mathcal{M}}$ is a history from $\mathcal{H}_{\mathrm{nil}}$. Observe that $\mathrm{succ}(\mathrm{nil}, h_{\mathcal{M}}) = \mathcal{S}(\mathrm{nil})$.

Proposition 18 *Let $\mathcal{M} = \langle \mathcal{R}, \mathcal{S}, \mathcal{V}\rangle$ be a* DL-PC *model. Then for every $\mathcal{L}_{\mathrm{Stit,X}}$ formula φ we have*

$$\mathcal{M} \models \varphi \textit{ if and only if } \mathrm{tr}(\mathcal{M}), \mathrm{nil}/h_{\mathcal{M}} \models \varphi$$

Proof We prove by induction on the structure of φ that for every model $\mathcal{M}$ and for every sequence σ we have

$$\mathcal{M}^\sigma \models \varphi \text{ if and only if } \mathrm{tr}(\mathcal{M}^\sigma), \mathrm{nil}/h_{\mathcal{M}^\sigma} \models \varphi$$

where $\mathcal{M}^\sigma$ is defined recursively as expected:

$$\begin{aligned} \mathcal{M}^{\mathrm{nil}} &= \mathcal{M} \\ \mathcal{M}^{\alpha \cdot \sigma} &= (\mathcal{M}^\alpha)^\sigma \end{aligned}$$

Observe that $\mathrm{succ}(\sigma, h_{\mathcal{M}^\sigma}) = \sigma \cdot \mathcal{S}^\sigma(\mathrm{nil})$.

The only interesting cases are the operators Stit_G and the operator X. For the 'next' operator we have:

$$\begin{aligned}\mathcal{M}^\sigma \models \mathrm{X}\psi \text{ iff } & (\mathcal{M}^\sigma)^{\mathcal{S}^\sigma(\text{nil})} \models \psi \\ \text{iff } & \mathcal{M}^{\sigma\cdot\mathcal{S}^\sigma(\text{nil})} \models \psi \\ \text{iff } & \text{tr}(\mathcal{M}^{\sigma\cdot\mathcal{S}^\sigma(\text{nil})}), \text{nil}/h_{\mathcal{M}^{\sigma\cdot\mathcal{S}^\sigma(\text{nil})}} \models \psi && \text{(by I.H.)} \\ \text{iff } & \text{tr}(\mathcal{M}^\sigma), \mathcal{S}^\sigma(\text{nil})/h_{\mathcal{M}^\sigma} \models \psi && (*) \\ \text{iff } & \text{tr}(\mathcal{M}^\sigma), \text{succ}(\text{nil}, h_{\mathcal{M}^\sigma})/h_{\mathcal{M}^\sigma} \models \psi \\ \text{iff } & \text{tr}(\mathcal{M}^\sigma), \text{nil}/h_{\mathcal{M}^\sigma} \models \mathrm{X}\psi\end{aligned}$$

The step $(*)$ is correct because for every model $\mathcal{M}$ and formula ψ, $\text{tr}(\mathcal{M}), \mathcal{S}(\text{nil})/h_{\mathcal{M}} \models \psi$ if and only if $\text{tr}(\mathcal{M}^\alpha), \text{nil}/h_{\mathcal{M}^\alpha} \models \psi$.

For the agency operator we have:

$$\begin{aligned}& \mathcal{M}^\sigma \models \text{Stit}_G\psi \\ \text{iff } & (\mathcal{M}^\sigma)' \models \psi \text{ for every } (\mathcal{M}^\sigma)' \text{ such that } (\mathcal{M}^\sigma)' \sim_G \mathcal{M}^\sigma \\ \text{iff } & \text{tr}((\mathcal{M}^\sigma)'), \text{nil}/h_{(\mathcal{M}^\sigma)'} \models \psi \text{ for every } (\mathcal{M}^\sigma)' \text{ such that } (\mathcal{M}^\sigma)' \sim_G \mathcal{M}^\sigma \\ & \text{(by I.H.)} \\ \text{iff } & \text{tr}(\mathcal{M}^\sigma), \text{nil}/h_{(\mathcal{M}^\sigma)'} \models \psi \text{ for every } (\mathcal{M}^\sigma)' \text{ such that } (\mathcal{M}^\sigma)' \sim_G \mathcal{M}^\sigma \\ & \text{(Prop.16)} \\ \text{iff } & \text{tr}(\mathcal{M}^\sigma), \text{nil}/h' \models \psi \text{ for every } h' \text{ such that } (h_{\mathcal{M}^\sigma}, h') \in \mathcal{C}^\sigma(G, \text{nil}) \\ & (**) \\ \text{iff } & \text{tr}(\mathcal{M}^\sigma), \text{nil}/h_{\mathcal{M}^\sigma} \models \text{Stit}_G\psi\end{aligned}$$

The step $(**)$ is correct because there is a history h' such that $(h_{\mathcal{M}^\sigma}, h') \in \mathcal{C}^\sigma(G, \text{nil})$ if and only if there is a successor function $(\mathcal{S}^\sigma)'$ such that for every sequence of group actions σ_1 we have $(\mathcal{S}^\sigma)'(\sigma_1) \subseteq \mathcal{R}$ and $((\mathcal{S}^\sigma)'(\sigma_1))_G = ((\mathcal{S}^\sigma)'(\sigma_1))_G$.

Corollary 19 For every formula $\varphi \in \mathcal{L}_{\text{Stit},\mathrm{X}}$, if φ is valid in the discrete Chellas stit logic then φ is valid in DL-PC.

We note that there exist $\mathcal{L}_{\text{Stit},\mathrm{X}}$ formulas that are DL-PC valid but invalid in the Chellas stit logic. An example is $\text{Stit}_i(p \vee q) \to (\text{Stit}_i p \vee \text{Stit}_i q)$. Among the $\mathcal{L}_{\text{Stit},\mathrm{X}}$ formulas, those that are valid in BT+AC are therefore a strict subset of those that are valid in DL-PC models. We leave it as an open question whether there is a set of schematic validities distinguishing DL-PC from discrete BT $+$ AC models.

6 Conclusion

We have introduced a Dynamic Logic of Propositional Control DL-PC having a stit operator. We have axiomatised DL-PC and have shown that the problem of satisfiability in models of propositional control is decidable. Our result is interesting because we know that in the set of BT+AC models, satisfiability of 'pure stit' formulas (formulas from $\mathcal{L}_{\mathrm{Stit},\mathrm{X}}$ without X) is already undecidable [21]. This makes DL-PC an interesting alternative to stit logics.

As the reader may have noticed, our logic is not a dynamic logic in the strict sense because it lacks sequential and nondeterministic composition, iteration and test. Their integration remains to be done.

Our logic is related to Segerberg's logic of bringing it about [22]. There, an operator μ is introduced whose argument is a formula. The expression $\mu\varphi$ denotes an action leading to states where φ holds, and the formula $[\mu\varphi]\psi$ reads "after an agent brings it about that φ it is the case that ψ". In Segerberg's logic the recursive structure of actions can be easily captured. For example, Jack's action of killing Joe by shooting him can be described by the formula $[\mu \mathit{JoeShot}]\mathit{JoeDead}$. The interesting aspect of Segerberg's logic—distinguishing it from other logics of agency such as the logic of seeing-to-it-that or the logic of bringing-it-about-that— is that it provides a clear separation between the result of the action and the means for achieving the result. This perspective is similar in spirit both to our logic, which also includes in the object language action labels making reference to the means leading to the result of the (individual or group) action: in the case of a single agent, our group actions α may be viewed as the bringing about of a conjunctions of literals. For example the group action $\{(i, +p), (i, -q)\}$ may be identified with $\mu(p \wedge \neg q)$.

7 Perspectives: Bringing Them All Together

The title of the present chapter is inspired from Krister Segerberg's chapter "Two traditions in the logic of belief: bringing them together" [3]. The aim of that work was to reconcile two different logical approaches to belief: epistemic logics à la Hintikka [23] and belief revision theory à la Alchourrón, Gärdenfors and Makinson [24]. His strategy was to couch the latter in the former by extending epistemic logic with modal operators from dynamic logic, where the programs of the latter are nothing but operations of belief revision. Obviously, a continuation of the present chapter would be to bring together DL-PC and Segerberg's approach. We leave this to future work.

Acknowledgments The first and third author acknowledge the support of the EU coordinated action SINTELNET. The fourth author acknowledges the support of the program Marie Curie People Action Trentino (project LASTS).

References

1. Segerberg, K. (1992). Getting started: Beginnings in the logic of action. *Studia Logica, 51*, 347–378.
2. Segerberg, K. (2000) Outline of a logic of action. In F. Wolter, H. Wansing, M. de Rijke, & M. Zakharyaschev (Eds.), *Advances in modal logic* (pp. 365–387). New Jersey: World Scientific.
3. Segerberg, K. (1999). Two traditions in the logic of belief: Bringing them together. In H. Jürgen Ohlbach, & U. Reyle (Eds.), *Logic, language and reasoning: Essays in honour of Dov Gabbay, volume 5 of Trends in Logic* (pp. 135–147). Dordrecht: Kluwer Academic Publishers.
4. Pörn, I. (1977). *Action theory and social science: Some formal models. Synthese library 120*. D. Reidel: Dordrecht.
5. Elgesem, D. (1993). Action theory and modal logic (Ph.D. thesis, Institut for filosofi, Det historiskfilosofiske fakultetet, Universitetet i Oslo, 1993).
6. Elgesem, D. (1997). The modal logic of agency. *Nordic Journal of Philosophy and Logic*, *2*(2), 1–46.
7. Governatori, Guido, & Rotolo, Antonino. (2005). On the axiomatization of elgesem logic of agency and ability. *Journal of Philosophical Logic*, *34*, 403–431.
8. Horty, John, & Belnap, Nuel. (1995). The deliberative stit: A study of action, omission, ability and obligation. *Journal of Philosophical Logic*, *24*(6), 583–644.
9. Horty, J. F. (2001). *Agency and deontic logic*. Oxford: Oxford University Press.
10. Belnap, N., Perloff, M., & Xu, M. (2001). *Facing the future: Agents and choices in our indeterminist world*. Oxford: Oxford University Press.
11. Thomason, R. H. (2012). Krister Segerberg's philosophy of action. *In this volume*.
12. McCarthy, J., & Hayes, P. J. (1969). Some philosophical problems from the standpoint of artificial intelligence. In B. Meltzer, & D. Mitchie (Eds.), *Machine intelligence* (Vol. 4, pp. 463–502). Edinburgh: Edinburgh University Press.
13. Reiter, Raymond. (1991). The frame problem in the situation calculus: A simple solution (sometimes) and a completeness result for goal regression. In Vladimir Lifschitz (Ed.), *Artificial Intelligence and Mathematical Theory of Computation: Papers in Honor of John McCarthy* (pp. 359–380). San Diego: Academic Press.
14. Reiter, R. (2001). *Knowledge in action: Logical foundations for specifying and implementing dynamical systems*. Cambridge: The MIT Press.
15. van Ditmarsch, Hans, Herzig, Andreas, & de Lima, Tiago. (2011). From situation calculus to dynamic logic. *Journal of Logic and Computation*, *21*(2), 179–204.
16. van Eijck, Jan. (2000). Making things happen. *Studia Logica*, *66*(1), 41–58.
17. Hans P., van Ditmarsch, Wiebe van der Hoek, & Barteld, P. Kooi. (2005). Dynamic epistemic logic with assignment. In F. Dignum, V. Dignum, S. Koenig, S. Kraus, M. P. Singh, & M. Wooldridge (Eds.), *Proceedings of the 4th International Conference on Autonomous Agents and Multi-Agent Systems (AAMAS)* (25–29 July 2005 , pp. 141–148). Utrecht, The Netherlands: ACM.
18. Blackburn, Patrick, de Rijke, Maarten, & Venema, Yde. (2001). *Modal logic. Cambridge tracts in theoretical computer science*. Cambridge: University Press.
19. Broersen, Jan, Herzig, Andreas, & Troquard, Nicolas. (2006). Embedding alternating-time temporal logic in strategic STIT logic of agency. *Journal of Logic and Computation*, *16*(5), 559–578.
20. Herzig, Andreas, & Lorini, Emiliano. (2010). A dynamic logic of agency I: STIT, abilities and powers. *Journal of Logic, Language and Information*, *19*(1), 89–121.
21. Herzig, A., & Schwarzentruber, F. (2008). Properties of logics of individual and group agency. In C. Areces, & R. Goldblatt (Eds.), *Advances in modal logic (AiML)* (pp. 133–149), Nancy: College Publications.
22. Segerberg, Krister. (1989). Bringing it about. *Journal of Philosophical Logic*, *18*(4), 327–347.
23. Hintikka, Jaakko. (1962). *Knowledge and belief*. Ithaca: Cornell University Press.
24. Alchourrón, Carlos, Gärdenfors, Peter, & Makinson, David. (1985). On the logic of theory change: Partial meet contraction and revision functions. *Journal of Symbolic Logic*, *50*, 510–530.

Deontic Logics Based on Boolean Algebra

Pablo F. Castro and Piotr Kulicki

Abstract Deontic logic is devoted to the study of logical properties of normative predicates such as *permission*, *obligation* and *prohibition*. Since it is usual to apply these predicates to actions, many deontic logicians have proposed formalisms where actions and action combinators are present. Some standard action combinators are action conjunction, choice between actions and *not doing* a given action. These combinators resemble boolean operators, and therefore the theory of boolean algebra offers a well-known mathematical framework to study the properties of the classic deontic operators when applied to actions. In his seminal work, Segerberg uses constructions coming from boolean algebras to formalize the usual deontic notions. Segerberg's work provided the initial step to understand logical properties of deontic operators when they are applied to actions. In the last years, other authors have proposed related logics. In this chapter we introduce Segerberg's work, study related formalisms and investigate further challenges in this area.

1 Introduction

The so-called *boolean operators* (*or*, *and*, *not*) are commonly used in ordinary language as basic connectors in phrases to put together propositions, subjects and verbs. George Boole in his famous text *An Investigation of the Laws of Thought* [5] was one of the first mathematicians (if not the first) to study the mathematical properties of these connectors, his work is considered a cornerstone of modern logic, and can be

P. F. Castro (✉)
Universidad Nacional de Río Cuarto, Ruta Nacional No. 36, Km. 601,
Río Cuarto, Cordoba, Argentina
e-mail: pcastro@dc.exa.unrc.edu.ar; castropf@mcmaster.ca

P. Kulicki
John Paul II Catholic University of Lublin, Al. Raclawickie 14, 20-950 Lublin, Poland
e-mail: kulicki@l3g.pl

R. Trypuz (ed.), *Krister Segerberg on Logic of Actions*,
Outstanding Contributions to Logic 1, DOI: 10.1007/978-94-007-7046-1_5,

thought of as capturing some universal laws of logic. One of the main contributions of George Boole to logic was the characterization of logical reasoning by means of algebraic equations. Since then, boolean algebra and its generalizations (boolean algebras with operators [16, 17]) have been used to study the mathematical properties of logics by means of algebras. A boolean algebra is made up of a non-empty set of elements, binary operators $+$, $\times$, the unary operator $-$ and two distinguished constants 0 and 1. Several (complete) axiomatizations of boolean algebras have been proposed in the literature; the following axiomatization comes from [12].

- $-0 = 1$ **and** $0 = -1$ *(Zero and One laws).*
- $x \times 0 = 0$ **and** $x + 1 = 1$ *(Absorption of zero and one laws).*
- $x \times 1 = x$ **and** $x + 0 = x$ *(Identity laws).*
- $x \times -x = 0$ **and** $x + -x = 1$ *(Inverse laws).*
- $-(-x) = x$ *(Involution law).*
- $x \times x = x$ **and** $x + x = x$ *(Idempotent laws).*
- $-(x \times y) = -x + -y$ **and** $-(x + y) = -x \times -y$ *(De Morgan laws).*
- $x \times y = y \times x$ **and** $x + y = y + x$ *(Commutativity laws).*
- $x \times (y \times z) = (x \times y) \times z$ **and** $x + (y + z) = (x + y) + z$ *(Associativity laws).*
- $x \times (y + z) = (x \times y) + (x \times z)$ **and** $x + (y \times z) = (x + y) \times (x + z)$ *(Distributivity laws).*

This set of axioms is not the smallest one possible, but it exposes the standard properties of boolean algebras. It is straightforward to see that these properties are true for set intersection, set union and set complement in any field of sets. One may think of logical propositions such as *it is raining* or *the wall is white* as elements of a boolean algebra; and therefore the boolean operators allow us to construct more complicate statements, such as: *it is raining or it is sunny*; *the wall is not white*; *it is raining and the wall is white*. As a consequence, propositional logic can be seen as a boolean algebra, the formal technique to connect both worlds is called Lindenbaum-Tarski algebra, which is a boolean algebra made up of equivalence classes of sentences and the corresponding operations [34].

Two useful concepts that we will use through this chapter are those of **ideal** and **filter**; an ideal I of a boolean algebra B is a non-empty set $I \subseteq B$ satisfying the following conditions:

1. If $x \in I$ and $y \in I$, then $x + y \in I$,
2. If $x \in I$ and $y \in B$, then $x \times y \in I$.

The dual notion of ideal is called filter: a filter is a non-empty subset $F \subseteq B$ such that it satisfies:

1. If $x \in F$ and $y \in F$, then $x \times y \in F$,
2. If $x \in F$ and $y \in B$, then $x + y \in F$.

An ideal that is not a (proper) subset of another ideal is called *maximal ideal*; on the other hand, maximal filters are called *ultrafilters*; and they are one of the key notions of boolean algebra, for instance, *ultrafilters* are usually used for proving

Stone's representation theorem [34]. We do not intend to introduce boolean algebras in detail in this chapter, good references are [12, 34].

Let us take another possible intuitive view of a boolean algebra: we may think of actions as elements of a boolean algebra, and so action combinators are the operations in this algebra. For instance, one may think of the action of driving as the set of all the ways in which one may drive: *driving fast*, *driving slow*, etc. Let us note that the boolean operators capture the way in which these sets can be combined; for example, consider the action of *driving* and the action of *drinking*, the boolean operators allow us to consider the following actions: *driving or drinking*; *driving and drinking*; *not driving*, etc. Roughly speaking, the first action expresses a choice between actions: one may perform any of these actions; the second one expresses an execution of two actions at the same time: one is driving and drinking; while the third one captures the notion of alternative action: one performs an action other then driving.

That is, at first sight, boolean algebras provide a useful mathematical framework to study basic properties of actions when they are combined in a simple way. In that framework different properties of actions can be analyzed. One type of such properties is the normative value of actions, which is investigated within deontic logic. Deontic logic can be most generally defined as a logic for rational agents acting in situations in which some kind of norms regulating their behaviour are present. The norms can be of a various nature—moral, legal, technical, organizational.

Deontic action logic is a branch of this discipline in which norms are applied to actions (alternatively norms might be linked with states of affairs). Within deontic action logic, the deontic value of boolean combinations of basic actions is worthy of being investigated. For example, if the action of drinking is permitted to be performed in any scenario (that is, it is allowed in a strong sense), then it is natural to think that we are allowed to drink while performing any other action (e.g., drinking while driving); in the interpretation of actions given above, this implies that permitted actions form an ideal in the algebra of actions. We discuss these ideas in detail in Sect. 3.

Let us remark that deontic logic is naturally related to the study of the logical properties of actions; St. Anselm, who investigated the properties of the Latin expressions *facere* and *non facere*, is considered the precursor of the formal study of actions and related concepts; his work has been an inspiration for contemporary authors, the reader can find a detailed introduction to the history of logic of actions in [33]. Modern logic of actions starts with the works of Belnap (*stit* logic) [3], Kanger [20], von Wright [41] and Segerberg [32] among others. In this text, we focus on those works where boolean algebras are used as a formalism to capture the properties of actions when combined with deontic predicates.

The chapter is organized as follows. In the next section we briefly review the history of deontic logic before Segerberg's work. In Sect. 3 we introduce Segerberg formalism with some remarks; in Sect. 4 we introduce review some contemporary works in deontic logic based on boolean algebra. Finally, in the last sections, we investigate future lines of research, and present some final remarks.

2 Deontic Action Logic Before Segerberg

Elements of logic of norms, preferences and imperatives were present all along the history of logic. First traces of formalization of deontic reasonings can be found already in the works of Aristotle, Aquinas and G.W. Leibniz. In modern times it was followed by the works of authors (philosophers, logicians and theorists of law) such as B. Bolzano, A. Hofler, E. Husserl, G.E. Moore, E. Westermarck, P. Lapie, E. Mally, K. Menger, W. Dubislav, J. Jorgensen, A. Ross, A. Hofstadter, J.C.C. McKinsey, R.M. Hare, R. Rand, but these works lack formal development or clarity in the understanding of the nature of norms. Thus, they cannot be treated as mature logical systems. We shall not present the details of those works, one can find a detailed presentation in [19].

The beginning of contemporary deontic logic is connected with von Wright's work published in 1951 [40], in which he presented the first system of that kind with the use of techniques of formal logic as we understand it by now.[1]

There are two main assumptions of this system. Firstly, deontic notions (from which von Wright is interested in obligation, permission and forbiddance) are applied to actions. Secondly, deontic notions are treated as modal operators along with alethic, epistemic and existential modalities. Thus, obligatory is understood by analogy to (alethic) necessary, (epistemic) known and (existential) for all, permitted—possible, undecided and for some, and finally forbidden—impossible, falsified and for some but not for all.

After von Wright's first paper, most of the work in deontic logic followed the second assumption neglecting the first one. What was created then is usually called standard deontic logic and is formally built in the same way as other modal systems, in which propositions are arguments of modal operators. It was Segerberg who reversed this tendency.

von Wright, already in his first paper, points out a few more important issues. He distinguishes types of actions from individual actions. He calls the first ones acts, and understands them as properties of individual actions defining a type and act-individuals—particular actions. In his system he uses the first ones. He assumes that there is a finite number of atomic acts from which one can create complex acts using boolean operators. He called such complex actions *molecular complexes*. The same symbols were used for the operators for creating complex acts as well as for truth functions. That made it easy to shift to standard deontic logic. However, at that stage they were intuitively divided and consequently the nesting of deontic operators was not possible.

von Wright did not introduce any formal semantics for his first deontic system. Instead, he formed several laws of deontic logic which he used as a foundation of his system. They were described as follows.

[1] von Wright in [42] lists three 'founding fathers' of modern deontic logic: himself, J. Kalinowski and O. Becker. All of them published their first papers on deontic logic in early 1950s we shall concentrate on the work of von Wright which is closest to our subject.

- A Principle of Deontic Distribution
  "If an act is a disjunction of two other acts, then the proposition that the disjunction is permitted is the disjunction of the proposition that the first act is permitted and the proposition that the second act is permitted" ([40], p. 7).
  Let us remark that an analogous principle for conjunction does not hold.
- A Principle of Permission
  "Any given act is either itself permitted or its negation is permitted" ([40], p. 9).
- A Principle od Deontic Contingency
  "A tautologous act [an act that is performed no matter what an agent does] is not necessarily obligatory, and a contradictory act is not necessarily forbidden" ([40], p. 11).

Since nesting of deontic operators is not allowed, the Principle of Deontic Distribution and the boolean character of operators on acts imply that every deontic proposition can be transformed to a form called by von Wright *absolutely perfect disjunctive normal form*. This normal form can be used for the verification of deontic propositions.

Some other contributions to deontic logic of action logic, which occurred between the first works of von Wright on deontic logic and Segerberg's works, are also worth mentioning. The first of them is a strict distinction between names of actions and propositions introduced by kalinowski in [18]. That was related to a division of the field to deontic logic of action (ought-to-do logic) and deontic logic of states (ought-to-be logic).

Another important contribution was the introduction of formal semantics into deontic action logic. It took the form of 3-valued matrices. In [18] a matrix for negation was presented and in [10] the idea was extended to conjunction and disjunction of actions (being the concept of action or 'inner' counterparts of operators of the propositional calculus). Aquist in [2] has shown that using matrices results in some intuitive difficulties, but nonetheless the general idea of applying formal semantics defining the meaning of deontic notions on the basis of the way that complex actions are constructed from basic ones is important for further development of the field. Recently some other proposals of multivalued semantics for deontic logic were presented in [22, 24].

Finally, it was pointed out that deontic logic must be closely related to the theory of action. An interesting formulation of that idea is given by von Wright in [42]. He concludes that there are branches of logic which are related to deontic logic to such extent that they may be regarded as extensions or offshoots of it. In particular, that applies to the formal theory of action and the logic of change.

The presentation of action logic introduced in the same paper of von Wright is also interesting and important for our further investigations. Actions are linked to and characterized by their results. The symbol '$[p]x$' is used to express the fact that the action x results in the state p. Then, deontic notions are applied to actions via states, which are the results of the actions.

In such a presentation, action theory and deontic logic are put in one system which for that reason can be regarded as a hybrid one. Segerberg, as we describe in details in the next section, divides it strictly, leaving the deontic part in the system itself and shifting action theory to the semantics of the system.

3 Segerberg's Deontic Logic

In [31], Segerberg proposes to study the properties of the standard deontic operators using the mathematical theory of boolean algebras. The basic idea behind Segerberg's work is to interpret actions as elements of a boolean algebra and deontic operators as sets of elements in this algebra; intuitively, deontic operators denote the set of elements that make them true. These sets satisfy some well-known properties: they are closed for boolean conjunction and boolean inclusion; that is, they are ideals of the corresponding algebra. As explained in the introduction, fields of sets are boolean algebras, and then, there is a, more or less, straightforward way of getting an intuitive semantics based on sets: actions are interpreted as sets of *outcomes*, and then the permission and prohibition operators are interpreted as sets of outcomes that fulfill some requirements; these conditions imply that these sets describe ideals in the underlying boolean algebra of sets; and so both approaches to the semantics are equivalent. In the following we introduce the syntax and semantics of Segerberg's logic with some remarks that will be useful in the next sections, the interested reader can find the details in [31].

Vocabularies are made up of a denumerable set of action letters: $\{a, b, c, \dots\}$[2], we consider two action constants **0** and **1**. Actions may be combined with the use of action operators: negation represented by an overline, parallel execution ($\sqcap$) and free choice ($\sqcup$). Atomic formulae are **Perm**(α) (*α is allowed*), **Forb**(α) (*α is forbidden*) and $\alpha = \beta$ (*α and β denote the same action*). We also have the standard propositional combinators: If φ and ψ are formulae, then $\varphi \wedge \psi$, $\varphi \vee \psi$, $\varphi \to \psi$ and $\neg\varphi$ are formulae. Segerberg provides two equivalent ways of providing the semantics of this logic: one is interpreting actions as elements of a boolean algebra, the other one is by interpreting them as subsets of a set of possible outcomes. Let us introduce both semantics.

Consider structures of the form $\mathscr{A} = \langle A, \times, +, -, 0, 1, F, P \rangle$, where $\langle A, \times, +, -, 0, 1 \rangle$ is a boolean algebra, F and P are ideals of this algebra and $F \cap P = \{0\}$ (i.e., they are disjoint ideals). We can define a valuation function, which maps actions to elements of the boolean algebra, as follows:

- $v(\mathbf{0}) = 0$.
- $v(\mathbf{1}) = 1$.
- $v(\alpha \sqcap \beta) = v(\alpha) \times v(\beta)$.
- $v(\alpha \sqcup \beta) = v(\alpha) + v(\beta)$.
- $v(\overline{\alpha}) = -v(\alpha)$.

[2] In [31], these letters are called event letters, since this terminology may cause some confusion with the meaning given to the word *event* in other related logics, we call them action letters.

Using v we define a satisfaction relationship $\models_A$ between boolean algebras, valuation functions, and formulae, as follows:

- $\mathscr{A}, v \models_A \alpha = \beta \iff v(\alpha) = v(\beta)$.
- $\mathscr{A}, v \models_A \mathbf{Forb}(\alpha) \iff v(\alpha) \in F$.
- $\mathscr{A}, v \models_A \mathbf{Perm}(\alpha) \iff v(\alpha) \in P$.
- $\mathscr{A}, v \models_A \varphi \wedge \psi \iff \mathscr{A}, v \models_A \varphi$ and $\mathscr{A}, v \models_A \psi$.
- $\mathscr{A}, v \models_A \varphi \vee \psi \iff \mathscr{A}, v \models_A \varphi$ or$\mathscr{A}, v \models_A \psi$ or both.
- $\mathscr{A}, v \models_A \neg\varphi \iff$ not $\mathscr{A}, v \models_A \varphi$.
- $\mathscr{A}, v \models_A \varphi \to \psi \iff$ not $\mathscr{A}, v \models_A \varphi$ or $\mathscr{A}, v \models_A \psi$, or both.

We say that $\models_A \varphi$ (φ is algebraically valid) iff $\mathscr{A}, v \models_A \varphi$ for every deontic action algebra $\mathscr{A}$ and every valuation v. Furthermore, given a set of formulae Γ, we say that $\Gamma \models_A \varphi$, if for every valuation v and every algebra $\mathscr{A}$, we have that, if $\mathscr{A}, v \models_A \psi$, for every $\psi \in \Gamma$, then $\mathscr{A}, v \models_A \varphi$.

Another interpretation of deontic operators is obtained by using set theory, we say that a structure $\mathscr{F} = \langle U, Ill, Leg \rangle$ is a deontic action frame (or deontic model) if U is a set and $Ill, Leg \subseteq U$ are two subsets of U such that $Ill \cap Leg = \emptyset$. We can think of U as the set of all possible outcomes. In this setting, the set Leg is the set of legal outcomes, and the set Ill is the set of illegal outcomes. A valuation is a function v from actions letters to the powerset of U. We can extend the definition of v using the usual set operators.

- $v(\mathbf{0}) = \emptyset$.
- $v(\mathbf{1}) = U$.
- $v(\alpha \sqcap \beta) = v(\alpha) \cap v(\beta)$.
- $v(\alpha \sqcup \beta) = v(\alpha) \cup v(\beta)$.
- $v(\overline{\alpha}) = U - v(\alpha)$.

We can define a relationship $\models$ between deontic models and formulae in a similar way that we defined $\models_{\mathscr{A}}$; we only introduce definitions for the deontic operators, the other ones are as usual.

- $\mathscr{F}, v \models \mathbf{Perm}(\alpha) \iff v(\alpha) \subseteq Leg$.
- $\mathscr{F}, v \models \mathbf{Forb}(\alpha) \iff v(\alpha) \subseteq Ill$.

We say that $\models \varphi$ if $\mathscr{F}, v \models \varphi$ for every valuation v and every model $\mathscr{F}$. Similarly, we define the relationship $\Gamma \models \varphi$ between formulae.

Segerberg proved that the two notions of validity coincide. We do not present the proof here, the interested reader can consult [31].

Theorem 1 *For every set of formulae Γ and formula φ, we have:*

$$\Gamma \models \varphi \Leftrightarrow \Gamma \models_A \varphi$$

The logic has a simple axiomatic system:

1. Axioms of boolean algebra for $=$.
2. Extensionality for equality.

3. $\mathbf{Forb}(\alpha \sqcup \beta) \leftrightarrow \mathbf{Forb}(\alpha) \wedge \mathbf{Forb}(\beta)$.
4. $\mathbf{Perm}(\alpha \sqcup \beta) \leftrightarrow \mathbf{Perm}(\alpha) \wedge \mathbf{Perm}(\beta)$.
5. $\alpha = 0 \leftrightarrow (\mathbf{Forb}(\alpha) \wedge \mathbf{Perm}(\alpha))$.

The unique deduction rule is the ancient *modus ponens*. If we have a proof (in the standard sense) of a formula φ, we say that $\vdash \varphi$; we also use this notation when we assume φ as an extra axiom. Note that axioms 3 and 4 state that prohibition and permission form ideals, while the last formula says that sets of prohibited and permitted actions are disjoint. Using Lindenbaum-Tarski algebras Segerberg proved the (strong) completeness of this system:

Theorem 2 $\Gamma \vdash \varphi \Leftrightarrow \Gamma \vDash \varphi$.

We do not reproduce the proof of this theorem, but it can be found in [31]. Let us explain the main technique used for the proof, since it will be useful in the next sections. Given a maximal consistent set of formulae Σ, we can define a relation of equivalence between actions, as follows:

$$\alpha \equiv_{\Sigma} \beta \Longleftrightarrow (\alpha = \beta) \in \Sigma$$

Since Σ is maximal, it is straightforward to prove that it is closed for the axiomatic system presented above, and therefore $=$ is an equivalence relation. Each action has an associated equivalence class:

$$\alpha_{\Sigma} = \{\beta \mid \alpha = \beta \in \Sigma\}$$

Using these ideas we can define the following algebra (the so-called Lindenbaum-Tarski algebra):

$$\langle \Delta/\Sigma, \sqcap_{\Sigma}, \sqcup_{\Sigma}, -_{\Sigma}, 0_{\Sigma}, 1_{\Sigma}, P_{\Sigma}, F_{\Sigma} \rangle$$

where:

- $\Delta/\Sigma = \{\alpha_{\Sigma} \mid \alpha \text{ is an action}\}$, is the set of equivalence classes of actions.
- $\alpha_{\Sigma} \sqcap_{\Sigma} \beta_{\Sigma} = (\alpha \sqcap \beta)_{\Sigma}$.
- $\alpha_{\Sigma} \sqcup_{\Sigma} \beta_{\Sigma} = (\alpha \sqcup \beta)_{\Sigma}$.
- $-_{\Sigma}\alpha_{\Sigma} = (-\alpha)_{\Sigma}$.
- $P_{\Sigma} = \{\alpha_{\Sigma} \mid \mathbf{Perm}(\alpha) \in \Sigma\}$.
- $F_{\Sigma} = \{\alpha_{\Sigma} \mid \mathbf{Forb}(\alpha) \in \Sigma\}$.

This algebra is a model for the set Σ, and therefore this proves the strong completeness of the system w.r.t. the algebraic models; to prove the completeness w.r.t. deontic models it is necessary to use the stone representation theorem to obtain a canonical model. Notice that the deontic operators induce ideals on the Lindebaum-Tarski algebra; these ideals are then used for defining the model. The Lindenbaum-Tarski construction will be useful for proving the completeness of related logics in Sect. 4.

An important principle in jurisprudence (and therefore in deontic logic) is the so-called *Closure Principle*: *what is not forbidden is allowed*. Note that this principle is not a theorem of the system shown above. Because of this, Segerberg calls this logic *Basic Open Deontic Logic* (or BOD for short). The non-validity of the closure principle in this logic can be proven by inspecting the deontic models where we may have some outcomes that do not belong to Ill or Leg. Deontic logics that satisfy the closure principle are called *closed*, one is tempted to add the following restriction to models to obtain a closed logic: $U = Ill \cup Leg$, which seems to guarantee the closure principle; however, as shown in [32], these kinds of models are equivalent to the standard models (that is, they satisfy the same formulae in BOD). This seems surprising at first sight; however, this is a consequence of the impossibility of capturing individual outcomes using terms—action terms denote sets of outcomes, and the syntactical construction of the logic do not allow us to distinguish between singleton sets and sets with many elements. In Sect. 4, we review some logics where it is possible to assert that individual outcomes are either permitted or forbidden. A possible solution to this issue is proposed by Segerberg using the following axiomatic schema:

$$\mathbf{Forb}(a) \vee \mathbf{Perm}(a) \qquad \text{(being } a \text{ an action letter)} \tag{1}$$

or, equivalently:

$$\neg\mathbf{Forb}(a) \rightarrow \mathbf{Perm}(a) \tag{2}$$

However, as stated in [37], this axiom induces some problems. Let us, for example, consider two actions $smoke$ and $drive$. We may say that:

$$\vdash smoke \sqcap drive \neq \emptyset$$

That is, driving while smoking is possible. Suppose now that driving is allowed, this fact is formalized as follows: $\vdash \mathbf{Perm}(drive)$. But, since $\vdash driving \sqcap smoke \sqsubseteq drive$, using the axioms we get:

$$\vdash \mathbf{Perm}(drive \sqcap smoke)$$

by formula 1 and the fact that $smoke \neq \emptyset$ we get:

$$\vdash \mathbf{Perm}(smoke)$$

Summarizing, we get the following property:

$$\alpha \sqcap \beta \neq \emptyset \wedge \mathbf{Perm}(\alpha) \rightarrow \mathbf{Perm}(\beta) \tag{3}$$

which is not intuitively true. In other words we can formulate this property stating that an agent can only perform parallel execution of two basic actions (actions described by action letters) if they are both permitted or both forbidden—otherwise parallel execution is impossible. In Sect. 4 we introduce some related logics that intend to tackle this issue.

It is possible to define other operators using permission and prohibition. One operator that is important in deontic logic is *obligation*; there are at least two ways of defining obligation in Segerberg's logic:

- $\mathbf{Obl}_P(\alpha) = \neg\mathbf{Perm}(\overline{\alpha})$.
- $\mathbf{Obl}_F(\alpha) = \mathbf{Forb}(\overline{\alpha})$.

The first one uses permission to define obligation, and the second one uses the prohibition operator. Intuitively, the first version of obligation says that an action is obligatory if and only if doing any other action is not allowed. In contrast, the second one says that an action is obligatory when it is forbidden to perform an alternative action. Let us write the satisfaction condition for the two versions of obligation:

- $\mathscr{F}, v \models \mathbf{Obl}_P(\alpha) \iff U - v(\alpha) \nsubseteq Leg$.
- $\mathscr{F}, v \models \mathbf{Obl}_F(\alpha) \iff U - v(\alpha) \subseteq Ill$.

A problematic issue with the first version of obligation (as already noted in [37]) is that strict refinements of forbidden actions are forbidden and obligatory at the same time, that is:

$$\alpha \sqsubseteq \beta \wedge \mathbf{Forb}(\beta) \wedge \alpha \neq \beta \rightarrow \mathbf{Forb}(\alpha) \wedge \mathbf{Obl}_P(\alpha)$$

For example, suppose the following statements:

- $\vdash \mathbf{Forb}(kill)$ (*it is forbidden to kill*).
- $\vdash kgently \sqsubseteq kill$ (*killing gently is a way of killing*).
- $\vdash kgently \neq kill$ (*there are some ways of killing that are not gentle*).

From these statements we can deduce: $\vdash \mathbf{Forb}(kgently) \wedge \mathbf{Obl}_P(kgently)$, the first part of the formula is intuitively true, but the second one does not fit with the intuitions: from the prohibition to kill we obtain that we are obliged to kill gently. This is a variation of the well-known paradox of the gentle killer, though no contrary-to-duty reasoning is involved in this case.

Let us take a look at the second version of obligation. Note that this version of obligation makes true the so-called Ross' paradox:

$$\mathbf{Obl}_F(\alpha) \rightarrow \mathbf{Obl}_F(\alpha \sqcup \beta)$$

which can be interpreted by saying: if you are obliged to send a letter, then you are obliged to send a letter or to burn it; which contradicts the common sense. Summarizing, the two versions of obligations described above do not capture the intuitive properties surrounding the concept of duty. In the next section we investigate other ways of defining obligation to avoid the problems explained above.

Segerberg presents his deontic logic of action just in a short paper. However, from today's perspective its content is important as well as inspiring. To sum up Segerberg's contribution to deontic action logic and his position towards problems occurring in it, let us point out the following issues.

- Segerberg's system is based on an action theory more sophisticated than truth value tables (as in Kalinowski's works); as a result, a deontic qualification of complex actions is not a simple function of generators. Thus, deontic qualification is essentially connected with complex actions.
- Segerberg introduces a novel semantics (defined using a domain of outcomes). He stresses the inspiration received from von Wright's paper [42], but in his paper he performs a strict separation between the axiomatic system and the semantics.
- Permission and forbiddance are not inter-definable in Segerberg's system. That creates the opportunity to discuss problems of openness and closedness of deontic action logic.
- Segerberg uses an infinite algebra of actions. Later works show that finite structures seems to be sufficient and much more handy.
- There is no operator corresponding to sequence of actions. Many things become much more interesting, but also complicated, when this combinator is introduced. We point out some ways of introducing it in the deontic context presented in later works.
- In Segerberg's paper obligation is a defined notion. However, both definitions given in it leads to some counterintuitive consequences. We shall discuss the issue of obligation in more details in the next section.

4 Contemporary Deontic Action Logics and Boolean Algebra

Several deontic logics with boolean operators have been proposed since the work of Segerberg. We distinguish between two kinds of logics; first, those logics that interpret deontic operators as sets of events/outcomes that fulfill these operators, among these logics we can cite those of Castro and Maibaum [7], R. van der Meyden [39] and Fiadeiro and Maibaum [9] as well as the work of Trypuz and Kulicki [37] enriching Segerberg's logic to obtain a more appealing version of obligation. On the other hand, the other kinds of logics are related to Dynamic Logic [13], this approach was initiated by J.J. Meyer in [27]; in this seminal work, Meyer relates modalities with deontic operators using violation markers. This line of research was followed by J. Broersen in his thesis [6], and by other authors. These works are related with Boolean Modal Logic defined by Gargov and Passy in [11], many of the properties of Dynamic Deontic Logics are inherited from the corresponding properties of Boolean Modal Logic, we present the details below. All these logics have a common feature of having terms for actions as well as operators to combine them; deontic operators can be used to state prescriptions over these action terms.

4.1 Deontic Dynamic Logics

Dynamic logic was introduced by Harel in [13]. This logic makes use of the box and diamond modalities to express the concepts of necessity and possibility, respectively. The novel part is that we have an infinite number of action letters; actions are combined with modalities to express the notion of causality, for example:

$$[a]\varphi$$

means: after executing action a, φ becomes true; on the other hand:

$$\langle a \rangle \varphi$$

says that it is possible to execute action a and finishing in a state of affairs where φ is true. Furthermore, we can combine actions as follows: if α and β are actions, then $\alpha; \beta$ is an action, α^* is an action and $\alpha \sqcup \beta$ is an action. Roughly speaking, ; expresses sequential composition (b is executed after a), $*$ expresses the Kleene operator: a is executed n times; and $\sqcup$ is the non-deterministic choice between actions α and β. The semantics of dynamic logic is given by models made up of a non-empty set of worlds W, a relationship $R_a \subseteq W \times W$ for each action letter a, and an interpretation function mapping propositional letters to sets of worlds. In this setting, the action combinators are interpreted as usual relational operators. For example, the sequential composition is interpreted as the relational composition; the non-deterministic choice is interpreted as the relational union and the star operator is interpreted as the reflexive-transitive closure of relations. There exist sound and complete axiomatic systems for dynamic logic, the first one was provided by Segerberg in [30]. However, as a consequence of the fact that the star operator is not elementary, the logic is not compact—the details can be found in [13].

One important variation of dynamic logic is the so-called Boolean Modal Logic [11] (or BML), where the boolean operators are used for combining actions. The semantics of these operators is given by means of the usual relational constructions. One important point about this logic is that the complement enables the introduction of the *window operator*, an operator that allows us to inspect any state related or not to the actual state, some authors have pointed out that this operator violates in some sense the principle of locality implicit in modal logics, see [4]. BML has sound and complete axiomatic systems, though this logic is not strongly complete nor compact.

John Jules Meyer uses the constructions of Dynamic Logic to define what he calls *Dynamic Deontic Logic* [27]; In this work, deontic constructions are reduced to dynamic logic constructions using a violation constant which indicates that a violation has been produced. Meyer proposes to use the following combinators: ; (composition), $\sqcup$ (non-deterministic choice), $\sqcap$ (parallel execution), and $-$ (alternative action). An algebra of actions, resembling boolean algebras, is proposed for these action combinators; however, the properties of this algebra of actions are not investigated by the author (indeed it is possible to prove that there is no decidable axiomatizations for these kinds of algebras [26]). Using modalities, Meyer defines:

$$\mathbf{Forb}(\alpha) \leftrightarrow [\alpha]\mathbf{V}.$$

That is, an action is forbidden if and only if every execution of this action yields a violation. Using prohibition, Meyer defines the rest of the deontic predicates:

- $\mathbf{Obl}(\alpha) \leftrightarrow \mathbf{Forb}(\overline{\alpha})$ (obligation) and,
- $\mathbf{Perm}(\alpha) \leftrightarrow \neg\mathbf{Forb}(\alpha)$ (permission).

Broersen [6] called this approach *goal oriented norms* since, for evaluating the truth value of a deontic predicate, only the resulting state of an action is important and not what happens during its execution. In [6] the boolean operators are used in combination with the deontic operators and the modalities; in this setting, Broersen obtains a sound and complete dynamic deontic logic with boolean operators; however, this logic is not compact.

Several criticisms have arisen to this approach. For example in [39], the following formula is exhibited as a paradox of dynamic deonticlogic: $\langle\alpha\rangle\mathbf{Perm}(\beta) \rightarrow \mathbf{Perm}(\alpha;\beta)$, which can be read as *if after shooting the president it is allowed to remain silent, then it is allowed to shoot the president and remain silent,* which is undoubtedly undesirable; these kinds of problems are inherent in goal oriented norms, Broersen has proposed the so-called process-oriented norms to deal with this problem, see [6] for the details.

In [1] these ideas are used to establish a more serious paradox: $\mathbf{Forb}(\alpha) \rightarrow [\alpha]\mathbf{Obl}(\beta \sqcap \overline{\beta})$, i.e., after executing a forbidden action, we are obliged to perform an impossible action, which is not intuitively true. In spite of these facts, Meyer's approach is interesting since in deontic dynamic logic a clear division between predicates and actions is established and, as Meyer argues, some paradoxes vanish in this approach, mainly since here we have a notion of time or state change. Moreover, some problematic statements, like nested deontic constraints, are no longer expressible. In the following section we introduce another branch of deontic action logic, initiated from the ideas of Segerberg, in which deontic operators are not captured by using modalities, instead an algebra is used to formalize the concept of norm.

4.2 Deontic Logics Based on Atomic Boolean Algebras

Segerberg used boolean algebra to give the semantics of deontic operators; in [7, 37] a variation of this approach is taken: the set of action letters is considered finite and therefore the underlying algebra of actions becomes atomic. Atomic boolean algebras have some good properties, from the topological point of view, the atoms allow us to refer to the points of the underlying space: there is an one-to-one mapping between the set of atoms of a boolean algebra and the set of its maximal ideals (or ultrafilters); the maximal ideals (or ultrafilters) can be thought of as points of the field of sets which is isomorphic to the boolean algebra (by the Stone theorem). Roughly speaking,

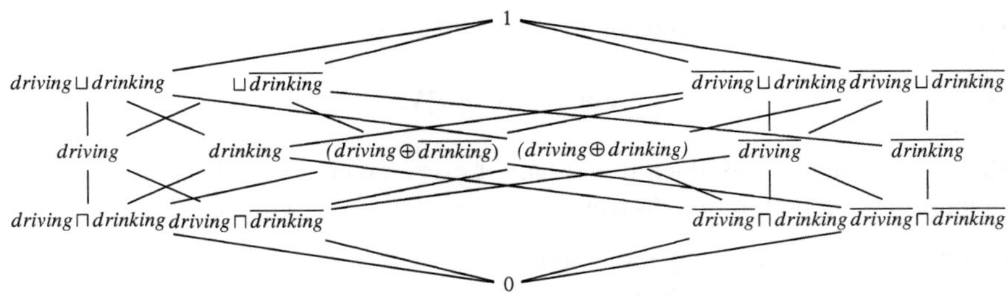

Fig. 1 Canonical Boolean algebra for three actions. For the case of simplicity we shall use the symbol $\oplus$ in the following way: $driving \oplus drinking = (driving \sqcap \overline{drinking}) \sqcup (\overline{driving} \sqcap drinking)$ (as the exclusive or between $drinking$ and $driving$)

we can refer in the language to the most specific actions that can be executed. For example, consider that we have two possible actions: $driving$ and $drinking$, if we abstract ourselves from the other possible actions, we obtain the (canonical) boolean algebra of Fig. 1. Note that the atoms in this algebra are: $driving \sqcap drinking$, $driving \sqcap \overline{drinking}$, $\overline{driving} \sqcap drinking$, $\overline{driving} \sqcap \overline{drinking}$. Every atom can be identified with an ultrafilter. For example, the atom $driving \sqcap drinking$ can be identified with the filter shown in Fig. 2. This filter can be thought of as stating a set of weakly allowed actions. In the same way, coatoms identify maximal ideals, and therefore sets of strongly allowed actions. Consider, for example, the coatom: $drinking \sqcup driving$, in this case we obtain the ideal shown in Fig. 3. This ideal may, for example, identify a set of strongly permitted actions. Let us note that atoms are monomials made up of atomic letters (or negation of them) composed by the $\sqcap$ operator; that is, it is straightforward to determine which action terms denote atoms in the corresponding boolean algebra and which do not. Let us note that, if we add the restriction $driving \sqcup drinking = 1$, then the diagrams above can be simplified, for example, the action $\overline{driving} \sqcap \overline{drinking}$ is an impossible action (that is, it is equal to 0). In some sense, this restriction says that no other actions are possible. This view of restricting ourselves to a finite number of action letters has many interesting consequences, and, of course, triggers philosophical questions. One may think that the number of possible actions is potentially infinite; however,

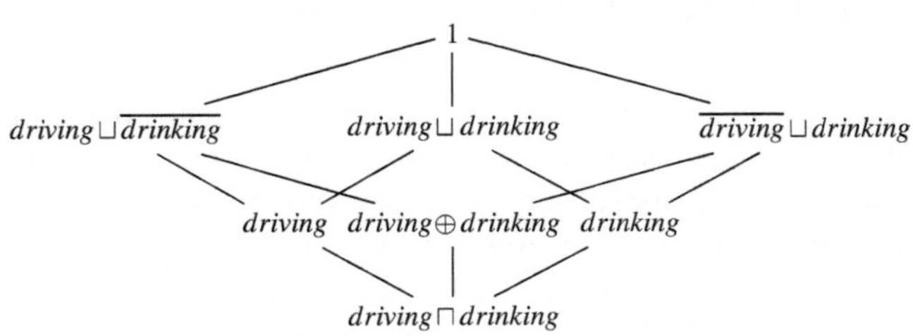

Fig. 2 Filter identified with atom $driving \sqcap drinking$

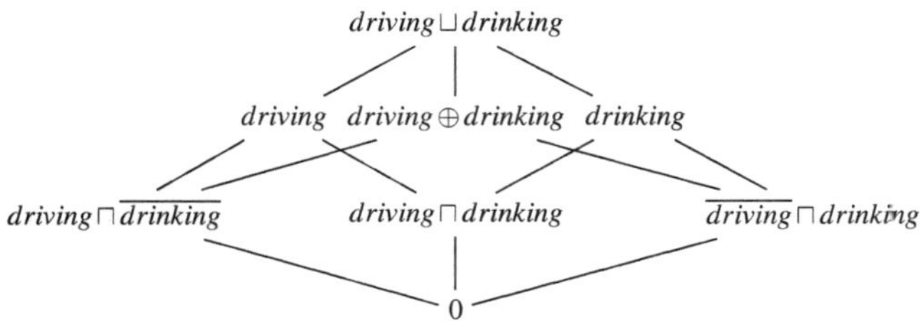

Fig. 3 Ideal corresponding to coatom $drinking \sqcup driving$

usually we are interested in reasoning about a particular set of actions, and a finite set (which may be very large) seems to be enough in most of the scenarios. No much expressivity is lost when the set of actions is restricted to a finite set, but the possibility of talking about atoms is gained, and this allows us to express interesting properties about the logic.

We shall first discuss some remarks about the semantics in the finite case. The semantics is given by means of structures: $\langle Out, Ill, Leg \rangle$, similar to the ones used by Segerberg. Note that atomic action terms are intended to express actions where no ambiguity is left, that is, each atomic action describes the actions letters involved during the execution of the action; an intuitive semantic restriction (in this case) is that atomic action terms denote at most one outcome; roughly speaking, these actions are deterministic. This restriction can be added as follows:

$$|\mathscr{I}(\delta)| = 1 \tag{4}$$

where $|-|$ denotes the cardinality of sets, and δ denotes an action term that is an atom in the boolean algebra of actions. The basic axioms of this logic are the following:

- $\textbf{Perm}(\alpha \sqcup \beta) \equiv \textbf{Perm}(\alpha) \wedge \textbf{Perm}(\beta)$.
- $\textbf{Forb}(\alpha \sqcup \beta) \equiv \textbf{Forb}(\alpha) \wedge \textbf{Forb}(\beta)$.
- $\alpha = 0 \equiv \textbf{Forb}(\alpha) \wedge \textbf{Perm}(\alpha)$.

Of course, we have the usual axioms for equality and boolean algebras. This system is equivalent to Segerberg's system (BOD). In addition to the standard operators we can define the weak versions of them:

- $\textbf{Perm}_w(\alpha) = \neg\textbf{Forb}(\alpha)$
- $\textbf{Forb}_w(\alpha) = \neg\textbf{Perm}(\alpha)$

Below we investigate the interpretation of the weak deontic operators.

We may use the atoms to introduce some further axioms. In the following we analyze the possible extensions of BOD, we follow the ideas of [37] to classify the systems.

4.3 Extensions of BOD

4.3.1 The Basic Closed System

As remarked above, Segerberg points out that closedness in BOD can be introduced by the following axiom:

$$\mathbf{Forb}(a_i) \vee \mathbf{Perm}(a_i) \qquad \text{for every action letter } a_i \tag{5}$$

as we shown in Sect. 3, this axiom has some paradoxical consequences, implying that actions that can be performed together must have the same deontic status. Furthermore, when we have a finite number of actions: $a_0, \ldots, a_n$, the atomic term:

$$\overline{a_0} \sqcap \ldots \sqcap \overline{a_n} \tag{6}$$

deserves special attention; note that this term can be interpreted as saying that no action of the actual agent is executed (this action may be thought of as denoting a behavior of an external agent). Let us note that formula 5 is not expressible enough to state that action term 6 is allowed or forbidden. Moreover, if we have an infinite number of actions, there is no way to capture the notion of such actions. If we want to ensure closedness in the finite case, we must add the following axiom:

$$\mathbf{Perm}(\overline{a_0} \sqcap \cdots \sqcap \overline{a_n}) \vee \mathbf{Forb}(\overline{a_0} \sqcap \cdots \sqcap \overline{a_n}) \quad \text{(being } a_0, \ldots, a_n \text{ all the action letters.)} \tag{7}$$

We call the system BOD+Axiom 5 **Basic Closed System** (BCS). In this system, any atomic action term δ is allowed or forbidden; that is, we have the following theorem: $\vdash \mathbf{Perm}(\delta) \vee \mathbf{Forb}(\delta)$

4.3.2 The Atomic Closed System

It is possible to use the atoms to state the closedness of the system at a low level, that is, we can state that the atomic actions are either allowed or forbidden:

$$\mathbf{Forb}(\delta) \vee \mathbf{Perm}(\delta) \quad \text{for every atomic term } \delta \tag{8}$$

This axiom, in contrast to axiom 5, avoids the paradox expressed by formula 3; note that, if two atomic actions have a non-empty intersection, then they are the same action. This axiom is adequate for models satisfying the following principle:

$$\mathscr{E} = Ill \cup Leg$$

We call the system BOD+Axiom 8 **Atomic Closed System** (ACS). Note that in this system the term $\overline{a_0} \sqcap \cdots \sqcap \overline{a_n}$ may denote some outcomes that can be interpreted as outcomes of external actions.

4.3.3 The Standard Atomic Closed System and Standard Closed System

As we remarked above, the action $\overline{a_0} \sqcap \ldots \sqcap \overline{a_n}$ may be thought of as the action of doing nothing; however, if we consider a special action $skip$ to denote this particular event, then the action $\overline{a_0} \sqcap \ldots \sqcap \overline{a_n}$ denotes an impossible action; that is, we have:

$$\overline{a_0} \sqcap \ldots \sqcap \overline{a_n} = 0 \tag{9}$$

or by duality:

$$a_0 \sqcup \ldots \sqcup a_n = 1 \tag{10}$$

We call the system ACS+Axiom 9 **Standard Atomic Closed System** or SACS. This system is presented in [7] under the name DPL, and in [37] is called DAL (see footnote 5). There are some interesting remarks about this logic; first, let us note that the Hasse diagram of the canonical boolean algebra for two actions ($driving$ and $drinking$).

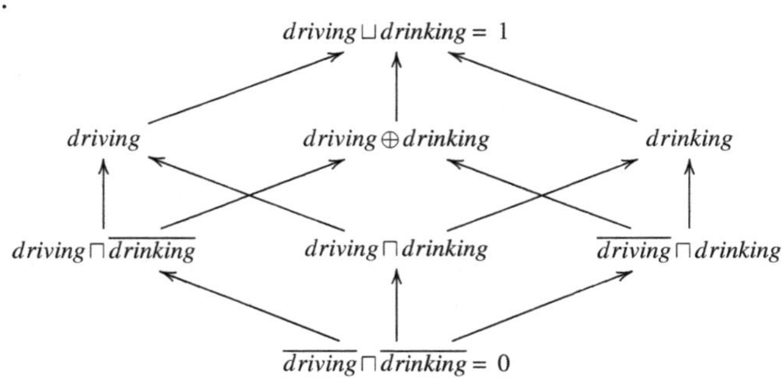

Note that, the definition of $\mathbf{Perm}_w(-)$ together with axiom 10, implies that the weak permission is semantically interpreted as the union of filters defined by the atoms which are strongly permitted. Weak permission does not define a filter since it is not closed for $\sqcap$.

In the analogical way, i.e by adding Axiom 9 we can obtain from BCS another system which we will call **Standard Closed System** or SCS.

4.3.4 The Relationship Between BOD, BCS, ACS, SACS, SCS

The relationship between these logics is shown by the diagram in Fig. 4 [37], where an arrow from one system to another means that all the theorems of the source system are theorems in the target system. The picture can be completed if we add subsystems

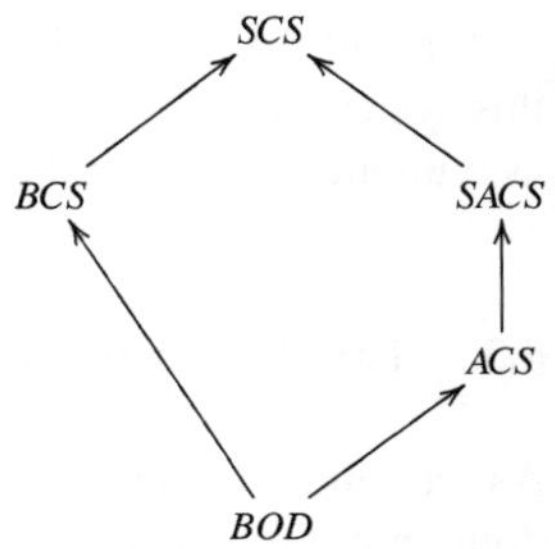

Fig. 4 Relation between the different logical systems

along the diagram; let us remark that the system *SCS* seems to be too strong to be accepted, as it is shown by formula 3, the other systems can be accepted or not, depending on the level of closure that we intend to capture.

4.4 The Obligation Operator

The formalization of the obligation has been controversial from the beginnings of deontic logic; in particular, in deontic action logicsthere exist several variations of the concept of obligation, in this section we review the usual ones. Meyer defines obligation as follows:

$$\mathbf{Obl}_F(\alpha) = \mathbf{Forb}(\overline{\alpha}) \tag{11}$$

That is, an action is obligatory iff doing any alternative action is forbidden. Obligation is defined as the complement of an ideal (prohibition) and therefore the interpretation of this operator defines a filter in the underlying boolean algebra. As a consequence, this version of obligation has the following properties:

- $\mathbf{Obl}_F(1)$
- $\mathbf{Obl}_F(\alpha \sqcap \beta) \equiv \mathbf{Obl}_F(\alpha) \wedge \mathbf{Obl}_F(\beta)$

Moreover, this obligation holds the so-called Ross' paradox:

$$\mathbf{Obl}_F(\alpha) \to \mathbf{Obl}_F(\alpha \sqcup \beta)$$

which admits the following reading: *if you are obliged to send a letter, then you are obliged to send a letter or to burn it.* Note that an obliged action (following this definition) may have some illegal outcomes, that is, an obliged action may not be allowed; this does not satisfy the principle: $\mathbf{Obl}(\alpha) \to \mathbf{Perm}(\alpha)$, which may be desirable in some contexts.

Another definition of obligation can be obtained by using the permission, as follows:

$$\mathbf{Obl}_P(\alpha) = \neg\mathbf{Perm}(\overline{\alpha})$$

Roughly speaking, an action is obligatory (following this definition) when some outcomes of alternative actions are not allowed. This operator has the following properties:

- $\mathbf{Obl}_P(\alpha \sqcup \beta) \equiv \mathbf{Obl}_P(\alpha) \vee \mathbf{Obl}_P(\beta)$.
- $\mathbf{Obl}_P(\alpha \sqcup \beta) \rightarrow \mathbf{Obl}_P(\alpha) \wedge \mathbf{Obl}_P(\beta)$.

As remarked in [37], a problematic property of this variation of obligation is the following one:

$$\mathbf{Forb}(\beta) \wedge \alpha \sqsubseteq \beta \wedge \alpha \neq \beta \rightarrow \mathbf{Obl}_P(\alpha)$$

That is, specific ways of performing forbidden actions are obligatory, which is paradoxical.

Let us present another possible definition of obligation, introduced in [7]. The definition is as follows:

$$\mathbf{Obl}_F^P(\alpha) = \mathbf{Perm}(\alpha) \wedge \mathbf{Forb}(\overline{\alpha})$$

Roughly speaking, an action is obligatory if it is allowed and any alternative action is forbidden. This definition does not hold the Ross' paradox, moreover it satisfies some intuitive properties [7]:

- $\mathbf{Obl}_F^P(\alpha) \rightarrow \mathbf{Perm}(\alpha)$
- $\mathbf{Obl}_F^P(\alpha) \wedge \mathbf{Obl}_F^P(\overline{\alpha}) \equiv (\alpha = 0)$

However, this definition of obligation satisfies the following property (called *extensionality* in [37]):

$$\mathbf{Obl}_F^P(\alpha) \wedge \mathbf{Obl}_F^P(\beta) \rightarrow \alpha = \beta$$

That is, only one action can be obligatory per time; this seems paradoxical as one can devise scenarios where this is not the case.

Trypuz and Kulicki have proposed another version of obligation which intends to improve the definitions of obligation given above. The idea is to add a new set *Req* of *required* outcomes, and therefore we can introduce the obligation as a new operator as follows:

$$\mathbf{Obl}_N(\alpha) \iff \mathscr{I}(\alpha) \subseteq Req$$

We may add the requirement that *Req* is not empty: $Req \neq \emptyset$. The properties of this new version of obligation are the following:

- $\mathbf{Obl}_N(\alpha) \wedge \mathbf{Obl}_N(\beta) \rightarrow \mathbf{Obl}(\alpha \sqcap \beta)$
- $\neg\mathbf{Obl}_N(0)$

Of course, if we want to obtain: $\mathbf{Obl}_N(\alpha) \rightarrow \mathbf{Perm}(\alpha)$, we should add the following requirement:

$$Req \subseteq Leg$$

However, the following principle cannot be proven for this version of obligation:

$$\mathbf{Obl}_N(\alpha) \rightarrow \mathbf{Forb}(\overline{\alpha})$$

To summarize, when we introduce the notion of atom in the basic logic we obtain several extensions of this logic, these extensions are obtained by adding different levels of closeness as well as different versions of obligation; it is not our intention to favor one deontic system over others, we leave this to the reader. In the following section we discuss some possible lines of future work; in particular, it seems interesting to extend deontic logics with boolean algebras with operators that also support the concept of atom and coatom.

4.5 A Deontic Logic Built on Synchronous Kleene Algebra

4.5.1 The Language of DAL Built on Synchronous Kleene Algebra

In a recent paper [29], another system (on the technical side inspired by the use of algebraic structures in the papers of Segerberg [31] and Castro and Maibaum [7]) based on intuitions similar to the system of Meyer from [27] is presented. Formally, the space of actions is represented there by an algebraic structure called synchronous Kleene algebra, defined in [28]. Such algebra differs from boolean algebra by having the operator of sequential composition on its elements instead of negation (complement). A kind of action complement is introduced into the system by definition, as a non-primitive notion. The work opens new possibilities for deontic action logic offering a new, interesting semantic tool.

Moreover, contratry-to-duty obligations, that are not expressible in the earlier mentioned systems, are introduced in the form of a *reparation* connected with obligation and prohibition. Thus, formulas $\mathbf{Obl}_{\mathscr{C}}(\alpha)$ and $\mathbf{Forb}_{\mathscr{C}}(\alpha)$ state respectively that α is obligatory (forbidden) and if an agent breaks such a norm it is bound by another norm expressed by $\mathscr{C}$, which is a reparation. Formulas $\mathbf{Obl}_{\perp}(\alpha)$ and $\mathbf{Forb}_{\perp}(\alpha)$ are understood as an absolute obligation and forbiddance.

Formally, we can define the language of the system as follows[3]:

$$\alpha := a \mid 0 \mid 1 \mid \alpha \sqcap \alpha \mid \alpha \sqcup \alpha \mid \alpha ; \alpha$$
$$\mathscr{C} := \perp \mid \mathbf{Perm}(\alpha) \mid \mathbf{Forb}_{\mathscr{C}}(\alpha) \mid \mathbf{Obl}_{\mathscr{C}}(\alpha) \mid \mathscr{C} \rightarrow \mathscr{C}$$

where a is an element of a finite set A of basic actions.

Let further $A^{\sqcap}$ be the set of actions composed from basic actions from A using only $\sqcap$ operator. Intuitively, the set $A^{\sqcap}$ contains actions that are parallel executions of an arbitrary number of basic actions. By analogy to boolean algebra of actions, we will call the elements of $A^{\sqcap}$ *quasiatoms*.[4] The difference is that atoms of BA can be described by parallel executions of basic actions or negation (complement) of them. Kleene algebra lacks boolean negation and quasiatoms contain only 'positive' parts of atoms. At this point we do not prejudge the semantic relation between atoms of

[3] We omit propositional constants originally used in [29].

[4] In [29] such formulas are called $\times$-formulas.

BA and quasiatoms, this can be figured out from the formal semantics of the system. We shall write that quasiatom α is contained in quasiatom β ($\alpha \subseteq \beta$), when the set of basic atoms from which α is composed is contained in the set of basic actions from which β is composed.

0 is interpreted, as in boolean algebra of actions, as an impossible action. In contrast 1 is understood differently, as 'skip' or 'doing nothing'.

4.5.2 Axioms of Synchronous Kleene Algebra

The following axioms of boolean algebra listed in our Introduction (applied to the language of the system) are also axioms of synchronous Kleene algebra:

- Absorption of Zero,
- Identity Laws,
- Commutativity Laws,
- Associativity Laws,
- Distributivity of $\sqcup$ over $\sqcap$,
- Idempotency of $\sqcup$.

Absorption of 1 does not hold since, as mentioned above, 1 has a different meaning here than in boolean algebra. The system does not include idempotency of $\sqcap$. Instead of the latter law, the following weak idempotency of $\sqcap$ (idempotency for basic actions) is used:
If $a \in A$, **then** $\alpha \sqcap \alpha = \alpha$

The following formulas complete the axiomatization of equality in synchronous Kleene algebra of actions:

- $\alpha; (\beta; \gamma) = (\alpha; \beta); \gamma$ *(Associativity of ;).*
- $\alpha; 1 = 1; \alpha = \alpha$ *(Identities of 1 with respect to ;).*
- $\alpha; 0 = 0; \alpha = 0$ *(Absorption of zero with respect to ;).*
- $\alpha; (\beta \sqcup \gamma) = (\alpha; \beta) \sqcup (\alpha; \gamma)$ **and** $(\alpha \sqcup \beta); \gamma = (\alpha; \gamma) \sqcup (\beta; \gamma)$ *(Distributivity of ; over* $\sqcup$*).*
- **If** $\alpha, \beta \in A^{\sqcap}$, **then** $(\alpha; \gamma) \sqcap (\beta; \delta) = (\alpha \sqcap \beta); (\gamma \sqcap \delta)$ *(Weak distributivity of* $\sqcap$ over ;).

The system of deontic logic from [29] is defined semantically (no axiomatization for deontic notions is given). The following notions and facts are used to define a valid deontic proposition. We use the content of the definitions from [29], slightly changing the way they are presented there.[5]

[5] As the present paper has a character of a review we refrain from criticizing particular intuitions behind the system and proposing alternative solutions. Preliminary results on an alternative proposal of one of the authors of the present paper and Robert Trypuz are presented in [23].

4.5.3 Canonical Form

The inductive definition of canonical forms is following:

(i) 0 is in canonical form.
(ii) If for all $i \in I$:

(1) either (a) $\beta^i = \alpha_1^i; \alpha_2^i$, (where $\alpha_1^i \in A^{\sqcap}$ and $\alpha_2^i \notin \{0, 1\}$ is in canonical form), or
(b) $\beta^i = \alpha_1^i$, where $\alpha_1^i \in A^{\sqcap} \cup \{1\}$
and
(2) for all $i, j \in I$ if $i \neq j$, then $\alpha_1^i \neq \alpha_1^j$,
then $\alpha = \bigsqcup_{i \in I} \beta^i$ is in canonical form.

Each α_1^i plays the role of a unique possible first step of compound action α—the first step of action β^1. Action α_1^i cannot be equal to 0, since in that case α would also be equal to 0. In case (a) it must be a quasiatom. In case (b), action β^1 is a one step action (α_1^i is its first and its last step). In that case α_1^i is a quasiatom or equals 1. Thus quasiatoms and 1 are in canonical form (when, in case (b), I is a singleton).

Each α_2^i is the rest of action β^i. Action α_2^i cannot equal 0 (for the same reasons as α_1^i) or 1 (because of identity of 1 w.r.t. ;).

For any action α there exists α' in canonical form s.t. $\alpha = \alpha'$ ([28] Th. 2.8).

4.5.4 Action Complement

Action complementis not a principal combinator but it is a function defined inductively as follows.

(i) Complement of 0 is 1, complement of 1 is 0, in symbols $\overline{0} = 1, \overline{1} = 0$.
(ii) Let $\alpha \notin \{0, 1\}$ be an action in canonical form, i.e. $\alpha = \bigsqcup_{i \in I} \beta^i$, where for all $i \in I$ $\beta^i = \alpha_1^i$ or $\beta^i = \alpha_1^i; \alpha_2^i$ as in the definition of canonical form.

Let further X_1 be the set of α_1^i s.t. $i \in I$ and $\beta^i = \alpha_1^i; \alpha_2^i$ (β^i is not a one step action), $\overline{X_1} = \{\gamma \in A^{\sqcap} \mid \neg\exists_{i \in I}\, \alpha_1^i \subseteq \gamma\}$. Moreover, let δ^j ($j \in J$) be all quasiatoms s.t. $\exists_{\alpha \in X_1}\, \alpha \subseteq \delta^j$ and $I_j \subseteq I$ be indexing set s.t. $I_j = \{i \in I \mid \alpha_1^i \subseteq \delta^j\}$.

Complement $\overline{\alpha}$ of action α is defined by the following equation:

$$\overline{\alpha} = \bigsqcup \overline{X_1} \sqcup \bigsqcup_{j \in J} \left(\delta^j; \overline{\bigsqcup_{i \in I_j} \alpha_2^i} \right)$$

Intuitively, a complement of a multiple step action is a free choice between different ways of not doing the first step of the action and doing the first step, and different ways of not doing the other steps. A complement of an action cannot have more steps then the original action. That makes the construction finite.

Proposition 2.8 from [29] states that the complement operation returns a deontic action which is in canonical form.

4.5.5 Rooted Tree

Let A be a set of basic actions. A rooted tree with labelled edges is an acyclic connected graph $\langle \mathcal{N}, \mathcal{E}, A \rangle$ with a designated node r. $\mathcal{N}$ is a set of nodes, $r \in \mathcal{N}$ is a designed node called root node. $\mathcal{E}$ is the set of directed labelled edges between nodes (in symbolical notation $m \xrightarrow{\alpha} n$ stands for the edge from node m to node n with label α), where labels are taken from the set $2^A \cup \{\Lambda\}$.

Intuitively, nodes represent states and edges—actions that can lead from one state to another by performing an action specified by a label. Empty label represents skip action 1, label Λ represents the impossible action 0 and all the other labels represent quasiatoms built from the elements of the label. For that reason, we use the same variables for labels as for actions. Multiple edges starting from one node represent the free choice operator.

A path in the rooted tree is understood in a way usual for graphs. A path which cannot be extended (there is no edge starting from its last node) is called *final*. The final nodes on each final path are called *leaf nodes*. When an edge e is an element of the set of edges $\mathcal{E}$ of a tree T we shall write in short that e is an element of T ($e \in T$).

Theorem 2.10 from [29] states that for any action in canonical form there exists a rooted tree corresponding to that action. For arbitrary action α we shall use the symbol $T(\alpha)$ to refer to the tree corresponding to the action in canonical form equal to α.

4.5.6 Normative Structure

Let A be a set of basic actions. A normative structure is a triple $K = (\mathcal{W}, R_A, \rho)$, in which:

- $\mathcal{W}$ is a set of worlds;
- R_A is a function returning a labelled patrial accessibility function $R_\alpha : \mathcal{W} \longrightarrow \mathcal{W}$ for each set of basic actions $\alpha \subseteq A$;
- ρ is a marking function which marks each world with markers from the set $\{\circ_a, \bullet_a \mid a \in A\}$ in such a way that no world can be marked by both $\circ_a$ and $\bullet_a$ for any $a \in A$.

A pointed normative structure $\langle K, i \rangle$ is a normative structure with designated world i ($i \in \mathcal{W}$). As for trees, we shall call an element $e = s \xrightarrow{\alpha} s'$ of a partial accessibility function R_α also an element of K (symbolically: $e \in K$).

K is deterministic as for each set of basic actions there is at most one world connected by the relation. The relation informs us what actions can be executed in each world. Markers on the successor world inform us which actions are obligtory

($\circ_a$) and which are forbidden ($\bullet_a$). Marking function ρ marks each world for each basic action $a \in A$ with $\circ_a$, $\bullet_a$ or nothing, that means that actions leading to that world can be obligatory, forbidden or neutral.

4.5.7 Relationship Between Normative Structures and Rooted Trees

For a tree $T = (\mathscr{N}, \mathscr{E}, A)$ and normative structure $K = (\mathscr{W}, R_A, \rho)$ let $\mathscr{S} \subseteq \mathscr{N} \times \mathscr{W}$ be the *simulation* relation of the tree node by the world of the structure s.t.:

$t\mathscr{S}s$ iff the following two conditions hold:

(i) for every edge $t \xrightarrow{\alpha} t' \in T$ there exists an element of a labelled accessibility relation $s \xrightarrow{\alpha'} s' \in K$ s.t. $\alpha \subseteq \alpha'$ and $t'\mathscr{S}s'$;

(ii) for every edge $t \xrightarrow{\alpha'} t' \in T$ and every element of a labelled accessibility relation $s \xrightarrow{\alpha'} s' \in K$ if $\alpha \subseteq \alpha'$, then $t'\mathscr{S}s'$.

We shall write that a tree T with root r is simulated by a normative structure K w.r.t. a world s ($T\mathscr{S}_s K$) if and only if $r\mathscr{S}s$.

In the definition, the label of the edge α of the tree is included in the label α' of the accessibility relation in the normative structure. Prisacariu and Schneider motivate this by the idea that, respecting an obligatory quasiatomic action constructed from elements of α means executing any quasiatomic action in which it is included. Intuitively a tree representing an action is represented by a normative structure if every possible way of executing any step of the action allows to execute another step of the action. Because the inclusion of α in α' is used, any step can be executed in parallel with any other quasiatomic action.

This simulation relation can be strengthened to a *strong simulation* by changing the conditions $\alpha \subseteq \alpha'$ in (i) and (ii) into the equivalence $\alpha = \alpha'$. Then, since K is a deterministic condition, (ii) is redundant. We shall use symbol $\mathscr{S}'$ for strong simulation. In this case, only the exact execution (with no other actions executed in parallel) of quasiatomic steps is considered.

The notion of simulation can be also weakened by dropping existential condition (i) from the definition. Such relation will be called *partial simulation* and it will be symbolically represented by $\widetilde{\mathscr{S}}$. In this case some steps of the action defining the simulated tree may not be executable, but if a step is executable, then the tree starting from the end of the step is partially simulated.

Now we define fragments of deontic structures, generated by rooted trees, which we shall call *simulating structure*[6] and *non-simulating reminder*.

Let T be a rooted tree, $K = \langle \mathscr{W}, R_A, \rho \rangle$ a deontic structure and $i \in \mathscr{W}$ a world s.t. $T\mathscr{S}_i K$.

$K^{T,i}_{sim} = (\mathscr{W}', R'_A, \rho')$ is a simulating structure w.r.t. T and i when it is the least sub-structure of K respecting the following conditions:

---

[6] In [29] it is called maximal simulating structure.

(i) $i \in \mathscr{W}'$;

(ii) if $t \xrightarrow{\alpha} t' \in T$ and $s \xrightarrow{\alpha'} s' \in K$ and $t\mathscr{S}s$ and $\alpha \subseteq \alpha'$, then $s' \in \mathscr{W}'$ and $s \xrightarrow{\alpha'} s' \in R'_A$;

(iii) $\rho' = \rho|\mathscr{W}'$.

$K_{rem}^{T,i} = (\mathscr{W}'', R''_A, \rho'')$ is a non-simulating reminder of K w.r.t. T and i when it is the least sub-structure of K respecting the following conditions:

(i) if $s \in K_{max}^{T,i}$ and there exist α' and s' s.t. $s \xrightarrow{\alpha'} s' \in K_{max}^{T,i}$ and $s \xrightarrow{\alpha} s'' \notin K_{max}^{T,i}$, then $s, s'' \in \mathscr{W}''$ and $s \xrightarrow{\alpha} s'' \in R''_A$;

(ii) $\rho'' = \rho|\mathscr{W}''$.

4.5.8 Validity

Now we are ready to define valid deontic formulae. The satisfaction of a deontic formula $\mathscr{C}$ w.r.t. a pointed normative structure $\langle K, i\rangle$ ($K, i \models \mathscr{C}$) is defined inductively as follows.

- $K, i \not\models \bot$
- $K, i \models \mathscr{C}_1 \to \mathscr{C}_2$ iff whenever $K, i \models \mathscr{C}_1$, then $K, i \models \mathscr{C}_2$
- $K, i \models \mathbf{Obl}_{\mathscr{C}}(\alpha)$ iff the following conditions hold:
  1. $T(\alpha)\mathscr{S}_i K$;
  2. if $t \xrightarrow{\beta} t' \in T(\alpha)$ and $s \xrightarrow{\beta'} s' \in K$ and $t\mathscr{S}s$ and $\beta \subseteq \beta'$ and $a \in \beta$, then $\circ_a \in \varrho(s')$;
  3. if $s \xrightarrow{\beta'} s' \in K_{rem}^{T(\alpha),i}$ and $a \in \beta'$, then $\circ_a \notin \rho(s')$;
  4. if t is a leaf of a final path of $T(\overline{\alpha})$ starting from its root and $t\mathscr{S}^s s$, then $K, s \models \mathscr{C}$.
- $K, i \models \mathbf{Forb}_{\mathscr{C}}\alpha$ iff the following conditions hold:
  1. $T(\alpha)\widetilde{\mathscr{S}_i} K$;
  2. if σ is a final path of $T(\alpha)$ s.t. $\sigma\mathscr{S}_i K$ and $t \xrightarrow{\beta} t' \in \sigma$ and $s \xrightarrow{\beta'} s' \in K$ and $t\mathscr{S}s$ and $\beta \subseteq \beta'$ and $a \in \beta'$, then $\bullet_a \in \rho(s')$;
  3. if σ is a final path of $T(\alpha)$ starting from its root s.t. $\sigma\mathscr{S}_i K$ and t is a leaf of σ and $t\mathscr{S}s$, then $K, s \models \mathscr{C}$.
- $K, i \models \mathbf{Perm}(\alpha)$ iff the following conditions hold:
  1. $T(\alpha)\mathscr{S}_i K$;
  2. if $t \xrightarrow{\beta} t' \in T(\alpha)$ and $s \xrightarrow{\beta'} s' \in K$ and $t\mathscr{S}s$ and $\beta \subseteq \beta'$ and $a \in \beta$, then $\bullet_a \notin \rho(s')$

We say that $\mathscr{C}$ is satisfied in normative structure K ($K \models \mathscr{C}$) iff it is satisfied in every world of K. A deontic formula $\mathscr{C}$ is valid ($\models \mathscr{C}$) if it is satisfied in any deontic structure.

Let us now examine briefly the intuitive meaning of the definition of satisfaction. The first condition for obligation states that an obligatory action must be executable. The second one states that at each step all alternative executions of the step (defined by the free choice operator) are indeed obligatory. The third one states that no other possible alternative transition from any world in the normative structure is obligatory. Finally, the fourth condition states that, at the end of any alternative path in the normative structure (violating the obligation defined in the considered proposition), a proposition defining a reparation holds.

In the first conditions for obligation only weak simulation is used. Thus, the impossible action is regarded as forbidden. The second condition states that, if the considered action can be executed in a certain way, described by a path in the respective tree, then any world, corresponding to a node in that path, marks the corresponding action as forbidden (according to the intuition that forbidding a sequence means forbidding all the actions on that sequence). The third and last condition states that a successful realization of a forbidden action leads to a world in which a proposition defining a reparation holds.

The two conditions for a permitted action state respectively that any permitted action is possible, and that any step of such an action is not forbidden (although it may be executable in parallel with a forbidden action).

4.5.9 Properties of Deontic Notions in the System

Most of the basic axioms of DAL based on BA concerning permission and forbiddance are valid in the discussed system based on Kleene algebra[7]:

$$\mathbf{Perm}(\alpha \sqcup \beta) \equiv \mathbf{Perm}(\alpha) \wedge \mathbf{Perm}(\beta);$$
$$\mathbf{Forb}_{\mathscr{C}}(\alpha \sqcup \beta) \equiv \mathbf{Forb}_{\mathscr{C}}(\alpha) \wedge \mathbf{Forb}_{\mathscr{C}}(\beta);$$
$$\mathbf{Forb}_{\mathscr{C}}(0).$$

Moreover, formula:

$$\mathbf{Forb}_{\mathscr{C}}(\alpha) \rightarrow \mathbf{Forb}_{\mathscr{C}}(\alpha \sqcap \beta)$$

is also valid. However, unlike in those systems, permission and forbiddance are not symmetrical here. The following formulas are not valid:

$$\mathbf{Perm}(0);$$
$$\mathbf{Perm}(\alpha) \rightarrow \mathbf{Perm}(\alpha \sqcap \beta).$$

The non-validity of the former makes it possible for the following formula to be valid:

$$\mathbf{Perm}(\alpha) \rightarrow \neg\mathbf{Forb}_{\mathscr{C}}(\alpha).$$

[7] Proofs of the facts concerning validity and non-validity of formulae stated here can be found in [29].

Let us now apply the criteria that were used in [36] to compare various deontic action logics of permission and forbiddance based on boolean algebra, esp. Segerberg's system: 'closedness' and treatment of 'doing nothing'. Although the set of basic action is finite, the absence of the classical complement makes it impossible to use the notion of atom from boolean algebra. Instead, the actions from $A^{\sqcap}$, which we called quasiatoms, can be used. The logic from [29] is closed neither for basic actions nor for quasiatoms. On the other hand 'doing nothing' is represented by action 1 which is quite different from the one considered in [36].

As for obligation the following formulas are valid:

$$\neg\mathbf{Obl}_{\mathscr{C}}(0);$$
$$\mathbf{Obl}_{\mathscr{C}}(1);$$
$$\mathbf{Obl}_{\mathscr{C}}(\alpha) \to \mathbf{Perm}(\alpha).$$

Moreover, the following formulas are not valid:

$$\mathbf{Obl}_{\mathscr{C}}(\alpha) \to \mathbf{Obl}_{\mathscr{C}}(\alpha \sqcap \beta);$$
$$\mathbf{Obl}_{\mathscr{C}}(\alpha \sqcap \beta) \to \mathbf{Obl}_{\mathscr{C}}(\alpha);$$
$$\mathbf{Obl}_{\mathscr{C}}(\alpha) \to \mathbf{Obl}_{\mathscr{C}}(\alpha \sqcup \beta);$$
$$\mathbf{Obl}_{\mathscr{C}}(\alpha \sqcup \beta) \to \mathbf{Obl}_{\mathscr{C}}(\alpha);$$
$$\mathbf{Obl}_{\mathscr{C}}(\alpha) \wedge \mathbf{Obl}_{\mathscr{C}}(\beta) \to \mathbf{Obl}_{\mathscr{C}}(\alpha \sqcap \beta).$$

The last formula, however, becomes valid if we add the following condition to the semantics of obligation:
there exists γ s.t. $T(\alpha \sqcap \gamma)$ is isomorphic to a simulating substructure of K w.r.t. $T(\alpha)$ and i.

The obligation modified in such a way is called in [29] a *natural obligation*.

For natural implication the following interesting formula is also valid:

$$\mathbf{Obl}_{\mathscr{C}_1}(\alpha) \wedge \mathbf{Obl}_{\mathscr{C}_2}(\beta) \to \mathbf{Obl}_{\mathscr{C}_1 \vee \mathscr{C}_2}(\alpha \sqcap \beta).$$

The way the definitions of obligation and prohibition are constructed guarantees that reparation is inevitable. Any possible execution of violating action by definition must end in a situation in which the deontic proposition describing a reparation holds. In particular for $\mathbf{Obl}_{\perp}(\alpha)$ there is no final path of $T(\overline{\alpha})$ strongly simulated by K. Intuitively, this means that it is impossible to violate absolute obligation and such an obligation can be understood as necessity. A similar fact holds for absolute forbiddance and consequently, it that can be interpreted as impossibility.

4.6 Conflicts Between Actions and Specialized Algebras

In the systems described above, we considered those action algebras generated by a finite set of basic actions. In the most straightforward situations all the combinations of basic actions are possible. However, it is not necessarily true. If actions a and b cannot be executed together, then their parallel combination is impossible, this can be expressed in symbols by the equation: $a \sqcap b = 0$. As an obvious example we can take actions: 'turn left' and 'turn right'. Moreover, some actions, essentially available for an agent, may be impossible in some situations. For example, we can consider the action 'turn left' when there is no left turn available on the crossroads.

The above mentioned facts can be used to enrich the expressive power of deontic logic based on boolean (or Kleene) algebra. In [29], the notion of conflict often found in legal contracts is introduced as a relation imposing more structure into the algebra.[8] It is defined as a symmetric and irreflexive relation over basic actions and symbolically represented by #. Its meaning is ensured by the following formula:

$$a\#b \rightarrow a \sqcap b = 0.$$

It can be further used in the deontic context to derive the following law:

$$\alpha\#\beta \rightarrow \neg(\mathbf{Obl}_{\mathscr{C}}(\alpha) \wedge \mathbf{Obl}_{\mathscr{C}}(\beta)).$$

In [38], the possibility of defining multiple action algebras based on the same set of basic actions was used to formulate a strategy of building a system of norms. By that strategy, first, each situation in which an agent can find itself should be analyzed. The possible actions for all situations should be recognized and formulated in a boolean algebra. The deontic notions can be then introduced for each situation separately, defining what in each situation is permitted, forbidden and obligatory. Finally, actions can be collected from specific situations and used to formulate a general algebra of actions for agents. It is shown how to construct the characteristics of deontic notions for this algebra from their specification in specific situations.

5 Future Challenges

In Sect. 3 we reviewed the logic defined by Segerberg, while in Sect. 4 we have described several related logics that use a boolean algebra of actions and provide different formalizations of the deontic operators. In this section we discuss some further work about deontic action logic based on boolean algebra.

[8] Similar ideas were also introduced in [35].

5.1 First-Order Deontic Action Logics

First, we review possible extensions of the logics described above aimed to embrace first-order reasoning. First-order deontic logics have been a topic of discussion since the beginning of deontic logic; for example, Hintikka [14] discusses the intuitive properties of first-order operators when combined with deontic operators; first-order operators are also explicit in the foundational work of Kanger about ethical theory [21]. More recently first order attempts to deontic logic are present in papers of Lokhorst [25] and Trypuz [35].

The main difficulty in deontic action logic to deal with first-order operators is the interplay between quantifiers and actions. In [8], the authors propose to introduce generalized boolean operators to deal with parameters, for example, consider the following term:

$$\bigsqcup_x a(x)$$

where a is an action letter. Roughly speaking, this operator is a non-deterministic execution of action a with some parameter x. For example, we may consider the following term:

$$\bigsqcup_x pay\_tax(x)$$

can be read as saying that some person pays its taxes. Some interesting questions arise when the first-order operators are introduced. For example, the proof of completeness in the propositional case relies on the fact that the underlying boolean algebra of terms (denoting actions) is atomic, and therefore the atoms in this algebra can be used to build a canonical model. It is not straightforward (at first sight) to preserve this property when the quantifiers are added; adding parameters to actions produces a boolean algebra of terms which is not atomic. The relationship between deontic operators and first-order predicates seems an interesting topic to investigate, for instance, it is not obvious at first sight which of this properties should be true:

- $\forall x : \mathbf{Perm}\,(\alpha(x)) \to \mathbf{Perm}\left(\bigsqcup_x \alpha(x)\right)$.
- $\mathbf{Perm}\left(\bigsqcup_x \alpha(x)\right) \to \forall x : \mathbf{Perm}(\alpha(x))$,

and similar properties for weak permission and the existential operator. For example, it seems obvious that the first property should be true: *if all the persons are permitted to drink, then any chosen person will be allowed to drink.* Similarly, the second property also seems true: *if a person (selected in a non-deterministic way) is allowed to drink, then all the person are allowed to drink.* These properties are more complicated when obligation is involved, we refer the reader to the discussion in [21] about this properties. For example, in the logic propose by Kanger, we can write $Ax : O(Px)$, this is a quantification over actions; the intuitive meaning of this expression is: every action of type P is obligatory to be performed. In the same way, we can write: $O(Ax : Px)$ which must be read as: *it is obligatory that every act of type A is performed.* The formula $Ax : O(Px) \to O(Ax : Px)$ is discarded with intuitive examples of the style: *in some settings, everyone ought to pay fines, but it is not true in every deontically perfect world, that everyone should pay fines.* As explained in [8], reasoning about these logics can be very hard. Introducing generalized boolean operators, on the other hand, can allow us to obtain logics expressive enough to capture interesting problems. In a similar way, cylindric algebras seem to be another possible way of extending boolean algebra of actions to obtain a framework where elementary operations can be captured; from our point of view these topics deserve further investigation and discussion.

5.2 Boolean Algebras with Operators

Boolean algebras with operators are obtained by enriching boolean algebras with a collection of additional operators f_i which satisfy:

- are join preserving:

$$f_i(x_0, \ldots, x_j \vee y_k, \ldots, x_n) = f_i(x_0, \ldots, x_j, \ldots, x_n) \vee f_i(x_0, \ldots, y_k, \ldots, x_n)$$

- are normal for each argument: $f_i(\ldots, 0, \ldots) = 0$.

These extra operators allow us to capture other intuitive combinators of actions. Many useful formalisms can be captured as BAO, for example: modal logics, relation algebras, relevance logics, geometries, etc. Between these algebras, relational algebras are those which are extension of boolean algebras and in addition they have the following operators:

- ;—composition of relations.
- $^{-1}$—converse of relations.
- e—identity for composition.

These operators satisfy the following axioms:

- $(x \sqcup y) \sqcup z = x \sqcup (y \sqcup z)$
- $x \sqcup y = y \sqcup x$
- $x = \overline{\overline{x} \sqcup y} \sqcup \overline{\overline{x} \sqcup \overline{y}}$
- $x; (y; z) = (x; y); z$
- $x; e = x$
- $(x \sqcup y); z = (x; z) \sqcup (y; z)$
- $(x^{-1})^{-1} = x$
- $(x; y)^{-1} = y^{-1}; x^{-1}$
- $x^{-1}; \overline{x; y} \sqcup y = \overline{y}$

All the axioms of boolean algebra can be deduced from this set of formulae. Relation algebras are very expressive; however, they are not representable and the axiomatic system shown above is not complete with respect to the calculus of relations (there do not exist finite axiomatizations of relation algebras); also the system is not decidable. If one intends to add operators such as ; or $^{-1}$, a correct way to start is looking at the theory of relation algebras [26]. It seems interesting to try to capture the meaning of the following predicates using algebraic methods:

$$\mathbf{Perm}(\alpha; \beta)$$

(which means that it is allowed to perform β after performing α), or:

$$\mathbf{Perm}(\alpha^{-1})$$

These kinds of operators have been discussed in the literature [6]; however, no algebraic methods are used by those authors; it seems an interesting trend of future research to investigate the interplay between deontic operators and these relational combinators. Another interesting algebras are the so-called *residuated boolean algebras* [15], there exist residuated algebras that have finite axiomatization and that support the notion of atom, and therefore they provides an expressive framework where it is possible to express action properties.

6 Further Remarks

In this chapter we have reviewed those deontic action logics that are based on boolean algebra; this line of research was initiated by Segerberg, and continued by several authors; the main characteristics of this approach is that deontic notions such as permission, prohibition and obligation can be captured using algebraic notions like ideals, filters, etc. However, one problematic issue of Segerberg' s logic is the lack of expressiveness to capture the closure principle of jurisprudence. We have introduced logics that use boolean atomic algebras to capture deontic operators; the main benefit of doing this is the possibility of using the atoms to state properties of the operators, in particular, this is important when capturing the closure principle. Future lines of research include the investigation of formalisms that allow one to introduce first-order reasoning and the use of boolean algebras with operators. We think that the main contribution of these formalisms is the possibility of studying the properties of deontic operators by means of well-known mathematical concepts like ideal, filters, etc. Furthermore, the use of algebraic tools seems to be a promising way of reasoning about more complicated action operators such as composition and iteration.

References

1. Anglberger, A. J. J. (2008). Dynamic deontic logic and its paradoxes. *Studia Logica*, *89*, 427–435.
2. Aquist, L. (1963). Postulate sets and decision procedures for some systems of deontic logic. *Theoria*, *29*, 154–175.

3. Belnap, N., Perloff, M., & Xu, M. (2001). *Facing the future: Agents and choices in our indeterminist world.* Oxford: Oxford University Press.
4. Blackburn, P., Rijke, M., & Venema, Y. (2001). *Modal logic. Cambridge tracts in, theoretical computer science* (vol. 53). Cambridge: Cambridge University Press.
5. Boole, G. (1854). *An investigation on the laws of though, on which are founded the mathematical theories of logic and probability*. London: Walton & Maberly.
6. Broersen, J. (2003). Modal action logics for reasoning about reactive systems. Ph.D. thesis, Vrije University.
7. Castro, P. F., & Maibaum, T. (2009). Deontic action logic, atomic boolean algebra and fault-tolerance. *Journal of Applied Logic*, *7*(4), 441–466.
8. Castro, P.F., & Maibaum, T. (2010). Towards a first-order deontic action logic. In *20th International Workshop in Recent Trends in Algebraic Development Techniques, Lectures Notes in Computer Science*. Heidelberg: Springer.
9. Fiadeiro, J. L., & Maibaum, T. S. E. (1991). Temporal reasoning over deontic specifications. *Journal of Logic and Computation*, *1*, 357–395.
10. Fisher, M. (1961). A three-valued calculus for deontic logic. *Theoria*, *27*, 107–118.
11. Gargov, G., & Passy, S. (1990). A note on boolean logic. In P. P. Petkov (Ed.) *Proceedings of the Heyting Summerschool*. New York: Plenum Press.
12. Givant, S., & Halmos, P. (2010). *Introduction to Boolean Algebras*. Heidelberg: Springer.
13. Harel, D., Kozen, D., & Tiuryn, J. (2000). *Dynamic logic*. Massachusetts: MIT Press.
14. Hintikka, J. (1957). Quantifiers in deontic logic. In: Societas Scientiarum Fennica, Commentationes Humanarum Litterarum.
15. Jipsen, P. (1992). Computer aided investigations of relational algebras. Ph.D. thesis, Vanderbilt University.
16. Jonsson, B., & Tarski, A. (1951). Boolean algebras with operators i. *American Journal of Mathematics*, *73*, 891–939.
17. Jonsson, B., & Tarski, A. (1952). Boolean algebras with operators ii. *American Journal of Mathematics*, *74*, 127–162.
18. Kalinowski, J. (1953). Theorie des propositions normativess. *Studia Logica*, *1*, 147–182.
19. Kalinowski, J. (1972). La logique des normes. Presses Universitaires de France.
20. Kanger, S. (1957). New foundations for ethical theory. Tech. rep., Stockholm University.
21. Kanger, S. (1971). New foundations for ethical theory. In R. Hilpinen (Ed.) *Deontic logic: Introductory and systematic readings*. Reidel: Dordrecht.
22. Kouznetsov, A. (2004). Quasi-matrix deontic logic. In A. Lomuscio, & D. Nute (Eds.) *Deontic logic in computer science, Lecture Notes in Computer Science* (vol. 3065, pp. 191–208). Berlin: Springer.
23. Kulicki, P., & Trypuz, R. (2012). A deontic action logic with sequential composition of actions. In T. Ågotnes, J. Broersen, & D. Elgesem (Eds.) *Deontic logic in computer science, Lecture Notes in Computer Science* (vol. 7393/2012, pp. 184–198). Berlin: Springer.
24. Kulicki, P., & Trypuz, R. (2012). How to build a deontic action logic. In *The Logica Yearbook 2011* (pp. 107–120). Upper Saddle River: College Publications.
25. Lokhorst, G. J. C. (1996). Reasoning about actions and obligations in first-order logic. *Studia Logica*, *57*, 221–237.
26. Maddux, R. (2006). Relation algebras. North-Holland: Elsevier Science.
27. Meyer, J. (1987). A different approach to deontic logic: Deontic logic viewed as variant of dynamic logic. *Notre Dame Journal of Formal Logic*, *29*(1), 109–136.
28. Prisacariu, C. (2009). Synchronous kleene algebra. *The Journal of Logic and Algebraic Programming*, *78*, 608–635.
29. Prisacariu, C., & Schneider, G. (2012). A dynamic deontic logic for complex contracts. *The Journal of Logic and Algebraic Programming*, *81*, 458–490.
30. Segerberg, K. (1977). A completeness theorem in the modal logic of programs. *Notices of the American Mathematical Society*, *24*(6), A-552.
31. Segerberg, K. (1982). A deontic logic of action. *Studia Logica*, *41*, 269–282.
32. Segerberg, K. (1984). A topological logic of action. *Studia Logica*, *43*(4), 415–419.

33. Segerberg, K. (1992). Getting started: Beginnings in the logic of action. *Studia Logica, 51*, 347–378.
34. Sikorski, R. (1969). *Boolean algebras*. Heidelberg: Springer.
35. Trypuz, R. (2011). Simple theory of norm and action. In A. Brożek, J. Jadacki, & B. Žarnić (Eds.) *Theory of imperatives from different points of view, logic, methodology and philosophy of science at Warsaw University* (vol. 6, pp. 120–136). Wydawnictwo Naukowe Semper.
36. Trypuz, R., & Kulicki, P. (2009). A systematics of deontic action logics based on boolean algebra. *Logic and Logical Philosophy, 18*, 263–279.
37. Trypuz, R., & Kulicki, P. (2010). Towards metalogical systematisation of deontic action logics based on boolean algebra. In *Proceedings of the 10th International Conference Deontic Logic in Computer Science, Lecture Notes in Computer Science* (vol. 6181). Heidelberg: Springer.
38. Trypuz, R., & Kulicki, P. (2011). A norm-giver meets deontic action logic. *Logic and Logical Philosophy, 20*, 59–72.
39. van der Meyden, R. (1996). The dynamic logic of permission. *Journal of Logic and Computation, 6*(3), 465–479.
40. von Wright, G. H. (1951). Deontic logic. *Mind, LX(237)*, 1–15.
41. von Wright, G. H. (1963). *Norm and action: A logical inquiry*. London: Routledge & Kegan Paul.
42. von Wright, G. H. (1980). Problems and prospects of deontie logic: A survey. In *Modern logic—a survey* (pp. 399–423). Dordrecht: Reidel.

Dynamic Deontic Logic, Segerberg-Style

John-Jules Ch. Meyer

Abstract In this chapter we'll review Krister Segerberg's approach to a dynamic deontic logic. In particular we will look at the logic that was the result of Segerberg's attempts to come up with a logic in line with ideas of Von Wright, Alchourrón and Ross. We first treat the basic core, which is a blend of temporal and dynamic logic. Then we add the deontic operators. Finally we briefly discuss an extension discussed by Segerberg, which adds deontic actions to install a new deontic status of actions.

1 Introduction

As is obvious from this very book, Krister Segerberg has a broad interest and expertise as to philosophical logic, and the logic of action, in particular. One of the topics he has occupied himself with is that of deontic logic. Inspired very much by the pioneers such as Von Wright, Alchourrón and Ross, he has made an attempt to come up with a deontic logic in the spirit of particularly Von Wright's work as "an effort to take seriously the existence of actions and the way we think about them" [24]. It appears that this attempt led him via some more preliminary publications [23–27] to a more definitive framework published in [28], which we will follow as a main guide in the present chapter.

His main interest thus is a deontic logic in which one can express the deontic status (prohibition, permission, obligation,...) of *actions*. Traditionally this branch of deontic logic has been dubbed '*Tunsollen*' or '*ought-to-do*'. If one is interested in this it thus makes sense to employ *a logic of action* as a base logic, and so taking *dynamic*

J.-J. Ch. Meyer (✉)
Intelligent Systems Group, Department of Information and Computing Sciences,
Faculty of Science, Utrecht University, P.O.Box 80.089, 3508 TB Utrecht, The Netherlands
e-mail: jj@cs.uu.nl; J.J.C.Meyer@uu.nl

J.-J. Ch. Meyer
Alan Turing Institute Almere, Louis Armstrongweg 78, 1311 RL Almere, The Netherlands

R. Trypuz (ed.), *Krister Segerberg on Logic of Actions*,
Outstanding Contributions to Logic 1, DOI: 10.1007/978-94-007-7046-1_6,

logic is an obvious choice. But Segerberg also mixes in elements of *temporal* logic, which results in a quite idiosyncratic but powerful framework. Moreover, the blend of dynamic and temporal logic is surprisingly smooth, as we will see.

In this chapter we'll briefly review Krister Segerberg's proposal for dynamic deontic logic, which, although Segerberg himself calls it a still rather meagre logic, is yet already quite expressive[1] and able to resolve a number of classical 'paradoxes' in deontic logic in an interesting way, including that of Ross. (It even appears to me that avoiding Ross' paradox was one of the main intentions of pursuing this work.). Furthermore, Segerberg distinguishes two types of actions: 'real' actions and 'deontic' actions. The former are actions that change the world, so to speak, or the 'brute facts' in terms of Anscombe [4] and Searle [22], while the latter modifies the institutional facts in the sense that permissions, obligations and prohibitions come into existence. This is a very interesting aspect of Segerberg's work. In some sense it gives another meaning to the term 'dynamic': not only can the logic be used to describe deontic aspects with respect to actions, it can also state properties about the change of deontic status of actions over time in the sense that it can express that deontic properties such as the obligation to do an action may commence to hold. This is not only interesting from a philosophical/analytical point of view but also very much so from the standpoint of the design of so-called normative systems in computer science, as I will explain!

2 The Basic Framework in a Nutshell

In this section I will sketch the basic framework that Segerberg sets up in order to add deontic notions. The latter we will see in the next sections.

2.1 Syntax

As mentioned in the introduction the basic logic used by Segerberg is a kind of blend of dynamic logic and temporal logic.

Let $PROP$ be a set of propositional letters with typical element P and E be a set of event letters with typical element e. The core language $\mathscr{L}$ (with typical elements φ and ψ) and the set $\mathscr{A}$ of actions terms (or actions for short, with typical elements α and β) are defined by the following simultaneously induced definition:

- for any propositional letter $P \in PROP$ we have that $P \in \mathscr{L}$
- for $\varphi, \psi \in \mathscr{L}$ we have that $\neg\varphi, \varphi \wedge \psi, \varphi \vee \psi \in \mathscr{L}$
- for $\varphi, \psi \in \mathscr{L}$ we have that $[F]\varphi, [P]\varphi, [H]\varphi, [UNTIL\psi]\varphi \in \mathscr{L}$

[1] As well as impressive for a computer scientist like myself. My own proposal for a dynamic deontic logic [18] was even more 'meagre'. But I appreciate Segerberg's view: in philosophy there is a lot of interesting related things that are not covered here such as agency, causality and intentionality.

- for any event letter $e \in E$ we have that $e \in \mathscr{A}$
- for $\varphi \in \mathscr{L}$ we have that $\partial\varphi \in \mathscr{A}$
- for $\alpha, \beta \in \mathscr{A}$ we have that $\alpha + \beta, \alpha; \beta, \alpha; ; \beta \in \mathscr{A}$
- for $\alpha \in \mathscr{A}$ we have that $occurs\alpha, occurring\alpha, occurred\alpha \in \mathscr{L}$
- for $\alpha \in \mathscr{A}$ and $\varphi \in \mathscr{L}$ we have that

$[after\alpha]\varphi, [after^*\alpha]\varphi, [during\alpha]\varphi, [before\alpha]\varphi, [before^*\alpha]\varphi \in \mathscr{L}$

The readings (intended meanings) of the operators in this language (apart form the usual logical ones) are as follows: $[F]$, $[P]$, $[H]$, $[UNTIL\psi]$ are temporal operators with readings "in the future", "in the past", "historically necessarily"/"unavoidably"/ "settled true", and "until", respectively; ∂ is the *result* operator, which might be read as "seeing to it that".[2] The action operators $+$, ; and ; ; are 'choice', 'immediately followed by', and '(loosely) followed by', respectively (we'll see the difference between ; and ; ; shortly below.) $occurs\alpha, occurring\alpha, occurred\alpha$ express that an action occurs (next), is occurring right now, and has (just) occurred, respectively. And finally we have $[after\alpha]\varphi$, $[after^*\alpha]\varphi$, $[during\alpha]\varphi$, $[before\,\alpha]\varphi$, and $[before^*\alpha]\varphi$, meaning that, respectively, 'after' (two versions), 'during' and 'before' (two versions) the performance of an action the property φ holds (we'll explain the differences between the two versions of 'after' and 'before' presently). Furthermore the abbreviation $\langle\ldots\rangle\varphi = \neg[\ldots]\neg\varphi$ is used.

2.2 Semantics

The semantics provided by Segerberg [28] is a bit non-standard, probably due to the mixture of temporal and dynamic logic elements. It is not a traditional modal Kripke semantics with accessibility relations for all the modal notions involved. Instead, it employs as semantical basis pairs (h, g) of paths, which are basically (finite or one-way or two-way infinite) sequences of states. In such a pair h denotes the past, while g denotes the future. As a convenient notation we use the following: $p(*)$ denotes the first element of the path p (if this exists) and $p(\#)$ denotes the last element of the path p (if this exists). We require of pairs (h, g) used in the semantics that it holds that $h(\#) = g(*)$, i.e., that the past and the future are connected via the 'now' represented by the last element of the past and the first element of the future. We furthermore employ the usual notions of subpath and (proper) initial subpath. (For the formal definitions the reader is referred to [28].)

We assume a given universe of states (possible worlds) $\mathscr{U}$ and set of events $\mathscr{E}$. $\mathscr{H}$ is the set of complete histories in $\mathscr{U}$, i.e., paths in $\mathscr{U}$ that are complete in the sense that proper subpaths of histories are not histories themselves. A valuation V is a function with domain $PROP \cup E$ such that elements of $PROP$ are mapped into $2^{\mathscr{U}}$, and elements of E are mapped into $\mathscr{E}$. We write $[\ldots]$ for the interpretation of formulas and action terms, and define $[P] = V(P)$ for $P \in PROP$, $[e] = V(e)$ for

[2] Seeing to it that or stit is in itself a very well-studied subject within philosophical logic, see e.g., [16].

$e \in E, [\neg\varphi] = \mathcal{U}\backslash[\varphi], [\varphi\wedge\psi] = [\varphi]\cap[\psi], [\varphi\vee\psi] = [\varphi]\cup[\psi], [\alpha+\beta] = [\alpha]\cup[\beta]$, $[\alpha; \beta] = \alpha \cdot \beta$ and $[\alpha; ; \beta] = \alpha \circ \beta$, where the functions $\cdot$, $\circ$ are defined as follows: if A and B are sets of path, then $A \cdot B = \{pq : p \in A, q \in B, p(\#) = q(*)\}$ and $A \circ B = \{prq : p \in A, q \in B, r$ paths with $p(\#) = r(*), r(\#) = q(*)\}$ (So $\cdot$ is path concatenation and $\circ$ is a diluted version of concatenation, where also things may be added in between the operands.) Finally, we need to define the meaning of the ∂ operator: $[\partial\varphi] = \{(u, v) : v \in Sel_u([\varphi])\}$, where $Sel_u(X)$ is a selection function dependent on the state u, picking out a subset of X. (So this definition essentially states that the action $\partial\varphi$ ends up in some state where φ holds; in general it is nondeterministic: there might be multiple states, all satisfying φ, where the action may end up, determined by the selection function. See [28] for more details on constraints that are reasonably imposed on Sel_u.)

Now we define the truth of a formula φ w.r.t. an articulated history, which is a pair (h, g) with $h(\#) = g(*)$, denoted $(h, g) \models \varphi$, as follows:

- for pure boolean formulas, $(h, g) \models \varphi$ iff $u \in [\varphi]$, where $u = h(\#) = g(*)$
- $(h, g) \models [F]\varphi$ iff, for all p, h', g' such that $hp = h'$ and $pg' = g$ it holds that $(h', g') \models \varphi$
- $(h, g) \models [P]\varphi$ iff, for all p, h', g' such that $h'p = h$ and $g' = pg$ it holds that $(h', g') \models \varphi$
- $(h, g) \models [H]\varphi$ iff, for all $g' \in \{g'' : hg'' \in \mathcal{H}\}$ it holds that $(h, g') \models \varphi$
- $(h, g) \models [UNTIL\psi]\varphi$ iff
  either for all h', g' such that $h'g' = hg$ and h is an initial subpath of h'[3] it holds that $(h', g') \not\models \psi$, or else there is a shortest path p such that $(h', g') \models \psi$ where $h' = hp$ and $pg' = g$, and, for all proper initial subpaths q of p, it holds that $(h'', g'') \models \varphi$, where $h'' = hq$ and $qg'' = g$.
- $(h, g) \models occurs\alpha$ iff for some finite path $p \in [\alpha]$ and future g' it holds that $g = pg'$
- $(h, g) \models occurring\alpha$ iff for some finite nonempty paths p, q with $pq \in [\alpha]$, past h' and future g' it holds that $h = h'p$ and $g = qg'$
- $(h, g) \models occurred\alpha$ iff for some finite path $p \in [\alpha]$ and past h' it holds that $h = h'p$
- $(h, g) \models [after\alpha]\varphi$ iff for all $p \in [\alpha], h', g'$ with $h' = hp$ and $pg' = g$ it holds that $(h', g') \models \varphi$
- $(h, g) \models [after^*\alpha]\varphi$ iff for all $p \in [\alpha], q, r$ (where q may be the null path) with $p = qr, hr = h', g = rg'$ it holds that $(h', g') \models \varphi$
- $(h, g) \models [during\alpha]\varphi$ iff for all h', g' such that for some paths $p \in [\alpha], q, r, x, y$ (where either q or r may be null) with $h = xq, h' = xq', g = ry, g' = r'y, p = qr = q'r'$ it holds that $(h', g') \models \varphi$
- $(h, g) \models [before\alpha]\varphi$ iff for all $p \in [\alpha], h', g'$ with $h'p = h, g' = pg$ it holds that $(h', g') \models \varphi$
- $(h, g) \models [before^*\alpha]\varphi$ iff for all $p \in [\alpha], q, r$ (where r may be null) with $p = qr, h = h'q, qg = g'$ it holds that $(h', g') \models \varphi$

---

[3] I've added the latter condition, since I believe it was accidentally omitted in [28]: surely for an until to hold we should look at the future and not at the past.

2.2.1 Comments

In the above semantics using pairs (h, g) where h refers to the past and g to the future, the current moment ('now') is represented by the element $h(\#)$ (the last element of the past sofar, which must be equal to $g(*)$, the first element of the future. This is used in the evaluation of pure boolean formulas, as can be seen from the first clause. The second and third clause say that a formula is true in the future (past) at (h, g) if it is true in all the pairs (h', g') representing the future (past). A formula is historically necessary/unavoidable/settled true, if the formula is true with respect to all possible futures. The $[H]$ operator thus very much resembles the universal path quantifier in branching-time temporal logics such as CTL and CTL* [12]. The $[UNTIL\psi]\varphi$ operator is a 'weak' until operator from (linear) temporal logic: either ψ never becomes true or ψ becomes true for the first time along a path, and then the operand φ should hold till then. The operator $occurs$ expresses that the action is about to occur/happen next. (It is similar to the operator HAPPENS in the work of Cohen and Levesque [8].) Similarly, the operator $occurred$ expresses that the action has just happened. It is similar to the DONE actions in the work of Cohen and Levesque [8] and Meyer et al. [20]. The operator $occurring$ means that the action is still in the process of being performed. The $[after\alpha]$ operator is a kind of 'local' version of the dynamic logic operator $[\alpha]$, stating that its operand φ holds (immediately) after the (direct) performance of the action α. With local I mean here that this formula is evaluated given a certain (history and) a future. The normal version of the dynamic logic formula $[\alpha]\varphi$ corresponds to the more global formula $[H](occurs\alpha \to [after\alpha]\varphi)$, where there is a quantification involved over all possible futures and not just the one is used for evaluation that is given. (This does justice to the kind of hypothetical reasoning aspect of traditional dynamic logic: "if I were to perform an action it would result in a state with the following property".) The starred version of this operator allows one to express that a formula holds after the performance of an action that has possible started already (as seen from the point of evaluation). Likewise, the before operator expresses that something holds (immediately) before the performance of an action that just has been done, while the starred version pertains to the situation in which possibly the action is still going on (at the moment of evaluation). Finally the during operator states that the operand holds while the action is being performed.

2.3 Properties

A few propertes listed in [28] are:

- $occurs\alpha \leftrightarrow \langle after\alpha\rangle\top$
- $occurring\alpha \leftrightarrow \langle during\alpha\rangle\top$
- $occurred\alpha \leftrightarrow \langle before\alpha\rangle\top$
- $occurs\alpha \to ([after^*\alpha]\varphi \leftrightarrow [after\alpha]\varphi)$
- $occurred\alpha \to ([before^*\alpha]\varphi \leftrightarrow [before\alpha]\varphi)$

2.4 Comments

The basic logic on which Segerberg bases his dynamic deontic logic is thus an interesting mix of temporal [13] and dynamic logic [15]. It combines the best of both worlds: it enables one to express temporal properties but also interesting properties of actions such as the distinction between an action occurring and having occurred. Naturally, also the semantics is a mix of that of temporal logic and dynamic logic. As to the temporal aspect it is a kind of branching-time temporal logic [12], which is in itself consists of elements of linear-time temporal logic [21] with operators such as 'in the future', 'in the past' and 'until', augmented by explicit branching (path) quantifiers such as the 'unavoidably' operator, so that it is possible to speak about truth across possible futures at a certain moment in time,

3 Adding Deontic Operators

In this section deontic operators will be added to the basic language. As mentioned before these operators are of the ought-to-do (*Tunsollen*) kind.

3.1 Syntax

The core language(s) $\mathscr{L}$ and $\mathscr{A}$ is (are) extended to $\mathscr{L}_\Delta$ (again with typical elements φ and ψ) and $\mathscr{A}_\Delta$ (with typical elements $\alpha.\beta$) by augmenting the clauses of $\mathscr{L}$ with the following:

- for $\alpha \in \mathscr{A}_\Delta$ we have that $Ob\alpha, Pm\alpha, Fb\alpha, Om\alpha \in \mathscr{L}_\Delta$
- for $\alpha \in \mathscr{A}_\Delta$ we have that $Ob^*\alpha, Pm^*\alpha, Fb^*\alpha, Om^*\alpha \in \mathscr{L}_\Delta$

The readings of these operators are obligatory, permissible, forbidden and omissible, respectively. The last operator is perhaps not very well-known in deontic logic. Omissible means that it can be omitted or waived. The starred versus non-starred versions of these operators refer to the issue whether they are 'local' (non-starred) or 'normal' (starred). As we will see in the semantics of these operators local operators only pertain to what is normative regarding the future seen from the perspective of the moment at hand, while the normal operators regard also what is normative in the future, and in fact in all possible futures. (I agree this may be a little hard to understand; it will become clear in the formal definition below.)

3.2 Semantics

The deontic operators get their meaning given a norm. In [28] a (simple) norm[4] is defined as follows. A norm N is a function such that $N(h)$ selects a set of futures

[4] Segerberg also gives a more refined notion. We leave this out here.

after h that are considered normal (legal) according to the norm. Segerberg imposes two conditions on the function N:

1. If $g = pg'$, for any finite path p, then $g \in N(h)$ implies $g' \in N(hp)$
2. for all h, $N(h) \neq \emptyset$

The semantics of the added operators are given as follows:

- $(h, g) \models Ob\alpha$ iff $\forall g' \in N(h) \exists q \in [\alpha] : q$ is a subpath of g', and $\forall q \in [\alpha] \exists g' \in N(h) : q$ is a subpath of g'
- $(h, g) \models Pm\alpha$ iff $\exists g' \in N(h) \exists q \in [\alpha] : q$ is a subpath of g', and $\forall q \in [\alpha] \exists g' \in N(h) : q$ is a subpath of g'
- $(h, g) \models Fb\alpha$ iff $\forall g' \in N(h) \forall q \in [\alpha] : q$ is not a subpath of g', and $\forall q \in [\alpha] \exists g' \in N(h) : q$ is not a subpath of g'
- $(h, g) \models Om\alpha$ iff $\exists g' \in N(h) \forall q \in [\alpha] : q$ is not a subpath of g', and $\forall q \in [\alpha] \exists g' \in N(h) : q$ is not a subpath of g'
- $(h, g) \models Ob^*\alpha$ iff, for all finite paths p with $h(\#) = p(*)$, either $\exists q \in [\alpha] : q$ is a subpath of p or $[\forall g' \in N(hp) \exists q \in [\alpha] : q$ is a subpath of g', and $\forall q \in [\alpha] \exists g' \in N(hp) : q$ is a subpath of $g']$
- $(h, g) \models Pm^*\alpha$ iff, for all finite paths p with $h(\#) = p(*)$, either $\exists q \in [\alpha] : q$ is a subpath of p or $[\exists g' \in N(hp) \exists q \in [\alpha] : q$ is a subpath of g', and $\forall q \in [\alpha] \exists g' \in N(hp) : q$ is a subpath of $g']$
- $(h, g) \models Fb^*\alpha$ iff, for all finite paths p with $h(\#) = p(*)$, either $\exists q \in [\alpha] : q$ is a subpath of p or $[\forall g' \in N(hp) \forall q \in [\alpha] : q$ is not a subpath of g', and $\forall q \in [\alpha] \exists g' \in N(hp) : q$ is not a subpath of $g']$
- $(h, g) \models Om^*\alpha$ iff, for all finite paths p with $h(\#) = p(*)$, either $\exists q \in [\alpha] : q$ is a subpath of p or $[\exists g' \in N(hp) \forall q \in [\alpha] : q$ is not a subpath of g', and $\forall q \in [\alpha] \exists g' \in N(hp) : q$ is not a subpath of $g']$

3.3 Comments

First we observe that these operators are defined by relating behaviour associated with the operand (the action at hand) to normative behaviour as represented by the norm N, and particularly the set $N(h)$ of normative/legal future paths given history h. In fact, we observe a relation in two directions: in all legal futures the behaviour as expressed by the operators is adhered to: obligatory actions will be performed in every legal future, permitted actions in at least one legal future, forbidden actions will not be performed in any legal future and omissible actions will not be performed in at least one legal future. But also a relation in the other direction is stipulated: for an obligatory or permissible action, any way of performing the action has to occur in at least one legal future, and for a forbidden or omissible action, any way of performing the action is excluded in at least one legal future. As Segerberg explains in [28], the requirement regarding this latter direction is more technical, and motivated by the desire to solve the Ross and free choice permission paradox. Finally note the difference in the semantics between the starred and the non-starred operators. The non-starred ones pertain to the "normative futures" in the set $N(h)$, so regarding the history (and moment) at hand, while the starred operators pertain to sets $N(hp)$ for any future path p, thus regarding sets of normative futures at any point in the future.

This is perhaps a good point to look at related work. Segerberg's semantics of deontic operators comes down to specifying what is normative or *good* behaviour (by means of the set $N(h)$ of normative/legal future path given history h). In the literature there have been proposed alternatives (and generalizations) of this approach. For example, my own approach [18], inspired by Anderson's work [3], uses a violation atom and primarily specifies *bad* behaviour: an action is forbidden if performing it leads to a bad (violation) state. Of course, by considering the negation of the violation atom, one is also able to express good states, but in a more indirect way than in Segerberg's approach. Note that Meyer's approach is based on good and bad *states*. Moreover, in this simple approach it is the end state after performing an action (assuming a deterministic settting here for convenience) that determines whether the action is permitted or not: if it is a violation state the action is forbidden, otherwise it is permitted. Dignum et al. [11] refine this by defining deontic operators that express whether an action leads from a non-violation state to a violation state, from a violation state to a non-violation state, remains in a violation state or remains in a non-violation state, respectively. On the other hand, Van der Meyden [30] proposes an approach in which directly *transitions* instead of states are classified as permitted (good)/non-permitted (bad). Recently Craven and Sergot [9] have generalized this idea, combining Meyer's approach with that of Van der Meyden. In Craven and Sergot's models one can specify so-called *red* and *green states* as well as *red* and *green (state) transitions* to express bad and good states and transitions, respectively. In this way one obtains refined notions of permission and prohibition for system specification. Furthermore, there is an intuitive relation postulated between green transitions and green states, viz. the so-called green-green-green (ggg) constraint, which expresses that a green transition in a green state always leads to a green state again. Finally, even more generally, in deontic logic there is also other work where there are multiple categories of states, such as ideal//sub-ideal states and transitions, of which we mention here Carmo and Jones [7].

3.4 Properties

Segerberg [28] gives a list of the following validities:

- $Ob\alpha \rightarrow Pm\alpha$
- $Fb\alpha \rightarrow Om\alpha$
- $\neg(Ob\alpha \wedge Fb\alpha)$
- $Ob(\alpha + \beta) \leftarrow (Ob\alpha \wedge Ob\beta)$
- $Pm(\alpha + \beta) \leftrightarrow (Pm\alpha \wedge Pm\beta)$
- $Fb(\alpha + \beta) \leftrightarrow (Fb\alpha \wedge Fb\beta)$
- $Om(\alpha + \beta) \rightarrow (Om\alpha \wedge Om\beta)$

Here $\leftarrow$ stands for the converse of material implication. It should be noted that the following are *non*-validities:

- $\neg(Pm\alpha \wedge Om\alpha)$
- $Ob\alpha \vee Fb\alpha$
- $Pm\alpha \vee Om\alpha$

As to the starred operators versus the non-starred ones: this difference is most easily seen by the observation that it holds that:

- $X^*\alpha \leftrightarrow [H][UNTIL\ occurs\alpha]X\alpha$

for $X \in \{Ob, Pm, Fb, Om\}$ and X^* the associated starred version. So for $X = Ob$ this means that no matter what happens (unavoidably) the action α is obligated until it occurs (happens). Similarly for the other operators.[5] This property is very helpful in understanding the difference between the difference between the local (non-starred) and normal (starred) operators: the local ones ($X\alpha$) are evaluated with respect to just one given past/history pair, while the normal ones ($X^*\alpha$) involve a historical necessity (which is a path quantifier!) aspect: along *every possible future path*, until α actually occurs, it holds that the local operator $X\alpha$ holds.

3.5 Comments

So an important thing to observe is that the resulting deontic logic is quite different from SDL (standard deontic logic, cf. e.g., [19], which is a normal modal logic inspired by Von Wright. In this logic, generally obligation is taken to be the primary modal operator of a 'necessity kind' ('box-like' for those who know modal logic), and the other operators (viz. prohibition and permission) are taken as abbreviations: $F\phi = O\neg\phi$ and $P\phi = \neg F\phi$. (Mind you, this is actually about ought-to-be, although there has been some confusion about this in the early history of deontic logic.) A consequence of this set-up is that it holds that

$$O(\phi \wedge \psi) \leftrightarrow (O\phi \wedge P\psi)$$
$$P(\phi \vee \psi) \leftrightarrow (P\phi \vee P\psi)$$
$$O(\phi \vee \psi) \leftarrow (O\phi \vee O\psi)$$
$$P(\phi \wedge \psi) \rightarrow (P\phi \wedge P\psi)$$

giving rise to problems like the Ross paradox

$$O(mail\_the\_letter) \rightarrow O(mail\_the\_letter \vee burn\_the\_letter)$$

and the paradox of free choice permission:

[5] Perhaps for e.g., Fb (forbidden) the starred version is a bit strange: the prohibition holds until the prohibition has been violated.

$$P(mail\_the\_letter) \rightarrow P(mail\_the\_letter \vee burn\_the\_letter)$$

(see, e.g., [17]).[6] (Here you see the abuse of ought-to-be as a kind of ought-to-do, although one can also just say $O(mailed\_the\_letter) \rightarrow O(mailed\_the\_letter) \vee O(burnt\_the\_letter)$, which is equally paradoxical. Now observe that in Segerberg's logic the analogues of the formulas pertaining to choice are quite different from the formulas above. In particular one has $Ob(\alpha + \beta) \leftarrow (Ob\alpha \wedge Ob\beta)$ and *not* $Ob(\alpha + \beta) \leftarrow (Ob\alpha \vee Ob\beta)$, so Ross' paradox is avoided. Likewise, the free choice permission paradox is avoided. So this is rather different from standard deontic logic. Furthermore, there is the temporal dimension, which enables one to express quite complicated norms.

For instance, we can now try to tackle the problem of expressing norms involving deadlines. In my own experience [5, 10] this has turned out to be a surprisingly tough and difficult topic. It seems that in Segerberg's logic one can conveniently express deadlines. For example, the obligation of doing an action α before a deadline denoted by a formula d, notated as $Ob(\alpha \leq d)$, can be expressed as

$$Ob(\alpha \leq d) = [H][until\ occurs\partial d]Ob\alpha$$

which states that the obligation to do α before d amounts to the assertion that unavoidably (along every possible future) the (local) obligation to do α persists until the action δd happens, i.e., d becomes true. Of course, although this seems to be a reasonable definition, this raises all kinds of questions such as: should the obligation persist when the action has already been done? Can similar definitions be given for the other deontic operators? For instance, the previous question seems to be even more important for prohibition: if you are forbidden to perform an action before a deadline, it appears reasonable that you are still forbidden to do the action (until the deadline occurs) after having violated this norm once by performing the action. Are there ramifications (sanctions, repairs) of not complying to the norm, that persist even beyond the deadline? And there are several more concerns as can be seen in the papers mentioned above.

4 Adding Deontic Actions

Finally Segerberg adds also deontic (or institutional) actions to the repertoire of actions.

---

[6] Interestingly, Segerberg's framework also seems to be able to cope with the infamous Chisholm paradox (again see for example [17]), the solutions of which are generally held to need nonmonotonic or defeasible logic. Treatment of this issue is beyond the scope of the present chapter.

4.1 Syntax

The action language $\mathscr{A}_\Delta$ (keeping the same name of the language) is extended with the clause:

- for $\alpha \in \mathscr{A}_\Delta$ we have that also $!\alpha$, $!!\alpha$, $\S\alpha$, $\S\S\alpha \in \mathscr{A}_\Delta$

Here !!, !, §§, and §are read as "ordering", "permitting", "forbidding" and "making omissible", respectively. So these are truly dynamic deontic actions: they create obligations, permissions, prohibitions and 'omissions' (waivers).

4.2 Semantics

For reasons of conciseness we omit the semantics of these operators here. The interested reader is referred to [28].

4.3 Properties

Segerberg [28] lists the following (intuitive) validities:

- $[after!!\alpha]Ob\alpha$
- $[after!\alpha]Pb\alpha$
- $[after\S\alpha]Fb\alpha$
- $[after\S\S\alpha]Om\alpha$
- $[after!!(\alpha+\beta)]\varphi \leftarrow ([after!!\alpha]\varphi \wedge [after!!\beta]\varphi)$
- $[after!(\alpha+\beta)]\varphi \leftrightarrow ([after!\alpha]\varphi \wedge [after!\beta]\varphi)$
- $[after\S\S(\alpha+\beta)]\varphi \leftrightarrow ([after!\S\S\alpha]\varphi \wedge [after\S\S\beta]\varphi)$
- $[after\S(\alpha+\beta)]\varphi \rightarrow ([after\S\alpha]\varphi \wedge [after\S\beta]\varphi)$

4.4 Comments

We thus have seen that in this logic there is a way of representing the installment of some deontic notions, viz. obligations, permission, prohibitions and omissions of *actions*. So this pertains again to ought-to-do norms. This is a good start. But besides addition of norms, we need also contraction and revision of norms, more in general. Furthermore, as I deem ought-to-be norms equally important to ought-to-do ones, we should also consider the dynamics of these. So then we should make situations described by formulas ϕ obligatory, permitted, forbidden and omissible. This seems completely different and also harder to accomplish. In fact, in my view this brings back Alchourrón's original motivation for the well-known AGM work [2]: changing (ought-to-be) norms is similar to belief revision. As far as I know there is still no consensus among researchers to what extent belief revision and (ought-to-be-type) norm revision are similar or distinct.

4.5 Norm Change in Multi Agent Systems

As mentioned earlier, I deem change of deontic aspect very important also for applications in computer science [31]. In particular in that subarea dealing with so-called multi-agent systems (or MAS). These are systems consisting of multiple intelligent (software) agents devised to perform certain ('intelligent') tasks. The agents in MAS are designed to act autonomously, i.e., without human intervention, as much as possible. However, of course, these autonomous agents should be restrained/constrained in order for the MAS as a whole to be able to function and perform its task appropriately. To this end norms may be used. (These systems are therefore called normative (multi-agent) systems.) There is currently a lot of research going on on the topic of normative systems [6, 14, 19], inspired by philosophical work by Alchourrón and Bulygin[1], who argue that a normative system should not be defined as a set of norms, as was commonly done, but in terms of consequences. A proper treatment of the topic of normative systems is beyond the scope of our present paper. But for our purposes it is interesting to note that one has realized that as things are constantly changing, also these norms should be able to change in such systems. In [29] we have made a first attempt of programming normative MAS in which norms may be changed. In that paper we offer a first, very simple language for changing norms. But this is only a start. I foresee that this issue will get more and more important in the near future, as normative systems will get used increasingly. And, since these systems may operate in critical applications involving a lot of money (such as space exploration) or even human lives (as in medical applications) there will also be a strong need to validate and verify such systems. Here logic comes in again, and a dynamic deontic logic à la Krister Segerberg could be a good start for devising logics for this societally important enterprise!

References

1. Alchourrón, C., & Bulygin, E. (1971). *Normative systems*. Vienna: Springer.
2. Alchourrón, C., Gärdenfors, P., & Makinson, D. (1985). On the logic of theory change. *Journal of Symbolic Logic*, *50*, 510–530.
3. Anderson, A. R. (1967). Some nasty problems in the formalization of ethics. *Noûs*, *1*, 345–360.
4. Anscombe, G. E. M. (1958). On Brute facts. *Analysis*, *18*, 69–72.
5. Broersen, J., Dignum, F., Dignum, V., & Meyer, J-J Ch. (2004). Designing a deontic logic of deadlines. In A. Lomuscio & D. Nute (Eds.). *Proceedings of the Deontic Logic in Computer Science (DEON 2004), LNAI*(vol. 3065 pp. 43–56). Berlin: Springer.
6. Brown, M. A., & Carmo, J. (Eds.). (1996). *Deontic Logic, Agency and Normative Systems: Proceedings of DEON'96. Workshops in Computing*(80–97). Berlin: Springer.
7. Carmo, J., & Jones, A. J. I. (1996). Deontic database constraints, violations and recovery. *Studia Logica*, *57*(1), 139–165.

8. Cohen, P. R., & Levesque, H. J. (1990). Intention is choice with commitment. *Artificial Intelligence, 42*, 213–261.
9. Craven, R., & Sergot, M. (2008). Agent strands in the action languages nC+. *Journal of Applied Logic, 6*, 172–191.
10. Dignum, F., Broersen, J., Dignum, V., & Meyer, J-J Ch. (2005). Meeting the deadline: Why, when and how. In M.G. Hinchey, J.L. Rash Formal, & W.F. Truszkowski (Eds.), *Approaches to Agent-Based Systems (FAABS 2004), Revised Selected Papers, Greenbelt, April 26–27, (2004), LNAI.* (Vol. 3228, pp. 30–40). Berlin: Springer.
11. Dignum, F., Meyer, J.-J. Ch., & R.J. Wieringa, R.J. (1994). A dynamic logic for reasoning about sub-ideal states. In J. Breuker (Ed.), *Proceeing of the ECAI'94 Workshop "Artificial Normative Reasoning"* (pp. 79–92), Amsterdam.
12. Emerson, E.A., (1990). Temporal and modal logic. In J. van Leeuwen (Ed.), *Handbook of Theoretical Computer Science. Vol. B. Chapter 16.* Cambridge: The MIT Press.
13. Galton, A. (2008). Temporal Logic. In E.N. Zalta (Ed.), *The Stanford Encyclopedia of Philosophy (Fall 2008 Edition).* Retrived Sep 9, 2008 from http://plato.stanford.edu/archives/fall2008/entries/logic-temporal/
14. Goble, L., & Meyer, J-J Ch., (Eds.). (2006). *Deontic Logic and Artificial Normative Systems: Proceedings of DEON,. (2006). LNAI* Vol. 4048. Berlin: Springer.
15. Harel, D. (1984). Dynamic logic. In D. Gabbay & F. Guenthner (Eds.). *Handbook of philosophical logic* (Vol. 2, pp. 497–604), Dordrecht and Boston: Reidel.
16. Kracht, M., Meyer, J.-J. Ch., & Segerberg, K. (2009). The logic of action. In E.N. Zalta (Ed.). *The stanford encyclopedia of philosophy (2009 Edition)*,p. 29. Retrived March 31 from http://plato.stanford.edu/entries/logic-action
17. McNamara, P. (2010). Deontic logic. In E. N. Zalta (Ed.). *The stanford encyclopedia of philosophy (Fall 2010 Edition)* Retrived July 7–9 from http://plato.stanford.edu/archives/fall2010/entries/logic-deontic
18. Meyer, J-J Ch. (1988). A different approach to deontic logic: Deontic logic viewed as a variant of dynamic logic. *Notre Dame Journal of Formal Logic, 29*(1), 109–136.
19. Meyer, J-J Ch., & Wieringa, R. J. (Eds.). (1993). *Deontic logic in computer science: Normative system specification.* Chichester: Wiley.
20. Meyer, J-J Ch., Weigand, H., & H. and Wieringa, R.J., (1989). A specification language for static, dynamic and deontic integrity constraints. In J. Demetrovics & B. Thalheim (Eds.). *Proceedings of the MFDBS 89*, Visegrad, Hungary, LNCS (pp. 347–366). Berlin: Springer.
21. Pnueli, A. (1977). The temporal logic of programs. In *Proceedings of 18th Annual Symposium on Foundations of Computer Science (FOCS).* pp. 46–57.
22. Searle, J. (1995). The Construction of Social Reality. Free Press: NewYork.
23. Segerberg, K. (1990). Validity and satisfaction in imperative logic. *Notre Dame Journal of Formal Logic, 31*(2), 203–221.
24. Segerberg, K. (2003). DΔL: a dynamic deontic logic, unpublished.
25. Segerberg, K. (2006). Trying to meet Rosss challenge. In E. Ballo & M. Franchella (Eds.) *Logic and philosophy in Italy: Some trends and perspectives. Essays in honor of corrado mangione on his 75th Birthday* (pp. 155–166) Monza, Italy: Polimetrica International Scientific Publisher.
26. Segerberg, K. Comments on "Trying to meet Rosss challenge", unpublished.
27. Segerberg, K. (2007). A blueprint for deontic logic in three (not necessarily easy) steps. In G. Bonanno, J. P. Delgrande, J. Lang, & H. Rott (Eds.), *Formal Models of Belief Change in Rational Agents, volume 07351 of Dagstuhl Seminar Proceedings. Internationales Begegnungs- und Forschungszentrum fuer Informatik (IBFI)*, Schloss Dagstuhl, Germany.
28. Segerberg, K. (2009). Blueprint for a dynamic deontic logic. *Journal of Applied Logic, 7*(4), 388–402.
29. Tinnemeier, N. A. M., Dastani, M., & Meyer, J.-J. Ch. (2010). Programming Norm Change. In W. van der Hoek, G. Kaminka, Y. Lesprance, M. Luck & S. Sen (Eds.). *Proceedings of 9th International Conference on Autonomous Agents and Multiagent Systems (AAMAS 2010).* (pp. 957–964) Toronto, Canada: IFAAMAS.

30. van der Meyden, R. (1996). The dynamic logic of permission. *Journal of Logic and Computation*, *6*(3), 465–479.
31. Wooldridge, M. (2009). *An Introduction to MultiAgent Systems* (2nd ed.,). John Wiley Sons, Chichester, UK.

Part II

Contraction, Revision, Expansion: Representing Belief Change Operations

Sven Ove Hansson

Abstract The underlying idealizations in Krister Segerberg's Dynamic Doxastic Logic (DDL) are investigated in comparison with other belief revision models. It is argued that the doxastic voluntarism of the proposed interpretation is problematic but can be discarded. The treatment of conditional operators in DDL is discussed, and it is proposed that the use of conditional operators not satisfying the Ramsey test should be further investigated.

1 Introduction

Krister Segerberg's Dynamic Doxastic Logic (DDL) is a major alternative to the AGM model that is the current standard in studies of belief change. In order to investigate its properties we need to have a clear view of the basic idealizations that are common to belief revision theories. That is the subject of Sects. 2 and 3. In Sect. 4, DDL is introduced. After that two of its major features are scrutinized, namely its doxastic voluntarism (Sect. 5) and its treatment of non-truthfunctional connectives such as conditionals (Sect. 6). Finally, some general conclusions are drawn (Sect. 7).

2 Sentences and Epistemic Priorities

Logic is an astoundingly efficient and versatile tool for modelling a wide array of phenomena. However, like any modelling tool it puts emphasis on some aspects of the object of modelling at the expense of others. One of the major characteristics of logical models is that they impose linguistic structure on their subject-matter. This is particularly prominent in logical modelling of belief and knowledge.

S. O. Hansson(✉)
Royal Institute of Technology (KTH), Stockholm, Sweden
e-mail: soh@kth.se

R. Trypuz (ed.), *Krister Segerberg on Logic of Actions*,
Outstanding Contributions to Logic 1, DOI: 10.1007/978-94-007-7046-1_7,

Just a few minutes ago I looked out of the window, saw two roe deer in the garden and believed what I saw. In standard models of belief change, this event is represented by the addition of some sentence p ("There are two roe deer in the garden") to my set of beliefs. My previous belief state is represented by a set K containing the sentences I believed to be true.[1] When I see the two deer, p is added to K. More precisely, assuming that the resulting set of beliefs is closed under logical consequence, K is exposed to the *input* p and is then replaced by $\mathrm{Cn}(K \cup p)$. This is the simplest form of belief change (expansion), but it involves massive idealizations. Most importantly, if by the input we mean that which makes me believe that there are two deer in the garden, then the input is neither p nor any other sentence or set of sentences; what affected me was a visual impression with no linguistic encoding whatsoever. Furthermore, the resulting belief change may not be perfectly representable by a sentence (or set of sentences). I may have a "mental picture" of how the deer moved around that is not primarily linguistic and may be difficult to translate into words.[2] This, by the way, is why the police use identity parades, photo-lineups and similar methods in addition to asking witnesses to verbally describe a suspect. A witness may know what the culprit looks like without being able to express this knowledge in words.

But in the belief change literature, both belief states and inputs are taken to be sentential. The totality of the beliefs held by an agent is taken to be represented by a belief set that is a logically closed set of sentences, mostly assumed to be consistent. The inputs refer to a sentence[3] that either has to be added to the belief set or removed from it. This gives rise to two basic types of input-based belief changes:

incorporation: The result is that a belief is accepted.
contraction: The result is that a belief is not accepted.

Four basic integrity constraints are usually imposed on the outcome of a belief change operation:

logical closure: The outcome is a logically closed set, just like the original belef set.
consistency preservation: The outcome is consistent, just like the original belief set.
success: (i) A sentence to be incorporated is included in the outcome. (ii) A sentence to be contracted is not included in the outcome.
conservatism: (i) In incorporation, no sentences are removed. (ii) In contraction, no sentences are added.[4]

---

[1] Or more precisely: the sentences I was committed to believe to be true (Cf. [18]).

[2] If belief change is interpreted as referring to other belief-holders than individual persons, then the sentential format may be less problematic. One example of this is database management. The contents of databases are more readily representable by sentences than human beliefs or memories. Another example is changes in collectively created and maintained stocks of information or knowledge, such as the corpus of scientific beliefs. Collective processes are usually based on sentential representations since these are needed for interindividual communication.

[3] Or set of sentences [9].

[4] These are the most elementary demands of conservatism. In addition the following, somewhat less precise, demands are common: (iii) In incorporation, no sentences are added unless this is needed to incorporate the input. (ii) In contraction, no sentences are removed unless this is needed to remove the input.

Fig. 1 The two alternative priorities among basic requirements on belief change that standard belief revision theory (such as AGM) vacillates between

Pattern A	Pattern B
logical closure	logical closure
∨	∨
success	success
∨	∨
conservatism	consistency preservation
∨	∨
consistency preservation	conservatism

In contraction, these four requirements are all compatible if the sentence to be removed is non-tautologous. If the sentence is a tautology, then *logical closure* and *success* are incompatible (but each of them is compatible with the other two conditions). The standard solution is to give higher priority to logical closure than to success, i.e. the outcome of contraction by a tautology is a logically closed set and therefore it does not satisfy the success criterion.

In incorporation, all four requirements are compatible if the sentence to be added is consistent with the original belief set (i.e. if $K \cup \{p\}$ is consistent). If p is inconsistent, then *consistency preservation* and *success* cannot both be satisfied. This is traditionally solved by giving priority to *success* (which is compatible with the other two conditions). If p is consistent but inconsistent with the original belief set, then any two of the three conditions *consistency preservation*, *success*, and *conservatism* are compatible, but not all three of them. (*Logical closure* is compatible with each of these combinations). There are two standard solutions to this. One is to give up *consistency preservation*, usually by just letting the outcome be $\mathrm{Cn}(K \cup \{p\})$. This form of incorporation is called expansion. The other solution is to give up *conservatism*, and remove enough elements from the original belief set K to ensure that p can be added without giving rise to inconsistency. This type of incorporation is called revision.

Summarizing this, the priorities inherent in these operations can be described as vacillating between the two patterns shown in Fig. 1. The standard operation of contraction is compatible with both patterns, whereas expansion is compatible only with Pattern A and revision with Pattern B.

3 Decomposing Belief Change

The standard framework of belief revision theory originates largely in Isaac Levi's [18] work from the 1960s and 1970s. He established a framework in which belief states are represented by logically closed belief sets. There are three types of changes: contraction ($\div$), expansion ($+$), and revision ($*$). Expansions are performed in the simple way already indicated, i.e. $K + p = \text{Cn}(K \cup \{p\})$. Furthermore, revisions are definable in terms of contractions and expansions through what is now called the Levi identity:

$$K * p = (K \div \neg p) + p. \tag{1}$$

The Levi identity can be seen as based on an underlying assumption of decomposability into simple operations. It can perhaps be defended as follows: Real-life belief change results in new beliefs being added and old ones being removed. Therefore, we can assume without losing generality that all operations of change consist of two suboperations: "pure" contraction that removes beliefs but does not add any new ones, and "pure" incorporation that adds new beliefs but removes no old ones.[5]

Segerberg somewhat cautiously endorsed this decomposition principle although in slightly different terms. After discussing straightforward cases in which only removals or additions of beliefs are needed, he said:

> There are certainly more complex cases when the agent will go to a new belief-set that is neither weaker nor stronger than the current one; but those can perhaps be seen as derivative, as achievable by a combination of weakenings and strengthenings. ([35], 143)

In the same paper he proposed as a desideratum for belief revision theory "that there be two basic kinds of doxastic action, *basic expansion* and *basic contraction*" (p. 144). Basic contractions (weakenings) of the belief set are representable in possible world models as retreats to sets of worlds that contain the set of worlds that represent the current belief state. Following [21] he called such retreats *fall-backs*. Basic expansions (strengthenings) could analogously be represented by sets of worlds included in the one representing the current belief state. Segerberg called them *push-ups*.

It is important to distinguish between two interpretations of the postulated decomposability of all belief changes into contraction and expansion. We can call them the "black box" and the "step-by-step" interpretation. According to the black box interpretation, the decomposition provides us with a convenient method to obtain the desired outcome, but it does not necessarily correspond to how changes in belief actually take place. According to the step-by-step interpretation the decomposition is a representation of how belief change actually takes place, specifying the actual suboperations and the order in which they take place. The black box interpretation is fairly plausible. Irrespectively of how a human being goes from a belief set K_1 to another belief set K_2, in a formal model we can go from K_1 to K_2 by performing first a contraction that takes us from K_1 to some K' such that $K' \subseteq K_1 \cap K_2$, and then an expansion that takes us from K' to K_2. For this to be feasible it is sufficient that there are two sentences p and q such that contraction of K_1 by p leads us to

[5] An alternative approach takes as primitive an operation that both removes some sentence(s) and adds some other sentence(s). It is then possible to develop a model of belief change on the basis of one single primitive operation instead of two as in Levi's model [13].

some K' that is also a subset of K_2 and that expansion of K' by q leads us further on to K_2.[6]

The step-by-step interpretation of the decomposition is much more problematic. One of the reasons for this is that the required composite operations, "pure" contraction (in which no sentences are added) and "pure expansion" (in which no sentences are removed) do not seem to be matched by actual operations of change. Although contraction is taken for granted as a building-block in belief change theory, it is not easily exemplified. Of course there are belief changes in real life that are driven by a need to give up a certain belief. However, such changes tend to be caused by the acquisition of some new information that is added to the belief set. Not long ago a friend said to me that he was quite sure that the Vatican City State is a member of the United Nations, which I believed it was not. This made me uncertain and induced me to enter a state of hesitation concerning the issue in question. I therefore removed the sentence "The Vatican City State is not a member of the United Nations" from my set of beliefs without adding its negation. In the belief revision literature, this would be treated as a contraction, but in fact it was not since I added the new belief that my friend believes that the Vatican City State is a member of the United Nations. The only credible examples of pure contraction that have been presented in the literature are hypothetical contractions such as contractions for the sake of argument [8, 20].[7] Pure incorporation, i.e. expansion, is also problematic, as will be seen in Sect. 6.

A crucial step in the theory of belief change was taken by Carlos Alchourrón, Peter Gärdenfors and David Makinson [1] who provided what is now the standard framework of belief revision. Their major invention was a formally precise account of contraction, namely partial meet contraction:

$$K \div p = \bigcap \gamma(K \perp p), \tag{2}$$

where $K \perp p$ is the set of inclusion-maximal subsets of K not implying p and γ is a selection function, such that $\varnothing \neq \gamma(K \perp p) \subseteq K \perp p$ whenever $K \perp p \neq \varnothing$, and $\gamma(K \perp p) = K$ when $K \perp p = \varnothing$. Revision is defined according to the Levi identity, i.e. $K * p = (K \div \neg p) + p$. This framework has turned out to be exceptionally fruitful, and AGM-style belief revision is a rapidly developing research area with a surprising number of ramifications and connections with other areas. [7]

But it should be remembered that the standard framework is the result of a whole series of idealizations and limitations. The belief changes of real-life human beings are often not sentential. Furthermore, even given the choice of sentential representations there are many other options than the three standard ones of contraction,

---

[6] For arbitrary K_1 and K_2, this recipe only works if the language is finite. In a framework with an infinite language, two operations on sentences are not sufficient to take us from a belief set K_1 to any other belief set K_2. If there is a countably infinite number of logical atoms, then the number of belief sets expressible in the language is uncountable. (This can be shown with a standard diagonalization argument.) On the other hand, there is only a countable number of sequences $\div p + q$ of a contraction by one sentence (p) followed by an expansion by another (q). This problem can be solved by introducing multiple contraction and expansion.

[7] This refers to the modelling of human beliefs. Pure contraction of databases is unproblematic.

expansion, and revision. Alternative types of operators that may better represent some real-life belief changes include the following:

- *consolidation*, an operation that makes an inconsistent belief state consistent by removing beliefs from it.
- *external revision*, revision by a sentence p that proceeds by first expanding by p and then contracting by $\neg p$, i.e. the two suboperations take place in the reverse order to that of the Levi identity.
- *semi-revision*, an operation that receives a sentence p and weighs it against old information, with no special priority assigned to the new information due to its novelty. The input may be either incorporated or rejected.
- *selective revision*, a generalization of semi-revision in which it is possible for only a part of the input information to be accepted. (Selective revision by $p\&q$ may for instance result in p being incorporated and q rejected.)
- *shielded contraction*, a variant of contraction in which some non-tautological beliefs are not retractable. The agent may hold a non-logical belief p that nothing can make her give up, so that $p \in K \div p$, and presumably also $p \in K \div q$ for all q.
- *lowering* and *raising*, operations in which the belief set is unchanged but the degrees of belief in some of its elements are either decreased or increased, which may have effects on the outcomes of subsequent changes.
- *replacement*, an operation that replaces one sentence by another in a belief set. Excepting limiting cases, the outcome of replacing p by q is a belief set $K \mid_q^p$ such that $p \notin K \mid_q^p$ and $q \in K \mid_q^p$. Replacement can serve as a "Sheffer stroke" for the standard belief revision operators.
- *reconsideration* reintroduces previously removed beliefs if there are no longer any valid reasons for their removal.
- *multiple contraction*, in which a set of sentences, rather than a single sentence, is (simultaneously) removed from the belief set.
- *indeterministic belief change*, in which there are several alternative outcomes of a change operation. In indeterminist contraction, $K \div p$ is typically a set of belief sets that are subsets of K and do not contain p, rather than a single such belief set.

(For references on these operations, see [15].)

In summary, belief revision theory is dominated by an elegant and highly idealized framework (AGM) that only covers some of the many aspects of actual belief change. This is the background against which we should study Krister Segerberg's contributions to belief revision theory. He has paid much attention to possible extensions of the framework, such as consolidation [33], semi-revision [33], external revision [33], and indeterministic change [34]. But most importantly, he has provided us with an alternative framework in which the very notion of an operation of change is explicated quite differently from the AGM framework.

4 Dynamic Doxastic Logic

Given his background as one of the major contributors to the development of modern modal logic, is should be no surprise that Segerberg took the lead in approaches that employ the resources of modal logic to increase the expressive power of belief change theory. This resulted in *dynamic doxastic logic* (DDL) that includes two major additions to the language that increase its expressive power [32, 35]. (The term "dynamic doxastic logic" is modelled after van Benthem's "dynamic modal logic", cf. [32], p. 535.)

The first of these additions is sentence formation with epistemic modal operators of the type introduced by Hintikka [16]. The sentence $B_i p$ denotes that the individual i believes that p. When only one agent is under consideration, the subscript can be deleted, and the operator B can be read "it is believed that" or "the agent believes that" ([32], p. 536).

A major difference between Bp and the formula $p \in K$ of AGM is that the former but not the latter is a sentence in the same language as p. This makes it possible to express in the object language that a sentence is believed. In Segerberg's own words, he tried to develop belief revision "as a generalization of ordinary Hintikka type doxastic logic", whereas in contrast "AGM is not really logic; it is a theory about theories" ([35], p. 136). The difference becomes crucial when beliefs about beliefs are introduced. Sentences such as "i believes that i does not believe that p" and "i believes that j believes that p" are readily expressible in DDL as $B_i \neg B_i p$ respectively $B_i B_j p$. The AGM framework does not have the corresponding resources. (Neither $(p \notin K_i) \in K_i$ nor $(p \in K_j) \in K_i$ is a well-formed formula.)

The other addition is the formalization of belief revision operations (expansion, revision, and contraction) with dynamic modal operators, similar to those used for program execution. This element of DDL was present also in publications by several other authors ([8, 28, 37, 38]). The standard notation used by Segerberg is as follows:

$[\div p]\alpha$ (α holds after contraction by p)
$[*p]\alpha$ (α holds after revision by p)
$[+p]\alpha$ (α holds after expansion by p)

The combination of these two elements, belief operators and dynamic operators, provides us with a framework that is in important respects more general than AGM. $[*p]Bq$ means that q is believed after revision by p, hence it conveys the same information as the AGM formula $q \in K * p$. ([17], 168) Similarly, $[\div p]\neg Bq$ says that q is not believed after contraction by p, i.e. $q \notin K \div p$. But in addition, the combined use of belief operators and dynamic operators makes it possible to express an agent's beliefs about her own patterns of belief revision. As an example of this, $B([*p]Bq)$ means that the agent believes that after revision by p she will believe that q, and the more complex formula $[*[*p]Bq]Br$ means that the agent will believe r if she revises her belief state by the belief that if she revises by p then she will believe q. ([17], 169)

The success criteria of the three operations are succinctly expressed as follows:

$[*p]Bp$ (Revision success)
$[+p]Bp$ (Expansion success)
If $p \notin \mathrm{Cn}(\varnothing)$ then $[\div p]\neg Bp$ (Contraction success)

According to the Levi identity, $[*p]$ can be read as an abbreviation of $[\div\neg p][+p]$ ([32], p. 357). In the same fashion, iterated operations can be expressed by repetition of the dynamic ([ ]) operators, such as $[*p][*q][\div r]$ etc.

The recasting of belief revision theory as modal-style dynamic logic has the important advantage that it "puts at our disposal the rich meta-theory developed in the study of modal and dynamic logic". Segerberg ([35],142) As a simple example of this, the analogy between $[\circ p]$ (where $\circ$ is any of $\div$, $+$, and $*$) and $\Box$ suggests the introduction of operators of the form $\langle \circ p \rangle$ that stand in the same relation to $[\circ p]$ as $\diamond$ to $\Box$, i.e.:

$$\langle \circ p \rangle q \ \text{ if and only if } \ \neg[\circ p]\neg q. \tag{3}$$

$\langle \alpha \rangle \beta$ is to be read "after the agent has carried out the action α, it may be the case that β, and consequently $\langle \circ p \rangle Bq$ should be read "after the agent has contracted/expanded/revised by p, it may be the case that the agent believes q" ([34], pp. 187, 189). In standard, deterministic belief revision models, the extension of the language with $\langle\ \rangle$-operators is not of much use. If $\circ p$ has a well-determined outcome, then $\langle \circ p \rangle Bq$ and $[\circ p]Bq$ have the same truth conditions. However, in indeterministic belief revision (that assigns to $\circ p$ a set of possible outcomes, rather than a single outcome) the $\langle\ \rangle$-operators provide a highly useful increase in expressive power. (On indeterministic belief revision, see [21].)

It should be mentioned, though, that although DDL has more expressive power than AGM in some respects, there are other respects in which the opposite relation seems to hold. In AGM we can easily express non-prioritized belief changes, i.e. changes in which the input is not always accepted. We can have a semi-revision operation $*$ such that $p \in K * p$ does not hold for all p or a screened contraction operator $\div$ such that $p \notin K \div p$ does not hold for all non-tautologous sentences p. Since $K * p$ simply represents the belief state obtained after receiving the information that p, this does not require any reinterpretation of the formalism. It is less obvious how to interpret $*p$ in DDL if $[*p]Bp$ does not hold; what type of action is then $*p$?

Important contributions to DDL have been made by Segerberg himself, by Sten Lindström and Wlodek Rabinowicz [22] who investigated formulas such $B([*p]Bq)$ that represent introspective agents, and by John Cantwell [6] who explored iterated change. In parallel, largely similar systems have been developed under the name of Dynamic Epistemic Logic, DEL ([5, 27, 40]). The original DEL models referred to belief expansion only, but in later work revision has been included ([3, 5, 37, 39]). A major difference between DDL and DEL is that the latter has mostly been studied in multiagent contexts.

DDL is a major alternative to the AGM-style formalisms that are currently the standard in belief revision theory. Since logical modelling of belief change operates with considerable idealizations, it is a wise strategy to promote the development of models that put emphasis on different aspects of the subject matter. ([12, 14]) It is also a wise strategy to subject each of these alternative formalisms to critical scrutiny. In what follows, I will discuss two possibly problematic aspects of DDL, namely its concept of doxastic agency and its treatment of non-truthfunctional sentences in the object langauge.

5 Doxastic Voluntarism

Should belief changes be seen as actions undertaken by the epistemic subject or as uncontrollable effects of external influences? There is one formulation in one of his early papers on the subject where Segerberg kept both options open, describing belief changes as something that the agent can have "undertaken (or undergone)". ([34], p. 183) However, in his development of DDL he settled for the former option, interpreting the interior of [ ] and $\langle\ \rangle$ (for instance $*p$ in $[*p]$) as a representation of action.

> "Suppose that you believe that a proposition P is true—thus $X \subseteq P$, where X is your current belief set—but that you have decided that this belief has to be given up... This means that you wish to replace X by a belief set Y such that P is no longer believed after the change. Call this operation *contraction* by P ...
>
> Suppose that you decide to accept the truth of P in the sense of simply adding it to your existing stock of beliefs. Again you are changing your views, you wish to replace your current belief set X by a belief set Y such that after the change you believe P as well as everything you already believe. We call this operation *expansion* by P. "([34], p. 185)

> "Now to expand or revise or contract is to do something. Thus it is possible to think of expansion, revision and contraction as actions of a certain kind—epistemic or doxastic actions." ([35], p. 137)

In Segerberg's theory, doxastic actions are a special type of actions. They differ from "real actions" in that they do not change the state of the world, as the latter may do. ([34], p. 187).[8]

Are there any doxastic (epistemic) actions? This is a much debated issue in philosophy, and the standpoint that there are such actions is usually called doxastic (epistemic) voluntarism. As these discussions have shown, it is important to distinguish between different variants of doxastic voluntarism. [26] First of all we need to identify the elements of human behaviour that are candidates for being such actions. Robert Audi [2] provided a useful distinction for this purpose, namely that between

[8] Heinrich Wansing is another prominent proponent of this view. He has proposed that developing the semantics of belief ascriptions from the viewpoint of doxastic voluntarism can be a way to avoid closure of belief under logical consequence. In his view, a variant of seeing-to-it-that (stit) logic of agency can be used to represent voluntary acquisition and abandonment of belief. [41] In later work he has further specified this as dstit-theory, where dstit stands for "deliberately sees to it that" [42]. He proposes the introduction of a belief formation operator to be read "α sees to it that α believes that p" (p. 212).

a behavioural and a genetic version of doxastic voluntarism. According to the behavioural version, believing, i.e. holding a belief, is (or can be) an action-type. According to the genetic version, forming (rather than holding) a belief is (or can be) an action-type.

Both behavioural and genetic doxastic voluntarism can be further subdivided. In what follows I will focus on the variants of genetic doxastic voluntarism. Many authors have referred to the distinction between a weak and a strong variant, but it has often been overlooked that voluntarism can be weak or strong in two senses that give rise to crossing distinctions: Doxastic voluntarism can be either complete or partial. It can also be either direct or indirect. Acccording to complete doxastic voluntarism all beliefs are voluntary, according to partial doxastic voluntarism only some of them. Doxastic voluntarism is direct if it implies that we can make ourselves adopt or give up a belief by just deciding to so. It is indirect if it indicates that we can do so only by performing will-controlled actions that cause, in ways that are not will-controlled, a change in belief. Obviously, both direct and indirect doxastic voluntarism can be either complete or partial.

What type of doxastic voluntarism does Segerberg need? Since his is a logic of belief change, rather than the statics of belief, the behavioural version is irrelevant for his theory. (It is also a version that has very rarely been defended by philosophers.) The doxastic actions that he refers to consist in the adoption or abandonment of beliefs. We should therefore focus on genetic doxastic voluntarism. This gives rise to two further questions: Should a genetic doxastic voluntarism that supports DDL be complete or partial, and should it be direct or indirect?

The answers to both these questions are quite obvious. DDL is a theory of belief change in general, not a theory intended to cover some fraction of the belief changes that epistemic subjects undertake. Therefore a doxastic voluntarism suitable for interpreting DDL will have to be complete. Furthermore, the framework is one of direct causation. $[*p]Bq$ means that the subject performs an action $(*p)$ that has Bq as a consequence. Alternatively she may perform some action such as letting another person indoctrinate or hypnotize her to believe that p, but then her own action is not a doxastic action but a "real action" (in Segerberg's terminology, quoted above) since it changes the state of the world rather than her own beliefs.

In summary then, the type of doxastic voluntarism that we need to support DDL is genetic, complete, and indirect. How credible is such a form of doxastic voluntarism?

If a student comes up to me after a lecture and tells me that my lecture was boring, I acquire the belief that she has said this to me. Reacting to such a sensory impression by questioning its veracity would be a sign of insanity rather than philosophical sophistication. This applies to most of the sensory evidence that we receive in everyday life. This is acknowledged by the majority of doxastic voluntarists. Philosophically credible argumentation in favour of direct doxastic voluntarism tends to stop short of defending the complete version of the thesis that would be necessary for Segerberg's purposes. Hence, Ronney Mourad [24] concedes that "most beliefs are involuntary" (p. 60) and that this applies in particular when we have conclusive evidence in support of either belief or disbelief (p. 62). Similarly, Philip Nickel acknowledges that "conclusive evidence, when grasped by a doxastic subject, must induce belief" ([25],

p. 313). These and most other defenders of direct doxastic voluntarism do not claim that all beliefs are formed at will, only that some of them are. Unfortunately, this is not sufficient for DDL.

Even the partial version of direct doxastic voluntarism is highly contestable. Proponents often point out that (some) beliefs are not completely determined by evidence. This is incontrovertible. ("[I]t is far from clear that all beliefs of all agents come into being as an inescapable response to some evidence", [42] p. 211.) However, there are many other influences on our beliefs than volition and evidence. Our beliefs are influenced by factors such as wishful thinking, intellectual sloppiness, and irrational trust in authorities. Influences such as these cannot in general be applied or deactivated at will in order to adopt or give up a particular belief. To substantiate (partial) direct doxastic voluntarism it would seem necessary to exhibit plausible examples of beliefs that are formed by direct volition-driven causation. Such examples do not seem easy to find. (Arguably the best attempts are so-called self-fulfilling beliefs that may arise for instance if someone credibly offers you $1.000.000 for forming the belief that you are a millionaire. [30], p. 83.)

A strong case can be made in favour of indirect doxastic voluntarism, especially its partial variant. There are things we can do to induce beliefs in ourselves. Someone who wishes to become a believer in a certain religious faith can expose herself to arguments and emotional influence that is expected to make her a believer. Someone who is plagued by her own jealousy may try in different ways to convince herself that her husband is faithful. However, such indirect causation is not always successful, as exemplified by the phenomenon of being plagued by religious doubt.

Ethical arguments have had an important role in argumentation for doxastic voluntarism. There are situations when it is plausible to hold a person responsible for incorrect beliefs that have negative consequences. It may seem as if we can only be responsible for our beliefs if we have some kind of control over them. [23] However, such responsibility can at least in most cases be accounted for in terms of indirect doxastic voluntarism. What we require of persons with wrongful beliefs is that they study the evidence, listen to the experts, and reconsider the issue in a rational fashion. We do not normally demand that they change their belief by *fiat*.

In summary, Segerberg's explication of DDL seems to require complete, direct doxastic voluntarism, which is an apparantly implausible standpoint with very few adherents. There is much to say in favour of partial, indirect doxastic voluntarism, but that is not sufficient for DDL. Is there a way out of this conundrum? Can DDL be saved?

There is indeed a fairly simple way out: The interior of $[\ ]$ and $\langle\ \rangle$ need not be interpreted as representing actions. Instead they may be taken to represent external influences, in much the same way as in AGM. $[*p]Bq$ will then be interpreted for instance as "after receiving the information that p, the epistemic subject believes that q. As far as I can see there is nothing in Segerberg's remarkably versatile formalism that precludes such an interpretation. However, it remains to investigate the more detailed consequences of its adoption.

6 Non-truthfunctional Connectives

Belief revision theory has primarily been concerned with beliefs expressed in an object language that contains no other resources than logical atoms and (the full set of) truth-functional connectives. This is a severe limitation since non-truthfunctional combinations are essential components of our belief systems, without which intentional actions as we know them would not be possible. This applies not least to conditional beliefs. I believe that I can light up the room by turning on the switch, and I also believe that consuming a bottle of wine will make me drunk. Such beliefs can usefully be formalized as conditional sentences. ("If I turn on that switch, then the room will be lit." "If I drink that bottle of wine then I will be drunk.") However, in spite of their essential role in our belief systems, such beliefs are disturbingly difficult to express in belief revision theory. In fact, any attempt to include non-truthfunctional expressions into the language seems to have drastic and often unwished-for effects on the formal system.

It is usually assumed that at least a large part of our conditional beliefs satisfy the so-called Ramsey test that is based on a suggestion by Ramsey that has been further developed by Robert Stalnaker [36] and others. The basic idea is that "if p then q" is taken to be believed by the epistemic subject if and only if she would believe in q after revising her present belief state by p. Let $p \Box\!\!\rightarrow q$ denote "if p then q", or more precisely: "if p were the case, then q would be the case". The Ramsey test says:

$$p \Box\!\!\rightarrow q \text{ holds if and only if } q \in K * p \tag{4}$$

In AGM, attempts have been made to include sentences of the form $p \Box\!\!\rightarrow q$ in the object language, which means that they will be included in the belief set when they are assented to by the agent, thus:

$$p \Box\!\!\rightarrow q \in K \text{ if and only if } q \in K * p \tag{5}$$

However, the step from (4) to (5), i.e. the inclusion in belief sets of conditionals that satisfy the Ramsey test, has turned out to require radical changes in the logic of belief change.[9] As one example of this, contraction cannot then satisfy the inclusion postulate ($K \div p \subseteq K$). The reason for this is that contraction typically generates support for conditional sentences that were not supported by the original belief state. If I give up my belief that John is mentally retarded, then I gain support for the conditional sentence "If John has lived 30 years in London, then he understands the English language" [11].

A famous impossibility theorem by Peter Gärdenfors [10] shows that the Ramsey test is incompatible with a set of plausible postulates for revision. This was shown by Gärdenfors to hold if the underlying logic is (or contains) classical propositional logic. Segerberg [31] generalized this result, showing that it holds whenever the con-

[9] Issac Levi [19] avoids most of the common difficulties with Ramsey test conditionals by accepting (4) but not (5).

sequence operator Cn of the underlying logic satisfies the three standard conditions $A \subseteq \mathrm{Cn}(A)$ (inclusion or reflexivity), If $A \subseteq B$, then $\mathrm{Cn}(A) \subseteq \mathrm{Cn}(B)$ (monotony or monotonicity), and $\mathrm{Cn}(\mathrm{Cn}(A)) \subseteq \mathrm{Cn}(A)$ (iteration or transitivity).

The crucial part of the proof consists in showing that the Ramsey test implies the following monotonicity condition.

$$\text{If } K \subseteq K' \text{ then } K * p \subseteq K' * p \tag{6}$$

The proof of this is straightforward: Let $K \subseteq K'$ and $q \in K * p$. The Ramsey test yields $p \Box\!\!\rightarrow q \in K$, then $K \subseteq K'$ yields $p \Box\!\!\rightarrow q \in K'$, and finally one more application of the Ramsey test yields $q \in K' * p$.

(6) is incompatible with the AGM postulates for revision, and it is also easily shown to be implausible.[10] Let K be a belief set in which you know nothing about Ellen's private life and K' one in which you know that she is a lesbian. Let p denote that she is married and q that she has a husband. Then we can have $K \subseteq K'$ but $q \in K * p$ and $q \notin K' * p$.

DDL was "introduced with the aim of representing the *meta*-linguistically expressed belief revision operator $*$ as an *object*-linguistic sentence operator $[*\_]$ in the style of dynamic modal logic" ([17], 167–168). In other words, the driving idea of DDL is that a formula such as $[*p]q$ should be treated on the same level as its components p and q. ([17], p. 171) Furthermore, since the intended semantics of DDL is a possible world semantics, sets of possible worlds will be assigned to formulas such as $[*p]q$, just as this will be done for p and q. Therefore, we should expect the equivalent of (5) to hold in DDL, i.e.:

$$B(p \Box\!\!\rightarrow q) \text{ if and only if } [*p]Bq \tag{7}$$

Unfortunately, this gives rise to the same type of problem that Gärdenfors showed to hold in the AGM model. This can be seen from the fact that a conditional property closely related to (6) can be obtained, namely the following:

$$\text{If } [*p]Bq \text{ and } \neg B \neg r \text{ then } [*r][*p]Bq \tag{8}$$

The derivation of (8) is straight-forward.

Postulates

- $B(p \Box\!\!\rightarrow q) \leftrightarrow [*p]Bq$ (Ramsey test)
- If $\neg B \neg r$ and Bs then $[*r]Bs$ (preservation)
- Logical equivalence is preserved after substitution of logically equivalent subformulas (extensionality)

[10] However, it is trivially unproblematic in an approach where it holds for all potential belief sets K_1 and K_2 that $K_1 \not\subseteq K_2$. In such a framework there cannot be any pure contraction, or any other operation that takes us from a belief set to one of its proper subsets. Furthermore, there cannot be any pure expansion, or any other operation that takes us from a belief set to one of its proper supersets. Cf. [11].

Derivation

(1) $[*p]Bq$ (assumption)
(2) $\neg B \neg r$ (assumption)
(3) $B(p \Box\!\!\rightarrow q)$ ((1) and Ramsey test)
(4) $[*r](B(p \Box\!\!\rightarrow q))$ ((2), (3), and preservation)
(5) $[*r][*p]Bq$ ((4), Ramsey test, and extensionality)

It is easy to show that (8) is starkly implausible. Consider my beliefs about Rebecca, a casual acquaintance whom I met at a party. Initially I know nothing about her profession or about what musical abilities she may have; in particular I do not know whether or not she is tonedeaf (r). However, if I acquire the belief that she has applied for a position as concertmaster in the Czech Philharmonic (p), then I will also believe that she is a first-rate violinist (q). Hence, $[*p]Bq$ and $\neg B \neg r$. However, it does not hold that $[*r][*p]Bq$. The reason for this is that if I acquire both the beliefs that she is tonedeaf and that she has applied for the position in question, then I may conclude that she is an unqualified but self-conceited fiddler, and thus not believe q to be true.

Leitgeb and Segerberg ([17], 172) mention two ways to avoid difficulties like this. One is to "not allow the derivation, for all p and q, of a formula of the form $B(\chi(p,q)) \leftrightarrow [*p]Bq$, where $\chi(p,q)$ is some formula that is built syntactically from p and q".[11] There will then be some formulas of the type $[*p]Bq$ that cannot be an argument of the B operator, in other words $B([*p]Bq)$ is not a well-formed formula. This means that there are certain revision patterns that an agent may have but may not believe herself to have. This might have been an acceptable limitation if it only affected beliefs of an uncommon type, or only beliefs with a paradoxical flavour. However, as we have seen it will arise also with respect to seemingly unparadoxical everyday beliefs such as "If I am made to believe that she has applied for a position as concertmaster of the Czech Philharmonic, then I will also believe that she is a first-rate violinist".

The second option that they mention is that the axioms and rules for $[*\ ]$ may not conform to the AGM postulates. This is a much more plausible option. The AGM postulates (and their counterparts in DDL) have been developed for a restricted language that contains simple factual statements but does not contain conditionals. This is why it can be taken for granted in AGM that for a given belief set K and some sentence p that is compatible with all the factual sentences in K there is some operation that, when applied to K, gives rise to some belief set K' such that $K \cup \{p\} \subseteq K'$ (scilicet an expansion or a revision by a sentence consistent with K). This is plausible as long as K and K' are restricted to the purely factual fraction of the language. However, if K also contains all the conditional beliefs that the agent holds, then the fact that p does not contradict any factual belief in K does not guarantee that it does not contradict any of the conditional beliefs held in K. For instance, suppose that originally I know nothing about John's profession. It seems as if any concrete belief that I can acquire about his profession will lead to the loss of some conditional belief. If I learn that he is a driver by profession, then I will lose my belief that if he

[11] The notation in the quoted formulas has been slightly modified.

goes home from work by taxi every day, then he is a rich man. If I learn that he is a policeman, then I will lose my conditional belief that if he drove past several speed cameras at 110 mph last evening then he will be cited for speeding. If I learn that he is a philosopher, then I will lose my belief that if he has spent most of the last two years thinking intensely about the meaning of life, then he is unemployed and depressed. Generally speaking, it is difficult to find a clear example of a belief that can be acquired without the loss of some previously held conditional belief. This has far-reaching implications for the project of developing belief revision models capable of housing conditional sentences. It may for instance be necessary to give up the use of expansion as one of the (idealized) operations by which we try to capture the mechanisms of belief change. [11, 29] This is a problem that seems to affect AGM and DDL alike.

DDL has the major advantage, as compared to AGM, of allowing us to express self-referential beliefs. This applies not only to beliefs about one's own current beliefs such as BBp or $B\neg B\neg p$ but also to the arguably much more interesting beliefs that refer to how one will change one's beliefs under certain influences. However, the condition that $B(p \Box\!\!\rightarrow q)$ is true if and only if $[*p]Bq$ appears to be in a sense trivializing since it equates two entities between which we have an interesting tension: an agent's conditional beliefs and her tendencies to change her beliefs.[12] One interesting further development of DDL would be to treat $B(p \Box\!\!\rightarrow q)$ and $[*p]Bq$ as separate entities with different truth conditions so that their truth values coincide sometimes but not always.

7 Conclusion

All belief change frameworks are the outcomes of far-reaching idealizations—otherwise they would be much too complex to work with. This applies to DDL as well as to the rival frameworks. In the above reflections on DDL I have focused on some of its limitations, but the remaining impression is that Krister Segerberg has provided us with an unusually versatile framework that is more suitable than most others for the introduction of new formal elements and new interpretations. Above, two such potential additions have been put forward: alternative interpretations in which the interior of [ ] and $\langle\ \rangle$ represents the effects of external influences rather than the performance of actions, and models that have separate, non-equivalent representations of conditional beliefs and tendencies to change beliefs. Another development for which DDL is unusually well suited is the introduction of non-sentential inputs, in order to capture some of the properties of actual belief change that are lost in models operating with sentences. We can for instance have a set $\mathcal{I}$ of non-sentential

[12] This conflation is perhaps stimulated by the standard theory of probabilities, in which two notions of degree of belief are merged: the current strength of a belief and the propensity to retain it when it is challenged are represented by the same number. However, this is a limitation that should not necessarily be transferred to other frameworks.

entities called inputs such that for any $\alpha \in \mathcal{I}$, we interpret $[\alpha]Bp$ as saying that after receiving the input α, the sentence p is believed.

References

1. Alchourrón, C., Gärdenfors, P., & Makinson, D. (1985). On the logic of theory change: Partial meet contraction and revision functions. *Journal of Symbolic Logic*, *50*, 510–530.
2. Audi, R. (2001). Doxastic voluntarism and the ethics of belief. In M. Setup (Ed.), *Knowledge, truth, and duty. Essays on epistemic justification, responsibility, and virtue* (pp. 93–111). Oxford: Oxford University Press.
3. Aucher, G. (2003). *A combined system for update logic and belief revision*, ILLC report MoL-2003-03. Amsterdam: ILLC, University of Amsterdam.
4. Baltag, A., Moss, L., & Solecki, S. (1998). The logic of public announcements, common knowledge, and private suspicions. In I. Gilboa (Ed.), *Proceedings of the 7th conference on theoretical aspects of rationality and knowledge (TARK 98)* (pp. 43–56). San Francisco: Morgan Kaufmann.
5. Baltag, A., & Smets, S. (2008). A Qualitative Theory of dynamic interactive belief revision. In G. Bonanno, W. van der Hoek, M. Wooldridge (Eds.) *Logic and the Foundations of Game and Decision Theory (LOFT 7)*, Texts in Logic and Games 3 (pp. 11–58). Amsterdam: Amsterdam University Press.
6. Cantwell, J. (1997). On the logic of small changes in hypertheories. *Theoria*, *63*, 54–89.
7. Fermé, E., & Hansson, S. O. (2011). AGM 25 years. Twenty-five years of research in belief change. *Journal of Philosophical Logic*, *40*, 295–331.
8. Fuhrmann, A. (1991). Theory contraction through base contraction. *Journal of Philosophical Logic*, *20*, 175–203.
9. Fuhrmann, A., & Hansson, S. O. (1994). A survey of multiple contraction. *Journal of Logic, Language, and Information*, *3*, 39–76.
10. Gärdenfors, P. (1986). Belief revisions and the Ramsey test for conditionals. *Philosophical Review*, *95*, 81–93.
11. Hansson, S. O. (1992). In defense of the Ramsey test. *Journal of Philosophy*, *89*, 522–540.
12. Hansson, S. O. (2000). Formalization in philosophy. *Bulletin of Symbolic Logic*, *6*, 162–175.
13. Hansson, S. O. (2009). Replacement—a Sheffer stroke for belief revision. *Journal of Philosophical Logic*, *38*, 127–149.
14. Hansson, S. O. (2010). Methodological pluralism in philosophy. *Theoria*, *76*, 189–191.
15. Hansson, S. O. (2011). Logic of belief revision. In *The Stanford Encyclopedia of Philosophy*. (http://plato.stanford.edu/entries/logic-belief-revision)
16. Hintikka, J. (1962). *Knowledge and belief: An introduction to the logic of the two notions*. Ithaca: Cornell University Press.
17. Leitgeb, H., & Segerberg, K. (2007). Dynamic doxastic logic: Why, how, and where to? *Synthese*, *155*, 167–190.
18. Levi, I. (1977). Subjunctives, dispositions and chances. *Synthese*, *34*, 423–455.
19. Levi, I. (1988). Iteration of conditionals and the Ramsey test. *Synthese*, *76*, 49–81.
20. Levi, I. (1991). *The fixation of belief and its undoing*. Cambridge: Cambridge University Press.
21. Lindström, S., & Rabinowicz, W. (1991). Epistemic entrenchment with incomparabilities and relational belief revision. In A. Fuhrmann & M. Morreau (Eds.), *The logic of theory change* (pp. 208–228). Berlin: Springer.
22. Lindström, S., & Rabinowicz, W. (1999). DDL unlimited. Dynamic doxastic logic for introspective agents. *Erkenntnis*, *51*, 353–385.
23. Montmarquet, J. (2008). Virtue and voluntarism. *Synthese*, *161*, 393–402.
24. Mourad, R. (2008). Choosing to believe. *International Journal for Philosophy of Religion*, *63*, 55–69.

25. Nickel, P. J. (2010). Voluntary belief on a reasonable basis. *Philosophy and Phenomenological Research*, *81*, 312–334.
26. Nottelmann, N. (2006). The analogy argument for doxastic voluntarism. *Philosophical Studies*, *131*, 559–582.
27. Plaza, J. (1989). Logics of public communications. In M. L. Emrich, M. S. Pfeifer, M. Hadzikadic, & Z. W. Ras (Eds.), *Proceedings of the 4th International Symposium on Methodologies for Intelligent Systems*, (pp. 201–216). Oak Ridge, Tennessee: Oak Ridge National Laboratory.
28. de Rijke, M. (1994). Meeting some neighbours. In J. van Eijck, & A. Visser (Eds.), *Logic and information flow*, (pp. 170–195). Cambridge: MIT Press.
29. Rott, H. (1989). Conditionals and theory change: Revisions expansions, and additions. *Synthese*, *81*, 91–113.
30. Scott-Kakures, D. (1994). On belief and the captivity of the will. *Philosophy and Phenomenological Research,54*, 77–103. [p. 83, to be checked.].
31. Segerberg, K. (1989). A note on an impossibility theorem of Gärdenfors. *Noûs*, *23*, 351–354.
32. Segerberg, K. (1995). Belief revision from the point of view of doxastic logic. *Logic Journal of the IGPL*, *3*, 535–553.
33. Segerberg, K. (1996). Three recipes for revision. *Theoria*, *62*, 62–73.
34. Segerberg, K. (1997). Proposal for a theory of belief revision along the lines of Lindström and Rabinowicz. *Fundamenta Informaticae*, *32*, 183–191.
35. Segerberg, K. (1999). Two traditions in the logic of belief: Bringing them together. In H. J. Ohlbach & U. Reyle (Eds.), *Logic, language and reasoning: Essays in honour of Dov Gabbay* (pp. 135–147). Dordrecht: Kluwer Academic Publishers.
36. Stalnaker, R. (1968). A theory of conditionals. In N. Rescher (Ed.), *Studies in logical theory. American philosophical quarterly monograph series* (Vol. 2). Oxford: Blackwell.
37. van Benthem, J. (1989). Semantic parallels in natural language and computation. InH.-D. Ebbinghaus, J. Fernandez-Prida, M. Garrido, D. Lascar, M. Rodrigues Artalejo *Logic Colloquium'87* (pp. 331–375). Amsterdam: North-Holland.
38. van Benthem, J. (1995). Logic and the flow of information. In *Proceedings of the 9th International Congress of Logic, Methodology and Philosophy of Science. Studies in Logic and the Foundations of Mathematics* (Vol. 134, pp. 693–724).
39. van Ditmarsch, H. (2005). Prolegomena to dynamic logic for belief revision,*Synthese (Knowledge, Rationality & Action)*, *147*, 229–275.
40. van Ditmarsch, H., van der Hoek, W., & Kooi, B. (2007). *Dynamic epistemic logic. Synthese Library*. Dordrecht: Springer.
41. Wansing, H. (2000). A reduction of doxastic logic to action logic. *Erkenntnis*, *53*, 267–283.
42. Wansing, H. (2006). Doxastic decisions, epistemic justification, and the logic of agency. *Philosophical Studies*, *128*, 201–227.

Segerberg on the Paradoxes of Introspective Belief Change

Sebastian Enqvist and Erik J. Olsson

Abstract The aim of the chapter is to provide a critical assessment of Krister Segerberg's solution to the problems of introspective belief change. We present three alternative ways in which the paradoxes may be avoided. The first is a solution due to Lindström and Rabinowicz, using a two-dimensional semantics for DDL. The second is found in a logic for belief change suggested by Bonanno, in which the operator for belief is replaced by a class of operators for belief, each supplied with a temporal index. The third solution consists in a logic for belief change due to van Benthem, founded on the method of Dynamic Epistemic Logic in which the dynamics is modelled by operations on entire models, rather than on some structure within the models. We argue that, while there are some differences between these approaches, there is a strong structural similarity between them, and they avoid the paradoxes of DDL in essentially the same way. Furthermore, this way of avoiding the paradoxes is both different from and, we think, more natural than Segerberg's own solution.

1 Introduction

Theories of rational belief change [1, 4, 5] are traditionally presented in a semi-formalized manner. While a formalized language is used to speak about the content of a state of belief, the theory of belief revision is, like most mathematical theories, presented in mathematical English rather than a formal language in the strict sense.

It is possible to formulate axioms of belief change, like the well-known AGM postulates [1], in a fully formalized language. This is the purpose of the socalled

S. Enqvist (✉), E. J. Olsson
Department of Philosophy, Lund University, Kungshuset, Lundagård, Lund 222 22, Sweden
e-mail: Sebastian.Enqvist@fil.lu.se

E. J. Olsson
e-mail: Erik_J.Olsson@fil.lu.se

R. Trypuz (ed.), *Krister Segerberg on Logic of Actions*,
Outstanding Contributions to Logic 1, DOI: 10.1007/978-94-007-7046-1_8,

Dynamic Doxastic Logic (henceforth DDL, or "full" DDL) developed by Krister Segerberg [10, 12], in which epistemic states are modelled using modal operators of belief in the style of Jaakko Hintikka's classic [7], and belief *changes* are modelled using dynamic operators reminiscent of those studied in propositional dynamic logic [6].

Reasoning about belief in a formal language has the advantage of added expressive strength. Rather than just speaking about beliefs about the external world, we can now also reason about *introspective* beliefs, i.e. beliefs that an agent has about her *own state of belief*. For instance, I can believe that the world is round, which presumably means that I don't believe it is flat. Suppose now that someone asks me whether I believe the Earth is round; I answer that I do believe it. In these circumstances I am apparently *aware* that I believe the Earth is round, that is, I *believe that I believe* that the world is round. In the same manner, I might be asked whether I believe the Earth is flat, and I answer that I do not believe that. In this case, I have revealed that I *believe that I do not believe* that the Earth is flat. If r stands for "the Earth is round" and f for "the Earth is flat", we can formalize these beliefs as

$$BBr$$

and

$$B\neg Bf$$

respectively.

In the case of DDL, where we have the capacity to speak about not only beliefs but also belief *change*, it turns out that this added expressive power comes with a price: given that we adopt the AGM postulate known as *Vacuity*, we arrive at some disturbing *paradoxes* of introspective belief change. These paradoxes are discussed at length by Sten Lindström and Wlodek Rabinowicz in [8], where a modification of the semantics of DDL is presented as a solution to the problem.

In this chapter, we present and criticize Krister Segerberg's own solution to this problem. We present three alternative ways that the paradoxes of introspective belief change may be avoided: the first is a solution due to Sten Lindström and Wlodek Rabinowicz, using a *two-dimensional* semantics for DDL. The second solution is found in a logic for belief change suggested by Giacomo Bonanno, in which the operator for belief is replaced by a *class* of operators for belief, each supplied with a temporal index [3]. The third solution we present is a logic for belief change due to Johan van Benthem [14], founded on the method of Dynamic Epistemic Logic where dynamics is modelled by operations on entire models, rather than some structure within the models. We shall argue that, while there are some differences between these approaches, there is a strong structural similarity between them, and the they avoid the paradoxes of DDL in essentially the same way. Furthermore, the way that these logics avoid the paradoxes is both different from and, we think, more natural than Segerberg's own solution.

Throughout the discussion we presuppose familiarity with the AGM model of belief revision, as well as the basics of modal logic.

2 DDL and the Paradoxes

We begin by introducing the system DDL and the paradoxes it gives rise to. Throughout the chapter, we work with a fixed, countably infinite supply of propositional variables *Prop*. The language of DDL is then defined in Backus-Naur form as follows, where $p \in Prop$:

$$\mathcal{L}_{DDL} : p \mid \neg\alpha \mid \alpha \vee \alpha \mid B\alpha \mid [*\alpha]\alpha$$

Classical connectives $\wedge, \rightarrow, \leftrightarrow$ are defined as usual. Informally, $B\alpha$ means "the agent believes α", and $[*\alpha]\beta$ means "after revision by α, it will be the case that β".

We now provide semantics for this language. Throughout the chapter, given a binary relation R over a set W and given an element $u \in W$, we use the notation

$$R(u) =_{df.} \{v \in W : uRv\}$$

The logic of revision inherent in the semantics will be rather minimal, since the details of belief revision are irrelevant to the problem we address and its solutions. All we shall require of revision in this semantics, and in the other semantics presented in the chapter, are the following conditions:

- after revision by α, the agent believes α
- revision by any consistent sentence results in a consistent belief state and
- Some semantic version of the *Vacuity* postulate holds.

We recall that, in the standard AGM framework for belief revision, the *Vacuity* postulate is:

$$\neg\alpha \notin K \Longrightarrow K * \alpha = Cn(K \cup \{\alpha\})$$

where Cn is the logical closure operator of the propositional logic underlying the epistemic states. This postulate says that if some input proposition is consistent with the agent's beliefs, then revision by that proposition amounts to simply adding the proposition to the initial stock of beliefs and forming the logical closure of the results; in other words, no information is *lost* in consistent revision.

Semantics for $\mathcal{L}_{DDL}$ is given as follows.

Definition 1 A *revision model* is a structure

$$\langle W, B, R^*, V \rangle$$

defined as follows: B is a binary relation over W, and $R^* : 2^W \rightarrow 2^{W\times W}$ is a function from subsets of W (sometimes called *propositions*) to relations over W. Furthermore we require that for each $X \subseteq W$, if $vR^*(X)w$ then

1. $B(w) \subseteq X$
2. if $X \neq \emptyset$ then $B(w) \neq \emptyset$

3. if $B(v) \cap X \neq \emptyset$ then $B(w) = B(v) \cap X$

Finally, $V : Prop \to 2^W$ is an evaluation function in the usual sense. A *pointed* revision model is a pair $(\mathfrak{A}, u)$ where $\mathfrak{A}$ is a revision model and $u \in W$.

The reader should note that the last item on the list in this definition is the obvious way to formulate the *Vacuity* postulate in the present framework. The truth definition for formulas of $\mathcal{L}_{DDL}$ in a pointed revision model is given as follows:

- $(\mathfrak{A}, u) \models p$ *iff* $u \in V(p)$
- standard clauses for Boolean connectives
- $(\mathfrak{A}, u) \models B\alpha$ *iff* $(\mathfrak{A}, v) \models \alpha$ for each v such that uBv
- $(\mathfrak{A}, u) \models [*\alpha]\beta$ *iff* $(\mathfrak{A}, v) \models \beta$ for each v such that $uR^*(\|\alpha\|)v$

Here, $\|\alpha\|$ denotes the set

$$\{w \in W : (\mathfrak{A}, w) \models \alpha\}$$

From this semantics we define the consequence relation $\models_{DDL}$ over $\mathcal{L}_{DDL}$ by setting, for all sets of formulas $\Gamma \cup \{\alpha\}$, $\Gamma \models_{DDL} \alpha$ *iff*

$$(\mathfrak{A}, u) \models \Gamma \Longrightarrow (\mathfrak{A}, u) \models \alpha$$

for any pointed revision model $(\mathfrak{A}, u)$. Here, $(\mathfrak{A}, u) \models \Gamma$ means that $(\mathfrak{A}, u) \models \beta$ for each $\beta \in \Gamma$.

We will need to be precise about what we mean by a logical system in this chapter. Formally, a *logic* will here be taken to be a pair $(\mathcal{L}, \models)$ where $\mathcal{L}$ is a set containing the set of variables *Prop* and $\models \subseteq 2^{\mathcal{L}} \times \mathcal{L}$. Thus, $(\mathcal{L}_{DDL}, \models_{DDL})$ is a logical system, which we denote by S_{DDL}.

To see why S_{DDL} is paradoxical, we ask the reader to verify that the following validity holds:

$$\models_{DDL} \neg B\neg\alpha \wedge B\beta \to [*\alpha]B\beta$$

and, furthermore, that we have the following validity:

$$\models_{DDL} [*\alpha]B\alpha$$

The former validity is called *Preservation* by Lindström and Rabinowicz, and the latter validity is called *Success*. The validity of *Preservation* is a direct consequence of the fact that the *Vacuity* postulate is built into the semantics. From *Preservation*, in turn, we derive the paradoxes: let α, β be any formulas. Then as an instance of *Preservation* we have

$$\models_{DDL} \neg B\neg\alpha \wedge B\neg B\alpha \to [*\alpha]B\neg B\alpha$$

On the other hand, from *Success* follows trivially by classical logic that:

$$\models_{DDL} \neg B\neg\alpha \wedge B\neg B\alpha \to [*\alpha]B\alpha$$

But clearly the operator $[*\alpha]$ is normal, so that we have

$$[*\alpha]B\alpha \wedge [*\alpha]B\neg B\alpha \vDash_{DDL} [*\alpha](B\alpha \wedge B\neg B\alpha)$$

By classical logic we can now derive:

$$\vDash_{DDL} \neg B\neg\alpha \wedge B\neg B\alpha \rightarrow [*\alpha](B\alpha \wedge B\neg B\alpha)$$

This is the formula deemed paradoxical by Lindström and Rabinowicz, and it would be hard to deny that it is quite bizarre. To see why, toss a coin, without looking at it when it lands. Presumably, given that the coin is fair, you now have no opinion at all on whether the coin landed heads or tails. Let α stand for the proposition that the coin landed heads. Since you have no opinion on whether the toss came out heads or tails, you do not believe that the coin did *not* land heads. That is, your current belief state satisfies the condition $\neg B\neg\alpha$. But you do not believe that the coin *did* land heads, and we think that you have the required powers of introspection to be aware of this fact. Thus, your current belief state also satisfies the condition $B\neg B\alpha$. But then, according to DDL, the condition $[*\alpha](B\alpha \wedge B\neg B\alpha)$ should also be true. This means that if you were to take a look at the coin and learn that it did in fact land heads, as a result you should believe that the coin landed heads, but at the same time you should *believe that you do not believe it*. Under perfectly ordinary circumstances, revision of beliefs has lead to a curious, or even incoherent, state of belief.

If we simply dropped the *Vacuity* postulate, then the problem would disappear. But for those who are strongly convinced of the validity of Vacuity, the more attractive route would be to try and retain some semantic version of the *Vacuity* postulate, while employing some strategy to avoid the paradoxes. In the following section, we present Segerberg's own strategy for doing so.

3 Segerberg's Solution

Segerberg treats the paradoxes of introspective belief change, which he refers to as "Moore problems", in a paper from 2006 [11]. In this paper, he proposes a solution based on Sorensen's notion of a *blindspot* from his 1988 book [13].

In Segerberg's terminology, an agent has a *Moore problem* (of rank 0) if $B(\phi \wedge \neg B\phi)$ or $B(\phi \wedge B\neg\phi)$ is true (in a certain situation and with respect to his beliefs). In the former case, the problem is said to be *acute*, in the latter *grave*. More generally, the agent has a Moore problem of rank n, where n is a nonnegative integer, if, for some formula ϕ, either $B^n(\phi \wedge \neg B\phi)$ or $B^n(\phi \wedge B\neg\phi)$, where B^n abbreviates

$$\underbrace{B \ldots B}_{n\ times}$$

Segerberg is very clear on the desirability of avoiding Moore problems:

> It is probably impossible to compile a complete list of all the ways in which a doxastic agent may be incoherent or exhibit some degree of inconsistency, but certainly an agent with a Moore problem of any rank is not perfect. Doxastically ambitious agents will stay clear of Moore problems as far as possible! ([11], p.96)

Segerberg's solution seems radical on first sight: he proposes to reject the assumption that the star operator correctly formalizes revision. Revision by ϕ is not to be formalized as $*\phi$ but rather as

$$\mathbf{R}\phi =_{df.} *(\phi \wedge B\phi)$$

As Segerberg points out, the Preservation and Success conditions are not affected by this definition, meaning that the derivations of the Moorean sentences are still valid inferences. Yet, the conclusions are no longer "an embarrassment":

> [...] for the fact that in a certain possible situation, a star change leads to a Moore problem is not embarrassing, however plausible the situation – why would one want to perform a star change anyway? ([11], p. 101).

What *would* be troublesome is if the corresponding sentences could be derived for revision, i.e. if we could derive

$$(\neg B\neg\phi \wedge B\neg B\phi) \rightarrow [\mathbf{R}\phi]B(\phi \wedge \neg B\phi)$$

and

$$(\neg B\neg\phi \wedge BB\neg\phi) \rightarrow [\mathbf{R}\phi]B(\phi \wedge B\neg\phi)$$

But these sentences are not derivable. Hence his new definition of revision avoids the Moore problems of rank 0. However, as Segerberg shows, some new problems crop up in their stead. Suppose ϕ is such that before revision by ϕ, $\neg B\neg(\phi \wedge B\phi)$ is true, and that, before revision, either $B\neg BB\phi$ or $BB\neg B\phi$ or $BBB\neg\phi$ is true. Then it follows, using Preservation and Success, that after revision by ϕ, on the new understanding of revision, at least one of $B(B\phi \wedge \neg BB\phi)$ or $BB(\phi \wedge \neg B\phi)$ or $BB(\phi \wedge B\neg\phi)$ is true. Thus the agent is confronted with a Moore problem of rank 1.

How can this situation be avoided? Segerberg's main idea is that the predicament can be avoided by making the problematic sets of sentences *inconsistent*, "for inconsistent sets describe (what according to the logic) are impossible situations, and it is of no concern that Moore problems arise in impossible situations" ([11], p. 100). In the present case, this strategy translates into finding a plausible underlying logic that makes each of the following sets inconsistent: $\{\neg B\neg(\phi \wedge B\phi), B\neg BB\phi\}$, $\{\neg B\neg(\phi \wedge B\phi), BB\neg B\phi\}$ and $\{\neg B\neg(\phi \wedge B\phi), BBB\neg\phi\}$. Segerberg notes that the weakest normal logic satisfying this condition is the normal extension of K by the following schemata:

(1A) $B\neg BB\phi \rightarrow B\neg(\phi \wedge B\phi)$
(1B) $BB\neg B\phi \rightarrow B\neg(\phi \wedge B\phi)$
(1C) $BBB\neg\phi \rightarrow B\neg(\phi \wedge B\phi)$

Segerberg shows that all three are derivable, for instance, in KD4 which "is a favorite with many doxastic logicians" ([11], p. 102). He then goes on to generalize this approach to Moore problems at rank n and of rank ω, showing that the problematic situations can be excluded by a reasonable choice of underlying doxastic logic. Finally, Segerberg connects his approach to Sorensen's concept of a blindspot by defining a *blindspot* as a sentence ϕ such that either ϕ is not entertainable or revision by it leads to an inconsistent state and showing that the following principle comes out as valid on his approach: revision by an entertainable proposition leads to a consistent doxastic state if and only if the sentence in question is not a blindspot. Since

$$[\mathbf{R}(\phi \wedge \neg B\phi)]B \perp$$

and

$$[\mathbf{R}(\phi \wedge B\neg\phi)]B \perp$$

are theorems in all logics recommended by Segerberg, in those logics the original Moore sentences $\phi \wedge \neg B\phi$ and $\phi \wedge B\neg\phi$ are blindspots.

This is certainly an impressive treatment of the Moore problems, especially considering the proposal, which we will grant, that the Moore problems arise in impossible situations where what is impossible or not is defined in a principled manner relative to logical frameworks that have an independent standing in the literature. Segerberg can hardly be accused of adhockery in that respect. However, Segerberg's strategy may still be ad hoc in another regard. Consider again Segerberg's new definition of revision by ϕ, i.e. $\mathbf{R}\phi =_{df.} *(\phi \wedge B\phi)$. First of all, it surely is less simple and striking than the old one. But second and more important, Segerberg does not give any independent motivation for his new definition of revision. Certainly, defining revision in this way does the job of providing a framework within which Moore problems can be avoided, but apart from this fact little speaks in favor of the new definition. And, one might ask, why should every revision by ϕ be, as it were, accompanied by a revision by $B\phi$? Suppose ϕ is an object level sentence such as "it is raining". Why should updating by "it is raining" involve updating by "I believe that it is raining"? Of course, it may often be the case that these two propositions are accommodated in one swoop, but it is less clear that it has to be that way. For certain kinds of introspective agents the new definition of revision may be fine. But what about agents that adopt beliefs routinely without reflecting on those beliefs at the time of adoption? So there is still a sense in which Segerberg's approach is, at least to some extent, ad hoc.

Another way of putting it is that Segerberg gives but a partial solution to the Moore problems, a solution that takes care of those problems for reflective agents (by which we mean agents for which an update by ϕ is always accompanied by an update by $B\phi$), but that he has little to say about the prospects of dealing with those problems from the perspective of unreflective agents.

In the light of these remarks, it is natural to ask whether there is some other way to treat the paradoxes of full DDL. In the next section, we present *three* different logics for belief revision that can be found in the literature, each of which can be shown to avoid the paradoxes of introspective belief change. We shall begin by introducing each variant formally, and then discuss what we believe is the common structure behind each approach.

4 Three Alternative Solutions

4.1 First Solution: Two-dimensional DDL

The first solution we consider is due to Sten Lindström and Wlodek Rabinowicz. The approach suggested by Lindström and Rabinowicz is to adopt a modified, two-dimensional semantics for DDL in which formulas are no longer evaluated at single worlds, but rather at *pairs* of worlds. Here, the idea is that in an evaluation point (u, v), the left component u serves as a *point of reference*, while v functions as a *point of evaluation*. In addition, rather than an accessibility relation B over the universe of a model, a class of accessibility relations is used, one relative to each world in the universe. Each accessibility relation B_v, where $v \in W$, represents the agent's beliefs *about* the point of reference v.

Formally, the definition of a model from the system S_{DDL} is modified as follows:
Definition 2 A *two-dimensional revision model* is a structure

$$\langle W, \{B_u\}_{u \in W}, \{R^*_u\}_{u \in W}, V\rangle$$

defined as follows: for each $u \in W$, B_u is a binary relation over W. For each $u \in W$ $R^*_u : 2^W \rightarrow 2^{W \times W}$ is a function from propositions to relations between possible worlds, such that for each $X \subseteq W$, if $vR^*_u(X)w$ then

1. $B_u(w) \subseteq X$
2. if $X \neq \emptyset$ then $B_u(w) \neq \emptyset$
3. if $B_u(v) \cap X \neq \emptyset$ then $B_u(w) = B_u(v) \cap X$

A *pointed* two-dimensional revision model is a triple $(\mathfrak{A}, u, v)$ where $\mathfrak{A}$ is a two-dimensional revision model and $u, v \in W$.

To speak about these models, we use an extension of the language $\mathcal{L}_{DDL}$. Formally, the language $\mathcal{L}_{2D}$ is given by the following definition where, again, $p \in Prop$:

$$\mathcal{L}_{2D} : p \mid \neg\alpha \mid \alpha \vee \alpha \mid B\alpha \mid [*\alpha]\alpha \mid \dagger\, \alpha$$

The truth definition for formulas is given as follows:

- $(\mathfrak{A}, u, v) \vDash p$ *iff* $v \in V(p)$
- standard Boolean clauses
- $(\mathfrak{A}, u, v) \vDash B\alpha$ *iff* $(\mathfrak{A}, u, w) \vDash \alpha$ for each w such that vB_uw
- $(\mathfrak{A}, u, v) \vDash [*\alpha]\beta$ *iff* $(\mathfrak{A}, u, w) \vDash \beta$ for each w such that $vR^*_u(\|\alpha\|_u)w$
- $(\mathfrak{A}, u, v) \vDash \dagger\, \alpha$ *iff* $(\mathfrak{A}, v, v) \vDash \alpha$

The consequence relation $\models_{2D}$ is defined from this semantics as before, and we let S_{2D} denote the logical system $(\mathcal{L}_{2D}, \models_{2D})$. The new component of the language of this logic is the †-operator, although the meanings of the modal operators present in $\mathcal{L}_{DDL}$ have changed. This operator has the effect of making the current point of evaluation the current point of reference as well. The formula $\dagger\ \alpha$ can informally be interpreted as saying that α is true *about* the present point of evaluation.

How does this avoid the paradoxes of DDL? As noted by Lindström and Rabinowicz, for each formula α the paradoxical formula of S_{DDL} which we recall was:

$$\neg B\neg\alpha \wedge B\neg B\alpha \rightarrow [*\alpha](B\alpha \wedge B\neg B\alpha)$$

is still valid in this semantics. *But*, as we said, the meaning of the connectives has changed. Consider an evaluation point (u, u) in a model $\mathfrak{A}$ (here, the point of reference and the point of evaluation is the same). Suppose that

$$(\mathfrak{A}, u, u) \models \neg B\neg\alpha \wedge B\neg B\alpha$$

so that the agent does not disbelieve α at (u, u) and she believes that she does not believe α. According to the validity of the previously deemed paradoxical formula, we must have

$$(\mathfrak{A}, u, u) \models [*\alpha](B\alpha \wedge B\neg B\alpha)$$

This means that

$$(\mathfrak{A}, u, v) \models B\alpha \wedge B\neg B\alpha$$

But this is not incoherent, since the righthand conjunct here means that at the *present* point of evaluation (v), the agent believes that the condition $\neg B\alpha$ holds for the point of evaluation *prior* to revision by α (u). By contrast, the formula

$$\neg B\neg\alpha \wedge B\neg B\alpha \rightarrow [*\alpha]\ \dagger\ \ (B\alpha \wedge B\neg B\alpha)$$

is paradoxical, since the beliefs described as resulting after revision by α are now beliefs about the point of evaluation after revision, not the one prior to it. But this formula is *not* valid in S_{2D}. Thus, the system S_{2D} is free of this paradoxical feature of S_{DDL}.

4.2 Second Solution: Temporally Indexed Beliefs

The second solution, present in Giacomo Bonanno's "simple" modal logic for belief revision, consists in letting a model represent an ω-ordered discrete time-line and use belief operators supplied with indexes representing points in the succession of time. Each move forward in time corresponds to an act of revision by some new piece of information. The expression $B_n\alpha$, where $n \in \omega$, says that the agent believes α *at* the nth point in the succession of time.

Formally, the language $\mathcal{L}_{Temp}$ for Bonanno's system is defined as follows, where n is any natural number:

$$\mathcal{L}_{Temp} : p \mid \neg\alpha \mid \alpha \vee \alpha \mid B_n\alpha \mid I_n\alpha$$

The new operator I_n is interpreted so that $I_n\alpha$ means, informally, that α is the last piece of information received at the nth point in time, or that α it is the input of the revision that results in the belief state at time n.

Semantics for $\mathcal{L}_{Temp}$ is given by the following definitions:

Definition 3 A *temporal belief model* is a structure

$$\langle W, \{B_n\}_{n\in\omega}, \{I_n\}_{n\in\omega}, V\rangle$$

such that:

1. $B_n(u) \subseteq I_n(u)$
2. if $I_n(u) \neq \emptyset$ then $B_n(u) \neq \emptyset$
3. if $B_n(u) \cap I_{n+1}(u) \neq \emptyset$ then $B_{n+1}(u) = B_n(u) \cap I_{n+1}(u)$

A *pointed* temporal belief model is a pair $(\mathfrak{A}, u)$ where $\mathfrak{A}$ is a temporal belief model and $u \in W$.

Truth definitions of formulas in a pointed temporal belief model are:

- $(\mathfrak{A}, u) \models p$ *iff* $u \in V(p)$
- standard clauses for Boolean connectives
- $(\mathfrak{A}, u) \models B_n\alpha$ *iff* $(\mathfrak{A}, v) \models \alpha$ for each v such that uB_nv
- $(\mathfrak{A}, u) \models I_n\alpha$ *iff* $I_n(u) = \|\alpha\|$

Here, as before, $\|\alpha\| = \{v \in W : (\mathfrak{A}, v) \models \alpha\}$. From this semantics we define the consequence relation $\models_{Temp}$ as before, and we define S_{Temp} to be the logical system $(\mathcal{L}_{Temp}, \models_{Temp})$. To get a grasp of how the language works, consider the syntactic form of the *Success* postulate in this system; this is captured by the validity

$$\models_{Temp} \; I_n\alpha \rightarrow B_n\alpha$$

This says that if the belief state at time n is the result of the revision of a prior belief state by α, then α is believed at time n.

The way that the paradoxes of DDL are avoided in this system is simple. We do have a form of the *Preservation* formula valid in S_{Temp}, namely:

$$\models_{Temp} \; \neg B_n\neg\alpha \wedge B_n\beta \rightarrow (I_{n+1}\alpha \rightarrow B_{n+1}\beta)$$

That is, if α is consistent with the agent's beliefs at time n, and the next revision at time $n+1$ has the input formula α, then everything the agent believes at time n she believes at time $n+1$ also. But we cannot derive any paradoxes from this formula, since belief operators come with temporal indexes. To see this, let's try to derive a paradox in the same manner as before. Consider any formula α. As an instance of the previous validity we get

$$\models_{Temp} \neg B_n \neg \alpha \wedge B_n \neg B_n \alpha \rightarrow (I_{n+1}\alpha \rightarrow B_{n+1} \neg B_n \alpha)$$

From this, using the S_{Temp}-version of *Success* above together with classical logic, we can derive

$$\models_{Temp} \neg B_n \neg \alpha \wedge B_n \neg B_n \alpha \rightarrow (I_{n+1}\alpha \rightarrow B_{n+1}\alpha \wedge B_{n+1} \neg B_n \alpha)$$

The informal content of this formula looks a lot like that of the paradoxical formula we derived in S_{DDL}. But of course, it is not paradoxical. It says that if α is consistent with the agents beliefs at time n, and the agent is aware that she does not believe α at time n, then after revision by α at time $n+1$, she believes α and *believes that she did not believe it* at time n. By contrast, the formula

$$\models_{Temp} \neg B_n \neg \alpha \wedge B_n \neg B_n \alpha \rightarrow (I_{n+1}\alpha \rightarrow B_{n+1}\alpha \wedge B_{n+1} \neg B_{n+1} \alpha)$$

is paradoxical but not valid.

4.3 Third Solution: The DEL Method

The third alternative way of getting out of the paradoxes of DDL we consider in this chapter is found in Johan van Benthem's dynamic logic for belief revision. The system is built on a method used in Dynamic Epistemic Logic (DEL), a framework for studying dynamics of multi-agent epistemic scenarios. The relevant aspect of DEL here is not the multi-agent feature, but rather the way in which dynamics is modelled semantically and reasoned about syntactically.

The method can be described in this way: to model changes of some type of *states*, one should first develop a *static base language* for reasoning about the states and provide it with a semantics, i.e. define *models* for it. Then, changes of states are modelled as operations on models for the static base language, which is extended with dynamic operators to reason about these operations. If the static base logic is rich enough in expressive strength, then it is often possible to translate any dynamic formula into a semantically equivalent formula of the static base logic via socalled *reduction axioms*.

For brevity we will present the static and the dynamic part of van Benthem's system all in one swoop. For a gentler presentation of the system we refer to [14]. For an introduction to DEL, see [15].

We begin by defining the models for the static part of the logic:

Definition 4 A *conditional belief model* is a structure

$$\langle W, \{\sigma_u\}_{u \in W}, V \rangle$$

defined as follows. For each $u \in W$, $\sigma_u : 2^W \to 2^W$ is called a *selection function* and satisfies the following properties:

1. $\sigma_u(X) \subseteq X$
2. $X \neq \emptyset$ implies $\sigma_u(X) \neq \emptyset$
3. if $\sigma_u(X) \cap Y \neq \emptyset$ then $\sigma_u(X \cap Y) = \sigma_u(X) \cap Y$

V is a valuation function as before, and pointed conditional belief models are defined as before.

The central component of these models is the set of selection functions, which can be thought of as encoding the *conditional beliefs* of the agent. The intuitive explanation is that, for each proposition $X \subseteq W$, the set $\sigma_u(X)$ consists of the "most plausible" worlds from the agent's point of view at the world u. *Actual beliefs* of the agent are defined as beliefs conditional on the trivial proposition. That is, the set of possible worlds compatible with the agent's actual beliefs at the world u is the set $\sigma_u(W)$. The semantics presented in [14] is a bit different from the presentation here and uses orders of plausibility rather than selection functions, but this is irrelevant to the current issue.

To model dynamics of the models, we will use an operation that van Benthem calls *lexicographic upgrade*. Or, rather, we use a version of this operation, adapted to the semantics here based on selection functions which is slightly more general than van Benthem's semantics. Consider a proposition $X \subseteq W$ in a model $\mathfrak{A}$; we want a way to *revise* the selection function u at a world u by X. This is provided by the following definition:

Definition 5

$$\sigma_u^{\Uparrow X}(Y) = \begin{cases} \sigma_u(Y) \cap X & \text{if } \sigma_u(Y) \cap X \neq \emptyset \\ \sigma_u(X) & \text{if } \sigma_u(Y) \cap X = \emptyset \end{cases}$$

Given a conditional belief model $\mathfrak{A} = \langle W, \{\sigma_u\}_{u \in W}, V \rangle$ and $X \subseteq W$, we define the revised model $\mathfrak{A} \Uparrow X$ by

$$\mathfrak{A} \Uparrow X =_{df.} \langle W, \{\sigma_u^{\Uparrow X}\}_{u \in W}, V \rangle$$

We leave it to the reader to check that this is always a well defined conditional belief model. Notice that we have

$$\sigma_u(W) \cap X \neq \emptyset \quad \Longrightarrow \quad \sigma_u^{\Uparrow X}(W) = \sigma_u(W) \cap X$$

With the definition of actual beliefs as beliefs conditional on the trivial proposition, this property can be seen as a semantic formulation of the *Vacuity* postulate.

Turning to the syntactic side of the system, we define the language $\mathcal{L}_{DEL}$:

$$\mathcal{L}_{DEL} : p \mid \neg\alpha \mid \alpha \vee \alpha \mid B(\alpha \mid \alpha) \mid A\alpha \mid [\Uparrow \alpha]\alpha$$

Here, $B(\alpha \mid \beta)$ says that α is believed conditionally on β, and $[\Uparrow \alpha]\beta$ says that the condition β will hold after revision by α. The operator A is the *global necessity* operator (see [2]). $A\alpha$ means that α holds in all possible worlds of a model; it can be thought of as expressing *logical* necessity. A *static* formula of $\mathcal{L}_{DEL}$ is a formula without any occurrences of the dynamic operators. We define an operator for actual beliefs by $B\alpha =_{df.} B(\alpha \mid p \vee \neg p)$, where p is a propositional variable.

Truth definitions for formulas in a pointed model are:

- $(\mathfrak{A}, u) \models p$ *iff* $u \in V(p)$
- standard clauses for Boolean connectives
- $(\mathfrak{A}, u) \models B(\alpha \mid \beta)$ *iff* $\sigma_u(\|\beta\|) \subseteq \|\alpha\|$
- $(\mathfrak{A}, u) \models A\alpha$ *iff* $(\mathfrak{A}, v) \models \alpha$ for each $v \in W$
- $(\mathfrak{A}, u) \models [\Uparrow \alpha]\beta$ *iff* $(\mathfrak{A} \Uparrow \|\alpha\|, u) \models \beta$

The consequence relation $\models_{DEL}$ and the system S_{DEL} are now defined as before.

It is instructive to look at the reduction axioms for S_{DEL}. These are as follows (we follow van Benthem's axiomatization almost without any modification):

$\Uparrow$1: $[\Uparrow\gamma]\, q \leftrightarrow q$, *q a propositional atom*
$\Uparrow$2: $[\Uparrow \gamma]\neg\alpha \leftrightarrow \neg[\Uparrow \gamma]\alpha$
$\Uparrow$3: $[\Uparrow \gamma](\alpha \vee \beta) \leftrightarrow ([\Uparrow \gamma]\alpha \vee [\Uparrow \gamma]\beta)$
$\Uparrow$4: $[\Uparrow \gamma]A\alpha \leftrightarrow A[\Uparrow \gamma]\alpha$
$\Uparrow$5: $[\Uparrow \gamma]B(\alpha \mid \beta) \leftrightarrow$
$\leftrightarrow (E(\gamma \wedge [\Uparrow \gamma]\beta) \wedge B([\Uparrow \gamma]\beta \rightarrow [\Uparrow \gamma]\alpha \mid \gamma)\vee$
$\vee(\neg E(\gamma \wedge [\Uparrow \gamma]\beta) \wedge B([\Uparrow \gamma]\alpha \mid [\Uparrow \gamma]\beta))$

The reader can check that these axioms are sound in the semantics for S_{DEL}. These axioms can be thought of as providing recursive *definitions* of the truth conditions of dynamic formulas in terms of static formulas. Together with a suitable set of complete axioms for the static fragment of S_{DEL} and a rule for substitution of equivalents, they provide a complete axiomatization of S_{DEL}. To prove this result, one exploits the soundness of the reduction axioms to prove the following proposition as a lemma. The proof is excluded here.

Proposition 1 *There exists a function $\rho : \mathcal{L}_{DEL} \rightarrow \mathcal{L}_{DEL}$ such that for each formula $\alpha \in \mathcal{L}_{DEL}$, the formula $\rho(\alpha)$ is a static formula and, furthermore, for each pointed conditional belief model* $(\mathfrak{A}, u)$,

$$(\mathfrak{A}, u) \models \alpha \Longleftrightarrow (\mathfrak{A}, u) \models \rho(\alpha)$$

To get a feel for the system, let us look at some validities. Here, p, q are two propositional variables and $\perp$ is any tautological contradiction. First, revision by p leads the agent to believe p:

$$\models_{DEL} [\Uparrow p]Bp$$

Second, revision by a consistent sentence results in a consistent belief state:

$$\models_{DEL} \neg A\neg p \rightarrow [\Uparrow p]\neg B \perp$$

What about *Preservation*? We do indeed have a form of the *Preservation* principle valid in this system:

$$(i) \quad \models_{DEL} \quad \neg B\neg p \wedge Bq \rightarrow [\Uparrow p]Bq$$

Now, if validity in S_{DEL} were closed under substitutions for propositional variables (as is the case in most logics), then obviously we could derive a paradox in the same manner as in S_{DDL}. However, this is not the case, and it is in fact this feature of S_{DEL} that makes it non-paradoxical. In particular, the following substition instance of (*i*):

$$(ii) \quad \neg B\neg\alpha \wedge B\neg B\alpha \rightarrow [\Uparrow \alpha]B\neg B\alpha$$

is invalid. This is exactly the formula that would be required to derive a paradox in S_{DEL}. By contrast, the following formula is valid:

$$(iii) \quad \neg B\neg\alpha \wedge B\neg B\alpha \rightarrow B(\neg B\alpha \mid \alpha)$$

Now, what does this formula say? it says that, if $\neg B\neg\alpha$ and $B\neg B\alpha$ are true at some world in a model, than from the point of view of the agent in that world, $\neg B\alpha$ will be *true in the most plausible worlds where* α *is true*. Now, the most plausible worlds where α is true, *prior* to revision by α, are exactly those worlds that are compatible with the agent's actual beliefs *after* revision. But since the truth values of formulas involving beliefs will change at *every* world in a model through the act of revision by α, it does *not* follow from this that $\neg B\alpha$ will be true at all worlds that are compatible with the agent's beliefs after the revision. This is why (*ii*) fails to be valid.

5 Comparison of the Solutions

5.1 What the Three Approaches Have in Common

The three solutions we have just presented are, we think, essentially one and the same. All three of them are based on making a distinction between two different perspectives, the state of affairs *prior* to revision and the one *after* revision. This is perhaps clearest in Lindström and Rabinowicz's system; it is embodied quite explicitly in the distinction between the point of *reference* (typically being the state *prior* to revision) and the point of *evaluation* (typically the state *after* revision).

But we see the same distinction very clearly in Bonanno's temporal system of belief revision, although in a different form. Here, it turns up through the temporally indexed belief operators. In particular, in the formula

$$\neg B_n \neg \alpha \wedge B_n \neg B_n \alpha \rightarrow (I_{n+1}\alpha \rightarrow B_{n+1}\alpha \wedge B_{n+1}\neg B_n \alpha)$$

which is provable in S_{Temp}, the state prior to revision corresponds to the time-point represented by the number n, and the state after revision corresponds to $n+1$.

It is perhaps a bit less obvious how van Benthem's system S_{DEL} fits into this picture, but we think it does. We postpone the task of explaining this to Sect. 5.3, where we will be better prepared to do so. The fact that the same solution to the paradoxes can be found in three seemingly rather different frameworks for belief revision counts, we think, as evidence in favor of this approach as a particularly natural way to resolve the paradoxes. Think of it in analogy with the case of various definitions of computable functions, for example in terms of recursive functions or in terms of Turing machines. The wellknown fact that these definitions turn out to be equivalent speaks strongly in favor of the idea that they all capture the pre-formal notion of computability in a natural way. The present situation, where three different formalisms can be seen to resolve the paradoxes of DDL in the same way, is similar.

To strengthen these claims, we shall establish a formal correspondence between the three logical systems S_{2D}, S_{Temp} and S_{DEL}. More specifically, we shall show that the system S_{2D} can in a precise sense be *interpreted* in S_{Temp}, and in turn, S_{DEL} can be interpreted in S_{2D}. From this will follow that S_{DEL} can be interpreted in S_{Temp} also. These interpretation results will help to clarify the deeper connection that we think exists between the different systems, particularly with respect to how they handle the paradoxes of DDL. In order to formally prove these claims, we need to make precise what it means that a logical system can be interpreted in another. This is captured by the following definition.

Definition 6 Given logical systems $S_1 = (\mathcal{L}_1, \models_1)$ and $S_2 = (\mathcal{L}_2, \models_2)$, an *interpretation* of S_1 in S_2 is any function $F : \mathcal{L}_1 \rightarrow \mathcal{L}_2$ such that $F(p) = p$ for any $p \in Prop$. The interpretation F is said to be a *sound* interpretation of S_1 if, for all sets of formulas $\Gamma \cup \{\alpha\} \subseteq \mathcal{L}_1$, we have

$$\Gamma \models_1 \alpha \Longrightarrow F(\Gamma) \models_2 F(\alpha)$$

So a sound interpretation of a logical system S_1 in S_2 is a translation that maps sentences of S_1 to sentences of S_2 in a way that preserves logically valid consequences. Just like when we interpret a logical system in a semantics, we might consider the question of whether an interpretation is *complete* in addition to being sound. We could say that an interpretation F of S_1 in S_2 is *sound and complete* if, for all $\Gamma \cup \{\alpha\} \subseteq \mathcal{L}_1$, we have

$$\Gamma \models_1 \alpha \Longleftrightarrow F(\Gamma) \models_2 F(\alpha)$$

The issue of completeness will not concern us in this chapter. Rather, we will focus on soundness. Completeness is a welcome property of any interpretation of a logical system, but soundness is absolutely crucial. If an interpretation is not sound, it is doubtful whether it can be called a proper interpretation at all. Also, as we shall see in the next section, the soundness property of the interpretations we provide is enough to make the correspondence quite enlightening.

5.2 Interpreting S_{2D} in S_{Temp}

Our first result is that, in the sense of Definition 6, there exists a sound interpretation F of S_{2D} in S_{Temp}. First, by induction over the complexity of formulas, we define the class of functions

$$\tau_{n,m} : \mathcal{L}_{2D} \rightarrow \mathcal{L}_{Temp}$$

where $n, m \in \omega$ as follows:

1. $\tau_{n,m}(p) = p$
2. $\tau_{n,m}(\neg\alpha) = \neg\tau_{n,m}(\alpha)$
3. $\tau_{n,m}(\alpha \vee \beta) = \tau_{n,m}(\alpha) \vee \tau_{n,m}(\beta)$
4. $\tau_{n,m}(B\alpha) = B_m\tau_{n,n}(\alpha)$
5. $\tau_{n,m}([*\alpha]\beta) = I_{m+1}\tau_{n,n}(\alpha) \rightarrow \tau_{n,m+1}(\beta)$
6. $\tau_{n,m}(\dagger\, \alpha) = \tau_{m,m}(\alpha)$

We then set $F =_{df.} \tau_{0,0}$. For this mapping F we have the following result, proved in Appendix A.1:

Theorem 1 *The translation F constitutes a sound interpretation of the system S_{2D} in the system S_{Temp}.*

To see how this interpretation relates the two systems to each other, let us consider the interpretation of the formula

$$\neg B\neg p \wedge B\neg Bp \rightarrow [*p](Bp \wedge B\neg Bp)$$

given by F. This formula is an instance of the paradoxical schema we derived in S_{DDL}. As we mentioned earlier, the formula is valid in S_{2D} also, and therefore by soundness its interpretation under F is valid in S_{Temp}. Now, Lindström and Rabinowicz claim that this formula is *not* paradoxical under the interpretation given to it in two-dimensional semantics. Then, its interpretation under F had better not be paradoxical either!

Indeed it is not. For the formula

$$(1) \quad F(\neg B\neg p \wedge B\neg Bp \rightarrow [*p](Bp \wedge B\neg Bp))$$

is identical to

$$(2) \quad (\neg B_0 \neg p \wedge \neg B_0 \neg B_0 p) \rightarrow (I_1 p \rightarrow B_1 p \wedge B_1 \neg B_0 p)$$

which is perfectly fine. We can derive this as follows: first, recalling that $F = \tau_{0,0}$ and using translation clauses for Boolean connectives, atomic formulas and B, the formula (1) becomes

$$\neg B_0 p \wedge B_0 \neg B_0 p \rightarrow \tau_{0,0}([*p](Bp \wedge B \neg Bp))$$

Carrying out the translation further, we get

$$\neg B_0 p \wedge B_0 \neg B_0 p \rightarrow (I_1 p \rightarrow \tau_{0,1}(Bp) \wedge \tau_{0,1}(B \neg Bp))$$

Applying the function $\tau_{0,1}$ to its arguments here, we get

$$\neg B_0 p \wedge B_0 \neg B_0 p \rightarrow (I_1 p \rightarrow B_1 p \wedge B_1 \tau_{0,0}(\neg Bp))$$

But $\tau_{0,0}(\neg Bp) = \neg B_0 p$, so now we arrive at (2) as desired.

By contrast, let's look at the translation of the formula

$$\neg B \neg p \wedge B \neg Bp \rightarrow [*p] \dagger (Bp \wedge B \neg Bp)$$

which *is* paradoxical. Applying the translation F to this formula, instead of (2) we will get the formula

$$(3) \quad (\neg B_0 \neg p \wedge \neg B_0 \neg B_0 p) \rightarrow (I_1 p \rightarrow B_1 p \wedge B_1 \neg B_1 p)$$

which is indeed paradoxical, and not valid in S_{Temp}. To see what happens here, we can carry out the translation step by step and check that we eventually arrive at the formula

$$\neg B_0 p \wedge B_0 \neg B_0 p \rightarrow (I_1 p \rightarrow \tau_{0,1}(\dagger(Bp \wedge B \neg Bp))$$

Applying the translation clause for $\dagger$, this becomes

$$\neg B_0 p \wedge B_0 \neg B_0 p \rightarrow (I_1 p \rightarrow \tau_{1,1}(Bp \wedge B \neg Bp)$$

But

$$\tau_{1,1}(Bp \wedge B \neg Bp) = B_1 p \wedge B_1 \tau_{1,1}(\neg Bp) = B_1 p \wedge B_1 \neg B_1 p$$

and so we arrive at (3).

5.3 Interpreting S_{DEL} in S_{2D}

We now show how to interpret S_{DEL} in S_{2D}. The central observation here is that, since we know that there is a translation ρ that sends every formula α to an equivalent *static* formula $\rho(\alpha)$, it suffices to interpret the static formulas of S_{DEL} in order to get a full interpretation of S_{DEL} in S_{2D}.

Formally, we define the mapping τ as follows:

1. $\tau(p) = p$
2. $\tau(\neg\alpha) = \neg\tau(\alpha)$
3. $\tau(\alpha \vee \beta) = \tau(\alpha) \vee \tau(\beta)$
4. $\tau(A\alpha) = [*\neg\tau(\alpha)]B\perp$
5. $\tau(B(\alpha \mid \beta)) = [*\tau(\beta)]B\tau(\alpha)$

Clearly, every *static* formula of $\mathcal{L}_{DEL}$ receives an interpretation by this mapping. Letting ρ be any translation function as specified in Proposition 1, we define an interpretation $F : \mathcal{L}_{DEL} \to \mathcal{L}_{2D}$ by setting

$$F(\alpha) = \tau(\rho(\alpha))$$

for each $\alpha \in \mathcal{L}_{DEL}$. As before, we have the following soundness result for this interpretation:

Theorem 2 *The translation F constitutes a sound interpretation of the system S_{DEL} in the system S_{2D}.*

The proof of this result is in Appendix A.2 Furthermore, the composition of two sound interpretations (whenever it is well defined) is obviously a sound interpretation. So by the existence of a sound interpretation of S_{DEL} in S_{2D} and a sound interpretation of S_{2D} in S_{Temp}, we get:

Corollary 1 *There exists a sound interpretation of S_{DEL} in S_{Temp}.*

An interesting aspect of the translation F presented in this section is that, clearly, for any $\mathcal{L}_{DEL}$-formula α, the corresponding $\mathcal{L}_{2D}$-formula $F(\alpha)$ will never contain any occurrence of the operator $\dagger$. Our analysis of this state of affairs is this: consider a formula

$$(A) \quad B(\alpha \mid \beta)$$

contrasted with

$$(B) \quad [\Uparrow \beta]B\alpha$$

What is the difference in meaning between these two formulas? We think it can be understood in terms of Lindström and Rabinowicz's distinction between point of *evaluation* and point of *reference*. Both (A) and (B) can be thought of as expressing that the formula α is believed after revision by β, but the formula α has different meaning in the two cases. In (A), the point of reference is held fixed, while in (B), the formula α is evaluated against a different point of reference than β. However, since the interpretation F takes a detour through the static fragment of the system S_{DEL}, in which no formulas of the form (B) occur, it makes sense that the operator † does not occur in the interpretation of any formulas: it has exactly the effect of changing the point of reference.

Thus, by extracting this insight from our interpretation of S_{DEL} in S_{2D}, we have managed to show how S_{DEL} also fits into the picture we described earlier. The distinction between a perspective corresponding to the states of affairs before and after revision, respectively, is mirrored in S_{DEL} by the distinction between expressions of the form (A) and (B). Expressions of the first kind describe our revised beliefs about the state prior to revision, and expressions of the second kind describe our revised beliefs about the state of affairs after revision. Really, we do not have three different solutions; we have three different logical systems, each of which solves the problem with full DDL in one and the same way.

6 Discussion

We have argued that the systems S_{2D}, S_{Temp} and S_{DEL} all solve the problems of full DDL by distinguishing between two perspectives, expressed most explicitly in Lindström and Rabinowicz's two-dimensional approach. Given this, it is striking to find that Segerberg himself has suggested a two-dimensional approach to resolve another well-known paradox, namely Fitch's paradox (in a paper from 1994 with Rabinowicz [9]). Given the obvious similarities between Fitch's paradox and the paradoxes of full DDL, and given that Segerberg argued for a two-dimensional approach to the former, one would have expected him to embrace a two-dimensional approach to the latter as well. Thus it is surprising that Segerberg instead bases his solution on Sorensen's notion of a blindspot, which is essentially unrelated to the two-dimensional approach.

In fact it is not only surprising but, we think, it is questionable from a methodological point of view. Given the affinities between these paradoxes it would be desirable to treat them in a uniform fashion. Thus, for Segerberg, who is associated with two-dimensional semantics and the blindspot approach, the following uniform approaches suggests themselves:

(1) Treating both paradoxes as involving blindspots
(2) Treating both paradoxes in a two-dimensional semantics

By contrast, the following would seem less attractive from a systematic perspective:

(3) Treating Fitch's paradox in a two-dimensional semantics and Moore's paradox as involving blindspots
(4) Treating Fitch's paradox as involving blindspots and Moore's paradox in a two-dimensional semantics

And yet, as we saw, Segerberg's published responses to the paradoxes correspond to option (3), a suboptimal strategy from a systematic perspective. Finally, the result of the present article suggests that option (2) is, in a sense, considerably more plausible than meets the eye. More precisely, (2) is but a specific variant of a more general approach:

(2′) Treating both paradoxes as arising from failure to distinguish between different perspectives

As we have argued, two-dimensional DDL, Bonanno's temporal system and van Benthem's DEL-style system are all instances of (2′). They all resolve the paradoxes by distinguishing between two different perspectives, in the two-dimensional case the point of reference and the point of evaluation, in Bonanno's case the time before and after revision, and in van Benthem's logic between conditional beliefs and beliefs after revision. Thus, the main competitor to the blindspot approach, as things must look from Segerberg's point of view, is more widely adopted, and thus has a stronger standing in the research community, than the apparent diversity could lead one to believe. Perhaps even more important is the fact that the main competitor—the perspectival strategy—is a very natural way of dealing with the problems, or else researchers with widely different starting points would not have converged on it. Furthermore, to reconnect with our discussion of Segerberg's own solution, the perspectival strategy is perfectly compatible with the traditional view that we often revise simply by α rather than by $\alpha \wedge B\alpha$, and are quite rational in doing so. Not only does this accord better with our pre-theoretical conceptions of things (at least those of the present authors), but it means that this strategy works for reflective agents and unreflective agents alike. Unlike the perspectival strategy, Segerberg's solution is dependent on the assumption that the agent in question is reflective. Thus, unless an independent motivation is provided for not taking unreflective agents into consideration, the perspectival strategy stands out as the more general solution.

Appendix: Proofs of Main Results

A.1 Proof of Theorem 1

The proof is based on constructing models for S_{2D} out of models for S_{Temp}, in the following manner:

Definition 7 Given a temporal belief model $\mathfrak{A} = \langle W, \{B_n\}_{n\in\omega}, \{I_n\}_{n\in\omega}, V\rangle$, we define the two-dimensional revision model

$$\mathfrak{A}_{2D} = \langle W^*, \{B_u\}_{u\in W}, \{R^*_u\}_{u\in W}, V^*\rangle$$

as follows. We set

$$W^* = \{(u, n) : u \in W \;\&\; n \in \omega\}$$

For all $(u, n), (v, m), (w, k) \in W^*$, we set $(u, n)B_{(v,m)}(w, k)$ iff $uB_n w$ and $k = m$. We set $(u, n)R^*_{(v,m)}(X)(w, k)$ iff

- $u = w$,
- $k = n + 1$ and
- $Z = I_k(u)$, where $Z = \{t \in W : (t, m) \in X\}$

Finally, we set $(u, n) \in V^*(p)$ iff $u \in V(p)$.

The construction is sound by the following proposition:

Proposition 2 *$\mathfrak{A}_{2D}$ is a two-dimensional revision model, for any temporal belief model $\mathfrak{A}$.*

Proof We need to check that, for each $X \subseteq W^*$, if $(u, m)R^*_{(v,n)}(X)(w, k)$ then

1. $B_{(v,n)}(w, k) \subseteq X$
2. if $X \neq \emptyset$ then $B_{(v,n)}(w, k) \neq \emptyset$
3. if $B_{(v,n)}(u, m) \cap X \neq \emptyset$ then $B_{(v,n)}(w, k) = B_{(v,n)}(u, m) \cap X$

So suppose $(u, m)R^*_{(v,n)}(X)(w, k)$. Then $u = w$, $k = m + 1$ and

$$I_{m+1}(u) = \{t \in W : (t, n) \in X\}$$

Now, since

$$B_{m+1}(u) \subseteq I_{m+1}(u)$$

item (1) follows easily by definition of the relation $B_{(v,n)}$: for if $(u, m + 1)B_{v,n}(w', k')$, then $k' = n$ and $uB_{m+1}w'$, so $w' \in I_{m+1}(u)$, so $(w', n) = (w', k') \in X$.

For (2), note that $X \neq \emptyset$ implies $I_{m+1}(u) \neq \emptyset$, so $B_{m+1}(u) \neq \emptyset$. Pick w' such that $uB_{m+1}w'$. Then $(u, m + 1)B_{v,n}(w', n)$ so $B_{(v,n)}(u, m + 1) \neq \emptyset$.

Lastly, for (3), suppose $B_{(v,n)}(u, m) \cap X \neq \emptyset$. Let $(w', k') \in B_{(v,n)}(u, m) \cap X \neq \emptyset$; then $k' = n$ and $uB_m w'$. Since $(w', n) \in X$, $w' \in I_{m+1}(u)$. So

$$B_m(u) \cap I_{m+1}(u) \neq \emptyset$$

and hence

$$B_{m+1}(u) = B_m(u) \cap I_{m+1}(u)$$

This means that

$$B_{(v,n)}(u, m + 1) = B_{(v,n)}(u, m) \cap X$$

To see this, suppose $(u, m + 1)B_{(v,n)}(s, i)$. Then $i = n$, and $uB_{m+1}s$. But then $uB_m s$ and $s \in I_{m+1}(u)$. So $(u, m)B_{(v,n)}(s, n)$ and $(s, n) \in X$.

Conversely, suppose $(u, m + 1)B_{(v,n)}(s, i)$ and $(s, i) \in X$. By definition of $B_{v,n}$, $i = n$. So $(s, n) \in X$ and therefore $s \in I_{m+1}(u)$. Furthermore, $uB_{m+1}s$. So $s \in B_m(u) \cap$

$I_{m+1}(u)$, hence $s \in B_{m+1}(u)$. By definition this means that $(u, m+1)B_{(v,n)}(s, n)$, i.e. $(u, m+1)B_{(v,n)}(s, i)$ as required.

We now define a mapping G from pointed temporal belief models to pointed two-dimensional revision models by setting

$$G(\mathfrak{A}, u) =_{df.} (\mathfrak{A}_{2D}, (u, 0), (u, 0))$$

for each pointed temporal revision model $(\mathfrak{A}, u)$. We then have the following result, which gives the key to the soundness result for F:

Lemma 1 *For any pointed temporal model* $(\mathfrak{A}, u)$ *and any* $\mathcal{L}_{2D}$*-formula* α*, we have*

$$(\mathfrak{A}, u) \models F(\alpha) \Longleftrightarrow G(\mathfrak{A}, u) \models \alpha$$

Proof We show, for any formula α, that for each world u in the universe of $\mathfrak{A}$, we have both

$$(1) \quad (\mathfrak{A}, u) \models \tau_{n,m}(\alpha) \Longrightarrow \forall v \in W : (\mathfrak{A}_{2D}, (v, n), (u, m)) \models \alpha$$

and

$$(2) \quad (\mathfrak{A}, u) \not\models \tau_{n,m}(\alpha) \Longrightarrow \forall v \in W : (\mathfrak{A}_{2D}, (v, n), (u, m)) \not\models \alpha$$

for all $v \in W$. From (1) and (2) together it follows that

$$(\mathfrak{A}, u) \models \tau_{0,0}(\alpha) \Longleftrightarrow (\mathfrak{A}_{2D}, (u, 0), (u, 0)) \models \alpha$$

i.e.

$$(\mathfrak{A}, u) \models F(\alpha) \Longleftrightarrow G(\mathfrak{A}, u) \models \alpha$$

as desired.

The proof goes by induction on the length of α. For propositional variables, both clauses are immediate, and the steps for Boolean connectives are easy.

Step for B: Suppose $(\mathfrak{A}, u) \models \tau_{n,m}(B\alpha)$, i.e. $(\mathfrak{A}, u) \models B_m\tau_{n,n}(\alpha)$. Let $v \in W$ and let (w, k) be such that $(u, m)B_{v,n}(w, k)$. Then by definition uB_mw and $k = n$, so we must have $(\mathfrak{A}, w) \models \tau_{n,n}(\alpha)$ and by clause (1) of the IH we get $(\mathfrak{A}_{2D}, (v, n), (w, n)) \models \alpha$. So we must have $(\mathfrak{A}_{2D}, (v, n), (u, m)) \models B\alpha$. This shows that

$$(1) \quad (\mathfrak{A}, u) \models \tau_{n,m}(B\alpha) \Longrightarrow \forall v \in W : (\mathfrak{A}_{2D}, (v, n), (u, m)) \models B\alpha$$

Suppose that $(\mathfrak{A}, u) \not\models \tau_{n,m}(B\alpha)$, i.e. $(\mathfrak{A}, u) \not\models B_m\tau_{n,n}(\alpha)$. Then there exists $w \in W$ such that uB_mw and $(\mathfrak{A}, v) \not\models \tau_{n,n}\alpha$. Let $v \in W$; then we have $(u, m)B_{(v,n)}(w, n)$ and by clause (2) of IH we have $(\mathfrak{A}_{2D}, (v, n), (w, n)) \not\models \alpha$, hence $(\mathfrak{A}_{2D}, (v, n), (u, m)) \not\models B\alpha$. We have shown that

$$(2)\quad (\mathfrak{A}, u) \not\models \tau_{n,m}(B\alpha) \Longrightarrow \forall v \in W : (\mathfrak{A}_{2D}, (v, n), (u, m)) \not\models B\alpha$$

as required.

Step for $*$: Suppose $(\mathfrak{A}, u) \models \tau_{n,m}([*\alpha]\beta)$, i.e.

$$(\mathfrak{A}, u) \models I_{m+1}\tau_{n,n}(\alpha) \rightarrow \tau_{n,m+1}(\beta)$$

We note that by the IH we have, for each $v \in W$,

$$(\ddagger)\quad \left\|\tau_{n,n}(\alpha)\right\|_{\mathfrak{A}} = \{t \in W : (t, n) \in \|\alpha\|_{(v,n)}\}$$

Suppose for $v \in W$ that $(u, m)R^*_{(v,n)}(\|\alpha\|_{(v,n)})(w, k)$. Then $k = m+1$. Furthermore, by definition and by ($\ddagger$) we get

$$I_{m+1}(u) = \{t \in W : (t, n) \in \|\alpha\|_{(v,n)}\} = \left\|\tau_{n,n}(\alpha)\right\|_{\mathfrak{A}}$$

So $(\mathfrak{A}, u) \models I_{m+1}(\tau_{n,n}(\alpha))$. Thus, we get $(\mathfrak{A}, u) \models \tau_{n,m+1}(\beta)$. By clause (1) of the IH, this gives $(\mathfrak{A}_{2D}, (v, n), (w, m+1)) \models \beta$, i.e. $(\mathfrak{A}_{2D}, (v, n), (w, k)) \models \beta$. So $(\mathfrak{A}_{2D}, (v, n), (u, m)) \models [*\alpha]\beta$. We have thus shown

$$(1)\quad (\mathfrak{A}, u) \models \tau_{n,m}([*\alpha]\beta) \Longrightarrow \forall v \in W : (\mathfrak{A}_{2D}, (v, n), (u, m)) \models [*\alpha]\beta$$

Suppose $(\mathfrak{A}, u) \not\models \tau_{n,m}([*\alpha]\beta)$, i.e. $(\mathfrak{A}, u) \models I_{m+1}\tau_{n,n}(\alpha)$ but $(\mathfrak{A}, u) \not\models \tau_{n,m+1}(\beta)$. Pick $v \in W$. Using ($\ddagger$) we obtain

$$I_{m+1}(u) = \left\|\tau_{n,n}(\alpha)\right\|_{\mathfrak{A}} = \{t \in W : (t, n) \in \|\alpha\|_{(v,n)}\}$$

From this we can conclude that $(u, m)R^*_{(v,n)}(\|\alpha\|_{(v,n)})(u, m+1)$. Furthermore, by clause (2) of the IH we have $(\mathfrak{A}_{2D}, (v, n), (u, m+1) \not\models \beta)$, so $(\mathfrak{A}_{2D}, (v, n), (u, m) \not\models [*\alpha]\beta)$. We have thus shown

$$(2)\quad (\mathfrak{A}, u) \not\models \tau_{n,m}([*\alpha]\beta) \Longrightarrow \forall v \in W : (\mathfrak{A}_{2D}, (v, n), (u, m)) \not\models [*\alpha]\beta$$

as required.

Step for $\dagger$: Given that the IH holds for α, suppose first that we have $(\mathfrak{A}, u) \models \tau_{n,m}(\dagger\, \alpha)$, i.e. $(\mathfrak{A}, u) \models \tau_{m,m}(\alpha)$. Then we have by clause (1) of IH: for all $v \in W$, $(\mathfrak{A}_{2D}, (v, m), (u, m)) \models \alpha$. In particular, $(\mathfrak{A}_{2D}, (u, m), (u, m)) \models \alpha$. This means that, for all $v \in W$, $(\mathfrak{A}_{2D}, (v, n), (u, m)) \models \dagger\, \alpha$. We have established:

$$(1)\quad (\mathfrak{A}, u) \models \tau_{n,m}(\dagger\, \alpha) \Longrightarrow \forall v \in W : (\mathfrak{A}_{2D}, (v, n), (u, m)) \models \dagger\, \alpha$$

On the other hand, suppose $(\mathfrak{A}, u) \not\models \tau_{n,m} \dagger\, \alpha$, i.e. $(\mathfrak{A}, u) \not\models \tau_{m,m}(\alpha)$. Then we have by clause (2) of IH: for all $v \in W$, $(\mathfrak{A}_{2D}, (v, m), (u, m)) \not\models \alpha$. In particular, $(\mathfrak{A}_{2D}, (u, m), (u, m)) \not\models \alpha$. This means that, for all $v \in W$, $(\mathfrak{A}_{2D}, (v, n), (u, m)) \not\models \dagger\, \alpha$. We have established:

$$(2)\quad (\mathfrak{A}, u) \nvDash \tau_{n,m}(\dagger\, \alpha) \Longrightarrow \forall v \in W : (\mathfrak{A}_{2D}, (v, n), (u, m)) \nvDash \dagger\, \alpha$$

This ends the proof.

We now prove Theorem 1 as follows: suppose $F(\Gamma) \nvDash_{Temp} F(\alpha)$. Then there is a pointed temporal belief model $(\mathfrak{A}, u)$ such that $(\mathfrak{A}, u) \vDash F(\Gamma)$ but $(\mathfrak{A}, u) \nvDash F(\alpha)$. By the previous theorem, $G(\mathfrak{A}, u) \vDash \Gamma$ but $G(\mathfrak{A}, u) \nvDash \alpha$. Hence $\Gamma \nvDash_{2D} \alpha$. This ends the proof of the theorem.

A.2 Proof of Theorem 2

We use the same strategy as in the previous section:

Definition 8 Given a two-dimensional model $\mathfrak{A}$ and a world v in the universe of $\mathfrak{A}$, we define the conditional belief model

$$\mathfrak{A}_{DEL}[v] = \langle W^*, \{\sigma_u\}_{u \in W^*}, V^* \rangle$$

as follows: we set $W^* = W$ and $V^* = V$. For each $u \in W$ and $X \subseteq W$, we set

$$\sigma_u(X) = \{w \in W : \exists p \in W[uR^*_v(X)p \text{ and } pB_v w]\}$$

It is easily checked that $\mathfrak{A}_{DEL}[v]$ is a conditional belief model. We define the mapping G from pointed two-dimensional revision models to pointed conditional belief models by setting $G(\mathfrak{A}, v, u) = (\mathfrak{A}_{DEL}[v], u)$ for a pointed two-dimensional revision model $(\mathfrak{A}, v, u)$. We have the following result:

Lemma 2 *For any pointed two-dimensional model* $(\mathfrak{A}, u, v)$ *and any* <u>*static*</u> $\mathcal{L}_{DEL}$-*formula* α *we have*

$$(\mathfrak{A}, u, v) \vDash \tau(\alpha) \Longleftrightarrow G(\mathfrak{A}, u, v) \vDash \alpha$$

Proof By induction over the length of static formulas we show that, for all $v \in W$ we have

$$(\mathfrak{A}, u, v) \vDash \tau(\alpha) \Longleftrightarrow (\mathfrak{A}_{DEL}[u], v) \vDash \alpha$$

The steps for atomic formulas and Boolean connectives are trivial.

Step for A: suppose $(\mathfrak{A}, u, v) \vDash \tau(A\alpha)$, i.e. $(\mathfrak{A}, u, v) \vDash [*\neg\tau(\alpha)]B\bot$. By seriality of $R^*_u(\|\neg\tau(\alpha)\|^{\mathfrak{A}}_u)$ there must be some w such that $vR^*_u(\|\neg\tau(\alpha)\|^{\mathfrak{A}}_u)w$. Furthermore, clearly we have $B_u(w) = \emptyset$, and this means that $\|\neg\tau(\alpha)\|^{\mathfrak{A}}_u = \emptyset$. Hence $\|\tau(\alpha)\|^{\mathfrak{A}}_u = W = W^*$. By the IH, $\|\alpha\|_{\mathfrak{A}_{DEL}[u]} = W^*$, and so we have $(\mathfrak{A}_{DEL}[u], v) \vDash A\alpha$ as required.

Conversely, suppose $(\mathfrak{A}, u, v) \nvDash \tau(A\alpha)$, i.e. $(\mathfrak{A}, u, v) \nvDash [*\neg\tau(\alpha)]B\bot$. Then there is some w such that $vR^*_u(\|\neg\tau(\alpha)\|^{\mathfrak{A}}_u)w$ and $B_u(w) \neq \emptyset$. Hence there is some s such that $wB_u s$. By the definition of a two-dimensional model, $s \in \|\neg\tau(\alpha)\|$ i.e.

$(\mathfrak{A}, u, s) \models \neg\tau(\alpha)$. Hence $(\mathfrak{A}, u, s) \not\models \tau(\alpha)$, and by the IH $(\mathfrak{A}_{DEL}[u], s) \not\models \alpha$. Hence $(\mathfrak{A}_{DEL}[u], v) \not\models A\alpha$ as required.

Step for B: suppose $(\mathfrak{A}, u, v) \models \tau(B(\alpha \mid \beta))$, i.e.

$$(\mathfrak{A}, u, v) \models [*\tau(\beta)]B\tau(\alpha)$$

Suppose $w \in \sigma_v(\|\beta\|_{\mathfrak{A}_{DEL}[u]})$. By the IH this means that $w \in \sigma_v(\|\tau(\beta)\|_u^{\mathfrak{A}})$, so there is some s such that $vR_u^*(\|\alpha\|_u^{\mathfrak{A}})s$ and sB_uw. Since $(\mathfrak{A}, u, v) \models [*\tau(\beta)]B\tau(\alpha)$ we have $(\mathfrak{A}, u, s) \models B\tau(\alpha)$ so $(\mathfrak{A}, u, w) \models \tau(\alpha)$. By IH we get $(\mathfrak{A}_{DEL}[u], w) \models \alpha$. We have thus shown that $(\mathfrak{A}, u, v) \models B(\alpha \mid \beta)$ as required.

Conversely, suppose that $(\mathfrak{A}, u, v) \not\models \tau(B(\alpha \mid \beta))$, i.e.

$$(\mathfrak{A}, u, v) \not\models [*\tau(\beta)]B\tau(\alpha)$$

Then there is some s such that $vR_u^*(\|\tau(\beta)\|_u^{\mathfrak{A}})s$ and $(\mathfrak{A}, u, s) \not\models B\tau(\alpha)$. This means that for some w we have sB_uw and $(\mathfrak{A}, u, w) \not\models \tau(\alpha)$. By the IH we have $vR_u^*(\|\beta\|_{\mathfrak{A}_{DEL}[u]})s$, and thus we have $w \in \sigma_v(\|\beta\|_{\mathfrak{A}_{DEL}[u]})$. Furthermore, by the IH again, we have $(\mathfrak{A}_{DEL}[u], w) \not\models \alpha$. Thus $(\mathfrak{A}_{DEL}[u], v) \not\models B(\alpha \mid \beta)$ as required.

Using the fundamental property of the translation ρ used in the construction of F, this lemma immediately entails:

Corollary 2 *For any pointed two-dimensional model* $(\mathfrak{A}, u, v)$ *and any* $\mathcal{L}_{DEL}$*-formula* α *we have*

$$(\mathfrak{A}, u, v) \models F(\alpha) \iff G(\mathfrak{A}, u, v) \models \alpha$$

From this result, we can prove Theorem 2 just like we proved Theorem 1.

References

1. Alchourrón, C. E., Gärdenfors, P., & Makinson, D. (1985). On the logic of theory change: Partial meet contraction and revision functions. *Journal of Symbolic Logic*, *50*, 510–530.
2. Blackburn, P., de Rijke, M., & Venema, Y. (2001). *Modal logic*. Cambridge: Cambridge University Press.
3. Bonanno, G. (2005). A simple modal logic for belief revision. *Synthese*, *147*, 193–228.
4. Gärdenfors, P. (1988). *Knowledge in flux: Modeling the dynamics of epistemic states*. Cambridge, MA: MIT Press.
5. Hansson, S.-O. (1999). *A textbook of belief dynamics: Theory change and database updating*. Dordrecht: Kluwer Academic.
6. Harel, D., Kozen, D., & Tiuryn, J. (2000). *Dynamic logic*. Cambridge: MIT Press.
7. Hintikka, J. (1962). *Knowledge and belief: An introduction to the logic of the two notions*. Ithaca: Cornell University Press.
8. Lindström, S., & Rabinowicz, W. (1999). DDL unlimited: Dynamic doxastic logic for introspective agents. *Erkenntnis*, *50*, 353–385.
9. Rabinowicz, W., & Segerberg, K. (1994). Actual truth, possible knowledge. *Topoi*, *13*, 101–115.

10. Segerberg, K. (1998). Irrevocable belief revision in dynamic doxastic logic. *Notre Dame Journal of Formal Logic*, *39*, 287–306.
11. Segerberg, K. (2006). Moore problems in full dynamic doxastic logic. In J. Malinowski, & A. Pietruszczak (Eds.), *Poznan studies in the philosophy of the sciences and the humanities, Essays in logic and ontology* (pp. 95–110). Amsterdam: Rodopi.
12. Segerberg, K., & Leitgeb, H. (2007). Dynamic doxastic logic—why, how and where to? *Synthese*, *155*, 167–190.
13. Sorensen, R. A. (1988). *Blindspots*. Oxford: Clarendon Press.
14. van Benthem, J. (2007). Dynamic logic for belief revision. *Journal of Applied Non-Classical Logics*, *17*, 129–155.
15. van Ditmarsch, H. P., van der Hoek, P., & Kooi, B. P. (2005). *Dynamic epistemic logic*. Dordrecht: Springer.

Equivalent Beliefs in Dynamic Doxastic Logic

Robert Goldblatt

Abstract Two propositions may be regarded as doxastically equivalent if revision of an agent's beliefs to adopt either has the same effect on the agent's belief state. We enrich the language of dynamic doxastic logic with formulas expressing this notion of equivalence, and provide it with a formal semantics. A finitary proof system is then defined and shown to be sound and complete for this semantics.

1 Introduction

When should two propositions be regarded as equivalent as adopted beliefs? In a theory of belief revision, we will understand this notion of *doxastic equivalence* as follows: ϕ and ψ are equivalent if revision of an agent's set of beliefs to include ϕ has exactly the same effect as revision of that belief set to include ψ. Our interest is in exploring formal logics that represent this notion in their object language, by allowing formation of formulas with syntax $\phi \bowtie \psi$, expressing 'ϕ is doxastically equivalent to ψ'.[1]

But what should we understand by 'has exactly the same effect'? We answer that in the context of the approach to *dynamic doxastic logic* (DDL) for belief revision that has been developed by Krister Segerberg in [11–14] and other papers.[2] This uses multi-modal logics that are designed to formalise reasoning about the beliefs of an agent. These logics have normal modalities of the form $[*\phi]$, generating formulas of type $[*\phi]\theta$ that can be read 'after revision of the agent's beliefs by ϕ, it must be

R. Goldblatt (✉)
School of Mathematics, Statistics and Operations Research,
Victoria University of Wellington, Kelburn Parade, 6012 Wellington, NZ
e-mail: rob.goldblatt@msor.vuw.ac.nz

[1] $\phi \bowtie \psi$ could conveniently be pronounced 'ϕ tie ψ', from the LaTeX control word `\bowtie` for the symbol $\bowtie$.

[2] An introduction to the modal logic of belief revision appears in [10], and a review of DDL in [9].

R. Trypuz (ed.), *Krister Segerberg on Logic of Actions*, 179
Outstanding Contributions to Logic 1, DOI: 10.1007/978-94-007-7046-1_9,

the case that θ'. The dual formula $\langle *\phi \rangle\theta$ can be read, 'after revision by ϕ, it may be that θ'. There are also normal modalities **B** for belief and **K** for 'commitment'. $\mathbf{B}\theta$ expresses that the agent believes θ, while $\mathbf{K}\theta$ asserts that θ is a 'hard-core' belief that the agent is committed to and is not prepared to revise. We follow the syntax of [14] in allowing $\mathbf{B}\theta$ and $\mathbf{K}\theta$ to be well-formed only when θ is a pure Boolean formula, whereas $[*\phi]\theta$ is well-formed when ϕ is pure Boolean and θ is *any* formula, one that may contain (iterations of) modalities.

A typical Kripkean relation semantics for the modalities $[*\phi]$ would assign to each a binary relation $R[\![\phi]\!]$ on a set S. The members of S may be thought of as *belief states* of an agent. Intuitively, a pair (s, t) belongs to $R[\![\phi]\!]$ if the agent may enter belief state t from state s after revising their beliefs to adopt ϕ. There may be more than one such accessible 'result state' compatible with revision by ϕ, so in general $R[\![\phi]\!]$ is a relation that is not a function.

We use such doxastic accessibility relations to interpret the equivalence formulas $\phi \bowtie \psi$, by declaring such a formula to be true in state s precisely when

$$\text{for all belief states t,}\quad (s, t) \in R[\![\phi]\!] \text{ iff } (s, t) \in R[\![\psi]\!]. \tag{1}$$

So $\phi \bowtie \psi$ asserts that revision by ϕ or by ψ leads to exactly the same alternative belief states. This is a *local* notion of equivalence, in that it is tied to a particular initial state s. Global equivalence would mean that $\phi \bowtie \psi$ is true at all states, which amounts to having $R[\![\phi]\!] = R[\![\psi]\!]$.

This chapter shows that there is a finitary axiomatisation of the systems produced by adding $\bowtie$ with the above interpretation to certain dynamic doxastic logics. The postulates for $\bowtie$ that are required are the axiom

$$\phi \bowtie \psi \to ([*\phi]\theta \leftrightarrow [*\psi]\theta);$$

and the inference rule

$$\frac{[*\phi]p \leftrightarrow [*\psi]p}{\phi \bowtie \psi},\quad \text{if the variable p does not occur in } \phi \text{ or } \psi;$$

along with variants of this rule in which its premiss and conclusion are embedded in other formulas (see Fig. 1 in Sect. 3).

The models of [14] have, in addition to S and R, a set U whose members are thought of as possible worlds, about which the agent may hold beliefs. Certain subsets of U are designated as being *propositions*. Each member of S is a 'selection function', a type of function that assigns to each proposition P a 'theory' representing the set of propositions that the agent comes to believe after revising their beliefs to include P. A selection function can be thought of as embodying the agent's overall disposition to respond to new information. A model has a truth relation $f, u \models \theta$, specifying when θ is true at a pair consisting of a selection function f and a world $u \in U$. A pure Boolean formula ϕ defines a proposition $[\![\phi]\!] \subseteq U$, with $f, u \models \phi$ iff $u \in [\![\phi]\!]$.

Axioms

(TF)	all truth-functional tautologies
($\Box$)	$\Box(\theta \to \omega) \to (\Box\theta \to \Box\omega)$, for each modality $\Box \in \{\mathbf{B}, \mathbf{K}, [*\phi]\}$.
(KB)	$\mathbf{K}\phi \to \mathbf{B}\phi$
($*$2)	$[*\phi]\mathbf{B}\phi$
($*$3)	$[*\top]\mathbf{B}\phi \to \mathbf{B}\phi$
($*$4)	$\mathbf{b}\top \to (\mathbf{B}\phi \to [*\top]\mathbf{B}\phi)$
($*$5)	$\mathbf{b}\top \to (\mathbf{k}\phi \to \langle *\phi\rangle\mathbf{b}\top)$
($*$6)	$\mathbf{K}(\phi \leftrightarrow \psi) \to ([*\phi]\mathbf{B}\chi \leftrightarrow [*\psi]\mathbf{B}\chi)$
($*$7)	$[*(\phi \wedge \psi)]\mathbf{B}\chi \to [*\phi]\mathbf{B}(\psi \to \chi)$
($*$8)	$\langle *\phi\rangle\mathbf{b}\psi \to ([*\phi]\mathbf{B}(\psi \to \chi) \to [*(\phi \wedge \psi)]\mathbf{B}\chi)$
($*$FB)	$\langle *\phi\rangle\mathbf{B}\psi \to [*\phi]\mathbf{B}\psi$
(K$*$)	$\mathbf{K}\psi \to [*\phi]\mathbf{K}\psi$
(BK)	$\mathbf{B}\bot \to \mathbf{K}\bot$
($\bowtie$)	$\phi \bowtie \psi \to ([*\phi]\theta \leftrightarrow [*\psi]\theta)$

Rules

(MP) $\dfrac{\theta, \theta \to \omega}{\omega}$

($\Box$N) $\dfrac{\theta}{\Box\theta}$, for $\Box \in \{\mathbf{B}, \mathbf{K}, [*\phi]\}$ ($\Box$-NECESSITATION)

(CR) $\dfrac{\phi \leftrightarrow \psi}{[*\phi]\theta \leftrightarrow [*\psi]\theta}$ (CONGRUENCE RULE)

($\bowtie$R) $\dfrac{\rho([*\phi]p \leftrightarrow [*\psi]p)}{\rho(\phi \bowtie \psi)}$, if the variable p does not occur in ϕ, ψ or the template ρ.

Fig. 1 Axioms and inference rules

Here we take a more abstract approach in which S can be any set, with each member $s \in S$ being assigned a selection function f^s, allowing the possibility that distinct members of S (belief states) are assigned the same selection function. Thus we may have $s \neq t$ but $f^s = f^t$. This provides flexibility in constructing models, and we will produce (in Sect. 3) a series of small examples that effectively differentiate a number of logics and their properties. Our models also have a function $\mathsf{ws} : S \to U$, with $\mathsf{ws}(s)$ being thought of as the *world state* corresponding to the belief state s. This makes it possible to introduce a simpler truth relation $s \models \theta$, specifying when θ is true at belief state s. For pure Boolean ϕ we have $s \models \phi$ iff $\mathsf{ws}(s) \in [\![\phi]\!]$.

The minimal logic we study, which we call L_{K}, is characterised by models in which ws is surjective, i.e. the image of ws is the whole of U (every possible world is the world state of some belief state). The $\bowtie$-free fragments of logics in general have a canonical model in which ws is surjective. But this condition is stronger than is strictly needed: it suffices that the image of ws is topologically dense in U, under the topology generated by the propositions. To provide every logic having $\bowtie$ with a characteristic canonical model we need to admit models having only this weaker topological condition.

The axiomatisation of the minimal logic L_K is in some respects weaker than that of [14]. We have left out the axioms

$$\begin{array}{ll} (*\mathrm{D}) & [*\phi]\theta \to \langle *\phi\rangle\theta \\ (*\mathrm{X}) & \psi \leftrightarrow [*\phi]\psi \\ (*\mathrm{K}) & \mathbf{K}\psi \leftrightarrow [*\phi]\mathbf{K}\psi. \end{array}$$

These can be consistently added to L_K (even simultaneously). But each of them is inconsistent with the formula $\neg\mathbf{B}\bot$ which holds of the belief state of a *rational* agent, one who does not believe a contradiction. Moreover, any logic containing (∗K) allows a direct derivation of $\mathbf{B}\bot$, somewhat limiting its interest. Our logic L_K does not include $\neg\mathbf{B}\bot$, but it can be consistently added.

On the other hand, we include the axiom

(K∗) $\mathbf{K}\psi \to [*\phi]\mathbf{K}\psi$

that weakens (∗K), and which appears to capture the essence of a hard-core belief as being one that cannot be revised. We also show that the scheme $\psi \to [*\phi]\psi$ can be consistently added, resulting in logics characterised by models satisfying

$$(s, t) \in R[\![\phi]\!] \quad \text{implies} \quad \mathsf{ws}(s) = \mathsf{ws}(t).$$

Moreover, $\psi \to [*\phi]\psi$ is consistent with $\neg\mathbf{B}\bot$.

The scheme (∗D) is equivalent to $\langle *\phi\rangle\top$. The obstacle to its inclusion is that any logic containing $\neg\mathbf{B}\bot$ must have $\neg\langle *\bot\rangle\top$ as a theorem. But we can use the equivalence connective $\bowtie$ to exclude contradictory formulas, and consider the weaker scheme

$$\neg(\phi \bowtie \bot) \to \langle *\phi\rangle\top. \tag{2}$$

This makes the plausible assertion about rational belief that revision by ϕ is possible provided that ϕ is not equivalent to a contradiction. The logic obtained by adding $\neg\mathbf{B}\bot$ and (2) to L_K is consistent. This is explained in Sect. 7, where we deal with all these issues about axiomatisation.

It is worth noting that the $\bowtie$ concept is not special to DDL. It could be added to any multi-modal logic. Given an indexed set $\{[\alpha] : \alpha \in I\}$ of normal modalities, interpreted by a set $\{R[\![\alpha]\!] : \alpha \in I\}$ of binary relations, we can extend the language by adding formulas $\alpha \bowtie \beta$ for all $\alpha, \beta \in I$, and define $\alpha \bowtie \beta$ to be true at a point s iff

$$\text{for all } t, \quad (s, t) \in R[\![\alpha]\!] \text{ iff } (s, t) \in R[\![\beta]\!].$$

A significant example is *dynamic program logic* [7], where I is a set of programs, and $R[\![\alpha]\!]$ is thought of as the set of input/output pairs of states of program α. Then $\alpha \bowtie \beta$ expresses the natural notion of equivalence of programs as meaning that execution of either program in a given input state induces the same possible output states.

It turns out that in that computational context, $\bowtie$ is a very powerful notion. Elsewhere [6] we have shown that addition of $\bowtie$ to the basic program logic PDL produces a system whose set of valid formulas is not recursively enumerable, and so cannot have a finitary axiomatisation. In fact this holds for any variant of PDL whose class of programs is closed under compositions of programs and formation of WHILE- DO commands. But for DDL, where the modalities $[*\phi]$ are indexed by the rather simpler class of Boolean propositional formulas, a finitary axiomatisation of logics with $\bowtie$ is possible, as we now proceed to show.

2 Syntax and Semantics

This section sets out the formal language and semantics that we use. A good deal of the notation and terminology is adapted from [14].

We take as given some denumerable set of propositional variables, for which the letters p, q are used. From these, *pure Boolean formulas* are constructed by the Boolean connectives, say taking $\to$ and the constant $\bot$ (Falsum) as primitive, and introducing $\wedge$, $\vee$, $\neg$, $\leftrightarrow$ by the usual abbreviations. The letters ϕ, ψ, χ will always denote pure Boolean formulas.

We use θ and ω for arbitrary formulas. These are generated from the propositional variables by the Boolean connectives and the specifications:

- If ϕ is pure Boolean and θ is any formula, then $\mathbf{B}\phi$, $\mathbf{K}\phi$ and $[*\phi]\theta$ are formulas.
- If ϕ and ψ are pure Boolean, then $\phi \bowtie \psi$ is a formula.

Further abbreviations are introduced by writing $\top$ for $\neg\bot$, $\mathbf{b}\phi$ for $\neg\mathbf{B}\neg\phi$, $\mathbf{k}\phi$ for $\neg\mathbf{K}\neg\phi$, and $\langle*\phi\rangle\theta$ for $\neg[*\phi]\neg\theta$.

A *Boolean structure* $(U, Prop)$ comprises a set U and a non-empty collection *Prop* of subsets of U that is closed under binary intersections $X \cap Y$ and complements $-X$, hence under binary unions $X \cup Y$ and Boolean implications $(-X) \cup Y$. So *Prop* is a Boolean subalgebra of the powerset algebra of U. The members of *Prop* are called the *propositions* of the structure. This is in accord with the view of U as a set of possible worlds, with a proposition being identified with the set of worlds in which it is true.[3] Members of U may be thought of as different possible states of the world about which an agent may hold various beliefs.

We make use of the topology on U generated by *Prop*. Since $U \in Prop$ and *Prop* is closed under binary intersections, *Prop* is a *base* for this topology, so every open subset of U is a union of propositions. Since *Prop* is closed under complements, every proposition is also closed, and every closed subset of U is an intersection of propositions. Hence a closed set can be viewed as representing a *theory*, in the sense of a set of propositions, i.e. the theory is identified with the set of worlds in which all of its propositions are true.

---

[3] The members of *Prop* are sometimes called the *admissible* propositions of the structure, to distinguish them from other subsets of U. See [5].

The topological *closure* of a set $X \subseteq U$ will be denoted $\mathbf{C}X$. This is the intersection of all closed supersets of X, and hence the smallest closed superset.

A *valuation* on a Boolean structure is a map $p \mapsto [\![p]\!]$ assigning to each propositional variable p a proposition $[\![p]\!] \in \mathit{Prop}$. This extends inductively to assign a proposition $[\![\phi]\!]$ to each pure Boolean ϕ in the usual way:

$$[\![\bot]\!] = \emptyset, \ [\![\phi \to \psi]\!] = (U - [\![\phi]\!]) \cup [\![\psi]\!].$$

Hence $[\![\phi \wedge \psi]\!] = [\![\phi]\!] \cap [\![\psi]\!]$, $[\![\phi \vee \psi]\!] = [\![\phi]\!] \cup [\![\psi]\!]$, and $[\![\top]\!] = U$.

The belief state of an agent is embodied, not just in their current set of beliefs, but also in their *doxastic dispositions*: how they would respond to new information [11], p. 288. These may be represented by the function assigning to each proposition P the theory representing all propositions that the agent comes to believe after revising their beliefs to include P. Formally, dispositions are modelled by a *selection function* in a Boolean structure (U, Prop), which is a function f assigning to each proposition $P \in \mathit{Prop}$ a closed set (theory) fP, such that for all propositions P and Q:

- $fP \subseteq P$. (INCL)
- if $P \subseteq Q$ and $fP \neq \emptyset$, then $fQ \neq \emptyset$. (MONEYS)
- if $P \subseteq Q$ and $P \cap fQ \neq \emptyset$, then $f(P \cap Q) = P \cap fQ$. (ARROW)[4]

The current belief set of the belief state represented by selection function f may be identified with fU, which corresponds to the set of propositions that the agent believes after revision by the tautologous $\top$.

Every selection function satisfies the stronger condition

- $P \cap fQ \neq \emptyset$ implies $f(P \cap Q) = P \cap fQ$. (STRONG ARROW)

This follows readily by replacing P by $P \cap Q$ in (ARROW) and using (INCL).

A selection function f will be called *null* if $fP = \emptyset$ for all propositions P. By (MONEYS), f is null iff $fU = \emptyset$. Note that every selection function has $f\emptyset = \emptyset$, by (INCL).

The *commitment set* of a selection function f is defined to be

$$\mathscr{C}f = \bigcup\{fP : P \in \mathit{Prop}\}.$$

We now introduce structures of the form

$$\mathfrak{F} = (U, \mathit{Prop}, S, \mathsf{ws}, \mathsf{sf}, R),$$

with (U, Prop) a Boolean structure; S a set; ws a function from S to U; sf a function assigning to each member s of S a selection function $\mathsf{sf}(s)$ on (U, Prop); and R a function assigning to each proposition $P \in \mathit{Prop}$ a binary relation $R(P)$ on S, i.e. $R(P) \subseteq S \times S$.

---

[4] INCL stands for 'inclusion', MONEYS for 'monotonicity for nonempty segments', and ARROW is named in honour of Kenneth Arrow. See [14], p. 232.

U may be thought of as a set of possible worlds, as above, and S as the set of possible belief states of an agent. $\mathsf{ws}(s)$ is the world state associated with belief state s. $\mathsf{sf}(s)$ is the selection function representing the agent's doxastic dispositions in belief state s. $R(P)$ is the accessibility relation representing possible changes of belief state resulting from revision to include the belief P.

The selection function $\mathsf{sf}(s)$ will usually be denoted f^s. The structure $\mathfrak{F}$ is called a *(selection) frame* if it satisfies the following conditions:

(F1) if $(s, t) \in R(P)$, then $f^t U = f^s P$.
(F2) if $(s, t) \in R(P)$, then $\mathscr{C} f^t \subseteq \mathbf{C}(\mathscr{C} f^s)$.
(F3) If $f^s P \neq \emptyset$, then there exists $t \in S$ with $(s, t) \in R(P)$.
(F4) The image $\mathsf{ws}(S)$ of the function ws is dense in U, i.e. $\mathbf{C}(\mathsf{ws}(S)) = U$.

Referring to the axioms and inference rules of Fig. 1 in Sect. 3, the frame conditions (F1) and (F3) will play a role in the soundness of several of them, particularly via Lemma 3(3), whose proof uses these conditions. (F2) on the other hand has a specific purpose: the soundness of axiom (K$*$).

(F3) is a weakening of the requirement that $R(P)$ be *serial*, which itself means that for all $s \in S$ there exists $t \in S$ with $(s, t) \in R(P)$.

Note that if ws is *surjective*, i.e. each $u \in U$ is $\mathsf{ws}(s)$ for some s, then (F4) holds. Surjectivity requires that each $u \in U$ belongs to the image-set $\mathsf{ws}(S)$. (F4) is a weakening of this to require only that each u be 'close to' $\mathsf{ws}(S)$, i.e. every open neighbourhood of u intersects $\mathsf{ws}(S)$.

We may call a frame *world-surjective* if its ws-function is surjective. Eventually we will see that the minimal logic we study, and the $\bowtie$-free fragments of all logics, are characterised by models on world-surjective frames. For now we focus on the weaker (F4) itself, and its role in a frame, which is contained in the following result.

Lemma 1 *Let P and Q be any propositions in a frame, such that for all $s \in S$, $\mathsf{ws}(s) \in P$ iff $\mathsf{ws}(s) \in Q$. Then $P = Q$.*

Proof Assume that $\mathsf{ws}(s) \in P$ iff $\mathsf{ws}(s) \in Q$ for all $s \in S$.

Now density of $\mathsf{ws}(S)$ as in (F4) is equivalent to the property that every non-empty open set intersects $\mathsf{ws}(S)$. So if $P - Q \neq \emptyset$, then since $P - Q$ is a proposition and therefore open, it must intersect $\mathsf{ws}(S)$, giving an s such that $\mathsf{ws}(s) \in P$ and $\mathsf{ws}(s) \notin Q$, contrary to assumption. Thus $P - Q = \emptyset$. Likewise $Q - P = \emptyset$, so we must have $P = Q$. ⊣

For the use of Lemma 1, and hence the need for (F4), see Lemma 3(2) below and its proof. Ultimately, (F4) is required to ensure the soundness of the Congruence Rule (CR) of Fig. 1.

A *(selection) model* $\mathfrak{M} = (\mathfrak{F}, [\![-]\!])$ on a frame $\mathfrak{F}$ is given by a valuation $[\![-]\!]$ on the Boolean structure of $\mathfrak{F}$. If $s \in S$, the relation 'θ is true at s in $\mathfrak{M}$', written $\mathfrak{M}, s \models \theta$, is defined by induction on the formation of the formula θ, as follows:

$\mathfrak{M}, s \models p$ iff $\mathsf{ws}(s) \in [\![p]\!]$, if p is a propositional variable.
$\mathfrak{M}, s \not\models \bot$, (i.e. not $\mathfrak{M}, s \models \bot$).
$\mathfrak{M}, s \models \theta \to \theta'$ iff $\mathfrak{M}, s \models \theta$ implies $\mathfrak{M}, s \models \theta'$.
$\mathfrak{M}, s \models \mathbf{B}\phi$ iff $f^s(U) \subseteq [\![\phi]\!]$.
$\mathfrak{M}, s \models \mathbf{K}\phi$ iff $\mathscr{C}f^s \subseteq [\![\phi]\!]$.
$\mathfrak{M}, s \models [*\phi]\theta$ iff for all t such that $(s, t) \in R[\![\phi]\!]$, $\mathfrak{M}, t \models \theta$.
$\mathfrak{M}, s \models \phi \bowtie \psi$ iff for all $t \in S$, $(s, t) \in R[\![\phi]\!]$ iff $(s, t) \in R[\![\psi]\!]$.

Writing $R^s[\![\phi]\!]$ for the set $\{t \in S : (s, t) \in R[\![\phi]\!]\}$, the semantics of $\bowtie$ can be given as

$$\mathfrak{M}, s \models \phi \bowtie \psi \quad \text{iff} \quad R^s[\![\phi]\!] = R^s[\![\psi]\!].$$

A formula θ is *true in model* $\mathfrak{M}$, written $\mathfrak{M} \models \theta$, if $\mathfrak{M}, s \models \theta$ for all $s \in S$. θ is *valid at s in frame* $\mathfrak{F}$, written $\mathfrak{F}, s \models \theta$, if $\mathfrak{M}, s \models \theta$ for all models $\mathfrak{M}$ on $\mathfrak{F}$. θ is *valid in* $\mathfrak{F}$, written $\mathfrak{F} \models \theta$, if $\mathfrak{F}, s \models \theta$, for all $s \in S$; this is equivalent to requiring that θ is true in all models on $\mathfrak{F}$.

A set Σ of formulas is *satisfied at s in* $\mathfrak{M}$, written $\mathfrak{M}, s \models \Sigma$, if $\mathfrak{M}, s \models \theta$ for all $\theta \in \Sigma$. Σ *semantically implies* a formula θ in $\mathfrak{M}$, written $\Sigma \models^{\mathfrak{M}} \theta$, if θ is true at every s satisfying Σ, i.e. $\mathfrak{M}, s \models \Sigma$ implies $\mathfrak{M}, s \models \theta$ for all s in $\mathfrak{M}$. Σ semantically implies θ in frame $\mathfrak{F}$, written $\Sigma \models^{\mathfrak{F}} \theta$, if every model $\mathfrak{M}$ on $\mathfrak{F}$ has $\Sigma \models^{\mathfrak{M}} \theta$.

Satisfaction of a formula is determined by the valuations of the variables that occur in the formula, in the following sense.

Lemma 2 *Let θ be any formula. Then for any models $\mathfrak{M} = (\mathfrak{F}, [\![-]\!])$ and $\mathfrak{M}' = (\mathfrak{F}, [\![-]\!]')$, on the same frame, such that $[\![p]\!] = [\![p]\!]'$ for all variables p that occur in θ, we have*

$$\mathfrak{M}, s \models \theta \quad \textit{iff} \quad \mathfrak{M}', s \models \theta$$

for all $s \in S$.

Proof A straightforward induction on the formation of θ. ⊣

The following facts are useful for proving validity of axioms and soundness of rules.

Lemma 3 *In any selection model $\mathfrak{M}$:*

(1) $\mathfrak{M}, s \models \phi$ iff $\mathsf{ws}(s) \in [\![\phi]\!]$.
(2) $\mathfrak{M} \models \phi \leftrightarrow \psi$ iff $[\![\phi]\!] = [\![\psi]\!]$.
(3) $\mathfrak{M}, s \models [*\phi]\mathbf{B}\psi$ iff $f^s[\![\phi]\!] \subseteq [\![\psi]\!]$.
(4) $\mathfrak{M}, s \models \langle *\phi \rangle \mathbf{b}\psi$ iff $(f^s[\![\phi]\!]) \cap [\![\psi]\!] \neq \emptyset$.
(5) $\mathfrak{M}, s \models \mathbf{K}(\phi \leftrightarrow \psi)$ implies $f^s[\![\phi]\!] = f^s[\![\psi]\!]$.

Proof (1) A straightforward induction on the formation of pure Boolean ϕ.
(2) Using (1), $\mathfrak{M} \models \phi \leftrightarrow \psi$ iff for all $s \in S$, $\mathsf{ws}(s) \in [\![\phi]\!]$ iff $\mathsf{ws}(s) \in [\![\psi]\!]$. But this condition implies $[\![\phi]\!] = [\![\psi]\!]$ by Lemma 1, and is evidently implied by $[\![\phi]\!] = [\![\psi]\!]$.

(3) Let $\mathfrak{M}, s \models [*\phi]\mathbf{B}\psi$. If $f^s[\![\phi]\!] = \emptyset$, then immediately $f^s[\![\phi]\!] \subseteq [\![\psi]\!]$. But if $f^s[\![\phi]\!] \neq \emptyset$, then by (F3) there is a t with$(s, t) \in R[\![\phi]\!]$, hence $\mathfrak{M}, t \models \mathbf{B}\psi$. Then by (F1) and the semantics of $\mathbf{B}$, $f^s[\![\phi]\!] = f^t U \subseteq [\![\psi]\!]$. Conversely, let $f^s[\![\phi]\!] \subseteq [\![\psi]\!]$. Then using (F1) again we argue that $(s, t) \in R[\![\phi]\!]$ implies $f^t U = f^s[\![\phi]\!] \subseteq [\![\psi]\!]$, which implies $\mathfrak{M}, t \models \mathbf{B}\psi$. Hence $\mathfrak{M}, s \models [*\phi]\mathbf{B}\psi$.

(4) By (3) and set algebra, because $\mathfrak{M}, s \models \langle *\phi \rangle \mathbf{b}\psi$ iff $\mathfrak{M}, s \not\models [*\phi]\mathbf{B}\neg\psi$.

(5) Let $\mathfrak{M}, s \models \mathbf{K}(\phi \leftrightarrow \psi)$. Then $\mathscr{C} f^s \subseteq [\![\phi \leftrightarrow \psi]\!]$. Take first the case $f^s[\![\phi]\!] \neq \emptyset$. Now

$$f^s[\![\phi]\!] \subseteq \mathscr{C} f^s \subseteq [\![\phi \leftrightarrow \psi]\!] \subseteq [\![\phi \to \psi]\!],$$

so $f^s[\![\phi]\!] \cap [\![\phi]\!] \subseteq [\![\psi]\!]$, which by (INCL) means that $f^s[\![\phi]\!] \subseteq [\![\psi]\!]$. Then $[\![\psi]\!] \cap f^s[\![\phi]\!] = f^s[\![\phi]\!] \neq \emptyset$, hence by (STRONG ARROW),

$$f^s([\![\psi]\!] \cap [\![\phi]\!]) = [\![\psi]\!] \cap f^s[\![\phi]\!] = f^s[\![\phi]\!] \neq \emptyset.$$

Therefore $f^s[\![\psi]\!] \neq \emptyset$ by (MONEYS).
Summing up so far: from $f^s[\![\phi]\!] \neq \emptyset$ we deduced that $f^s[\![\phi]\!] = f^s([\![\psi]\!] \cap [\![\phi]\!])$ and $f^s[\![\psi]\!] \neq \emptyset$. But then from $f^s[\![\psi]\!] \neq \emptyset$, interchanging ϕ and ψ in the above, we can go on to deduce that $f^s[\![\psi]\!] = f^s([\![\phi]\!] \cap [\![\psi]\!])$, which is $f^s([\![\psi]\!] \cap [\![\phi]\!])$, i.e. $f^s[\![\phi]\!]$.
Overall, we showed that if $f^s[\![\phi]\!] \neq \emptyset$, then $f^s[\![\phi]\!] = f^s[\![\psi]\!]$. Likewise, interchanging ϕ and ψ in the overall argument shows that if $f^s[\![\psi]\!] \neq \emptyset$, then $f^s[\![\psi]\!] = f^s[\![\phi]\!]$. That leaves the case that $f^s[\![\phi]\!] = \emptyset$ and $f^s[\![\psi]\!] = \emptyset$, whence of course $f^s[\![\phi]\!] = f^s[\![\psi]\!]$. ⊣

To axiomatise the logic determined by selection frames, we need the notion of a *template*, which can be thought of, approximately, as an expression of the form

$$\theta_0 \to \Box_1(\theta_1 \to \Box_2(\theta_2 \to \cdots \to \Box_n(\theta_{n-1} \to \#)\cdots),$$

where the new symbol # is a place holder for a formula, the θ_i's are formulas, and each $\Box_j$ is a sequence $[*\phi_{j_1}]\cdots[*\phi_{j_{m_j}}]$ of belief revision modalities. Formally, the set of templates is defined inductively by the following stipulations.

- # is a template.
- If ρ is a template, then $\theta \to \rho$ is a template for all formulas θ.
- If ρ is a template, then $[*\phi]\rho$ is a template for all pure Boolean ϕ.

Each template ρ has a single occurrence of the symbol #. We write $\rho(\theta)$ for the formula obtained from ρ by replacing # by the formula θ. Inductively, $\#(\theta) = \theta$, $(\varphi \to \rho)(\theta) = \varphi \to \rho(\theta)$, and $([*\phi]\rho)(\theta) = [*\phi]\rho(\theta)$. The notion of template was introduced in [4], under the name 'admissible form', in order to axiomatise certain dynamic program logics.

In Fig. 1 in Sect. 3 there is an inference rule (⋈R) involving templates. This rule need not preserve truth in a model. Rather, it preserves validity in a frame, as the following result shows.

Lemma 4 *Let ρ be any template; ϕ, ψ any pure Boolean formulas; and p any variable not occurring in ϕ, ψ or ρ. Then for any $s \in S$ in a frame $\mathfrak{F}$, if $\mathfrak{M}, s \not\models \rho(\phi \bowtie \psi)$ for some model $\mathfrak{M} = (\mathfrak{F}, [\![-]\!])$, then $\mathfrak{M}', s \not\models \rho([*\phi]p \leftrightarrow [*\psi]p)$ for some model $\mathfrak{M}' = (\mathfrak{F}, [\![-]\!]')$ that has $[\![q]\!]' = [\![q]\!]$ for all variables $q \neq p$.*

Proof By induction on the formation of ρ.

For the case $\rho = \#$, suppose p does not occur in ϕ or ψ, and $\mathfrak{M}, s \not\models \phi \bowtie \psi$. Then there exists a $t \in S$ with, say, $(s, t) \in R[\![\phi]\!]$ but $(s, t) \notin R[\![\psi]\!]$. Define $\mathfrak{M}'$ by putting $[\![p]\!]' = \{t' \in S : (s, t') \in R[\![\psi]\!]\}$, and $[\![q]\!]' = [\![q]\!]$ for all variables $q \neq p$.

Now $[\![-]\!]$ and $[\![-]\!]'$ agree on all variables of ϕ, since p is not in ϕ. A simple induction then shows that $[\![\phi]\!] = [\![\phi]\!]'$. Likewise, $[\![\psi]\!] = [\![\psi]\!]'$. Thus $(s, t') \in R[\![\psi]\!]'$ implies $(s, t') \in R[\![\psi]\!]$, which implies $t' \in [\![p]\!]'$. This shows that $\mathfrak{M}', s \models [*\psi]p$. On the other hand, $t \notin [\![p]\!]'$, and so as $(s, t) \in R[\![\phi]\!] = R[\![\phi]\!]'$, this shows $\mathfrak{M}', s \not\models [*\phi]p$. Therefore $\mathfrak{M}', s \not\models [*\phi]p \leftrightarrow [*\psi]p$. The same conclusion follows if, instead, $(s, t) \in R[\![\psi]\!]$ but $(s, t) \notin R[\![\phi]\!]$. That completes the proof that the result holds when $\rho = \#$.

Now assume the result inductively for ρ, and consider a template $\theta \to \rho$ with p not in ϕ, ψ or $\theta \to \rho$. If $\mathfrak{M}, s \not\models \theta \to \rho(\phi \bowtie \psi)$, then $\mathfrak{M}, s \models \theta$ and $\mathfrak{M}, s \not\models \rho(\phi \bowtie \psi)$. But p is not in ϕ, ψ or ρ, so the induction hypothesis gives that $\mathfrak{M}', s \not\models \rho([*\phi]p \leftrightarrow [*\psi]p)$ for some model $\mathfrak{M}'$ on $\mathfrak{F}$ that differs from $\mathfrak{M}$ only on p. Since p is not in θ, we then get $\mathfrak{M}', s \models \theta$ by Lemma 2. It follows that $\mathfrak{M}', s \not\models \theta \to \rho([*\phi]p \leftrightarrow [*\psi]p)$, showing that the result holds for template $\theta \to \rho$.

Finally, again assume the result inductively for ρ, and consider a template $[*\chi]\rho$, with p not in ϕ, ψ or $[*\chi]\rho$. If $\mathfrak{M}, s \not\models [*\chi]\rho(\phi \bowtie \psi)$, then there is a t with $(s, t) \in R[\![\chi]\!]$ and $\mathfrak{M}, t \not\models \rho(\phi \bowtie \psi)$. By the induction hypothesis, $\mathfrak{M}', t \not\models \rho([*\phi]p \leftrightarrow [*\psi]p)$ for some $\mathfrak{M}'$ differing from $\mathfrak{M}$ only on p. Since p is not in χ, we have $[\![\chi]\!] = [\![\chi]\!]'$, so $(s, t) \in R[\![\chi]\!]'$, implying that $\mathfrak{M}', s \not\models [*\chi]\rho([*\phi]p \leftrightarrow [*\psi]p)$. Thus the result holds for template $[*\chi]\rho$. ⊣

Corollary 1 *Let ρ, ϕ, ψ and p be as in the Lemma. Then for any frame $\mathfrak{F}$, and any $s \in S$, if $\mathfrak{F}, s \models \rho([*\phi]p \leftrightarrow [*\psi]p)$, then $\mathfrak{F}, s \models \rho(\phi \bowtie \psi)$.*

Hence if $\rho([*\phi]p \leftrightarrow [*\psi]p)$ is valid in $\mathfrak{F}$, then so is $\rho(\phi \bowtie \psi)$. ⊣

3 Logics

Axioms and rules of inference appear in Fig. 1. There, as usual, ϕ, ψ, χ are pure Boolean formulas, while θ, ω are general formulas.[5] A *selection logic*, or more briefly a *logic*, is defined to be a set L of formulas that contains all instances of these axioms and is closed under these inference rules. The members of L are the *L-theorems*. The *smallest* logic will be denoted L_K. This is the intersection of all

[5] Except that in (□) and (□N), θ and ω must be pure Boolean when □ is **B** or **K**.

logics. Since the proof theory is finitary (all rules have finitely many premisses), L_{K} can also be described as the set of formulas that can be obtained from the axioms by finitely many applications of the inference rules.

The $\bowtie$-free axioms of Fig. 1 are a sub-list of those in [14], except that (K$*$) has replaced ($*$K), as mentioned in the Introduction. The Congruence Rule (CR) is an addition which in fact makes the axiom ($*$6) redundant. In Sect. 7 we discuss this, and explore the consequences of adding a variety of axioms to L_{K}.

The axiom ($\Box$) and the rule ($\Box$N) define $\Box$ as a *normal* modality, and we use the phrase 'by modal logic' to mean that some conclusion has been obtained by properties of a normal $\Box$ together with tautological reasoning. Note that ($\Box$) and ($\Box$N) hold not just for $\Box \in \{\mathbf{B}, \mathbf{K}, [*\phi]\}$, but also for combinations of these modalities. For instance they hold when $\Box$ denotes the combination $[*\phi]\mathbf{B}$, in the sense that any formula

$$[*\phi]\mathbf{B}(\psi \to \chi) \to ([*\phi]\mathbf{B}\psi \to [*\phi]\mathbf{B}\chi)$$

is an L-theorem; and if ψ is an L-theorem, then so is $[*\phi]\mathbf{B}\psi$.

Axioms ($*$2)–($*$8) are intended to formalise certain postulates of the AGM theory (and preserve their numbering). In the presence of (BK) some of these axioms can be simplified or strengthened. For instance, the consequent of ($*$4) is derivable, and this is the converse of ($*$3). Also the consequent of ($*$5) is derivable, and this can be used to show that the modality $\mathbf{K}$ is definable in L, in the sense that $\mathbf{K}\phi$ is equivalent to $[*\neg\phi]\mathbf{B}\bot$. We record these and other derivability facts now:

Theorem 1 *In any selection logic L:*

(1) $(*4)'$: $\vdash_L \mathbf{B}\phi \to [*\top]\mathbf{B}\phi$.
(2) $(*5)'$: $\vdash_L \mathbf{k}\phi \to \langle *\phi\rangle\mathbf{b}\top$. *Equivalently*, $\vdash_L [*\phi]\mathbf{B}\bot \to \mathbf{K}\neg\phi$.
(3) $\vdash_L \mathbf{K}\phi \leftrightarrow [*\neg\phi]\mathbf{B}\bot$.
(4) If $\vdash_L \phi \leftrightarrow \psi$, then $\vdash_L [*\phi]\mathbf{B}\chi \leftrightarrow [*\psi]\mathbf{B}\chi$.
(5) If $\vdash_L \phi \to \psi$, then $\vdash_L [*\psi]\mathbf{B}\bot \to [*\phi]\mathbf{B}\bot$.
(6) ($*$BH): $\vdash_L \mathbf{B}\bot \to [*\phi]\mathbf{B}\bot$.
(7) $\vdash_L \rho(\phi \bowtie \psi) \to \rho([*\phi]\theta \leftrightarrow [*\psi]\theta)$.

Proof For (1), from (BK) and (K$*$) we obtain $\vdash_L \mathbf{B}\bot \to [*\top]\mathbf{K}\bot$. Since (KB) and modal logic gives $\vdash_L [*\top]\mathbf{K}\bot \to [*\top]\mathbf{B}\bot$ and modal logic gives $\vdash_L [*\top]\mathbf{B}\bot \to [*\top]\mathbf{B}\theta$, this all leads to $\vdash_L \mathbf{B}\bot \to [*\top]\mathbf{B}\phi$, and hence by Boolean logic to

$$\vdash_L \mathbf{B}\bot \to (\mathbf{B}\phi \to [*\top]\mathbf{B}\phi).$$

But ($*$4) is equivalent to $\neg\mathbf{B}\bot \to (\mathbf{B}\phi \to [*\top]\mathbf{B}\phi)$, and these last two L-theorems yield $\vdash_L \mathbf{B}\phi \to [*\top]\mathbf{B}\phi$.

For (2), from (BK) and modal logic we obtain $\vdash_L \mathbf{B}\bot \to \mathbf{K}\neg\phi$, hence by Boolean logic $\vdash_L \mathbf{B}\bot \to ([*\phi]\mathbf{B}\bot \to \mathbf{K}\neg\phi)$. But ($*$5) is equivalent by modal logic to $\neg\mathbf{B}\bot \to ([*\phi]\mathbf{B}\bot \to \mathbf{K}\neg\phi)$, and these last two L-theorems yield $\vdash_L [*\phi]\mathbf{B}\bot \to \mathbf{K}\neg\phi$.

For (3), by (K$*$), (KB) and modal logic we get $\vdash_L \mathbf{K}\phi \to [*\neg\phi]\mathbf{B}\phi$. By this, ($*$2) and modal logic, $\vdash_L \mathbf{K}\phi \to [*\neg\phi](\mathbf{B}\phi \wedge \mathbf{B}\neg\phi)$ and then $\vdash_L \mathbf{K}\phi \to [*\neg\phi]\mathbf{B}\bot$. But from (2) we can derive the converse $\vdash_L [*\neg\phi]\mathbf{B}\bot \to \mathbf{K}\phi$, leading to (3).

(4) is just an instance of the Congruence Rule (CR) (and also follows by axiom ($*$6) and **K**-Necessitation).

For (5), $\vdash_L \phi \to \psi$ implies $\vdash_L \mathbf{K}\neg\psi \to \mathbf{K}\neg\phi$ by modal logic, and this in turn implies $\vdash_L [*\neg\neg\psi]\mathbf{B}\bot \to [*\neg\neg\phi]\mathbf{B}\bot$ by (3). Then $\vdash_L [*\psi]\mathbf{B}\bot \to [*\phi]\mathbf{B}\bot$ follows by (4).

The 'Black Hole' principle ($*$BH) of (6) is derived in [14, Appendix A], using (BK), (K$*$), (KB) and modal logic, similarly to the arguments for (1).

(7) is shown by induction on the formation of ρ. When $\rho = \#$, this is just axiom ($\bowtie$). Assuming inductively that (7) holds for ρ, then it holds with $[*\psi]\rho$ in place of ρ by modal logic, and with $\omega \to \rho$ in place of ρ by Boolean logic. $\dashv$

Remark 1 A simpler axiom set could be given by taking the derivable schemes $(*4)'$ and $(*5)'$ in place of ($*$4) and ($*$5), and deleting (BK), which is itself derivable from the simple cases $\mathbf{B}\bot \to [*\top]\mathbf{B}\bot$ of $(*4)'$ and $[*\top]\mathbf{B}\bot \to \mathbf{K}\neg\top$ of $(*5)'$. $\dashv$

A formula θ is *L-derivable* from a set Σ of formulas, in symbols $\Sigma \vdash_L \theta$, if there is some finite subset Σ_0 of Σ such that $(\bigwedge \Sigma_0) \to \theta$ is an L-theorem. The empty conjunction $\bigwedge \emptyset$ is taken to be the formula $\top$. We write $\vdash_L \theta$ when $\emptyset \vdash_L \theta$, which holds iff $\theta \in L$, i.e. iff θ is an L-theorem.

The fundamental derivability fact for a normal modality $\Box$ is the following (see e.g. [1], p. 159).

Lemma 5 **($\Box$-Lemma)** *If* $\{\theta : \Box\theta \in \Sigma\} \vdash_L \omega$, *then* $\Sigma \vdash_L \Box\omega$. $\dashv$

A set Σ is *L-consistent* if $\Sigma \nvdash_L \bot$, and is *L-maximal* if it is maximally L-consistent. Familiarity is assumed with the properties of an L-maximal Γ, including that it contains all L-theorems; is closed under tautological consequence; has $\Gamma \vdash_L \theta$ iff $\theta \in \Gamma$; $\neg\theta \in \Gamma$ iff $\theta \notin \Gamma$, etc.

The logic L is called *consistent* if it is L-consistent as a set of formulas. This holds iff $\bot$ is not an L-theorem, or equivalently, iff there is at least one formula that is not an L-theorem.

A set Σ is said to *respect* $\bowtie$ *in* L if, for all templates ρ and all pure Boolean ϕ, ψ,

$$\text{if } \Sigma \vdash_L \rho([*\phi]\theta \leftrightarrow [*\psi]\theta) \text{ for all formulas } \theta, \text{ then } \Sigma \vdash_L \rho(\phi \bowtie \psi). \tag{3}$$

If Σ is L-maximal, this is equivalent to requiring that for all ρ, ϕ, ψ,

$$\{\rho([*\phi]\theta \leftrightarrow [*\psi]\theta) : \theta \text{ is any formula}\} \subseteq \Sigma \quad \text{implies } \rho(\phi \bowtie \psi) \in \Sigma. \tag{4}$$

The set Σ is *L-saturated* if it is L-maximal and satsfies (3), or equivalently (4). The set of L-saturated sets will be denoted S_L.

Lemma 6 *Let Σ be a set that respects $\bowtie$ in L. Then*

(1) For each finite set Γ of formulas, $\Sigma \cup \Gamma$ respects $\bowtie$ in L.
(2) $[*\phi]^{-L}\Sigma = \{\theta : \Sigma \vdash_L [*\phi]\theta\}$ respects $\bowtie$ in L.

Proof (1) Let $\Sigma \cup \Gamma \vdash_L \rho([*\phi]\theta \leftrightarrow [*\psi]\theta)$ for all formulas θ. If ω is the conjunction of the members of Γ, then $\Sigma \vdash_L \omega \rightarrow \rho([*\phi]\theta \leftrightarrow [*\psi]\theta)$ for all θ. Applying the fact that Σ respects $\bowtie$ to the template $\omega \rightarrow \rho$ then gives $\Sigma \vdash_L \omega \rightarrow \rho(\phi \bowtie \psi)$. Hence $\Sigma \cup \Gamma \vdash_L \rho(\phi \bowtie \psi)$.

(2) Let $[*\phi]^{-L}\Sigma \vdash_L \rho([*\chi]\theta \leftrightarrow [*\psi]\theta)$ for all formulas θ. Then by the $\Box$-Lemma 5 with $\Box = [*\phi]$, $\Sigma \vdash_L [*\phi]\rho([*\chi]\theta \leftrightarrow [*\psi]\theta)$ for all θ. Applying the fact that Σ respects $\bowtie$ to the template $[*\phi]\rho$ then gives $\Sigma \vdash_L [*\phi]\rho(\chi \bowtie \psi)$, hence $\rho(\chi \bowtie \psi) \in [*\phi]^{-L}\Sigma$, and so $[*\phi]^{-L}\Sigma \vdash_L \rho(\chi \bowtie \psi)$. $\dashv$

We turn now to the question of the existence of saturated sets, and indeed the existence of 'sufficiently many' of them. The following variant of Lindenbaum's Lemma and related results depend on the fact that our propositional language is countable.

Theorem 2 (1) *Every L-consistent set that L-respects $\bowtie$ has an L-saturated extension.*
(2) *If Σ is L-consistent, and there are infinitely many variables that do not occur in any member of Σ, then Σ has an L-saturated extension.*
(3) *Every finite L-consistent set has an L-saturated extension.*
(4) *$\vdash_L \theta$ iff θ belongs to every L-saturated set.*
(5) *If L is a consistent logic, then the set S_L of L-saturated sets is non-empty.*

Proof (1) Let Σ_0 be L-consistent and respect $\bowtie$ in L. Since there are countably many formulas, there is an enumeration $\{\theta_n : n \geq 0\}$ of the set of all formulas of the form $\rho(\phi \bowtie \psi)$. We define a nested sequence $\Sigma_0 \subseteq \cdots \subseteq \Sigma_n \subseteq \cdots$ of L-consistent sets such that $\Sigma_n - \Sigma_0$ is finite for all $n \geq 0$.
Suppose inductively that we have defined Σ_n that is L-consistent and has $\Sigma_n - \Sigma_0$ finite. Then Σ_n respects $\bowtie$ by part (1) of Lemma 6. If $\Sigma_n \vdash_L \theta_n$, put $\Sigma_{n+1} = \Sigma_n \cup \{\theta_n\}$. If however $\Sigma_n \nvdash_L \theta_n$, with $\theta_n = \rho(\phi \bowtie \psi)$, since Σ_n respects $\bowtie$ there is some formula θ with $\Sigma_n \nvdash_L \rho([*\phi]\theta \leftrightarrow [*\psi]\theta)$. Put

$$\Sigma_{n+1} = \Sigma_n \cup \{\neg\rho([*\phi]\theta \leftrightarrow [*\psi]\theta)\}.$$

In both cases we get that Σ_{n+1} is L-consistent, with $\Sigma_{n+1} - \Sigma_0$ finite.
Now put $\Sigma = \bigcup_{n\geq 0} \Sigma_n$. Then Σ is L-consistent, so extends to an L-maximal set Γ in the usual way. It remains to show that Γ respects $\bowtie$. But if $\Gamma \nvdash_L \rho(\phi \bowtie \psi)$, with $\rho(\phi \bowtie \psi) = \theta_n$, then $\Sigma_n \nvdash_L \theta_n$ as $\Sigma_n \subseteq \Gamma$, so by our construction there is a θ with $\neg\rho([*\phi]\theta \leftrightarrow [*\psi]\theta) \in \Sigma_{n+1} \subseteq \Gamma$, so $\Gamma \nvdash_L \rho([*\phi]\theta \leftrightarrow [*\psi]\theta)$ as Γ is L-consistent.

(2) Suppose there are infinitely many variables that do not occur in Σ. Then we show that Σ respects $\bowtie$ in L. For, if $\Sigma \vdash_L \rho([*\phi]\theta \leftrightarrow [*\psi]\theta)$ for all θ,

then we choose a variable p that does not occur in Σ or in ρ, ϕ or ψ. Then $\Sigma \vdash_L \rho([*\phi]p \leftrightarrow [*\psi]p)$, so $\vdash_L \omega \to \rho([*\phi]p \leftrightarrow [*\psi]p)$ where ω is the conjunction of some finite subset of Σ. Since p also does not occur in ω, the rule ($\bowtie$R) then applies to the template $\omega \to \rho$ to give $\vdash_L \omega \to \rho(\phi \bowtie \psi)$. It follows that $\Sigma \vdash_L \rho(\phi \bowtie \psi)$.
This confirms that Σ respects $\bowtie$. So if Σ is also L-consistent, by part (1) it has an L-saturated extension.

(3) From part (2), for if Σ is finite, there are infinitely many variables that do not occur in Σ.

(4) If $\vdash_L \theta$, then θ belongs to every L-maximal set, and in particular to the L-saturated ones. But if $\nvdash_L \theta$, then $\{\neg\theta\}$ is L-consistent and finite, hence by (3) there is an L-saturated Γ with $\neg\theta \in \Gamma$, hence $\theta \notin \Gamma$.

(5) If L is consistent, then $\nvdash_L \bot$, so by (4) there is a L-saturated set. $\dashv$

Theorem 3 *Let Σ be L-saturated, and ϕ a pure Boolean formula. Then*

$$[*\phi]\omega \in \Sigma \quad \textit{iff} \quad \textit{for all } \Delta \in S_L \textit{ such that } \{\theta : [*\phi]\theta \in \Sigma\} \subseteq \Delta,\ \omega \in \Delta.$$

Proof The result from left to right is immediate. For the converse, note first that since Σ is L-maximal,

$$\{\theta : [*\phi]\theta \in \Sigma\} = \{\theta : \Sigma \vdash_L [*\phi]\theta\} = [*\phi]^{-L}\Sigma.$$

Now if $[*\phi]\omega \notin \Sigma$, then $\Sigma \nvdash_L [*\phi]\omega$, so by the $\Box$-Lemma 5 with $\Box = [*\phi]$, we have $[*\phi]^{-L}\Sigma \nvdash_L \omega$. Hence $\Delta_0 = [*\phi]^{-L}\Sigma \cup \{\neg\omega\}$ is L-consistent.

But $[*\phi]^{-L}\Sigma$ respects $\bowtie$ by part (2) of Lemma 6, hence by part (1) of that Lemma, Δ_0 respects $\bowtie$. It follows by Theorem 2(1) that Δ_0 has an L-saturated extension Δ. Then $\neg\omega \in \Delta$, so $\omega \notin \Delta$, and $[*\phi]^{-L} \subseteq \Delta$, as required to complete the proof. $\dashv$

4 Soundness

First we briefly account for the truth of axioms in models, identifying the model-theoretic properties needed in each case.

Lemma 7 *The axioms in Fig. 1 are true in all models, hence valid in all frames.*

Proof We work in a given model, suppressing its name and writing $s \models \theta$ for its truth relation.

($\Box$): For $\Box = [\![\phi]\!]$, this is true in the model as in standard Kripkean semantics. For $\Box = \mathbf{B}$, observe that if $f^s U \subseteq [\![\phi \to \psi]\!]$ and $f^s U \subseteq [\![\phi]\!]$, then

$$f^s U \subseteq [\![\phi \to \psi]\!] \cap [\![\phi]\!] \subseteq [\![\psi]\!].$$

For $\Box = \mathbf{K}$ the argument is similar, with $\mathscr{C} f^s$ in place of $f^s U$.

(∗2): $f^s[\![\phi]\!] \subseteq [\![\phi]\!]$ by (INCL), so $s \models [\![\phi]\!]\mathbf{B}\phi$ by Lemma 3(3).

(∗3): If $s \models [*\top]\mathbf{B}\phi$, then $f^s[\![\top]\!] \subseteq [\![\phi]\!]$ (Lemma 3(3)), i.e. $f^s U \subseteq [\![\phi]\!]$, and so $s \models \mathbf{B}\phi$.

(∗4): We show that the stronger (∗4)′ is true. If $s \models \mathbf{B}\phi$, then $f^s[\![\top]\!] = f^s U \subseteq [\![\phi]\!]$, hence $s \models [*\top]\mathbf{B}\phi$. Thus $s \models \mathbf{B}\phi \to [*\top]\mathbf{B}\phi$.

(∗5): We show that the stronger (∗5)′ is true. If $s \models \mathbf{k}\phi$, then $s \not\models \mathbf{K}\neg\phi$, so $\mathscr{C} f^s \not\subseteq -[\![\phi]\!]$, so there is a ψ with $[\![\phi]\!] \cap f^s[\![\psi]\!] \neq \emptyset$. Hence $f^s([\![\phi]\!] \cap [\![\psi]\!]) \neq \emptyset$ by (STRONG ARROW), and so $f^s[\![\phi]\!] \neq \emptyset$ by (MONEYS). Thus $(f^s[\![\phi]\!]) \cap [\![\top]\!] \neq \emptyset$, and so $s \models \langle *\phi\rangle\mathbf{b}\top$ by Lemma 3(4). Thus $s \models \mathbf{k}\phi \to \langle *\phi\rangle\mathbf{b}\top$.

(∗6): If $s \models \mathbf{K}(\phi \leftrightarrow \psi)$, then $f^s[\![\phi]\!] = f^s[\![\psi]\!]$ by Lemma 3(5). So in general $f^s[\![\phi]\!] \subseteq [\![\chi]\!]$ iff $f^s[\![\psi]\!] \subseteq [\![\chi]\!]$, hence by Lemma 3(3), $s \models [*\phi]\mathbf{B}\chi$ iff $s \models [*\psi]\mathbf{B}\chi$, showing $s \models [*\phi]\mathbf{B}\chi \leftrightarrow [*\psi]\mathbf{B}\chi$.

(∗7): Let $s \models [*(\phi \wedge \psi)]\mathbf{B}\chi$. Then $f^s[\![\phi \wedge \psi]\!] \subseteq [\![\chi]\!]$.
First, if $(f^s[\![\phi]\!]) \cap [\![\psi]\!] \neq \emptyset$ then, using (STRONG ARROW),

$$(f^s[\![\phi]\!]) \cap [\![\psi]\!] = f^s([\![\phi]\!] \cap [\![\psi]\!]) = f^s[\![\phi \wedge \psi]\!] \subseteq [\![\chi]\!],$$

so $f^s[\![\phi]\!] \subseteq [\![\psi \to \chi]\!]$, and hence $s \models [*\phi]\mathbf{B}(\psi \to \chi)$.
But if $(f^s[\![\phi]\!]) \cap [\![\psi]\!] = \emptyset$, then $(f^s[\![\phi]\!]) \cap [\![\psi]\!] \subseteq [\![\chi]\!]$, anyway, and we get the same conclusion $s \models [*\phi]\mathbf{B}(\psi \to \chi)$.

(∗8): Let $s \models \langle *\phi\rangle\mathbf{b}\psi$. Then by Lemma 3(4), $(f^s[\![\phi]\!]) \cap [\![\psi]\!] \neq \emptyset$, so by (STRONG ARROW), $f^s[\![\phi \wedge \psi]\!] = (f^s[\![\phi]\!]) \cap [\![\psi]\!]$.
Now if $s \models [*\phi]\mathbf{B}(\psi \to \chi)$, then $f^s[\![\phi]\!] \subseteq [\![\psi \to \chi]\!]$, and hence $(f^s[\![\phi]\!]) \cap [\![\psi]\!] \subseteq [\![\chi]\!]$. Thus $f^s[\![\phi \wedge \psi]\!] \subseteq [\![\chi]\!]$, implying $s \models [*(\phi \wedge \psi)]\mathbf{B}\chi$. Altogether this shows that $s \models [*\phi]\mathbf{B}(\psi \to \chi) \to [*(\phi \wedge \psi)]\mathbf{B}\chi$.

(∗FB): If $s \models \langle *\phi\rangle\mathbf{B}\psi$, there exists t with $(s, t) \in R[\![\phi]\!]$ and $t \models \mathbf{B}\psi$. Then by (F1), $f^s[\![\phi]\!] = f^t U \subseteq [\![\psi]\!]$, implying $s \models [*\phi]\mathbf{B}\psi$.

(K∗): Let $s \models \mathbf{K}\psi$. Then $\mathscr{C} f^s \subseteq [\![\psi]\!]$, hence $\mathbf{C}(\mathscr{C} f^s) \subseteq [\![\psi]\!]$ as $[\![\psi]\!]$ is closed. If $(s, t) \in R[\![\phi]\!]$, then by (F2), $\mathscr{C} f^t \subseteq \mathbf{C}(\mathscr{C} f^s) \subseteq [\![\psi]\!]$, hence $t \models \mathbf{K}\psi$. This shows that $s \models [*\phi]\mathbf{K}\psi$.

(KB): If $s \models \mathbf{K}\phi$, then $f^s U \subseteq \mathscr{C} f^s \subseteq [\![\phi]\!]$, hence $s \models \mathbf{B}\phi$.

(BK): If $s \models \mathbf{B}\bot$, then $f^s U = \emptyset$, so for all propositions $P \subseteq U$, $f^s P = \emptyset$ by (MONEYS), hence $\mathscr{C} f^s = \emptyset = [\![\bot]\!]$, implying $s \models \mathbf{K}\bot$.

(⋈): If $s \models \phi \bowtie \psi$, then for all t, $(s, t) \in R[\![\phi]\!]$ iff $(s, t) \in R[\![\psi]\!]$. Hence $s \models [*\phi]\theta$ iff $s \models [*\psi]\theta$, and so $s \models [*\phi]\theta \leftrightarrow [*\psi]\theta$. ⊣

Theorem 4 *For any frame $\mathfrak{F}$, the set $L_{\mathfrak{F}} = \{\theta : \mathfrak{F} \models \theta\}$ of formulas valid in $\mathfrak{F}$ is a logic. If $S \neq \emptyset$ in this frame, then $L_{\mathfrak{F}}$ is consistent.*

Proof By the Lemma just proved, all axioms belong to $L_{\mathfrak{F}}$. So we need to check that $L_{\mathfrak{F}}$ is closed under the inference rules.

The rules (MP) and (□N) are readily seen to preserve truth in each model on $\mathfrak{F}$, hence preserve validity in $\mathfrak{F}$, so $L_{\mathfrak{F}}$ is closed under these rules.

For closure of $L_{\mathfrak{F}}$ under the Congruence Rule (CR), suppose that $\mathfrak{M} \models \phi \leftrightarrow \psi$ where $\mathfrak{M}$ is any model on $\mathfrak{F}$. Then $[\![\phi]\!] = [\![\psi]\!]$ by Lemma 3(2), and therefore $R[\![\phi]\!] = R[\![\psi]\!]$. Hence for any θ we get $\mathfrak{M}, s \models [*\phi]\theta$ iff $\mathfrak{M}, s, \models [*\psi]\theta$ for all s in $\mathfrak{M}$, and so $\mathfrak{M} \models [*\phi]\theta \leftrightarrow [*\psi]\theta$. Thus (CR) preserves truth in each model on $\mathfrak{F}$, hence preserves validity in $\mathfrak{F}$.

Finally, Corollary 1 states that $L_{\mathfrak{F}}$ is closed under the rule ($\bowtie$R), completing the proof that $L_{\mathfrak{F}}$ is a logic.

Now suppose there exists some $s \in S$ (so also $U \neq \emptyset$ as then $\mathsf{ws}(s) \in S$). Then $\bot$ is falsified at s, showing that $\bot \notin L_{\mathfrak{F}}$, as need for consistency of this logic. $\dashv$

We can now demonstrate the soundness of the minimal logic L_{K} with respect to our semantics. From the Theorem just proved we infer that

$$If \vdash_{L_{\mathrm{K}}} \theta, \text{ then } \theta \text{is valid in all frames.}$$

For if $\vdash_{L_{\mathrm{K}}} \theta$, then θ belongs to every logic, and hence belongs to the logic $L_{\mathfrak{F}}$ of any frame $\mathfrak{F}$. We can then extend this to Strong Soundness results:

Theorem 5 *Let $\mathfrak{F}$ be any selection frame.*

(1) *If $\Sigma \vdash_{L_{\mathfrak{F}}} \theta$, then $\Sigma \models^{\mathfrak{F}} \theta$.*
(2) *If Σ is satisfiable in $\mathfrak{F}$, then it is $L_{\mathfrak{F}}$-consistent.*

Proof For (1): Let $\Sigma \vdash_{L_{\mathfrak{F}}} \theta$. Then $\vdash_{L_{\mathfrak{F}}} \omega \to \theta$, where ω is the conjunction of some finite subset of Σ. Thus $\omega \to \theta$ is valid in $\mathfrak{F}$.

To show that $\Sigma \models^{\mathfrak{F}} \theta$, suppose that $\mathfrak{M}, s \models \Sigma$ in some model $\mathfrak{M}$ on $\mathfrak{F}$. Then $\mathfrak{M}, s \models \omega$. But as $\mathfrak{F} \models \omega \to \theta$, it follows that $\mathfrak{M}, s \models \theta$. This shows that $\Sigma \models^{\mathfrak{M}} \theta$ for all models $\mathfrak{M}$ on $\mathfrak{F}$, as required.

For (2): If Σ is satisfiable at some point s in some model on $\mathfrak{F}$, then since $s \not\models \bot$ we get $\Sigma \not\models^{\mathfrak{F}} \bot$, hence $\Sigma \nvdash_{L_{\mathfrak{F}}} \bot$ by (1). $\dashv$

Corollary 2 (1) *If $\Sigma \vdash_{L_{\mathrm{K}}} \theta$, then $\Sigma \models^{\mathfrak{F}} \theta$ for all frames $\mathfrak{F}$.*
(2) *If Σ is satisfiable, then it is L_{K}-consistent.* $\dashv$

Next we give a series of examples of frames and models, designed to demonstrate various properties of logics and their maximal sets.

Example 1 This is a frame with one world and two belief states.

Put $U = \{u\}$, $Prop = \{\emptyset, U\}$, $S = \{0, 1\}$, $R(U) = \{(0, 0), (1, 1)\}$ and $R(\emptyset) = \{(0, 1), (1, 1)\}$. ws is the unique function from S onto U, while f^0 and f^1 are defined by the following table.

P	f^0P	f^1P
$\emptyset$	$\emptyset$	$\emptyset$
U	U	$\emptyset$

In other words, f^0 is the identity function and f^1 the null function. They are both selection functions, and this structure is a frame.

Now $\mathscr{C} f^1 = \emptyset$ while $\mathscr{C} f^0 = U \neq \emptyset$, so $1 \models \mathbf{K}\bot$ but $0 \not\models \mathbf{K}\bot$. By definition of $R[\![\bot]\!]$, this gives $0 \models [*\bot]\mathbf{K}\bot$ (actually $[*\bot]\mathbf{K}\bot$ is valid in all frames). Hence

$$0 \not\models [*\bot]\mathbf{K}\bot \to \mathbf{K}\bot.$$

Also, as $f^0 U \neq \emptyset$ we get $0 \not\models \mathbf{B}\bot$, while $f^1 U = \emptyset$ and so $1 \not\models \neg\mathbf{B}\bot$.

Thus the logic $L_{\mathfrak{F}}$ determined by this frame contains none of the formulas $\mathbf{B}\bot$, $\neg\mathbf{B}\bot$, $\mathbf{K}\bot$, $[*\bot]\mathbf{K}\bot \to \mathbf{K}\bot$. Therefore L_{K} contains none of them. ⊣

In Example 1, the relations $R(P)$ are serial, so the frame validates the (∗D)-scheme $\langle *\phi \rangle \top$. We now show that this can fail. To do so requires only one world and one belief state, in which case we may as well identify them. Such a structure will be called a *singleton frame*.

The main purpose of the example is to show that $\neg\mathbf{B}\bot$ can be consistently added to L_{K}. As already mentioned, we will see in Sect. 7 that a logic cannot contain both $\neg\mathbf{B}\bot$ and scheme (∗D).

Example 2 The Rational Singleton Frame

Define a frame $\mathfrak{F}_r$ by putting $U = S = \{r\}$, $Prop = \{\emptyset, U\}$, $\mathsf{ws}(r) = r$, f^r = the identity function on *Prop*, $R(\emptyset) = \emptyset$, and $R(U) = \{(r, r)\}$.

Since $f^r U \neq \emptyset$, $\mathbf{B}\bot$ is false at r in any model on the frame. Thus the frame validates $\neg\mathbf{B}\bot$. The logic of the frame is consistent and contains $\neg\mathbf{B}\bot$, and hence the smallest logic containing $\neg\mathbf{B}\bot$ is consistent.

The formula $\langle *\phi \rangle \top$ is false in any model on this frame that has $R[\![\phi]\!] = \emptyset$. In particular, $\mathfrak{F}_r$ validates $\neg\langle *\bot \rangle \top$.

$\mathfrak{F}_r$ is the only singleton frame (up to isomorphism) that validates $\neg\mathbf{B}\bot$. For, in any singleton frame based on $\{r\}$, from $r \models \neg\mathbf{B}\bot$ we infer that $f^r U \neq \emptyset$, so $f^r U = U$ and f^r is the identity function on $\{\emptyset, U\}$. Moreover, if we had $(r, r) \in R(\emptyset)$, then by (F1) we would get the contradictory $f^r U = f^r \emptyset = \emptyset$. Hence we must have $R(\emptyset) = \emptyset$. Also from $f^r U \neq \emptyset$, by (F3) we infer $R(U) \neq \emptyset$, so we must have $R(U) = \{(r, r)\}$.

In summary, a singleton frame validates $\neg\mathbf{B}\bot$ iff its single selection function is the identity function, and if this condition holds, then the structure of the frame is uniquely determined as being that of $\mathfrak{F}_r$. Therefore, any different kind of singleton frame must have a null selection function. There are four such "null frames", which we describe in Example 5 below. ⊣

The next example validates every formula of the form $[*\phi]\mathbf{B}\psi$. Nonetheless its points can be distinguished by other kinds of formulas. The construction will serve a signficant purpose at at the end of the chapter, where we use it to show that in the canonical models we construct in the next section, distinct belief states may have the same selection function and the same associated world state.

Example 3 As in Example 1, put $U = \{u\}$, $Prop = \{\emptyset, U\}$, $S = \{0, 1\}$, and ws = the unique function $S \to U$. But now, for both $s \in S$, let f^s be the null function, i.e. $f^s(\emptyset) = f^s(U) = \emptyset$. Thus $\mathscr{C} f^s = \emptyset$. Let $R(\emptyset) = R(U) = \{(1, 1)\}$. It is readily checked that this is a frame. In particular, (F3) holds vacuously, as there is no case of $f^s P \neq \emptyset$.

By definition of R, for every pure Boolean ϕ, the formula $\langle *\phi \rangle \top$ is true at 1 in every model on the frame, but false at 0 in every model. Also, in any such model, since $f^s P = \emptyset \subseteq [\![\psi]\!]$ for all s and P, we have $[*\phi]\mathbf{B}\psi$ true in the model for all ϕ and ψ by Lemma 3(3).

Now fix a model $\mathfrak{M}$ on this frame, and let $\Gamma_s = \{\theta : \mathfrak{M}, s \models \theta\}$. Then by the Strong Soundness Theorem 5(2), Γ_0 and Γ_1 are both L-consistent, where L is the logic of this frame. Since in general $\neg\theta \in \Gamma_s$ iff $\theta \notin \Gamma_s$, both are L-maximal. Moreover, both are closed under the rule ($\bowtie$R). This is because the conclusion $\rho(\phi \bowtie \psi)$ of a such a rule is true in $\mathfrak{M}$, hence belongs to Γ_s, since $R[\![\phi]\!] = R[\![\psi]\!]$. Thus Γ_0 and Γ_1 are both L-saturated. Hence they are L_{K}-saturated.

Since $\mathsf{ws}(0) = \mathsf{ws}(1)$, Γ_0 and Γ_1 contain exactly the same pure Boolean formulas (Lemma 3(1)). They both contain all formulas of the form $[*\phi]\mathbf{B}\psi$, since these are all valid in the frame.

On the other hand, Γ_1 contains all formulas $\langle *\phi \rangle \top$, while Γ_0 contains none of them. ⊣

The next example in this series shows that there are maximal sets that are not saturated.

Example 4 Let $U = \{u\}$, *Prop* $= \{\emptyset, U\}$, $S = \{0, 1, 2\}$, ws = the unique function $S \to U$, f^s = the null function for all $s \in S$, $R(\emptyset) = \{(0, 1)\}$ and $R(U) = \{(0, 2)\}$. Again we have a frame.

In any model $\mathfrak{M}$ on this frame, the points 1 and 2 are semantically indistinguishable, i.e.

$$\mathfrak{M}, 1 \models \theta \quad \text{iff} \quad \mathfrak{M}, 2 \models \theta \tag{5}$$

for all formulas θ. This is shown by induction on the formation of θ. The fact that $\mathsf{ws}(1) = \mathsf{ws}(2)$ ensures that (5) holds when θ is a variable, and the inductive cases for the Boolean connectives are routine. The fact that f^1 and f^2 are null ensures that every formula of the form $\mathbf{B}\chi$ or $\mathbf{K}\chi$ is true at both 1 and 2. The fact that there are no pairs $(1, t)$ or $(2, t)$ in any $R[\![\phi]\!]$ ensures that every formula of the form $[*\phi]\chi$ or $\phi \bowtie \psi$ is true at both 1 and 2. Thus (5) holds in all cases.

Since $(0, 1)$ is the only member of $R[\![\bot]\!]$, in $\mathfrak{M}$ we have $0 \models [*\bot]\theta$ iff $1 \models \theta$, for all θ. Similarly, $0 \models [*\top]\theta$ iff $2 \models \theta$. Hence by (5), $0 \models [*\bot]\theta$ iff $0 \models [*\top]\theta$, and therefore $0 \models ([*\bot]\theta \leftrightarrow [*\top]\theta)$ for all θ. But since $(0, 1)$ is in $R[\![\bot]\!] - R[\![\top]\!]$, we have $0 \not\models \bot \bowtie \top$.

Now let Γ be the L_{K}-maximal set $\{\theta : \mathfrak{M}, 0 \models \theta\}$. What we have just shown is that

$$\{[*\bot]\theta \leftrightarrow [*\top]\theta : \theta \text{ is any formula}\} \subseteq \Gamma,$$

while $\bot \bowtie \top \notin \Gamma$. So Γ does not respect $\bowtie$ (i.e. (4) fails with $\rho = \#$), and therefore Γ is not L_{K}-saturated. ⊣

Besides the frame $\mathfrak{F}_r$ of Example 2, there are four other singleton frames. They all validate $\mathbf{B}\bot$:

Example 5 The Null Singleton Frames.

Let $U = S = \{\nu\}$, $Prop = \{\emptyset, U\}$, $\mathsf{ws}(\nu) = \nu$, and f^ν = the null function on *Prop*. Since $f^\nu U = \emptyset$, any frame on this structure is going to have $\nu \models \mathbf{B}\bot$. There are four such frames, according to their definitions of the relations $R(P)$:

Name	$R\emptyset$	RU	Validates
$\mathfrak{F}_\nu$	$\emptyset$	$\emptyset$	$\neg\langle *\phi\rangle\top$
$\mathfrak{F}_\top$	$\emptyset$	$\{(\nu,\nu)\}$	$\langle *\phi\rangle\top \leftrightarrow (\phi \bowtie \top)$
$\mathfrak{F}_\bot$	$\{(\nu,\nu)\}$	$\emptyset$	$\langle *\phi\rangle\top \leftrightarrow (\phi \bowtie \bot)$
$\mathfrak{F}_D$	$\{(\nu,\nu)\}$	$\{(\nu,\nu)\}$	$\langle *\phi\rangle\top$

The frame $\mathfrak{F}_D$ validates all three of the schemes ($*$D), ($*$X) and ($*$K) mentioned in the Introduction. ⊣

The following fact about models on singleton frames will be used in Theorem 7 in the next section.

Theorem 6 *If $\mathfrak{M}$ is any model on a singleton frame, then the set $\{\theta : \mathfrak{M} \models \theta\}$ is closed under the rule* ($\bowtie$ R).

Proof We need to show of any template ρ that for all ϕ, ψ:

$$\text{if } \mathfrak{M} \models \rho([*\phi]\theta \leftrightarrow [*\psi]\theta) \text{for all formulas } \theta, \text{then} \mathfrak{M} \models \rho(\phi \bowtie \psi).$$

For this it suffices that for any ρ,

$$\mathfrak{M} \models \rho([*\phi]\bot \leftrightarrow [*\psi]\bot) \quad \text{implies} \quad \mathfrak{M} \models \rho(\phi \bowtie \psi). \tag{6}$$

We show this by induction on ρ. (Note that the converse of (6) holds in any model, by soundness—see Theorem 1(7)).

Now if s is the single element of $\mathfrak{M}$, then in general $\mathfrak{M} \models \theta$ iff $\mathfrak{M}, s \models \theta$, and $R[\![\phi]\!]$ is either $\emptyset$ or $\{(s,s)\}$. From these facts we see that

$$\begin{array}{ll} R[\![\phi]\!] = \emptyset & \text{iff } \mathfrak{M} \models [*\phi]\bot. \\ R[\![\psi]\!] = \emptyset & \text{iff } \mathfrak{M} \models [*\psi]\bot. \\ R[\![\phi]\!] = R[\![\psi]\!] & \text{iff } \mathfrak{M} \models [*\phi]\bot \leftrightarrow [*\psi]\bot. \end{array}$$

Since $\mathfrak{M} \models \phi \bowtie \psi$ iff $R[\![\phi]\!] = R[\![\psi]\!]$ (in any model), this confirms that (6) holds when $\rho = \#$.

Now assume inductively that (6) holds for a template ρ. Then for any χ, if $\mathfrak{M} \not\models [*\chi]\rho(\phi \bowtie \psi)$, then $R[\![\chi]\!] \neq \emptyset$ and $\mathfrak{M} \not\models \rho(\phi \bowtie \psi)$. By induction hypothesis on ρ, $\mathfrak{M} \not\models \rho([*\phi]\bot \leftrightarrow [*\psi]\bot)$. This implies $\mathfrak{M} \not\models [*\chi]\rho([*\phi]\bot \leftrightarrow [*\psi]\bot)$, since $R[\![\chi]\!] = \{(s,s)\}$. Hence (6) holds with $[*\chi]\rho$ in place of ρ.

Also, if $\mathfrak{M} \not\models \omega \to \rho(\phi \bowtie \psi)$, then $\mathfrak{M} \models \omega$ and $\mathfrak{M} \not\models \rho(\phi \bowtie \psi)$, so by induction hypothesis, $\mathfrak{M} \not\models \rho([*\phi]\bot \leftrightarrow [*\psi]\bot)$, and thus $\mathfrak{M} \not\models \omega \to \rho([*\phi]\bot \leftrightarrow [*\psi]\bot)$. Hence (6) holds with $\omega \to \rho$ in place of ρ. That completes the proof of (6). ⊣

5 Canonical Model for L

Fix a logic L. We will construct a model $\mathfrak{M}_L$, based on the set S_L of L-saturated sets, such that the formulas true in $\mathfrak{M}_L$ are precisely the L-theorems.

A *Boolean L-maximal set* is a set u of pure Boolean formulas that is maximally L-consistent within the set of all pure Boolean formulas. Equivalently, u is L-consistent and *negation complete* in the sense that for all pure Boolean ϕ, either $\phi \in u$ or $\neg\phi \in u$. Let U_L be the set of all Boolean L-maximal sets. Any L-consistent set of pure Boolean formulas can be extended to a member of U_L.

For each pure Boolean ϕ, define $[\![\phi]\!]_L = \{u \in U_L : \phi \in u\}$. Put

$$Prop_L = \{[\![\phi]\!]_L : \phi \text{ is pure Boolean}\}.$$

Then $Prop_L$ is a Boolean set algebra, since $U_L - [\![\phi]\!]_L = [\![\neg\phi]\!]_L$; $[\![\phi]\!]_L \cap [\![\psi]\!]_L = [\![\phi \wedge \psi]\!]_L$; $[\![\phi]\!]_L \cup [\![\psi]\!]_L = [\![\phi \vee \psi]\!]_L$; $U_L = [\![\top]\!]_L$, $\emptyset = [\![\bot]\!]_L$ etc. Thus $(U_L, Prop_L)$ is a Boolean structure.[6]

Moreover, $\vdash_L \phi \to \psi$ iff $[\![\phi]\!]_L \subseteq [\![\psi]\!]_L$, and hence $\vdash_L \phi \leftrightarrow \psi$ iff $[\![\phi]\!]_L = [\![\psi]\!]_L$. The only part of that which is not routine is to observe that if $\nvdash_L \phi \to \psi$, then $\{\phi, \neg\psi\}$ is L-consistent and so extends to some $u \in U_L$ with $u \in [\![\phi]\!]_L - [\![\psi]\!]_L$.

Each L-maximal set Γ gives rise to a function f^Γ on *Prop* by putting

$$f^\Gamma [\![\phi]\!]_L = \{u \in U_L : \{\psi : [*\phi]\mathbf{B}\psi \in \Gamma\} \subseteq u\}.$$

f^Γ is well-defined, in the sense that the definition of $f^\Gamma [\![\phi]\!]_L$ does not depend on how the proposition $[\![\phi]\!]_L$ is named. For if $[\![\phi]\!]_L = [\![\phi']\!]_L$, then $\vdash_L \phi \leftrightarrow \phi'$, so by the rule (CR), $\vdash_L [*\phi]\mathbf{B}\psi \leftrightarrow [*\phi']\mathbf{B}\psi$ for any ψ; hence as Γ is an L-maximal set, $\{\psi : [*\phi]\mathbf{B}\psi \in \Gamma\} = \{\psi : [*\phi']\mathbf{B}\psi \in \Gamma\}$.

We also use the fact that, by normal modal logic,

$$u \in f^\Gamma [\![\phi]\!]_L \quad \text{iff} \quad \{\langle *\phi \rangle \mathbf{b}\psi : \psi \in u\} \subseteq \Gamma. \tag{7}$$

Lemma 8 *If Γ is L-maximal, then for any ϕ the following are equivalent.*

(1) $f^\Gamma [\![\phi]\!]_L = \emptyset$.
(2) $\{\psi : [*\phi]\mathbf{B}\psi \in \Gamma\}$ *is L-inconsistent.*

---

[6] In the models of [14], *Prop* is taken to be the set of clopen subsets of a topology on U that makes it a *Stone space*, i.e. compact and totally separated. It can be shown that $Prop_L$ generates a Stone topology on U_L, for which the clopen sets are precisely the members of $Prop_L$. But we do not make any use of those additional properties.

(3) $[*\phi]\mathbf{B}\bot \in \Gamma$.

Proof (1) implies (2): If $\{\psi : [*\phi]\mathbf{B}\psi \in \Gamma\}$ is L-consistent, then it is included in a Boolean L-maximal set u, which then belongs to $f^\Gamma[\![\phi]\!]_L$, so $f^\Gamma[\![\phi]\!]_L \neq \emptyset$.

(2) implies (3): If $\{\psi : [*\phi]\mathbf{B}\psi \in \Gamma\} \vdash_L \bot$, then by the $\Box$-Lemma 5 with $\Box = [*\phi]\mathbf{B}$ we have $\Gamma \vdash_L [*\phi]\mathbf{B}\bot$, hence $[*\phi]\mathbf{B}\bot \in \Gamma$.

(3) implies (1): If $[*\phi]\mathbf{B}\bot \in \Gamma$, then any $u \in f^\Gamma[\![\phi]\!]_L$ would have $\bot \in u$, contrary to L-consistency, so in fact $f^\Gamma[\![\phi]\!]_L = \emptyset$. ⊣

Lemma 9 *f^Γ is a selection function on $(U_L, Prop_L)$.*

Proof (INCL): By (∗2), $[*\phi]\mathbf{B}\phi \in \Gamma$. Hence if $u \in f^\Gamma[\![\phi]\!]_L$, then $\phi \in u$, so $u \in [\![\phi]\!]_L$. This confirms that $f^\Gamma[\![\phi]\!]_L \subseteq [\![\phi]\!]_L$.

(MONEYS): Let $[\![\phi]\!]_L \subseteq [\![\psi]\!]_L$. Then $\vdash_L \phi \to \psi$, so by Theorem 1(5), $[*\psi]\mathbf{B}\bot \to [*\phi]\mathbf{B}\bot$ belongs to Γ. But now if $f^\Gamma[\![\phi]\!]_L \neq \emptyset$, then by Lemma 8, $[*\phi]\mathbf{B}\bot \notin \Gamma$, hence $[*\psi]\mathbf{B}\bot \notin \Gamma$, and so $f^\Gamma[\![\psi]\!]_L \neq \emptyset$.

(STRONG ARROW): Suppose that $[\![\psi]\!]_L \cap f^\Gamma[\![\phi]\!]_L \neq \emptyset$. Then we have to show that

$$f^\Gamma([\![\psi]\!]_L \cap [\![\phi]\!]_L) = [\![\psi]\!]_L \cap f^\Gamma[\![\phi]\!]_L. \tag{8}$$

Note that $f^\Gamma([\![\psi]\!]_L \cap [\![\phi]\!]_L) = f^\Gamma[\![\psi \wedge \phi]\!]_L = f^\Gamma[\![\phi \wedge \psi]\!]_L$.

By assumption, there is some element of $f^\Gamma[\![\phi]\!]_L$ that contains ψ, which by (7) implies

$$\langle *\phi\rangle \mathbf{b}\psi \in \Gamma. \tag{9}$$

Now take $u \in f^\Gamma([\![\psi]\!]_L \cap [\![\phi]\!]_L)$. Then as (INCL) holds, $u \in f^\Gamma([\![\psi]\!]_L)$. Also if $[*\phi]\mathbf{B}\chi \in \Gamma$, then by modal logic $[*\phi]\mathbf{B}(\psi \to \chi) \in \Gamma$, which by (∗8) and (9) gives $[*(\phi \wedge \psi)]\mathbf{B}\chi \in \Gamma$. Hence $\chi \in u$ as $u \in f^\Gamma[\![\phi \wedge \psi]\!]_L$. This shows that $u \in f^\Gamma[\![\phi]\!]_L$, and altogether that the left-right inclusion of (8) holds.

Conversely, let $u \in [\![\psi]\!]_L \cap f^\Gamma[\![\phi]\!]_L$. If $[*(\phi \wedge \psi)]\mathbf{B}\chi \in \Gamma$, then $[*\phi]\mathbf{B}(\psi \to \chi) \in \Gamma$ by (∗7), so $\psi \to \chi \in u$ as $u \in f^\Gamma[\![\phi]\!]_L$. But $\psi \in u$ as $u \in [\![\psi]\!]_L$, so then $\chi \in u$. This shows that $u \in f^\Gamma[\![\phi \wedge \psi]\!]_L$, completing the proof of the right-left inclusion of (8). ⊣

If Γ is any L-maximal set, let $\mathsf{ws}_L(\Gamma) = \{\psi : \psi \in \Gamma\}$, the set of all pure Boolean formulas that belong to Γ. This is the *world state* of Γ, and is evidently a Boolean-maximal set, i.e. $\mathsf{ws}_L(\Gamma) \in U_L$. Restricting this to L-saturated sets Γ gives a function $\mathsf{ws}_L : S_L \to U_L$.

The *canonical frame* of L is the structure

$$\mathfrak{F}_L = (U_L, Prop_L, S_L, \mathsf{sf}_L, R_L),$$

based on the Boolean structure $(U_L, Prop_L)$, such that S_L is the set of all L-saturated sets; $\mathsf{ws}_L : S_L \to U_L$ is the function just defined; $\mathsf{sf}_L(\Gamma) = f^\Gamma$ for all $\Gamma \in S_L$; and for any $[\![\phi]\!]_L \in Prop_L$,

$$(\Gamma, \Delta) \in R_L[\![\phi]\!]_L \quad \text{iff} \quad \{\theta : [*\phi]\theta \in \Gamma\} \subseteq \Delta.$$

The definition of $R_L[\![\phi]\!]_L$ does not depend on how the proposition $[\![\phi]\!]_L$ is named. For if $[\![\phi]\!]_L = [\![\phi']\!]_L$, then $\vdash_L \phi \leftrightarrow \phi'$, hence by the rule (CR), $\vdash_L [*\phi]\theta \leftrightarrow [*\phi']\theta$ for all formulas θ, so $\{\theta : [*\phi]\theta \in \Gamma\} = \{\theta : [*\phi']\theta \in \Gamma\}$.

By standard modal logic,

$$(\Gamma, \Delta) \in R_L[\![\phi]\!]_L \quad \text{iff} \quad \{\langle *\phi\rangle\theta : \theta \in \Delta\} \subseteq \Gamma. \tag{10}$$

Lemma 10 *$\mathfrak{F}_L$ is a selection frame.*

Proof We verify the four defining frame conditions.

(F1): Let $(\Gamma, \Delta) \in R_L[\![\phi]\!]_L$. We have to show that $f^\Delta U_L = f^\Gamma[\![\phi]\!]_L$. Note that $U_L = [\![\top]\!]_L$. Suppose that $u \in f^\Delta[\![\top]\!]_L$. Then if $[*\phi]\mathbf{B}\psi \in \Gamma$, since $(\Gamma, \Delta) \in R_L[\![\phi]\!]_L$ we have $\mathbf{B}\psi \in \Delta$, hence $[*\top]\mathbf{B}\psi \in \Delta$ by $(*4)'$ (see Theorem 1(1)), so $\psi \in u$ as $u \in f^\Delta[\![\top]\!]_L$. This shows that $\{\psi : [*\phi]\mathbf{B}\psi \in \Gamma\} \subseteq u$, i.e. $u \in f^\Gamma[\![\phi]\!]_L$.

Conversely, let $u \in f^\Gamma[\![\phi]\!]_L$. Then if $[*\top]\mathbf{B}\psi \in \Delta$, by axiom $(*3)$ we have $\mathbf{B}\psi \in \Delta$, hence $\langle *\phi\rangle\mathbf{B}\psi \in \Gamma$ by (10), so $[*\phi]\mathbf{B}\psi \in \Gamma$ by $(*\text{FB})$, and therefore $\psi \in u$ as $u \in f^\Gamma[\![\phi]\!]_L$. This shows that $u \in f^\Delta[\![\top]\!]_L$ as required.

(F2): Let $(\Gamma, \Delta) \in R_L[\![\phi]\!]_L$. We have to show that $\mathscr{C} f^\Delta \subseteq \mathbf{C}(\mathscr{C} f^\Gamma)$. So suppose that $u \in U_L$ has $u \notin \mathbf{C}(\mathscr{C} f^\Gamma)$. Since $\mathbf{C}(\mathscr{C} f^\Gamma)$ is topologically closed, there must then be some basic open set $P \in \mathit{Prop}$ that contains u and is disjoint from $\mathbf{C}(\mathscr{C} f^\Gamma)$. Then the complement of P is also a basic open set, hence of the form $[\![\psi]\!]_L$, that includes $\mathbf{C}(\mathscr{C} f^\Gamma)$ and does not contain u. Now

$$f^\Gamma[\![\neg\psi]\!]_L \subseteq \mathscr{C} f^\Gamma \subseteq \mathbf{C}(\mathscr{C} f^\Gamma) \subseteq [\![\psi]\!]_L.$$

But $f^\Gamma[\![\neg\psi]\!]_L \subseteq [\![\neg\psi]\!]_L = -[\![\psi]\!]_L$ by (INCL) (Lemma 9), so we conclude that $f^\Gamma[\![\neg\psi]\!]_L = \emptyset$. Hence by Lemma 8, $[*\neg\psi]\mathbf{B}\bot \in \Gamma$. Thus by Theorem 1(3), $\mathbf{K}\psi \in \Gamma$. It follows by axiom $(\mathrm{K}*)$ that $[*\phi]\mathbf{K}\psi \in \Gamma$. So $\mathbf{K}\psi \in \Delta$ as $(\Gamma, \Delta) \in R_L[\![\phi]\!]_L$.

Then for every χ we get $[*\chi]\mathbf{K}\psi \in \Delta$ by $(\mathrm{K}*)$, while $\psi \notin u$ as $u \notin [\![\psi]\!]_L$, showing that $u \notin f^\Delta[\![\chi]\!]_L$. Hence $u \notin \bigcup_\chi f^\Delta[\![\chi]\!]_L = \mathscr{C} f^\Delta$, completing the proof that $\mathscr{C} f^\Delta \subseteq \mathbf{C}(\mathscr{C} f^\Gamma)$.

(F3): Suppose $f^\Gamma[\![\phi]\!]_L \neq \emptyset$. Then by Lemma 8, $[*\phi]\mathbf{B}\bot \notin \Gamma$. Therefore by Theorem 3, there is some $\Delta \in S_L$ (with $\mathbf{B}\bot \notin \Delta$) such that $\{\theta : [*\phi]\theta \in \Gamma\} \subseteq \Delta$ and hence $(\Gamma, \Delta) \in R_L[\![\phi]\!]_L$.

(F4): To show that $\mathsf{ws}_L(S_L)$ is dense in U_L, it is enough to show that it is intersected by every non-empty basic open set. Since *Prop* is a base for the topology, a basic open set has the form $[\![\phi]\!]_L$, and if this is non-empty, then $\{\phi\}$ is L-consistent, and obviously finite. So by Theorem 2(3), there is a $\Gamma \in S_L$ with $\{\phi\} \subseteq \Gamma$. Then $\phi \in \mathsf{ws}_L(\Gamma)$, so $[\![\phi]\!]_L \cap \mathsf{ws}_L(S_L)$ contains $\mathsf{ws}_L(\Gamma)$ and is therefore non-empty as required. ⊣

Concerning (F4), we now give a sufficient criterion for $\mathfrak{F}_L$ to be world-surjective, a criterion that holds when $L = L_{\mathrm{K}}$.

Theorem 7 *If a logic L is validated by some singleton frame, then in the canonical frame $\mathfrak{F}_L$, the function $\mathsf{ws}_L : S_L \to U_L$ is surjective.*

Proof Let L be validated by some singleton frame $\mathfrak{F}$ having $S = U = \{s\}$. Given any Boolean L-maximal set $u \in U_L$, define a valuation $[\![-]\!]_u$ on $\{s\}$ by declaring that $s \in [\![p]\!]_u$ iff $p \in u$, for all variables p. This gives a model $\mathfrak{M}_u = (\mathfrak{F}, [\![-]\!]_u)$ on $\mathfrak{F}$, for which $\mathfrak{M}_u, s \models p$ iff $p \in u$.

Let $\Gamma_u = \{\theta : \mathfrak{M}_u \models \theta\} = \{\theta : \mathfrak{M}_u, s \models \theta\}$. Since $\mathfrak{F} \models L$ we have $L \subseteq \Gamma_u$, and so Γ_u is L-maximal. A straightforward induction shows that for all pure Boolean ψ, $\psi \in \Gamma_u$ iff $\psi \in u$. Hence $\mathsf{ws}_L(\Gamma_u) = u$.

But by Theorem 6, Γ_u is closed under the rule ($\bowtie$R), and so is L-saturated by (4). Hence $\Gamma_u \in S_L$ as required to conclude that ws_L maps S_L onto U_L. ⊣

The *canonical L-model* is $\mathfrak{M}_L = (\mathfrak{F}_L, [\![-]\!]_L)$, with $[\![p]\!]_L = \{u \in U_L : p \in u\}$, as above, for all variables p.

Theorem 8 (The 'Truth Lemma')
Let θ be any formula. Then for all $\Gamma \in S_L$,

$$\mathfrak{M}_L, \Gamma \models \theta \quad \textit{iff} \quad \theta \in \Gamma.$$

Proof By induction on the formation of θ. In considering each case, we suppress the symbol $\mathfrak{M}_L$, writing $\Gamma \models \theta$ etc.

- For the case of a variable p we have $\Gamma \models p$ iff $\mathsf{ws}(\Gamma) \in [\![p]\!]_L$ iff $p \in \mathsf{ws}(\Gamma)$ iff $p \in \Gamma$ as p is pure Boolean.
- For the case of a formula $\phi \bowtie \psi$, suppose that $\Gamma \models \phi \bowtie \psi$. Take a formula $[*\psi]\omega$ in Γ. If $\Delta \in S_L$ has $\{\theta : [*\phi]\theta \in \Gamma\} \subseteq \Delta$, then $(\Gamma, \Delta) \in R_L[\![\phi]\!]_L$ by definition, hence $(\Gamma, \Delta) \in R_L[\![\psi]\!]_L$ as $\Gamma \models \phi \bowtie \psi$, so $\{\theta : [*\psi]\theta \in \Gamma\} \subseteq \Delta$, and thus $\omega \in \Delta$. This shows that $\{\theta : [*\phi]\theta \in \Gamma\} \subseteq \Delta$ implies $\omega \in \Delta$, which by Theorem 3 means that $[*\phi]\omega \in \Gamma$.
  Altogether we showed that $[*\psi]\omega \in \Gamma$ implies $[*\phi]\omega \in \Gamma$. Similarly $[*\phi]\omega \in \Gamma$ implies $[*\psi]\omega \in \Gamma$. Hence $([*\phi]\omega \leftrightarrow [*\psi]\omega) \in \Gamma$ for all formulas ω. By the case $\rho = \#$ of (4), this ensures that $\phi \bowtie \psi \in \Gamma$, since Γ is L-saturated.
  Conversely, suppose $\phi \bowtie \psi \in \Gamma$. Let $(\Gamma, \Delta) \in R_L[\![\psi]\!]_L$. Then if $[*\phi]\theta \in \Gamma$, since $([*\phi]\theta \leftrightarrow [*\psi]\theta) \in \Gamma$ by axiom ($\bowtie$), we get $[*\psi]\theta \in \Gamma$, and hence $\theta \in \Delta$ as $(\Gamma, \Delta) \in R_L[\![\psi]\!]_L$. This shows that $(\Gamma, \Delta) \in R_L[\![\phi]\!]_L$. Similarly, $(\Gamma, \Delta) \in R_L[\![\phi]\!]_L$ implies $(\Gamma, \Delta) \in R_L[\![\psi]\!]_L$. Thus in general, $(\Gamma, \Delta) \in R_L[\![\phi]\!]_L$ iff $(\Gamma, \Delta) \in R_L[\![\psi]\!]_L$, which means that $\Gamma \models \phi \bowtie \psi \in \Gamma$.
- For the case of a formula $\mathbf{B}\phi$, assume first that $\Gamma \models \mathbf{B}\phi$, and so $f^{\Gamma}[\![\top]\!]_L \subseteq [\![\phi]\!]_L$. Suppose then, for the sake of contradiction, that $\{\psi : \mathbf{B}\psi \in \Gamma\} \nvdash_L \phi$. Then $\{\psi : \mathbf{B}\psi \in \Gamma\} \cup \{\neg\phi\}$ is L-consistent, so extends to a Boolean-maximal set u. But now $u \notin [\![\phi]\!]_L$ as $\phi \notin u$, while for any formula $[*\top]\mathbf{B}\psi \in \Gamma$ we have $\mathbf{B}\psi \in \Gamma$ by (∗3), hence $\psi \in u$ by construction. But this shows that $u \in f^{\Gamma}[\![\top]\!]_L$, contradicting $f^{\Gamma}[\![\top]\!]_L \subseteq [\![\phi]\!]_L$. So we must conclude that $\{\psi : \mathbf{B}\psi \in \Gamma\} \vdash_L \phi$. Hence by the $\Box$-Lemma 5 with $\Box = \mathbf{B}$ we get $\Gamma \vdash_L \mathbf{B}\phi$, and therefore $\mathbf{B}\phi \in \Gamma$.

Conversely, suppose $\mathbf{B}\phi \in \Gamma$. Then by (∗4′), $[*\top]\mathbf{B}\phi \in \Gamma$, so if $u \in f^{\Gamma}[\![\top]\!]_L$ we have $\phi \in u$ and hence $u \in [\![\phi]\!]_L$. This shows that $f^{\Gamma}[\![\top]\!]_L \subseteq [\![\phi]\!]_L$, implying that $\Gamma \models \mathbf{B}\phi$.

- The case of $\bot$ and the inductive case of an implicational formula $\theta \to \omega$ are standard, given the semantics for $\bot$ and $\to$ and the properties of Γ as a maximal set.
- For the inductive case of a formula $[*\phi]\omega$, make the induction hypothesis that the Theorem holds for ω. Then by this hypothesis and Theorem 3, we have $[*\phi]\omega \in \Gamma$ iff

$$\text{for all } \Delta \in S_L \text{ such that } (\Gamma, \Delta) \in R_L[\![\phi]\!]_L,\ \Delta \models \omega,$$

which is precisely the condition for $\Gamma \models [*\phi]\omega$. Hence the Theorem holds for $[*\phi]\omega$.

- Finally, we can apply the proof thus far to deal with the case of a formula $\mathbf{K}\phi$, using its equivalence to $[*\neg\phi]\mathbf{B}\bot$. The formula $\mathbf{K}\phi \leftrightarrow [*\neg\phi]\mathbf{B}\bot$ is a theorem of every selection logic (Theorem 1(3)), so is valid in every frame, and in particular is true at every point in $\mathfrak{M}_L$. Moreover, as this formula is an L-theorem, it belongs to every member of S_L. Since the present Theorem holds for $[*\neg\phi]\mathbf{B}\bot$ from the above, we can then argue that

$\Gamma \models \mathbf{K}\phi$
iff $\Gamma \models [*\neg\phi]\mathbf{B}\bot$ as $\Gamma \models \mathbf{K}\phi \leftrightarrow [*\neg\phi]\mathbf{B}\bot$,
iff $[*\neg\phi]\mathbf{B}\bot \in \Gamma$ as the Theorem holds for $[*\neg\phi]\mathbf{B}\bot$,
iff $\mathbf{K}\phi\bot \in \Gamma$ as $(\mathbf{K}\phi \leftrightarrow [*\neg\phi]\mathbf{B}\bot) \in \Gamma$.

That completes the proof of all cases. ⊣

Corollary 3 *For any formula θ, $\mathfrak{M}_L \models \theta$ iff $\vdash_L \theta$.*

Proof $\mathfrak{M}_L \models \theta$ iff θ belongs to every L-saturated set, iff $\vdash_L \theta$ by Theorem 2(4). ⊣

6 Strong Completeness for L_{K}

The Corollary just proven leads to the completeness of L_{K} with respect to frame validity:

Theorem 9 *For any formula θ:*

(1) *If θ is valid in all frames, then $\vdash_{L_{\mathrm{K}}} \theta$.*
(2) *If θ is L_{K}-consistent, then it is true at some point of some model.*

Proof (1) If θ is valid in all frames, then in particular it is true in the model $\mathfrak{M}_{L_{\mathrm{K}}}$, hence $\vdash_{L_{\mathrm{K}}} \theta$ by Corollary 3.

(2) If θ is L_{K}-consistent, then $\nvdash_{L_{\mathrm{K}}} \neg\theta$, so by part (1), $\neg\theta$ is false at some point of some model. ⊣

Now *Strong Completeness* of L_{K} would state that

$$\textit{If } \Sigma \models^{\mathfrak{F}} \theta \textit{ for all frames } \mathfrak{F}, \textit{ then } \Sigma \vdash_{L_{\mathrm{K}}} \theta.$$

This is equivalent to:

Every L_{K}-consistent set of formulas is satisfiable in some model.

We can prove that by carrying out the canonical model construction for an expanded language, along the following lines. Suppose that Σ is an L_{K}-consistent set of formulas of the present language. Add a countably infinite set of new variables, and let L'_{K} be the smallest set of formulas of the enlarged language that constitutes a logic.

Then Σ is L'_{K}-consistent, by a well known argument. For, if Σ were not L'_{K}-consistent, we would have $\vdash_{L'_{\mathrm{K}}} \neg\theta$, where θ is the conjunction of some finite subset of Σ. Since our proof theory is finitary, this means that there is some finite sequence of formulas that is an L'_{K}-derivation of $\neg\theta$ by axioms and rules of L'_{K}. This sequence involves only finitely many of the new variables, so we can uniformly replace them by variables from the old language that do not occur in the sequence (there are infinitely many such old variables). This replacement does not alter $\neg\theta$, and it provides a new sequence demonstrating that $\vdash_{L_{\mathrm{K}}} \neg\theta$, contradicting the L_{K}-consistency of Σ.

Thus Σ is L'_{K}-consistent, and there are infinitely many variables in the new language that do not occur in Σ (all the new variables at least). Hence by Theorem 2(2), Σ has an L'_{K}-saturated extension Γ. Then in the model $\mathfrak{M}_{L'_{\mathrm{K}}}$, since $\Sigma \subseteq \Gamma$, the Truth Lemma implies that $\mathfrak{M}_{L'_{\mathrm{K}}}, \Gamma \models \Sigma$, showing that Σ is satisfiable, as required.

In conclusion, we note that the minimal logic L_{K} is strongly complete with respect to the world-surjective frames. The singleton frames validates L_{K} (since every frame does), so by Theorem 7, the canonical frame of L_{K} is world-surjective. Thus

Every L_{K}-consistent set of formulas is satisfiable in a model on a world-surjective frame.

7 Commentary

The main objective of this chapter has been to show how the equivalence construct $\bowtie$ can be incorporated into a multi-modal logic. But our work has consequences for the non-$\bowtie$ part of this kind of doxastic logic, and we provide here some observations about additions and adjustments to its axioms, simplification of its semantics, and properties of its models.

Avoiding Inconsistency

The scheme $[*\phi]\mathbf{K}\psi \to \mathbf{K}\psi$, converse to to axiom (K$*$), can be consistently added to L_{K}, as shown by any of the frames of Examples 3, 4 and 5, which validate the scheme since they validate $\mathbf{K}\psi$.

But this scheme is inconsistent with the rational-agent formula $\neg\mathbf{B}\bot$. Even the instance $\psi = \bot$ of the converse is incompatible, as shown by the following derivation.

1. $[*\bot]\mathbf{K}\bot \to \mathbf{K}\bot$	converse to (K*)
2. $\mathbf{B}\bot \to \mathbf{K}\bot$	axiom (BK)
3. $[*\bot]\mathbf{B}\bot \to [*\bot]\mathbf{K}\bot$	from 2 by modal logic
4. $[*\bot]\mathbf{B}\bot$	axiom (*2)
5. $[*\bot]\mathbf{K}\bot$	3, 4, modus ponens
6. $\mathbf{K}\bot$	1, 5, modus ponens
7. $\mathbf{K}\bot \to \mathbf{B}\bot$	axiom (KB)
8. $\mathbf{B}\bot$	6, 7, modus ponens.

This shows that any logic containing $[*\bot]\mathbf{K}\bot \to \mathbf{K}\bot$ must contain $\mathbf{K}\bot$ and $\mathbf{B}\bot$, and be inconsistent with $\neg\mathbf{B}\bot$.

Now axiom (BK) is a tautological consequence of $\neg\mathbf{B}\bot$, so even without assuming (BK), we see from the derivation that:

if a modal logic contains the axioms $(*2)$ *and* (KB), *as well as the formula* $[*\bot]\mathbf{K}\bot \to \mathbf{K}\bot$, *then adding* $\neg\mathbf{B}\bot$ *to it would allow derivation of* $\mathbf{B}\bot$, *hence yield an inconsistency.*

Example 1 showed that none of $\mathbf{B}\bot$, $\neg\mathbf{B}\bot$ and $[*\bot]\mathbf{K}\bot \to \mathbf{K}\bot$ is a theorem of L_{K}.

A similar situation applies to the seriality scheme $\langle *\phi\rangle\top$, equivalent as an axiom to the $(*\mathrm{D})$-scheme $[*\phi]\theta \to \langle *\phi\rangle\theta$. The logic of the frame of Example 1 contains $(*\mathrm{D})$ (as does the logic of the frame $\mathfrak{F}_{\mathrm{D}}$ of Example 5). This shows that $(*\mathrm{D})$ can be consistently added to L_{K}. But consider the derivation

1. $\neg\mathbf{B}\bot$	
2. $[*\bot]\neg\mathbf{B}\bot$	from 1 by $[*\bot]$-Necessitation
3. $[*\bot]\mathbf{B}\bot$	axiom (*2)
4. $[*\bot]\bot$	from 2, 3 by modal logic
5. $\neg\langle *\bot\rangle\top$	from 4 by modal logic.

This shows that a logic cannot consistently contain both $\langle *\bot\rangle\top$ and $\neg\mathbf{B}\bot$.

It is also revealing to look at this semantically. Suppose that $\neg\mathbf{B}\bot$ is true in a model $\mathfrak{M}$. Then at each point $t \in S$ we have $f^tU \neq \emptyset$. Now if there were a pair (s, t) in $R(\emptyset)$, by (F1) and (INCL) we would have $f^tU = f^s\emptyset = \emptyset$, contradicting $f^tU \neq \emptyset$. Therefore the relation $R(\emptyset)$ is empty, so $\langle *\bot\rangle\top$ is false at every point.

In the Introduction we proposed the scheme (2), i.e.

$$\neg(\phi \bowtie \bot) \to \langle *\phi\rangle\top,$$

as a suitable weakening of $(*\mathrm{D})$. The rational singleton frame $\mathfrak{F}_r$ of Example 2 validates this scheme as well as $\neg\mathbf{B}\bot$, showing that the two can be jointly added to L_{K} to produce a consistent logic. (2) itself is not a theorem of L_{K}, as it is not valid in the null frame $\mathfrak{F}_\bot$ of Example 2, and indeed is false in any model on that frame that has $[\![\phi]\!] = U$.

Status of Axiom$(*6)$

Axiom $(*6)$ was not used in our completeness proof. It *could have* been used to prove that $f^{\Gamma}[\![\phi]\!]_L$ is well defined, since this requires the result

$$\vdash_L \phi \leftrightarrow \psi \quad \text{implies} \quad \vdash_L [*\phi]\mathbf{B}\chi \leftrightarrow [*\psi]\mathbf{B}\chi$$

of Theorem 1(4), which, as we noted, follows by $(*6)$ and **K**-Necessitation. But the result itself is just an instance of the Congruence Rule (CR).

Thus (CR) supersedes $(*6)$, which can be dropped from the axiomatisation of L_{K}. But $(*6)$ is valid (Lemma 7), so it must then be derivable from the rest of the axiomatisation. It would be an interesting exercise to formulate such a derivation.

Adding $\psi \to [*\phi]\psi$

It is readily checked that the axiom

$$\psi \to [*\phi]\psi \tag{11}$$

is valid in all frames that satisfy

$$(s,t) \in R[\![\phi]\!] \quad \text{implies} \quad \mathsf{ws}(s) = \mathsf{ws}(t), \tag{12}$$

a condition expressing that 'belief revision does not affect the world' [14],p. 231. Moreover, the presence of (11) in a logic forces its canonical frame to satisfy (12):

Lemma 11 *Let L be any logic that contains the scheme (11). Then in $\mathfrak{F}_L$, if $(\Gamma, \Delta) \in R_L[\![\phi]\!]_L$, then $\mathsf{ws}_L(\Gamma) = \mathsf{ws}_L(\Delta)$.*

Proof Let $(\Gamma, \Delta) \in R_L[\![\phi]\!]_L$. If $\psi \in \Gamma$, then $[*\phi]\psi \in \Gamma$ by axiom (11), so $\psi \in \Delta$. But if $\psi \notin \Gamma$, then $\neg\psi \in \Gamma$, hence $[*\phi]\neg\psi \in \Gamma$ by (11) again, so $\neg\psi \in \Delta$ and thus $\psi \notin \Delta$. This shows that Γ and Δ contain the same pure Boolean formulas. $\dashv$

It follows from these observations that the smallest logic containing (11) is strongly sound and complete for validity in all frames satisfying (12). Moreover, this logic is valid in all singleton frames, which satisfy (12). Hence this logic has a world-surjective canonical frame, and is characterised by validity in the world-surjective frames satisfying (12). Note that (11) is valid in the frame of Example 2, and so is consistent with $\neg\mathbf{B}\bot$.

The converse of (11) is $[*\phi]\psi \to \psi$. This is consistent with L_{K}, since it is validated by the frame of Example 1. But any logic containing the scheme $[*\phi]\psi \to \psi$ is inconsistent with $\neg\mathbf{B}\bot$, since when $\psi = \bot$ the scheme becomes $[*\phi]\bot \to \bot$, equivalent to $\langle *\phi\rangle\top$. We saw above that even $\langle *\bot\rangle\top$ is inconsistent with $\neg\mathbf{B}\bot$.

Simpler $\bowtie$-Free Semantics

For the $\bowtie$-free fragment of L_{K}, we can replace frame condition (F4) in general by the stronger, and simpler, condition that the function $\mathsf{ws} : S \to U$ is surjective.

For the canonical model construction, we take S_L to be the set of all L-maximal sets (and not L-saturated ones, as $\bowtie$ is no longer present). U_L remains as the set of

Boolean L-maximal sets, and we define $\mathsf{ws}_L : S_L \to U_L$, as before, by

$$\mathsf{ws}_L(\Gamma) = \{\psi : \psi \in \Gamma\}.$$

But now ws_L is surjective, because every $u \in U_L$ is L-consistent hence extends to an L-maximal $\Gamma \in S_L$ with $\mathsf{ws}_L(\Gamma) = u$.

This construction can be used to show that the class of $\bowtie$-free formulas that are valid in all world-surjective frames is axiomatised by the $\bowtie$-free fragment of L_{K}.

Γ is not determined by $\mathsf{sf}_L(\Gamma)$ and $\mathsf{ws}_L(\Gamma)$
In a canonical model $\mathfrak{M}_L$, there is more to a belief state $\Gamma \in S_L$ than its associated selection function f^Γ and and world state $\mathsf{ws}_L(\Gamma)$. There may be other L-saturated (or L-maximal in the $\bowtie$-free case) sets with the same selection function and world state.

This is illustrated by the two sets Γ_0 and Γ_1 defined in Example 3 of Sect. 4. These belong to S_L when L is the logic of the frame of that Example, and also when $L = L_{\mathrm{K}}$. Γ_0 and Γ_1 both contain all formulas of the form $[*\phi]\mathbf{B}\psi$. In particular they contain all formulas $[*\phi]\mathbf{B}\bot$, which ensures that $f^{\Gamma_0} = f^{\Gamma_1} =$ the null function (Lemma 8). Also Γ_0 and Γ_1 contain the same Boolean formulas, so $\mathsf{ws}_L(\Gamma_0) = \mathsf{ws}_L(\Gamma_1)$.

But as was shown in Example 3, $\Gamma_0 \neq \Gamma_1$.

Acknowledgments The $\bowtie$ notation is due to Tim Stokes, who introduced the study of the concept it denotes as an operation in the algebra of binary relations [2, 3, 8, 15]. I am obliged to him for posing the question of its axiomatisation in the context of mult-modal logics, and for illuminating explanations and discussions about this. This paper also owes much to Krister Segerberg's innovative contributions to the modelling of dynamic doxastic modalities, and indeed to his approach to the model-theoretic analysis of modalities in general.

References

1. Chellas, B. F. (1980). *Modal logic: An introduction*. New York: Cambridge University Press.
2. Fearnley-Sander, D., & Stokes, T. (1997). Equality algebras. *Bulletin of the Australian Mathematical Society*, *56*(2), 177–191.
3. Fearnley-Sander, D., & Stokes, T. (2003). Varieties of equality structures. *International Journal of Algebra and Computation*, *13*(4), 463–480.
4. Goldblatt, R. (1982). *Axiomatising the logic of computer programming, Lecture Notes in Computer Science* (Vol. 130). Berlin: Springer.
5. Goldblatt, R. (2011). *Quantifiers, propositions and identity: Admissible semantics for quantified modal and substructural logics. Lecture Notes in Logic*, (Vol. 38). Cambridge: Cambridge University Press and the Association for Symbolic Logic.
6. Goldblatt, R., & Jackson, M. (2012). *Well structured program equivalence is highly undecidable. ACM Transactions on Computational Logic*. Retrived 2011, from http://tocl.acm.org/accepted.html.
7. Harel, D., Kozen, D., & Tiuryn, J. (2000). *Dynamic logic*. Cambridge: MIT Press.
8. Jackson, M., & Stokes, T. (2011) Modal restriction semigroups: Towards an algebra of functions and deterministic computation. *International Journal of Algebra and Computation*.
9. Leitgeb, H., & Segerberg, K. (2007). Dynamic doxastic logic: Why, how, and where to? *Synthese*, *155*(2), 167–190.

10. Lindström, S., & Segerberg, K. (2007). Modal logic and philosophy. In: P. Blackburn, J.V. Benthem, & F. Wolter (Eds.), *Handbook of modal logic, studies in logic and practical Reasoning*, (Vol. 3, pp. 1149–1214). Amsterdam: Elsevier.
11. Segerberg, K. (1998). Irrevocable belief revision in dynamic doxastic logic. *Notre Dame Journal of Formal Logic*, *39*(3), 287–306.
12. Segerberg, K. (1999). A completeness proof in full DDL. In: R. Sliwinski (Ed.), *Philosophical Crumbs. Essays Dedicated to Ann-Mari Henschen-Dahlquist on the Occasion of her Seventy-Fifth Birthday, Uppsala Philosophical Studies*, (Vol. 49, pp. 195–207). Swedan: Department of Philosophy, Uppsala University
13. Segerberg, K. (2001). The basic dynamic doxastic logic of AGM. In M. A. Williams & H. Rott (Eds.), *Frontiers in Belief Revision, Applied Logic Series* (Vol. 22, pp. 57–84). Dordrecht: Kluwer Academic Publishers.
14. Segerberg, K. (2010). Some completeness theorems in the dynamic doxastic logic of iterated belief revision. *The Review of Symbolic Logic*, *3*(2), 228–246.
15. Stokes, T. (2006). On EQ-monoids. *Acta Scientiarum Mathematicarum (Szeged)*, *72*(3–4), 481–506.

On Revocable and Irrevocable Belief Revision

Hans van Ditmarsch

Abstract Krister Segerberg proposed irrevocable belief revision, to be contrasted with 'standard' belief revision, in a setting wherein belief of propositional formulas is modelled explicitly. In standard belief revision one can unmake ('revoke') belief in any formula, given yet further information that contradicts it. But irrevocable formulas remain believed forever. We compare traditional AGM belief revision with Segerberg's dynamic doxastic logic, and with dynamic epistemic logical approaches to belief revision. Our work falls in the latter category. In that context with explicit belief operators and dynamic modal operators $[*\varphi]$ for belief revision with φ, we define *revocable belief revision* as belief revision satisfying that $\psi \leftrightarrow [*\varphi][*\neg\varphi]\psi$ is valid; such that irrevocable means not revocable. Segerberg's irrevocable belief revision is indeed irrevocable in that sense. We give semantic constraints (on multi-agent Kripke models) for revocable belief revision. In order for belief revision to be revocable: (i) the agents should consider the same states possible before and after revision, (ii) states that are non-bisimilar before revision may not be bisimilar after revision (if states are non-bisimilar, they can be distinguished from one another in the logical language), and (iii) it should be possible that states that are not equally

I had the pleasure to be introduced by Greg Restall to Krister Segerberg at the Logic, Methodology and Philosophy of Science conference in 2003 in Oviedo, Spain. This was not entirely coincidental. I presented at that LMPS my first steps in modelling belief revision in dynamic epistemic logic, joint work with my Otago colleague Willem Labuschagne, rather an abstract than a formal publication: [47]. But from that initial study I had become acquainted with Segerberg's work, and I was therefore eager to meet him. Our relationship has developed since. With great pleasure I recall the event organized at the University of Amsterdam by Olivier Roy where we met again in 2006. This was the 4th Paris-Amsterdam Logic Meeting of Young Researchers (PALMYR-4): Logics for Belief Dynamics. In 2008 we both became editors of the Journal of Philosophical Logic. In 2012 I still am, this a position I cherish, and I tend to feel that I owe it to Krister. The hospitality offered by Krister and Anita Segerberg, wherever they reside, is legendary. It need hardly be mentioned. But one should, on occasion..

H. van Ditmarsch
University of Seville, Seville, Spain
e-mail: hvd@us.es

R. Trypuz (ed.), *Krister Segerberg on Logic of Actions*,
Outstanding Contributions to Logic 1, DOI: 10.1007/978-94-007-7046-1_10,

plausible before revision become equally plausible after revision. We reformulate four well-known belief revision operators (hard update, soft update, conservative revision, severe revision) as qualitative dynamic belief revision operators. They are irrevocable in the (strong) sense above, because they violate one or more of these three requirements. However, single-agent severe revision is revocable in a weaker sense that following a revision $*\varphi$ there is a *sequence* of further revisions recovering the initial state of belief. The work may be relevant for restricted-memory or other bounded rationality approaches to belief revision, e.g., when only a finite number of plausibility distinctions may be stored in memory. Therefore, it may be relevant for the study of logic and cognition.

1 Introduction

1.1 Belief Revision and Dynamic Epistemic Logic

Both belief revision and dynamic epistemic logic have been on the research agenda for quite a while [1, 22, 30, 39].

Belief revision has been studied from the perspective of structural properties of reasoning about changing beliefs [15], from the perspective of changing, growing and shrinking knowledge bases, and from the perspective of models and other structures of belief change wherein such knowledge bases may be interpreted, or that satisfy assumed properties of reasoning about beliefs. A typical approach involves preferential orders to express increasing or decreasing degrees of belief [14, 22, 26, 27] (such works provided a basis for [45]), where these works refer to the 'systems of spheres' in [19, 24]. Within this tradition multi-agent belief revision has also been investigated, e.g., belief merging [20]. Belief operators are normally not explicit in the logical language, so that higher-order beliefs (I know that you are ignorant) cannot be formalized. Iterated belief revision may be also be problematic.

Dynamic epistemic logic has developed more or less since the late 1980s, with seminal publications by [6, 17, 30, 43, 44]. Precursors with dynamic but without epistemic operators are [12, 38]. Such logics have epistemic operators (or any other base modality, e.g. a doxastic operator) to formalize knowledge or belief, and dynamic modal operators to formalize change of knowledge or belief. They are typically multi-agent logics. Initially, e.g. in all the seminal publications mentioned above, change of knowledge always meant some kind of *growth* of knowledge or *strengthening* of belief, and not belief revision in the sense of incorporating otherwise inconsistent novel beliefs. Research in dynamic epistemic logic was mainly driven by the attempt to model higher-order phenomena of belief change, and was initially motivated by the attempt to model so-called 'unsuccessful updates', as in the well-known muddy children problem [28]: from a public update with 'nobody knows whether he/she is muddy', the muddy children may learn that they are muddy.

Dynamic doxastic logic was proposed and investigated by Krister Segerberg and collaborators in works such as [25, 34–36]. From the biased viewpoint of dynamic epistemic logic these works are seen as its direct forerunners; as such, they are distinct from yet (many) other approaches to belief revision in modal logics but without dynamic modal operators, such as [2, 9, 10, 23], that also influenced the development of dynamic logics combining knowledge and belief change. In dynamic doxastic logics belief operators are in the logical language, and belief revision operators are dynamic modalities. Higher-order belief change, i.e., to revise one's beliefs about one's own or other agent's beliefs and ignorance, are considered problematic in dynamic doxastic logic, see [25]. In [34, 36] belief revision is restricted to propositional formulas (factual revision). There are dynamic doxastic logics wherein $[*\varphi]$ merely means belief revision with φ according to some externally defined strategy, as in AGM style (this is the general setup in [36], not unlike the non-epistemic/doxastic modal setup in [38]), but there are also dynamic doxastic logics, such as the irrevocable belief revision that is the topic of this investigation [34], wherein $[*\varphi]$ is a recipe operating on a semantic structure and outputting a novel structure, the standard approach in dynamic epistemic logic.

Belief revision in dynamic epistemic logic (in short: dynamic belief revision) was initiated by a group of researchers all more or less in contact with one another and in various and changing relations of collaborator, student, and supervisor, active all over the globe. The initial publications are [4, 7, 40, 45] (where we should note that [4] is based on Aucher's Master of Logic thesis [3], that was written under the supervision of van Benthem and van Ditmarsch). From these, [4, 45] propose a treatment involving degrees of belief and based on degrees of plausibility among states in structures interpreting such logics, so-called quantitative dynamic belief revision; whereas [7, 40] propose a treatment involving comparative statements about plausibilities (a binary relation between states denoting more/less plausible), so-called qualitative dynamic belief revision. The latter is clearly more suitable for *logics* of belief revision, and for notions such as conditional belief. Given the usual prewellorders for plausibility, qualitative and quantitative approaches are interdefinable (see [46] for details)—but that amounts to saying that propositional logic might as well be written with Sheffer strokes. Qualitative approaches are much more succinct. Quantitative approaches may have special uses in artificial intelligence. The analogue of the AGM postulate of 'success' must be given up when one incorporates higher-order belief change as in dynamic epistemic logic, where again a prime mover are Moore-sentences of the form 'proposition p is true but you don't know it', which cannot after acceptance be believed by you. Many more works and whole PhD theses [5, 13, 18] on dynamic belief revision have appeared since, and the work has greatly developed towards philosophical logic and formal epistemology [8], that we do not wish to give a comprehensive overview of. For that we refer to [41].

1.2 Irrevocable Belief Revision in Dynamic Doxastic Logic

In [34] Krister Segerberg coined the term *irrevocable belief revision*.

> Ordinary theories of belief change do not seem suited to handle the sort of hypothetical belief change that goes on, for example, in debates where the participants agree, "for the sake of argument," on a certain common ground on which possibilities can be explored and disagreements can be aired. One need not actually believe what one accepts in this way. Nevertheless such acceptance amounts to what may be called a doxastic commitment, one that cannot be given up within the perimeter of the debate.

He then proceeds to explain that for such belief change one does not expect a further revision with another formula to be executable. That would merely be a different common ground for debate. It is not puzzling, nor required that argument assumed for the sake of argument are consistent. He then proceeds to call this irrevocable belief revision, and proposes a logic, in the setting with dynamic modalmodal logic operators for revision and explicit belief and knowledge (conviction) operators. For that, we have to explain how Segerberg's setting relates to the standard AGM setting.

In AGM belief revision, a given set of formulas incorporated in a deductive closed theory $\mathcal{K}$ is revised with a formula φ resulting in a revised theory $\mathcal{K}*\varphi$. Typically, $\neg\varphi$ is in $\mathcal{K}$, one has to give up belief in $\neg\varphi$ by a process of retraction, and φ is in $\mathcal{K}*\varphi$. In the setting of dynamic doxastic logic, formulas $B\varphi$ or $K\varphi$ with explicit modal belief or knowledge operators, and where φ is a propositional formula, are interpreted on systems of algebras that are so-called hypertheories. For our purposes it is sufficient to think of them as 'systems of spheres' M with certain additional properties, and where truth is defined relative to a point s in the system. Instead of writing $\neg\varphi \in \mathcal{K}$ for 'the agent believes $\neg\varphi$, we have that $M, s \models B\neg\varphi$ for the $\neg\varphi \in \mathcal{K}$ as above (and, indeed, M, s should be such that $\psi \in \mathcal{K}$ iff $M, s \models \psi$). 'Revision with φ' is now a program $*\varphi$ that transforms the structure (M, s) into another structure (M', s'). The transformation is described in the logical language by a dynamic modal operator $[*\varphi]$, that is interpreted as a binary relation between structures. In irrevocable belief revision (but not in all other dynamic doxastic logics), $M^{*\varphi}$ is computed from M by standard restriction of the model to the φ-states, and $s' = s$. So in that sense, the semantic operation is like 'hard update', 'public announcement', etc. The crucial aspect of this update is that the most plausible states in M may no longer be 'believable' (namely because they did not satisfy φ), but the construction makes the most plausible φ-states now the overall most plausible states. (Examples are given in the following sections. For dynamic epistemic logic the procedure is quite similar.) We now have that $\psi \in \mathcal{K} * \varphi$ iff for all M, s, if $M, s \models B\chi$ for all $\chi \in \mathcal{K}$, then $M^{*\varphi}, s \models B\varphi$. In this framework, knowledge or convinced belief plays the role of background knowledge. Unlike standard AGM, iterated belief revision is quite natural in this setting. Expansion and revision are combined in this update. If the revision formula φ is consistent with the current beliefs, we have expansion, otherwise revision.

1.3 Overview

We have already reviewed the literature in the area: AGM belief revision, dynamic epistemic logic, dynamic doxastic logic, and more recent approaches to belief revision in dynamic epistemic logic. We also recalled Segerberg's irrevocable belief revision in dynamic doxastic logic. In the next section we compare revocable to irrevocable belief revision, and illustrate the dynamic epistemic logic approach to belief revision in a number of extended examples. Section 3 contains the more technical part of our contribution. First, we define structures with plausibility relations, and a logical language for belief, knowledge, and belief change (i.e, nearly exactly as in Segerberg's original proposal). Then, we demonstrate that various well-known kinds of belief revision are irrevocable in a strict sense, and only one is revocable in a limited sense. The conclusion outlines why our study is relevant for modelling bounded rationality and the area of logic and cognition.

2 An Example of Revocable Belief Revision

> I have this electric water heater, to make cups of tea and such. It has a heating element that is a metal coil, and also a light to indicate when the heater is turned on. Normally, they work in tandem, the light is on exactly when the element heats the water. But the following malfunctions are known to happen: the element still heats the water but the light is off, because it's blown; and dually, the light may still be on indicating that the element is heating the water up, but in fact it doesn't due to malfunction. Then, very rarely when there it's turned on while there is a current, both might be gone. Let p stand for 'the coil is heating' and let q stand for 'the light is on'. The default is that both are true when I turn on the heater: $p \wedge q$. It seems somewhat less likely, but very possible, that at least one is OK: $p \vee q$. And least plausible is that they are both malfunctioning: $\neg p \vee \neg q$. That is depicted in Fig. 1. Observing that the coil does not work, more or less (I am impatient, and the typical sizzling noise accompanying the water heating up may not yet have started) makes us want to revise the belief in $p \wedge q$ *with* $*\neg p$ into belief in $\neg p \wedge q$. Such a transition is depicted in Fig. 2. And so on... With a fair stretch of the imagination for the wilder transitions we can thus accommodate the belief revision examples provided in this section.

Consider one agent and two factual propositions p and q that the agent is uncertain about. The state of uncertainty is represented in Fig. 1. There are four states of the world, $\{00, 01, 10, 11\}$. Atom p is only true in $\{10, 11\}$, and atom q is only true in $\{01, 11\}$. The agent has preferences among these states. He considers it most plausible

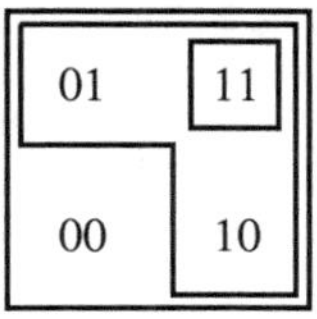

Fig. 1 Knowledge, belief and plausibility about two propositions p and q. The agent believes that p and q are true

that 11 is the actual state, i.e., that both p and q are true, slightly less plausible that 01 or 10 are the actual state, and least plausible that 00 is the actual state. (We assume that this perspective on plausibilities is the same in all states.) We write

$$11 < 01 = 10 < 00$$

The agent *believes* propositions when they hold in the most plausible states. For example, she believes that p and q are true. This is formalized as

$$B(p \wedge q)$$

As usual we write B for belief, and honouring Segerberg-style we will write B for its dual. E.g., the truth of both propositions is also believable: $b(p \wedge q)$. Her belief in the slightly weaker proposition $p \vee q$ is slightly stronger than his belief in $p \wedge q$. Note that p or q are true in all three of 11, 01, and 10, i.e., including state 11.

Her strongest beliefs, or knowledge, involve in this case only tautologies such as $p \vee \neg p$ and $q \vee \neg q$. This is described as

$$K(p \vee \neg p)$$

As usual K stands for knowledge. We will also, less usual, let it stand for conviction, or, as Segerberg playfully and appropriately writes: *K*onviction. Also as in Segerberg we write k for the dual of knowledge. For example, we have that the state of affairs where p and q are both false is considered possible: $k(\neg p \wedge \neg q)$, but also the state of affairs where they are both true $k(p \wedge q)$. The last already follows from the fact that this was believable $b(p \wedge q)$. Her strong beliefs are also about her plausibilities. For example, she knows that she believes p and q

$$KB(p \wedge q)$$

This is, because whatever the actual state of the world is, $B(p \wedge q)$ is true.

Now imagine that the agent wants to revise her current beliefs. She believed that p and q are both true, but has been given sufficient reason to be willing to revise her beliefs with $\neg p$ instead. We can accomplish that when we allow a model transformation. On the right in Fig. 2 the agent believes that p is false and that q is true. So in particular, in modal terms, $B\neg p$ is true. Therefore, the revision was successful. This can already be expressed in the model on the left, by using a dynamic

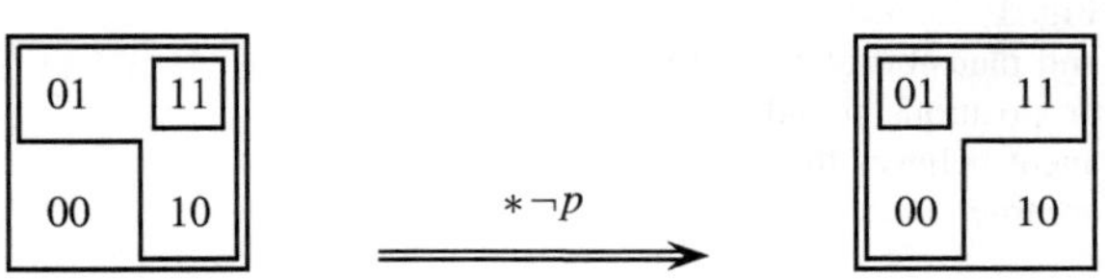

Fig. 2 The agent changes hes belief in p and q by revising with $\neg p$. After the revision, the agent believes $\neg p$ instead. She still believes q

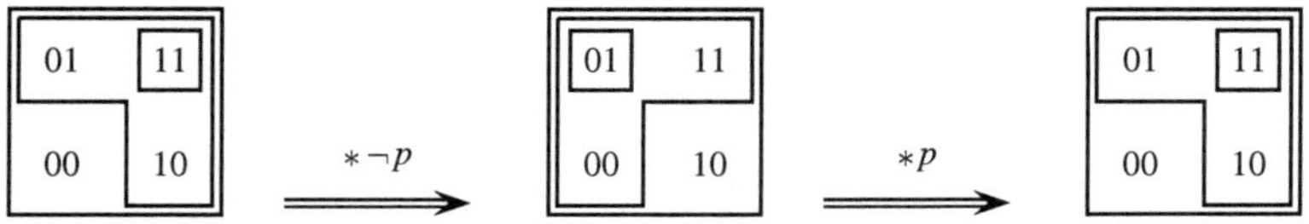

Fig. 3 Subsequent to revision $*\neg p$, the agent revises with $*p$. The original state of belief is recovered

modal operator $[*\neg p]$ for the relation induced by the program "belief revision with $\neg p$", followed by what should hold after that program is executed. On the left, it is true that the agent believes p and that after belief revision with $\neg p$ the agent believes that $\neg p$. In a dynamic modal setting this is described as $Bp \wedge [*\neg p]B\neg p$.

To prolong the comparison with standard belief revision of sets of formulas, we observe that the plausibility order $11 < 01 = 10 < 00$ on the states in this model reflects the order $\{p, q\} < \{p \vee q\} < \{\top\}$ on belief bases, or the order $Cl(\{p, q\}) < Cl(\{p \vee q\}) < Cl(\{\top\})$ on theories, i.e., deductively closed sets of formulas that are believed by the agent. In dynamic epistemic logic, beyond the original Segerberg setting, beliefs and knowledge can also be about modal formulas. For example, we not only have that $B(p \wedge q)$, because $p \wedge q \in Cl(\{p, q\})$, but we also have that $B\neg B(\neg p \wedge \neg q)$: $\neg p \wedge \neg q \notin Cl(\{p, q\})$ means that $\neg B(\neg p \wedge \neg q)$ is valid on the model, which by introspection delivers $B\neg B(\neg p \wedge \neg q)$; so that $\neg B(\neg p \wedge \neg q)$ is in the set of formulas believed by the agent. As another example we already mentioned that $KB(p \wedge q)$.

The revision above is obtained as follows—we prefer an informal description as we will not further develop this line of quantitative belief revision. Given the belief revision formula, $\neg p$, (i) *increase* the plausibility of the states satisfying it sufficiently so that the most plausible $\neg p$ states becomes the overall most plausible state, and (ii) simultaneously *decrease* the plausibility of the p states sufficiently so that the most plausible p states are no longer the overall most plausible states. The order $11 < 01 = 10 < 00$ defines degrees of plausibility 0, 1, 2. In order to make a $\neg p$ state the most plausible, we increase the plausibility of those states by 1: 01 then gets degree of plausibility 0 and 00 gets degree of plausibility 1. In order to undo that a p state is the most plausible, we decrease the plausibility of those states by 1: 11 then gets degree of plausibility 1 and 10 gets degree of plausibility 2. In the revision process, states 00 and 11 have become equally plausible, and the new order is therefore $01 < 00 = 11 < 10$. This proposal was named *successful minimal belief revision* in [45], it is a particular case of the proposal in [4], and like that it is inspired by the ordinal conditional functions in [37]. It comes close to what is known in the AGM community as *conservative revision*, see e.g. [32]. It defies an elegant qualitative formulation. But it serves our purpose wonderfully: it is revocable.

Subsequently to the revision $*\neg p$ we perform a revision $*p$. Now, we increase the degree of plausibility of the p states 10 and 11 from 2 and 1 to 1 and 0, and decrease the degree of plausibility of the $\neg p$ states 10 and 11 from 1 and 0 to 2 and 1. The original model, encoding the original beliefs, reappears. See Fig. 3.

Fig. 4 Segerberg irrevocable belief revision

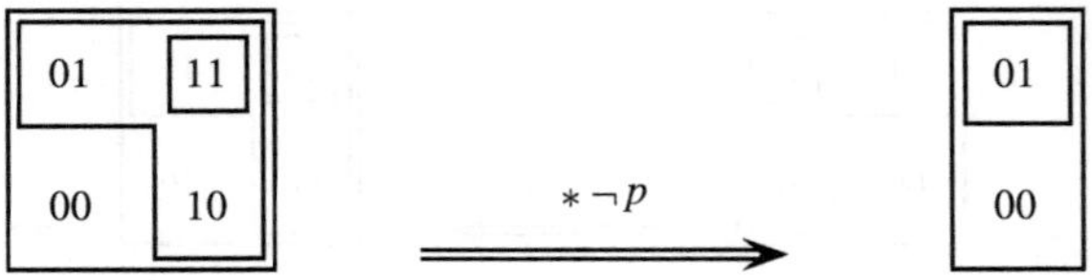

It is clear that the depicted model satisfies

$$B(p \wedge q) \to [*\neg p][*p]B(p \wedge q).$$

As the two revision operations return the original model we also have that, for any ψ,

$$\psi \to [*\neg p][*p]\psi.$$

It will be obvious that this works for any form of plausibility change on this model, so that

$$\psi \to [*\varphi][*\neg\varphi]\psi$$

is valid on the model for all formulas φ. This seems an interesting principle, formalizing that belief revision $*\varphi$ is 'revocable', undone, by the additional belief revision $*\neg\varphi$. Let us investigate this principle a bit further.

Segerberg irrevocable belief revision is indeed not revocable. Figure 4 shows the effect of Segerberg irrevocable belief revision with $*\neg p$. All p-states are eliminated. Before the revision, both Bp and Bq hold, afterwards, $B\neg p$ and Bq, but also that $K\neg p$: prior belief in p is irrecoverable indeed. This form of belief revision is called *maximal belief revision* in [45], *hard update* in [40], and is clearly based on the semantics of truthful public announcement [6, 30]. Subsequent belief revision $*p$ is not even executable, as there are no p-states left that are considered possible by the agent. Diagnosing the illness, the crucial feature making the belief revision irrevocable is that in the process of the revision some states are eliminated, or, putting it in even more general terms also compatible with arrow-eliminating update: some states have become inaccessible (unbelievable) from the actual state.

We have demonstrated that Segerberg irrevocable belief revision does not satisfy the principle $\psi \to [*\varphi][*\neg\varphi]\psi$. Does successful minimal belief revision satisfy this principle? We worked our way towards suggesting that it does, but in fact it does not. The beliefs that the agents have, are not merely about factual propositions but also about each others' beliefs. It is then perfectly conceivable that an agent finds one state more plausible than another one even though they have the same valuations. They simply differ in their belief properties.

Consider two agents Anne (a) and Bill (b), say, that have different access to the state of a light. Proposition p stands for 'the light is on'. Bill knows whether the light is on, but he is uncertain if Anne believe that the light is on, or that she believes that the light is off. This situation is depicted in Fig. 5. Access for a is solid and access

Fig. 5 Bill knows the value of p but does not know what Anne believes about p

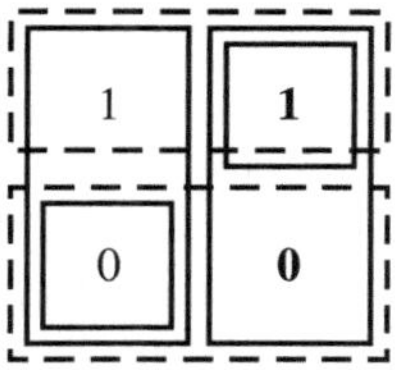

for b is dashed. We distinguish the plain 0 and 1 states from the bold **0** and **1** states. Proposition p is true in 1 and in **1**.

Again, we can now evaluate various statements about knowledge and belief, where we now label the K and B operators with the agents (a for Anne, and b for Bill) whose modalities they represent. In state **0** the light is off but Anne (incorrectly) believes that it is on:

$$\neg p \wedge B_a p,$$

whereas Bill does not know that, knows that the light is off, and also considers it possible that Anne correctly believes that:

$$\neg K_b(\neg p \wedge B_a p) \wedge K_b \neg p \wedge k_b B_a \neg p$$

We now execute belief revision with $*p$ according to the successful minimal belief revision policy explained above. This does not affect Bill's knowledge or beliefs. If the actual states are 1 or **1** he is already convinced of p, and otherwise he is already convinced of $\neg p$. (And no evidence to the contrary will make him change his mind—according to the procedure for belief revision described above, the 0 and **0** states will get degree of plausibility 1 for agent b, but given the absence of states with degree of plausibility 0 in that b-equivalence class, they still remain the most plausible states.) But it affects the plausibilities for agent a. Proceeding as above, state 1 will become more plausible than state 0 for agent a. The transition is as follows.

However, the states 1 and **1** can no longer be distinguished in the logical language from each other: they share the same value of the proposition p and are also both more plausible than a $\neg p$ state. We can therefore identify them. Similarly, for states 0 and **0**. (We will see that 1 and **1**, and 0 and **0**, respectively, are *bisimilar*.) The following structure results.

A further revision with $*\neg p$ will now not return the original state of information, but instead a model wherein, in state 0: Bill knows that $\neg p$, and Anne believes that $\neg p$, and Bill knows that Anne believes that $\neg p$. The transitions in sequence are as follows.

However, single-agent successful minimal belief revision is revocable. Our B and K operators satisfy the standard KD45 properties for belief, and (at least) those properties for conviction/knowledge. For single-agent KD45 and stronger it cannot be that different states in the same equivalence class have the same valuation but satisfy different modal properties. It follows that states that are not equally plausible must have a different valuation.

Again diagnosing the illness here, this time the crucial feature making the two-agent successful minimal belief revision irrevocable is that in the process of the revision some states that could be distinguished by a formula in the logical language (that were not bisimilar) have become indistinguishable after the revision (are now bisimilar). Then, the original distinction cannot be recovered by subsequent belief revision with the negation of the revision formula (or by any other formula).

We now continue with the formal presentation of such results, for a number of well-known qualitatively defined forms of belief revision.

3 A Language and Logic for Dynamic Belief Revision

We present a fairly standard multi-agent dynamic doxastic logic. The language is presented Segerberg-style [34], the structures are presented as in our [45], and the dynamic belief revision operators are presented Baltag/Smets qualitative style [7]. The four belief revision operators presented in that style are: soft update / lexicographic belief revision [7, 40], hard update / public announcement / irrevocable revision / radical revision [30, 34], conservative revision [11, 31], and severe revision [32] (based on various severe belief contraction proposals).

Definition 1 *(Doxastic model)* Given are countable sets of agents A and propositional variables P. A *doxastic model* is a triple $(S, \leq, V)$. The set S is a *domain* of factual states, and *valuation* V is a function $V : P \to \mathcal{P}(S)$ such the subset $V(p)$ denotes the states where p is true. The *plausibility function* $\leq$: $A \to S \to \mathcal{P}(S \times S)$ defines a plausibility relation $\leq^s_a$ for each agent $a \in A$ and for each $s \in S$, that is a prewellorder.[1] We require that $t \leq^s_a t'$ implies $\leq^s_a = \leq^t_a = \leq^{t'}_a$. If $t \leq^s t'$ we say that t is more plausible than t' given / from the perspective of s. The set $Plaus_a(s) := \{t \mid t' \leq^s t \text{ or } t \leq^s t'\}$ defines the *plausible states* for agent a given s. The set $\min_a(s) := \{t \mid t' \leq^s t \text{ implies } t \leq^s t'\}$ are the *most plausible states* for agent a given s. If $s \in Plaus_a(s)$ for all states s, $(S, \leq, V)$ is a *doxastic epistemic model*.⊣

For "$t' \leq^s t$ or $t \leq^s t'$" we write $t \sim^s_a t'$. For $t \sim^s_a t'$ and $t \leq^s_a t'$ we can respectively write $t \sim_a t'$ and $t \leq_a t'$ without ambiguity, because $\leq^s_a = \leq^t_a = \leq^{t'}_a$. For $t \leq_a t'$ and not $(t' \leq_a t)$ we write $t <_a t'$ (strictly more plausible), and for $t \leq_a t'$ and $t' \leq_a t$ we write $t \equiv_a t'$ (equally plausible).

The relation $\sim_a$ 'almost' defines an equivalence relation for agent a. The domain can be partitioned in $\sim_a$ equivalence classes, that constitute disjoint sets of plausible states, plus some isolated states. From an isolated state only the states in one such class are considered plausible. (It is a multi-agent KD45 structure, partitioned into, for each agent, 'KD45 balloons': a balloon is a prewellorder.)

[1] A prewellorder is a total, transitive and well-founded binary relation. A prewellorder induces an equivalence relation and a wellorder of equivalence classes.

Definition 2 *(Bisimulation)* Let doxastic models $M = (S, \leq, V)$ and $M' = (S', \leq', V')$ be given, $u \in S$ and $u' \in S'$. A relation $\mathfrak{R} \subseteq S \times S'$ is a *bisimulation* iff for all $(s, s') \in \mathfrak{R}$:

- **[atoms]** for all $p \in P$, $s \in V(p)$ iff $s' \in V'(p)$;
- **[forth]** for all $a \in A$, if $t, u \in S$ and $t \leq_a^s u$ then there are $t', u' \in S'$ such that $t' \leq_a^{s'} u'$ and $(t, t'), (u, u') \in \mathfrak{R}$;
- **[back]** for all $a \in A$, if $t', u' \in S'$ and $t' \leq_a^{s'} u'$ then there are $t, u \in S$ such that $t \leq_a^s u$ and $(t, t'), (u, u') \in \mathfrak{R}$.

A *total bisimulation* between M and M' is a bisimulation with domain S and codomain S' (all states are related). For a bisimulation between doxastic states (M, s) and (M', s') it is required that $(u, u') \in \mathfrak{R}$. ⊣

For doxastic epistemic models, back and forth reduce to the more intuitive (for all $a \in A$):

- **[forth]** if $s \leq_a u$ then there is a $u' \in S'$ such that $s' \leq_a u'$ and $(u, u') \in \mathfrak{R}$;
- **[back]** if $s' \leq_a u'$ then there is a $u \in S$ such that $s \leq_a u$ and $(u, u') \in \mathfrak{R}$.

Definition 3 *(Language of doxastic logic)* Given are countable sets of agents A and propositional variables P. The language $\mathcal{L}$ of doxastic logic is defined as

$$\varphi ::= p \mid \neg\varphi \mid \varphi \wedge \psi \mid B_a\varphi \mid K_a\varphi \mid [*\varphi]\varphi$$

where $a \in A$ and $p \in P$. ⊣
We allow for the usual abbreviations of proposotional connectives and also define $b_a\varphi \leftrightarrow \neg B_a\neg\varphi$ and $k_a\varphi \leftrightarrow \neg K_a\neg\varphi$.

Definition 4 *(Semantics of doxastic logic)* Let $(S, \leq, V)$ be a doxastic model, $s \in S$, and $\varphi \in \mathcal{L}$.

$$\begin{array}{ll} M, s \models B_a\varphi & \text{iff for all } t, t' \text{ such that } t \leq_a^s t' \text{ and } t \text{ is minimal} : M, t \models \varphi \\ M, s \models K_a\varphi & \text{iff for all } t, t' \text{ such that } t \leq_a^s t' \text{ or } t' \leq_a^s t : M, t \models \varphi \\ M, s \models [*\psi]\varphi & \text{iff } M^{*\psi}, s \models \varphi \quad \text{where } M^{*\psi} \text{ is defined below} \end{array}$$

We denote $[\![\psi]\!]_M = \{s \in S \mid M, s \models \psi\}$. ⊣

Definition 5 *(Belief revision)* Let $M = (S, \leq, V)$ be a doxastic model and $\psi \in \mathcal{L}$. We give four different constructions for $M^{*\psi} = (S, \leq^*, V)$, defining four belief revision policies. For convenience of presentation we write $t \leq t'$ for $t \leq_a^s t'$ and $t \leq^* t'$ for $t {\leq^*}_a^s t'$ (all the below are for arbitrary states s and agents a), and we write $s \models \varphi$ for $M, s \models \varphi$, and $s, s' \models \varphi$ for $s \models \varphi$ and $s' \models \varphi$.

hard revision $t \leq^* t'$ iff $t \leq t'$ and $s, t' \models \psi$

soft revision $t \leq^* t'$ iff $t \leq t'$ and $t, t' \models \psi$
or
$t \models \psi$ and $t' \not\models \varphi$
or
$t \leq t'$ and $t, t' \not\models \psi$

conservative revision $t \leq^* t'$ iff $t \models \varphi$ and for all $t'' < t : t'' \not\models \varphi$
or
$t \leq t'$ otherwise

severe revision $t \leq^* t'$ iff $t \leq t'$ and $t, t' \models \varphi$
or
$t \models \varphi$ and $t' \not\models \varphi$
or
$(t \leq t'$ or $t' \leq t)$ and $t, t' \not\models \varphi$ ⊣

Examples of the different effects of these belief revision strategies are shown in Fig. 9.

Hard revision is also known under the names: public announcement [30] (although without the aspect of plausibility), hard update [40], and (Segerberg) irrevocable revision [34]. In this contribution, we will merely see the latter as one kind of irrevocable belief revision. We presented hard revision in the version of the semantics known as 'believed public announcement' [16, 21], not in the more standard version 'truthful public announcement' [6, 30]. This why in the example the 01 and 00 states remain there after revision. If these were the actual states, the agent would now incorrectly believe that p is false: $01 \models Bp$. She would also be convinced (*k*onvinced) that p is true: $01 \models Kp$. A further revision with $*\neg p$ would 'drive her mad': her accessibility relation would become empty. Soft revision also goes under the name of lexicographic update (a proposal with many old roots), or Spohn-maximal revision. Conservative revision [11] is also known as Spohn-minimal revision (see [46] for the exact relation to Spohn's [37]). Severe revision is taken from [32] that also lists other forms of severe revision. Their unifying trait is that unequally plausible states become equally plausible. It therefore carries stronger aspects of contraction in it than other belief revision operators. As we will see, merging of plausibilities while retaining (the conceivability of) all states is a requirement for revocable belief revision.

In the standard AGM sense, hard revision, i.e., Segerberg irrevocable belief revision, can be revision but also expansion. In the dynamic epistemic logic setting (that is more semantic than syntactic) it is a mere change of perspective whether something counts as revision or expansion, and not a radically different method. Consider yet another Segerberg style irrevocable update, now with $*p$ instead of $*\neg p$, on a similar model. Before the revision, the agent believes $p \vee q$, the new information p is consistent with those beliefs. As a consequence of the expansion with $*p$ the agent now believes p (Bp is true in any state of the model). This is an example of expansion.

Definition 6 *(Revocable belief revision)* A belief revision operator is revocable iff $\psi \rightarrow [*\varphi][*\neg\varphi]\psi$ is valid for all $\varphi, \psi \in \mathcal{L}$. A belief revision operator is irrevocable iff it is not revocable. ⊣

We observe that from the validity of $\psi \rightarrow [*\varphi][*\neg\varphi]\psi$ also follows the validity of $B_a\psi \rightarrow [*\varphi][*\neg\varphi]B_a\psi$ that spells out the belief change for an individual agent. Therefore the principle formalizes exactly that the beliefs of the agent do not change. For this to hold in the dynamic epistemic logic setting wherein also higher-order beliefs are relevant, we also need the additional principle that $K_a\psi \rightarrow [*\varphi][*\neg\varphi]K_a\psi$. Obviously that is valid as well.

Definition 7 *(Restrictive)* A belief revision operator is *restrictive* iff there is a doxastic model M, a state s in M and an agent a such that the plausible states after revision are strictly contained in the plausible states before the revision: $Plaus_a^*(s) \subset Plaus_a(s)$. ⊣

The next proposition needs no proof.

Proposition 8 *Hard update is restrictive. The other three belief revision operators are not restrictive.* ⊣

Proposition 9 *A restrictive belief revision operator is irrevocable.* ⊣

Corollary 10 *Hard update is irrevocable.* ⊣

Definition 11 *(Merging)* A belief revision operator is *merging* iff it does not preserve non-bisimilarity of states. ⊣

Proposition 12 *A merging belief revision operator is irrevocable.* ⊣

Proof If belief revision is merging, non-bisimilar states may become bisimilar, and can then no longer be distinguished from one another in the logical language. □

If a revision operator preserves non-bisimilarity, one might say that it preserves structural complexity. The revision operator may jumble plausibilities around as it pleases, but not to the extent that two states with the same valuation become equally plausible for all agents. We recall Definition 2 of bisimilarity: two states are bisimilar if they have the same valuation and the same 'relation to plausible states', i.e., for doxastic epistemic models, the same valuation and equal plausibility.

Proposition 13 *All four belief revision operators are merging.* ⊣

Proof The revision executed in Fig. 6, on page xx would also be the result for soft, conservative, and severe revision. For hard revision, only the 1 and **1** states remain plausible, but the structures are again bisimilar. In all four cases, the total bisimulation is: $\mathfrak{R} = \{(0, \mathbf{0}), (1, \mathbf{1})\}$). □

Corollary 14 *All four belief revision operators are irrevocable.* ⊣

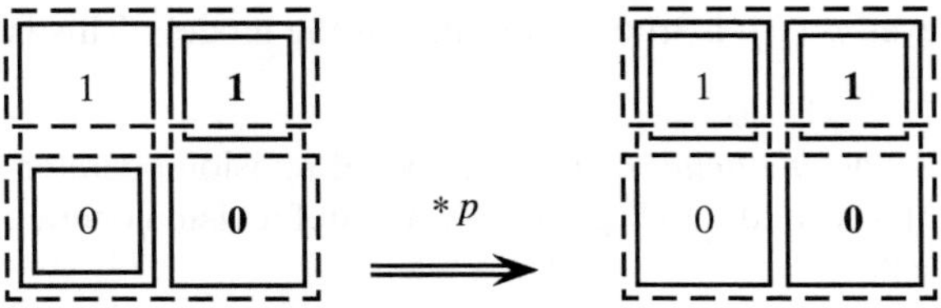

Fig. 6 A revision with $*p$

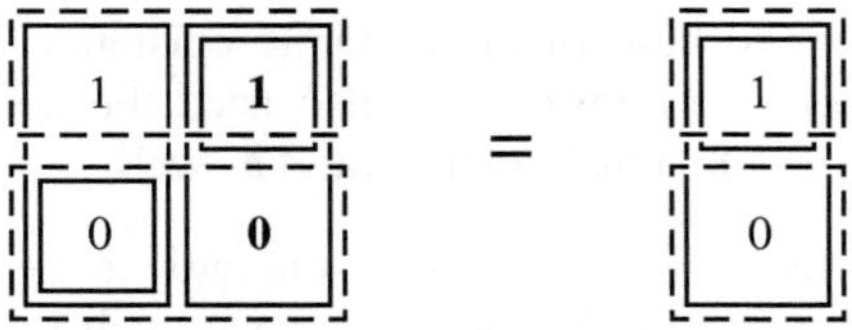

Fig. 7 Identification of bisimilar states

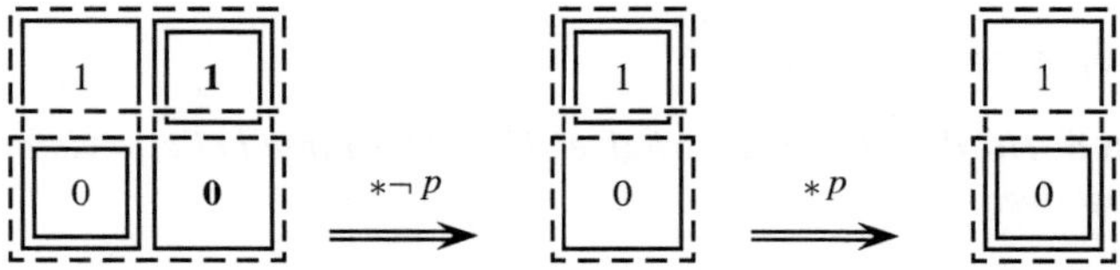

Fig. 8 An example of irrevocable belief revision

Given this result, surely 'merging' is a trivial notion. Not really. The multi-agent versions of the logics are pathological in the sense that bisimilarity resulting from revision is (always) a consequence of identification of equivalence classes (or KD45 balloons). Within a given equivalence class we cannot have such merging. Non-bisimilar states in a KD45 (or S5) equivalence class must have a different valuation, because all states in the class satisfy the same modal formulas (formulas of form $B\psi$ or $K\psi$).

Proposition 15 *In the single-agent case, all four belief revision operators are not merging.* $\dashv$

Proof We show that all four belief operators preserve non-bisimilarity. We check the clauses on the right-hand side of the four belief revision operators in Definition 5. We recall that there are *two* reasons for non-bisimilarity: different valuation, or different degree of plausibility. Or else, combining one or the other, satisfying different formulas of the logic (bisimilarity implies logical equivalence, so logical difference implies non-bisimilarity).

Hard revision: $t \leq^* t'$ on the left follows from $t \leq t'$ on the right. If there was a different degree of plausibility, it will remain so.

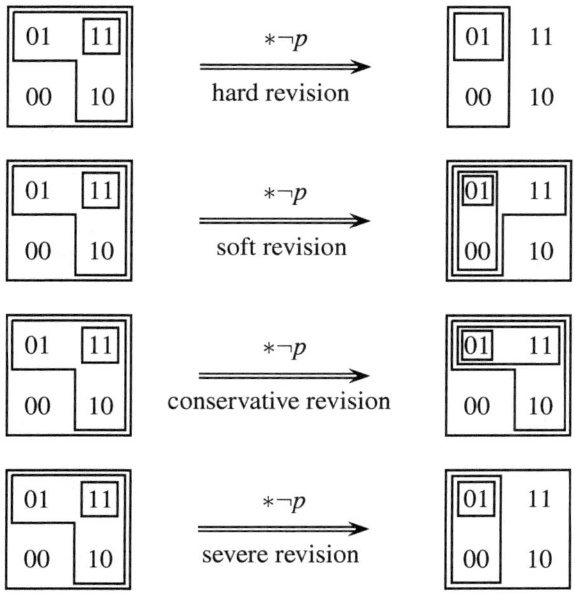

Fig. 9 Belief revision with $*\neg p$ according to the four different revision strategies

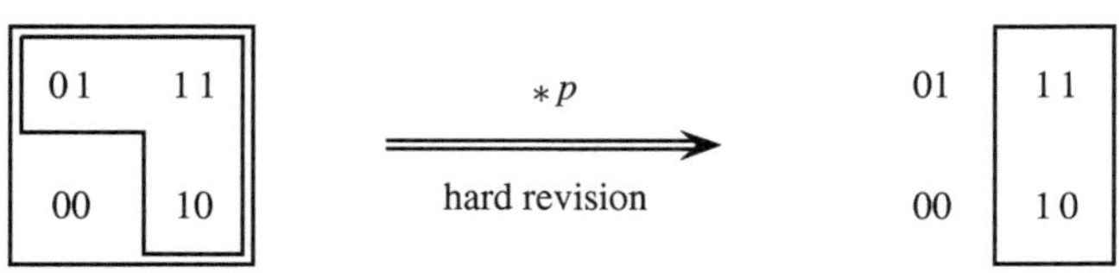

Fig. 10 Segerberg irrevocable belief revision can be expansion or revision. This is an example of expansion: belief in $p \vee q$ is strengthened to belief in p

Soft revision: $t \leq^* t'$ follows from one of three clauses on the right. In the first clause it follows from $t \leq t'$, which preserves non-bisimilarity. In the second clause non-bisimilarity is preserved because the states t and t' satisfy ψ and $\neg\psi$, respectively: states satsifying different formulas are non-bisimilar. The third clause is as the first.

Conservative revision: In the first clause, first assume that t and t' are both minimal. They both satisfy ψ. If t and t' are not bisimilar (in M), they must have a different valuation (see the explanation prior to the proposition), so in $M^{*\psi}$ they still have that different valuation: the two states remain non-bisimilar. Or else, the equally plausible and minimal t and t' already were bisimilar. If t and t' are both minimal but not equally plausible, they remain so. The second clause is also as before.

Severe revision: The first two clauses are as before. In the third clause, states t and t' may become equally plausible. They both satisfy $\neg\psi$. Either they already were bisimilar, or they have a different valuation (as for conservative revision), so they still carry that valuation in $M^{*\psi}$ and despite being now equally plausible they still remain non-bisimilar. □

We have shown that all four belief operators preserve non-bisimilarity in the single-agent case, but do not preserve it in the multi-agent case. Note that they all preserve bisimilarity, single-agent or multi-agent. This is a standard requirement for such dynamic modal operators. We have not yet shown that they are revocable.

Definition 16 (Plausibility Merging) A belief revision operator is *plausibility merging* iff states with unequal plausibility before revision may become equally plausible after revision. ⊣

Proposition 17 *A revocable belief revision operator must be plausibility merging.* ⊣

Proof If a belief revision operator is not plausibility merging, it preserves unequal plausibility. Now, maybe somewhat obviously, no belief revision operator that is not restrictive preserves *equal* plausibility. For any form of belief revision $*\varphi$, the effect of a revision is not merely change of belief or knowledge but also that 'φ has become an issue': a refinement of, or different treatment in the model, of the φ-states and $\neg\varphi$-states. So belief revision $*\varphi$ may make two equally plausible states unequally plausible after revision. In order for a belief revision operator to be revocable, it should be able that these states become equally plausible again. □

Proposition 18 *Single-agent severe revision is plausibility merging. Single-agent hard, soft and conservative revision are not plausibility merging.* ⊣

Proof Single-agent severe revision is plausibility merging because two states t, t' not satisfying the revision formula φ become equally plausible after revision. In the third clause of Definition 5 of severe revision, we get both $t \leq^* t'$ and $t \leq^* t'$ from the given '$(t \leq t'$ or $t' \leq t')$'.

It is trivial that the other three belief revision operators are not plausibility merging. (A proof would be similar to that of Proposition 15.) □

Corollary 19 *Single-agent soft and conservative revision are irrevocable.* ⊣

Hard revision was already shown to be irrevocable because it is restrictive. We are not left with a small window of opportunity. The only remaining candidate for revocable belief revision is single-agent severe belief revision. In order to be revocable, a belief revision operator must not be merging, but on the other hand it must be plausibility merging. Merging implies plausibility merging, but plausibility merging does not imply merging, as we have seen in the case of severe revision. Unfortunately also single-agent severe revision is irrevocable (see next proposition) but we can still obtain that severe revision is irrevocable in a slightly weaker sense.

Definition 20 *(Weakly revocable)* A belief revision operator is weakly revocable iff for all ψ, φ, there are $\varphi_1, \ldots, \varphi_n$ such that $\psi \to [*\varphi][*\varphi_1], \ldots, [*\varphi_n]\psi$ is valid. ⊣

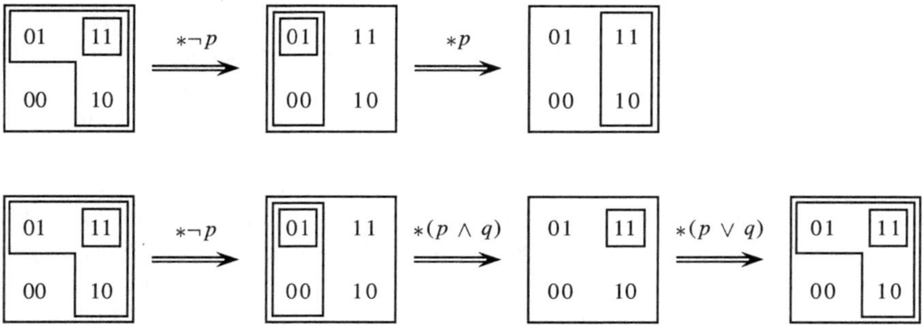

Fig. 11 Severe revision is weakly revocable

Proposition 21 *Single-agent severe revision is irrevocable, but it is weakly revocable on models with a finite number of degrees of plausibility.* ⊣

Proof Single-agent severe revision is irrevocable. For a counterexample see Fig. 11, upper part.

Single-agent severe revision is weakly revocable if there is only a finite number of degrees of plausibility. After the initial revision $*\varphi$, we can recover the original model by successively revising with the formulas characterizing the 'onions' from the inside out—and for the finite-degree single-agent model these characterizations are simply the disjunctions of the valuations of the states in these onion bits. An example of this general procedure is given in Fig. 11, lower part. □

The successful minimal belief revision that guided us through Sect. 2 is revocable (in the single agent case). It is plausibility merging, but not merging, and the recipe to increase/decrease levels of plausibility is simply reversed by having the revision $*\varphi$ followed by a revision $*\neg\varphi$. However, as we already observed, it does not allow an elegant reformulation as a qualitatively defined belief revision operator.

4 Conclusion and Further Research

Guided by a proposal by Krister Segerberg on irrevocable belief revision, we defined four belief revision operators, hard/soft/conservative/severe revision, in the setting of dynamic epistemic logic, and investigated whether they are revocable. Belief revision that is restrictive (arrow or state eliminating) and belief revision that is merging (non-bisimilar states become similar) is irrevocable. However, a requirement for revocable belief revision is that it is plausibility merging. Single-agent severe belief revision is revocable on models with a finite number of plausibility distinctions.

It is unclear to us if there are common belief revision operators that are revocable. Is a revocable belief revision operator desirable? It seems a very intuitive concept to us. An undo-button, so to speak. But maybe we have not looked in the proper direction. Instead of looking forward—given a model that is the result of belief revision, what *further* belief revision restores the original state of information—we should maybe be looking backward: the real undo. In a dynamic epistemic logic with history-based structures [29, 42] and history-operators [33] undoing belief revision $[*\varphi]$ should not be much else then going back one step in the temporal tree-unfolding, a real sort of $[*\varphi]^{-1}$ operator.

We think that our work may be relevant for restricted-memory or other bounded rationality approaches to belief revision, e.g., when only a finite number of plausibility distinctions may be stored in memory. A real disadvantage of an otherwise elegant framework like soft update (soft belief revision) is that in the course of iterated revision, the number of belief distinctions only increases and never decreases. For a closer correspondence between logic and cognition, one would like to stick to structures with seven non-bisimilar states, say, corresponding to what the average human can juggle in his or her mind at the same time. Another way to reduced complexity than the plausibility merging that we investigated here, would be awareness/unawareness changing logics, e.g., abstraction as vocabulary restriction (propositional variable restriction). Logics for knowledge, plausibility and awareness have been proposed in [48].

References

1. Alchourrón, C. E., Gärdenfors, P., & Makinson, D. (1985). On the logic of theory change: Partial meet contraction and revision functions. *Journal of Symbolic Logic*, *50*, 510–530.
2. Asheim, G. B., & Søvik, Y. (2005). Preference-based belief operators. *Mathematical Social Sciences*, *50*(1), 61–82.
3. Aucher, G. (2003). A combined system for update logic and belief revision. (Master's thesis, ILLC, University of Amsterdam, Amsterdam, The Netherlands), ILLC report MoL-2003-03.
4. Aucher, G. (2005). A combined system for update logic and belief revision. In M.W. Barley & N. Kasabov (Eds.), *Intelligent agents and multi-agent systems: 7th pacific rim international workshop on multi-agents (PRIMA 2004)*, (pp. 1–17). Berlin: Springer, LNAI 3371.
5. Aucher, G. (2008). Perspectives on belief and change. (PhD thesis, University of Otago and Institut de Recherche en Informatique de Toulouse, New Zealand and France).
6. Baltag, A., Moss, L. S. & Solecki, S. (1998). The logic of public announcements, common knowledge, and private suspicions. In I. Gilboa (Ed.), *Proceedings of the 7th conference on theoretical aspects of rationality and knowledge (TARK 98)*, (pp. 43–56).
7. Baltag, A., & Smets, S. (2006). Dynamic belief revision over multi-agent plausibility models. In *Proceedings of 7th conference on logic and the foundations of game and decision theory (LOFT 2006)*.
8. Baltag. A.,& Smets, S. (2008). The logic of conditional doxastic actions. In K. R. Apt & R. van Rooij (Eds.), *New perspectives on games and interaction*, Texts in Logic and Games 4. Amsterdam: University Press.
9. Board, O. (2004). Dynamic interactive epistemology. *Games and Economic Behaviour*, *49*, 49–80.
10. Bonanno, G. (2005). A simple modal logic for belief revision. *Synthese Knowledge, Rationality and Action*, *147*(2), 193–228.
11. Boutilier, C. (1993). Revision sequences and nested conditionals. In *Proceedings of the 13th IJCAI* (Vol. 1, pp. 519–525). Burlington: Morgan Kaufmann.
12. de Rijke, M. (1994). Meeting some neighbours. In J. van Eijck & A. Visser (Eds.), *Logic and information flow*, (pp. 170–195). Cambridge: MIT Press.

13. Dégremont, C. (2011). The Temporal Mind. Observations on the logic of belief change in interactive systems. (PhD thesis, University of Amsterdam, ILLC Dissertation Series DS-2010-03).
14. Ferguson, D., & Labuschagne, W. A. (2002). Information-theoretic semantics for epistemic logic. In *Proceedings of LOFT 5*, Turin: ICER.
15. Gärdenfors, P. (1988). *Knowledge in Flux: Modeling the dynamics of epistemic states*. Bradford Books, Cambridge: MIT Press.
16. Gerbrandy, J. D. (1999). *Bisimulations on planet kripke*. (PhD thesis, University of Amsterdam, ILLC Dissertation Series DS-1999-01).
17. Gerbrandy, J. D., & Groeneveld, W. (1997). Reasoning about information change. *Journal of Logic, Language, and Information, 6*, 147–169.
18. Girard, P. (2008). *Modal logic for belief and preference change*. (PhD thesis, ILLC Dissertation Series DS-2008-04). Palo Alto: Stanford University.
19. Grove, A. (1988). Two modellings for theory change. *Journal of Philosophical Logic, 17*, 157–170.
20. Konieczny, S., & Pino Pérez, R. (2002). Merging information under constraints: A logical framework. *Journal of Logic and Computation, 12*(5), 773–808.
21. Kooi, B. (2007). Expressivity and completeness for public update logics via reduction axioms. *Journal of Applied Non-Classical Logics, 17*(2), 231–254.
22. Kraus, S., Lehmann, D., & Magidor, M. (1990). Nonmonotonic reasoning, preferential models and cumulative logics. *Artificial Intelligence, 44*, 167–207.
23. Laverny, N. (2006). *Révision, mises à jour et planification en logique doxastique graduelle*. PhD thesis, Toulouse: Institut de Recherche en Informatique de Toulouse (IRIT).
24. Lewis, D. K. (1973). *Counterfactuals*. Cambridge: Harvard University Press.
25. Lindström, S., & Rabinowicz, W. (1999). DDL unlimited: Dynamic doxastic logic for introspective agents. *Erkenntnis, 50*, 353–385.
26. Meyer, T. A. (2001). Basic infobase change. *Studia Logica, 67*, 215–242.
27. Meyer, T. A., Labuschagne, W. A., & Heidema, J. (2000). Refined epistemic entrenchment. *Journal of Logic, Language, and Information, 9*, 237–259.
28. Moses, Y. O., Dolev, D., & Halpern, J. Y. (1986). Cheating husbands and other stories: A case study in knowledge, action, and communication. *Distributed Computing, 1*(3), 167–176.
29. Parikh, R., Ramanujam, R., & Distributed processing and the logic of knowledge. In *Logic of programs*, volume 193 of *Lecture Notes in Computer Science*, (pp. 256–268). Springer. A newer version appeared in *Journal of Logic, Language and Information*, (Vol. 12, 453–467), (2003).
30. Plaza, J. A. (1989). Logics of public communications. In M. L. Emrich, M. S. Pfeifer, M. Hadzikadic, & Z. W. Ras (Eds.), *Proceedings of the 4th international symposium on methodologies for intelligent systems: Poster session program*, (pp. 201–216). Oak Ridge: Oak Ridge National Laboratory.
31. Rott, H. (2003). Coherence and conservatism in the dynamics of belief ii: Iterated belief change without dispositional coherence. *Journal of Logic and Computation, 13*(1), 111–145.
32. Rott, H. (2006). Shifting priorities: Simple representations for twenty-seven iterated theory change operators. In H. Lagerlund, S. Lindström, & R. Sliwinski (Eds.), *Modality matters: Twenty-Five essays in honour of krister segerberg*, (Vol. 53, pp. 359–384). Uppsala: Uppsala Philosophical Studies, Uppsala Universitet.
33. Sack, J. (2007). *Adding temporal logic to dynamic epistemic logic*. PhD thesis, Bloomington: Indiana University.
34. Segerberg, K. (1998). Irrevocable belief revision in dynamic doxastic logic. *Notre Dame Journal of Formal Logic, 39*(3), 287–306.
35. Segerberg, K. (1999). Default logic as dynamic doxastic logic. *Erkenntnis, 50*, 333–352.
36. Segerberg, K. (1999). Two traditions in the logic of belief: Bringing them together. In H. J. Ohlbach & U. Reyle (Eds.), *Logic language, and reasoning* (pp. 135–147). Dordrecht: Kluwer Academic Publishers.

37. Spohn, W. (988). Ordinal conditional functions: A dynamic theory of epistemic states. In W. L. Harper & B. Skyrms (Eds.), *Causation in decision, belief change, and statistics*, (Vol. 2, pp. 105–134).
38. van Benthem, J. (1989). Semantic parallels in natural language and computation. In *Logic colloquium '87*, Amsterdam: North-Holland.
39. van Benthem, J. (1996). *Exploring logical dynamics*. Stanford: CSLI Publications.
40. van Benthem, J. (2007). Dynamic logic of belief revision. *Journal of Applied Non-Classical Logics*, *17*(2), 129–155.
41. van Benthem, J. (2011). *Logical dynamics of information and interaction*. Cambridge: Cambridge University Press.
42. van Benthem, J., Gerbrandy, J. D., Hoshi, T., & Pacuit, E. (2009). Merging frameworks for interaction. *Journal of Philosophical Logic*, *38*, 491–526.
43. van Benthem, J., van Eijck, J., & Kooi, B. (2006). Logics of communication and change. *Information and Computation*, *204*(11), 1620–1662.
44. van Ditmarsch, H. (2002). Descriptions of game actions. *Journal of Logic, Language and Information*, *11*, 349–365.
45. van Ditmarsch, H. (2005). Prolegomena to dynamic logic for belief revision. *Synthese Knowledge, Rationality and Action*, *147*, 229–275.
46. van Ditmarsch, H. (2008). Comments on 'the logic of conditional doxastic actions'. In K. R. Apt & R. van Rooij (Eds.), *New perspectives on games and interaction*, Texts in Logic and Games 4, (pp. 33–44). Amsterdam: Amsterdam University Press.
47. van Ditmarsch, H. & Labuschagne, W. A. (2003). A multimodal language for revising defeasible beliefs. In E. Álvarez, R. Bosch, & L. Villamil (Eds.), *Proceedings of the 12th international congress of logic, methodology, and philosophy of science (LMPS)*, (pp. 140–141). Oxford: Oviedo University Press.
48. Velazquez-Quesada, F. R. (2011). *Small steps in dynamics of information*. (PhD thesis, ILLC Dissertation Series DS-2011-02), Amsterdam: University of Amsterdam.

Actions, Belief Update, and DDL

Jérôme Lang

Abstract Two prominent topics in Krister Segerberg's works are, on the one hand, actions, and on the other hand, belief change. Both topics are connected in multiple ways; one of these connections is via KGM belief update, since, as we argue, belief update is a specific case of feedback-free action progression. We discuss the links between update and action, and, starting from Segerberg's works, discuss further other possible interpretations of belief update, its differences with AGM belief revision, and why it is interesting to develop further KGM-based Dynamic Doxastic Logic.

1 Introduction

Krister Segerberg has introduced and developed a powerful and influential way of dealing with belief change: dynamic doxastic logic (DDL). DDL aims at expressing belief change actions at the same language level as factual sentences, using dynamic modalities $[\star\varphi]$, where $\star\varphi$ is the action of adding φ to the agent's belief. Nesting such belief change modalities allows us to reason about an agent's beliefs about how her beliefs are changed. For instance, borrowing from [25], p. 169, $\mathbf{B}[\star\varphi]B\theta$ expresses that the agent believes that after adding φ to her body of knowledge she will believe θ, and $[\star[\star\varphi]\mathbf{B}\theta]\mathbf{B}\chi$ expresses that the agent believes χ after adding to her belief state the information that adding φ to it would lead to a belief in θ.

In the paragraph above I deliberately avoided using the "to revise", and used the more neutral, but less elegant verbs "to change" or "to add". However, most of the work on DDL assumes that the belief change operation $\star$ corresponds to a *belief revision*, in the sense of Alchourrón, Gärdenfors and Makinson [1]; see for instance

A significant part of this article is a revised version of [23].

J. Lang (✉)
LAMSADE-CNRS, Paris, France
e-mail: Jerome.Lang@irit.fr

R. Trypuz (ed.), *Krister Segerberg on Logic of Actions*,
Outstanding Contributions to Logic 1, DOI: 10.1007/978-94-007-7046-1_11,

[33, 34]. Other parts of this special issue deal with DDL and its relationship with AGM-style belief revision (as well as its iterated versions), and the rôle played by the Ramsey rule and Gärdenfors' impossibility theorem in the development of DDL. Segerberg however noticed that moving belief change actions from the linguistic meta-level to the object level makes also perfectly sense for other paradigms of belief change, be it other operations in AGM-style belief change such as expansion and contraction, and also other non-AGM notions of belief change, the most prominent example being *belief update*, in the sense of Katsuno and Mendelzon [21] and Grahne [13]—which Segerberg calls the KGM paradigm. Developing a KGM version of DDL and highlighting its main differences with the traditional, AGM version of DDL is mentioned first in Lindström and Segerberg [28] and developed further by Leitgeb and Segerberg [25] of which it is one of the main topics.

Now, although many chapters about belief update have been written, including many chapters addressing its differences with belief revision, its precise scope still remains unclear. Part of the reason is that the first generation of chapters on belief update contain a number of vague and ambiguous formulations, such as "belief revision has to do with static worlds, while belief update has to do with dynamic worlds", or "belief update incorporates into a belief base some notification of a change in the world".

Friedman and Halpern [11] were perhaps the first to argue that this is not as simple as that. The issue is also addressed by Leitgeb and Segerberg [25], pages 183 and 184:

> In the literature of belief change the distinction between static and dynamic environments has become important. (...) it seems right to say that that belief change due to new information in an unchanging environment has come to be called *belief revision* (the static case, in the sense that the "world" remains unchanged), while it is fairly accepted to use the term *belief update* for belief change that is due to reported changes in the environment itself (the dynamic case, in the sense that the "world" changes).(...) The established tradition notwithstanding, it would be interesting to see a really convincing argument for tying AGM revision to static environments. (...) But it is also not clear that belief update has to be interpreted as reflecting a proper change in the environment.

Leitgeb and Segerberg also address an important ramification of this major question, which has to do with the role and the meaning of rankings of worlds in revision and in update. They give a very convincing line of argumentation towards the following conclusion: in revision, rankings are subjective and correspond to relative plausibilities (they can be thought of as an ordinal counterpart of subjective probabilities). In belief update, rankings are objective (agent-independent) and correspond to similarity between worlds. Let me quote Leitgeb and Segerberg [25], pp. 184–185:

> (...) Given new evidence, we find that in the case of belief revision the agent tries to change his beliefs in a way such that the worlds that he subsequently believes to be in comprise the *subjectively most plausible deviation* from the worlds he originally believed to inhabit. However, when confronted in the same evidence in belief update, the agent tries to change his beliefs in a way such that the worlds that he subsequently believes to be in are *as objectively similar as possible* to the worlds he originally believed to be the most plausible candidates for being the actual world.

This question about the role of rankings can be pushed even further, as we may even question the need for rankings in belief update. Accordingly, a series of chapters defined and studied families of update operators that, in contrast to the original model by Grahne, Katsuno and Mendelzon, are not based on minimization and thus do not need any rankings at all. This is extensively discussed by Herzig and Rifi [18]. This is in sharp contrast with belief revision, and this may be part of the explanation why the Ramsey test, to which AGM revision does not escape, seems perfectly escapable with belief update. This question of the compatibility of KGM update with the Ramsey test is addressed in detail by Leitgeb and Segerberg, pp. 179–187. It is further linked to the question of iteration, which appear to be much less problematic in belief update in with belief revision.

This chapter addresses all of these questions and develops on them (several more than others; in particular, there will be no emphasize at all on the Ramsey test), and discusses in detail some of the answers given in [25]. It is partly based on a previous conference chapter of mine [23]. The main question of this chapter is the identification of the precise scope of belief update, i.e., the conditions (expressed by properties of the world and of the agent's beliefs) under which update is a suitable process for belief change. After recalling some background on KGM belief update in Sect. 2, we give in Sect. 3 an informal discussion about the role of time in revision and update. In Sect. 4, we relate update to the field of reasoning about action (another issue in which Krister Segerberg is a major contributor). Our main claim is that updating a knowledge base by α corresponds to progressing it by a specific "purely physical", feedback-free action "make α true" whose precise meaning depends on the chosen update operator. This in turn raises the following question, addressed in Sect. 5: if update is progression, are there belief change operators corresponding to regression? In Sect. 6 we discuss another important (and different?) interpretation of belief update, which has to do with counterfactuals and causality; we address the question of whether this interpretation is really different from action progression, or only a variation of it. In Sect. 7 we come back to where the chapter started, namely DDL, and show why it is highly promising to develop further an update-based version of DDL. Further issues are briefly addressed in Sect. 8.

2 Belief Update

Let L^V be the propositional language generated from a finite set of propositional variables V, the usual connectives and the Boolean constants $\top$, $\bot$. $S = 2^V$ is the set of *states* (i.e., propositional interpretations). For any $\varphi \in L^V$, $Mod(\varphi)$ is the set of states satisfying φ. For any $X \subseteq S$, $for(X)$ is the formula of L^V (unique up to logical equivalence) such that $Mod(for(X)) = X$. If $X = \{s\}$, we write $for(s)$ instead of $for(\{s\})$. We use $\varphi \oplus \psi$ as a shorthand for $\varphi \leftrightarrow \neg\psi$.

As in [21], a belief update operator $\diamond$ is as mapping from $L^V \times L^V$ to L^V, i.e., mapping two propositional formulas φ (the initial belief state) and α (the "input") to a propositional formula $\varphi \diamond \alpha$ (the resulting belief state). We recall here the Katsuno-Mendelzon (KM for short) postulates for belief update [21].

U1 $\varphi \diamond \alpha \models \alpha$.
U2 If $\varphi \models \alpha$ then $\varphi \diamond \alpha \equiv \varphi$.
U3 If φ and α are both satisfiable then $\varphi \diamond \alpha$ is satisfiable.
U4 If $\varphi \equiv \psi$ and $\alpha \equiv \beta$ then $\varphi \diamond \alpha \equiv \psi \diamond \beta$.
U5 $(\varphi \diamond \alpha) \wedge \beta \models \varphi \diamond (\alpha \wedge \beta)$.
U6 If $\varphi \diamond \alpha \models \beta$ and $\varphi \diamond \beta \models \alpha$ then $\varphi \diamond \alpha \equiv \varphi \diamond \beta$.
U7 If φ is complete then $(\varphi \diamond \alpha) \wedge (\varphi \diamond \beta) \models \varphi \diamond (\alpha \vee \beta)$.
U8 $(\varphi \vee \psi) \diamond \alpha \equiv (\varphi \diamond \alpha) \vee (\psi \diamond \alpha)$.

Although we have recalled all postulates for the sake of completeness, we should not accept them unconditionally. They have been discussed in several chapters, including [18] in which it was argued that not all these postulates should be required, and that the "uncontroversial" ones (those deeply entrenched in the very notion of update and satisfied by most operators studied in the literature) are (U1), (U3), (U8), and (U4) to a lesser extent. We therefore call a *basic update operator* any operator $\diamond$ from $L^V \times L^V$ to L^V satisfying at least (U1), (U3), (U4) and (U8). In addition, $\diamond$ is said to be *syntax-independent* if it also satisfies (U4), *inertial* if it also satisfies (U2), and $\diamond$ is a *KM update operator* if it satisfies (U1)–(U8).[1] In this chapter we refer to some specific update operators such as the PMA [36]; see [18] for a compendum of belief update operators that date, and [17] for an update on the literature about update since then.

The first goal of this chapter consists in identifying is the exact scope of belief revision and belief update, and more generally belief change operators. To assess the scope of belief change operators, we need to be able to talk about the properties of the system (the world and the available actions) and the properties of the agent's state of knowledge, as in the taxonomy for reasoning about action and change from [31]. However, unlike reasoning about action, belief change processes have never (as far as we know) been analyzed from the point of view of such a taxonomy. A first step is taken towards this direction (for belief revision only) in [11]. We aim at identifying further the precise scope of belief update, i.e., the conditions (expressed by properties of the world and of the agent's beliefs) under which update is a suitable process for belief change.

3 Time, Revision, and Update

As already quoted in the Introduction, Leitgeb and Segerberg write in [25], pp. 183 and 184:

[1] (U5), (U6) and (U7) are much more controversial than the other ones (see [18]); they characterize the specific class of updates based on a similarity-based minimization process (which is known to lead to several counterintuitive results).

> The established tradition notwithstanding, it would be interesting to see a really convincing argument for tying AGM revision to static environments. (...) But it is also not clear that belief update has to be interpreted as reflecting a proper change in the environment.

Their diagnosis is definitely right: the discourse, seen so often, that the difference between the scope of revision and that of update should be seen as an opposition between static and dynamic environments, is wrong indeed. Belief revision, AGM style, has been developed as a qualitative counterpart of probabilistic conditionalisation; tying AGM to "static environments" would thus implicitly mean that the probability calculus does not apply to dynamic environments—which would be absolutely nonsense. And indeed, nothing in the AGM theory of belief revision implies that we should restrict its application to static worlds. Belief revision [10] is meant to map a belief set (a closed logical theory, or equivalently, since the language is finitely generated, a propositional formula[2]) and a new piece of information α (a consistent propositional formula) whose truth is held for sure, into a new belief set $K * \alpha$ taking account of the new piece of information without rejecting too much of the previous beliefs. The initial belief set as well as the new piece of information may talk about the state of an evolving world at different time points. As remarked already by Friedman and Halpern [11], what is essential in belief revision is not that the world is static, but that *the language used to describe the world* is static. Thus, if an evolving world is represented using time-stamped propositional variables of the form v_t (v true at time t), we can perfectly revise a belief set by some new information about the past or the present (or even, sometimes, the future), and infer some new beliefs about the past, the present, or the future.

Example 3.1 On Monday, Alice is the head of the computer science lab while Bob is the head of the math lab. On Tuesday I learned that one of them resigned (but without knowing which one). On Wednesday I learn that Charles is now the head of the math lab, which implies that Bob isn't. (It is implicit that heads of labs tend to keep their position for quite a long time.) What do I believe now?

Example 3.1 contains a sequence of two "changes". Both are detected by observations, and the whole example can be expressed as a revision process (with time-stamped variables). Let us identify Monday, Tuesday and Wednesday by the time stamps 1, 2 and 3. On Monday I believe A_1, B_1, as well as the persistency laws $A_1 \leftrightarrow A_2$, $A_2 \leftrightarrow A_3$, $B_1 \leftrightarrow B_2$ etc., therefore I also believe A_2, B_2 etc.: I expect that Alice and Bob will remain the heads of their respective labs on Tuesday and Wednesday. The revision by $\neg A_2 \vee \neg B_2$ (provided that the revision operator minimizes change) leads me to believe A_1, B_1, $A_2 \oplus B_2$, $A_3 \oplus B_3$ etc.: on Tuesday, I still believe that Alice and Bob were heads of their labs on Monday, and that now *exactly one* of them is. Then the revision by $\neg B_3$ (at time 3) makes me believe A_1, B_1, A_2, $\neg B_2$, A_3, $\neg B_3$: on Wednesday, I understand that Bob was the one to resign on

---

[2] Our assumption that the language is finite allows us to consider revision operators as acting on propositional formulas as in [22] (instead of belief sets).

Tuesday, and therefore that Alice was still head of the CS lab on Tuesday, and is still now.[3]

Now, the fact that belief revision can deal with (some) evolving worlds suggests that the opposition between revision and update relies on the possibility or not that the state of the world may evolve is not accurate. In particular, claiming that belief update is the right belief change operation for dealing with evolving worlds is unsufficient and ambiguous. The literature on belief update abounds in ambiguous explanations such as "update consists in bringing the knowledge base up to date when the world is described by its changes".[4] Especially, the expressions "describing the world by its changes" and "notification of change", appearing in many chapters, are particularly ambiguous. The problem is not that much, as it has been observed sometimes, that in these expressions "change" has to be understood as "possibility of change" (we'll come back to this point). The main problem is the status of the input formula α. To make things clear, here is an example.

Example 3.2 My initial belief is that either Alice or Bob is in the office (but not both). Both tend to stay in the office when they are in. Now I see Bob going out of the office. What do I believe now?

Trying to use belief update to model this example is hopeless. For all common update operators seen in the literature, updating $A \oplus B$ by $\neg B$ leads to $\neg B$, and not to $\neg A \wedge \neg B$. The culprit is (U8), which, by requiring that all models of the initial belief set be updated separately, forbids us to infer new beliefs about the past from later observations. Indeed, because of (U8), we have $(A \oplus B) \diamond \neg B \equiv [(A \wedge \neg B) \diamond \neg B] \vee [(\neg A \wedge B) \diamond \neg B] \equiv (A \wedge \neg B) \vee (\neg A \wedge \neg B) \equiv \neg B$. The only way to have $\neg A \wedge \neg B$ as the result would be to have $(A \wedge \neg B) \diamond \neg B \equiv \neg A \wedge \neg B$, which can hold only if there is a causal relationship between A and B, such as B becoming false entails A becoming false—which is not the case here.

Example 3.2 definitely deals with an evolving world and contains a "notification of change", and still it cannot be formulated as a belief update process. On the other hand, like Example 3.1, it can be perfectly expressedas is a time-stamped belief revision process.[5]

The key point is (U8) which, by requiring that all models of the initial belief set be updated separately, *forbids us from inferring new beliefs about the past from later observations*: indeed, in Example 3.2, belief update provides no way of eliminating the world $(A, \neg B)$ from the set of *previously* possible worlds, which in turn, does not allow for eliminating $(A, \neg B)$ from the list of possible worlds *after* the update:

---

[3] Note that this scenario is also a case for belief extrapolation [8], which is a particular form of time-stamped revision.

[4] This formulation appears in [21], which may be one of the explanations for such a long-lasting ambiguity.

[5] Note that without time stamps (and in particular within the framework of belief update), we cannot distinguish between "B has become false" (as in "I see Bob go out of the office") and "the world has evolved in such a way that B is now false" (as in "I now see Bob out of his office"). Anyway, for Example 3.2, the expected outcome is the same in both cases (provided that A and B are expected to persist with respect to the granularity of time considered).

if $(A, \neg B)$ is a possible world at time t, then its update by $\neg B$ *must* be in the set of possible worlds at time $t+1$. In other terms, update fails to infer that Alice wasn't in the office and still isn't.

Belief update fails as well on Example 3.1: updating $A \wedge B \wedge \neg C$ by $\neg A \vee \neg B$ gives the intended result, but only by chance (because the agent's initial belief state is complete). The second step fails: with most common update operators, updating $(A \oplus B) \wedge \neg C$ by $\neg B \wedge C$ leads to $\neg B \wedge C$, while we'd expect to believe A as well.

The diagnosis should now be clear: the input formula α is not a mere observation. An observation made at time $t+1$ leads to filter out some possible states at time $t+1$, which in turn leads to filter out some possible states at time t, because the state of the world at time t and the state of the world at time $t+1$ are correlated (by persistence rules or other dynamic rules.[6]). And finally, the successor worlds (at time $t+1$) of these worlds at time t that update failed to eliminate can not be eliminated either. Such a backward-forward reasoning needs a proper generalization of update (and of revision), unsurprisingly called *generalized update* [3].

One could try to argue that such scenarios (such as Example 3.1 or 3.2) are both a case for revision and update, depending whether the formulation of the problem uses time-stamped variables or not. This line of argumentation fails: expressing Example 3.2 as a belief update still leads to the counterintuitive results that we do not learn anything about Alice. Besides, several authors remarked that, unless belief bases are restricted to complete bases, a belief update operator cannot be a belief revision operator. For instance, it is shown in [15, 30] that the AGM postulates are inconsitent with U8 as soon as the language contains at least two propositional symbols.

4 Update as Action Progression

We now investigate in further detail the belief change interpretation of belief update. (There is at least one other interpretation, which deals with causality and counterfactuals, on which we shall come back in Sect. 6.) Since standard belief update precludes any possibility of feedback, the input formula α has to be understood as an *action effect*, and certainly not as an observation. If α has to be understood as an action effect, update is a particular form of *action progression* for *feedback-free actions*. Action progression (as considered in the literature of reasoning about action and logic-based planning) consists in determining the belief state obtained from an initial belief state after a given action is performed, this action corresponding to a transition graph (an automaton) between states of the world.

---

[6] The only case where belief update could be compatible with interpreting α as an observation would therefore be the case where not the faintest correlation exists between the state of the world at different time points; in this case, we would have $\varphi \diamond \alpha \equiv \alpha$ whenever α is consistent—a totally degenerate and uninteresting case.

This connection between belief update and action progression was first mentioned by Del Val and Shoham [5], who argued that updating an initial belief state φ by a formula α corresponds to one particular action; they formalize such actions in a formal theory of actions based on circumscription, and their framework for reasoning action is then used to derive a semantics for belief update. The relationship between update and action progression appears (more or less explicitly) in several other chapters, including [27], who expresses several belief update operators in a specific action language. Still, the relationship between update and action progression still needs to be investigated in more detail.

We first need to give some background on reasoning about action. Generally speaking, an action A has two types of effects: an *ontic (or physical) effect* and an *epistemic effect*. For instance, if the action consists in tossing a coin, its ontic effect is that the next value of the fluent *heads* may change, whereas its epistemic effect is that the new value of the fluent is observed (this distinction between ontic and epistemic effects is classical in most settings). Complex actions (with both kinds of effects) can be decomposed into two actions, one being ontic and feedback-free, the other one being a purely epistemic (sensing) action.

The simplest model for a purely ontic (i.e., feedback-free) action A consists of a *transition graph* R_A on S.[7] $R_A(s, s')$ means that s' is accessible from s after A. $R_A(s) = \{s' \mid R_A(s, s')\}$ is the set of states that can obtain after performing A in s. If $R_A(s)$ is a singleton for all s then A is *deterministic*. If $R_A(s) = \emptyset$ then A is *inexecutable* in s. A is *fully executable* iff $R_A(s) \neq \emptyset$ for every s.

An epistemic action e corresponds to a set of possible *observations*, plus a *feedback function* f_e from S to 2^O, where O is a finite *observation space*. $o \in f_e(s)$ means that observation o may be obtained as feedback when performing e in state s. Observations are of course correlated with states (for instance, an observation can be a propositional formula, or equivalently a set of states.) For the sake of simplicity, we identify O with L_V, that is, we consider that observations are propositional formulas (note however that this implies a loss of generality. The simplest possible epistemic actions are *truth tests*, and correspond to two possible observations, φ and $\neg\varphi$, for some propositional formula φ. An epistemic action e is *truthful* iff for all $s \in S, o \in O, o \in f_e(s)$ implies $s \models o$, *deterministic* iff for all $s \in S$, $f_e(s)$ is a singleton, and *fully executable* iff for all $s \in S$, $f_e(s) \neq \emptyset$.

Let A be a purely ontic action modelled by a transition graph R_A on S. For any formula $\varphi \in L^V$, the *progression of* φ *by* A is the propositional formula (unique up to logical equivalence) whose models are the states that can obtain after performing A in a state of $Mod(\varphi)$: $prog(\varphi, A)$ is defined by

$$prog(\varphi, A) = for\left(\bigcup_{s \models \varphi} R_A(s)\right) \tag{1}$$

[7] More sophisticated models may involve graded uncertainty such as probabilities, delayed effects etc.

Remark that the probabilistic variant of action progression is the well-known action progression operator for stochastic actions: let p is a probability distribution over S and A a stochastic action described by a stochastic matrix $p(.|., A)$, where $p(s'|s, A)$ is the probability of obtaining s' after performing A in s. Then $prog_P(p, A)$ is the probability distribution over S defined by

$$prog_P(p, A)(s') = \sum_{s \in S} p(s)p(s'|s, A)$$

Mapping each probability distribution p into the belief state $B(p) = for(\{s | p(s) > 0\})$ consisting of those states deemed possible by p, i.e., $B(prog_P(p, A)) = prog(B(p), A)$. As argued by Dubois and Prade [7], the probabilistic variant of belief update is Lewis' imaging [26]: $p(.|., \alpha)$ is then defined by

$$p(s'|s, \alpha) = \begin{cases} \frac{1}{|Proj(s,\alpha)|} & \text{if } s' \in proj(s, \alpha) \\ 0 & \text{otherwise} \end{cases}$$

where $proj(s, \alpha)$ is the set of states closest to α (according to some proximity structure).

Lastly, for any action A, $Inv(A)$ is the set of *invariant states* for A, i.e. the set of all states s such that $R_A(s) = \{s\}$.

Clearly enough, (1) is identical to (U8). Therefore, for any update operator (and more generally any operator satisfying (U8)) and any input formula α, *updating by α is an action progression operator*. This raises several questions: (a) Which action is this exactly? (b) What is the class of actions that correspond to updates? (c) If update is progression, are there belief change operators corresponding to regression?

Question (a) first. As argued above, (U8) and (1) mean that the action is feedback-free. Indeed, a feedback would allow us to eliminate some states after the action has been performed, which in turn would lead us to eliminate some states before the action took place (see [3, 8]).[8] This comes down to saying that belief update assumes *unobservability*: the set of possible states after A is performed is totally determined by the set of possible states before it is performed and the transition system corresponding to A. In other words, *what you foresee is what you get* (WYFIWYG): once we have decided to perform A, waiting until it has actually been performed will not bring us any new information. Expressed in a modal language, the WYFIWIG principle is nothing but the (RR) axiom of Grahne [13], of which we give Leitgeb and Segerberg's formulation ([25], p. 181):

$$\mathbf{B}(\varphi \Box\!\!\rightarrow \psi) \leftrightarrow [\diamond\varphi]\mathbf{B}\psi$$

[8] Unless the state of the world after the action is performed is totally disconnected from the state of the world before the action is performed, which only happens if $R_A(s) = S$ for all s. In this case, a feedback never allows for learning anything about the past state of the world. Clearly, this case is a very degenerated one.

(RR) can be seen the syntactical counterpart of (U8). Leitgeb and Segerberg consider it as the key axiom of KGM, and I do agree.

Note that using update in Example 3.2 would correspond to performing an action whose effect is to make Bob go out of his office (when he is initially not in the office, this action has no effect). Likewise, in Example 3.1, updating $A \oplus B \wedge \neg C$ by $\neg B \wedge C$ corresponds to performing the action "demote Bob from his position and appoint Charles instead".

Therefore, updating by α is a purely ontic (feedback-free) action. Can we now describe this action in more detail? (U1) means that the action of updating by α has to be understood as "make α true". Such actions (or events[9] have been given some attention for long by Segerberg, and are referred to in [25] (pp. 182–183) as

> "resultative" events': events describable in terms of their results (...). The intended meaning of a term $\delta\varphi$ would be "the event resulting in (its being the case that) φ". Accordingly, the intended meaning of a formula $[\delta\varphi]\psi$ would be "after the event resulting in (its being the case that) φ, it is the case that ψ, or more briefly, "after φ has just been realized, ψ."

More precisely, Segerberg studied in [32] a class of actions *bringing about that* α, or simply, *doing* α. In the light of the discussion above, comparing this class of actions *do* α and KGM belief update appears is more than worth doing. One of the main axioms for *do* α *is* $[do\ \alpha]\alpha$, which is obviously equivalent to (U1), modulo reformulation. Axioms (E1) and (E2) ([32], p. 333) are together equivalent to (U4). Where the two frameworks depart is with the last main axiom of *do* α, namely,

$$[do\ \alpha]\beta \rightarrow ([do\ \beta]\gamma \rightarrow [do\ \alpha]\gamma)$$

whose reformulation in the language of belief update is

$$\varphi \diamond \alpha \models \beta \rightarrow ((\varphi \diamond \beta \models \gamma) \rightarrow (\varphi \diamond \alpha \models \gamma))$$

This axiom (which, incidentally, implies the KM axiom (U6)), cannot be satisfied by a belief update operator satisfying (U1) and (U2). Indeed, take $\gamma = \varphi$, $\alpha = \neg\varphi$, and $\beta = \top$. Trivially, $\varphi \diamond \alpha \models \beta$ holds. Due to (U2), we have $\varphi \diamond \beta \equiv \varphi$, thus $\varphi \diamond \beta \models \gamma$ holds. Lastly, due to (U1), $\varphi \diamond \alpha \models \alpha$, which implies that $\varphi \diamond \alpha \models \gamma$ cannot hold. This fact is intriguing, as the axiom seems natural. I leave a deeper discussion for further research, but still, I am convinced that early works by Segerberg on *do* α actions (which appeared several years before the first chapters on belief update)—was very close to belief update, and, probably due to the fact that both streams of work were developed in different communities, very few works mention that.

[9] The distinction between actions and events is mostly irrelevant to our discussion. Actions are usually thought of as agent-trigerred, whereas events don't, or don't necessarily (see for instance [31]). Who triggers what has no impact on our discussion: an action performed consciously and intentionally by an agent, or a nature-trigerred event, or an action performed by another agent, have the same effects on the agent's belief state *provided* that, in all cases, the agent is perfectly aware of the action or the event taking place.

Back to interpreting "updating by α" as "make α true". More precisely, due to the absence of feedback reflected by (U8), updating φ by α could be understood as a dialogue between an agent and a robot: "All I know about the state of the world is that is satisfies φ. Please, go to the real world, see its real state, and whatever this state, act so as to change it into a world satisfying α, following some rules" (given that the robot does not communicate with the agent once it is the real world.) The rules to be followed by the robot are dictated by the choice of the update operator $\diamond$. If $\diamond$ satisfies (U2), then the rules state that if the α is already true then the robot must leave the world as it is. If $\diamond$ is the PMA [36], then the rules are "make α true, without changing more variables than necessary". More generally, when $\diamond$ is a Katsuno-Mendelzon operator, associated with a collection of similarity preorders (one for each world), the robot should make α true by changing s into one of the states that are most similar to it notion (s being closer to s_1 than to s_2 may, in practice, reflect that from s it is easier to go to s_1 than to s_2) and not as an epistemic notion of similarity, as it would be the case for belief revision. When $\diamond$ is a forgetting-based operation, such as WSS [14, 36] or the MPMA [6], then the rules are "make α true, without changing the truth values of a given set of variables (those that do not appear in α, or those that play no role in α)." And so on.

It is the right place to discuss the rôle of minimisation in belief update. It has been remarked already by several authors (see [18] for a synthetic discussion) that requiring minimisation of change is not always the right thing to do, and that many well-behaved update operators do not need it, nor do they need these KM faithful orderings around worlds—which strongly departs with AGM belief revision. These rankings are optional; when relevant, they correspond to *objective similarity* between worlds. Peppas et al. [30], argue that this similarity has be understood as *ontological*, which agrees with our view of $update(\diamond, \alpha)$ as an ontic action. Leitgeb and Segerberg go further in this direction by giving this illuminating argument ([25], pp. 184–185):

> We think that the actual difference between the intended interpretation of revision and update is given by the fact that the former belief change follows a *doxastic* order of "fallback positions" [29] while the latter conforms to a *worldly* similarity order of states of affairs—the one rides on a subjective structure, the other as an objective one. (...) Thus, given new evidence, we find that in the case of belief revision the agent tries to change his beliefs in a way such that he subsequently believes to be in the *subjectively most plausible deviation* from the worlds he originally believed to inhabit. However, confronted with the same evidence in belief update, the agent tries to change his beliefs in a way such that the worlds that he subsequently believes to be are *as objectively similar as possible* to the worlds he originally believed to be the most plausible candidates to be the actual world.

Writing things more formally: given an update operator $\diamond$ and a formula α, let $update(\diamond, \alpha)$ be the ontic action whose transition graph is defined by: for all $s, s' \in S$,

$$s' \in R_{update(\diamond,\alpha)}(s) \quad \text{iff} \quad s' \models for(s) \diamond \alpha$$

The following characterizations are almost straightforward, but worth mentioning, as they shed some light on the very meaning of the KM axioms.

Proposition 4.1 *Let $\diamond$ satisfy (U8).*

1. $\varphi \diamond \alpha \equiv prog(\varphi, update(\diamond, \alpha))$;
2. $\diamond$ *satisfies (U1) if and only if for any formula* $\alpha \in L^V$ *and any* $s \in S$, $R_{update(\diamond,\alpha)}(s) \subseteq Mod(\alpha)$;
3. $\diamond$ *satisfies (U2) if and only if for any formula* $\alpha \in L^V$, $Inv(update(\diamond, \alpha)) \supseteq Mod(\alpha)$;
4. $\diamond$ *satisfies (U3) if and only if for any satisfiable formula* $\alpha \in L^V$, $update(\diamond, \alpha)$ *is fully executable.*

Proof For point 1, (U8) implies that $Mod(\varphi \diamond \alpha) = \cup_{s \models \varphi} for(s) \diamond \alpha$, which, by definition of $update(\diamond, \alpha)$, is equal to $\cup_{s \models \varphi} R_{update(\diamond,\alpha)}(s)$, which, by definition of progression, is equal to $Mod(prog(\varphi, update(\diamond, \alpha)))$.

For point 2, let $\diamond$ satisfying (U1). Then $R_{update(\diamond,\alpha)}(s) = Mod(for(s) \diamond \alpha) \subseteq Mod(\alpha)$. Conversely, if for any α and any $s \in S$, $R_{update(\diamond,\alpha)}(s) \subseteq Mod(\alpha)$ holds, then $Mod(\varphi \diamond \alpha) = \cup_{s \models \varphi} for(s) \diamond \alpha = \cup_{s \models \varphi} R_{update(\diamond,\alpha)}(s) \subseteq Mod(\alpha)$, therefore $\varphi \diamond \alpha \models \alpha$.

For point 3, we have that for all s and α, $for(s) \diamond \alpha = for(s)$ if and only if $R_{update(\diamond,\alpha)}(s) = \{s\}$ if and only if $s \in Inv(update(\diamond, \alpha))$. Now, if $\diamond$ satisfies (U2) then for any α and $s \in Mod(\alpha)$, by (U2) we get $for(s) \diamond \alpha = for(s)$, therefore $s \in Inv(update(\diamond, \alpha))$. Conversely, if $Inv(update(\diamond, \alpha)) \supseteq Mod(\alpha)$ holds then for any φ such that $\varphi \models \alpha$ we have $Mod(\varphi \diamond \alpha) = \cup_{s \models \varphi} R_{update(\diamond,\alpha)}(s) = \cup_{s \models \varphi} s$ (because $for(s) \models \alpha$), therefore $Mod(\varphi \diamond \alpha) = Mod(\varphi)$, hence (U2) is satisfied.

For point 4, let α be a satisfiable formula. For any s, $for(s) \diamond \alpha$ is satisfiable if and only if $R_{update(\diamond,\alpha)}(s) \neq \emptyset$. If $\diamond$ satisfies (U3) then because $for(s)$ is satisfiable, $for(s) \diamond \alpha$ is satisfiable, therefore $R_{update(\diamond,\alpha)}(s) \neq \emptyset$; this being true for all s, $update(\diamond, \alpha)$ is fully executable. Conversely, assume $update(\diamond, \alpha)$ is fully executable, then for any satisfiable φ, $Mod(\varphi \diamond \alpha) = \cup_{s \models \alpha} R_{update(\diamond,\alpha)}(s) \neq \emptyset$; hence $\diamond$ satisfies (U3). □

From point 4 of Proposition 4.1, (U3) corresponds to full executability of $update(\diamond, \alpha)$. We may wonder what new properties of $update(\diamond, \alpha)$ obtain when other postulates are required. (U2) is particularly interesting in this respect. Indeed, the inertia postulate (U2) together with (U1) and (U8), reinterpreted in terms of action progression, means that any state that can be reached by $update(\diamond, \alpha)$ is an invariant state. More precisely:

Proposition 4.2 *Let $\diamond$ satisfying (U1), (U2) and (U8). Then*

$$R_{update(\diamond,\alpha)}(S) = Inv(update(\diamond, \alpha)) \cap Mod(\alpha)$$

Proof By (U1), $update(\diamond, \alpha)$ maps any state to a set of states satisfying α; then by (U2), any of these states is invariant by $update(\diamond, \alpha)$; therefore, $R_{update(\diamond,\alpha)}(S) \subseteq Inv(update(\diamond, \alpha))$. $R_{update(\diamond,\alpha)}(S) \subseteq Mod(\alpha)$ is a direct consequence of (U1). Finally, let $s \in Inv(update(\diamond, \alpha)) \cap Mod(\alpha)$. Then, by (U2), $for(s) \diamond \alpha =$

$for(s)$, hence $R_{update(\diamond,\alpha)}(s) = \{s\}$ and thus $s \in R_{update(\diamond,\alpha)}(S)$, which proves $Inv(update(\diamond, \alpha)) \cap Mod(\alpha) \subseteq Inv(update(\diamond, \alpha)) \cap Mod(\alpha)$. □

Note that if $R_{update(\diamond,\alpha)}(s) \subseteq Inv(update(\diamond, \alpha))$ for all s, then $update(\diamond, \alpha)$ is involutive, i.e., $R_{update(\diamond,\alpha)} \circ R_{update(\diamond,\alpha)} = R_{update(\diamond,\alpha)}$, but the converse fails to hold.

The other postulates do not have any direct effect on the properties of $update(\diamond, \alpha)$ considered *as an isolated action*, but they relate different actions of the form $update(\diamond, \alpha)$. Noticeably, requiring (U4) corresponds to the equality between $update(\diamond, \alpha)$ and $update(\diamond, \beta)$ when α and β are logically equivalent. The characterizations of (U5), (U6) and (U7) in terms of reasoning about action are purely technical and do not present any particular interest.

Let us now consider question (b). Obviously, given a *fixed* update operator $\diamond$ satisfying (U1), (U3), (U4) and (U8), some fully executable actions are not of the form $update(\diamond, \alpha)$. This is obvious because there are 2^{2^n} actions of the form $update(\diamond, \alpha)$ and 2^{n+2^n-1} fully executable actions, where $n = |V|$. Here is another proof, more intuitive and constructive: let $V = \{p\}$, thus $S = \{p, \neg p\}$, and consider the actions $A = switch(p)$, such that $R_A(p) = \{\neg p\}$ and $R_A(\neg p) = \{p\}$. Assume there is a formula α such that $A = update(\diamond, \alpha)$; then $U1$ enforces $\alpha \equiv \top$; therefore, if $A = update(\diamond, \alpha)$ then by (U4), $A = update(A, \top)$. Now, let A' be the identity action; we also have that if A' can be expressed as an update action for $\diamond$, then $A' = update(\diamond, \top)$. Therefore, at most one of A and A' can be expressed as an update action for $\diamond$.

Now, what happens if we allow $\diamond$ to vary? The question now is, what are the actions that can be expressed as $update(\diamond, \alpha)$, for *some* update operator $\diamond$ and some α?

Proposition 4.3 *Let A be a fully executable ontic action such that $R_A(s) \subseteq Inv(A)$ for all $s \in S$. Then there exists a KM-update operator, and a formula α, such that $A = update(\diamond, \alpha)$.*

Proof The proof is constructive. Let us take any formula $\alpha = for(Inv(A))$, and the collection of faithful orderings in the sense of [21] defined by $s_1 <_s s_2$ if and only if $s = s_1 \neq s_2$ or $(s \neq s_1, s \neq s_2, s_1 \in R_A(s), s_2 \notin R_A(s))$; and $s_1 \leq_s s_2$ iff not $(s_2 <_s s_1)$.

Because A is fully executable, $R_A(s) \neq \emptyset$ for any s, therefore $Inv(A) \neq \emptyset$ and α is satisfiable.

Let $s \models \alpha$. Because $\alpha = for(Inv(A))$ we have $R_A(s) = \{s\}$. By (U2), because $for(s) \models \alpha$, we have $for(s) \diamond \alpha = for(s)$, therefore $R_{update(\diamond,\alpha)}(s) = \{s\} = R_A(s)$.

Let $s \models \neg\alpha$. Then $s \notin R_A(s)$, which implies that $Min(\leq_s, Mod(\alpha)) = R_A(s)$, from which we have $for(s) \diamond \alpha = for(R_A(s))$ and $R_{update(\diamond,\alpha)}(s) = R_A(s)$.

We have established that $R_{update(\diamond,\alpha)}(s) = R_A(s)$ holds for all $s \in S$. Because of (U8), $\diamond$ is fully determined by $\{R_{update(\diamond,\alpha)}(s), s \in S\}$, therefore $A = update(\diamond, \alpha)$.

From Propositions 4.1 and 4.3 we get □

Corollary 4.4 *Let A be an ontic action. There exists a KM-update operator* $\diamond$*, and a formula* α *such that* $A = update(\diamond, \alpha)$*, if and only if A is fully executable and* $R_A(s) \subseteq Inv(A)$ *for all* $s \in S$.

A variant of Proposition 4.3 (and Corollary 4.4) can be obtained by not requiring $R_A(s) \subseteq Inv(A)$: in that case there exists an update operator $\diamond$ satisfying all the KM postulates except (U3), and a formula α such that $A = update(\diamond, \alpha)$. α can be taken as $\top$ and $s \leq_s s_2$ iff $s_1 \in R_A(s)$ or $s_2 \notin R_A(s)$.

Note that if (U2) is not required in Proposition 4.3 then we have the meaningless result that any action is expressible as an update.

5 Reverse Update

Now, question (c). Is there a natural notion which is to action regression what update is to progression? The point is that we do not have one, but two notions of action regression. The *weak* (or *deductive*) *regression* (also called *weak preimage* in the AI planning literature) of ψ by A is the formula whose models are the states from which the execution of A *possibly* leads to a model of ψ, while the *strong* (or *abductive*) *regression* (also called *strong preimage*) of ψ by A is the formula whose models are the states from which the execution of A *certainly* leads to a model of ψ:

$$reg(\psi, A) = form\,(\{s, R_A(s) \cap Mod(\psi) \neq \emptyset\})$$
$$Reg(\psi, A) = form\,(\{s, R_A(s) \subseteq Mod(\psi)\})$$

While weak regression is the suitable operator for *postdiction* (given that ψ now holds and that α has been performed, what can we say about the past state of the world?), strong regression is better understood as *goal regression* (what are the states in which it is guaranteed that performing α will lead to a goal state, i.e. a state satisfying ψ?) See for instance [24] for the interpretation of these two notions of regression in reasoning about action. This naturally leads to two notions of reverse update.

Definition 5.1 Let $\diamond$ be an update operator.

- the *weak reverse update* $\odot$ associated with $\diamond$ is defined by: for all $\psi, \alpha \in L^V$, for all $s \in S$,

$$s \models \psi \odot \alpha \text{ iff } for(s) \diamond \alpha \not\models \neg\psi$$

- the *strong reverse update* $\otimes$ associated with $\diamond$ is defined by: for all $\psi, \alpha \in L^V$, for all $s \in S$,

$$s \models \psi \otimes \alpha \text{ iff } for(s) \diamond \alpha \models \psi$$

Equivalently, $\psi \odot \alpha = for(\{s \mid for(s) \diamond \alpha \not\models \neg\psi\})$ and $\psi \otimes \alpha = for(\{s \mid for(s) \diamond \alpha \models \psi\})$.

Intuitively, weak reverse update corresponds to (deductive) postdiction: given that the action "make α true" has been performed and that we now know that ψ holds, what we can say about the state of the world before the update was performed is that it satisfied $\psi \odot \alpha$. As to strong reverse update, it is an abductive form of postdiction, better interpreted as goal regression: given that a rational agent has a goal ψ, the states of the world in which performing the action "make α true" is guaranteed to lead to a goal states are those satisfying $\psi \otimes \alpha$.

The following result shows that $\odot$ and $\otimes$ can be characterized in terms of $\diamond$:

Proposition 5.2 *1.* $\psi \odot \alpha \models \varphi$ *iff* $\neg\varphi \diamond \alpha \models \neg\psi$;
2. $\varphi \models \psi \otimes \alpha$ *iff* $\varphi \diamond \alpha \models \psi$;

Proof For point 1, assume $\neg\varphi \diamond \alpha \not\models \neg\psi$. Then there exists s and s' such that $s \models \neg\varphi$, $s' \in R_A(s)$ and $s' \models \psi$. This implies that $for(s) \diamond \alpha \not\models \neg\psi$, *i.e.*, $s \models \psi \odot \alpha$, and since $s \models \neg\varphi$, we have $\psi \odot \alpha \not\models \neg\varphi$. Conversely, assume $\psi \odot \alpha \not\models \varphi$. Then there exists $s' \models \psi$ and $s \models \neg\varphi$ such that $s' \in R_A(s)$, which implies that $\neg\varphi \not\models \neg\psi$. For point 2, assume $\varphi \diamond \alpha \not\models \psi$. Then there exists s' such that $s' \models \varphi \diamond \alpha$, and $s' \models \neg\psi$. This implies that there exists an s such that $s' \in R_A(s)$ and $s \models \varphi$, hence $for(s) \diamond \alpha \not\models \psi$, *i.e.*, $s \not\models \psi \otimes \alpha$. Conversely, assume $\varphi \not\models \psi \otimes \alpha$. Then there exists $s \models \varphi$ such that $s \not\models \psi \otimes \alpha$, *i.e.*, $for(s) \diamond \alpha \not\models \psi$, which implies that there is a s' such that $s' \in R_A(s)$ and $s' \models \neg\psi$, therefore $\varphi \diamond \alpha \not\models \psi$. □

As a consequence of Proposition 5.2, $\psi \odot \alpha$ is the *weakest formula* φ *such that* $\neg\varphi \diamond \alpha \models \neg\psi$, *and* $\psi \otimes \alpha$ *is the strongest formula* φ *such that* $\varphi \diamond \alpha \models \psi$.

Example 5.3 Let $\diamond = \diamond_{PMA}$ [36]. Let b and m stand for "the book is on the floor" and "the magazine is on the floor". The action $update(\diamond, b \vee m)$ can be described in linguistic terms by "make sure that the book or the magazine is on the floor". Then $b \odot (b \vee m) \equiv b \vee (\neg b \wedge \neg m) \equiv b \vee \neg m$, which can be interpreted as follows: if we know that the book is on the floor after $update(\diamond, b \vee m)$ has been performed, then what we can say about the previous state of the world is that either the book was already on the floor (in which case nothing changed) or that neither the book nor the magazine was on the floor (and then the update has resulted in the book being on the floor). On the other hand, $b \otimes (b \vee m) \equiv b$: if our goal is to have the book on the floor, the necessary and sufficient condition for the action $update(\diamond, b \vee m)$ to be guaranteed to succeed is that the book is already on the floor (if neither of them is, the update might well leave the book where it is and move the magazine onto the floor).

An interesting question is whether weak and strong reverse update can be characterized by some properties (which then would play the role that the basic postulates play for "forward" update). Here is the answer (recall that a basic update operator satisfies U1, U3, U4 and U8).

Proposition 5.4 $\odot$ *is the weak reverse update associated with a basic update operator* $\diamond$ *if and only if* $\odot$ *satisfies the following properties:*

W1 $\neg\alpha \odot \alpha \equiv \bot$;

W3 *if α is satisfiable then* $\top \odot \alpha \equiv \top$;
W4 *if* $\psi \equiv \psi'$ *and* $\alpha \equiv \alpha'$ *then* $\psi \odot \alpha \equiv \psi' \odot \alpha'$;
W8 $(\psi \vee \psi') \odot \alpha \equiv (\psi \odot \alpha) \vee (\psi' \odot \alpha)$.

In addition to this, $\diamond$ *satisfies (U2) if and only if* $\odot$ *satisfies*

W2 $(\psi \odot \alpha) \wedge \alpha \equiv \psi \wedge \alpha$.

Proof Note first that (W4) and (W8) are *exactly* the same properties as (U4) and (U8), replacing $\diamond$ by $\odot$.

Let $\odot$ be the weak reverse update associated with a basic update operator $\diamond$. Let us show that $\odot$ satisfies (W1), (W3), (W4) and (W8).

From Proposition 5.2, $\neg\alpha \odot \alpha \equiv \bot$ is equivalent to $\top \diamond \alpha \models \alpha$, *i.e.*, for all s, $for(s) \diamond \alpha \models \alpha$, which in turns is equivalent to: for all φ, $\varphi \diamond \alpha \models \alpha$, which is (U1). Therefore, $\odot$ satisfies (W1).

Let α be a satisfiable formula. Assume that $\odot$ does not satisfy (W3), that is, $\top \odot \alpha \not\equiv \top$: from (U8), there is a s such that $s \not\models \top \odot \alpha$, which is equivalent to $\top \odot \alpha \models for(S \setminus \{s\})$, i.e., using Proposition 5.2, $\neg for(S \setminus \{s\}) \diamond \alpha \models \bot$, equivalent to $for(s) \diamond \alpha$ unsatisfiable, which contradicts the assumption that $\diamond$ satisfies (U3). Therefore, $\odot$ satisfies (W3).

Assume $\psi \equiv \psi'$ and $\alpha \equiv \alpha'$. For any s, $s \models \psi \odot \alpha$ holds if only if $for(s) \diamond \alpha \not\models \neg\psi$, which using (U4) is equivalent to $for(s) \diamond \alpha' \not\models \neg\psi'$, therefore $s \models \psi' \odot \alpha'$, which implies that $\odot$ satisfies (W4).

It holds that $s \models (\psi \vee \psi') \odot \alpha$ if and only if $for(s) \diamond \alpha \not\models \neg(\psi \vee \psi')$, which is equivalent to $for(s) \diamond \alpha \not\models \neg\psi$ and $for(s) \diamond \alpha \not\models \neg\psi')$, *i.e.*, to $s \models \psi \odot \alpha$ or $s \models \psi \odot \alpha$, which shows that $\odot$ satisfies (W8).

Conversely, let $\odot$ satisfying (W1), (W3), (W4) and (W8). Let us show that there exists an operator $\diamond$ satisfying satisfies (U1), (U3), (W4) and (U8), such that $\odot$ is the weak reverse update associated with $\diamond$. We first note that definition of $\odot$ from $\diamond$ is symmetric: let us call the *conjugate* of a belief change operator $\star$ the belief change operator $\overline{\star}$ defined by

$$s \models for(s')\overline{\star}for(s) \text{ iff } for(s) \star \alpha for(s')$$

Then we see that if the weak reverse operator $\odot$ associated with $\diamond$ is its conjugate, *i.e.*, $\odot = \overline{\diamond}$, but also *vice versa*: $\diamond = \overline{\odot}$. Therefore, if we define $\diamond$ as the conjugate of $\odot$, $\odot$ is the weak reverse update associated with $\diamond$.

Let us now show that $\diamond = \overline{\odot}$ satisfies (U1), (U3), (U4) and (U8). Since (W4) and (W8) coincide with (U4) and (U8), exchanging $\diamond$ and $\odot$, together with the first half of the proof we immediately get that $\diamond$ satisfies (U4) and (U8).

Recall from above that in presence of (U8), $\diamond$ satifies (U1) if and only if $\odot$ satisfies (W1). Therefore, $\odot$ satisfies (W1).

As to the point concerning (U2) and (W2), assume furthermore that $\diamond$ satisfies (U2). Assume $s \models (\psi \odot \alpha) \wedge \alpha$. Suppose $s \not\models \psi$. Then there exists s' such that $s' \in R_A(s)$ and $s' \models \psi$, which implies $s \neq s'$, therefore $R_A(s) \neq \{s\}$; this, together with $for(s) \models \alpha$, violates (U2). Therefore, $s \models \psi \wedge \alpha$. Now, assume $s \models \psi \wedge \alpha$. By (U2), $R_A(s) = \{s\}$, therefore there is a $s'(= s)$ such that $s' \models \psi$ and $s' \in R_A(s)$, which shows that $s \models \psi \odot \alpha$. Therefore, $\odot$ satisfies (W2). Conversely, assume that $\diamond$ does not satisfy (U2). Then, by (U8), there exist two states s, s' and a formula α such that $s' \neq s$, $s \models \alpha$, and $s' \models for(s) \diamond \alpha$. Take $\psi = for(s')$, we have $s \models (\psi \odot \alpha) \wedge \alpha$ but $s \not\models \psi \wedge \alpha$; therefore $\odot$ does not satisfy (W2). □

Properties (U5), (U6) and (U7) do not seem seem to have meaningful counterparts for $\odot$ (and anyway, as already argued, these three postulates are controversial).

Proposition 5.5 *The strong reverse update $\otimes$ associated with a basic update operator $\diamond$ satisfies the following properties:*

S1 $\alpha \otimes \alpha \equiv \top$;
S3 *if α is satisfiable then* $\bot \otimes \alpha \equiv \bot$;
S4 *if $\psi \equiv \psi'$ and $\alpha \equiv \alpha'$ then* $\psi \otimes \alpha \equiv \psi' \otimes \alpha'$;
S8 $(\psi \wedge \psi') \otimes \alpha \equiv (\psi \otimes \alpha) \wedge (\psi' \otimes \alpha)$.

In addition to this, $\diamond$ satisfies (U2) if and only if $\otimes$ satisfies

S2 *if $\psi \models \alpha$ then* $\psi \models \psi \otimes \alpha$.

Note that, unlike weak reverse update, strong reverse update does generally not satisfy modelwise decomposability (U8/W8), but a symmetric, conjunctive decomposability property (S8).

Moreover, if $\diamond$ is a basic update operator then

SIW if α is satisfiable then $\psi \otimes \alpha \models \psi \odot \alpha$

Proof By Proposition 5.2, $\alpha \otimes \alpha \equiv \top$ is equivalent to $\top \diamond \alpha \models \alpha$, which is equivalent to (U1), therefore $\otimes$ satisfies (S1).

Assume $\bot \otimes \alpha \not\equiv \bot$, *i.e.*, $\bot \otimes \alpha$ is satisfiable. Then there exists s such that $s \models \bot \otimes \alpha$, which by Proposition 5.2 implies $for(s) \diamond \alpha \models \bot$, which by (U3) implies that α is unsatisfiable.

Assume $\psi \equiv \psi'$ and $\alpha \equiv \alpha'$. For any φ, by Proposition 5.2, $\varphi \models \psi' \otimes \alpha'$ is equivalent to $\varphi \diamond \alpha' \models \psi'$, which by (U4) is equivalent to $\varphi \diamond \alpha \models \psi$, which again by Proposition 5.2 is equivalent to $\varphi \models \psi \otimes \alpha$. This being true for all φ, we get that $\psi' \otimes \alpha'$ and $\psi \otimes \alpha$ are equivalent: $\otimes$ satisfies (S4).

It is straightforward from the definition of $\otimes$ that $(\psi \wedge \psi') \otimes \alpha \models \psi \otimes \alpha$; therefore, $(\psi \wedge \psi') \otimes \alpha \models (\psi \otimes \alpha) \wedge (\psi' \otimes \alpha)$. Now, let $s \models (\psi \otimes \alpha) \wedge (\psi' \otimes \alpha)$. Then by Proposition 5.2, $for(s) \diamond \alpha \models \psi$ and $for(s) \diamond \alpha \models \psi'$, therefore $for(s) \diamond \alpha \models \psi \wedge \psi'$, which again by Proposition 5.2 is equivalent to $s \models (\psi \wedge \psi') \otimes \alpha$. Hence $\otimes$ satisfies (S8).

Finally, let ψ and α be such that $\psi \models \alpha$. Then by Proposition 5.2, $\psi \models \psi \otimes \alpha$ is equivalent to $\psi \diamond \alpha \models \psi$, which is entailed by (U2). Therefore, if $\diamond$ satisfies (U2) then $\otimes$ satisfies (S2). For the converse, assume $\otimes$ satisfies (S2) and $s \models \psi$. Then $s \models \alpha$, and by (S2) we get $for(s) \models for(s) \otimes \alpha$, which by definition of $\otimes$ is equivalent to $for(s) \diamond \alpha \models for(s)$. Now, by (U3), $for(s) \diamond \alpha \models for(s)$ implies that $for(s) \diamond \alpha \equiv for(s)$, which by (U8) implies $\psi \diamond \alpha \equiv \psi$: $\diamond$ satisfies (U2). □

Note that (SIW) fails without (U3). Example 5.3 shows that the converse implication of (SIW) does not hold in general. Finally, $\otimes$ and $\odot$ coincide if and only if $update(\diamond, \alpha)$ is deterministic.

One may wonder whether reverse update has something to do with erasure [21]. An erasure operator $\blacklozenge$ is defined from an update operator $\diamond$ by $\psi \blacklozenge \alpha \equiv \psi \vee (\psi \diamond \neg\alpha)$. Erasing by α intuitively consists in making the world evolve (following some rules) such that after this evolution, the agent no longer believes α. A quick look suffices to understand that erasure has nothing to do with weak and strong reverse update. Erasure corresponds to action progression for an action $erase(\alpha)$ whose effect is be epistemically negative (*make* α *disbelieved*). This implies in particular that $\top \blacklozenge \top$ is always unsatisfiable ($\top$ cannot be made disbelieved) whereas $\top \odot \top \equiv \top \otimes \top \equiv \top$. To give another short example: if $\diamond = \diamond_{PMA}$, then $(a \leftrightarrow \neg b) \blacklozenge_{PMA} b \equiv (\neg a \vee \neg b)$, whereas $(a \leftrightarrow \neg b) \odot_{PMA} b \equiv (a \leftrightarrow \neg b) \otimes_{PMA} b \equiv \neg a$.

Pursuing the investigation on reverse update does not only have a theoretical interest: weak (deductive) reverse update allows for postdiction, and strong (abuctive) reverse update allows for goal regression (when the actions performed are updates) and is therefore crucial if we want to use an update-based formalism for planning (see [25]).

6 Update as Counterfactual Reasoning

There is another prominent interpretation of belief update, which *a priori* does not seem to be related to feedback-free action progression: counterfactual reasoning and causality. Let me quote Leitgeb and Segerberg [26], pp. 184–185:

> The intended interpretation of the semantics for belief update depends crucially on the manner in which selection functions are interpreted. The standard interpretation is in terms of environmental change; but there is another plausible way of interpreting selection functions, one that enables us to demonstrate that update does not necessarily correspond to environmental changes. Lewis famously considered objective similarity relations between possible worlds to be determinable from the objective spheres systems (...). This, given new evidence, we find that in the case of belief revision the agent tries to change his beliefs in a way such that the worlds that he subsequently believes to be in comprise the *subjectively most plausible deviation* from the worlds he originally believed to inhabit. However, when confronted in the same evidence in belief update, the agent tries to change his beliefs in a way such that the worlds that he subsequently believes to be in are *as objectively similar as possible* to the worlds he originally believed to be the most plausible candidates for being the actual world.

This is in agreement with Grahne's relationship between updates and counterfactuals [13]. Dupin de Saint-Cyr [9] goes further and argues that belief update is the right operation to deal with causality: the fact that α was true (respectively, that some event ϵ took place) at some time point t causes φ to be true at $t' > t$ is equivalent to saying that updating the past of the system by the fact that α was false (respectively, that ϵ did not take place) at t allows to derive that $\neg\varphi$ holds at t'. Updating the past in such a way requires selecting objectively most similar worlds that satisfy the condition part of the counterfactual ($\neg\varphi_t$ or $\neg\epsilon_t$).

Is counterfactual reasoning a radically different interpretation from feedback-free action progression? The traditional view of action progression only involves reasoning about the agent's future beliefs given her current beliefs and the knowledge of the action that is taking place now. Performing an action whose effects take place in the past does not look particularly intuitive at first sight. We argue that updating the past (in order to assess a causality statement) does however correspond to some form of action progression.

Technically, this is clear. The actions involved here act on the whole history. As in [9], consider a time-stamped language generated by propositional variables of the form v_t. A world τ is a full trajectory $\langle s_t, t \in T \rangle$ consisting of a full state at each time point. A temporal formula is a formula α built on the alphabet $\{v_t, t \in T\}$. Updating τ by α is conceptually no different from updating a world by a propositional formula in standard belief update. Updating a temporal formula β by a temporal formula α consists in taking the union of all $\tau \diamond \alpha$ for all trajectories τ satisfying β.

From a philosophical point of view, this is less obvious and we proceed by giving first an analogy between time and space. Consider the following counterfactual statement: if event ϵ had occurred at time point t, would p had been true at time point t'? This is equivalent to check whether (a) $\beta \models \neg p_t$ and (b) $\beta \diamond \epsilon_t \models p_{t'}$. Clearly, the part of the knowledge history β that takes place before t should remain unchanged: for every temporal formula γ involving only time-stamped variables $p_{t''}$ with $t" < t$, we should have $\beta \diamond \epsilon_t \models \gamma$ if and only if $\beta \models \gamma$. Now, consider a series of cells, horizontally connected, with a gate between cell i and cell $i + 1$ that can be pushed and opened from i but not from $i + 1$: when pushed from the left side towards the right, they open, but when pushed from the right towards the left, they do not. Suppose now that we perform an action in cell i that may increase the pressure, which in turn can lead to increase the pressure in cells $i + 1, i + 2$ etc. and possibly other side effects. Because the doors cannot open from right to left, nothing changes in cells $j < i$. (One can also imagine some information passing between cells that is possible only from the left to the right). It is not difficult to see that the strong left-to-right orientation of space is analogous to the past-to-future orientation of time. Asking whether making α true at cell i results in ψ holding at cell $j > i$ corresponds to asking whether the event of making α true at time t would result in ψ holding at time $t' > t$.

As a second example, consider a fiction writer who has built a scenario for a novel; the temporal formula β represents the beliefs of the reader at each time point (obviously, β is not necessarily complete). We assume here that these beliefs are correct, *i.e.*, the reader is never misled. The author is then asked by the publisher to change the scenario so that a particular temporal formula α be true (and known by the reader). This requires the writer to update β by α. Making α true is an action that can have effects on the whole history, *including maybe at time points earlier to those concerned by* α: it may indeed be simpler for the writer to adapt his novel so that x_t now holds by changing facts at time points $t' < t$. Although this is another example of updating the past, the possible influence from future to past make it radically different from updates used in counterfactual reasoning.

7 Updates and DDL

As developed in length in Krister Segerberg's works on Dynamic Doxastic Logic, there are many reasons why it is tempting to "express doxastic actions such as belief revision on the object language level". This, however, raises a serious issue: the failure of the Ramsey test. Quoting [25], p. 171:

> (...) DDL is bound to face a serious challenge: the danger of getting entangled in the potentially paradoxical of combining belief revision for an object language F with a representation of the revision operator in terms of formulæ in F.
>
> The possibly devastating effects of such a combination first showed up when Gärdenfors considered a doxastic interpretation of conditionals in terms of the so-called Ramsey test for conditionals.
>
> $$\varphi \Rightarrow \theta \text{ iff } \theta \in K \star \varphi$$

Indeed, Gärdenfors shows in [12] that as soon as the language contains at least three propositions that are pairwise consistent but jointly inconsistent, the AGM axioms of $\star$ are inconsistent with the Ramsey test for conditionals. The implications of Gärdenfors' impossibility result, to DDL, and the two ways to escape it, are discussed in [25], p. 172. As noticed by Herzig [16] and by Leitgeb and Segerberg [15], Gärdenfors' impossibility result does not carry over to belief update, and indeed, quoting from [15], "most standard systems of conditional logic support update operations". The intuitive reason for this lies in this ([25], p. 186):

> (...) given a body of beliefs [about the ways in which the environment may change] and an initial state of beliefs [about the current state of the environment], in KGM all future beliefs [about the current state of the environment] are determined by reports of what happens. So KGM, unlike basic AGM, is a theory of iterated belief change.

And indeed, iteration in belief update does not cause any particular problem. In the view of the discussion of Sect. 4, this should not be seen as surprising: recall that belief update is a particular kind of action progression, and action progression is naturally iterated. More than that, belief update can, just as action progression, be generalized not only to sequences of updates but also to *conditional updates*, *nondeterministic updates*, and *concurrent updates*. A *nondeterministic update* [4, 16] $\alpha \cup \beta$ corresponds to the nondeterministic choice of the two updates α and β. A *conditional update* [16] $\mathsf{if}\ \varphi\ \mathsf{then}\ \alpha\ \mathsf{else}\ \beta$ corresponds to an update by α if φ holds and by β otherwise. A *concurrent update* [16] $\alpha || \beta$ corresponds to the simulatenous execution of an update by α and an update by β. These constructs, which can be applied recursively, considerable enrich the language of belief update and makes it more suitable to express planning problems.

Now that we know that updates are a specific class of feedback-free actions, associated with transition systems, it makes even more sense to use DDL-KGM for expressing interactions between actions and beliefs, where $\diamond\alpha$ denotes the action of updating by α. As we argued already, the specificity of feedback-free actions is the *what you foresee is what you get* axiom, which is expressed in DDL by

$$\mathbf{B}[\diamond\alpha]\varphi \equiv [\diamond\alpha]\mathbf{B}\varphi$$

which, of course, does not hold for sensing actions or more generally actions that may bring some feedback. Progression and regression can also be expressed in DDL-KGM. The axiom

$$(Prog) \quad (\mathbf{B}\varphi \rightarrow \mathbf{B}[\diamond\alpha]\psi) \equiv (prog(\varphi, \alpha) \rightarrow \psi)$$

actually gives a *definition* of progression, i.e., a unique characterization of $prog(\varphi, \alpha)$ up to logical equivalence; and similarly for weak and strong regression:

$$(WR) \quad ([\diamond\alpha]\mathbf{B}\psi \rightarrow \mathbf{B}\varphi) \rightarrow (reg(\psi, \alpha) \rightarrow \varphi)$$

$$(SR) \quad (\mathbf{B}\varphi \rightarrow [\diamond\alpha]\mathbf{B}\psi) \rightarrow (\varphi \rightarrow Reg(\psi, \alpha))$$

There is no reason to stop here. For instance, we may integrate DDL-AGM and DDL-KM and express something like that

$$[\star([\diamond\alpha]\mathbf{B}\psi)]\mathbf{B}\varphi$$

expressing that after learning that updating by α would make ψ true, I now believe that it is the case that φ. (As an example, take $\diamond$ to be $\diamond_{PMA}$, and $\alpha = a \vee b$, $\psi = a \leftrightarrow \neg b$, $\varphi = \neg a \vee \neg b$.)

8 Summary and Conclusion

Let us try to summarize what we have said so far. Both revision and update deal with dynamic worlds, but they strongly differ in the nature of the information they process. Belief revision (together with the introduction of time stamps in the propositional language) aims at correcting some initial beliefs about the past, the present, and even the future state of the world by some newly *observed* information about the past or the present state of the world. Belief update is suitable only for (some specific) action progression without feedback: updating φ by α corresponds to progressing (or projecting forward) φ by the action $update(\diamond, \alpha)$, to be interpreted as *make α true*. The "input formula" α is the effect of the action $update(\diamond, \alpha)$, and definitely not an observation. Expressed in the terminology of Sandewall [31], the range of applicability of update is the class $\mathcal{K}_\mathrm{p}$-**IA**: correct knowledge,[10] no observations after the initial time point, inertia if (U2) is assumed, and alternative results of actions.

In complex environments, especially planning under incomplete knowledge, actions are complex and have both ontic and epistemic effects; the belief change

[10] However, this point is somewhat debatable: update would work as well if we don't assume that the agent's initial beliefs is correct—of course, in this case the final beliefs may be wrong as well.

process then is very much like the feedback loop in partially observable planning and control theory: perform an action, project its effects on the current belief state, then get the feedback, and revise the projected belief state by the feedback. Clearly, update allows for projection only. Or, equivalently, if one chooses to separate the ontic and the epistemic effects of actions, by having two disjoint sets of actions (ontic and epistemic), then ontic actions lead to projection only, while epistemic actions lead to revision only. Therefore, if one wants to extend belief update so as to handle feedback, there is no choice but integrating some kind of revision process, as in [3, 19, 20, 35]. Another possibility is to generalize update so that it works in a language that distinguishes facts and knowledge, such as epistemic logic S5: this *knowledge update* process is investigated by Baral and Zhang [2]. Here, effects of sensing actions are handled by *updating* (and not revising) formulas describing the agent's knowledge. Such a framework takes the point of view of a modelling agent O who reasons an the state of knowledge of another agent ag. Thus, for instance, updating a S5 model by $K_{ag}\varphi$ means that the O updates her beliefs about ag's knowledge; considering ag's mental state as part of the *outside world* for agent O, this suits our view of update as a feedback-free action for O (updating by $K_{ag}\varphi$ corresponds as "make $K_{ag}\varphi$ true", which can for instance be implemented by telling ag that φ is true).

Acknowledgments In my conference paper [23], I wrote that I would never have thought of writing that chapter without these years of discussion with Andreas Herzig about the very meaning of belief update. This is still true now, with a few more years in the count.

References

1. Alchourrón, C. E., Gärdenfors, P., & Makinson, D. (1985). On the logic of theory change: Partial meet contraction and revision functions. *Journal of Symbolic Logic*, *50*(2), 510–530.
2. Baral, C., & Zhang, Y. (2005). Knowledge updates: Semantics and complexity issues. *Artificial Intelligence*, *164*(1–2), 209–243.
3. Boutilier, C. (1998). A unified model of qualitative belief change: A dynamical systems perspective. *Artificial Intelligence*, *98*(1–2), 281–316.
4. Brewka, G., & Hertzberg, J. (1993). How to do things with worlds: On formalizing actions and plans. *Journal of Logic and Computation*, *3*(5), 517–532.
5. del Val, A., & Shoham, Y. (1994). Deriving properties of belief update from theories of action. *Journal of Logic, Language, and Information*, *3*, 81–119.
6. Doherty, P., Łukasziewicz, W., & Madalińska-Bugaj, E. (1998) The PMA and relativizing change for action update. In *Proceedings of the KR'98*, pp. 258–269.
7. Dubois, D., & Prade, H. (1993). Belief revision and updates in numerical formalisms: An overview, with new results for the possibilistic framework. In *Proceedings of IJCAI'93*, pp. 620–625.
8. Dupin de Saint-Cyr, F., & Lang, J. (2011). Belief extrapolation (or how to reason about observations and unpredicted change). *Artificial Intelligence*, *175*(2), 258–269.
9. Dupin de Saint-Cyr, F. (2008). Scenario update applied to causal reasoning. In *Proceedings of the Eleventh International Conference on the Principles of Knowledge Representation and Reasoning (KR 2008)* (pp. 188–197). AAAI Press.

10. Friedman, N., & Halpern, J. Y. (1999). Modelling beliefs in dynamic systems. Part ii: Revision and update. *JAIR*, *10*, 117–167.
11. Friedman, N., & Halpern, J. Y. (1996). Belief revision: A critique. In *Proceedings of the KR'96*, pp. 421–431.
12. Gärdenfors, P. (1986). Belief revisions and the Ramsey test for conditionals. *Philosophical Review*, *95*, 81–93.
13. Grahne, G. (1991). Updates and counterfactuals. In *KR*, pp. 269–276.
14. Herzig, A. (1996). The PMA revisited. In *Proceedings of the KR'96*, pp. 40–50.
15. Herzig, A. (2000). Logics for belief base updating. In D. Gabbay & Ph. Smets (Eds.), *Handbook of defeasible reasoning and uncertainty management systems*. Dordrecht: Kluwer Academic Publishers.
16. Herzig, A., Lang, J., Marquis, P., & Polacsek, T. (2001). Updates, actions, and planning. In *Proceedings of IJCAI'01*, pp. 119–124.
17. Herzig, A., Lang, J., & Marquis, P. (2011). Propositional update operators based on formula/literal dependence. Technical report.
18. Herzig, A., & Rifi, O. (1999). Propositional belief update and minimal change. *Artificial Intelligence*, *115*, 107–138.
19. Hunter, A., & Delgrande, J. (2005). Iterated belief change: A transition system approach. In *Proceedings of IJCAI'05*, pp. xxx–yyy.
20. Jin, Y., & Thielscher, M. (2004). Representing beliefs in the fluent calculus. In *Proceedings of ECAI-04*, pp. 823–827.
21. Katsuno, H., & Mendelzon, A. (1991). On the difference between updating a knowledge base and revising it. In *Proceedings of KR'91*, pp. 387–394.
22. Katsuno, H., & Mendelzon, A. (1991). Propositional knowledge base revision and minimal change. *Artificial Intelligence*, *52*, 263–294.
23. Lang, J. (2007). Belief update revisited. In *Proceedings of IJCAI'07*, pp. 2517–2522.
24. Lang, J., Lin, F., & Marquis, P. (2003). Causal theories of action: A computational core. In *Proceedings of IJCAI-03*, pp. 1073–1078.
25. Leitgeb, H., & Segerberg, K. (2007). Dynamic doxastic logic: Why, how, and where to? *Synthese (Knowledge, Rationality and Action)*, *155*, 167–190.
26. Lewis, D. (1973). *Counterfactuals*. Cambridge: Harvard University Press.
27. Liberatore, L. (2000). A framework for belief update. In *Proceedings of JELIA'00*, pp. 361–375.
28. Lindström, S., & Segerberg., K. (2006). *Modal logic and philosophy*. Dordrecht: Elsevier.
29. Lindström, S., & Rabinowicz, W. (1990). Epistemic entrenchment with incomparabilities and relational belief revision. In A. Fuhrmann & M. Morreau (Eds.), *The logic of theory change, Lectures Notes in Artificial Intelligence* (Vol. 645, 93–126). Berlin: Springer
30. Peppas, P., Nayak, A., Pagnucco, M., Foo, N., Kwok, R., & Prokopenko, M. (1996). Revision versus update: Taking a closer look. In *Proceedings of ECAI96*.
31. Sandewall, E. (1995). *Features and fluents*. Oxford: Oxford University Press.
32. Segerberg, K. (1989). Bringing it about. *Journal of Philosphical Logic*, *18*, 327–347.
33. Segerberg, K. (1998). Irrevocable belief revision in dynamic doxastic logic. *Notre Dame Journal of Formal Logic*, *39*, 287–306.
34. Segerberg, K. (2001). *The basic dynamic doxastic logic of AGM* (pp. 57–84). Dordrecht: Kluwer.
35. Shapiro, S., & Pagnucco, M. (2004). Iterated belief change and exogeneous actions in the situation calculus. In *Proceedings of the ECAI04*.
36. Winslett, M. (1990). *Updating logical databases*. Cambridge: Cambridge University Press.

DDL as an "Internalization" of Dynamic Belief Revision

Alexandru Baltag, Virginie Fiutek and Sonja Smets

Abstract In this chapter we re-evaluate Segerberg's "full DDL" (Dynamic Doxastic Logic) from the perspective of Dynamic Epistemic Logic (DEL), in its belief-revision-friendly incarnation. We argue that a correct version of full DDL must give up the Success Postulate for dynamic revision. Next, we present (an appropriately generalized and simplified version of) full DDL, showing that it is a generalization of the so-called Topo-logic of Moss and Parikh. We construct AGM-friendly versions of full DDL, corresponding to various revising/contracting operations considered in the Belief Revision literature. We show that DDL can internalize inside one model the "external" doxastic dynamics of DEL, as well as the evidential dynamics investigated by van Benthem and Pacuit. In our Conclusions section, we compare three styles of modeling doxastic dynamics: DDL, DEL and PDL/ETL (the Propositional Dynamic Logic approach, with its Epistemic Temporal Logic variant).

1 Introduction

Following the seminal work of Hintikka [11], the field of epistemic/doxastic logic generated a series of interesting logical systems which have sparkled the interest of several groups of researchers: the philosophers interested in using logical formalism to address the questions raised in the traditional study of epistemology, the researchers in AI studying agency, attitudes, non-monotonic reasoning and knowledge representation, and the computer scientists investigating distributed systems.

A. Baltag (✉) · V. Fiutek · S. Smets
University of Amsterdam, ILLC, Amsterdam, Netherlands
e-mail: thealexandrubaltag@gmail.com

V. Fiutek
e-mail: fiutek.virginie@gmail.com

S. Smets
e-mail: S.J.L.Smets@uva.nl

R. Trypuz (ed.), *Krister Segerberg on Logic of Actions*,
Outstanding Contributions to Logic 1, DOI: 10.1007/978-94-007-7046-1_12,

The interaction with these other areas of research gave a boost to the further development of epistemic/doxastic logic and raised the interest in the logical study of belief change and knowledge update.

It is at this point of time in the development of modal doxastic logic that we place the important contributions of Krister Segerberg: his idea was to enhance traditional epistemic and doxastic logics with specific dynamic-modal operators for "belief revision", thus linking modal logic with Belief Revision Theory (BRT). Looking the other way around, Segerberg's work provided BRT with a new syntax and formal semantics. Note that traditionally, the work on belief revision [1] focuses on the way in which a given theory (or belief base, consisting of sentences in a given object language) gets revised, but it does *not* treat "belief revision" itself as an ingredient in the object language under study. Segerberg's work opened up a new perspective by taking the very act of belief revision itself and placing it on an equal (formal) footing with the doxastic attitudes such as "knowledge" and "belief".

Dynamic doxastic logic (DDL) has been introduced and developed by Krister Segerberg in [19–26]. The system's main syntactic construct is the use of a dynamic modal operator $[*\varphi]\psi$ whose intended meaning is that "ψ holds after (the agent performs a) revision with φ". As explained in [26], the main added value of treating belief revision in this way (in contrast with the AGM approach [1]) is that we gain all the well-known advantages provided by working in a modal logic setting. Modal logics have turned into a rich area of investigation with applications to several other domains, hence casting Belief Revision Theory into a modal framework holds a great promise for its future development.

Segerberg distinguished between "basic DDL" and "full DDL": while basic DDL is about the way an agent revises her beliefs about the world, full DDL deals with the way in which an agent revises her beliefs about the world *and* about her own beliefs. Syntactically, this distinction is captured by restricting all the operators of the basic DDL language to Boolean formulas (while full DDL is not subject to this restriction).

In this chapter we take a fresh look at full DDL from the new perspective of "soft DEL" (the belief-revision-friendly version of Dynamic Epistemic Logic [2–7]), as a modern semantic embodiment of the AGM paradigm. DEL shares with DDL the modal logic approach to belief and belief-revision. However, DEL treats dynamic revision as an "external" operation (representing actions as changes of the current model), while in DDL the dynamics is "internal" to the model (i.e., actions are represented as changes of doxastic structure within the same model). One of our goals in this chaper is to show that the DDL approach is at least as powerful as the DEL approach: it can internalize all the recent DEL developments.

We start, in Sect. 2, by borrowing from DEL the distinction between static and dynamic revision, in order to correct an old conceptual error that plagued all attempts to develop a full DDL: the assumption that the AGM Success Postulate is tenable (and desirable) for dynamic revision. We show that (due to Moore-type paradoxes) a correct version of full DDL must give up the unrestricted dynamic version of the Success Postulate (keeping it only for static revision, or for the restriction of dynamic revision to non-doxastic sentences).

Next, in Sect. 3, we present an appropriately generalized and simplified version of full DDL. In Sect. 4 we show that DDL can be considered to be a generalization of the so-called Topo-logic of Moss and Parikh [15, 17]. In Sect. 5, we deal with static revision in DDL, by adopting the conditional belief logic *CDL* from [3].

Further, in Sect. 6, we develop and axiomatize (in "constructive", DEL-style) three versions of DDL, that internalize three of the revision operations considered in the Belief Revision literature. In Sect. 7, we analyze Segerberg's constructive treatment of expansion and contraction in DDL, and comment on their non-AGM nature. Next, we introduce and axiomatize three AGM-friendly versions of contraction and expansion in DDL. Based on this work, we argue that (if appropriately generalized), the DDL approach is at least as powerful as the DEL approach. In Sect. 8, we exemplify this point further by showing that Segerberg's generalized "hypertheory" version of DDL can internalize, not only belief dynamics, but also the *evidential dynamics* of van Benthem and Pacuit [8].

Finally, in Sect. 9, we compare three ways of doing dynamic belief revision: DDL, DEL, and PDL/ETL (i.e. the Propositional Dynamic Logic style of modeling belief changes, and its Epistemic Temporal Logic variant). Both PDL/ETL and DDL are ways to "internalize" the doxastic dynamics inside one model, but we argue that the DDL style is the most natural, most elegant and most "economical" way to do this internalization.

2 Static Versus Dynamic Belief Revision

Before developing full DDL, we first need to correct what we think to be a conceptual mistake of its founder, concerning the validity of the so-called Success Axiom in a dynamic setting. To address this, we follow the DEL literature in *distinguishing between "static" and "dynamic" belief revision*. Though it is often explained in syntactic terms (as referring to two different kinds of behaviour under revision with higher-level doxastic sentences), from a semantic point of view this distinction is in fact related to (though distinct from) the traditional dichotomy between *one-step* revision and *iterated* revision.

To model one-step revision, it is enough to specify, for every proposition P, the result of doxastic revision with P, either syntactically (as a set of sentences) or semantically (as a set of states, the ones that are most plausible after revising with P). *Semantically*, this can be uniformly done in three different ways: by giving a *selection function*, in Stalnaker's style; by giving a *family of spheres* (in Lewis-Grove style), i.e. an "onion" in the sense of Segerberg (or a "hypertheory", in his generalized semantics); or by giving a *plausibility relation* (or equivalently, an entrenchment relation). As far as modal (dynamic doxastic) logic can tell, these three semantic styles are equivalent, if considered at an appropriate level of generality.

Syntactically, one can capture static revision by specifying, in AGM-style, a set $T * P$ of revised beliefs, for each original set T of beliefs and each proposition P; or alternatively, on can enconde static revision using conditional belief operators $B^P Q$

(or $B(Q|P)$), whose meaning is that "after revision with P, the agent will come to believe that Q *was* the case (*before the revision*)".

The "static" character of this revision is reflected in the fact that, after the revision, Q is still evaluated according to the original state of affairs; in terms of Grove spheres, this is reflected in the fact that the same onion is used for evaluating Q (though not the same sphere): $B^P Q$ holds iff the smallest sphere in the current onion that intersects P is included in Q.

In contrast, dynamic revision involves a *change of onion*, or a change of plausibility relation (or a change of model). Semantically, it requires a binary relation between onions (in DDL-style), or between states with different plausibility (in PDL/ETL style), or between models (in DEL-style). Again, these three styles of doing doxastic dynamics are equivalent, if considered at an appropriate level of generality. Syntactically, dynamic revision can be captured by the use of dynamic modalities $[*P]Q$. More precisely, $[*P]B\,Q$ captures the fact that Q is believed to hold after revision with P. The "dynamic" character is reflected in the fact that, after the revision, $B\,Q$ is evaluated using the *new* onion (to which the old onion is related by the dynamic binary relation R^{*P}).

The "static" character of conditional belief operators $B^P Q$ can be made more explicit by expressing them in terms of dynamic operators ("weakest preconditions") $[*\phi]\psi$ and their *Galois adjoints*, i.e. the "reversed" dynamic operators $\langle *^{-1}\phi\rangle\psi$ (also known as "strongest postconditions"). While dynamic operators $[*\phi]\psi$ are (in the Segerberg's onion semantics) the universal (Box) modalities for some binary revision relation $R^{*\phi}$ between onions, the reversed dynamic operators $\langle *^{-1}\phi\rangle\psi$ are the existential (Diamond) modalities for the converse relation $(R^{*\phi})^{-1}$ (going *backwards* in time from of the revised doxastic state to the initial, unrevised doxastic state). It is easy to see that we have the following equivalence:

$$B^{\phi}\psi \Leftrightarrow [*\phi]B\langle *^{-1}\phi\rangle\psi.$$

This equivalence fully captures our above explanation of static revision $B^{\phi}\psi$, as reflecting the *revised beliefs* (after a revision with ϕ) about a sentence ψ's truth value *before* the revision.

Nevertheless, in our logics we chose *not* to reduce static revision to dynamic revision (and its converse); instead, we take static revision as basic, in the shape of primitive conditional belief operators $B^{\phi}\psi$, interpreted as *belief-revision plans*: "if *in the future* I ever would have to revise with ϕ, I would then come to believe that ψ *was true now*". And we follow the DEL tradition by recursively reducing any instance of dynamic revision to the static revision statements (via so-called Reduction laws, or Recursion laws). We choose this option because we think that, from a semantic point of view, static belief revision is a *simpler* concept than the dynamic one. Indeed, recall that to specify static revision one only needs to give *one onion* (together with a specific way to move between its spheres). While dynamic belief revision is given by a specific type of *onion change* (i.e. a specific way of moving between onions): a relation between onions! So in fact, dynamic belief revision does not involve only a simple revision of *beliefs*, but rather a *revision of (static) belief revision plans*!

Indeed, to syntactically describe in full a given type of dynamic belief revision, we do not need only statements of the form $[*P]B\,Q$ (describing dynamic revision of beliefs), but rather sentences of the form $[*P]B^R Q$ (describing dynamic revision of static belief-revision plans).

Luckily, this distinction does *not* need to be iterated: since (to use van Benthem's expression) static belief revision $B^R Q$ "pre-encodes" dynamic belief revision $[*R]BQ$, it is enough to know the behaviour $[*P]B^R Q$ of static revision plans under dynamic revision in order to be able to calculate the result of *iterated dynamic revision* $[*P][*R]B\,Q$. More generally, for each specific type of doxastic dynamic revision $*$, the statement $[*P]Q$ can be recursively reduced to a statement involving only static revision operators $B^R Q$: these are the well-known Reduction (or Recursion) Laws, from Dynamic Epistemic Logic.

Thus, dynamic revision, by its very semantic modelling, can be straightforwardly *iterated*; while static belief revision is just a *one-step* revision of (simple) beliefs.

But the distinction of static versus dynamic revision is *not the same* as the distinction between one-step and iterated revision! Dynamic revision fully "keeps up" with the doxastic change, while static revision looks back at the old doxastic state from the perspective of the new one.

To see this, note that *dynamic revision with higher-level doxastic sentences behaves differently than static revision.* Take a Moore sentence, of the form $\phi := p \wedge \neg Bp$. An introspective agent will obviously *not* come to believe ϕ after she learns ϕ; indeed, believing ϕ would amount to a lack of introspection, since it would mean to believe *both p and* the fact that one doesn't believe p. So, after learning ϕ, an introspective agent will clearly come to believe p, but not ϕ itself. This is correctly reflected by dynamic revision: as we will see, for any reasonable dynamic interpretation of the revision operation $*$ as a binary relation on doxastic states (onions), the formula $[*\phi]B\phi$ is *false* for any Moore sentence ϕ: indeed, even if ϕ was true in the old doxastic state, after revision with ϕ the sentence $B\phi$ is evaluated according to the new doxastic state, in which ϕ is false, and (known to be false, hence) disbelieved. In contrast, static revision with any sentence ϕ will always produce belief in that sentence, since after static revision, the sentence is still evaluated according to the original doxastic state: this is reflected by the conditional-belief validity $B^\phi \phi$, which is a version of the AGM "Success" Postulate $\phi \in T * \phi$.

This distinction is an important one, that DDL needs to learn from DEL, in order to deal correctly with higher-level doxastic sentences. Ignoring this distinction leads to what we think to be a conceptual "mistake", made by Lindstrom and Rabinowicz in their papers [13, 14] on DDL for introspective agents, as well as by Segerberg himself in [24]. Namely, these authors assume (mistakenly, in our view) that a dynamic version of the Success postulate (in the form of the axiom $[*\phi]B\phi$) is desirable, or even tenable, in full DDL (i.e. when ϕ is itself a doxastic sentence). As we argue below (and as was already argued before in the DEL literature), this assumption is wrong,

We should stress that this conceptual problem affects *only* the *first* solution to the Moore "paradox" proposed by Lindstrom and Rabinowicz (in the first part of their paper [13]). There, they define a semantics for revision, which together with their (standard PDL-like) semantics for dynamic modalities, can be shown to immediately lead to a *semantic failure of the Success Postulate for any (positively) introspective agent*. Indeed, in a Lindstrom-Rabinowicz model, formulas are evaluated at "total states" x, each coming with an ontic state ("world") $w(x)$ and a doxastic state $d(x)$. In their turn, doxastic states $d(x)$ are Segerberg "onions" (or more generally hypertheories): these are families of "spheres" (i.e., of closed sets of total states). If we put $b(x) := \bigcap d(x)$ for the "smallest sphere" of the onion $d(x)$, then belief is defined as usually in Grove models: $x \models B\phi$ iff $b(x) \subseteq \|\phi\|$. Take now any Lindstrom-Rabinowicz model M in which the following two conditions are satisfied: (a) the agent is *positively introspective with respect to some specific fact p* (at *all* the states of the model); and (b) there exists *some* total state x in which *the agent doesn't believe p and she doesn't believe* $\neg p$. It seems clear that, no matter what additional restrictions one might want to impose on Lindstrom-Rabinowicz models, situations satisfying (a) and (b) should still be allowed.[1] So, even if we add further conditions, a model M of the above kind should still be in the intended class of models. As a consequence of (b), the smallest sphere $b(x) := \bigcap d(x)$ (at total state x) contains both p and $\neg p$ worlds. In this situation, the Moore sentence $\phi := p \wedge \neg Bp$ is semantically consistent with the agent's (semantic) beliefs; indeed, ϕ is true at all the p-worlds belonging to the smallest sphere: $b(x) \cap \|\phi\| \subseteq \|p\|$. Hence, this smallest sphere $b(x)$ has a non-empty intersection $b(x) \cap \|\phi\| = b(x) \cap \|p\| \neq \emptyset$ with the extension $\|\phi\|$ of ϕ in this model. The Lindstrom-Rabinowicz semantic conditions (or more precisely, their postulates on semantic contraction and their Levi-style definition of revision) ensure that in this situation a revision with ϕ is the same as an expansion with ϕ (as is also prescribed by the AGM theory): so, the total state y obtained after revision (i.e. such that $xR^{*\psi}y$) is the same as the state obtained by expansion, i.e. we have $xR^{+\phi}y$. But unlike revision (or contraction), the expansion operation is completely determined by the AGM axioms, which are accepted by Lindstrom and Rabinowicz, who in fact explicitly assume that the expanded state y is the unique total state satisfying the conditions $w(y) = w(x)$ (stability of ontic state) and $d(y) = d(x) + \|\phi\| =: d(x) \cup \{X \cap \|\phi\| : X \in d(x)\}$. This means that the smallest sphere of the new "onion" $d(y)$ must be $b(y) = \bigcap d(y) = \bigcap d(x) \cap \|\phi\| = b(x) \cap \|\phi\| = b(x) \cap \|p\| \subseteq \|p\|$. As a consequence, in the new total state y, the agent believes p: $y \models Bp$. Since Positive Introspection with respect to p holds in this model, we also have $y \models BBp$. If the Success Postulate would also hold, in its dynamic form $x \models [*\phi]B\phi$, then by the standard PDL semantics for dynamic operators (accepted by Lindstrom and Rabinowicz in this part of their paper), we would have $y \models B\phi$. Using the normality of the operator B (which is another immediate consequence of the Lindstrom-Rabinowicz semantic definition of belief) and the fact that $\phi := p \wedge \neg Bp$, it follows that $y \models B\neg Bp$. So we have that $y \models (BBp \wedge B\neg Bp)$, and by normality again, we conclude that $y \models B(p \wedge \neg Bp)$, which by the semantic definition of B, entails that $b(y) \subseteq \|Bp \wedge \neg Bp\| = \emptyset$. But this contradicts the above-mentioned fact that $b(y) = \bigcap d(y) = \bigcap d(x) \cap \|\phi\| = b(x) \cap \|\phi\| = b(x) \cap \|p\| \neq \emptyset$.

[1] Even if one doesn't accept Positive Introspection as a general axiom, one certainly shouldn't exclude situations in which the agent *is* introspective, at least with respect to *some particular fact p*.

Observe that this contradiction is obtained only using the Lindstrom-Rabinowicz semantics for belief and revision, the Success Postulate, and the natural and innocuous assumptions (a) and (b) (i.e. that there occasionally may exist some agent who is introspective with respect to some fact p, while the fact p itself is currently neither believed nor disbelieved by the agent). Since the title of one of the papers presenting their setting is *Belief Change for Introspective Agents* [14], it seems to us that Lindstrom and Rabinowicz do not aim to give up even the mere *possibility* of Positive Introspection (with respect to even just one factual statement). So it follows that they must give up the Success Postulate.

However, Lindstrom and Rabinowicz resist this conclusion. They do prove a "Moore paradox" (namely, that the agent's beliefs are inconsistent), but only *syntactically* (axiomatically), using an additional (unnecessary) assumption (the so-called Preservation Principle). Their conclusion is that this last-mentioned assumption (rather than the Success axiom) is to be blamed for the paradox. So they propose giving up Preservation, without apparently noticing that the above clear-cut semantic argument shows already (without any use of Preservation, but using only the local assumptions (a) and (b)) that the Success postulate is conceptually incompatible with their dynamic semantics.

It is true that, in the *second* part of their paper [13], Lindstrom and Rabinowicz propose a second solution to the Moore paradox, their so-called bidimensional semantics, which is in fact very close to our (i.e. the DEL) solution. Indeed, their rendering in English of their proposal is essentially the same as our solution: they point out that the Success Postulate makes sense for doxastic sentences ϕ *only* if it is interpreted in terms of *the revised beliefs about* ϕ*'s truth value before the revision*. However, they formally package this solution in a different way, in order to maintain the appearance (at a purely syntactic level!) that the Success Postulate is maintained. Namely, they do this by adopting a bidimensional semantics in terms of pairs of states (x, y), in order to refer to both doxastic states (before and after the revision), and they *radically change the PDL semantics of dynamic operators to a non-standard one*: roughly speaking, their new semantics amounts to evaluating any doxastic expression $B\psi$ that comes in the scope of a dynamic operator $[*\phi]$ as capturing the revised beliefs (after revision with ϕ) about ψ's truth value before the revision.

We fully agree with the conceptual analysis underlying the second solution of Lindstrom and Rabinowicz, but we disagree with their non-standard, and completely ad-hoc, modification of the semantics of dynamic operators. We think dynamic modalities should be left to express what they always did: a one-way move in time, from the state before the (revision) action to the state after the action. Instead of twisting the meaning of dynamic operators, we think one should simply recognize the plain, inescapable truth: the Success Postulate does not (and should not) hold for dynamic revision with doxastic sentences.

In most of his papers on DDL, Segerberg himself is cautious not to fall into the above mentioned conceptual mistake, by almost always limiting himself to "basic DDL": no revision with doxastic sentences. However, in [24] he proposes an axiomatic system for full DDL. Unfortunately, this converts a conceptual mistake into a logical error: the proposed system is *not sound* with respect to the proposed semantics. The reason is that the proposed Success Axiom $[*\phi]B\phi$ is not a validity in this semantics: essentially, the above model provides a counterexample to this. The semantic setting in [24] differs slightly from the version of DDL presented in our paper (since we follow [21, 26]), in that it is actually closer to the Lindstrom-Rabinowicz setting: formulas are evaluated at *states* (called "points"), not at pairs of a state and an onion, and so the dynamics is given via binary relations between states (similarly to the standard *PDL* semantics), rather than via relations between onions. The resulting relational frame is called a revision space. However, in this setting (from [24]), each state is assigned an onion, via an "onion determiner", which paired with a revision space gives an "onion frame". Completeness (for an axiomatic system that includes the dynamic version of the Success Axiom) is claimed with respect to the class of "AGM onion frames" (i.e. onion frames satisfying some additional AGM-like semantic conditions). Introspection is *not* assumed by Segerberg in this setting, neither as a semantic condition nor as an axiomatic one. But it is easy to see that (Positive) Introspection is consistent with this setting: there exist AGM onion frames that are positively introspective. More precisely, the above counterexample (an introspective onion model in which neither p nor $\neg p$ are believed) can be easily repackaged as an AGM onion model in the sense of [24]. The dynamic version of the Success Axiom, when instantiated to the Moore sentence $p \wedge \neg Bp$, fails in this model. So this axiom is simply not sound.[2]

The lesson is that in DDL (as in DEL) we can really make sense of dynamic revision with doxastic sentences by an introspective agent *only* if we drop (the unrestricted, dynamic version of) the Success Postulate. A weakened version of this postulate can be retained either by (a) restricting it to (dynamic revision with) simple, Boolean, *non-doxastic* sentences (as in the AGM literature, as well as in many of Segerberg's papers), or by (b) interpreting it in terms of *static* revision (i.e. as a conditional-belief statement $B^{\phi}\phi$).

3 General DDL Semantics

We present here a generalized (and simplified) version of the "General Model Theory" for DDL introduced by Segerberg in Sect. 3 of [21]. The semantics is based on Segerberg's "hypertheories" (i.e. families of sets of states, called "fallbacks"), which are generalizations of Segerberg's "onions" (which are families of *nested* sets of states, called "spheres", in accordance to the Lewis-Grove tradition). As a formal language to describe these models, we use the slightly extended syntax for DDL introduced in [26], having (in addition to belief operators B and dynamic modalities) operators K for what Leitgeb and Segerberg call "nonrevisable belief" or "knowledge". We call this "irrevocable knowledge", to distinguish it from other,

2 While soundness of the given axiomatic system is not explicitly claimed in [24], its completeness is claimed. But from a conceptual point of view, a completeness result (with respect to a class of frames) is of course of no use if the axioms are not sound (with respect to that same class of frames).

"softer" notions of knowledge considered in the philosophical literature (e.g. defeasible knowledge). To ensure that the K operator is factive (as it is expected from "knowlewdge"), we make a slight change to the definition of validity, inspired from the Moss-Parikh semantics of Topo-logic: validity is obtained by quantifying only over pairs (s, H) of ontic states and hypertheories such that $s \in H$. We further simplify Segerberg's setting from [21], by dropping all the topological assumptions (Stone spaces, compactness assumptions), as well as all the closure assumptions on hypertheories (e.g. Lewis' famous Limit Assumption, or the assumption from [26] of closure under nonempty intersections). The price for this generality is that the definition of belief is more complicated: we adopt the definition of B introduced by van Benthem and Pacuit [8]. But we show that, whenever hypertheories do satisfy closure under intersection, this definition boils down to Segerberg's notion of belief (which is the same as Grove's definition: belief equals truth in all the states of the smallest sphere). Moreover, we show that in the special case of onions, this definition amounts to a natural generalization of Grove's definition (belief equals truth in all the states of all the spheres that are "small enough"), that was already proposed in the Belief Revision literature (and which validates the same modal formulas as Grove's standard definition). Finally, it is easy to see that, in case of onions satisfying Lewis' Limit assumption, this definition boils down again to the standard (Grove-Segerberg) notion of belief.

Let U be a set of states (a *universe*). A *hypertheory* in U is a nonempty family $H \subseteq \mathscr{P}(U)$ of nonempty subsets of U, called *fallbacks*. An *onion* (or "sphere system") in U is a hypertheory $O \subseteq \mathscr{P}(U)$, that is "nested", i.e. linearly ordered by set-inclusion: $X, Y \in O$ implies that either $X \subseteq Y$ or $Y \subseteq X$. The elements of an onion (its fallbacks) are sometimes called "spheres".

We think of each $s \in U$ as an "ontic state": a possible description of all the ontic (i.e. non-doxastic) facts of the world. We think of a hypertheory H as representing the agent's "doxastic state". In particular, as we will see in the next section, an onion O will represent a doxastic state that satisfies the AGM postulates (when these postulates are appropriately stated, as axioms about *static* revision).

An onion O is *standard* (or "well-founded") if there is no infinite descending chain of spheres in O; i.e. there is no infinite sequence $X_1 \supset X_2 \supset X_3 \supset \ldots$, with all $X_i \in O$.

Given a hypertheory $H \subseteq \mathscr{P}(U)$, a family $F \subseteq H$ of fallbacks has the **finite intersection property** (f.i.p.) if every *finite* subfamily $F' \subseteq F$ has a non-empty intersection $\bigcap F' \neq \emptyset$. We say that a family $F \subseteq H$ of fallbacks has the **maximal f.i.p.** if F has the f.i.p. but no proper extension $F \subset G \subseteq H$ does. Observe that, if O is an onion,such that $P \cap (\cup 0) \neq \emptyset$ then O has itself the maximal f.i.p.; and moreover O is the only family $F \subseteq O$ having the maximal f.i.p.

An *A-doxology* is a structure (U, D, R), where U is a universe, D is a set of hypertheories in U and $R = \{R^\alpha\}_\alpha$ is a set of binary relations $R^\alpha \subseteq D \times D$ on D, labeled with names $\alpha \in A$ coming from a given set A of *action terms*. The elements $R^\alpha \in R$ are called *doxastic actions*, and R itself a *repertoire*. Observe that each R^α is a binary relation between hypertheories (or onions), *not* between states.

Intuitively, each R^α describes a specific type of change which may affect the agent's epistemic/doxastic state (but which *does not change the "ontic state"*).

Assume now given any object language $\mathscr{L}$ containing *propositional letters* coming from a set Φ, Boolean connectives, a *belief* operator B, an *irrevocable knowledge* operator K, a set A of *action terms*, as well as and the dynamic modalities $[\alpha]$ ("after action α") of Propositional Dynamic Logic (one for each action term $\alpha \in A$). Any such language $\mathscr{L}$ is called *a DDL-language*. The *minimal language of ("full") DDL* has *only* the above operators. (But later we will add conditional belief operators, to describe static revision.)

A *DDL model* $M = (U, D, R, V)$ for any *DDL* language $\mathscr{L}$ (with propositional letters in Φ and action terms in A) consists of an A-doxology (U, D, R) together with a valuation V, mapping every propositional letter $p \in \Phi$ to a set $V(p) \subseteq U$ of states. An *onion model* is a *DDL* model (U, D, R, V) in which D consists only of onions. A *static (DDL) model* is a *DDL* model with $R = \emptyset$.

A *semantics* for $\mathscr{L}$ is a map that, for each *DDL* model $M = (U, D, R, V)$ and each hypertheory $H \in D$, assigns to each formula $\phi \in \mathscr{L}$ some set of states $\|\phi\|_{M,H} \subseteq \bigcup H$, and assigns to each action term $\alpha \in A$ some doxastic action $\|\alpha\|_{M,H} \in R$, in such a way that a number of conditions (to be given below) are satisfied. Our restriction to $\bigcup H$ is motivated by the intuition that the states $s \notin \bigcup H$ represent "impossible states": ontic states that are excluded by the doxastic state H. In other words, $\bigcup H$ encompasses the agent's "hard information" about the world. As a consequence, the operator K (given by quantifying over $\bigcup H$) is *factive* (unlike in the usual setting of DDL): we can think of K as representing the agent's "knowledge", in the absolute sense of infallible, absolutely certain, and absolutely unrevisable knowledge. We use the notation

$$s, H \models_M \phi$$

whenever we have $s \in \|\phi\|_{M,H}$, and we delete the subscript(s) whenever it is possible to do this without ambiguity, writing e.g. $\|\phi\|_H$ and $s, H \models \phi$ when M is fixed, or even $\|\phi\|$ when both M and H are fixed. (Note that $s, H \models \phi$ can only hold for $s \in H$.) A semantics for $\mathscr{L}$ is required to satisfy the following constraints:

$$\begin{array}{ll}
s, H \models p & \text{iff } s \in V(p) \\
s, H \models \neg\phi & \text{iff } s, H \not\models \phi \\
s, H \models \phi \wedge \psi & \text{iff } (s, H \models \phi) \wedge (s, H \models \psi) \\
s, H \models B\phi & \text{iff } \forall \text{ maximal f.i.p.} F \subseteq H\, \exists F' \text{ finite} \subseteq F\, \forall t \in \bigcap F'\, (t, H \models \phi) \\
s, H \models K\phi & \text{iff } \forall t \in \bigcup H\, (t, H \models \phi) \\
s, H \models [\alpha]\phi & \text{iff } \forall H' \in D\, \big((H, H') \in \|\alpha\|_H \wedge s \in \bigcup H' \implies s, H' \models \phi\big)
\end{array}$$

For a class $\mathscr{C}$ of (*DDL*) models, we write $\mathscr{C} \models \phi$ and we say that ϕ is *valid* on $\mathscr{C}$, if $\|\phi\|_{M,H} = U$ for every model $M = (U, D, R, V) \in \mathscr{C}$ and every $H \in D$; equivalently, iff $s, H \models_M \phi$ holds for all models $M = (U, D, R, V) \in \mathscr{C}$, all hypertheories $H \in D$ and all states $s \in \bigcup H$.

An onion model (U, D, R, V) is *standard* if all the onions $O \in D$ are standard. A weakening of the standardness condition, which has the disadvantage of being language-dependent is the so-called Lewis Limit Assumption: an onion model (U, D, R, V), together with a semantics $\| \bullet \|$ is said to *satisfy the Limit Assumption* if, for every formula $\phi \in \mathscr{L}$ and every onion $O \in D$, we have that: $\|\phi\| \cap \bigcup O \neq \emptyset$ implies $\bigcap\{X \in O : \|\phi\| \cap X \neq \emptyset\} \in O$.

It is easy to see that *standard onion models always satisfy the Limit Assumption* (for *every* language $\mathscr{L}$); but the converse is false. In fact, standard onion models satisfy a stronger condition, that we call the Strong Limit Assumption: for every *set* $P \subseteq U$ of states and every onion $O \in D$, $P \cap \bigcup O \neq \emptyset$ implies $\bigcap\{X \in O : P \cap X \neq \emptyset\} \in O$. This means that, in a standard model, every onion intersecting a given set P contains a unique smallest sphere intersecting P.

Any fallback H in a DDL model induces a corresponding relation of plaubility between states. We say that *state s is at least as plausible as state t according to H*, and we write $s \leq_H t$, if s belongs to all the fallbacks in H that contain t:

$$s \leq_H t \text{ iff } \forall X \in H (t \in X \Rightarrow s \in X).$$

Obviously, the plausibility relation $\leq_H$ is a *preorder* (reflexive and transitive relation) on the set $\bigcup H$. Moreover, if O is an onion, then $\leq_O$ is a *total* (i.e. connected) preorder on $\bigcup O$: for all $s, t \in \bigcup O$, we have either $s \leq_O t$ or $t \leq_O s$ (or both).

Our definition of irrevocable knowledge K is essentially the same as in [26], except that our modified definition of validity entails the *factivity* of K, making it to behave indeed like a notion of "knowledge" (in contrast to [26]). Our definition of belief B is a generalization of the Grove-Segerberg definition, due to van Benthem and Pacuit [8]. But it can be simplified in onion models (where it boils down to a widely used generalization of Grove's), and it can be simplified further when we have either the Limit Condition or closure under intersection (where it boils down to the Grove-Segerberg definition):

Proposition In DDL models in which the set D of hypertheories is closed under non-empty intersections, *ϕ is believed iff it is true in all the "most plausible states"* (i.e. the states of the smallest fallback):

$$s, H \models B\phi \text{ iff } \forall t \in \bigcap H \, (t, O \models \phi).$$

In *onion models*, ϕ is believed iff ϕ is true in all the states that are "plausible enough" (i.e. throughout all the spheres that are "small enough"):

$$s, O \models B\phi \text{ iff } \exists X \in O \forall t \in X \, (t, O \models \phi).$$

Moreover, in *onion models satisfying the Limit Condition*, this boils down to the usual Grove definition:

$$s, O \models B\phi \text{ iff } \forall t \in \bigcap O \, (t, O \models \phi).$$

(And, as a consequence, this equivalence holds in standard onion models.)

4 DDL as a Generalization of Topo-logic

The language of Topo-logic, proposed by Moss and Parikh [15, 17], is a modal logic with two modalities: K (for "knowledge"), and $\Box$ (for "effort"). The box modality stands for *stability under information increase:* the sentence $\Box\varphi$ means that φ (is true and) *stays true no matter what the agent increases her information with*. Using its De Morgan dual $\Diamond$, one can define "learnability" as $\Diamond K\varphi$ (i.e. φ *might come to be known* after learning some further information). Topo-logic frames $(U, \mathcal{T}, V)$ consists of a universe (set of points, or "states") U, a family $\mathcal{T} \subseteq \mathcal{P}(U)$ of sets of states (called "opens")[3] and a valuation V for the atomic sentences of the above language. While the points $s \in U$ represent possible ontic states, the opens $V \in \mathcal{T}$ represent possible *information states*: when the agent's information state is V, this means that the only thing that she knows about the state of the world is that it belongs to V. Sentences are evaluated at pairs (s, V) of an ontic state $s \in U$ and and information state $V \in \mathcal{T}$, with the restriction that $s \in V$ (so that "knowledge" is factual: indeed, these are information states, rather than doxastic states!). The semantics is given by putting

$$s, V \models K\phi \quad \text{iff} \quad t, V \models \phi \text{ for every } t \in V,$$
$$s, V \models \Box\phi \quad \text{iff} \quad t, V' \models \phi \text{ for every } V' \in \mathcal{T} \text{ such that } V' \subseteq V.$$

If we think of $V, V' \in \mathcal{T}$ as possible information states, then $V' \subseteq V$ means that V' is a *refinement* of V: it contains at least as much information (about the real state $s \in V'$) as V does. So we can think of the move from V to $V' \subseteq V$ as an increase of information: a form of (correct, accurate, infallible) "learning".

It is easy to see that Topo-logic is a special case of Generalized *DDL*: we can reinterpret a *topo-logic model* as a special kind of onion model $M = (U, D, R)$ in which all the onions are singletons ($D = \{\{V\} : V \in \mathcal{T}\}$), each consisting of only one fallback $V \in \mathcal{T}$, and in which the repertoire is a singeton $R = \{R_\Box\}$, where the relation $R_\Box$ is given by:

$$\{V\}R_\Box\{V'\} \text{ iff } V \supseteq V' \qquad (\text{for all } V, V' \in \mathcal{T}).$$

We can similarly reinterpret the *language* of topo-logic as simply the minimal *DDL* language for the above kind of (topo-logic) DDL models. *The distinction between the belief and knowledge operators B and K vanishes* in this case (so that we can follow Moss and Parikh and denote them both by the same letter K), and the (only) dynamic modality is denoted by $\Box$.

---

[3] Although the family $\mathcal{T}$ of all opens is not in general required to be a topology in the mathematical sense, Moss and Parikh do consider and axiomatize various possible closure conditions on $\mathcal{T}$, including the ones defining a topology.

5 Complete Axiomatization of Static Revision: The Logic CDL

To capture static revision, we follow the DEL tradition, by borrowing from conditional logic a *conditional belief operator* $B^{\phi}\psi$. Our semantic clauses can be naturally extended to this enlarged language.

But first, following Segerberg [21], we introduce the notation

$$H \Cap P \;:=\; \{X \in H : X \cap P \neq \emptyset\}$$

for all hypertheories $H \in D$ and sets $P \subseteq U$ of states, and moreover we generalize to any families $F \subseteq H$ of fallbacks (of a hypertheory H):

$$F \Cap P \;:=\; \{X \in F : X \cap P \neq \emptyset\}.$$

The *relativization of a family $F \subseteq H$ of fallbacks (of a hypertheory H) to a set $P \subseteq U$* of states is the family

$$F^{P} \;:=\; \{X \cap P : X \in F \Cap P\} = \{P \cap X : X \in F, P \cap X \neq \emptyset\}.$$

Of course, this operation can be applied in particular to an hypertheory H or onion O, producing a *relativized hypertheory* H^P or *relativized onion* O^P. A family $F \subseteq H$ of fallbacks has the **finite intersection property relative to** P (P-f.i.p.) if every *finite* subfamily (of its relativization to P) $F' \subseteq F^P$ has non-empty intersection $\bigcap F' \neq \emptyset$. We say that a family $F \subseteq H$ of fallbacks has the **maximal** P**-f.i.p.** if F has the P-f.i.p. but no proper extension $F \subset G \subseteq H$ has the P-f.i.p. Observe that, if O is an *onion* such that $P \cap (\cup O) \neq \emptyset$, then O has itself the maximal P-f.i.p.; and moreover O is the only family $F \subseteq O$ having the maximal P-f.i.p.

When $P = \|\phi\|_H$ for some formula ϕ, we write "maximal ϕ-f.i.p." for "maximal $\|\phi\|_H$-f.i.p." and so on. Now we define conditional belief by putting:

$$s, H \models B^{\theta}\phi \text{ iff } \forall \text{ maximal } \theta - \text{f.i.p.} F \subseteq H\, \exists F' \text{ finite } \subseteq F^{\|\theta\|_H}\, \forall t \in \bigcap F'\, (t, H \models \phi)$$

Proposition In *onion models*, ϕ is believed conditional on θ iff ϕ is true in all the most plausible states satisfying θ:

$$s, O \models B^{\theta}\phi \text{ iff } \exists X \in O^{\|\theta\|_O}\, \forall t \in X\, (t, O \models \phi).$$

Moreover, in *onion models satisfying the Limit Condition*, this boils down to the usual Grove semantics for static revision:

$$s, O \models B^{\theta}\phi \,\text{iff}\, \forall t \in \bigcap O^{\|\theta\|_O}\, (t, O \models \phi).$$

The language of *conditional doxastic logic* CDL is the smallest set of formulas containing the atomic sentences $p \in \Phi$, the tautological formula $\top$ and is closed under conditional belief operators $B^{\theta}\phi$. It can be considered as a variant of the DDL language, in which we take $R = \emptyset$ (so there are no dynamic modalities), while B and K are defined as abbreviations: indeed, by putting

$$B\phi := B^{\top}\phi,$$
$$K\phi =: B^{\neg\phi}\bot$$

(where $\bot := \neg\top$), we can easily see that these abbreviations are semantically equivalent to the belief and knowledge operators, as defined in the previous section.

Theorem The following proof system *CDL* for conditional doxastic logic is sound and complete w.r.t. the class of *all onion models*, the class of *standard onion models*, and the class of *finite onion models*:

Necessitation Rule:	From $\vdash \varphi$ infer $\vdash B^{\psi}\varphi$
Normality:	$\vdash B^{\theta}(\varphi \to \psi) \to (B^{\theta}\varphi \to B^{\theta}\psi)$
Truthfulness of Knowledge:	$\vdash K\varphi \to \varphi$
Persistence of Knowledge:	$\vdash K\varphi \to B^{\psi}\varphi$
Full Introspection:	$\vdash B^{\psi}\varphi \to KB^{\psi}\varphi$
	$\vdash \neg B^{\psi}\varphi \to K\neg B^{\psi}\varphi$
Hypotheses are (hypothetically) accepted:	$\vdash B^{\varphi}\varphi$
Superexpansion:	
Subexpansion (=Rational Monotonicity)	$\vdash B^{\varphi\wedge\psi}\theta \to B^{\varphi}(\psi \to \theta)$
	$\vdash \neg(B^{\varphi}\neg\psi \wedge B^{\varphi}(\psi \to \theta)) \to B^{\varphi\wedge\psi}\theta$

(where in all the above axioms, K is just the abbreviation $K\varphi := B^{\neg\varphi}\bot$).

As a consequence, it is easy to see that *onion models satisfy all the AGM postulates for "static" belief revision*, except for the Vacuity Postulate ($T * \varphi = \bot$ iff $\vdash \neg\varphi$), which is valid only modulo a natural epistemic restriction: $T * \varphi = \bot$ iff $T \vdash K\neg\varphi$. This restriction is unavoidable in the presence of any "unrevisable belief" operator K: it seems to us to be the natural *epistemic* version of the Vacuity principle. Hence, the resulting theory was called "epistemic AGM" in [3].

Corollary If we take the initial AGM theory T to be the set $T = \{\psi : s, O \models_M B\psi\}$ of all beliefs held in (a given ontic state s and a given onion O of) an onion model M, and interpret the statically-revised theory $T * \phi$ as the set $T * \phi = \{\psi : s, O \models B^{\phi}\psi\}$ of all conditional beliefs held (conditional on ϕ) in (the same state s and same onion O of the same model) M, then all the postulates of the "epistemic AGM" theory are satisfied.

In contrast, static revision in general DDL models does *not* satisfy the (epistemic) AGM postulates (since the Subexpansion principle fails in general DDL models). In conclusion, general DDL does *not* support an AGM-type theory of belief revision; but *onion models are the natural AGM-friendly version of DDL.*

6 Dynamic Revision in DDL: Internalizing Doxastic Upgrades

It is sometimes said that the main difference between Dynamic Epistemic Logic and the traditional Epistemic Temporal Logic approach to information change is that *DEL* is *constructive*, while *ETL* is purely *descriptive*: in *DEL*, one actually defines in a constructive way the new doxastic/epistemic relation after a given doxastic action. But this constructive approach can be internalized in *DDL* models, and in fact [21] anticipated this! As we will see in the next section, in that paper Segerberg used a *constructive* DDL approach to expansion and contraction.

In this section we will use such a constructive DDL approach to belief *revision*. We give constructive definitions of binary relations between onions, that internalize three different revision operations considered in the literature. We adopt from DEL the method of using Reduction/Recursion laws to give complete axiomatizations of the dynamic logics of these three kinds of revision. Indeed, our laws are identical to the ones considered in the DEL literature: in effect, this section is a concrete example of how the DEL-style of modeling and axiomatizing belief revision can be "internalized" in DDL.

One can think of many ways to change the beliefs of an agent according to the information she receives. She can receive *hard information* (unrevisable and irrevocable, since received from an infallible source), or she can receive *soft information* (fallible and potentially revisable).

Receiving "hard" information φ corresponds to what in the DEL literature [2, 7, 9] is called an *update*[4] $!\varphi$, and in Belief Revision literature is known as a "radical revision" (or irrevocable revision), with φ. This operation changes the model by eliminating all the $\neg\varphi$-worlds. The result of this elimination is a submodel only consisting of φ-worlds.

A second, softer kind of revision is given by the DEL operation of *lexicographic upgrade* $\Uparrow \varphi$ [6, 5], known in Belief Revision literature as "moderate revision" (or lexicographic revision). It changes the model by making all φ-worlds become more plausible than all $\neg\varphi$-worlds:

Finally, the DEL operation of *conservative upgrade* $\uparrow \varphi$ [6, 5] is known as "conservative revision" (or natural revision) in the Belief Revision literature. It changes the model by making the most plausible φ-worlds become the most plausible overall (while leaving everything else unchanged) (Figs. 4, 5 and 6).

Dynamic Epistemic Logic *DEL* (in its single-agent version) for the above-mentioned three types of upgrades can now be obtained as a *special case* of Generalized *DDL*. For this, we reuse the "relativized onion" notation

$$O^P := \{P \cap X : X \in O, P \cap X \neq \emptyset\}$$

introduced in Sect. 5, to define binary relations $R^{!P}$ (for update), $R^{\Uparrow P}$ (for lexicographic upgrade) and $R^{\uparrow P}$ (for conservative upgrade) between onions $O \in D$ (of

[4] Unfortunately, this terminology diverges from the one in Belief Revision literature, where "update" refers to a completely different type of operation, namely to the Katsuno-Mendelson revision.

some onion model (U, D, R)) and sets of sets of states $O' \subseteq \mathscr{P}(U)$, as follows:

$$(O, O') \in R^{!P} \text{ iff } O' = O^P \neq \emptyset$$
$$(O, O') \in R^{\Uparrow P} \text{ iff } O' = O^P \cup \left\{X \cup \bigcup O^P : X \in O\right\}$$
$$(O, O') \in R^{\uparrow P} \text{ iff } O' = \left\{\bigcap O^P : \bigcap O^P \neq \emptyset\right\} \cup \left\{X \cup \bigcap O^P : X \in O\right\}$$

To visualize these doxastic actions, see Figs. 1, 2 and 3 in the Appendix.

Next, we define a *DEL onion model* to be a standard onion model $M = (U, D, R)$ such that

$$R = \{R^{!P} : P \subseteq U\} \cup \{R^{\Uparrow P} : P \subseteq U\} \cup \{R^{\uparrow P} : P \subseteq U\}$$

and such that *D is closed under all the relations in R*.

The *language* of (this version of) *DEL* is obtained by adding to *CDL* dynamic modalities for all the above types of upgrades. The *semantics* is obtained by defining the interpretation maps $\|\varphi\|$ and $\|\alpha\|$ by double recursion: the static propositional clauses are as in *CDL*, the semantics of dynamic modalities is as in the generalized *DDL*, while the clauses for $\|\alpha\|$ are given by

$$\|!\varphi\| = R^{!\|\varphi\|}$$
$$\| \Uparrow \varphi\| = R^{\Uparrow \|\varphi\|}$$
$$\| \uparrow \varphi\| = R^{\uparrow \|\varphi\|}$$

Theorem A sound and complete proof system for *DEL* onion models can be obtained by adding to the above proof system of *CDL* the van Benthem Reduction/Recursion laws [6]. We give here only the reduction laws for conditional belief:

$$[!\varphi]B^{\psi} \iff \varphi \Rightarrow B^{\varphi \wedge [!\varphi]\psi}[!\varphi]\theta,$$
$$[\Uparrow\varphi]B^{\psi}\theta \iff B^{\varphi \wedge [\Uparrow\varphi]\psi}[\Uparrow\varphi]\theta \wedge \left(K^{\varphi}[\Uparrow\varphi]\neg\psi \Rightarrow B^{[\Uparrow\varphi]\psi}[\Uparrow \varphi]\theta\right),$$
$$[\uparrow\varphi]B^{\psi}\theta \iff B^{\varphi}([\uparrow\varphi]\psi \Rightarrow [\uparrow \varphi]\theta) \wedge \left(B^{\varphi}[\uparrow \varphi]\neg\psi \Rightarrow B^{[\uparrow\varphi]\psi}[\uparrow \varphi]\theta\right),$$

where we used the abbreviation $K^{\varphi}\psi := K(\varphi \Rightarrow \psi)$.

Strongest Postcondition Modalities The standard dynamic modalities $[\alpha]\varphi$ are known in Computer Science as *weakest preconditions*: indeed, they capture the weakest condition that can be imposed on an input information state (s, H) to ensure that, after performing action α in that state, φ will become true in the output-state. The dual modalities (in the sense of Galois duality, rather than De Morgan duality) are the *strongest postcondition* modalities $\langle\alpha^{-1}\rangle\varphi$, capturing the weakest condition that is ensured to hold in an output-state after performing action α on an input state satisfying φ.

While standard *DEL* cannot represent strongest postconditions,[5] *DDL* models contain enough information to define them, as *existential (Diamond) modalities for the converse relations* R_α^{-1}: equivalently, just put

$$s, H \models \langle \alpha^{-1} \rangle \varphi \text{ iff } \exists H' \left((H', H) \in \|\alpha\|_H \wedge s, H' \models \varphi \right)$$

It is obvious that these operators are indeed the Galois duals of the standard dynamic modalities, and that the same holds for their corresponding de Morgan duals: i.e. we have the validities

$$\varphi \Rightarrow [\alpha]\langle \alpha^{-1} \rangle \varphi,$$
$$\varphi \Rightarrow [\alpha^{-1}]\langle \alpha \rangle \varphi.$$

Finally, using the strongest postcondition modality for lexicographic upgrade, we can check the semantic equivalence:

$$B^{\varphi}\psi \iff [\Uparrow \varphi] B \langle (\Uparrow \varphi)^{-1} \rangle \psi.$$

This equivalence confirms our interpretation of conditional beliefs $B^{\varphi}\psi$ as embodiments of "static revision": the agent's *revised beliefs* (after revision with φ) about ψ's truth value *before* the revision.

7 Expansion and Contraction in Full DDL

In [21], Krister Segerberg used a constructive approach (similar to the one we used above for revision) for modeling expansion and contraction in DDL. Assuming some additional conditions on the hypertheories (namely that they are closed under non-empty intersections and satisfy the Strong Limit Assumption,[6] Segerberg puts, for hypertheories H and sets $P \subseteq U, X \in H$:

$$H/P := H \cup \{X \cap P : X \in H, X \cap P \neq \emptyset\},$$
$$H|P := \{Y \in H : X \subseteq Y\},$$

and requires the doxology D to be closed under these operations. Using these notations, Segerberg says that a fallback $Z \in H$ is *a contraction with* $P \subseteq U$ *in* H iff Z is a minimal fallback (with respect to inclusion) in the family $H \Cap (U - P)$ (where recall that $H \Cap (U - P) := \{X \in H : X \cap (U - P) \neq \emptyset\}$). Note that such a contraction

[5] But extensions of *DEL* which can define strongest postconditions have been proposed by G. Aucher and H. van Ditmarsch.

[6] Segerberg calls *LR hypertheories* (from Lindstrom and Rabinowicz) the hypertheories that satisfy these two conditions.

with P in H might not exist,[7] and even if it exists it might not be unique! Segerberg then explicitly defines an *expansion action* $+P$ and a *contraction action* $-P$ (for any given set $P \subseteq U$ of states), given by the following relation on hypertheories in D:

$$(H, H') \in R^{+P} \text{ iff } H' = H/P,$$
$$(H, H') \in R^{-P} \text{ iff } H' = H|Z \text{ for } \textit{some} \text{ contraction } Z \text{ with } P \text{ in } H.$$

Now, these two operations, as defined by Segerberg, do not fit the *AGM* framework. This was a conscious decision by Segerberg, since his aim in [21] was to give a semantics to the Lindstrom-Rabinowicz theory of contraction (in which contraction is *not* unique), rather than the *AGM* theory. In order to try to accommodate AGM, first we have of course to restrict the above definitions to *onion models*: as we saw, these are the AGM-friendly models for DDL. On onion models, contractions with P (as defined above) might still not exist; but, if they do, then they are unique (as required by AGM). To ensure existence, we have to further restrict to *onion models satisfying the Limit condition*; or (for simplicity) to the even more restricted case of *standard onion models*. As we'll see, this restriction does ensure that Segerberg's contraction satisfies the AGM principles. But, even in this case, we still have problems with Segerberg's definition of *expansion*: this operation does not preserve the "nestedness" property, so it does not map (standard) onions into onions! Moreover, there is no reasonable additional condition that would ensure that the expansion (in the sense of Segerberg) of an onion O with a set P is an onion whenever $P \cap \bigcup O \neq \emptyset$. Since "onionhood" (i.e. nestedness of the hypertheories) is essential for satisfying *AGM* postulates, this means that one should look for a different definition for *AGM* expansion.

AGM-type Expansion Operations on Standard Onion Models

In fact, any of the known semantic proposals for expansion (as an operation on Grove sphere models) considered in the Belief Revision literature can be internalized in *DDL*. In particular, *for each of the three types of revision defined above there is a corresponding expansion action* on standard onion models:

$$(O, O') \in R^{+!P} \text{ iff } (O, O') \in R^{!P} \text{ and } X \cap P \neq \emptyset \text{ for all } X \in O,$$
$$(O, O') \in R^{+\Uparrow P} \text{ iff } (O, O') \in R^{\Uparrow P} \text{ and } X \cap P \neq \emptyset \text{ for all } X \in O,$$
$$(O, O') \in R^{+\uparrow P} \text{ iff } (O, O') \in R^{\uparrow P} \text{ and } X \cap P \neq \emptyset \text{ for all } X \in O.$$

See the Appendix (Figs. 4, 5 and 6) for visualizations of these operations. Since expansion is a special case of revision (namely the case in which the new information does not contradict any prior beliefs), the corresponding expansion modalities can be reduced to the revision ones, e.g.

$$[+!\varphi]\theta \iff (\neg B\neg\varphi \Rightarrow [!\varphi]\theta)\,.$$

---

[7] Though the additional closure assumptions made by Segerberg in [21] do ensure the existence of contractions.

Segerberg Contraction on Standard Onion Models: "Severe Withdrawal"
It is easy to see that, on standard onion models, contractions with P exist and are unique whenever P is not irrevocably known (i.e. whenever $(\bigcup O) \cap (U - P) \neq \emptyset$). Moreover, on standard onion models, Segerberg's definition is equivalent to putting:

$$(O, O') \in R^{-P} \text{ iff } O' = O \Cap (U - P) := \{X \in O : X \cap (U - P) \neq \emptyset\}.$$

This semantic contraction operation was called "mild contraction" by Levi [12], "severe withdrawal" by Pagnuco and Rott [16] and "Rott contraction" by Ferme and Rodriguez [10]. See the Appendix (Fig. 7) for a picture of severe withdrawal.

Static Withdrawal To axiomatize the dynamic logic of contraction, we need to introduce a *"static" contraction modality* $B^{-P}Q$ that pre-encodes Segerberg's dynamic contraction in the same way in which conditional belief $B^P Q$ pre-encodes dynamic revision. We call this operator "withdrawn belief" and we read $B^{-P}Q$ as saying that *Q is believed conditionally on the withdrawal of P*. We do this by putting:

$$s, O \models B^{-\theta}\phi \text{ iff } \forall \text{maximal} \neg\theta\text{–f.i.p.} F \subseteq O \, \exists F' \text{ finite } \subseteq F \Cap \|\neg\theta\|_O \, \forall t \in \bigcap F' \, (t, O \models \phi)$$

Proposition In onion models, *withdrawn belief (after withdrawing P) is the same as truth in all the states of some sphere not included in P*:

$$s, O \models B^{-\theta}\phi \text{ iff } \exists X \in O \, (X \not\subseteq \|\theta\|_O \text{ and } \forall t \in X \, (t, O \models \phi)) .$$

Moreover, in onion models satisfying the Limit Condition (and in particular, in *standard* onion models), *withdrawn belief (after withdrawing P) is the same as truth in all the states of the smallest sphere not included in P*:

$$s, O \models B^{-\theta}\phi \text{ iff } \forall t \in \bigcap (O \Cap \|\neg\theta\|_O) \, (t, O \models \phi).$$

Observation (*"Static" Levi Identity*) It is easy to see that standard conditional belief can in fact be defined in terms of the withdrawn belief operator, via the following semantic equivalence:

$$B^{\theta}\varphi \iff B^{-\neg\theta}(\theta \Rightarrow \varphi).$$

The converse is false: *one cannot define withdrawn belief only in terms of conditional belief.*

Open Question Finding a complete axiomatization for (static) withdrawn belief is still an open problem.

Reducing Segerberg's Dynamic Contraction to Static Withdrawal However, if given such a complete axiomatization for static withdrawal, then we could immediately obtain a complete axiomatization for Segerberg's dynamic contraction logic, by adding a number of Recursion laws, the most important being:

$$[-\varphi]B^{-\psi}\theta \iff K\varphi \vee B^{\varphi\vee[-\varphi]\psi}[-\varphi]\psi$$

However, many authors consider severe withdrawal to be a bad candidate for modeling contraction. In addition to *not* satisfying the Recovery principle, it *does* satisfy a highly implausible property, called *Expulsiveness*: for ontic facts p, q, we have that $\neg Bp \wedge \neg Bq$ implies $[-p]Bq \vee [-q]Bp$. This property does not allow unrelated beliefs to be undisturbed by each other's contraction!

To this objection, we can add another one, based on dynamic logic. Namely, although severe withdrawal satisfies a dynamic version of the so-called *Levi identity* with respect to irrevocable revision (DEL update)

$$R^{-\neg P}; R^{+!P} = R^{!P}$$

(where $R; R'$ is relational composition and $P \subseteq U$ is an arbitrary set of states), the corresponding Levi identies for lexicographic revision or minimal revision are *not* satisfied:

$$R^{-\neg P}; R^{+\Uparrow P} \neq R^{\Uparrow P},$$
$$R^{-\neg P}; R^{+\uparrow P} \neq R^{\uparrow P}.$$

Since update (irrevocable revision) is a rather implausible operation when dealing to belief change in daily life, this throws more doubt on the appropriateness of Segerberg's definition of contraction.

Other AGM-type Contractions

But severe withdrawal is not the only AGM-friendly semantic contraction operation in the literature. Other options include *conservative contraction* $-_c P$ and *moderate contraction* $-_m P$ (see the pictures). We give below the formal definition over onion models in DDL (but see the pictures for a better intuitive explanation): if we put $O_{-P} := \bigcap O^{U-P}$ (for the smallest non-empty intersection of an O-sphere with $U - P$) whenever $O^{U-P} \neq \emptyset$ (i.e. whenever $\bigcup O \not\subseteq P$), and $O_{-P} := \emptyset$ otherwise, then for any two standard onions $O, O' \in D$ we define

$$(O, O') \in R^{-_c P} \text{ iff } O' = \{X \cup O_{-P} : X \in O\},$$
$$(O, O') \in R^{-_m P} \text{ iff } O' = \{Y \cup \bigcap O : Y \in O^{U-P}\} \cup \{X \cup \bigcup O^{U-P} : X \in O\}.$$

See the Appendix for visualizations of these operations (Figs. 8 and 9). They are much better behaved than severe withdrawal. They satisfy the Recovery postulate, and moreover *they satisfy the dynamic versions of Levi identity for all the above-mentioned revision operators*: e.g. for all sets $P \subseteq U$ of states, we have

$$R^{-_c\neg P}; R^{+!P} = R^{!P}, \qquad R^{-_m\neg P}; R^{+!P} = R^{!P},$$
$$R^{-_c\neg P}; R^{+\Uparrow P} = R^{\Uparrow P}, \qquad R^{-_m\neg P}; R^{+\Uparrow P} = R^{\Uparrow P},$$
$$R^{-_c\neg P}; R^{+\uparrow P} = R^{\uparrow P}, \qquad R^{-_m\neg P}; R^{+\uparrow P} = R^{\uparrow P}.$$

Even better, there is no need to introduce the "static" counterparts of these operators as new primitive operators: *their static versions are definable in terms of conditional beliefs*. This means that the logic of conditional beliefs, conservative contraction and moderate contraction can be directly axiomatized, in a similar way that the logic of (various types of) dynamic revision was axiomatized:

Theorem There exists a sound and complete proof system for conservative contraction and moderate contraction over the class of DDL onion models that are closed under these operations. The system consists of the axioms of conditional doxastic logic *CDL*, together with the following Recursion laws:

$$[-_c\varphi]p \iff p, \qquad [-_m\varphi]p \iff p,$$
$$[-_c\varphi]\neg\theta \iff \neg[-_c\varphi]\theta, \qquad [-_m\varphi]\neg\theta \iff \neg[-_m\varphi]\theta,$$
$$[-_c\varphi](\theta \wedge \psi) \iff [-_c\varphi]\theta \wedge [-_c\varphi]\psi, \qquad [-_m\varphi](\theta \wedge \psi) \iff [-_m\varphi]\theta \wedge [-_m\varphi]\psi,$$
$$[-_c\varphi]B^{\psi}\theta \iff B([-_c\varphi]\psi \Rightarrow [-_c\varphi]\theta) \wedge B^{\neg\varphi}([-_c\varphi]\psi \Rightarrow [-_c\varphi]\theta) \wedge \left(B^{\neg\varphi}[-_c\varphi]\neg\psi \Rightarrow B^{[-_c\varphi]\psi}[-_c\varphi]\theta\right),$$
$$[-_m\varphi]B^{\psi}\theta \iff B([-_m\varphi]\psi \Rightarrow [-_m\varphi]\theta) \wedge B^{\neg\varphi\wedge[-_m\varphi]\psi}[-_m\varphi]\theta \wedge \left(K^{\neg\varphi}[-_m\varphi]\neg\psi \Rightarrow B^{\varphi\wedge[-_m\varphi]\psi}[-_m\varphi]\theta\right)$$

8 Evidential Dynamics in DDL

In the Chapter [8], van Benthem and Pacuit develop a very interesting extension of DEL aimed to deal with evidential dynamics. Their evidence models are based on the well-known neighbourhood semantics for modal logic, in which the neighbourhoods are interpreted as "evidence sets": pieces of evidence (possibly false, possibly mutually inconsistent) possesed by the agent. In this section we briefly sketch how their setting can be internalized in DDL.

Belief modality, revisited (in general DDL models) We revert here to general DDL models, based on hypertheories H whose fallbacks are not necessarily nested. But now the fallbacks $X \in H$ is interpreted as "evidence sets", and each hypertheory H is interpreted as a possible "evidential state" (rather than just a doxastic state): one in which the agent possesses a piece of evidence X iff $X \in H$. Our general definition of belief operators B (and their conditional-belief generalizations) in terms of maximal f.i.p. families is in fact taken from [8]. But now this definition has a clearer justification: when confronted with mutually inconsistent pieces of evidence, a rational agent believes the sentences that are implied by *all* the maximally consistent bodies of available evidence. So belief $B\varphi$ is defined as "truth in all the states that are contained in any maximally consistent family of evidence sets".

Evidence Modality In addition, van Benthem and Pacuit introduce a $\Box$ operator, such that $\Box\varphi$ means that *the agent has evidence for* φ. We adopt this notion in general DDL models, except that we denote it by $\boxminus$ (to distinguish from the "effort" modality $\Box$ from Topo-logic):

$$s, H \models \boxminus\varphi \text{ iff } \exists X \in H \forall t \in X\, (t, H \models \varphi).$$

Note that, by a previous Proposition, $\boxminus\varphi$ and $B\varphi$ are equivalent in onion models. This is natural: onion models represent situations in which all the available pieces of evidence are mutually consistent; hence, in an onion model belief in φ is the same as "having evidence for φ", while in general these two notions are distinct.

Conditional Evidence Again, we can follow van Benthem and Pacuit and generalize $\boxminus$ to a conditional evidence modality $\boxminus^{\theta}\varphi$, expressing the fact that *the agent has some evidence for* ϕ *that is compatible with* θ:

$$s, H \models \boxminus^{\theta}\varphi \text{ iff } \exists X \in H^{\|\theta\|_H} \forall t \in X\, (t, H \models \varphi).$$

Evidence Management Actions Further, Van Benthem and Pacuit proceed to formalize a number of "evidence management" actions: they denote *evidence addition* by $+\varphi$, *evidence removal* by $-\varphi$, *evidence upgrade* by $\Uparrow\varphi$ and *evidence combination* by #. We briefly sketch here how can these be defined in DDL models. To distinguish the first three of these evidential operations from the doxastic operations that we previously considered, we add a subscript *e* (from "evidence").

$$(H, H') \in R^{+_e P} \text{ iff } H' = H \cup \{P\},$$
$$(H, H') \in R^{-_e P} \text{ iff } H' = H - \{X \in H : X \subseteq P\},$$
$$(H, H') \in R^{\Uparrow_e P} \text{ iff } H' = \{X \cup P : X \in H\} \cup \{P\},$$
$$(H, H') \in R^{\#} \text{ iff } H' \text{ is the closure of } H \text{ under non-empty intersections.}$$

An *evidential DDL model* is one whose doxology is closed under these relations. As before, we introduce universal modalities $[+_e\varphi]$, $[-_e\varphi]$, $[\Uparrow_e \varphi]$, $[\#]$ for the binary relations $R^{+_e\|\varphi\|}$ etc. Essentially, evidence addition $+_e\varphi$ is the action by which φ *comes to be accepted as an addmissible piece of evidence*; evidence removal $-_e\varphi$ is the action by which *all evidence entailing* φ *is removed*; evidence upgrade $\Uparrow_e \varphi$ *incorporates* φ *into each piece of available evidence* (thus making φ the most important piece of evidence); finally, evidence combination # is the action by which the agent *combines all the mutually consistent pieces of evidence.*

Proposition All the Recursion laws for evidence management actions presented in [8] are valid on evidential DDL models.

9 Conclusions: Comparing DDL, DEL and PDL/ETL

Three Styles of Doing Static Belief Revision As already mentioned, in the literature we encounter three styles of modelling "static" belief revision: Stalnker's *selection functions*, *plausibility relations*, and the Grove-Lewis *sphere models*. When considered at an appropriate level of generality, these settings are equivalent. In this paper, we followed Segerberg in considering only sphere models. At a syntactic level, we followed the DEL approach (inspired from the Conditional Logic tradition) of using conditional belief operators to express static revision.

Three Styles of Doing Doxastic Dynamics As also mentioned, we are aware of three different styles of modeling doxastic changes. The first is the DEL approach, in which the dynamics is *external* to the models: doxastic actions are seen as model-changing actions, and represented as relations *between models*. The second style is the (doxastic version of the) old PDL (Propositional Dynamic Logic) approach: the dynamics is internalized simply by adding enough states to the model to represent the results of all the possible doxastic actions, which are thus represented *internally*, as binary relations *between states*. A variant is the ETL style (of Epistemic Temporal Logic), obtained by unravelling PDL models into trees, and by lumping together all the dynamic relations into one single temporal relation (going from a state to the possible next states). Finally, the third style is given by Segerberg's DDL: this approach keeps the actual states unchanges (as "*ontic* states") and internalizes the dynamics by representing doxastic actions as binary relations *between doxastic structures* ("onions", "hypertheories", "*doxastic* states") living in a fixed space of possible such structures (the "doxology").

Again, if considered at an appropriate level of generality, these three approaches are equivalent. However, there are some conceptual (and practical) differences. The DEL approach is the most "open-ended", well-suited for open systems, in which there are innumerable doxastic actions that might happen. It is also the most "economical", as only the states and the doxastic structures that are currently epistemically possible are "given": only they are represented in a given model; hence, the DEL models can be easily visualized and drawn. It is also a "constructive" approach: the doxastic dynamics is *not given* in this approach, but is to be *constructed* (in the form of various model transformers, or "upgrades").

The PDL/ETL approach has the advantage that it internalizes all the possible dynamics, in a clear way, using an almost flat structure (with only two levels: states, and relations between them). But the price, especially in the ETL version, is that the models are typically huge and quickly risk becoming unamanagable. This is the most un-economical of the three dynamic styles: we cannot actually draw PDL/ETL models for almost any realistic scenario involving iterated belief change.

The DDL style is somewhere in between. It is much more economical than the ETL approach, since it keeps the states fixed and only multiplies the doxastic structure. It also brings conceptual clarity: doxastic changes *are* after all only changes of belief, so they shouldn't multiply the states of the world. It is an elegant and natural way to internalize doxastic changes. As shown in this paper, it is potentially at least as expressive and powerful as the (single-agent version of the) DEL approach: everything that was ever done in DEL style can be done in DDL style.

However, there is still a price to pay. DDL models are very high-level, involving fourth-order entities (not only states, but also fallbacks as sets of states, and hypertheories as sets of fallbacks, and doxologies as sets of hypertheories..., as well as doxastic actions as binary relations between hypertheories!). As a result, these models are hard to visualize. Their economy of resources is also relative: in complex dynamic-doxastic scenarios, the number of needed hypertheories explodes. Finally, it seems to us that, although in the end equivalent to the DEL style, the DDL approach lacks some of the heuristic value of DEL. As we saw, all the conceptual clarifications and settings that were developed in (single-agent) DEL style (such as the distinction between static and dynamic revision, the use of static conditional-belief modalities to "pre-encode" the dynamics, the axiomatization of various types of belief upgrades, the development of evidential dynamics) *can* be done in DDL style. We are confident that other such developments (such as the doxastic dynamics of questions studied in Interrogative DEL) *can* also be done in DDL style. But there might be a reason for which these developments were first done in DEL style: the inherent complexity of DDL models, their higher-order nature and the difficulty of visualizing them may reduce their heuristic value and may risk becoming obstacles to the intuitive pursuit of new developments in the field. An open-ended approach such as DEL, which keeps to a minimum the number of entities (and the number of higher-order concepts) in a given model and keeps the dynamics outside the models, may be easier to use when pursuing new developments. But this is just the context of discovery. At a later stage, in the context of presentation and justification, it may again become important, at least for the sake of conceptual clarity, to *re-internalize* these new dynamic developments, using the elegant DDL style. As indeed we attempted here, in this paper.

Acknowledgments Sonja Smets' contribution to this paper was funded by the European Research Council under the European Community's Seventh Framework Programme (FP7/2007–2013) / ERC Grant agreement nr 283963.

Appendix: Pictures of the Main Operations on Onions

The pictures drawn here are following Hans Rott's presentation [18]. The spheres of the initial onion are drawn as usual, as nested circles. The numbers represent the spheres of the new onion, *after* the revision/expansion/contraction: e.g. all regions labeled with one form the first sphere of the new onion, the regions labeled with two form the second sphere etc. Finally, the regions labeled with ω contain the states that are outside the union of all the spheres of the onion (the "impossible states").

Fig. 1 Radical revision ($!\varphi$)

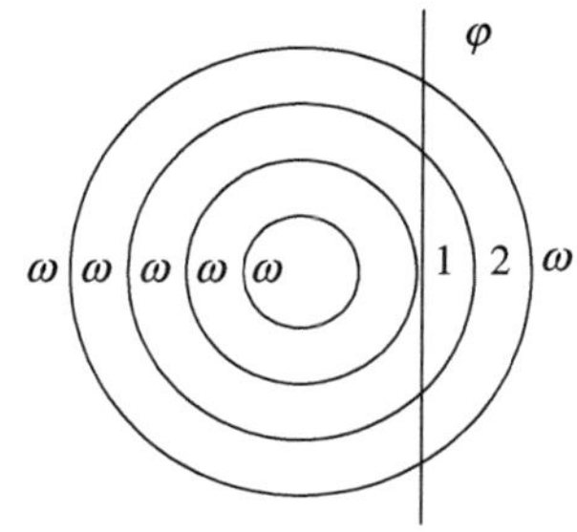

Fig. 2 Conservative revision ($\uparrow \varphi$)

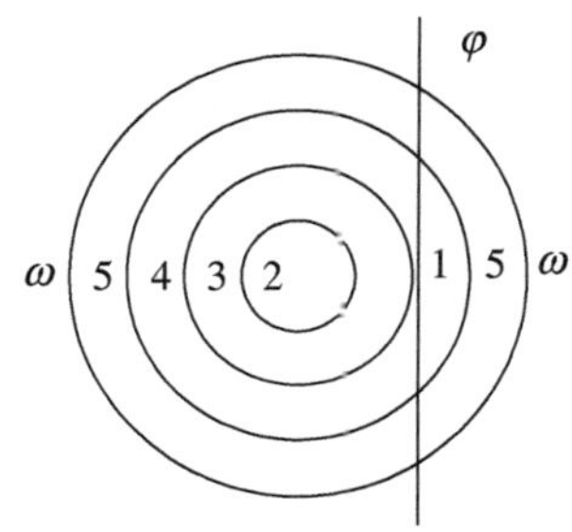

Fig. 3 Moderate revision ($\Uparrow \varphi$)

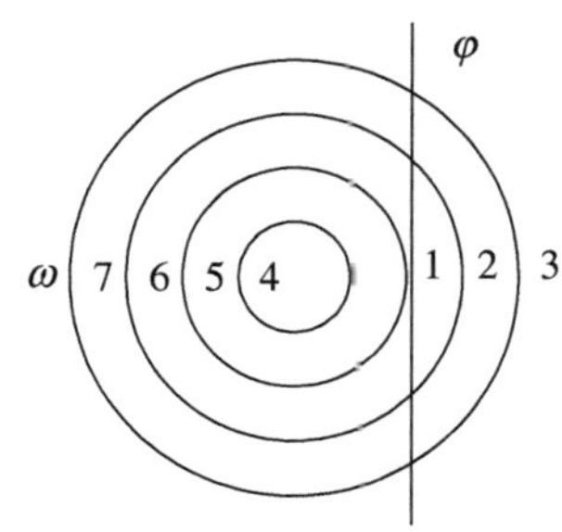

Fig. 4 Conservative expansion ($+\uparrow\varphi$)

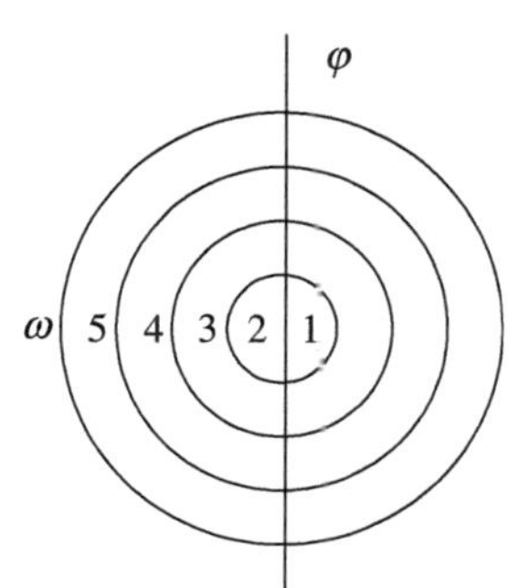

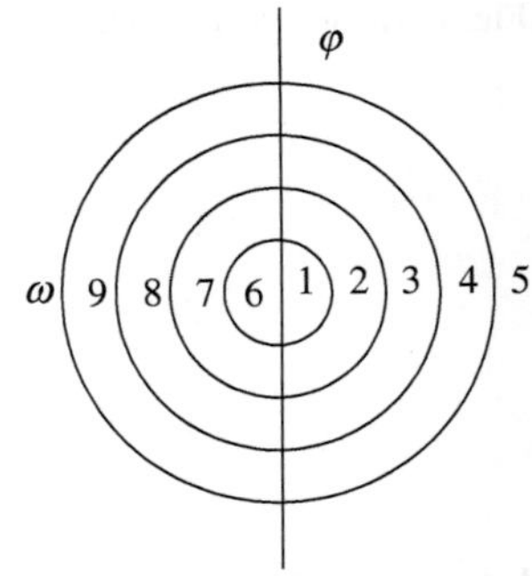

Fig. 5 Moderate expansion ($+\Uparrow\varphi$)

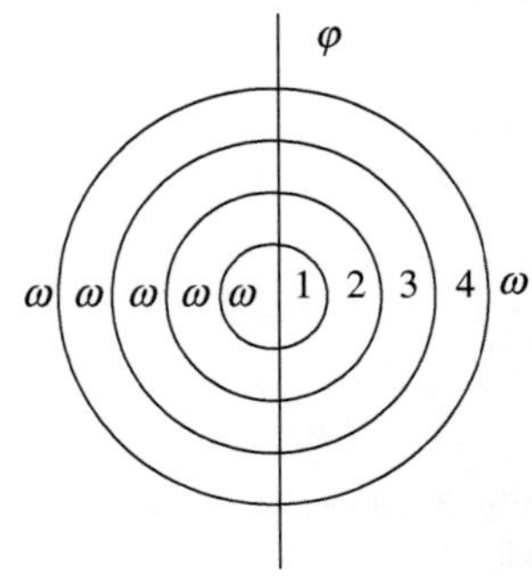

Fig. 6 Radical expansion ($+!\varphi$)

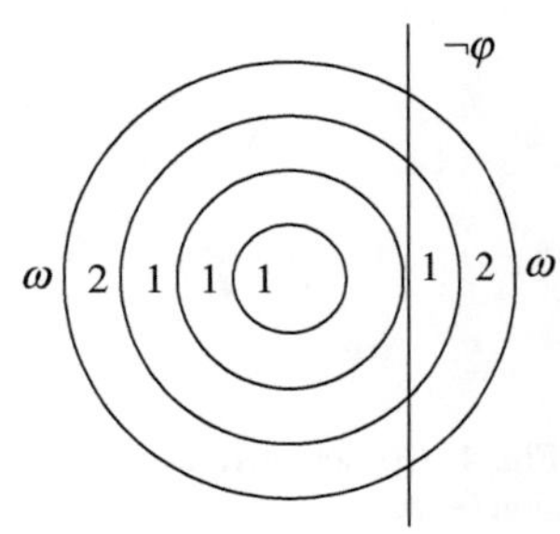

Fig. 7 Severe withdrawal ($-\varphi$)

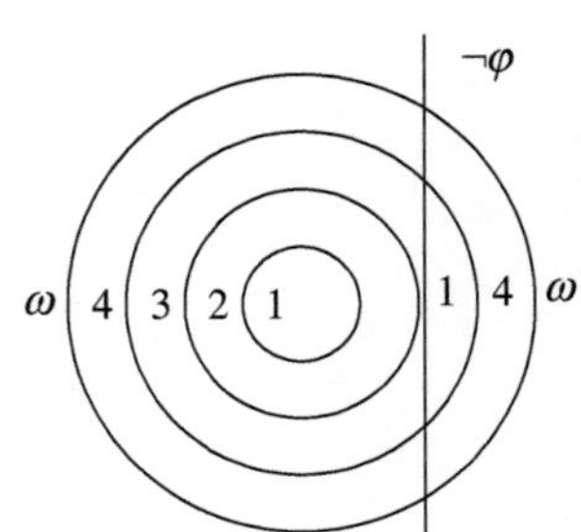

Fig. 8 Conservative contraction ($-_c\varphi$)

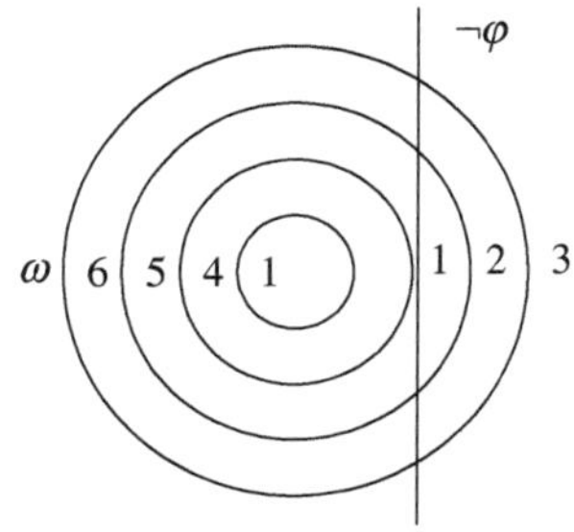

Fig. 9 Moderate contraction ($-_m\varphi$)

References

1. Alchourron, C. E., Gardenfors, P., & Makinson, D. (1985). On the logic of theory change: Partial meet contraction and revision functions. *The Journal of Symbolic Logic*, *50*(2), 510–530.
2. Baltag, A., Moss, L. S., & van Ditmarsch, H. P. (2008). Epistemic logic and information update. In P. Adriaans & J. van Benthem (Eds.), *Philosophy of information, part of handbook of the philosophy of science* (Vol. 8, pp. 361–465). New York: Elsevier.
3. Baltag, A., & Smets, S. (2006). Conditional doxastic models: A qualitative approach to dynamic belief revision. In G. Mints & R. de Queiroz (Eds.), *Proceedings of WOLLIC 2006. Electronic Notes in Theoretical Computer Science*, *165*, 5–21.
4. Baltag, A., & Smets, S. (2006). Dynamic belief revision over multi-agent plausibility models. In G. Bonanno, W. van der Hoek, & M. Woolridge (Eds.), *Proceedings of LOFT 2006* (pp. 11–24). Liverpool: University of Liverpool.
5. Baltag, A., & Smets, S. (2008). A Qualitative Theory of Dynamic Interactive Belief Revision. In (eds.) G. Bonanno, W. van der Hoek, and M. *Wooldridge, Texts in Logic and Games, Amsterdam University Press*, *3*, 13–60.
6. van Benthem, J. (2007). Dynamic logic for belief change. *Journal of Applied Non-Classical Logics*, *17*(2), 129–155.
7. van Benthem, J. (2011). *Logical Dynamics of Information and Interaction*. Cambridge University Press.
8. van Benthem, J., & Pacuit, E. (2011). Dynamic logics of evidence-based belief. *Studia Logica*, *99*(1), 61–92.
9. van Ditmarsch, H., van der Hoek, W., & Kooi, B. (2008). *Dynamic epistemic logic, Springer coll* (p. 337). Dordrecht: Synthese Library: Studies in Epistemology, Logic, Methodology, and Philosophy of Science.
10. Ferme, E., & Rodriguez, R. (1998). A brief note about rott contraction. *Logic Journal of the IGPL*, *6*, 835842.
11. Hintikka, J. (1962). *Knowledge and belief*. Ithaca, NY: Cornell University Press.
12. Levi, I. (2004). *Mild Contraction: Evaluating loss of information due to loss of belief*. Oxford: Oxford University Press.
13. Lindström, S., & Rabinowicz, W. (1999). DDL unlimited: Dynamic doxastic logic for introspective agents. *Erkenntnis*, *50*, 353–385.
14. Lindström, S., & Rabinowicz, W. (1999). Belief change for introspective agents. In *Spinning Ideas*, Electronic Essays Dedicated to Peter Gärdenfors on His Fiftieth Birthday.
15. Moss, L. S., & Parikh, R. (1992). Topological reasoning and the logic of knowledge. In Moses, Y.(Ed.), Theoretical aspects of reasoning about knowledge (pp. 95–105). Los Altos: Morgan Kaufmann.
16. Pagnucco, M., Rott, H. (1999). Severe withdrawal—and recovery. *Journal of Philosophical Logic*, *28*, 501–547. (Corrected reprint in issue February 2000).

17. Parikh, R., Moss, L. S., & Steinsvold, C. (2007), Topology and Epistemic Logic. In M. Aiello, I. Pratt-Hartmann, & J. van Benthem (Eds.), Handbook of Spatial Logics. Netherlands: Springer.
18. Rott, H. (2006). Shifting priorities: Simple representations for twenty-seven iterated theory change operators. In D. Makinson, J. Malinowski & H. Wansing (Eds.), Towards mathematical philosophy (Trends in Logic) (Vol. 4, pp. 269–296). Dordrecht: Springer.
19. Segerberg, K. (1995). Belief revision from the point of view of doxastic logic. *Bulletin of the IGPL*, *3*, 535–553.
20. Segerberg, K. (1996). A general framework for the logic of theory change. *Bulletin of the section of logic*, *25*, 2–8.
21. Segerberg, K. (1997). Proposal for a theory of belief revision along the lines of Lindström and Rabinowicz. *Fundamenta Informaticae*, *32*, 183–191.
22. Segerberg, K. (1998). Irrevocable belief revision in dynamic doxastic logic. *Notre Dame Journal of Formal Logic*, *39*(3), 287–306.
23. Segerberg, K. (1999). Two traditions in the logic of belief: bringing them together, In H. J. Ohlbach, & U. Reyle (Eds.), Logic, language and reasoning: Essays in honour of Dov Gabbay (pp. 135–147), Dordrecht: Kluwer.
24. Segerberg, K. (2001a). A completeness proof in full DDL. *Logic and Logical Philosophy*, *9*, 77–90.
25. Segerberg, K. (2001b). The basic dynamic doxastic logic of AGM. In M.A. Williams & H. Rott, Frontiers in belief revision (pp. 57–84), Dordrecht: Kluwer.
26. Segerberg, K., & Leitgeib, H. (2007). Dynamic doxastic logic—why, how and where to? *Synthese*, *155*, 167–190.

Two Logical Faces of Belief Revision

Johan van Benthem

Abstract This piece proposes a style of thinking using modal frame correspondence that puts Segerberg's dynamic doxastic logic and 'Dutch' dynamic-epistemic logic for belief change in one setting. While our technical results are elementary, they do suggest new lines of thought.

1 Two Modal Logics for Belief Change

Belief revision theory is a small corner of the world of philosophy and computer science, and modal logic is a small corner of the world of logic. When two specialized topics come together, surely, there can be only one way of doing that? The dynamic-doxastic logic *DDL* of Segerberg's [24, 25] [1] has abstract modal operators describing transitions in abstract universes of models to describe changes in belief, and then encodes basic postulates on belief change in modal axioms that can be studied by familiar techniques. But there is also another line in the logical literature, started in [3, 31][2] that works differently. Here belief changes are modeled in the framework of dynamic-epistemic logic (*DEL*) as acts of changing a plausibility ordering in a current model, and the update rule for doing that is made explicit,

[1] See also [16] for extensive discussion of the research program.
[2] Relevant predecessors to this work are [28, 33].

Krister Segerberg's seminal work has been a beacon in modal logic ever since the late 1960s. Add the attractive personality to the deep intellect, and one understands why my writing in this volume is a case of duty coinciding, not just with Kantian inclination, but with active desire.

J. van Benthem (✉)
University of Amsterdam, Amsterdam, The Netherlands
e-mail: johan.vanbenthem@uva.nl

J. van Benthem
Stanford University, Stanford, USA

R. Trypuz (ed.), *Krister Segerberg on Logic of Actions*,
Outstanding Contributions to Logic 1, DOI: 10.1007/978-94-007-7046-1_13,

while its properties are axiomatized completely in modal terms. The contrast may be stated as follows. Segerberg follows *AGM* belief revision theory [9] in its *postulational* approach constraining spaces of all possible belief changes, while the *DEL* approach is *constructive*, studying specific update rules and the complete logics of their corresponding dynamic model-changing modalities. Stated this way, there need not be any conflict between the two approaches—and in fact, there is not. Still, there are many differences in their subsequent technical agenda.[3] One could spend much time analyzing these differences, but my aim in this paper is modest. I want to suggest that, for colleagues from modal logic, *DDL* and *DEL* fit very well, if we use the method of *frame correspondence*. This suggestion occurs in [36], but I will pursue it more systematically here. My results are simple technically, but they suggest new perspectives. I start with knowledge in Sect. 2, exploring frame correspondences for 'public announcement logic' *PAL*. Many general methodological points can be made at this level, as they are not specific to belief. Next, I give modal correspondence for logics of belief change in Sect. 3. In Sect. 4, I discuss two generalizations: full dynamic-epistemic logic with product update over event models, and an extension of correspondence analysis to neighborhood models, using the *DEL* treatment in van [36]. Section 5 lists new general issues coming to light in my analysis, all of them 'to be explored'. Section 6 states the conclusion of this paper, though it will already be clear right here at the start: the two existing styles of modal logic for belief revision live well together, and analyzing their connections actually reveals some interesting issues that will unfold in due course.

2 Correspondence for Information Update and Knowledge

We start with a phenomenon that is not very interesting in the *AGM* style, though it becomes wildly exciting when we study it in a constructive setting: update with new hard information that shrinks agents' current ranges of epistemic options for the actual situation.

2.1 Hard Information, Knowledge, and Public Announcement Logic

Basic epistemic logic We start by recalling some basics. Standard epistemic logic *EL* describes semantic information encoded in agents' ranges of uncertainty. The

[3] *DEL*-style logics of belief revision depart from the *AGM*-format in a number of ways. (i) The content of new beliefs need not be factual, but it can itself consist of complex statements about beliefs. (ii) What changes in acts of revision is not just beliefs, but crucially also conditional beliefs. (iii) Infinitely many types of triggering event can be analyzed structurally in the logic by mechanisms like 'event models' or 'model-change programs'. (iv) The setting is essentially multi-agent, making, in principle, social acts of belief merge as crucial to the logical system as individual acts of revision (cf. the logics for merging in [11, 18]).

language extends propositional logic with modal operators $K_i\varphi$ (i knows that φ), for agents i, and $C_G\varphi$ (φ is common knowledge in group G). Epistemic models $\boldsymbol{M} = (W, \{\sim_i\}_{i\in I}, V)$ have a set of worlds W, accessibility relations $\sim_i$ for agents i in some total group I, and a valuation V for proposition letters. Pointed models $(\boldsymbol{M}, s)$ mark a actual world s.[4] The key truth condition is that $\boldsymbol{M}, s \models K_i\varphi$ iff for all worlds t with $s \sim_i t : \boldsymbol{M}, t \models \varphi$.[5,6] Complete logics capturing epistemic reasoning about oneself and others are known [8]. The base system is a minimal modal logic. A restriction to equivalence relations adds *S5* axioms of positive and negative introspection, while the complete logic of common knowledge can be axiomatized with *PDL*-techniques.

Information update by elimination Now for the logical dynamics of information flow. An event $!\varphi$ yielding the information that φ is true shrinks the current model to just those worlds that satisfy φ. This is the well-known notion of *public hard information*. More precisely, for any epistemic model $\boldsymbol{M}$, world s, and formula φ true at s, the new $(\boldsymbol{M}|\varphi, s)$ (*$\boldsymbol{M}$ relativized to φ at s*) is the sub-model of $\boldsymbol{M}$ whose domain is the set $\{t \in \boldsymbol{M} | \boldsymbol{M}, t \models \varphi\}$. This mechanism models public communication, but also public observation. There is much more to this dynamics than meets the eye in standard views of 'mere update' with factual formulas. For instance, crucially, truth values of complex epistemic formulas may change after update: agents who did not know that φ now do. Therefore, it makes sense to get clear on the exact dynamic logic behind this.

Public announcement logic The language of *public announcement logic PAL* adds action expressions to *EL*, plus matching modalities, defined by the syntax rules:

Formulas	$F : p \mid \neg\varphi \mid \varphi\vee\psi \mid K_i\varphi \mid C_G\,\varphi \mid \langle A\rangle\varphi$
Action expressions	$A : !F$

The semantic clause for the dynamic action modality looks ahead between models:

$$\boldsymbol{M}, s \models \langle !\varphi\rangle\psi \quad \text{iff} \quad \boldsymbol{M}, s \models \varphi \; \textit{and} \; \boldsymbol{M}|P, s \models \psi$$

PAL is axiomatized by any complete logic over static models plus *recursion axioms*

[4] Further relational conditions on $\sim_i$ encode special assumptions about agents' powers of observation and introspection: very common is the special case of equivalence relations.

[5] As for common knowledge, $\boldsymbol{M}, s \models C_G\varphi$ iff for all worlds t that are reachable from s by some finite sequence of arbitrary $\sim_i$ steps $(i \in G) : \boldsymbol{M}, t \models \varphi$.

[6] In what follows, for convenience, we mostly suppress agent indices, and use standard modal notation for the epistemic modality of one accessibility relation R. Also for convenience, we will work mostly with existential modalities $\Diamond$ instead of universal boxes $\Box$.

$$\langle !\varphi \rangle q \leftrightarrow (\varphi \wedge q) \text{ for proposition letters } q$$
$$\langle !\varphi \rangle (\psi \vee \chi) \leftrightarrow (\langle !\varphi \rangle \psi \vee \langle !\varphi \rangle \chi)$$
$$\langle !\varphi \rangle \neg \psi \leftrightarrow (\varphi \wedge \neg \langle !\varphi \rangle \psi)$$
$$\langle !\varphi \rangle \diamond \psi \leftrightarrow (\varphi \wedge \Diamond \langle !\varphi \rangle \psi)$$

Intuitively, the final recursion axiom for knowledge captures the essence of getting hard information. We will see in just which sense this is true in our further analysis. For further theory and applications of *PAL* and related systems, cf. [1, 3, 28, 36].

2.2 Switching Directions: From Valid Axioms to Constraints

PAL is about one constructive way of taking incoming hard information: elimination of incompatible worlds. Now we reverse the perspective. Let us ask which postulates look plausible for hard update, of course, always keeping in mind that our intuitions need to be valid for arbitrary propositions, bringing the logic in harmony.[7] Having done that, we can see which transformations of models validate them. This sounds grand. In what follows, however, I take a simple approach, investigating the recursion axioms of *PAL* themselves as postulates, since they have a lot of general appeal. To make this work, we need a suitably abstract setting—close to the models of *DDL*.[8]

Update universe and update relations Consider any family $\boldsymbol{M}$ of pointed epistemic models $(\boldsymbol{M}, s)$, viewed as an 'update universe' where model changes can take place. Possible changes are given as a family of update relations $R_P(\boldsymbol{M}, s)(\boldsymbol{N}, t)$ relating pointed models, where the index set P is a subset of $\boldsymbol{M}$: intuitively, the proposition triggering the update. One can think of the R as recording the action of some update operation ♥ occurring in the syntax of our language that depends on the proposition P. Here different operations can have different effects: from our hard updates $!\varphi$ to the soft updates $\Uparrow\varphi$ to be discussed below. As just said, this is essentially the semantic setting of Krister Segerberg's dynamic doxastic logic, where each transition relation has a matching modality.[9] Now, for each formula φ, let $[[\varphi]]$ be the set of worlds in $\boldsymbol{M}$ satisfying φ. We set, for the update modality matching the relation R:

---

[7] It is a curiously overlooked mismatch that modal logics for philosophical notions are often based on philosophers' intuitions about factual statements only, whereas the logic itself also deals with complex assertions that make good sense, for which the philosophers' intuitions might have to be different. Other imbalances of this sort occur in logics for non-standard consequence relations, and accounts of knowledge proposed in formal epistemology.

[8] The setting chosen here is more abstract and flexible than that used in the correspondence analaysis of [36], and it removes some infelicities in that earlier treatment.

[9] This is not the only possible format, and one can experiment with others. In particular, making the relational transition depend on just an extensional set of worlds reflects the valid *PAL* rule of *Replacement of Provable Equivalents*. Stated as one axiom in a language extended with a universal modality U ranging over the whole universe, this is the following implication making announced propositions 'extensional': $U(\varphi \leftrightarrow \psi) \to (\langle !\varphi \rangle \alpha \leftrightarrow \langle !\psi \rangle \alpha)$.

$$\boldsymbol{M}, s \models \langle \heartsuit\varphi \rangle \psi \text{ iff } \textit{there exists a model } (\boldsymbol{N}, t) \textit{ in } \mathbf{M} \textit{ with } R_{[[\varphi]]}(\boldsymbol{M}, s)(\boldsymbol{N}, t) \textit{ and } (\boldsymbol{N}, t) \models \psi$$

Remark To be yet more precise, we are really interpreting our language in a *three-index format* $\mathbf{M}, \boldsymbol{M}, s$, and for the accessibility relations R in this update universe $\mathbf{M}$, we have that $(\boldsymbol{M}, s)R(\boldsymbol{M}, t)$ iff Rst in $\boldsymbol{M}$, without any jumps out of the model $\boldsymbol{M}$. This precision can be ignored for most of what follows, but it will come up occasionally.

2.3 A Correspondence Theorem for Eliminative Update

In what follows, the reader is supposed to know how modal frame correspondence works: cf. the textbooks van Blackburn, [5, 34]. We will analyze the *PAL* recursion axioms one by one in this style to see what they say, as a way of determining their total content as a correspondence constraint on update operations. But before doing so, we need to address a subtlety.

Substitution closure Correspondence arguments use frame truth of modal formulas, i.e., truth under all possible valuations for the proposition letters. Thus, if a formula is true, so are all its substitution instances: proposition letters are schematic variables for arbitrary propositions. But this sits badly with the system *PAL*, whose valid principles are not closed under substitution. In particular, the base axiom $\langle !\varphi \rangle q \leftrightarrow (\varphi \wedge q)$ is only valid for proposition letters q. Substituting to the general form $\langle !\varphi \rangle \psi \leftrightarrow (\varphi \wedge \psi)$ yields obviously invalid instances for epistemic assertions ψ. Much can be said about this phenomenon (cf. [14]), but in this paper, we take a simple line. We will first analyze the substitution-closed principles of *PAL*, and then return to the correspondence status of the base axiom. Thus, for the moment, we only look at the following obviously substitution-closed special case:

$$\langle !\varphi \rangle T \leftrightarrow \varphi$$

In our correspondence setting, substitution failures relate to the semantics of atomic propositions p. Inside one epistemic model $\boldsymbol{M}$, the obvious choice seems to be sets of worlds. But in an update universe $\mathbf{M}$ as above, propositions range over all *pairs* $(\boldsymbol{M}, s)$, and hence one p could have different truth values at pairs $(\boldsymbol{M}, s)$, $(\boldsymbol{N}, s)$. We will view Greek letters in axioms as standing for such general context-dependent propositions in what follows, returning to the original view of *PAL*-atoms as sets of worlds later on. Finally, here is one more important convention in what follows:

Remark Throughout, we will fix announced formulas φ in contexts $\langle !\varphi \rangle \psi$, refraining from varying these in correspondence. Think of distinguished fixed propositions.

Now we are ready to go through the axioms:

Base axiom The axiom $\langle !\varphi \rangle T \leftrightarrow \varphi$ says that, given any model $\boldsymbol{M}$, the domain of the transition relation $R_{[[\varphi]]}$ is the set of worlds satisfying φ in $\boldsymbol{M}$. In other words, our abstract update action has the truth of φ as a necessary and sufficient precondition.

Disjunction axiom There is no special constraint expressed by the modal formula $\langle !\varphi\rangle(\psi\vee\chi) \leftrightarrow \langle !\varphi\rangle\psi\vee\langle !\varphi\rangle\chi$, since this law holds for any transition relation.

Negation axiom One direction of this axiom expresses no constraint on the update operation: $(\varphi\wedge\neg\langle !\varphi\rangle\psi) \rightarrow \langle !\varphi\rangle\neg\psi$ is valid, given that ϕ is equivalent to $\langle !\varphi\rangle T$.But the converse $\langle !\varphi\rangle\neg\psi \rightarrow (\varphi\wedge\neg\langle !\varphi\rangle\psi)$, even just $\langle !\varphi\rangle\neg\psi \rightarrow \neg\langle !\varphi\rangle\psi$, says by a standard correspondence argument that the transition relation is a *partial function*[10]:

$$\text{if}(\boldsymbol{M}, s)R_{[[\varphi]]}(\boldsymbol{N}, t) \text{ and } (\boldsymbol{M}, s)R_{[[\varphi]]}(\boldsymbol{K}, u), \text{ then } (\boldsymbol{N}, t) = (\boldsymbol{K}, u).$$

Using this observation, we now simplify the original transition relations R_P in the update universe to *partial functions* F_P on pointed models. In particular, given any model $\boldsymbol{M}$ with a subset P, we can meaningfully talk about its image $F_P[\boldsymbol{M}]$.

Knowledge axiom So far, we were just doing preliminaries. The heart of the matter is evidently the recursion axiom for knowledge: $\langle !\varphi\rangle\Diamond\psi \leftrightarrow (\varphi\wedge\Diamond\langle !\varphi\rangle\psi)$. The two directions of this clearly express two constraints on the update function—and together, they enforce a well-known notion from modal logic [23]:

Fact The update function satisfies frame truth of $\langle !\varphi\rangle\Diamond\psi \leftrightarrow (\varphi\wedge\Diamond\langle !\varphi\rangle\psi)$ iff every map F_P is a *p-morphism* between $\boldsymbol{M}$ and $F_P[\boldsymbol{M}]$.

Proof We do this first proof in a bit of detail, mainly to show how simple correspondence arguments for update functions are. Consider any model $\boldsymbol{M}$, with $[[\varphi]] = P$. First we show that F_P is a homomorphism. Suppose that *Rst* in $\boldsymbol{M}$, with *s, t* both in the domain of F_P. Now set $V(\psi) = \{F_P(t)\}$. Then $(\boldsymbol{M}, s) \models \varphi\wedge\Diamond\langle !\varphi\rangle\psi$, and therefore also, $(\boldsymbol{M}, s) \models \langle !\varphi\rangle\Diamond\psi$. By the definition of $V(\psi)$, this implies that $R\ F_P(s)F_P(t)$. Next, for the backward clause of being a *p*-morphism, suppose that $R\ F_P(s)u$, and now set $V(\psi) = \{u\}$. Then we have $(\boldsymbol{M}, s) \models \langle !\varphi\rangle\Diamond\psi$. It follows from the truth of our axiom that $(\boldsymbol{M}, s) \models \varphi\Diamond\langle !\varphi\rangle\psi$, and hence there exists a point *t* in $\boldsymbol{M}$ with *Rst* and $F_P(t) = u$. ■

Collecting all our observations so far, we have the following result:

Theorem An update universe satisfies the substitution-closed principles of *PAL* iff its transition relations F_P are partial *p*-morphisms defined on the sets P.

Discussion This is not quite the formation of submodels in standard elimination. Here is why. First, having a *p*-morphism is enough for validity of the *PAL* axioms, so we found a generalization of the standard semantics that may be of independent interest. Also, contracting several worlds into one during update occurs naturally in the setting of *PAL*: cf. [36] on the use of bisimulation contractions in updating.[11]

---

[10] The above comment on interpreting propositions is crucial here: in the argument, we use the singleton set of the pointed model $(\boldsymbol{N}, t)$ as the denotation of ψ in the update universe $\boldsymbol{M}$.

[11] If one insists on making the maps one-to-one, this can be done by enriching the modal language, and enforcing one more reduction axiom for public announcement, namely, for the *difference modality* $D\psi$ *saying that* ψ holds in a least one different world.

The base axiom once more Still, the above outputs enforced by our update mechanism are relational subframes, rather than submodels. What about the atomic propositions? *PAL* update assumes that these stay the same when a world does not change. Here is how we can think of this. Consider the usual proposition letters of epistemic logic as distinguished atomic propositions. The base axiom tells us that these special propositions have a special behavior: if they hold for an pointed model $(\boldsymbol{M}, s)$, they also hold for any of its update images under a map F_P, and vice versa:

$$(\boldsymbol{M}, s) \models p \quad \text{iff} \quad F_P(\boldsymbol{M}, s) \models p$$

This might be the only content to the base axiom: update maps respect distinguished atomic propositions. But we can say a bit more in correspondence style. We assumed that proposition letters ranged over all sets of pointed models in the update universe. Now introduce special 'context-independent' proposition letters q ranging only over special sets of pointed models, with the property that they only depend on worlds:

$$(\boldsymbol{M}, s) \models q \quad \text{iff} \quad (\boldsymbol{N}, s) \models q, \quad \text{for all models } \boldsymbol{M}, \boldsymbol{N} \text{ in } \mathbb{M}$$

Fact An update universe satisfies the base axiom $\langle !\varphi \rangle q \leftrightarrow (\varphi \wedge q)$ for all context-independent q iff the update maps are the identity on worlds:

$$F_P(\boldsymbol{M}, s) = (\boldsymbol{N}, s) \text{ for some model } \boldsymbol{N}.$$

Proof Consider any pointed model $(\boldsymbol{M}, s)$ in the domain of F_P. Now set $V(q) = \{(\boldsymbol{N}, s) | (\boldsymbol{N}, s) \text{ is in } \mathbb{M}\}$. This is clearly a context-independent predicate. With this particular $V(q)$, the true implication $(\varphi \wedge q) \rightarrow \langle \varphi \rangle q$ then says that $F_P(\boldsymbol{M}, s) = (\boldsymbol{N}, s)$ for some model $\boldsymbol{N}$. ■

Even so, models $\boldsymbol{N}$ occurring in F_P-values for pointed models $(\boldsymbol{M}, t)$ with the same $\boldsymbol{M}$ could still differ. We will soon see a further recursion law making this uniform.[12]

This concludes our discussion of the correspondence content of the *PAL* axioms.[13]

2.4 Variations, Extensions, and a Provocation

Recursion axioms as general postulates We have determined the update content of one specific axiom for update. But there is more to this. Dynamic-epistemic recursion axioms are not just 'any sort of principle'. They have several features that

---

[12] For an analogy, think of correspondence theory for intuitionistic logic [21], where axioms are only valid for all 'hereditary propositions'.

[13] Readers who like open problems may ponder this: how should the above analysis be modified to allow *factual change*, as in [29]?

make them candidates for general postulates on information update.[14] In particular, our analysis says that the *PAL* recursion axiom for knowledge expresses a sort of *partial bisimulation* between the original model and the output of an update rule applied to it. I find abstract simulation behavior very appealing as a general semantic constraint on update functions, though I am not sure how to define it in its proper generality.[15]

Protocols Update universes also suggest a different setting, that has been proposed in dynamic-epistemic logic for independent reasons. So far, we had that $\langle !\varphi\rangle T \leftrightarrow \varphi$. This says that executing an action $!\varphi$ requires truth of the precondition φ, but also, whenever φ is true, $!\varphi$ can be executed. But in civilized conversation or regimented inquiry, the latter assumption is often untenable. To represent this, 'protocol models' make restrictions on propositions that can be announced or observed. [15] shows how *PAL* changes in this setting, since the earlier recursion axioms will now be valid only with $\langle !\varphi\rangle T$ in the place of φ on their right-hand sides. This move has many technical repercussions, though the system remains axiomatizable and decidable. From our correspondence perspective, nothing much changes: the only new thing is that the domain of an update map F_P will now be a subset of P, but not necessarily all of P. Our analysis of the modified recursion axioms remains essentially as before.

Language extensions We analyzed update axioms for the epistemic base language. But *PAL* also has a complete version for the full epistemic language with common knowledge. The recursion axiom then requires a new notion of 'conditional common knowledge' [29]. Since the axiom for single-agent knowledge already fixed the *PAL* update rule, as we have seen, no further constraints arise. We will return later to what this 'passive behavior' of common knowledge vis-à-vis single-agent knowledge means in terms of definability or derivability.[16] A useful language extension whose recursion axiom does add to our correspondence analysis introduces an *existential modality* $E\psi$ saying that ψ is true in some world in the current model, accessible or not. In update universes $\boldsymbol{M}$, we interpret this as saying, at a pointed model $(\boldsymbol{M}, s)$, that there is some t in $\boldsymbol{M}$ with ψ true at $(\boldsymbol{M}, t)$.

Fact On update universes $\boldsymbol{M}$ satisfying the earlier *PAL* update conditions, the axiom $\langle\varphi\rangle E\psi \leftrightarrow (\varphi \wedge E\langle !\varphi\rangle\psi)$ is frame-true iff, for every model $\boldsymbol{M}$, the update images of worlds in $\boldsymbol{M}$ have the same model $\boldsymbol{N}$ throughout.

Proof First, the axiom is clearly valid in the intended update universes. Conversely, its right to left direction implies the stated property. Consider any two worlds

[14] The commutation of action and knowledge in the key *PAL* recursion axiom has an appealing interpretation in terms of desirable features of logically well-endowed agents. It expresses notions of *Perfect Recall* and *No Miracles* in the sense of [13].

[15] A relevant analogy here may be with the modal logic of a *bisimulation* Z itself, viewed as a relation on a universe whose worlds are models. The key back-and-forth clause of bisimulation is precisely a commutation axiom $\langle Z\rangle\Diamond\psi \leftrightarrow \Diamond\langle Z\rangle\psi$.

[16] There is also the question whether the recursion axiom for conditional common knowledge by itself fixes world elimination as the update rule—but we will consider this issue only with an analogous case in the dynamic logic of belief change.

$(\boldsymbol{N}, t)$, $(\boldsymbol{K}, u)$ in the image $F_P\boldsymbol{M}$. Set $V(\psi) = \{(\boldsymbol{K}, u)\}$. Then the F_P-original of $(\boldsymbol{N}, t)$ in $\boldsymbol{M}$ satisfies $\varphi \wedge E\langle !\varphi\rangle\psi$. It follows that $\langle !\varphi\rangle E\psi$, and by the preceding definition, this only happens when $(\boldsymbol{N}, t)$ and $(\boldsymbol{K}, u)$ share the same model component. ■

Finally, update universes suggest yet further language extensions. For instance, there is also a natural relation $(\boldsymbol{M}, s) \sim (\boldsymbol{N}, s)$ holding between different models sharing the same distinguished world. Its modality would make sense, even though it does not inside single epistemic models, the way basic epistemic logic works.

What is the right version of PAL? We conclude with a more provocative feature of our analysis. We started by analyzing what standard public announcement says about update, and then determined its force in update universes. But doing so involved a natural distinction between the substitution-closed principles of *PAL* and the more 'accidental' base axiom holding only for a restricted class of valuations. So, what is 'public announcement logic' after all? Is its base semantics perhaps the one on update universes with context-dependent propositions and substitution-closed validities? And if so, is what we call the 'standard version' perhaps an accident of formulation?

2.5 Other Natural Operations: Link Cutting

Update with hard information that φ does show variety beyond the above elimination. In a well-known *link-cutting* variant, the operation $|\varphi$ performed announces *whether* φ is the case. This means that the domain of worlds stays the same, but all epistemic links get cut between φ-worlds and $\neg\varphi - worlds$ in the current model—an operation used by many authors. The changes induced in the *PAL* axioms are mainly these:

$$\langle|\varphi\rangle q \leftrightarrow q \text{ (this implies the substitution-closed instance} \langle|\varphi\rangle T)$$

$$\langle|\varphi\rangle\Diamond\psi \leftrightarrow (\ (\varphi \wedge \Diamond(\varphi \wedge \langle|\varphi\rangle\psi)) \vee (\neg\varphi \wedge \Diamond(\neg\varphi \wedge \langle|\varphi\rangle\psi))\ )$$

The following result can be proved in the same correspondence style as before:

Fact Link cutting is the only model-changing operation that satisfies the reduction axioms for the dynamic modality $\langle|\varphi\rangle$.

Proof We merely give a sketch of the substitution-closed part. Start from any pointed model $\boldsymbol{M}$, s. The modified base axiom tells us that the update map is now total on the whole domain of $\boldsymbol{M}$. Next, the recursion axiom for knowledge, read from left to right, says that the only links in the image come from already existing links between either φ–worlds, or $\neg\varphi$–worlds. Finally, from right to left, the axiom says that all links of the two mentioned types existing in $\boldsymbol{M}$ get preserved into the image. ■

3 Correspondence Analysis of Modal Logics for Belief Change

Now that we have seen how to analyze principles of knowledge update by changing domains or accessibility relations, an extension to belief revision is straightforward. We mainly need to decide what models we will be working with.

3.1 Soft Information and Belief

Doxastic models are structures $\boldsymbol{M} = (W, \{\leq_i\}_{i \in I}, V)$ where the $\leq_i$ are binary comparison relations $\leq_i xy$ saying that agent i considers x at least as plausible as y. As before, for convenience, we drop agent indices henceforth. These plausibility relations are usually taken to be reflexive and transitive, making the modal base logic *S4*—or also connected, like the 'Grove models' of belief revision theory, making the logic *S4.3*. Such options are important in practice, but they do not affect the analysis to follow.

These models encode varieties of information. While the whole domain represents our current hard information in the earlier sense, the most plausible worlds in the ordering $\leq$ represent our *soft information* about the actual world. This soft information is the basis of our beliefs and actions based on these, but it is defeasible: the actual world may lie outside of the most plausible area, and we may learn this as a scenario unfolds. In this setting, belief is commonly interpreted as truth in all most plausible worlds[17]:

$$\boldsymbol{M}, s \models B\varphi \text{ iff } \boldsymbol{M}, t \models \varphi \textit{ for all worlds } t \textit{ that are minimal in the ordering } \leq$$

But absolute belief does not suffice for most purposes. We need *conditional belief*[18]:

$$\boldsymbol{M}, s \models B^{\psi}\varphi \text{ iff } \boldsymbol{M}, t \models \varphi \textit{ for all } \leq -\textit{minimal worlds in } \{u | \boldsymbol{M}, u \models \psi\}$$

This point returns with recursion axioms for belief change. From a systematic logical perspective, we should not analyze changes in beliefs only (the usual practice in belief revision theory), but also changes in conditional belief.

Conditional logic Complete logics for conditional belief can be found in close analogy with *conditional logic* based on similarity semantics [17]. One difference is that conditional models usually involve a *ternary* comparison ordering $\leq_z xy$: world x is closer to world z then world y. A generalization from binary to ternary relation also makes sense for plausibility semantics of belief, but we forego this here.[19]

---

[17] We disregard some modifications of truth clauses needed with infinite models.

[18] Absolute belief can be retrieved as the special case of $\psi = T$.

[19] Another natural generalization are *epistemic-doxastic models* $\boldsymbol{M} = (W, \{\sim_i\}_{i \in I}, \{\leq_{i,s}\}_{i \in I}, V)$ allowing for both knowledge update and belief revision. Our methods also work there.

Safe belief While the preceding belief modalities are interesting, it has become clear recently that the plain base modality of plausibility models has independent interest.

$$\boldsymbol{M}, s \models \langle\leq\rangle\varphi \quad \text{iff} \quad \textit{there exists a point } t \geq s \textit{ with } \boldsymbol{M}, t \models \varphi$$

The matching universal modality offers an interesting doxastic notion in between knowledge and belief. Consider this picture with the actual world s in the middle:

$K\varphi$ describes what we know: φ must be true in all three worlds in the range, less or more plausible than the current one. $B\varphi$ describes beliefs, which have to be true in the right-most world only. Now $[\leq]\varphi$ describes our *safe beliefs*, referring to the actual s plus the right-most world. These cannot be refuted by any future correct observations. Technically, safe belief can also define the other kinds of belief [6]:

$$\text{on finite pre-orders, } B^{\psi}\varphi \text{ is defined by } U(\psi \rightarrow \langle\leq\rangle(\psi\wedge[\leq](\psi \rightarrow \varphi)))$$

with U the universal modality, or in epistemic-doxastic models, an appropriate knowledge modality. Thus, at least technically, an analysis of belief change might focus on safe belief without losing much.

3.2 Dynamic Logics of Belief Change

Now we can write complete logics for belief change. Indeed, there are several systems for this, depending on what kind of new information triggers the change.[20]

Hard information For hard information, the complete dynamic logic is as follows:

Theorem The logic of conditional belief under public announcements is axiomatized completely by

(a) any complete static logic for the model class chosen,
(b) the *PAL* recursion axioms for atomic facts and Boolean operations,
(c) an axiom for conditional belief: $\langle!\varphi\rangle B^{\alpha}\psi \leftrightarrow (\varphi \wedge B^{\langle!\varphi\rangle^{\alpha}}\langle\varphi\rangle\psi)$.

A similar analysis can be given for safe belief, with a simpler key recursion axiom

$$\langle!\varphi\rangle\langle\leq\rangle\psi \leftrightarrow (\varphi \wedge \langle\leq\rangle\langle!\varphi\rangle\psi)$$

Formally, this is just the earlier recursion axiom for a modality $\Diamond$.

---

[20] The results cited in this subsection and the next are from [31].

Soft information and plausibility change Now comes a major further step. Triggers for belief change can be of many kinds, and we do not always expect the same model changes. In particular, incoming new information may be soft rather than hard, which means that it does not eliminate worlds, but merely *rearranges the current plausibility order*. A common example is a *radical upgrade* $\Uparrow\varphi$ changing the current ordering $\leq$ between worlds in a model $(\boldsymbol{M}, s)$ to a new model $(\boldsymbol{M}\Uparrow\varphi, s)$ as follows:

> all φ–worlds in the current model become better than all $\neg\varphi$–worlds,
> while, within those two zones, the old plausibility ordering remains.

Like for public announcement, we introduce an upgrade modality into our language:

$$\boldsymbol{M}, s \models \langle\Uparrow\varphi\rangle\psi \quad \text{iff} \quad \boldsymbol{M}\Uparrow\varphi, s \models \psi$$

The earlier techniques extend. Again there is a complete set of recursion axioms:

Theorem The dynamic logic of lexicographic upgrade is axiomatized by

(a) any complete static logic for the model class chosen,
(b) the following recursion axioms:

$$\begin{aligned}
\langle\Uparrow\varphi\rangle q &\leftrightarrow q \quad \textit{for all atomic proposition letters } q\\
\langle\Uparrow\varphi\rangle\neg\psi &\leftrightarrow \neg\langle\Uparrow\varphi\rangle\psi\\
\langle\Uparrow\varphi\ \rangle(\psi \vee \chi) &\leftrightarrow \langle\Uparrow\varphi\rangle\psi\vee\langle\Uparrow\varphi\rangle\chi\\
\langle\Uparrow\varphi\rangle B^{\alpha}\psi &\leftrightarrow (\mathrm{E}(\varphi \wedge \langle\Uparrow\varphi\rangle\alpha) \wedge B^{\varphi\,\wedge\,\langle\Uparrow\varphi\rangle\alpha}\langle\Uparrow\varphi\rangle\psi)\\
&\qquad \vee(\neg(\mathrm{E}(\varphi\wedge\langle\Uparrow\varphi > \alpha)\wedge B^{\langle\Uparrow\varphi\rangle\alpha}\langle\Uparrow\varphi\rangle\psi))
\end{aligned}$$

Again, there is also an evident valid recursion axiom for changes in safe belief:

$$\langle\Uparrow\varphi\rangle\langle\leq\rangle\psi \leftrightarrow E\ (\varphi \wedge \langle\Uparrow\varphi\rangle\psi) \vee (\neg\varphi\wedge\langle\leq\rangle\langle\Uparrow\varphi\rangle\psi)$$

Given the earlier modal definition of absolute and conditional belief in terms of safe belief, one can even derive the preceding recursion axioms from this one. Other belief change policies can be treated in the same style, using the relation transformers of [31] or the priority product update of [1].

3.3 Correspondence for Axioms of Belief Change

As before with knowledge, we can now invert the preceding results and use the key recursion axioms as constraints to determine the space of possible update operations. For update operations transforming plausibility relations only, leaving domains of models the same, a more complex correspondence proof than earlier ones shows:

Theorem The recursion axioms of the dynamic logic of radical upgrade hold universally for an update operation on a universe of pointed plausibility models iff that operation is in fact radical upgrade.[21]

It is important to realize what is going on here. *AGM*-style postulates on changes in beliefs will not fix the relational transformation: we need to constrain the changes in *conditional beliefs*, since the new plausibility order encodes all of these. A similar analysis works for other revision policies, such as 'conservative' belief change. But actually, there is an easier road to such results, closer to earlier arguments.

Theorem Radical upgrade is the only update operation validating the given recursion axioms for atoms, Booleans plus safe belief.

Proof Suppose that the axiom is valid on a universe of plausibility models. The axiom for atoms tells us in particular that our update function is defined everywhere. Now consider any model $(\boldsymbol{M}, s)$. From left to right, taking ψ to denote just one world $(\boldsymbol{N}, t)$ with $F_P(\boldsymbol{M}, s) \leq (\boldsymbol{N}, t)$, it follows that $(\boldsymbol{N}, t)$ was either the image of some φ–world in $\boldsymbol{M}$, or $s \leq \mathrm{u}$ in $\boldsymbol{M}$ for some world u mapped to $(\boldsymbol{N}, t)$, i.e., the new $\leq$-link came from an old one originating in a $\neg\varphi$–world. This means that each new relational link comes from the set defined by radical upgrade. That in fact all such links occur in the F_P-image of $\boldsymbol{M}$ follows by similar unpacking of the reverse implication of the recursion axiom. ■

Given this last correspondence result, the earlier more complex ones seem less urgent, since safe belief defines absolute and conditional belief. Indeed, philosophically plausible *AGM*-style postulates on 'safe-belief change' might be easier conceptually than those for regular belief.[22]

3.4 Discussion: Generality of the Analysis

We have seen how recursion laws in constructive logics of belief change can serve as general postulates to constrain, and almost uniquely fix, possible updates. As before, this relates the *DDL* and *DEL* approaches to modal logics of belief change, softening a contrast that we started out with. Also as before, issues of generality arise. Are the recursion axioms too specific for belief change postulates? Here we repeat our earlier intuition of 'simulation' between input and output models of the transformation. One might add that a recursive postulate may itself be philosophically attractive as providing the core 'dynamic equation' driving the process of update or revision. Finally,

---

[21] Here as before, we work with the substitution-closed version of the logic. In particular, the atomic case simplifies to just $\langle\Uparrow\varphi\rangle T$: radical upgrade is defined everywhere.

[22] Still, it is interesting that recursion axioms for conditional belief fix radical upgrade, too. This might imply further definability and proof-theoretic connections between the various doxastic notions mentioned. If one recursion axiom fixes update, it looks as if others should be derivable in some way. We cannot explore this technical line here.

here is an issue more specific to belief. Given the overwhelming variety of belief revision policies, what is the general thrust of correspondence results like ours? We will return to this issue in Sect. 5, when discussing product update and other general mechanisms replacing a host of separate revision rules by one master rule plus richer input.[23,24]

4 Richer Formats as a Test Case

The style of analysis proposed here works on richer semantic formats for update than modal relational models. In this brief digression, we sketch two examples. These will also raise some issues about the scope and limitations of our earlier analysis.

4.1 Event Models and Product Update

While public announcement logic *PAL* is a good pilot system, its restriction to public information makes it unsuitable for analyzing individual differences in observation and communication. A much richer dynamic-epistemic logic for the latter tasks is true *DEL* [10, 3]. It uses *action models* $\boldsymbol{E}$ that collect events with attached 'preconditions', with epistemic uncertainty links between events representing agents' observational access to what actually happens. Action models have been used to represent a wide variety of triggers for information change. Next, by performing *product update* of an action model E with the current epistemic or doxastic model $\boldsymbol{M}$ one obtains a new updated information model $\boldsymbol{M} \times E$ displaying the right information for all agents involved after the event has taken place.

We assume that the reader knows how *DEL* update works, including its complete set of recursion axioms (cf. [36, 37] for details). We display two of these for later reference—suppressing agent indices as before, and using the letter R to denote the agent's accessibility relation:

$$\langle \boldsymbol{E}, e\rangle T \quad \leftrightarrow \quad Pre_e$$
$$\langle \boldsymbol{E}, e\rangle \Diamond\psi \leftrightarrow (Pre_e \wedge \vee_{eRf\ in E} \Diamond\langle \boldsymbol{E}, f\rangle\psi)$$

This mechanism changes epistemic or doxastic models much more drastically than the earlier world elimination or relation change. In particular, the set of new worlds

---

23 This argument still ignores some key features of product update, like its use of ordered pairs *(s, e)* of worlds and events by themselves without marking the context s *in* $\boldsymbol{M}$, e *in* $\boldsymbol{E}$.

24 Here is a more technical issue. We have only analyzed single update mechanisms so far. But some *AGM*-postulates mix update and revision. Can we use modal versions of such postulates to get correspondence results for axioms with two update modalities simultaneously?

$\{(s,e)|s \in \boldsymbol{M}, e \in \boldsymbol{E}, \boldsymbol{M}, s \models Pre_e\}$ in $\boldsymbol{M} \times E$ may grow beyond the size of the initial model $\boldsymbol{M}$.

Theorem The recursion axioms for the dynamic modality $\langle \boldsymbol{E}, e\rangle\varphi$ of *DEL* determine product update uniquely modulo *p*-morphism.

The precise sense in which this definability assertion is true will emerge from the following discussion.

Proof sketch As in our study of *PAL*, we analyze the impact of the *DEL* recursion axioms on an update universe of epistemic models with an abstract transition relation for the update for the pointed event model $(\boldsymbol{E}, e)$. The negation axiom of *DEL* tells us that this is a partial function $F_{E,e}$. This functionality means that we can think of values $F_{E,e}(\boldsymbol{M}, s)$ as pairs (s, e) without loss of information. Next, the substitution-closed base axiom tells us that $F_{E,e}$ is defined on those models $(\boldsymbol{M}, s)$ whose s satisfies the precondition of e in $\boldsymbol{E}$. Finally, also as before, the *DEL* recursion axiom for individual knowledge puts constraints on the function $F_{E,e}$. First, if $s\ R\ t$ in $\boldsymbol{M}$, and $e\ R f$ in $\boldsymbol{E}$, while $F_{E,e}(\boldsymbol{M}, s)$, $F_{E,e}(\boldsymbol{M}, t)$ are both defined, then $(s, e)R(t, f)$ holds by the direction from right to left in the axiom. Vice versa, any link in the image of the model $\boldsymbol{M}$ must also arise in this way, if we unpack the left-to-right direction of the axiom.[25]

One update logic to bind them all? The preceding analysis may still be too piecemeal, ignoring a key innovation of *DEL* in the area of constructive update logics. An earlier trend had been to define specific model changes for particular kinds of informational event: 'announcements that', link cutting 'announcements whether', or more complex types of private information flow, such as sending a *bcc* message over email. One gets different complete logics for each case. But *DEL* changed the game. All relevant structure triggering different updates is put in matching event models $\boldsymbol{E}$, and the logic for the special case is then a direct instance of the above 'mother logic' of $\langle \boldsymbol{E}, e\rangle\varphi$. In this light, characterizing specific update functions may have some value, but the real logical insight is the general product update mechanism. Is the latter perspective, then, the best constructive counterpart to a postulational approach to update?

Belief and priority update Similar points can be made about belief revision. One can capture complete logics for specific revision policies, as we have shown. But one can also work at the level of product update with 'plausibility event models', where agents now may think it more plausible that one event occurred rather than another. Update works with the priority rule that strict event plausibility overrides prior plausibility[26]:

$$(s, e) \leq (t, f) \quad \text{iff} \quad (s \leq t \wedge e \leq f) \quad \vee e < f$$

[25] As an illustration, an event model with two signals $!\varphi$, $!\neg\varphi$, with the first more plausible than the second, generalizes the above radical upgrade $\Uparrow\varphi$, which typically also had this over-ruling character for worlds that satisfied the distinguished triggering proposition φ.

[26] Here E is the earlier existential modality over all worlds in the model, accessible or not.

The key recursion axiom for the 'mother logic' is given in [1]:

$$\langle \boldsymbol{E}, e\rangle\langle\leq\rangle\varphi \quad \leftrightarrow (Pre_e \wedge (\vee_{e\leq finE}\langle\leq\rangle\langle \boldsymbol{E}, f\rangle\varphi \vee (\vee_{e<finE} E\langle \boldsymbol{E}, f\rangle\varphi))$$

We will not analyze this approach further, but as observed in our earlier discussion, this seems this seems the most general dynamic-epistemic counterpart to the postulational approach of dynamic doxastic logic.[27]

4.2 Updating Neighborhood Models for Evidence

It is hard to roam for long in modal logic without finding Krister Segerberg's traces. Another long-standing interest of his are *neighborhood models* [23] that have been used recently as a model for the epistemological notion of *evidence* and its dynamics (cf. [35] for technical details of what follows).

Static neighborhood logic An epistemic accessibility relation encodes an agent's current range of worlds after some history of informational events. If we want to retain some of the latter 'evidence', a set of neighborhoods (sets of worlds) does well—where we think of the current range as the intersection of all evidence sets.[28] The simplest neighborhood models, and all that we consider here, have just one family $\boldsymbol{N}$ of sets on a domain of worlds. We then interpret a matching evidence modality as follows:

$$\boldsymbol{M}, s \models \Box\varphi \quad \text{iff} \quad \textit{there is a set } X \textit{ in } \boldsymbol{N} \textit{ with } \boldsymbol{M}, t \models \varphi \textit{ for all } t \in X$$

The base logic of this notion is that of a monotone modality that does not necessarily distribute over either disjunction or conjunction. This generalization of modal logic supports correspondence analysis.[29] Neighborhood models support many epistemic notions. At least in finite models, one can define (cautious evidence-based) *belief* as what is true in all intersections of maximally overlapping families of evidence.[30]

Evidence dynamics: two samples In this setting, our pilot system *PAL* for information update can be seen as mixing different update actions into its public announcements $!\varphi$. The first is *evidence addition* $+\varphi$, adding the denotation $[[\varphi]]$ in the current model as one more piece of evidence to the current evidence family $\boldsymbol{N}$. The dynamic logic of this action can be determined completely. Here is one key recursion axiom:

---

27 Other ways of achieving generality in constructive update logics include the *PDL*-style *program format* of [30], specifying intended relation changes in models. [12] defines a merge of action models and programs that represents realistic social scenarios. We leave a correspondence analysis to another occasion.

28 If not all given sets overlap, we need more subtle views of conflicting evidence.

29 For instance, the *K*-axiom $\Box\wedge_i\psi_i \leftrightarrow \wedge_i\Box\psi_i$ forces *N* to be generated from a binary accessibility relation—provided we read it with an infinitary conjunction.

30 There are links with modeling beliefs in relational plausibility models here that we ignore.

$$\langle +\varphi \rangle \Box \psi \quad \leftrightarrow \quad (\Box \langle + \rangle \varphi \quad \vee U(\varphi \to \psi))$$

Again, the content of this principle can be determined by a correspondence argument:

Fact
An abstract update function on a universe of neighborhood models satisfies the recursion axiom for evidence addition iff each new evidence set is a superset of either some old evidence set or of the set $[[\varphi]]$.[31]

A second aspect of a public announcement $!\varphi$ that now gets into its own is *removal of the evidence* for $\neg\varphi$. The general new operation $-\psi$ removes all evidence sets from the current family $\boldsymbol{N}$ that are included in $[[\psi]]$. Complete recursion axioms are known for removal and the evidence modality, as well as belief, though a considerable extension of the standard static modal base languages over evidence models is required.[32] Here is one relevant principle, using a notion of evidence conditional on $\neg\varphi$ being true:

$$\langle -\varphi \rangle \Box \psi \leftrightarrow (E\neg\varphi \ \to \ \Box_{\neg\varphi} \langle -\varphi \rangle \psi)$$

We leave a correspondence analysis of recursion axioms for removal to future work.

Clearly, we have only scratched the surface here, but hopefully, the reader has seen that our analysis still makes sense when the semantic modeling of dynamic epistemic logic undergoes a drastic neighborhood extension of a sort that Krister Segerberg has long ago proposed for dynamic doxastic logic [11, 24].

5 Further Directions

We have shown how modal correspondence brings together the postulational format of *AGM* theory and dynamic doxastic logic with the constructive model transformation style of dynamic-epistemic logic. Our technical illustrations were very simple, and we opened up more new problems than closing old ones. Several technical and conceptual issues were already raised in the text. In this section we briefly mention a few more.

Extended semantic formats We have worked with binary accessibility relations for knowledge and belief. This analysis should be extended to ternary relational models, where plausibility can be world-dependent. Likewise, the analysis needs to be taken to the realm of neighborhood models, a natural finer modeling for belief and evidence.

---

[31] Recursion axioms for new beliefs under evidence addition extend the base language for evidence models to *conditional belief* in two basic varieties that had not surfaced so far.

[32] This is remarkable, since dealing with operations of contraction or removal has long been considered a stumbling block to constructive update logics. The reason why it works in the neighborhood setting after all is the richer model structure one is working on.

Group knowledge and belief At the start of this paper, we said that a multi-agent perspective is crucial to *DEL*-style logics, but soon this social aspect vanished. One should also analyze update postulates for common knowledge or belief in our style.[33]

'Dancing with the stars': propositional dynamic logic Common knowledge or belief go beyond the modal base language, being iterated modalities as found in dynamic logic *PDL*: another lifelong interest of Krister Segerberg. Iteration occurs naturally in dynamic-epistemic logic, also in the dynamic action component, as with repeated announcement or measurement. The resulting logical systems can be highly complex: cf. [19] on *PAL* with iteration, and [2] on limit phenomena with iterated radical update. Still *PDL* is no obstacle to our analysis. There have been some striking advances in the treatment of modal frame correspondence for non-first-order principles like Löb's Axiom for provability logic of Segerberg's Axiom for dynamic logic, making them fall under an extended Sahlqvist syntax matching the system *LFP+FO*, first-order logic with added fixed-point operators. New results and references are found in [27, 36].

Temporal setting and procedural information Both dynamic doxastic logic and *DEL* focus on single update steps. But equally essential is the temporal horizon. We make sense of local event in terms of global scenarios: a conversation, a process of inquiry, or a game. This 'procedural information' [15] suggests interfacing dynamic logics with temporal logics of knowledge and belief [1, 4, 20]. Existing results at interface take the form of *representation theorems* for 'update evolution': cf. [32]. One obvious question is how our correspondence results relate to representation theorems in the area of logics of belief. cf. [7].

General model theory The proofs in this paper were very simple. The recursion axioms all had Sahlqvist syntax (cf. the textbook [5]). One would like a correspondence analysis of axioms for belief change at the latter level of generality. Moreover, correspondence is not the only abstract analysis of concrete modal logics. The mechanism of model change behind the dynamic-epistemic logics in this paper invites reflection on their general features as modal logics. In an earlier book for Krister Segerberg, I gave a Lindström Theorem capturing basic modal logic in terms of bisimulation invariance and compactness. It would be of interest to take this further to capture the essentials of dynamic modal logics of model change.

Coda: have we really dealt with all logics of belief change? Do our two protagonists of dynamic-doxastic and dynamic-epistemic logic exhaust the field? My first attempt at doing modal logic of belief revision in [26] worked over a universe of information stages in the style of Beth or Kripke models for intuitionistic logic. An update with hard information was defined as a *minimal upward move* to a stage where the new information holds, while revision involved backtracking to the past and then going forward again to incorporate new information in conflict with what we thought so

[33] No complete dynamic logic has been given yet for changes in common belief produced by radical upgrade. Technical difficulties here might require a redesign of the base language to an analogue of the 'epistemic *PDL*' of [29], a system defined for the purpose of stating recursion axioms for common knowledge with product update.

far. I am not sure how this third view relates to either *DDL* or *DEL*, though it, too, offers abstract spaces for a wide array of update actions.

6 Conclusion

We have shown how the two main logic approaches to belief change, Segerberg's dynamic doxastic logic and the *DEL* tradition, co-exist in the perspective of modal frame correspondence. Indeed, 'modal logic of belief revision' has two dual aspects that belong together. This much was our contribution to translatability and interaction between frameworks. Our evidence was a set of very simple technical observations—but around these, many new problems came to light. To me, this agenda of unknowns seems a virtue of the proposed analysis. Krister and I have our work cut out for us. Finally, a confession is in order. In starting this study, I thought the main beneficiary would be *DDL*, as it could now import new ideas from the pressure-cooker of *DEL*. But as will be clear at various places in the paper, I now feel that a correspondence perspective also raises serious issues about best design for dynamic-epistemic logics, rethinking their striking deviant feature of being non-substitution-closed. And hence, I submit that both sides will benefit from the style of analysis presented here.

References

1. Baltag, A., & Smets, S. (2008). A qualitative theory of dynamic interactive belief revision. In G. Bonanno, W. van der Hoek, & M. Woolridge (Eds.), *Texts in logic and games* (Vol. 3). (pp. 9–58). Amsterdam: Amsterdam University Press.
2. Baltag, A., & Smets, S. (2009). Group belief dynamics under iterated revision: fixed points and cycles of joint upgrades. *Proceedings TARK XII* (pp. 41–50). Stanford.
3. Baltag, A., Moss, L., & Solecki, S. (1998). The logic of public announcements common knowledge and private suspicions. *Proceedings TARK 1998* (pp. 43–560). Los Altos: Morgan Kaufmann Publishers.
4. Belnap, N., Perloff, M., & Xu, M. (2001). *Facing the future*. Oxford: Oxford University Press.
5. Blackburn, P., de Rijke, M., & Venema, Y. (2000). *Modal logic*. Cambridge: Cambridge University Press.
6. Boutilier, C. (1994). Conditional logics of normality: A modal approach. *Artificial Intelligence*, *68*, 87–154.
7. Dégrémont, C. (2010). The temporal mind: observations on belief change in temporal systems. *Dissertation* ILLC, University of Amsterdam.
8. Fagin, R., Halpern, J., Moses, Y. & Vardi, M. (1995). *Reasoning about knowledge*. Cambridge, MA: The MIT Press
9. Gäerdenfors, P. (1988). *Knowledge in flux*. Cambridge, MA: The MIT Press.
10. Gerbrandy, J. (1999). Bisimulations on planet kripke. *Dissertation* ILLC, University of Amsterdam.
11. Girard, P. (2008). Modal logics for belief and preference change, *Dissertation* Department of Philosophy, Stanford University (ILLC-DS-20008-04).
12. Girard, P., Liu, F. & Seligman, J. (2011) *A product model construction for PDL*. Departments of Philosophy, Auckland University, and Tsinghua University.

13. Halpern, J., & Vardi, M. (1989). The complexity of reasoning about knowledge and time, I: Lower bounds. *Journal of Computer and System Sciences*, *38*, 195–237.
14. Holiday, W., Hoshi, T., & Icard, Th. (2011). Schematic validity in dynamic epistemic logic: decidability. In H. van Ditmarsch, J. Lang & S. Ju, (Eds.) *Proc's LORI-III, Guangzhou*, Springer Lecture Notes in Computer Science (Vol. 6953) (pp. 87–96).
15. Hoshi, T. (2009). Epistemic dynamics and protocol information. *Ph.D. thesis* Department of Philosophy, Stanford University (ILLC-DS-2009-08).
16. Leitgeb, H., & Segerberg, K. (2007). Dynamic doxastic logic: why, how, and where to? *Synthese*, *155*, 167–190.
17. Lewis, D. (1973). *Counterfactuals*. Oxford: Blackwell.
18. Liu, F. (2011). *Reasoning about preference dynamics*. Springer, Heidelberg: Synthese Librray.
19. Miller, J., & Moss, L. (2005). The undecidability of iterated modal relativization. *Studia Logica*, *97*, 373–407.
20. Parikh, R., & Ramanujam, R. (2003). A knowledge-based semantics of messages. *Journal of Logic, Language and Information*, *12*, 453–467.
21. Rodenburg, P. (1986). Intuitionistic correspondence theory. *Dissertation* Mathematical Institute, University of Amsterdam.
22. Rott, H. (2007). Information structures in belief revision. In P. Adriaans & J. van Benthem (Eds.), *Handbook of the philosophy of information* (pp. 457–482). Amsterdam: Elsevier Science Publishers.
23. Segerberg, K. (1971). *An essay in classical modal logic*. Philosophical Institute: University of Uppsala.
24. Segerberg, K. (1995). Belief revision from the point of view of doxastic logic. *Bulletin of the IGPL*, *3*, 534–553.
25. Segerberg, K. (1999). Default logic as dynamic doxastic logic. *Erkenntnis*, *50*, 333–352.
26. van Benthem, J. (1989) Semantic parallels in natural language and computation. In H-D. Ebbinghaus et al. (Eds.), Logic colloquium, Granada 1987 (pp. 331–375). North-Holland, Amsterdam.
27. van Benthem, J., Bezhanishvili, G., & Hodkinson, I. (2011). Sahlqvist correspondence for modal μ-calculus. *Studia Logica*, to appear.
28. van Ditmarsch, H. (2005). Prolegomena to dynamic logic for belief revision. *Synthese*, *147*, 229–275.
29. van Benthem, J., van Eijck, J., & Kooi, B. (2006). Logics of communication and change. *Information and Computation*, *204*, 1620–1662.
30. van Benthem, J., & Liu, F. (2007). Dynamic logic of preference upgrade. *Journal of Applied Non-Classical Logics*, *17*, 157–182.
31. van Benthem, J. (2007). Dynamic logic of belief revision. *Journal of Applied Non-Classical Logics*, *17*, 129–155.
32. van Benthem, J., Gerbrandy, J., Hoshi, T., & Pacuit, E. (2009). Merging frameworks for interaction. *Journal of Philosophical Logic*, *38*(2009), 491–526.
33. Aucher, G. (2004). A combined system for update logic and belief revision. *Master of Logic Thesis*, ILLC, University of Amsterdam.
34. van Benthem, J. (2010). *Modal logic for open minds*. Stanford: CSLI Publications.
35. van Benthem, J., & Pacuit, E. (2011). Dynamic logic of evidence-based beliefs. *Studia Logica*, *99*(1), 61–92.
36. van Benthem, J. (2011). *Logical dynamics of information and interaction*. Cambridge: Cambridge University Press.
37. van Ditmarsch, H., van der Hoek, W., & Kooi, B. (2007). *Dynamic epistemic logic*. Cambridge: Cambridge University Press.

Appendix A
Curriculum Vitæ

All my life I have been in education: as a student, as a teacher, as a researcher. An account of my life may therefore naturally be divided into periods corresponding to the institutions of learning where I have been active and the people I met there.

Early Years (1936–54)

I was born in 1936 in Skövde, a small city in the southern part of Sweden. Between the ages of six and ten I lived in Stensele, a village of a few hundred inhabitants in the North on the Ume river. My parents were both apothecaries—my mother no less than my father—and in order to obtain a royal privilege to operate an *apotek* (roughly, a big pharmacy) my parents had decided to try a part of the country where no member of our family had ever been before. My first school was of a type long since abandoned: in each class-room there were two classes each covering one of two consecutive years and both taught at the same time by one and the same teacher. Thus one teacher had years 1 and 2, another had years 3 and 4, and yet another had years 5 and 6. It was not a big school: three teachers and altogether certainly fewer than one hundred children, including a substantial number of children from even more isolated villages. (The teacher for the years 3 and 4, Margareta Ljunglöf, was the aunt of Lars Svenonius who, much later, was to teach me recursion theory in Uppsala (before ending up at the University of Maryland).)

In 1946 I was sent down the Ume river some 200 km to Umeå, the city on the Baltic where that magnificent river ends. This was necessary in order for me to receive my secondary school education, in those days reserved for the privileged classes. It was far from home, but I was well taken care of by a family. with whom I was lodged.

Then my parents moved with me, my brother and my sister to Kiruna in the Far North where my father had applied for and been given a bigger *apotek*. Kiruna, politically one of the reddest cities of Sweden, was a mining town of, what can it have been?, some 10,000. Here we belonged in the bourgeois class along with doctors (and one veterinarian), lawyers, teachers, engineers, clergy, army officers.

R. Trypuz (ed.), *Krister Segerberg on Logic of Actions*,
Outstanding Contributions to Logic 1, DOI: 10.1007/978-94-007-7046-1,

Our next door neighbour, a colonel, was the commander of the famous Jägarskolan, an elite regiment specially trained for warfare in the high mountain area. In those days only some 5 % of the population would send their children to what was then called *läroverk* (high school), something that created a certain tension with the other children; there were areas of the city I would be afraid to visit on my own. The adults seemed unaware of this: to them the city was safe, but for me, as a child, it was not. It always surprised me that one of my socialist friends would often speak, with expectant relish, of the day when the Revolution would come and I and my family would be dealt with. (Yes, he is still a friend; it is hard to explain.)

Kiruna is situated about one hour by train north of the Arctic Circle. Nowadays it is possible to drive all the way across the mountains to Narvik in Norway, but in those days the road ended in Kiruna. But, thanks to the mining industry, the railway to Narvik was already there (something that was important during the Second World War). In the summer there are some thirty days when the sun never sets in Kiruna, and in the winter equally many days when it never rises. Actually I did not experience the mid-night sun that much since my family would spend most of the summer school breaks in the south of Sweden. In those days one didn't fly; train was the only possibility. The journey would take up to 30 h—twenty-four to Stockholm, then change trains. Kiruna was an isolated place. For me, those summer months were a lifeline to civilization. This division between normal life most of the time and privileged life during a limited periods was somehow reflected later in my studies and my career.

I had decided early on that I was going to become an astronomer; I owned a couple of books on astronomy which I read and reread. But then music came into my life when at twelve or thirteen I was given a violin by my parents, and a couple of years later a piano. It took me a long time to realize that my playing would never amount to much: I had started too late. *(Much later the importance of starting early was brought home to me when I sat in on a course at Stanford with Paul J. Cohen, the Fields medallist: he and some friends had started a Club for Group Theory while still in high school.)*

Military Years (1954–56)

In 1954 I graduated from high-school. In those days military service was compulsory in Sweden. I was "sentenced" to 15 months with the coast artillery, but I actually ended up doing 2 years. The additional 9 months, by my own free choice, were spent at the Royal Swedish Naval College outside Stockholm. I didn't much mind the military training. Perhaps it was even good in some respects: it may have induced a modicum of discipline in a rather immature young man.

On the other hand it may have been a liability when much later I became Head of a Philosophy Department. There is of course something one may call intellectual discipline, but military discipline is something else. Academics are not good at taking orders!

Undergraduate Years (1956–59)

Uppsala I. With military service finally over, Uppsala was next. What I remember most from my first year at that venerable university (founded in 1477) was the loneliness. The math courses I followed were mainly delivered *ex cathedra* and taken by over 300 students. The teachers were good, no criticism there. But the way things were set up in Swedish universities (and still are) one normally takes one subject at the time. Thus the only students I met were other math students, most of them first-year students like myself. I don't know if math students are different from other students, but *for me* it was not a good year. Perhaps it was I who was not very good at making friends.

In any case it was a god-send when one day I ran into a girl who, full of enthusiasm, had just returned from a year on a scholarship in an American college. It would be easy for me to get one too, she said: just write to the Sweden America Foundation. Which I did. The result: a scholarship at Columbia College. I could not believe my luck!

Columbia. So I spent the following 2 years, 1957–59, at Columbia, getting my B.A. in mathematics (or A.B., as it is called at Columbia). The scholarship was actually given for as many years as it would take to get my degree, but I decided two would be enough. I now think that that may have been the wrong decision: I should have accepted to enter as a sophomore and got 3 years. But I thought I was already getting too old.

I spent my first week at Columbia as a chemistry major. But when I found out how much lab work was required for a degree in that subject, I changed to physics where it would be possible to stay theoretical. The two physics courses I took that fall semester were interesting and well taught (one of the professors was a Nobel Prize winner!), but for some reason I decided to switch once more, this time to mathematics. Of the professors in the math department I fondly remember two older gentlemen, de Lorche and Kolchin. (From the former I learnt the definition of a compact topological space: one that can be policed by a finite number of arbitrarily near-sighted cops.) Yet another interesting professor was Serge Lang, whose personal teaching style was enjoyable but demanding; at least I found it quite a challenge.

At Columbia I studied not just mathematics: in order to get my degree I also had to fulfill a number of general requirements. The ones I particularly liked were a 1 year sequence of literature/fine-arts/music and a 1 year course in what was called Western Civilization, a course for which Columbia College is famous. Both courses were excellent, but the one that I found particularly interesting was the latter. The Western Civ readings were all original texts, from the Greeks through the ages up until the present, including not only philosophers but also people like Darwin, Weber, Toynbee, Freud, Marx and even Lenin, Stalin and Hitler. The pace was horrific: one author a week. (Homer one week! Plato one week! Aristotle one week! ...) I remember later telling one of my Swedish philosophy professors about this; he shuddered. Why not rather one semester per author? The answer is of course that by doing it the Columbia way we were dragged through a lot of material that we may never have come across otherwise—this way we would at least become aware of it and so be able to re-visit it if there was ever a reason to do so. I understand my professor's reaction, but I am still extremely grateful to my *alma mater* for the rudiments of an education outside philosophy.

But it was not only an academic eduction I received at Columbia. There is a component in the U.S. undergraduate education, at least as I experienced it, that the whole person should be developed. Thus I was expected to work two hours a day during the week as part of my scholarship; it was in return for this that I got my three meals a day. My job was to work in one of the student eating halls, either waiting at tables or standing behind a counter serving coffee or other items. For me this was a novel but not unpleasant experience.

Another experience was living in dorms. In the military I had of course done this before—then we could be up to 24 men to a room, while here we were only two or three. During both my Columbia years, Ole Kristian Grimnes, now an emeritus professor of history at Oslo University, was one of my room-mates. Another acquaintance from this time was Johan Jørgen Holst. One striking thing about Holst was that he would always carry a copy of Foreign Affairs with him. Therefore I should not have been surprised that he later ended up foreign minister of Norway.

Graduate Years: Uppsala (1959–1965)

Uppsala II. When I returned to Uppsala in 1959 the next task was to get the *fil. kand.* degree, the Swedish counterpart of the B.A. As Uppsala required a minimum of three subjects, I had to find two more in addition to the math I had already done. Theoretical physics was a natural choice for one subject; in effect, it was just more math, and I did it but without enormous enthusiasm. For my third subject, influenced by my Columbia experience, I decided to choose philosophy. And, as it turned out, never looked back.

I found the environment in the small philosophy department at Villavägen 7 congenial. Here the pace was slower, there was a common room, and the teachers would sometimes have time for conversation, especially the legendary Thorild Dahlquist. There were two chairs, one in Theoretical Philosophy (Konrad Marc-Wogau), the other in Practical Philosophy (Ingemar Hedenius). Marc-Wogau (who conducted his seminars in the afternoon) would always have a "post-seminar" at Kajsa's Kafferum, a small café in downtown Uppsala, whereas Hedenius (who had his seminar Saturday morning), would go with his disciples to a restaurant or, sometimes, invite them to his home, where Mrs Hedenius would have prepared lunch. These were important watering-holes for young thirsty students.

Yet another member of the philosophy department in those days was Lennart Åqvist, who may have been the one who introduced me to deontic logic. It may also have been he who told me about a summer school of logic in Vasa (Vaasa), Finland in the summer of 1963.[1] In any case, we both went there. The other participants consisted of a group of silent Finnish students who kept to themselves and never said a word. (Evidently that group included Risto Hilpinen, Juhani Pietarinen and Raimo Tuomela, who much later would become my friends.) The main attraction was Andrzej Mostowski who gave a week-long series of lectures on the development of

[1] Finland is a bilingual country: "Vasa" in Swedish, "Vaasa" in Finnish.

modern logic. But there were also lectures by Jaakko Hintikka and Georg Henrik von Wright. It was exciting for us young students to meet these well-known philosophers and to be able to talk to them. Mostowski gave his lectures in the morning and would not participate in the more philosophical programme in the afternoon. I remember von Wright, playfully, suggesting that Mostowski be invited to participate—might it not be interesting to hear what a great mathematician would have to say about our philosophical problems? And I remember Hintikka's dismissive attitude: no, just let him do what he is good at doing—he would probably have nothing of interest to say about the philosophical questions that we were discussing. I thought it was interesting that of the two famous Finnish philosophers it was the the younger who stood for decorum in contrast with the playfulness of the older.

But the Vasa adventure was an exception to my ordinary student life. Looking back I wonder what I really did during all those years: 1959–65. In the words of the poet[2]:

All those days that came and went:
little did I know that that was my life.

Six years! I worked alone. After having passed enough required courses I embarked on writing two theses, first one for the *fil. kand.* degree and then one for the *fil. lic.* degree. The former, on intuitionistic mathematics, was immature and bizarre, I now realize, and certainly not very good; I can only hope that no copies survive. The other was on what Sören Halldén has called the logic of nonsense, a three-valued logic first invented by the Russian mathematician Bochvar [1].

*

As I will probably never write a proper biography, let me take this opportunity to say something about four Swedish academics whom I met during my formative years and who in different ways were important for my development as a philosopher.

Konrad Marc-Wogau (1902–91). When I became a student in the Uppsala philosophy department in 1959 there were only two permanent staff members, the professor of Theoretical Philosophy and the professor of Practical Philosophy. "My" professor, the former of the two, was Konrad Marc-Wogau ("Marc" was his father's last name, "von Wogau" his mother's maiden name). He had an interesting background in pre-revolutionary Moscow, which he left in his late teens. (In his home there was a portrait of him as a young boy painted by Pasternak, a well-known portrait painter and the father of the later Nobel Prize winning author.) I think of Marc-Wogau as a historian of philosophy, particularly as a Kant scholar, but he had also written on the topic of sense-data when that was in vogue and later on historical explanation, and he maintained an interest in psychology throughout his life. Unlike many he was philosophically tolerant. He would of course stand up against nonsense—he belonged to those who protested against Nazism in the thirties—but, important to me, he welcomed my interest in logic even though (as he would say) he himself was

[2] "Alla dessa dagar som kom och gick / inte visste jag att det var livet." (Stig Johansson)

not a logician. (But he did write a high-school textbook in logic.) Like several of the people mentioned in this article he was a private man, and I cannot pretend I knew him well. But he exercised some intellectual virtues which he taught by example: careful in argumentation, critical of nonsense, yet tolerant of honest efforts.

Ingemar Hedenius (1908–1982). The other full professor in the department was Ingemar Hedenius, a professor of practical philosophy who cared deeply about morality. He came from an upper-class family in Stockholm; his father was a medical doctor and *livmedicus* to the King; his grandfather, a professor of medicin, was for a while the rector of Uppsala University. As an adult Ingemar Hedenius revolted against this highly bourgeois back-ground. Through books, essays and newspaper articles he became nationally very well known. Before and during the Second World War he was an important critic of Nazism, then he became an influential critic of the Church, and during the last part of his life he was involved in the debate about euthanasia. Personally eloquent, he was a brilliant writer and a relentless polemicist. His attitude towards logic and logicians was ambivalent.On the one hand he valued logic (for example, it was useful in shooting down the bishops) and he was a friend of Anders Wedberg (professor at Stockholm University and the person who may be said to have brought modern logic to Sweden). But he was also suspicious of formal logic and formal logicians, as if he feared that they might take jobs away from real philosophers. I am not sure exactly why I think he was important for me; I suppose he fascinated me, as he fascinated many. I was impressed, sometimes chocked, by the ferocity with which he would attack opponents in public debate, not afraid to use words one would have thought to be unprintable (I am talking about the 1950s and 1960s).

Thorild Dahlquist (1923–2009). One striking thing about Socrates as a philosopher was that he never published. It is more difficult nowadays to make it as a professional academic philosopher if you don't publish, yet even today some departments will have their own Socrates: a member who enjoys enormous prestige locally, a "holy man" fawned on by students, yet one who publishes little or nothing. In Uppsala, Thorild Dahlquist was such a person. Thorild—everyone would always use his first name—was one of the first staff members I met when I came to the department as a student, and he died only after I had retired. He was a living legend already when I first met him, the confessed *amor intellectualis* of one Swedish novelist as well as of generations of students. Thorild had read everything, he remembered everything, and he could explain, analyze, defend and criticize everything. He was one of these enigmatic figures students will never tire of trying to understand: who was he really? His erudition was unmatched, and he was always accessible: if you had a question about anything philosophical, you could always approach him and get an answer, for example at Café Alma where he would maintain something like a *Stammtisch.* He was also very much engaged in moral matters. For example, like Hedenius he was fervently anti-anti-semitic. He would speak in complete sentences (like David Lewis, the only other person I have met who would do this). His memory was unmatched (of this he was proud). The only problem was that he did not publish. It is not as if he could not write: he wrote more letters than most people, always precisely formulated, and they could be long. The honorary doctorate he eventually got, thanks to Stig Kanger, was richly deserved.

Sören Halldén (1923–2010). Another person who played a rôle in my career as a student was Sören Halldén, professor at Lund University but educated in Stockholm and Uppsala. Like several other people mentioned in this article, he was also a very private person: a scholar who would sit at home and write book after book and rarely be seen. But even if I never saw much of him he was still a great support. Our first real meeting was when he was the opponent at the defence of my dissertation for the degree of *filosofie licentiat* in 1964. Later it was he who encouraged me to publish a number of articles in *Theoria*, a journal of which he was the editor, and then told me to collect them and use them as a doctoral dissertation in Uppsala. Doctoral disputations were a big deal in Sweden in those days, and I had taken it for granted that I would have to try to compose some massive tome in the traditional way—how, I had no idea. But in the faculties of medicine and the natural sciences, doctorands had begun to use a handful of published papers in place of a traditional treatise. It had not occurred to me that my papers would be enough for a doctorate, but as it turned out when they were presented in 1968 they were. It was also Sören Halldén who later designated me as editor of *Theoria*, which I was to edit during part of the 1970s. Without him my academic career would have been different.

Graduate Years: Stanford (1965–68)

My thesis for the *fil. lic.* degree was nothing to write home about, but it earned me my first publication and was perhaps one reason why I was accepted at Stanford. Here is how it happened.

In 1962 I had married Anita Forslund, and by 1965 we had two sons. Anita was the one to suggest that we should try to get me an education in the U.S.; in particular, she wanted for us to go to California. I accordingly wrote to two philosophy departments, Stanford and U.C. Berkeley, asking for advice and hoping for the best. The result was interesting: Patrick Suppes personally wrote a response the same day he got my letter, welcoming me to his department. Berkeley never answered. Which is perhaps just as well: we went to Stanford with our boys and had a wonderful 3 years there (1965–1968). (Our first daughter was born during that time.)

Why was Stanford so wonderful? Or more carefully, why did I find Stanford so wonderful? For one thing, it was a feast, a 3 years intellectual party. What an impressive cast of professors: in philosophy Suppes, Hintikka, Føllesdal, in mathematics Feferman, Kreisel, Paul Cohen, in economics Kenneth Arrow, in statistics Herman Chernoff. I took or audited courses with all of them. And there were interesting visitors, for example, Dick Jeffrey. One other visitor was Stig Kanger, who was later to have a big influence on me and my career.[3] (For the record: it was thanks to Kanger that Brian Chellas and I became friends, Brian having been assigned as his teaching assistant. Among the other Ph.D. candidates were Raimo Tuomela and Zoltan Dömötör. (The latter arrived as *Dömötör* but left as *Domotor*, six dots lost in transition.) Yet another friend was David Miller, an expert on croquet as well as on Popper.)

[3] For a collection of reminiscences of Stig Kanger, see [6].

But of course the greatest experience at Stanford was meeting Dana Scott, who became my thesis adviser. The beginning of our acquaintance was not auspicious. I still don't know exactly what happened, but evidently we had agreed on meeting in Scott's office on a certain day, only somehow we had different ideas of which day. In those days Scott lived in San Francisco and would have to drive down the Bayshore each time he was to visit the Stanford campus. Somehow I got it wrong and did not show up as expected. I suppose having had to make that extra drive in vain must have been irritating—this was a few days before the beginning of term—for Scott was not in a good mood when we finally met. For that meeting I had brought with me a specimen of my work, a completeness proof for a simple tense-logic proposed by von Wright. I stated the result. Scott leaned back in his chair and thought for a while. Yes, the result seemed correct. Then, after a short pause: "But isn't that obvious?" Not obvious to von Wright. Not obvious to me. But, yes, of course, as I came to realize, obvious. At that time I did not feel so good; this was the nadir of our relationship. But for some reason he didn't give up on me; instead he gave me something to read and asked me to come back when I had. I did, and I was on. I remember other students saying they had found Scott difficult. I never did. Even this first time, he was entitled to feeling peeved over the missed appointment, and right in his evaluation of the proof.

It was through Scott that I became aware of the great amount of then unpublished work in modal logic that had been carried out in California, especially at U.C.L.A. but also by E. J. Lemmon and Scott himself. Of my 3 years at Stanford, the first one was dominated by preparing for the prelims and generally settling in. But at some time in what must have been the second year Scott gave me what is now known as the "Lemmon notes" to read. Lemmon had died in July 1966, just 3 days after having completed a draft of what was meant to be the first chapter of a monograph on intensional logic that he and Scott had planned together. I found this draft congenial, and they inspired, not to say formed, much of my work in modal logic. For some reason Scott was in no hurry to get them published. When eventually they were published more than 10 years later, the momentum was gone [2].

Yes, working with Scott was the high point of my intellectual career. I never again met anyone with whom it was so interesting and so fruitful to talk philosophy. By the way, I still think of Scott as "Scott". Everyone else who came to know him, including my fellow students, would after a while call him "Dana". But to me Scott was always "Scott". I remember Kanger—Stig—would make jokes about it. I wonder whether Scott may have had a similar thing about Church: he would speak of him as "Professor Church". But then I guess most people did. I remember Mary Meyerhoff saying that Mrs Church was the only one who called Church "Alonzo". Mary should know since she worked for him in the J.S.L. office for several years.

Looking back I cannot help thinking that the best years of my professional life were the student years at Columbia and Stanford. I am extremely grateful for having had the privilege of receiving an education in the U.S. at a time when there was nothing better.

Intermediate Years (1968–72)

In May 1968 I returned briefly to Uppsala in order to defend my doctoral dissertation, consisting of five papers published in *Theoria* together with a thirty-page printed summary paid for by myself [3].[4] (My Stanford dissertation was completed in 1971 only after I had left Stanford [4].)

U.C.L.A. After little more than a month in Sweden I was back in the U.S., this time in Los Angeles, where I had been fortunate enough to get a 1-year combined position as half-time lecturer in the philosophy department and half-time assistant editor of *The Journal of Symbolic Logic* under Church.

I never saw much of Church, though. No one did: he would come into the J.S.L. office after 5 p.m. when everyone had left. In the morning we would find instructions for further work on slips of paper, written in his characteristic, round, almost child-like hand-writing. I sat in on his lectures, which were delivered from the manuscript of the never published vol. 2 of his classic textbook; he read them out as written, using the blackboard extensively but never once looking at us in the audience.

The rest of the department was more accommodating and extremely interesting, with a star-studded staff that included David Kaplan, David Lewis and Richard Montague. I was surprised but of course flattered that David Lewis would sit in on a course in modal logic that I gave one quarter. After having witnessed how Montague dealt with Erik Stenius, professor of philosophy at the University of Helsinki, who came through and gave a talk, I am glad it did not occur to Montague to join Lewis. What happened was this: Montague arrived 5 min late into Stenius's talk and took a seat at the back of the room. Almost immediately he interrupted Stenius, saying something like, "Is such-and-such what you are saying?" No, said Stenius. "Then is such-and-such what you are saying?" Again, no. "But then it must be that what you are saying is such-and-such?" For a third time, no. Then Montague got up, agitated: "In that case you are saying nothing!" And stormed out of the room. Probably feeling pleased with himself. At the time I did not know Stenius, but looking back, it is interesting to remember him as for once at the receiving end.

Åbo I. After my 4 years in California, given that I had come on an Exchange Student Visa, I had to leave the U.S. Not unexpectedly, Sweden had nothing to offer. Even today the academic career is difficult; young Ph.D.s wishing to remain in a university environment still worry about their future. But jobs were even more scarce in those days. My saving angel turned out to be Stig Kanger. He had had the same problem, and he had been able to solve it by becoming acting professor for many years (and ordinary professor only just before leaving) at the Åbo Academy after Erik Stenius, the incumbent—the very Stenius who was insulted by Montague—had been given the Swedish language chair of philosophy at Helsingfors University (Helsingin Yliopisto). Now that the Stenius-Kanger chair was vacant, I was appointed acting professor. (This chair was actually one of the original chairs when the Åbo Academy was founded in late 1917; its first holder was Edvard Westermarck, for whom it was created.)

---

[4] See above under the section on Halldén.

This first encounter with Finland was memorable and in many ways unrepresentative. Housing was difficult at the time, and we had been lucky to get the opportunity of being housed in a former summer home, a spacious two storey villa in the forrest on the shore of the Baltic. It was like something taken out of a Russian novel. Just one detail: when we arrived with all our furniture—no problem! We put it all at one end of the enormous drawing room, including our grand-piano, never mind that there already was one there. When my wife was hanging laundry outside one morning on a clothes line between two trees (there were no dryers in those days) one neighbor came over and greeted her by kissing her on the hand. In a completely natural fashion. Just like that! After a year we moved to a humbler abode, a town house in the city.

In those days the Swedish speaking Åbo was like a time capsule. The university was ruled by the professors. At faculty and senate meetings we were always seated in the order of *anciennitet*, a concept of seniority defined by rank and date of appointment, ordinary professors before acting professors before the few representatives of non-professorial teachers before the one or two student representatives (at those meetings when the latter three categories were allowed to attend). These were days when ceremonial things were taken seriously. [Later, in 1973 when I had become a *professor ordinariter*, I edited a miniature *Festschrift* in honour of Georg Henrik von Wright's 60th birthday named *Wright and wrong* [8], one professor sent me a handwritten letter officially terminating our friendship: he was outraged at the title which he felt was insulting to von Wright, and he vowed that he would never speak to me again. He kept his word. von Wright himself did not seem to mind.]

It was during this first sojourn in Åbo that I finally completed my Stanford dissertation. As it happened, the position as ordinary professor of philosophy at Åbo Academy had been declared vacant and applications invited. I did not have many publications; without the publication of my Stanford dissertation I would not have a chance. Here, once again, Kanger came to my rescue. In a matter of days he had my thesis retyped and mimeographed (there were no computers in those days, let alone LaTeX) and issued in his in-house series of publications [4]. Still, it had become a race against time. At Åbo Academy formalities were never to be trifled with. There was a last day for handing in specimina, as they were called (before noon, if I remember correctly), and it was clear that without my Stanford dissertation I would not stand a chance of being appointed. Copies of my master-piece as produced by Uppsala had to be delivered in Åbo, and the timing was not auspicious. I was saved by one of the other applicants for the chair, Ingmar Pörn, who was going to hand in his own papers in person at the very last minute and who happened to be in Uppsala. Ingmar was travelling from Uppsala to Åbo by the night-boat that arrived in the morning of the last day, and he agreed to take a copy of my *Essay* with him. As a result both our specimina were handed in on time. This was a magnanimous thing for a competing applicant to do! A few years later, Ingmar got the chair in Helsingfors after Stenius, but at the time there was of course no guarantee that that would happen.

As it turned out, this was the end of that dissertation. I foolishly declined an offer to publish it as it was, but I was not a student of Dana Scott for nothing. Scott's papers were always extremely well-written: . brilliant of content and elegant of style. I suppose I set my standards too high. When some time in the mid-seventies I had finally come around to a version I thought would be publishable, publishers were no longer interested.

Pittsburgh. *At this point let me mention an Andrew Mellon post-doctoral fellowship at the University of Pittsburgh 1971-72. This was a very unexpected boon that suddenly came my way. I still remember the excitement connected with the notification. We were having a faculty meeting of the Humanities Faculty in the Åbo Academy, seated in the usual order and behaving at our usual formal. Suddenly, in breach of all decorum the door is thrust open and a breathless young secretary, without waiting for her turn to speak, cries out, "Telephone from America for Acting Professor Segerberg". We would not have been more surprised if she had cried "Fire!". Transatlantic phone calls are not a big deal today, but forty years ago they were unheard of. Wondering what this was all about but full of self-importance I rose with as much calm and dignity as I could muster and followed the secretary, leaving my colleagues to wonder what on earth was going on.*

Pittsburgh, despite its reputation then, was a very liveable city. The department was a distinguished one, and it was a privilege to meet celebrities like Alan Ross Anderson, Nuel Belnap, Adolf Grünbaum, Nicholas Rescher in person. I attended Belnap's seminar but without being able to contribute much; I was very much in classical mood, as I still am. I had hoped to be allowed to sit in on Kurt Baier's seminar in ethics, but permission was denied—Baier did not want to compromise the intimacy of his group (I would have raised the number of students from, say, 15 to 16). Personally, the most important event during this year was the birth of our fourth child, another daughter.

Tenured Years (1972–2001)

During my career I have held, successively, three tenured jobs: at Åbo (Turku), Auckland, and Uppsala.[5]

Åbo II. Compared with the universities I already knew, Åbo Academy (in English today re-named the Åbo Academy University) provided a totally different surrounding. Totally different! It was almost surreal to be thrown into this environment which, although founded in 1917—the year of Finland's liberation from Russia "as a bulwark for Swedish speaking culture in Finland"—still retained a nineteenth century (and very pleasant) atmosphere. Åbo Academy is a small university, in those days even smaller than today: a singleton department! That is to say, when I arrived in 1969 I was the only staff member of the philosophy department. Trying to offer the few students something, I gave lectures in a number of areas where I have little or no formal competence, for example, history of philosophy, ethics, æsthetics, and philosophy of religion. It was not unpleasant; in fact, it was quite interesting. But of course it delayed my "real" work.

Finland is a country with two official languages, Finnish and Swedish, the former dominating: during my time, Finnish was the first language of 94 % of the population, while Swedish was the first language of the remaining 6 %. (I understand that today those figures are 95 and 5, respectively.) In Åbo there is also a Finnish language university (Turun Yliopisto, the University of Turku) with a very good philosophy

[5] "Åbo" is the Swedish, "Turku" the Finnish name. Cf. footnote 1.

department—actually, two good philosophy departments in two different faculties. In my day, when a department would have only one full professor, the two professors were Risto Hilpinen and Juhani Pietarinen. The collaboration with Hilpinen was particularly stimulating during the too few years that he was in town. Finnish professors at the time had a lot of authority, and I have the impression that Risto simply marched his students from the top of the hill where T.Y. is located to down by the river where my philosophy department was housed in a late nineteenth century villa. There was no language problem since we always used English—only natural, given that most of the relevant literature would be written in English and that we would write our papers in English anyway. Those were happy years!

One aspect of living in Finland was the relationship with the Soviet Union. In daily life it was not visible, but it was there, as a memory and as an unconscious consciousness. Finland was a part—an arch duchy—of Czarist Russia from 1809 to 1917, and during WWII Finland carried out two wars with the Soviet Union, the Winter War and the Continuation War. Against this background it was interesting that in the 1970s a certain academic contact was begun. In 1973 Finland's two eminent, internationally famous philosophers, Georg Henrik von Wright and Jaakko Hintikka, were invited to visit Moscow. The following year I was invited to what was called an All-Societ Conference in Logic in Moscow along with Dag Prawitz, a fellow Swede but at the time professor in Oslo (the successor of Arne Næss). I still remember the train ride, how at the border, when we were leaving Finland and entering Soviet territory, troops stormed the train and began to examine everyting—everything!—in our luggage. One detail: I have a habit of saving scrap paper with a clean reverse page (such as old non-personal letters, old drafts of papers) in order to use them for making temporary notes or sketching ideas. True to this custom I had brought a ream of such papers. It confused the soldiers who had to go through the entire material in order to ascertain that it contained nothing that could threaten the security of the Soviet Union.

Of the conference itself I don't remember much. The most important thing was to meet our Russian colleagues, for example, V. A. Smirnov; I also remember a very young G. E. Mints. But most important for me was the contact with Leo Esakia, who led a group in Tbilisi devoted to modal logic. This contact led to several visits in Tbilisi, where I also got to know Slava Meskhi and Rezo Gregolia. I shall never forget the long railway journey from Åbo via Moscow to Tbilisi with my family at a month long visit in 1978, which required three nights in a train. Our personal conductor in the train from Moscow served delicious tea round the clock and told us repeatedly what a great man Stalin had been. In Tbilisi I was invited to give two lectures, but after having given the first I was told that the second was cancelled. I never found out the reason for this change: was it because I had mentioned Hegel in my lecture, or was it something else I had said or done?

But the most important contact with the outside world during my Finnish years was with some colleagues in the U.S. After a 2-year stint as Dean of the Humanities Faculty 1974–76, a chore I found endurable and even mildly enjoyable (partly thanks to my wonderfully supportive and efficient secretary Maja Anckar) I was given a sabbatical, which I decided to spend at the University of Kansas, Lawrence. I had met Rex Martin of that department during his sabbatical in Helsinki, and it did not take him long to persuade me to come. As a result I spent a very pleasant year and a half in Lawrence.

The main events during the K.U. interlude were one workshop in Vancouver in early 1977 and one informal meeting in Boston, January 1978, both important, not to say pivotal, for my future research. Steve Thomason at Simon Fraser University, having decided he was done with recursion theory, the subject of his doctoral dissertation, had discovered modal logic. A man of action, and with a generous research grant, he invited some modal logicians he knew or knew about for an informal workshop: Kit Fine, Rob Goldblatt, and me. This turned out to be a memorable meeting in more ways than one. One memory is the fog which enveloped us throughout the entire week that we stayed together. It is a strange experience to live in fog—to be surrounded by fog day after day. And this was real fog, fog of nineteenth century London quality: people further away than ten feet might be conjectured but could not be visually identified. The more important memory is of a seminar conducted by Richard Ladner, who gave a talk about the new logic of programs that he and Michael Fischer had just developed at M.I.T. The modal logicians in the audience realized at once that this was really "just modal logic". Fischer and Ladner had solved the decision problem of their logic, but the problem of axiomatizing it remained. Kit became very enthusiastic and felt we should be able to solve it on the spot. But the problem turned out to be more difficult than so. When the fog lifted and the week was over, we still had not solved it. I seem to have been the only one of us to have pursued this research problem after we left. Eventually I was able to solve it and announced the result [5].

That summer of 1977 I was invited by Brian Chellas to teach summer school at the University of Calgary, and it was in Brian's seminar that I presented my response to the Ladner/Fischer challenge for the first time. (I remember Vera Dyson was in the audience, which made me a bit nervous, never having met her before.) Unfortunately there was a gap in the proof of one of the lemmas, but that I was to discover only in the evening on one of the the first days of 1978, the night before going up to Boston to give a presentation at a private meeting with Vaughan Pratt and Rohit Parikh. Patching up the proof later was not difficult, but the priority was lost, for in the meantime both Parikh and Dov Gabbay (and perhaps others) had developped their own (correct) proofs. *The matter does not seem so important today—the proof was after all only a small step forward, and much has happened since. Nevertheless, I found the experience humiliating* at the time, and the memory is still painful. Even today a scar remains—the embarrassment of having erred, the chagrin of having lost something irretrievable.

This experience is probably typical of (many? most? all?) academics. Ever since the days of the Greeks, academics will say that the most important thing is to seek the truth. But once you start looking for it, you quickly become committed, and before you know it, all that matters is that *you* find it. For the mountaineers who climbed Mount Everest and other peaks that had not been climbed before, being first was essential. Columbus would have been sorry if he had encountered a sign "Kilroy was here" when he came ashore in the Great Western Continent.

Auckland. Ah, the joys of being recruited! Of my three tenured jobs, this is the only one that was given to me on a silver platter. At least that is how it felt. When the University of Auckland offered me the chair of philosophy—Max Cresswell was the philosophy expert on the search committee—I happily accepted. Being in the same country as Cresswell, Rob Goldblatt and Robert Bull was a privilege. However, we were not in the same city, so unfortunately, even though we met numerous times, I did not see as much of them as I would have wanted.

I came to Auckland because the department needed a new H.O.D. (Head Of Department). The department had been ailing for a number of years, torn by strife. A directionless department, older staff members frustrated by not having received the academic recognition they felt was their due, younger staff members unhappy about their lack of influence—this is how I read the situation. The Vice-Chancellor told me in no uncertain terms that he expected me to clean up the mess (I am not sure his used those words, but that was the idea). I quickly found that the three difficult questions were: agreeing on the budget, dividing the teaching, and appointing new staff members. Of these questions, the last turned out to be the most difficult one. I have been surprised talking to American colleagues who have explained that appointments is usually not a problem in their departments, one main difference being that in the U.S. the standing of the department, nationally and internationally, is of overriding importance to all of its members. In New Zealand the ambition to be number one seemed to be less urgent. "But we *don't want* to be number one!", is a comment I would actually meet. It is interesting how conflicts have a life of their own, how long they can last, and how important they can be to the people involved. (Gulliver's Travels!) I am still convinced that if we had been not just the teaching staff of a philosophy department but the cabinet of a country with more violent traditions than New Zealand, the only question would have been who would manage to be first: I to have my colleagues arrested, or they to have me assassinated. Nowadays bygones are bygones and I like to think that we have all made up, but it took years. The Auckland philosophy department, I am proud to say, looks good today.

Among the many happy memories from this period of my life, to turn to them, are the encounters with two students, both unusually gifted, who since have made names for themselves, Adam J. Grove, an advanced student in computer science, and Michael Strevens, one of our own philosophy students. Each took one course ("paper", as it is called in New Zealand) with me. That all teaching had been so rewarding!

The interaction with Grove is relevant here. I had become interested in the theory of belief revision (having been privately tutored by David Makinson in Paris 1984), and that became the topic of the "paper". My own idea was that the theory that had been proposed by Peter Gärdenfors and then developed by him, Makinson and Carlos Alchourrón (the famous AGM trio) could be re-cast as an extension of modal logic. My research problem was to develop a model theoretic semantics for this theory. Following my own intuitions for what "natural" models would look like, I had arrived at a certain modelling; the snag was that it did not fit AGM. I was at my wit's end: AGM seemed so eminently plausible, my model theory seemed like the obvious candidate; so why did they not agree? That is, my modelling *almost* fitted

AGM, but the fit was not perfect—why? One morning when I came into the classroom we would use, Grove was there before me. "I think I have solved it", he said simply. And he had! I could not believe it: here he had a modelling that exactly fitted the AGM postulates. It was not that different from the modelling that I had developed; the difference was really just one detail, yet that detail made all the difference. I felt at the time—as I still do—that I would never have found Grove's modelling on my own, even though I had been so close. Later I realized the my modelling fitted KGM, the alternative logic of belief revision proposed by three computer scientists, Hirofumi Katsuno, Gösta Grahne and Alberto O. Mendelzon.

Digression: Why is it that even someone who tries very hard to keep an open mind may fail to do so? Why is it that one's own prejudices are so difficult to spot? In moral matters it is easier to understand. Certain moral ideas may define who we are, who we want to be; certain prejudices may somehow be integral to our identity—to question them would be to cut the ground from under our feet. In æsthetics we may be aware of prejudice, but sometimes we don't care. This is true also of culinary matters—if others don't care for what I consider a delicacy, I may still ask for a second helping; and however much some people in my family like red hot chili, I still don't. (I once met a Norwegian professor of anthropology, specializing in the ethnology of food, who assured me that the most delicious dish in the world is cow's head prepared in the old Norwegian way and served cut in half. What is particularly wonderful, according to this expert—who seemed very reliable, I must say—are some tiny pieces of flesh right behind the eyes.) But in formal work, prejudice of this kind presumably does not apply. So why is it so difficult to be aware of one's intellectual preconceptions, let alone to shed them? Why is it so difficult to keep an open mind?

Of contacts with the outside world during my Auckland years let me list some. Among those in New Zealand I have already mentioned Max Cresswell and Rob Goldblatt in Wellington and Robert Bull in Chirstchurch. But Pavel Tichý in Dunedin was also a friend and, after all, a fellow European. He was a hard man; whether he had been born hard or his unusually difficult life had made him hard, I don't know. I spent 2 weeks in his home in 1994 when I had been invited to his department as a Daniel Taylor Visiting Fellow. He had just been offered a chair in the Charles University in Prague, and he was torn between the alternatives: continuing his life in New Zealand, or returning to his country which he had left (illegally!) as a young man and which now offered him a future one did not know much about—this was still early days for the young Czech Republic. Just weeks after I left he was found dead in a stream in Dunedin. I miss Tichý as I miss Kanger.

The contact with Australia was never as intimate as I had thought it would be before coming to Auckland. However, the distance between New Zealand and Australia is greater than you may think from just looking at a globe or large-scale map (and, in those days at least, greater from Australia to New Zealand than from New Zealand to Australia). However, Richard Sylvan, *né* Routley, New Zealand born, provided friendship that was warm under the rough surface. I remember his surprise when my wife and I sawed up some logs and branches for firewood at his ranch outside Canberra; after that we seemed to have risen in his esteem. (I might add that our presence in Canberra was due to my wife's writing her Ph.D. dissertation on Christina Stead, an Australian author whose papers are kept in the A.N.U. library.)

Thanks to Hiroakira Ono my wife and I had the great privilege of spending many weeks on more than one occasion in Japan, and not only in Japan but in their home. Japan was extremely expensive in those days, and I suppose that that is why the Onos opened their delightful home to let us stay with them, a incomparable experience. Not only was the stay at J.A.I.S.T. (the Japan Advanced Institute of Scientific Research in Kanazawa) stimulating, but the setting—the cultural heritage, the Japanese cuisine, the beautiful bamboo forests—fascinating.

Among shorter visits from this period I would like to mention three. Biswambar Pahi invited me to spend 3 weeks lecturing at an Indian logic summer school in Jaipur, Rajasthan, that he arranged. To be able to visit this old cultural city and meet these intelligent and pleasant students from all over India was a great privilege. Furthermore, Anne Preller and Gisèle Fischer-Servi arranged for month-long visits to their departments in, respectively, Montpellier and Parma. On the non-professional side I particularly remember, from Montpellier, the nightingales in the garden outside our bed-room in Anne's house which she so generously let us use and, from Parma, the spaghetti that Gisèle's husband Mario, professor of mathematics, personally made from scratch.

And how could I not mention Futa Helu. founder and director in the Atenisi Institute of Tonga. His life's work, the establishment of an institution of learning in Tonga on the lines of the ancient Greeks, deserves to survive.

Uppsala III. In 1988 Stig Kanger unexpectedly died (at only sixty-four, on his way to Germany to receive a Humboldt Prize). When the Uppsala chair of theoretical philosophy was then advertized, it posed a big question for my wife and myself—bigger for me than for her. Uppsala was never my favorite city. I had a good job in a university I liked, and the difficulties in the department were now in the past. My New Zealand salary was considerably higher than what Uppsala would be able to offer. We owned a wonderful house directly on the Pacific Ocean, with three palm trees on a sandy beach, a ten foot tide coming and going twice a day, all this thirty minutes from campus and downtown Auckland. Wouldn't we be crazy to leave all that? (My colleagues at Victoria University said that we would.)

Perhaps we were. But we did. What decided the matter was perhaps our relatives. However much we liked New Zealand, we had no roots there. It didn't seem likely that our children would stay there. And retirement at 65 was mandatory in those days (it has changed since then).

So I applied for the Uppsala job and, in the end, got it, thus becoming the 49th incumbent of that chair (one of the oldest in the university, which itself was founded in 1477). At the time there was a good deal of student opposition against the appointment. It is true that Kanger pushed logic and its applications very far ("if it cannot be formalized, then it is not philosophy"—I cannot guarantee that this is a verbatim quote, but I believe it would be close to his position). It is also true that he liked to provoke, shock and, on occasion, antagonize philosophers who did not share his outlook. Since I was also a logician and it was known that I had been a friend and sometime protegé of his, many in Uppsala were worried: worried that my appointment would spell the death of philosophy in Uppsala. The conflict even spilled over into the national newspapers.

However, once I got there, the bruhaha died down, and I spent ten good years in the Uppsala department. That is to say, they were all good, but in one way the first few years were particularly good: the years when both Wlodek Rabinowicz and Sten Lindström were still there. At that time we shared an interest in belief dynamics, and we had numerous seminars together, formal as well as informal, and we wrote some joint papers. But then Wlodek was appointed to a full professorship in Lund and Sten to one in Umeå. My solace was some students with whom I was still able to discuss beliefs, norms, change and other things close to my heart. Of those students, John Cantwell and Tor Sandqvist are now professional philosophers. Having gifted students is in some ways even better than having gifted colleagues!

Last Years: Since 2001

I was retired (not "retired": "was retired") in 2001 when I hit the then mandatory retirement age of 65. I thought at the time that this was the end. But in fact it turned out to be more like a new beginning. By what seemed like a miracle I was immediately invited to spend a year at the Uppsala think tank, in those days called S.C.A.S.S.S. and later renamed S.C.A.S. After that I was invited to spend a quarter at U.S.C. thanks to Jim Higginbotham to whom I shall remain forever grateful. I sought in vain for a new department in the U.S. to take me in, a country where age limits are illegal. But even in a country where it is illegal to fire people because of old age, it is of course not illegal not to hire them.

And perhaps I should be grateful that I never received another permanent position; for what I got was something that may in the end have been better: a string of a term- or year-long appointments at U.C.L.A., Stanford, Amsterdam, N.I.A.S. (the Dutch think-tank outside Wassenaar), Calgary. And, to top it all, thanks to the Humboldt foundation, a year at the Goethe University in Frankfurt-am-Main.

Last Words

Parting is difficult: to get to know and like other people, and then perhaps never see them again. In fact, there are people I did not particularly like at the time whom I would be happy to meet now, many years later. This is perhaps a professional hazard in our kind of job: that of the quasi-itinerant scholar. We go some place, and for a limited time we develop an intense relationship with colleagues who feel like friends for life; and then we may never see them again. There is of course the kind of person who is all professional and no more interested in a personal relationship than your dentist is. There is also the kind of person who lives wrapped up in his or her own cocoon, constitutionally unable to have closer contact with others. And there is always the trivial but undeniable matter of time: just keeping the inbox clear may feel like enough contact with the outside world.

But making allowances for all that, there are still many I wish I could have kept in touch with. Paraphrasing the poet:

All those friends who came and went
little did I know we'd never meet again.

Parting from research is also difficult. In principle one should be able to go on indefinitely; and some lucky ones do. But for many of us, age sets limits. No students, no colleagues. Reduced input, not knowing what goes on. Less energy and, let's face it, less brain power. Perhaps best, then, to take the poet's advice and be "a well-mannered guest/who knows when to say thanks and leave".

A quote from the Western Civ source-book we used at Columbia (the value of a liberal arts eduction!) about the philosopher Georg Santayana, who was appointed in 1889 to teach at Harvard:

> He retired from teaching in 1912, an old legend telling us that on a beautiful April afternoon he rose from his chair, said to his students, "Gentlemen, it is spring," and walked slowly from the classroom, never to be seen there again. [7, p. 1033]

References

1 Halldén, S. (1949). *The logic of nonsense.* (p. 9) Uppsala: Uppsala Universitets Årsskrift.
2 E. J. Lemmon in collaboration with Dana Scott. (1977). *An introduction to modal logic.* In Segerberg, K. (Ed.) *American Philosophical Quarterly* monograph series, no. 11. Oxford: Basil Blackwell.
3 Segerberg, K. (1968). *Results in non-classical propositional logic.* Doctoral dissertation, Uppsala University, 30 pp.
4 Segerberg, K. (1971). An essay in classical modal logic. Doctoral dissertation, Stanford University, 250 pp. Mimeographed edition published by the Philosophical Society at Uppsala University.
5 Segerberg, K. (1977). A completeness theorem in the modal logic of programs. *Notices of the American Mathematical Society*, vol. 24 , A-552, no. 77T-E69.
6 Segerberg, K. (Ed.). (2001). Stig Kanger as we remember him: nine biographical sketches. In Holmström-Hintikka, G., Lindström, S., & Sliwinski, R. (Eds.) *Collected papers of Stig Kanger with essays on his life and work* (Vol. 2, pp. 3–30). Dordrecht, The Netherlands: Kluwer.
7 (1955). *Man in contemporary society* (Vol. 2). Morningside Heights, NY: Columbia University Press.
8 Segerberg, K. (Ed.). (1976). *Wright and wrong: Mini-essays in honor of Georg Henrik von Wright.* Åbo: Department of Philosophy, Åbo Akademi.

Appendix B
Some Metaphilosophical Remarks

The editor wants me to say something about my philosophical ideas. I don't suppose my ideas, if you can call them that, can be of much interest except in so far as what they say about me. But as the present essay is in the same category as income tax returns and customs declarations, a reasonable degree of honesty and completeness is expected, and so I ought to try to say something.[6] I will divide my remarks into three parts.

Logic and Truth

Several evenings that we had off during our military service in the mid-1950s my comrade-in-arms Gunnar Sohlenius, later professor and ultimately rector of the Royal Technical Institute in Stockholm, took me along to a series of private lectures in philosophy. They were given by Erik Jonson, an excentric older man who had been a student of Axel Hägerström and later *docent* in Uppsala. The lectures were mainly on Kant, but it was Hägerström and the idea that ethical terms and judgements lack theoretical meaning that fascinated me. Coming from Kiruna, as I did, I had never heard anything like it. Perhaps this first encounter with serious philosophical thought—thinking that does not compromise and does not necessarily balk at conclusions common sense finds unacceptable—was one reason why I ended up in philosophy.

In Uppsala several years later we studied, among others, the ethicists Richard Brandt and Charles Stevenson, big names at the time. Stevenson's division of meaning into descriptive and emotive, seemed reasonable. So when, still later, I was appointed to Edvard Westermarck's chair in the Åbo Academy and felt a responsibility to read his *Ethical relativism*, his (different but somewhat related) ideas were not entirely foreign to me [3].

I mention this background since problems concerning concepts like truth and validity are found in logic and science as well as in moral philosophy. We study

such concepts as they are expressed in language, but we also use them in the meta-language. Whenever we think systematically, it should be possible to give the

[6] For a previous effort in the same vein, see [1].

R. Trypuz (ed.), *Krister Segerberg on Logic of Actions*,
Outstanding Contributions to Logic 1, DOI: 10.1007/978-94-007-7046-1,

thought a rigorous formulation; then to ask whether the formulation is acceptable is to raise a further question. It seems that I—perhaps what German philosophers have called *das Ich*—is forever outside any model. It is one thing to formulate or study a theory or a model, another to decide whether to accept it and use it.

Actually there are four different things a researcher or scholar may do with respect to formal theories or models: (1) define one, (2) examine one that has been defined, (3) accept one that has been examined, and (4) use one that has been accepted. It is the third step that is of interest here: on what grounds do we (can we, should we) accept or reject a proposed theory or model? What makes us choose one rather than the other? Is there any sense in which we, as rational beings, should or must accept a theory? Exactly what features distinguish theories in logic from theories in physics, biology and political science? There is of course an overwhelming amount of literature on this topic: I only mention it here to confess my own bewilderment. (And this after a lifetime in philosophy departments!)

In other words: the modellings that I have devoted a life-time to studying—what use are they really?[7]

Logic and the Individual

There is a difference between theories and people, between disciplines and researchers. A discipline goes on even if individual researchers do not. A discipline may come to a temporary end, but there is always the possibility of a revival (in some form); whereas human life necessarily ends. So researchers, even philosophers (when they are at their best), are like pioneer soldiers fighting in no man's land. Or, to make a less martial comparison: like explorers or adventurers going into unknown continents. But in either case, the individual soldier/explorer/adventurer, having prepared the way for others who will come later, disappears.

So here is what might be called a paradox of progress: everyone wants to contribute, but when all do (almost) all are left behind. It is like going into a forrest in the autumn and hit upon a pristine patch of mushrooms: the feeling of being there first! Others who come later may still find some mushrooms, and picking them will still be worthwhile, but the beautiful feeling of being first is not there. This picture illustrates what may be called a me-me theory about research—a theory perhaps generalizable to all creative efforts, scientific and scholarly as well as activities like cooking and carpentry. There is something special about being able to contribute something new! It can of course feel good to be at the receiving end, as when we are taught by others and benefit from their creative efforts. Still, giving is different from receiving, as already children know: it is more fun to do something than to see it being done by others: "Let me! Let me!" The contrast between producer and consumer perspectives is reflected in the biblical claim that it is better to give than to receive.

Logic and the Future

It is an old idea that philosophy was the beginning of systematic knowledge. In an even wider perspective, magic comes into it: in both cases it must have been the

---

[7] Cf. [2].

human desire to understand (or control or manipulate) the environment. Philosophy was perhaps simply a spin-off.

Consider the well-worn idea that whenever a philosophical discipline has reached a certain degree of maturity it breaks off and starts a new discipline on its own, much as in many cultures young people leave their parental home to set up their own. Perhaps Kant was the last philosopher who had something really important to say about all the three main areas of philosophy: theoretical, practical, and æsthetical. Specialization is at work all the time. Like our universe, which astronomers tell us about, the universe of philosophy seems to be forever expanding, even at accelerating speeds. Isn't this what is happening to philosophical logic?

Here is a quote from Georg Henrik von Wright's address at the 1991 LMPS meeting in Uppsala:

> Big shifts in the centre of philosophy signalize changes in the general cultural atmosphere which in their turn reflect changes in political, economic and social conditions. The optimistic mood and belief in progress, fostered by scientific and technological developments, which has been our inheritance from the time of the Enlightenment, is giving way to a sombre mood of self-critical scrutiny of the achievements and foundation of our civilization. No attempt to survey the overall situation in contemporary philosophy can fail to notice this and to ponder over its significance.
>
> I shall not try to predict what will be the leading trends in the philosophy of the first century of the 2000s. But I think they will be markedly different from what they have been in this century, and that logic will not be one of them. If I am right, the twentieth century will even clearer than now stand out as another Golden Age of Logic in the history of those protean forms of spirituality we call Philosophy. [4 p. 23].

This statement was not well received at the conference; most dismissed it, some were upset. But to me there seemed to be some truth in it. Philosophical thought begins as inchoate reflexion on something or other and then, by and by, develops into something more concrete, perhaps eventually, in areas congenial to formalization, even rigorous. If this development is successful and runs its full course there will be a stage when the philosophers are replaced by others who are not philosophers but experts. And this is what may be happening with my own particular field, modal logic.

In this connexion one may discuss the value of formalization: how important is it that philosophical theories are formalized? It was obviously important for the foundation of mathematics that mathematical logic was invented and could be used to formalize arithmetic. In a more modest perspective, it is probably good to have certain idealized epistemic and deontic notions studied with the help of formal methods. But, in accordance with the more general observation in the preceding paragraph, epistemic logic and deontic logic are now in the process of being taken over by computer scientists. This is the way it always goes: if a theme in philosophical logic seems worth playing, then it will be taken over by specialists from another discipline. And in the process the subject matter will change in both content and form. This is something von Wright may have agreed with.

If modal logic, including epistemic and deontic logic, is to remain at least in part in philosophy we would perhaps need another Copernicus to replace the increasingly Ptolemaian proliferation of systems.

References

1 Segerberg, K. (2005). Krister Segerberg. In Hendricks, V. F. & Symons, J. (Eds.) *Formal philosophy: Aim, scope, direction* (pp. 159-167). Copenhagen: Automatic Press.
2 Segerberg, K. (2008). A conversation about epistemic logic. In Hendricks, V. F. & Pritchard, D. (Eds.) *Epistemology: 5 questions* (pp. 283–304). Copenhagen: Automatic Press/VIP.
3 Westermarck, E. (1932). *Ethical relativism.* New York: Littlefield.
4 von Wright, G. H. (1993). Logic and philosophy in the twentieth century. In Prawitz, D., Skyrms, B. & Westerståhl, D. (Eds.) *Logic, methodology and philosophy of science IX* (pp. 9–25). Amsterdam: Elsevier, 1994. Reprinted in *idem, The tree of knowledge and other essays*. Leiden: Brill.

Appendix C
Bibliography of Krister Segerberg

The works listed below have been divided into nine categories: books (B), editions (E), papers (P), abstracts (A), reprints (X), reviews (R), translations (T), verba (V), and miscellaneous (M). Only select abstracts are included.

1965

P1 "A contribution to nonsense-logics." *Theoria*, vol. 31, pp. 199–217.

1966

P1 "Axiomsystem för en av Mac Leod föreslagen satslogik." [Axiomatization of a propositional logic proposed by Mac Leod.] (Swedish) In *Analyser och argument*, edited by Ann-Mari Henschen-Dahlquist, pp. 112–116. (Uppsala, mimeographed)

1967

P1 "On the logic of 'to-morrow'." *Theoria*, vol. 33, pp. 45–52.
P2 "Some modal logics based on a three-valued logic." *Theoria*, vol. 33, pp. 53–71.

1968

P1 "Decidability of S4.1." *Theoria*, vol. 34, pp. 7–20.
P2 "Decidability of four modal logics." *Theoria*, vol. 34, pp. 21–25.
P3 "Propositional logics related to Heyting's and Johansson's." *Theoria*, vol. 34, pp. 26–61.
P4 "Antalet modaliteter i det Brouwerska systemet förstärkt med axiomschemat $CL^n aL^{n+1}a$." [The number of modalities in the Brouwer system supplemented by the axiom schema $CL^n aL^{n+1}a$.] (Swedish) In *Nio filosofiska studier tillägnade Konrad Marc-Wogau*, edited by Hjalmar Wennerberg, pp. 21–30. (Uppsala, mimeographed)
M1 *Results in non-classical propositional logic*. Doctoral dissertation, Uppsala University.

R. Trypuz (ed.), *Krister Segerberg on Logic of Actions*,
Outstanding Contributions to Logic 1, DOI: 10.1007/978-94-007-7046-1,

1969

R1 Review of Alan Rose's "Caractérisation, au moyen de la théorie des treillis, du calcul de propositions à foncteurs variables." *The journal of symbolic logic*, vol. 34, p. 121.
R2 Review of Henryk Skolimowski's *Polish analytical philosophy*. Ibid., p. 141.
R3 Review of Takeo Sugihara's "The number of modalities in T supplemented by the axiom CL^2pL^3p." Ibid., p. 305.
R4 Review of Raymond L. Wilder's *Introduction to the foundations of mathematics*. Ibid., p. 310.
R5 Review of Leon W. Cohen and Gertrude Ehrlich's *The structure of the real number system*. Ibid., p. 642.

1970

E1 *In memory of Arthur Prior*. Issue of *Theoria* (vol. 36, no. 3).
P1 "En anmärkning beträffande Brouwersystemet." [A remark concerning the Brouwer system.] (Swedish) In *Proceedings of the First Scandinavian Logic Symposium*, edited by Stig Kanger, pp. 166–169. (Uppsala, mimeographed)
P2 "Modal logics with linear alternative relations." *Theoria*, vol. 36, pp. 301–322.
P3 "Kripke-type semantics for preference logic." In *Logic and value*, edited by Tom Pauli, pp. 128–134. (Uppsala)
A1 "On some extensions of S4." *The journal of symbolic logic*, vol. 35, p. 363.
R1 Review of A. N. Prior's "On the calculus MCC". *Zentralblatt für Mathematik*, vol. 188, p. 317.
R2 Review of Richard G. Hull's "Counterexamples in intuitionistic analysis using Kripke's schema". Ibid., vol. 193, p. 290.
R3 Review of M. J. Cresswell's "Note on a system by Åqvist" and M. K. Rennie's "S3(S) = S3.5". *The journal of symbolic logic*, vol. 35, p.137.
R4 Review of Richard T. Garner and Bernard Rosen's *A systematic introduction to normative ethics and meta-ethics*. Ibid., p. 459.
R5 Review of Julius Stone's *Legal systems and lawyers' reasonings*. Ibid., p. 578.

1971

M1 "An essay in classical modal logic." Doctoral dissertation, Stanford University.
B1 *An essay in classical modal logic*. Mimeographed edition of M1, published by the Philosophical Society at Uppsala University.
P1 "Some logics of commitment and obligation." In *Deontic logic: Introductory and systematic readings*, edited by Risto Hilpinen, pp. 148–158. (Dordrecht, The Netherlands: Reidel)
P2 "Qualitative probability in a modal setting." In *Proceedings of the Second Scandinavian Logic Symposium*, edited by Jens-Erik Fenstad, pp. 341–352. (Amsterdam: North-Holland)
A1 "Qualitative probability in a modal setting." *The journal of symbolic logic*, vol. 36, p. 384.

A2 "On the extensions of S4.4." Ibid., pp. 590–591.
A3 "On some extensions of K4." Ibid., p. 697.
A4 "Two Scroggs Theorems." Ibid., pp. 697–698.
R1 Review of D. H. J. de Jongh's "Essay on I-valuations". *Zentralblatt für Mathematik*, vol. 213, p. 12.
R2 Review of Robert Blanché's "Sur l'interpretation du $\kappa\upsilon\rho\iota\varepsilon\upsilon\omega\nu\ \lambda o\gamma o\sigma$". *The journal of symbolic logic*, vol. 36, p. 175.

1972

P1 "Post completeness in modal logic." *The journal of symbolic logic*, vol. 37, pp. 711–715.
A1 "On Post completeness in modal logic." Ibid., p. 781–782.
R1 Review of M. K. Rennie's "On postulates for temporal order". Ibid., p. 629.

1973

P1 "Two-dimensional modal logic." *Journal of philosophical logic*, vol. 2, pp. 77–96.
P2 "Halldén's Theorem on Post completeness." In *Modality, morality, and other problems of sense and nonsense*, edited by Bengt Hansson et al., pp. 206–209. (Lund: Gleerup)
P3 "Harrison on ethical subjectivism." In *Studia philosophica in honorem Sven Krohn*, edited by Timo Airaksinen and Risto Hilpinen, pp. 191–198. *Annales Universitatis Turkuensis*, ser. B, vol. 126.
R1 Review of G. F. Schumm's "Solutions to four modal problems of Sobocinski". *Mathematical reviews*, vol. 46, #5110.
R2 Review of C. G. McKay's "A note on the Jaskowski sequence". *The journal of symbolic logic*, vol. 38, pp. 520–521.
M1 "Disproof of a conjecture of Rescher and Urquhart." In *P and Q: Mini-essays in honor of Risto Hilpinen*, pp. 18–23. (Åbo/Turku, mimeographed)
M2 "Moores kritik av Westermarck." [Moore's criticism of Westermarck.] (Swedish) Inaugural lecture. *Årsskrift utgiven av Åbo Akademi*, vol. 56, pp. 74–80.

1974

P1 (With David Makinson) "Ultrafilters and Post completeness." *Zeitschrift für mathematische Logik und Grundlagen der Mathematik*, vol. 20, pp. 385–388.
P2 "Franzén's proof of Bull's Theorem." *Ajatus*, vol. 35, pp. 216–221.
P3 "Proof of a conjecture of McKay." *Fundamenta mathematicæ*, vol. 81, pp. 267–270.
A1 "On binary trees in intermediate logic." *The journal of symbolic logic*, vol. 39, p. 208.
R1 Review of Peter Gärdenfors's "Positionalist voting functions". *Theoria*, vol. 40, pp. 211–212.

R2 Review of Peter Gärdenfors's "Assignment problem based on ordinal preferences". *Theoria*, pp. 212–214.
R3 Review of Dov M. Gabbay's "Selective filtration in modal logic I". *Mathematical reviews*, vol. 47, #1575.
M1 "Montague grammar with and without transformations." In *Kangerille: Mini-essays in honor of Stig Kanger*, pp. 25–32. (Åbo/Turku, mimeographed)
T1 "Logiche modali con relazioni di accessibilità lineari." In *La logica del tempo*, edited by Claudio Pizzi, pp. 187–210. (Turin). Italian translation of 1970 P2.

1975

P1 "That every extension of S4.3 is normal." In *Proceedings of the Third Scandinavian Logic Symposium*, edited by Stig Kanger, pp. 194–196. (Amsterdam: North-Holland)

1976

P1 "The truth about some Post numbers." *The journal of symbolic logic*, vol. 41, pp. 239–244.
P2 "A neglected family of aggregation problems in ethics." *Noûs*, vol. 10, pp. 221–244.
P3 "Discrete linear future time without axioms." *Studia logica*, vol. 35, pp. 273–278.
R1 Review of Brian F. Chellas and Audrey McKinney's "The completeness of monotonic modal logics". *Mathematical reviews*, vol. 51, #12480.
M1 "'Somewhere else' and 'some other time'." In *Wright and wrong: Mini-essays in honor of Georg Henrik von Wright*, pp. 61–64. (Åbo/Turku)

1977

A1 "The assignment problem as a problem of social choice." In *Filosofiska smulor tillägnade Konrad Marc-Wogau*, edited by Ann-Mari Henschen-Dahlquist, pp. 152–157. (Uppsala, mimeographed)
A2 "A completeness theorem in the modal logic of programs." *Notices of the American Mathematical Society*, vol. 24, p. A-552, #77T-E69.
R1 Review of M. J. Cresswell's "Frames and models in modal logic". *Mathematical reviews*, vol. 53, #2629.
R2 Review of Martin Gerson's "A neighborhood frame for T with no equivalent relational frame". Ibid., #2632.
R3 Review of George Epstein and Alfred Horn's "Propositional calculi based on subresiduation". Ibid., #5264.
R4 Review of Kit Fine's "Some connections between elementary and modal logic". Ibid., #5265.
A "A completeness theorem in the modal logic of programs." *Notices of the American Mathematical Society*, vol. 24 (1977), A-552, no. 77T-E69.
M1 "Editor's preface." In *The "Lemmon Notes": An introduction to modal logic* by E. J. Lemmon, in collaboration with Dana Scott, pp. v-x.

1978

M "A conjecture in dynamic logic." In *Odds and ends: Mini-essays in honor of Juhani Pietarinen*, pp. 23–26. (Åbo/Turku, mimeographed)

1979

P1 "Some reflections on method in the theory of social choice." In *Essays in honour of Jaakko Hintikka*, edited by E. Saarinen et al., pp. 147–159. (Dordrecht, The Netherlands: Reidel)

P2 "Epistemic considerations in game theory." *Theory and decision*, vol. 11, pp. 363–373.

P3 "På spaning efter det carrollska elementet." [Search for the Carrollian element.] (Swedish) In *Pegas och snöbollskrig*, edited by Roger Holmström et al., pp. 247–265. (Åbo/Turku)

T1 "Vremennaya logika fon Vrigta." [von Wright's tense logic.] In *Logicheskij vyvod*, edited by V. A. Smirnov et al., pp. 173-205. (Moscow: The Academy of Sciences of the U. S. S. R.) Russian translation of 1989:P3.

1980

E1 *Trends in modal logic*. Issue of *Studia logica* (vol. 39, no. 2–3).

1981

E1 *Philosophy in New Zealand*. Issue of *Theoria* (vol. 46 (for 1980), nos. 2–3).

P1 "A note on the logic of elsewhere." *Theoria*, vol 46, pp. 183–187.

P2 "Action-games." *Acta philosophica fennica*, vol. 32, pp. 220–231.

P3 "'After' and 'during' in dynamic logic." *Atti del Convegno Nazionale di Logica, Montecatini Terme, 1-5 Ottobre 1979*, pp. 273–294. (Naples: Bibliopolis).

X1 "'After' and 'during' in dynamic logic." *Acta philosophica fennica*, vol. 35, pp. 203–228. Reprint of 1981:P3.

T1 "Modalnye logiki s linejnymi otnosheniami alternativnosti." In *Semantika modalnych i intensionalnych logik*, edited by V. A. Smirnov, pp. 180–204. (Moscow) Russian translation of 1970:P2.

1982

B1 *Classical propositional operators: An exercise in the foundations of logic*. (Oxford: Clarendon Press)

P1 "The logic of deliberate action." *Journal of philosophical logic*, vol. 11, pp. 233–254.

P2 "Natural deduction and truth-functional operators." In < 320311 >: *Philosophical essays dedicated to Lennart Åqvist on his fiftieth birthday*, edited by Tom Pauli, pp. 330–336. (Uppsala)

P3 "A completeness theorem in the modal logic of programs." In *Universal algebra and applications*, edited by T. Tradczyk, pp. 31–46. Banach Center Publications, vol. 9. (Warsaw: PWN)

P4 "A deontic logic of action." *Studia logica*, vol. 61, pp. 269–282.

1983

P1 "Could have but did not." *Pacific philosophical quarterly*, vol. 64, pp. 230–241.

P2 "Arbitrary truth-functions and natural deduction." *Zeitschrift für mathematische Logik und Grundlagen der Mathematik*, vol. 29, pp. 557–564.

M1 Autobiographical remarks in *Research in Australia, New Zealand and Oceania: Its brief history and its present state*, edited by Richard Routley, pp. 43–45. Research Papers in Logic, vol. 14. (Canberra: Logic Group, R. S. S. S., A. N. U.) (Routley's article was later published in *Ruch filozoficzny*, vol. 41 (1984).)

1984

P1 (With ROBERT BULL) "Basic modal logic." In *Handbook of philosophical logic*, edited by F. Guenthner and D. Gabbay, vol. 2, pp. 1–88. (Dordrecht, The Netherlands: Reidel)

P2 "Towards an exact philosophy of action." *Topoi*, vol. 3, pp. 75–83.

A1 "A small corner of the big lattice of modal logics." *The journal of symbolic logic*, vol. 49, p. 1428.

1985

P1 "Models for actions." In *Studies in analytical philosophy*, edited by B. K. Matilal and J. L. Shaw, pp. 161–171. (Dordrecht: Holland: Reidel)

P2 "A topological logic of action." *Studia logica*, vol. 43, pp. 415–419.

P3 "Routines." *Synthese*, vol. 65, pp. 185–210.

P4 "On the question of semantics in the logic of action: Some remarks on Pörn's logic of action." *Acta philosophica fennica*, vol. 38, pp. 282–298.

1986

P1 "Modal logics with functional alternative relations." *Notre Dame journal of formal logic*, vol. 27, pp. 504–522.

P2 "Defining triage." In *Logic and abstraction*, edited by Mats Furberg et al., pp. 207–251. *Acta philosophica gothoburgensia*, vol. 1.

1988

P1 "On the logic of small changes in theories II." In *Mathematical logic and applications*, edited by Dimiter Skordev et al., pp. 205–211. (New York: Plenum)

P2 "Talking about actions." *Studia logica*, vol. 47, pp. 347–352.

P3 "Conditional logic and the logic of theory change." In *Logical consistency and dialectical contradiction*, edited by Bogdan Dyankov, pp. 99–116. (Sofia: Unified Centre for Philosophy and Sociology)

T1 "O logike malich izmeneniy v teoriach I". In *Intensionalnye logiki i logicheskaya struktura teoriy*, edited by V. A. Smirnov, pp. 105–115. (Tbilisi: Metsniereba) Translation of a paper never published in English.

A1 "Logics of change." *The journal of symbolic logic*, vol. 53, p. 331.

1989

P1 "A note on an impossibility theorem of Gärdenfors." *Noûs*, vol. 23, pp. 351–354.

P2 "Reflexions on a paper by Brown." In *In so many words*, edited by Sten Lindström and Wlodzimierz Rabinowicz, pp. 285–291. (Uppsala)

P3 "von Wright's tense-logic." In *The philosophy of Georg Henrik von Wright*, edited by P. A. Schilpp and L. E. Hahn, pp. 603–635. (La Salle, Ill.: Open Court)

P4 "Getting started: Beginnings in the logic of action." In *Le teorie delle modalita: Atti del convegno internazionale di storia della logica*, edited by G. Corsi, C. Mangione and M. Mugnai, pp. 221–250. (Bologna: CLUEB)

P5 "Bringing it about." *Journal of philosophical logic*, vol. 18, pp. 327–347.

P6 "Notes on conditional logic." *Studia logica*, vol. 48, pp. 157–168.

1990

P1 "Validity and satisfaction in imperative logic." *Notre Dame journal of formal logic*, vol. 31, pp. 203–221.

1991

A1 "To do and not to do." Abstract. *The journal of symbolic logic*, vol. 56, p. 379.

1992

E1 *Logic of action*. Double issue of *Studia logica*. (vol.51, no.3–4).

P1 "Action incompleteness." *Studia logica*, vol. 51, pp. 533–550.

P2 "Representing facts." In *Knowledge, belief and strategic interaction*, edited by Cristina Bicchieri and Maria Luisa Dalla Chiara, pp. 239–256. (Cambridge: Cambridge University Press)

P3 "How many logically constant actions are there?" *Bulletin of the Section of Logic*, vol. 21, pp. 134–139.

X1 "Getting started: Beginnings in the logic of action." *Studia logica*, vol. 51, pp. 347–378. Reprint of 1989:P4.

1993

P1. "Perspectives on preferences." *Proceedings of the Aristotelian Society*, vol. 20 (1993), pp. 263–278.

T1 "Logica modale di base." [Italian translation of the Segerberg part of 1984:P1.] In *Letture di logica: Fondamenti della matematica—linee di ricerca attuali*, edited by Corrado Mangione and Miriam Franchella, pp. 217–256. Milan: CEA.

M1 "Någonting barnsligt men mycket naturligt." ["Something childish but very natural."] Inaugural lecture. In *Forskningsprofiler* (Uppsala: University of Uppsala, 1993), pp. 96–101.

A1 "Remarks on some operators in dynamic logic." Abstract. *The journal of symbolic logic*, vol. 58 (1993), pp. 1483–1484.

1994

A1 "Trying to understand the logic of theory change in terms of modal logic." Extended abstract. In Norman Foo et al. (eds), *Record of the workshop on logic and action*, December 13-14, 1993, pp. 1–12. (Sydney: University of Sydney, 1994)

P1 (With Brian F. Chellas) "Modal logics with the MacIntosh rule." *Journal of philosophical logic*, vol. 23 (1994), pp. 67–86.

P2 "A model existence theorem in infinitary modal propositional logic." *Journal of philosophical logic*, vol. 23 (1994), pp. 337–367.

P3 (With Wlodek Rabinowicz) "Actual truth, possible knowledge." *Topoi*, vol. 13 (1994), pp. 101–115.

P4 "Accepting failure in dynamic logic." In Dag Prawitz, Brian Skyrms and Dag Westerståhl, *Logic, methodology and philosophy of science IX*, pp.327-349. Proceedings of the Ninth International Congress of Logic, Methodology and Philosophy of Science, Uppsala, Sweden, August 7–14, 1991. (Amsterdam: Elsevier, 1994)

1995

P1 "Belief revision from the point of view of doxastic logic." *Bulletin of the I. G. P. L.* (Interest Group in Pure and Applied Logics), vol. 3 (1995), pp. 535–553.

P2 "Conditional action." In *Conditionals: from philosophy to computer science*, edited by G. Crocco, L. Fariñas and A. Herzig, pp. 241–265. Studies in logic and computation, vol. 5. Oxford: Clarendon Press, 1995.

P3 "A festival of facts." *Logic and logical philosophy*, vol. 2 (for 1994, publ. 1995), pp. 9–22.

P4 "Some questions about hypertheories." In *Logic for a change: Essays dedicated to Sten Lindström*, edited by Sven Ove Hansson and Wlodek Rabinowicz, pp. 136–154. Uppsala Prints and Preprints in Philosophy, 1995:9. Uppsala, 1995.

A1 "Belief revision from the point of view of doxastic logic." *The bulletin of symbolic logic*, vol. 1 (1995), p. 357.

A2 "AGM as a dynamic, doxastic logic." *The bulletin of symbolic logic*, vol. 1 (1995), p. 387.

V1 "dynamic logic" In *The Cambridge dictionary of philosophy*, edited by Robert Audi, pp. 214–215. Cambridge: Cambridge University Press, 1995.

1996

P1 "A general framework for the logic of theory change." *Bulletin of the Section of Logic*, vol. 25 (1996), pp. 2–8.

P2 (With BRIAN F. CHELLAS) "Modal logics in the vicinity of S1." *Notre Dame journal of formal logic*, vol. 37 (1996), pp. 1–24.

P3 "The delta operator at three levels of analysis." In *Logic, action, and information*, edited by André Fuhrmann and Hans Rott, pp. 63–75. Walter de Gruyter: Berlin, 1996.

P4 "To do and not to do." In *Logic and reality: Essays on the legacy of Arthur Prior*, edited by B. J. Copeland, pp. 301–313. Oxford: Clarendon Press, 1996.

V1 "Modal logic." In *The encyclopedia of philosophy supplement*, edited by ......, pp. 350-351. Macmillan Reference USA: New York and Simon & Schuster and Prentice Hall International: London, etc., 1996.

V2 "Wright, Georg Henrik von." In *The encyclopedia of philosophy supplement*, edited by ......, pp. 593–594. Macmillan Reference USA: New York and Simon & Schuster and Prentice Hall International: London, etc., 1996.

1997

P1 "Further questions about hypertheories." In *Odds and ends: Philosophical essays dedicated to Wlodek Rabinowicz*, edited by Sten Lindström, Rysiek Sliwinski and Jan Österberg, pp. 171–184. Uppsala Philosophical Studies, vol. 45. Uppsala, 1997.

P2 "Delta logic and Brown's logic of ability." In *Logic, action and cognition*, edited by Eva Ejerhed and Sten Lindström, pp. 29–45. Dordrecht, The Netherlands: Kluwer, 1997.

P3 "A doxastic walk with Darwiche and Pearl." *Nordic journal of philosophical logic*, vol. 2 (1997), pp. 63–66.

P4 "The deontic logic of actual obligation." In *For good measure: philosophical essays dedicated to Jan Odelstad on the occasion of his fiftieth birthday*, edited by Lars Lindahl, Paul Needham and Rysiek Sliwinski, pp. 210–217. Uppsala Philosophical Studies, vol. 46. Uppsala, 1997.

1998

P1 "Three recipes for revision." *Theoria*, vol. 62 (for 1996, publ. 1998), pp. 62–73.

P2 "Belief revision along the lines of Lindström and Rabinowicz." *Fundamenta informaticæ*, vol. 32 (for 1997, publ. 1998), pp. 183–191.

A1 "Irrevocable revision." Abstract. *The bulletin of symbolic logic*, vol. 3 (for 1997, publ. 1998), p. 393.

X1 "The deontic logic of actual obligation." In *The Logica Yearbook 1997*, edited by Timothy Childers, pp. 251–258. Prague: Institute of Philosophy, Academy of Sciences of the Czech Republic, 1998. Reprint of 1997: P4.

P3 "Updating hypertheories." In *Not without cause*, edited by Lars Lindahl, Jan Odelstad & Rysiek Sliwinski, pp. 216–223. Uppsala Philosophical Studies, vol. 48. Uppsala, 1998.

1999

P1 "Results, consequences, intentions." In *Actions, norms, values: discussion with Georg Henrik von Wright*, edited by Georg Meggle, pp. 147–157. Berlin & New York: Walter de Gruyer, 1999.

P2 "A completeness proof in full DDL." In *Philosophical crumbs: essays dedicated to Ann-Mari Henschen-Dahlquist on the occasion of her seventy-fifth birthday*, edited by Rysiek Sliwinski, pp. 195–207. Uppsala Philosophical Studies, vol. 49. Uppsala, 1999.

P3 "Two traditions in the logic of belief: bringing them together." In *Logic, language and reasoning: essays in honour of Dov Gabbay*, edited by Hans Jürgen Ohlbach and Uwe Reyle, pp. 135–147. Dordrecht, The Netherlands: Kluwer, 1999.

P4 "Default logic as dynamic doxastic logic." *Erkenntnis*, vol. 50 (1999), pp. 333–352.

2000

P1 "Irrevocable belief revision in dynamic doxastic logic." *Notre Dame journal of formal logic*, vol. 39 (for 1998, publ. 2000), pp. 287–306.

P2 "The lattice of basic modal logics." In *Between words and worlds: a Festschrift for Pavel Materna*, edited by Timothy Childers and Jari Palomäki, pp. 170–183. Prague: Filosofia, 2000.

2001

P1 "A question about distribution." In *Omnium-gatherum: philosophical essays dedicated to Jan Österberg on the occasion of his sixtieth birthday*, edited by Eric Carlson and Rysiek Sliwinski, pp. 309–313. Uppsala Philosophical Studies, vol. 50. Uppsala, 2001.

P2 (With Michael Zakharyaschev, Maarten de Rijke & Heinrich Wansing) "The origins of modern modal logic." In *Advances in modal logic*, vol. 2, edited by Michael Zakharyaschev, Krister Segerberg, Maarten de Rijke & Heinrich Wansing, pp.xi–xxviii. CSLI Lecture Notes # 119. Stanford, Calif.: CSLI Publications, 2001.

P3 "The basic dynamic doxastic logic of AGM." In *Frontiers in belief revision*, edited by Mary-Anne Williams and Hans Rott, pp.57–84. Applied Logic Series, vol. 22. Dordrecht, The Netherlands: Kluwer, 2001.

X1 (With R. A. Bull) "Basic modal logic." In *Handbook of philosophical logic*, 2nd edition, edited by D. M. Gabbay & F. Guenthner, vol. 3, pp. 1–81. Dordrecht, The Netherlands: Kluwer, 2001. Reprint of 1984: P1.

X2 "Default logic as dynamic doxastic logic." In *Dynamics and management of reasoning processes*, edited by J.-J. Ch. Meyer and J. Treur, pp. 159-176. *Handbook of defeasible reasoning and uncertainty management systems*, vol. 6. Dordrecht, The Netherlands; Kluwer: 2001. Reprint of 1999: P4.

M1 "Professor Saul A. Kripke." In *The Rolf Schock Prizes 2001*, pp. 10–13. Stockholm: Stiftelsen The Schock Foundation, 2001.

M2 "Stig Kanger (1924–1988)." In *Collected papers of Stig Kanger with essays on his life and work*, vol. 2, edited by Ghita Holmström-Hintikka, Sten Lindström & Rysiek Sliwinski, pp. 3–9. Dordrecht, The Netherlands: Kluwer, 2001.

2002

P1 "Outline of a logic of action." In *Advances in modal logic*, vol. 3, edited by F, Wolter, H. Wansing, M. de Rijke & M. Zakharyaschev, pp. 365–387. River Edge, New Jersey & London: World Scientific, 2002.

X1 "A completeness proof in full DDL." *Logic and logical philosophy*, vol. 9 (2002), pp. 77–90. Reprint of 1999: P2.

2003

E1 With RYSIEK SLIWINSKI. *Logic, law, morality: thirteen essays in practical philosophy in honour of Lennart Åqvist.* Uppsala Philosophical Studies, vol. 51. 244 pp.

E2 With RYSIEK SLIWINSKI. *A philosophical smorgasbord: essays on action, truth, and other things in honour of Frederick Stoutland.* Uppsala Philosophical Studies, vol. 52. 362 pp.

P1 "Some Meinong/Chisholm theses." In 2003: E1, pp.67–77.

P2 "Modellings for two types of action." In 2003: E2, pp.151–156,

P3 "Axioms for a logic of actual knowledge." <http://www.cse.unsw.edu.au/~ksg /Norman>

2004

P1 "Deconstruction of epistemic logic." In *Knowledge and belief / Wissen und Glauben,* pp. 103-119. Proceedings of the 26th International Wittgenstein Symposium, Kirchberg am Wechsel, 2003, edited by Winfred Löffler & Paul Weingartner. Vienna: Österreichischer Bundesverlag & Hölder-Pichler-Tempsky, Vienna, 2004.

2005

P1 "Intension, intention." In *Intensionality*, edited by Reinhard Kahle, pp. 174-186. Lecture Notes in Logic. LaJolla, CA: Association for Symbolic Logic and Wellesley, MA: A. K. Peters, 2005.

P2 "Philosophy: what it is and why it matters." In *Polynesian paradox: essays in honour of Futa Helu*, edited by Ian Campbell & Eve Coxon, pp. 235–242. Suva, Fiji: University of the South Pacific, 2005.

M "Krister Segerberg." In *Formal philosophy*, edited by Vincent F. Hendricks & John Symons, pp. 159–167. Automatic Press, 2005.

2006

P1 "Trying to meet Ross's challenge." In *Logic and philosophy in Italy: some trends and perspectives*, edited by Edoardo Ballo & Miriam Franchella, pp. 155-166. Monza, Italy: Polimetrica International Scientific Publisher, 2006.

P2 "Moore problems in full dynamic doxastic logic". In *Essays in logic and ontology: dedicated to Jerzy Perzanowski*, edited by J. Malinowski and A. Pietruszczak, pp. 11-25. Poznan Studies in the Philosophy of the Sciences and the Humanities, vol. 91, pp. 95-110. Amsterdam/New York, NY: Rodopi, 2006.

P3 (With Sten Lindström) "Modal logic and philosophy." In *Handbook of modal logic*, edited by P. Blackburn, J. van Benthem & F. Wolter, pp. 1149–1214. Elsevier, the Netherlands: Amsterdam, 2006.

V1 "modal logic." In the *Encyclopedia of Philosophy*, edited by Donald Borchert, second edition. Detroit, Mich.: Macmillan Reference USA, 2006.

V2 "Wright, Georg Henrik von." In the *Encyclopedia of Philosophy*, edited by Donald Borchert, second edition. Detroit, Mich.: Macmillan Reference USA, 2006.

2007

P1 "Fallbacks and push-ons." In *Hommage à Wlodek: Philosophical papers dedicated to Wlodek Rabinowicz*, an electronic Festschrift in honour of Wlodek Rabinowicz, 14 January 2007 (http://www.fil.lu.se/hommageawlodek).

P2 (With Hannes Leitgeb) "Doxastic dynamic logic: why, whether, how." *Knowledge, rationality & action,* vol. 155 (2007), pp. 167–190.

P3 "Iterated belief revision in dynamic doxastic logic." In *Logic at the crossroads: an interdisciplinary view*, edited by Amitabha Gupta, Rohit Parikh & Johan van Benthem, pp. 331-343. New Delhi: Allied Publishers Pvt. Ltd., 2007. Reissued in *Proof, computation and agency: logical at the crossroads*, pp. 217–227. Dordrecht: Springer, 2011.

A1 "A blueprint for deontic logic in three (not necessarily easy) steps." Extended abstract. In *Formal models of belief change in rational agents*, edited by G. Bonnano, J. Delgrande, J. Lang & H. Rott. Dagstuhl Seminar Proceedings 07351. (http://drops.dagstuhl.de/opus/volltexte/2007/1218)

2008

P1 "Något om en paradox." I *Advocatus scientiae: en filosofisk vänbok tillägnad Hans Rosing*, redigerad av Kim-Erik Berts, Martin Nybom & Kim Solin, pp. 89–95. Åbo: Ämnet filosofi vid Åbo Akademi, 2008

M1 "A conversation about epistemic logic." In *Epistemology: 5 questions*, edited by Vincent F, Hendricks & Duncan Pritchard, pp. 283–304. Automatic Press/VIP, 2008.

2009

P1 "von Wright and the logic of the practical syllogism." In *Philosophical probings: essays on von Wright's later work*, edited by Frederick Stoutland, pp. 93–109. Automatic Press / VIP, 2009.

P2 "Introductory conversation." In *Discourses on social software*, edited by Jan van Eijck & Rineke Verbrugge, pp. 15–28. Texts in logic and games, vol. 5. Amsterdam: Amsterdam University Press, 2009.

P3 "Blueprint for a dynamic deontic logic." *Journal of applied logic*, vol. 7 (2009), pp. 388–402.

P4 "Real change, deontic action." In *Logic, ethics and all that jazz: essays in honour of Jordan Howard Sobel*, edited by Lars-Göran Johansson, Jan Österberg & Rysiek Sliwinski, pp. 295-298. Uppsala: Uppsala Philosophical Studies, vol. 57 (2009). Reprinted in *Dynamic formal epistemology*, edited by Patrick Girard, Olivier Poy & Mathieu Marion, pp. 223–226. Synthese Libary, vol. 351. Dordrecht: Springer, 2011.

V (With Marcus Kracht & John-Jules Meyer.) "The logic of action." *The Stanford Encyclopedia of Philosophy.*

M Foreword in *The picture theory of language: a philosophical investigation into the genesis of meaning* by John Roscoe, pp. i–iv. The Edwin Mellen Press, 2009.

2010

P "Some completeness theorems in the dynamic doxastic logic of iterated belief revision." *Review of symbolic logic*, vol 3 (2010), pp. 228–246,

2011

P1 "A report from the desert of deontic logic." In *Neither/nor: Philosophical papers dedicated to Eric Carlsson on the occasion of his fiftieth birthday.* edited by Rysiek Sliwinski and Frans Svensson, pp. 259–262. Uppsala: Uppsala Philosophical Studies, vol. 58 (2011).

P2 "A modal logic of metaphor." *Studia Logica*, vol. 99 (2011), pp. 337–347.

2012

P1 "DΔL: a dynamic deontic logic." *Synthese*. vol. 185 (1), pp. 1–17.

Forthcoming

P3 "Strategies for belief revision." In *Games, actions and social software 2011*, edited by Jan van Eijck & Rineke Verbrugge, pp. 73-95. In "Texts in logic and games", a FoLLI subseries of LNCS, vol. 7010. Berlin & Heidelberg: Springer Verlag, 2012.

P "Trying to model metaphor." To appear in *The Logica Yearbook 2011.*

MIX
Papier aus verantwortungsvollen Quellen
Paper from responsible sources
FSC® C105338

If you have any concerns about our products,
you can contact us on
ProductSafety@springernature.com

In case Publisher is established outside the EU,
the EU authorized representative is:
Springer Nature Customer Service Center GmbH
Europaplatz 3, 69115 Heidelberg, Germany

Printed by Libri Plureos GmbH
in Hamburg, Germany